FISCAL POLITICS

EDITORS

VITOR GASPAR • SANJEEV GUPTA

CARLOS MULAS-GRANADOS

INTERNATIONAL MONETARY FUND

Cataloging-in-Publication Data
Joint Bank-Fund Library

Names: Gaspar, Vitor. | Gupta, Sanjeev. | Mulas-Granados, Carlos.
Title: Fiscal politics / Vitor Gaspar, Sanjeev Gupta, and Carlos Mulas-Granados, editors.
Description: Washington, DC : International Monetary Fund, 2017. | Includes bibliographical references and index.
Identifiers: ISBN 9781475547900 (paper)
Subjects: LCSH: Fiscal policy. | Political science—Economic aspects.
Classification: LCC HJ192.5.F576 2017

978-1-47554-790-0 (paper)
978-1-47558-956-6 (PDF)
978-1-47558-952-8 (ePub)
978-1-47558-953-5 (Mobipocket)

Please send orders to

International Monetary Fund, Publication Services
P.O. Box 92780, Washington, DC 20090, U.S.A.
Tel.: (202) 623-7430 Fax: (202) 623-7201
E-mail: publications@imf.org
Internet: www.elibrary.imf.org
www.imfbookstore.org

Contents

Foreword v

Acknowledgments vii

Contributors ix

INTRODUCTION

1 Fiscal Politics ... 3
Vitor Gaspar, Sanjeev Gupta, and Carlos Mulas-Granados

PART I ELECTIONS, IDEOLOGY, AND POLITICAL FRAGMENTATION

2 Governments and Promised Fiscal Consolidations: Do They Mean What They Say? ... 25
Sanjeev Gupta, João Tovar Jalles, Carlos Mulas-Granados, and Michela Schena

3 Fiscal Policy over the Election Cycle in Low-Income Countries ... 63
Christian Ebeke and Dilan Ölçer

4 Economic and Political Determinants of Tax Policies in OECD Countries ... 83
Mark Hallerberg and Jürgen von Hagen

5 Now or Later? The Political Economy of Public Investment in Democracies ... 111
Sanjeev Gupta, Estelle X. Liu, and Carlos Mulas-Granados

6 Do Elections Affect the Wage Bill? ... 137
Yehenew Endegnanew, Mauricio Soto, and Geneviève Verdier

7 Energy Subsidies and Public Social Spending: Theory and Evidence ... 153
Christian Ebeke and Constant Lonkeng Ngouana

8 It's Politics, Stupid! Political Constraints Determine Governments' Reactions to the Great Recession ... 177
Fabian Gunzinger and Jan-Egbert Sturm

9 Fragmented Politics and Public Debt ... 213
Ernesto Crivelli, Sanjeev Gupta, Carlos Mulas-Granados, and Carolina Correa-Caro

PART II | INSTITUTIONS, RULES, AND FISCAL COUNCILS

10 | Political Institutions, State Building, and Tax Capacity: Crossing the Tipping Point 241
Vitor Gaspar, Laura Jaramillo, and Philippe Wingender

11 | Fiscal Discipline and Exchange Rates: Does Politics Matter? 271
João Tovar Jalles, Carlos Mulas-Granados, and José Tavares

12 | Expenditure Rules: Effective Tools for Sound Fiscal Policy? 299
Till Cordes, Tidiane Kinda, Priscilla Muthoora, and Anke Weber

13 | Fiscal Rules to Tame the Political Budget Cycle: Evidence from Italian Municipalities 327
Andrea Bonfatti and Lorenzo Forni

14 | On the Determinants of Fiscal Noncompliance: An Empirical Analysis of Spanish Regions 345
Mar Delgado-Téllez, Victor D. Lledó, and Javier J. Pérez

15 | Budget Institutions in Low-Income Countries 377
Sanjeev Gupta, Sami Yläoutinen, Brian Olden, Holger van Eden, Teresa Curristine, Tom Josephs, Eliko Pedastsaar, and Johann Seiwald

16 | Fiscal Watchdogs and Sound Fiscal Policy: Is the Barking Loud Enough to Tame Politicians? 399
Xavier Debrun, Marc Gérard, and Jason Harris

PART III | SUPRANATIONAL FISCAL POLITICS

17 | The Making of a Continental Financial System: Lessons for Europe from Early American History 427
Vitor Gaspar

18 | Fiscal Politics in the Euro Area 439
Luc Eyraud, Vitor Gaspar, and Tigran Poghosyan

19 | IMF Conditionality and Revenue Performance 477
Ernesto Crivelli and Sanjeev Gupta

Index 507

Foreword

Politics lie at the heart of the role that the state plays in the economy. Decisions to allocate resources, redistribute income, or stabilize the economy have a strong political component. Political developments can therefore have a powerful impact on economic outcomes.

For example, sudden policy shifts, uncertainty from political gridlock, or stalled budget negotiations can lead to market volatility and bad economic outcomes.

For this reason, analyzing the influence of political economy on policy outcomes is essential for the IMF's macroeconomic surveillance and policy analysis.

A deeper understanding of domestic and international constraints faced by policymakers facilitates our interactions with country authorities. By incorporating the understanding of a political dimension in its analysis, the IMF can also tailor its policy recommendations more closely to its mission of serving our member countries.

In particular, I believe that a better understanding of fiscal policy decisions can help us come up with more inclusive—and therefore more sustainable—macroeconomic policies.

I welcome the work done in the Fiscal Affairs Department in this area. It examines rigorously the impact of politics on fiscal decisions and presents compelling evidence that strong institutions and smart rules can have a positive effect on macroeconomic outcomes.

This book is a first step to further integrate political economy issues into the IMF's policy analysis. I hope it will also spark further debate and research on this topic, both inside and outside the IMF.

Christine Lagarde
Managing Director
International Monetary Fund

Acknowledgments

This book has been a collective endeavor and has been enriched by contributions from both inside and outside the IMF. We would like to thank the contributing authors for their close collaboration and enthusiasm for the topic. The research presented here has benefited from the comments of staff in the IMF's Fiscal Affairs Department and other departments. Comments presented at seminars hosted by other institutions have also made a valuable contribution to several chapters.

Michael Harrup and Rumit Pancholi of the IMF's Communications Department efficiently managed all aspects related to the production of the book, and we are grateful for their excellent work. We also thank Michela Schena and Elijah Kimani for their excellent research assistance in putting together a broad political economy database used in many chapters of the book. Juliet Narsiah and Leigh Huffman also provided excellent administrative assistance during the many steps needed to bring a book into completion.

Vitor Gaspar
Sanjeev Gupta
Carlos Mulas-Granados
Editors

Contributors

Andrea Bonfatti is a postdoctoral fellow at the University of Padua currently working on the SHARE (Survey of Health, Ageing and Retirement in Europe) project. He previously worked in the Statistics Division of the United Nations Food and Agriculture Organization in Rome. His research focuses on the analysis of risk, aging, economic development, applied political economy, and commodity market modeling. He holds a PhD in economics from the University of Verona.

Till Cordes is a policy officer at the Federal Ministry of Finance and is responsible for bank resolution in the Directorate-General for financial market policy. He was previously an economic and financial officer at the British Embassy in Berlin and a Carlo Schmid Fellow at the IMF. He holds a BA in philosophy and economics from the University of Bayreuth, an MSc in international political economy from the London School of Economics and Political Science, and a PhD from the Hertie School of Governance. He has taught seminars at undergraduate and graduate levels on sovereign debt and international economics. His research focuses on fiscal policy and the political economy of sovereign debt.

Carolina Correa-Caro is a consultant in the Inter-American Development Bank's Social Sector Department. She was previously a research analyst in the IMF's Fiscal Affairs Department and research assistant for governmental organizations in Colombia.

Ernesto Crivelli is an economist in the IMF's European Department. He is the desk economist on Romania and has worked on emerging economies in Central, Eastern, and South-Eastern Europe. He has previously worked in the IMF's Fiscal Affairs Department. Before joining the IMF, he was a senior fellow at the Max Planck Institute in Germany. He has published on tax policy, aid, and fiscal decentralization issues. He received a PhD from the University of Bonn in Germany.

Teresa Curristine is a senior economist in the IMF's Fiscal Affairs Department, where she provides advice to governments on managing their public finances. She leads projects and teams working on a variety of public financial management issues in Asia and Latin America, including medium-term budgeting, performance budgeting, managing fiscal risks, and developing independent fiscal councils. She has previously worked for the Organization for Economic Co-Operation and Development (OECD), where she was responsible for the OECD Senior Budget Officials Network on Performance and Results. She has also managed the cross-directorate project on improving public sector efficiency for the Germany Presidency of the European Union and a directoratewide project on public sector modernization. She has published several articles and edited three books: *Public Financial Management and Its Emerging Architecture*, *Performance Budgeting in*

OECD Countries, and *Modernising Government: The Way Forward*. She was also previously a lecturer at Oxford University, where she received a PhD.

Xavier Debrun is chief of the Systemic Issues Division in the IMF's Research Department. He has previously worked in the IMF's Fiscal Affairs Department, contributing to *Fiscal Monitor* and to policy papers on fiscal governance. In 2006–07, he was a visiting fellow at Bruegel (Brussels' leading think tank on European economic issues) and a visiting professor of economics at the Graduate Institute of International Studies in Geneva. He held various visiting professor positions, notably at the University of Geneva and at the CERDI-University of Auvergne. He received a PhD in international economics from the Graduate Institute in Geneva in 1999 and was a postdoctoral fellow in the Economics Department at Harvard University from 1999 to 2000. His research interests include international policy coordination, the economics of monetary unions, and macrofiscal issues, including the design and effectiveness of fiscal policy rules, and the stabilizing (or destabilizing) role of fiscal policy. His work has been published in prominent IMF series—notably the *World Economic Outlook* and *Fiscal Monitor*—as well as in various conference volumes and professional journals, including *The Economic Journal*, *The European Economic Review*, *The Canadian Journal of Economics*, and *Economic Policy*. In 2007 he was the first non-French national nominated for the Prize of the Best French Economist under 40 by the newspaper *Le Monde*.

Mar Delgado-Téllez is an economist in the Fiscal Policy Unit of the Directorate-General of Economics and Statistics at Banco de España. Her research focuses on public economics—in particular, federalism, subnnational financing, and regional debt. Before joining the Spanish central bank in 2011, she worked for the Fundación de las Cajas de Ahorros.

Christian Ebeke is an economist in the IMF's European Department, where he is part of the euro area team. He previously worked with the European Department's Poland team, covering the fiscal and the real sectors. Mr. Ebeke has published a number of papers on a range of topics in macroeconomic stability, international finance, fiscal policy, natural resources, and international migration. He holds a PhD in economics from the University of Auvergne in France.

Yehenew Endegnanew is an economist in the IMF's Fiscal Affairs Department. Before joining the IMF, he was a researcher at the National Bank of Ethiopia. His research interests and published works primarily focus on fiscal issues in developing countries. He holds a PhD from the Autonomous University of Barcelona.

Luc Eyraud is a deputy division chief in the Fiscal Policy Division of the IMF's Fiscal Affairs Department. He has also worked in the IMF's African Department and the Western Hemisphere Department. Before joining the IMF in 2007, Mr. Eyraud served as a civil servant at the French Treasury. He has published extensively on various fiscal issues, in particular the reform of fiscal rules in Europe, the design of fiscal decentralization, and fiscal multipliers.

Lorenzo Forni is currently a professor of economics at the University of Padua in Italy. He worked in the IMF's Fiscal Affairs Department from 2010 to 2016 and previously at the Research Department of the Bank of Italy. He has written on a number of macroeconomic topics, ranging from the economic impact of fiscal policy to the role of public debt, from the effects of structural reforms to inflation convergence in the European monetary union. He has published in important journals such as the *American Economic Review* and the *Journal of Public Economics*. He holds a master's in political economy and a PhD in economics from Boston University (2001) and has been visiting scholar at Harvard University (2005–06).

Vitor Gaspar is the director of the IMF's Fiscal Affairs Department. Before joining the IMF, he held a variety of senior policy positions in Banco de Portugal, including most recently as a special adviser. He served as Minister of State and Finance of Portugal from 2011 to 2013. He was head of the European Commission's Bureau of European Policy Advisers from 2007 to 2010 and director-general of research at the European Central Bank from 1998 to 2004. Mr. Gaspar holds a PhD and a postdoctoral agregado in economics from Universidade Nova de Lisboa. He has also studied at Universidade Católica Portuguesa.

Marc Gérard is an economist at the IMF, where has been working on macrofiscal and financial sector issues on low-income emerging market and advanced economies. He holds a PhD in economics from the University of Paris Ouest.

Sanjeev Gupta is a deputy director in the IMF's Fiscal Affairs Department and previously worked in the IMF's African Department and European Department. Mr. Gupta has led IMF missions to about 25 countries in Africa, Asia, Europe, and the Middle East. Before joining the IMF, he was a fellow of the Kiel Institute of World Economics, Germany; a professor in the Administrative Staff College of India, Hyderabad; and Secretary of the Federation of Indian Chambers of Commerce and Industry. Mr. Gupta has authored or coauthored more than 150 papers on macroeconomic and fiscal issues, many of which are published in well-known academic journals. He has also has authored, coauthored, or coedited 11 books, including three recently published by the IMF: *The Economics of Public Health Care Reform in Advanced and Emerging Economies* (2012), *Energy Subsidy Reform: Lessons and Implications* (2013), *Equitable and Sustainable Pensions: Challenges and Experiences* (2014), and *Fiscal Policy and Inequality* (2015).

Fabian Gunzinger is a graduate student at Oxford University, where he focuses of financial stability and financial networks. He was previously an economist at the Swiss National Bank and has received a BSc and a MSc in economics from the University of Bern.

Mark Hallerberg is a professor of public management and political economy at the Hertie School of Governance. His research focuses on fiscal governance, tax competition, financial crises, and European Union politics. He previously held academic positions at Emory University, where he maintains an affiliation with the political science department, as well as at the University of Pittsburgh and Georgia Institute of Technology. He received a PhD from the University of California–Los Angeles in 1995.

Jason Harris is an economist in the Public Financial Management Division I of the IMF's Fiscal Affairs Department. He previously worked in the Australian Treasury preparing the Commonwealth Budget, and as an economic and fiscal adviser to the Australian Prime Minister. He has also spent 2 years at the Papua New Guinea Treasury, helping to prepare the country's budget.

João Tovar Jalles is an economist in the IMF's Fiscal Affairs Department. He was previously an economist in the OECD's Economics Department where he was responsible for Portugal and Brazil. Before that, João was a fiscal economist at the European Central Bank, responsible for Malta and part of the Troika team for the Portuguese bailout program. João has also held visiting positions such as visiting scholar at the IMF's Research Department and at the Bank of Portugal's Research Department. He was an invited lecturer at Sciences Po in France and an assistant professor at the University of Aberdeen in the United Kingdom. He has also taught at the University of Cambridge in the United Kingdom and Universidade Nova de Lisboa in Portugal. João has worked mainly on fiscal-related topics and has published more than 50 academic papers in refereed journals. He has received a BSc, MSc, and PhD in economics from Universidade Nova de Lisboa, University of Warwick in the United Kingdom, and the University of Cambridge, respectively.

Laura Jaramillo is a deputy division chief in the Fiscal Operations II Division in the IMF's Fiscal Affairs Department. Since joining the IMF, she has worked on advanced, emerging market, and low-income economies in Africa, Europe, and Latin America. Her latest research focuses on the nexus between taxation, productivity, and growth, and on the drivers of public debt. She also worked at the Ministry of Finance of Colombia in the aftermath of the 1998 financial crisis. She completed graduate studies at the Princeton University Woodrow Wilson School of Public and International Affairs and undergraduate studies at Universidad Externado de Colombia and Science Po.

Tom Josephs leads the Trade Policy Directorate at the United Kingdom's Department of International Trade. He has previously worked in the Public Financial Management Division of the IMF's Fiscal Affairs Department.

Tidiane Kinda is a special assistant to the director in the Asia and Pacific Department of the IMF. He previously worked in the IMF's African Department and Fiscal Affairs Department, including in country teams covering the euro area, Canada, Chad, Croatia, Mali, Moldova, and Swaziland. Mr. Kinda previously worked in the Research Department of the World Bank and in the Research Division of the Central Bank of West African States. He has published widely on various topics, including capital flows, fiscal policy, and income inequality. He holds a PhD in economics from CERDI-Université de Clermont in France, where he taught macroeconomics and applied econometrics.

Estelle X. Liu is an economist in the IMF's Fiscal Affairs Department. She has extensive experience in fiscal issues and has worked on country-specific fiscal issues in Brazil, Nepal, and Vietnam. She has worked on global financial market issues in the IMF's Monetary and Capital Market Department; she was also the desk economist for the South Africa country team. Ms. Liu joined the IMF in 2010 and had previously worked at Hong Kong Monetary Authority.

Victor D. Lledó is a senior economist in the IMF's Fiscal Affairs Department. He is one of the IMF experts on fiscal rules, fiscal councils, and fiscal federalism, having published regularly on these topics. Mr. Lledó was the IMF Resident Representative in Mozambique, and, until recently, the Fiscal Affairs Department economist for Spain. Mr. Lledó has worked extensively with both advanced and developing economies in a number of IMF departments as well as consultant for the United Kingdom's Department for International Development and for the Brazilian government. Mr. Lledó holds a doctorate in development studies and a master's in economics from the University of Wisconsin–Madison, a master in economics from the Getúlio Vargas Foundation School of Economics, and a bachelor in economics from the University of Brasilia.

Constant Lonkeng Ngouana is currently the IMF Resident Representative for Jamaica. Before this field position, he was an economist in the IMF's Fiscal Affairs Department, where he worked on various issues including fiscal risks, the interaction between fiscal and monetary policy, and fiscal space, and contributed to *Fiscal Monitor*. He was the Fiscal Affairs Department economist for Indonesia and Jamaica. He has also worked in the IMF's African Department, where he covered several countries under IMF-supported programs, and in the Institute for Capacity Development. He holds a master's degree in international and development economics from the Economics School of Louvain, Belgium, and a PhD in economics from the University of Montreal in Canada.

Carlos Mulas-Granados is a senior economist in the IMF's Fiscal Affairs Department. Since joining the IMF in 2012, he has led research for flagship publications such as *Fiscal Monitor* and the *World Economic Outlook* and has worked on country-specific fiscal issues in Brazil, Costa Rica, Portugal, Senegal, and the euro area. He is also a tenured professor of applied economics at Complutense University (on leave) and has served as a deputy director of the Spanish Prime Minister's Economic Office. He is the author/editor of four books and has published dozens of articles in areas including political economy, fiscal adjustments, debt reduction, public investment, research and development, and inequality. He holds a PhD in economics from Cambridge University (United Kingdom), a European doctor degree in economics from Complutense University (Spain), and a master's degree in international political economy from Columbia University (United States). In 2015, he received an IMF Global Award for his research on inequality issues.

Priscilla Muthoora is an economist in the African Division of the IMF Institute for Capacity Development. She joined the IMF in 2009 and has previously worked in the IMF's Fiscal Affairs Department and in the Western Hemisphere

Department. She received a PhD in economics from the University of Oxford. Her research focuses on fiscal policy and institutions and development macroeconomics.

Dilan Ölçer is a senior economist at Riksbank, where she works on issues related to financial stability and macroprudential policy. She is also consulted by the IMF as an expert in these areas. Before joining Riksbank, she held positions at international organizations such as the IMF, World Bank, and OECD. Her research focuses on political economics, development economics, fiscal politics, and oil- and gas-rich economies. She obtained a PhD in economics from Sciences Po Paris in 2013 and was a visiting fellow at Harvard University during 2009–10. She holds a master's degree in international economics and business from the Stockholm School of Economics and a CEMS master's degree in international management jointly from HEC Paris and the Stockholm School of Economics.

Brian Olden is a deputy division chief in the Public Financial Management Division I of the IMF's Fiscal Affairs Department. Before joining the IMF, he was a regional public financial management advisor to South-East Europe and a senior economist. He has previously worked for FTI Management, Ltd., and the National Treasury Management Agency. He holds degrees from the University College of the Dublin and Dublin City University.

Eliko Pedastsaar is an economist in the Public Finance Management Division II of the IMF's Fiscal Affairs Department. She has delivered technical assistance missions to the countries in Asia, Europe, the Middle East, and the Caribbean. Before joining the IMF, she worked as a deputy budget director in the Estonian Ministry of Finance and as a member of the executive board in the Estonian Health Insurance Fund. She has taught various courses in public administration in Tallinn University. Her main areas of expertise are budget management and medium-term planning. She holds master's degrees in business administration from the Estonian Business School and in public administration from Tallinn University.

Javier J. Pérez is the head of division at the Directorate-General Economics and Statistics of Banco de España, the Spanish central bank. Before joining the Spanish central bank in 2008, he was a principal economist in the Fiscal Policies Division of the European Central Bank. Among other previous positions, he has been associate professor at University Pablo de Olavide of Seville and University Complutense of Madrid. He holds a PhD in economics from University Complutense of Madrid. He contributes regularly to international and national publications in the fields of macroeconomics, fiscal policies, fiscal federalism, and economic forecasting.

Tigran Poghosyan is an economist in the IMF's Fiscal Affairs Department, where he covers fiscal issues in the euro area and serves as an assistant to the director. He has also covered Ireland, Jordan, Lithuania, Ukraine, and Yemen in his previous assignments at the IMF and was a principal contributor to five issues of *Fiscal Monitor* over 2012–16. Before the IMF, he worked at the Central Bank of

Armenia and was a visiting researcher at the Deutsche Bundesbank. His work on banking, international finance, asset pricing, and public finance is featured in IMF research and policy publications, books, and peer-reviewed journals, including the *Journal of Money, Credit, and Banking*, the *Journal of Banking and Finance*, *Economics of Transition*, and *Empirical Economics*. He holds two PhDs in economics—one from CERGE-EI and the other from the University of Groningen.

Michela Schena is a research analyst in the IMF's Fiscal Affairs Department. She graduated from Tufts University in 2015 with a BA in international relations and economics.

Johann Seiwald has been a senior economist in the IMF's Fiscal Affairs Department since 2012. Before joining the IMF, he was the head of the Austrian Performance Management Office, where he implemented the performance budgeting and management system in Austria. Before this, he was a senior expert in the Ministry of Finance, responsible for developing the Austrian Budget Reform, and the head of the Finance Department for the penitentiary system in the Ministry of Justice.

Mauricio Soto is a senior economist at the IMF, where he has assessed the fiscal impact of social insurance programs in advanced and emerging economies (largely pensions and health). He has collaborated with the authorities of more than a dozen countries in analyzing fiscal issues over the past 5 years. Before joining the IMF, he worked as a researcher on retirement issues—first at the Center for Retirement Research at Boston College and most recently at the Urban Institute. He has authored and coauthored several papers on age-related spending, and his research has been published in *Labour*, the *Journal of Pension Economics and Finance*, and the *Journal of Financial Planning*.

Jan-Egbert Sturm is a professor of applied macroeconomics as well as the director of the KOF Swiss Economic Institute at ETH Zurich. He was previous Chair of Monetary Economics in Open Economies at the University of Konstanz in Germany, which was coupled with the position of director of the Thurgau Institute of Economics in Kreuzlingen, Switzerland from 2003 to 2005. During 2001–03, he was a professor of economics at the University of Munich and the head of the Department for Economic Forecasting and Financial Markets at the Ifo Institute for Economic Research. He is editor of the *European Journal of Political Economy* and a member of several advisory committees in Switzerland and abroad. His research relies heavily on empirical methods and statistics, concentrating on monetary economics, macroeconomics, as well as political economy and with a special interest in fields that are closely related to practical and current problems. He has published several books and has contributed articles to various anthologies and internationally renowned journals. He received a PhD from the University of Groningen in 1997.

José Tavares is professor of economics at Universidade Nova de Lisboa and an affiliate researcher at the Centre for Economic Policy Research in London. He received a PhD in economics from Harvard University, where he specialized in political economy and macroeconomics. In addition, he has taught at Harvard University, the University of California–Los Angeles, and Universidade Católica Portuguesa. His research spans a broad set of issues, including the relation between democracy and economic growth, the macroeconomic cost of gender discrimination, and the role of globalization in countering corruption. His work has been published in academic journals, including the *Journal of Monetary Economics*, the *Economics Journal*, the *Review of Economics and Statistics*, and the *Journal of Public Economics*. He has also received coverage in media outlets such as *Time* magazine, the *New York Times*, and *Handelsblatt*.

Holger van Eden recently joined the IMF's Technical Assistance Office in Thailand as a regional public financial management advisor for Southeast Asia, covering four emerging market economies—Indonesia, Malaysia, Philippines, Thailand—and four developing economies—Cambodia, Lao PDR, Myanmar, and Vietnam. He was previously the deputy division chief in the Public Financial Management II Division of the IMF's Fiscal Affairs Department. He has worked extensively with ministries of finance in Eastern Europe, Asia, and Latin America and the Caribbean. His main focus areas are budget preparation, ministry of finance institutional restructuring, budget and fiscal responsibility laws, public investment management, and government treasury and cash management. Mr. van Eden has led and participated in more than 50 IMF technical assistance missions, including to Belgium, Bhutan, Brazil, China, Colombia, Greece, India, Indonesia, Japan, Mexico, Netherlands, Mongolia, and Thailand. At the IMF he has had a leadership role in developing IMF research and board papers on reform of budget institutions, public investment management, and fiscal transparency. Before joining the IMF, he worked as team leader and project coordinator in international consultancy, as an economic journalist and editor, and as a financial consultant for a global accounting firm. He started his career in the Dutch Ministry of Finance.

Geneviève Verdier is the deputy division chief of the Expenditure Policy Division of the IMF's Fiscal Affairs Department. Before joining the IMF, she was an assistant professor at Texas A&M University. She also previously worked as an economist in the Research Department of the Bank of Canada, as well as the IMF's Strategy, Policy, and Review Department; the African Department; and the Institute for Capacity Development. She earned a PhD from the University of British Columbia. Her work to date and publications in IMF research and policy publications, books, and peer-reviewed journals cover a wide range of macroeconomic issues related to public spending efficiency, public investment, sovereign debt restructuring, economic growth, international macroeconomics, and financial development.

Jürgen von Hagen is a professor of economics and the director of the Institut für Internationale Wirtschaftspolitik at the University of Bonn. He is also the vice president of the Public Finance Council of Portugal. He has previously been the director of the Center for European Integration in Bonn, a research fellow of the Centre for Economic Policy Research , a senior fellow of Bruegel, and a member of the Academic Advisory Council to the German Federal Minister of Economics and Labor. He has been a consultant or a visiting scholar at the European Commission, the European Parliament, the World Bank, the Inter-American Development Bank, the Federal Reserve of Saint Louis, and the IMF. His teaching appointments include the University of Bonn, Indiana University, and the University of Mannheim. His research interests include macroeconomics of European integration and the euro area and European public finance. He has published in major international economic journals, and his acclaimed work on European integration addresses public finance and political economy issues has been widely cited. He holds a master's and PhD in economics from the University of Bonn.

Anke Weber is an economist in the IMF's European Department and previously was in the IMF's Fiscal Affairs and Middle East and Central Asia departments. Before joining the IMF, Ms. Weber obtained a PhD in macroeconomics from the University of Cambridge. She has published articles on fiscal policy and growth, fiscal rules, central bank communication, and the role of expectations in macroeconomics.

Philippe Wingender is an economist in the IMF's Fiscal Affairs Department. Mr. Wingender joined the IMF after obtaining his PhD in economics from the University of California, Berkeley. His research interests include the incidence of tax reform, taxation and informality and the macroeconomic effects of fiscal policy. His articles have appeared in the *National Tax Journal* and a number of books. As an IMF economist, he has worked in several countries, including China, as well as on Uganda, Bosnia and Herzegovina, Kosovo, and Trinidad and Tobago.

Sami Yläoutinen is the director general in charge of economic policy coordination in the Finnish Ministry of Finance. Previously employed by the Bank of Finland, he joined the Ministry in 1999 and has since held several positions at the Ministry. During 2011–14 he worked in the IMF's Fiscal Affairs Department. He holds a Doctor of Sciences in economics, and his dissertation focused on fiscal frameworks.

Introduction

CHAPTER 1

Fiscal Politics

VITOR GASPAR, SANJEEV GUPTA, AND
CARLOS MULAS-GRANADOS

INTRODUCTION

Fiscal Politics seeks to capture the politics of fiscal policymaking, and thus revives a tradition in political economy that gradually left the mainstream. This tradition takes economic, social, and political processes as co-determined and co-evolutionary.[1] The inspiration for the book's title comes from the work of the Austrian economist Joseph Schumpeter, drawing on his two seminal contributions: a theory of democracy and the concept of the tax state.

In *Capitalism, Socialism and Democracy*, Schumpeter (1942) defines democratic regimes as a set of institutions leading to a struggle for political power—a competition to win the people's vote and gain the right to exercise that power. This view influenced the work of subsequent political economists, most notably Downs (1957), who portrayed electoral politics as a fight for the median voter.

A second fundamental source of inspiration for the book is Schumpeter's concept of the modern tax state, which reflects an underlying tension between two forces.[2] On the one hand, the modern state is intertwined with social and political dynamics; on the other, it requires that private and civil spheres be allowed to develop separately from it. In Schumpeter's view, public finances go beyond economics narrowly defined, as captured in his statement, "The spirit of a people, its cultural level, its social structure, the deeds its policy may prepare—all this and more is written in its fiscal history" (Schumpeter 1991, 101).

Several authors have since given political and institutional factors a key role in the analysis of state building, taxation, and economic development. Most notably, Besley and Persson (2011, 2013, 2014a, 2014b) expand the concept of minimal state capacity originally developed by Adam Smith and add a Schumpeterian flavor to the range of capabilities that any modern state needs to function effectively.[3]

[1] For further details on this concept, see Hayek (1978, 1988).

[2] In 1918, Joseph Schumpeter wrote *The Crisis of the Tax State* (Schumpeter 1991), where he affirmed that the expression "tax state" could be considered a pleonasm.

[3] "Smith listed 'peace, easy taxes, and a tolerable administration of justice' as sufficient conditions for prosperity. His three pillars of prosperity are broadly the same as ours although with a somewhat different emphasis" (Besley and Persson 2011, 10). In Besley and Persson's view, peace refers to the

In the contributions of these authors, the capacities that define modern states are both economic and political in nature.

In a similar vein, this book is based on the premise that economics and politics are profoundly intertwined. For example, when the economy performs poorly, incumbent governments find it difficult to implement their policy agendas and are likely to lose power in the next elections. The opposite tends to be true during good times. When political uncertainty increases, investment decisions are postponed and markets can become volatile (Alesina and Perotti 1996b; Brandon and Yook 2012; Pastor and Veronesi 2013; Chang and others 2013). When combined with low growth and rising inequality, which fuel populism and protectionism, political uncertainty can become a serious threat to economic prosperity (Alesina and others 1996; IMF 2016).

Even during times of political stability, electoral outcomes and political polarization can affect economic policies and the state of the economy (Alesina and Rosenthal 1995; Acemoglu and Robinson 2013). Different political parties running for office target different economic outcomes of output growth and income equality. These distinctive objectives, coupled with uncertainty about the election results, make macroeconomic outcomes unpredictable and could generate unexpected recessions or expansions. Politics influences economic outcomes through various channels, including structural reforms and monetary and fiscal policies.

This book is about how politics affects policies on the fiscal front. Do elections affect budgetary policies? Is political fragmentation associated with the degree of fiscal discipline? What is the role of political ideology? If politics affects fiscal outcomes, can fiscal rules and institutions make a difference?

To address these questions, the chapter authors rely on past findings and offer new perspectives. Although the details vary and depend on country-specific circumstances, scholars have identified specific political patterns that have improved our understanding of fiscal outcomes.[4] The main lesson is that politics, whether at the national or supranational level, matters for fiscal policymaking. Unfortunately, this topic was neglected during the years of prosperity before the global crisis and, in light of the ongoing difficulties in implementing growth-friendly fiscal policies in the aftermath of the financial meltdown, further work is needed in this area. Minimizing political distortions to fiscal policy requires a sound understanding of the mechanisms through which political activity affects the budget. This book makes a contribution to this effect, motivated by the need to adapt fiscal policy advice to evolving political and economic circumstances.

---

absence of internal conflict and political repression; easy taxes means taxes that are easily extracted and broad based; and justice means finding ways of ensuring that the state supports contracts, enforces property rights, and limits (public or private) predation. These authors consider that modern state capacity involves three key dimensions: (1) fiscal capacity for tax collection; (2) legal capacity to secure market functioning, enforce contracts, and protect property rights; and (3) collective capacity to supply public goods.

[4] For recent literature reviews on the political economy of fiscal policy, see Katsimi and Sarantides (2012); Klomp and de Haan (2013a, 2013b); and Alesina and Passalacqua (2015).

Although the book's coverage of topics is comprehensive, it does not delve into issues such as the electoral consequences of fiscal adjustments, the impact of budget cuts on inequality, or the relationship between austerity and the recent wave of populist politics.

The book makes four contributions. First, in contrast to most of the existing literature on the political economy of fiscal policy that focuses on developed economies, this book also presents empirical evidence from advanced, emerging, and developing countries. Second, it goes beyond the typical concentration on electoral politics and uses a combination of electoral calendar variables, measures of political fragmentation, and indicators of ideological polarization to explain how political factors affect fiscal outcomes. Third, it examines the relevance of deeper political, historical, and institutional forces that influence the budget at the national and international levels. Finally, this volume not only describes the political bias embedded in fiscal policy decisions, but also proposes smart rules and strong fiscal institutions to bring fiscal outcomes closer to their optimum.

HOW POLITICS AFFECTS FISCAL POLICY

Fiscal policy, which was once defined as "the matter of who gets what, when, and how" (Laswell 1936, 19), is heavily influenced by political factors. A typical government performs three core functions: allocation, distribution, and stabilization (Musgrave 1959).[5] All of these functions are intrinsically political. Politics has a direct impact on the provision of public goods and is of particular relevance with regard to stabilization and redistributive policies. For example, when the executive branch of government runs a fiscal deficit to stabilize the economy, a political decision with intergenerational implications is involved. Similarly, subsequent discussions in the parliament about the composition of revenues and expenditures are the result of bargaining in the political process that has an impact on income distribution and can generate unintended economic outcomes.

The literature on the political economy of fiscal policy dates back to the nineteenth century when the Italian and Swedish schools of public finance began to analyze how governments choose policies (Alesina and Tabellini 1990). During the twentieth century, the Public Choice school continued this work and focused on the political incentives and constraints in policy formulation. For example, the work of Buchanan (1960) and Buchanan and Wagner (1976) stressed the inability of voters to understand the intricacies of fiscal policy and the government's tendency to deviate from the optimal path. This discussion revived the interest of scholars in the political determinants of fiscal policy. Initially, the new political economy models sought to explain deviations from the tax-smoothing framework (Barro 1979), under which public debt was the result of an optimal fiscal

[5]The stabilization function works to ensure the achievement of high employment and price stability; the redistribution function aims to achieve an equitable distribution of income; and the allocation function sees that resources are used efficiently.

policy aimed at smoothing tax rates over time. These political economy models aimed to explain observed fluctuations in deficits and public debt arising from institutional factors mediated by electoral constraints. These new models varied substantially in the type of electoral system,[6] the degree of fiscal centralization,[7] and the budgetary laws[8] under which fiscal policy decisions were made. But in general, their most important contribution was to develop a framework by which the effect of political factors on fiscal economic decisions could be empirically tested.[9] Since then, three sets of factors have systematically been shown to influence fiscal policies: (1) the date of elections when voters have the opportunity to reward or punish the government for its economic policies; (2) the ideology of the party in government with respect to the size and role of the state in the economy; and (3) the degree of political fragmentation, which determines how many actors participate in fiscal policy decisions.

Proximity of Elections

Elections mainly affect the stabilization and redistribution functions of the government. Proximity of elections can influence the government's budget decisions in various ways.

First, if the government believes that its prospects of getting reelected will be better when the economy is growing, it may consider launching a fiscal expansion before the elections. Such behavior would generate political budget cycles.[10] Moreover, if this action is not fully compensated for during the incumbent's tenure, it will lead to debt accumulation from one political cycle to the next. This bias requires two assumptions: fiscal illusion among voters, according to which they overestimate the benefits of current expenditures and underestimate the future tax burden that will be needed to finance current expenditure;[11] and voter ignorance, implying that voters find it difficult to fully understand the details of the budget's composition and its long-term impact.

The second type of electoral effect on fiscal policies is related to the first and has to do with the strategic use of debt by the incumbent government. For example, a conservative government that dislikes the provision of public goods, and is certain that it is going to be followed by a leftist government that is in favor of expanding the provision of such goods, may strategically leave less funds for

[6] For the effects of electoral systems on fiscal policy, see Grilli, Masciandaro, and Tabellini (1991); Hallerberg and von Hagen (1997); and Milesi-Ferretti, Perotti, and Rostagno (2002).

[7] For a review of theories of fiscal federalism, see Ter-Minassian (1997), and for a political economy perspective on fiscal decentralization, see Lockwood (2005).

[8] For the effects of different budgetary rules related to spending limits, see Hallerberg and von Hagen (1997) and Perotti (1998).

[9] For a literature review on the political economy of budget deficits and debt, see Alesina and Perotti (1995); de Wolff (1998); Persson and Tabellini (2002); Franzese (2002); Mulas-Granados (2006); and Alesina and Passalacqua (2015).

[10] See Nordhaus (1975) and Alesina, Roubini, and Cohen (1997).

[11] See Buchanan and Wagner (1976) for fiscal illusion.

the incoming government. By leaving a sizable debt for the successor government, the conservative government would tie the hands of the leftist government and oblige it to raise new taxes (which is unpopular), not comply with its electoral program of expansion of public services (which will cause strong disappointment among its supporters), or both. With this strategic use of the debt, the incumbent conservative government would dramatically increase its chances of defeating the new government in the next elections.[12]

We find support for this type of fiscal behavior in chapters included in this volume. As other scholars have noted, the intensity of political budget cycles is higher in younger democracies and in less transparent systems (Klomp and de Haan 2013a, 2013b), and is behind the delay in implementing necessary fiscal adjustments (Mierau, Jong-A-Pin, and de Haan 2007).[13]

In addition to proximity of elections, deviations from optimal behavior are explained by other political variables, such as the cabinet's ideology and, most important, by political fragmentation.

Ideology of the Cabinet

Parties in government are motivated by the objective of remaining in office and by their specific policy agenda following (in part) from their political ideology (Muller and Strom 1999).[14] Ideology of the party in government tends to surface in tax-and-spend policies linked to the government's redistribution function, but it can also influence fiscal policy decisions about macroeconomic stabilization.

The first contributions to the literature on stabilization policies date back to the 1970s, when Hibbs (1977, 1987) supported the thesis that left-wing governments fought unemployment while right-wing governments were especially worried about inflation. Subsequent studies provided empirical evidence that left-wing

---

[12] See Persson and Svensson (1989) for a concrete example. For a more general overview of the models that analyze the strategic use of debt, see de Wolff (1998) and Franzese (2002).

[13] Broad empirical evidence on the existence of political budget cycles can be found in Persson and Tabellini (2002); Drazen and Eslava (2010); or Alesina and Paradisi (2015). Klomp and de Haan (2013b) introduce some nuances and show that the size of political budget cycles is higher in developing countries than in advanced economies. Similarly, other papers report evidence suggesting that the occurrence and strength of manipulation of fiscal policy for electoral purposes depend on a variety of accompanying factors, such as the level of development and institutional quality (Shi and Svensson 2006), the maturity and age of democracy (Brender and Drazen 2005), constitutional provisions determining electoral rules and form of government (Persson and Tabellini 2002, 2003), transparency of the political process (Alt and Lassen 2006a, 2006b), the presence of checks and balances (Streb and Torrens 2013), or credible fiscal rules (Rose 2006; Alt and Rose 2009).

[14] We depart from Downs' statement that political parties "formulate policies in order to win elections, rather than win elections in order to formulate policies" (Downs 1957, 28). The chapters in the present volume assume that political parties are guided by two objectives at the same time: the pursuit of policy and the pursuit of office. This approach contrasts with pure policy seekers and pure office seekers (Muller and Strom 1999). The collective view underlying the different contributions in this book is that parties in government seek to maximize both objectives simultaneously, because staying in office guarantees further influence on the policy agenda, and delivering on the policies preferred by citizens typically increases the chances of remaining in office.

cabinets favored expansionary fiscal policies to accelerate aggregate demand as a means of reaching full employment, while right-wing cabinets maintained small and balanced budgets favoring market-led full employment equilibrium (Alesina and Rosenthal 1995; Boix 1997). In parallel, evidence showed that fiscal policies on the demand side had only temporary effects (Alesina 1989; Alesina and Roubini 1992), were inflationary (Álvarez, Garrett, and Lange 1991), and were difficult to implement in open economies (Alt 1985; Alesina and Summers 1993; Frieden and Rogowski 1996; Hall 1986; Garrett 1998).[15] Thus, political parties were only left with the possibility to affect economic policies on the supply side. Here again, some partisan differences in macroeconomic policies were found, indicating that left-wing governments were likely to implement interventionist supply-side policies, through the public provision of human and physical capital, to increase growth and the competitiveness of the economy (Boix 2000; Franzese 2002; Notermans 2000; Mulas-Granados 2006). This book presents some evidence that left-wing governments are associated with higher rates of growth in public investment.

Ideology heavily influences fiscal policies that pertain to redistribution. Left-wing parties draw their support from workers and the middle- and low-income segments of the population. Thus, they pay particular attention to income inequality, redistribution, social benefits, and interventionist supply-side policies in the form of public provision of human and physical capital. One would expect left-wing governments to be associated with higher public expenditures on welfare policies and a sizable public administration. To finance these expenditures, these governments would be expected to tax more and to tax more progressively (Angelopoulos, Economides, and Kammas 2012).[16] The book shows that after banking crises and during fiscal adjustment episodes, left-wing governments are associated with different revenue-raising measures than right-leaning governments.

In contrast, right-wing governments would prefer a less activist role for the government and would favor a stronger role for the private sector. Right-wing parties obtain their votes mostly from the economically stronger segments of the population (or at least with average income above the median voter's income). These voters have more private resources to smooth their personal consumption in periods of economic downturn; they are more concerned about inflation; and as potential private investors, they suffer most from the crowding-out effect of public intervention in the economy. Thus, right-wing governments would prefer to run balanced and small budgets. Lower levels of public spending would require lower levels of public revenue, meaning less distortionary taxes on market

[15] For a longer review of the initial literature on partisan economic policy management, see Boix (1997).

[16] Higher public expenditures financed by higher public revenues do not mean that left-wing governments run deficits more often than right-wing governments (Boix 1997; Franzese 2002; Notermans 2000). According to these authors, to intervene on the supply side of the economy through public investment, left-wing governments would prefer surplus or close to balanced budgets.

activities. The implication is that right-wing governments would tax and spend less than left-wing governments (Volverink and de Haan 2001).

Although the cabinet's ideology is an important predictor of fiscal policy, it does not always play the same role, especially when the government's credibility is at stake and they need to reassure financial markets. In this context, Tavares (2004) and Kraft (2016) show that cabinets signal commitment and gain credibility by pursuing fiscal adjustments in ways not favored by their constituents (that is, the left cuts expenditures and the right increases taxes). According to Starke, Kaasch, and van Hooren (2014), partisanship may play a different role than expected depending on the degree of development of the underlying welfare state (that is, in more developed welfare states, ideology is a weaker predictor of government's likely actions).

Political Fragmentation

Most studies focusing on the political economy of fiscal deficit and public debt find that fragmentation in decision making is damaging for expenditure control and eventually for fiscal discipline. Political fragmentation affects the three government functions—the provision of public goods, stabilization, and income redistribution. In the presence of multiple parties with different ideologies, achieving consensus on balanced budgets is difficult because every party will have its favorite spending program, but it will only internalize a part of the costs and distortions of the associated increase in revenues needed to finance spending. This is the "common pool problem" put forward by Weingast, Shepsle, and Johnsen (1981).[17]

The larger the number of actors with a voice in the fiscal decision-making process, the stronger the pressure for more expenditures, and thus the greater the deviation from optimal fiscal policy. Political fragmentation affects the stabilization function of the government because the pace and size of fiscal consolidations can be contentious. For example, coalition governments or big cabinets (with many spending ministries) would be less likely to undertake a fiscal adjustment. Alesina and Drazen (1991) show how the distributional struggle among different interest groups delays the adoption of the efficient policy of balancing the budget. They further show that the more polarized the groups are in a country, the longer stabilization is delayed. The predictions arising from this theoretical work have been confirmed by empirical studies. For example, Roubini and Sachs (1989); Grilli, Masciandaro, and Tabellini (1991); and Volverink and de Haan (2001) find that fragmented governments tend to be associated with larger public deficits. Perotti and Kontopoulos (2002) and Illera and Mulas-Granados (2008) show that the size and duration of fiscal consolidations is negatively affected by political fragmentation. In general,

[17] The origin of this idea can be traced to Hardin (1968). In addition, note that many studies link the electoral system (majoritarian, proportional, and so on) with the subsequent degree of political fragmentation. See Persson and Tabellini (2002) and Golosov (2015) for an overview of this literature.

minority governments, divided legislatures, coalitions, and multiparty cabinets, along with a weak coordinating role for the ministry of finance, are associated with fiscal profligacy and low productive investment (Hallerberg and von Hagen 1997; von Hagen, Hallett, and Strauch 2001; Hallerberg, Strauch, and von Hagen 2007).

The number and strength of political and institutional veto players helps explain why spending cuts are so difficult to implement. A government system with a large number of veto players (Tsebelis 1995, 2000, 2002) tends to preserve the status quo. Changes only materialize when a certain number of institutional or partisan actors agree. As the number of veto players increases, spending cuts and fiscal adjustment become slower, leading to suboptimal public debt accumulation (Spolaore 2004). Similarly, as the ideological distance between the government players increases, the likelihood of any policy change from the status quo decreases (Franzese 2007; Tsebelis and Chang 2004). The presence of a large number of veto players and sharp ideological polarization reduces the chances of agreeing on policy changes and stabilizing the magnitude of excessive public debt (Cox and McCubbins 2001; MacIntyre 2001; Mian, Sufi, and Trebbi 2014).

This book examines the role of political constraints and finds that strong parliamentary opposition weakens the capacity of governments to implement fiscal policies during recessions, confirming previous findings that decisive countercyclical action happens under unified governments (Armingeon 2012). It shows that political fragmentation (measured by both "common pool" and "veto players" indicators) is associated with higher public debt accumulation.

WHAT CAN BE DONE ABOUT THE INFLUENCE OF POLITICS ON FISCAL POLICY?

To date, the main response intended to reduce the influence of political factors on fiscal policymaking has been the introduction of fiscal rules and frameworks to restrain the budgetary discretion of politicians. The book presents mixed evidence on the role of these institutions.

Fiscal rules to constrain political distortions in the budget were introduced in many countries from the 1990s onward (IMF 2009). According to Solow (2004, 30–31), the main reason for imposing rules is, "Whenever discretionary fiscal policy rises to the top of the political agenda, special interests come out of the woodwork. Every tax change, every increase or decrease in public spending is fought over by the potential winners and losers, their lobbyists and elected representatives. The final outcome may often be distributionally and allocationally, and even macroeconomically, perverse. . . . Note that this is not some kind of minor flaw in the system; it *is* the system."

Those who argue in favor of rules-based fiscal policy also support reliance on automatic stabilizers to smooth macroeconomic shocks (Buti and van den Noord 2004). Because political factors could always force sovereign governments to violate fiscal rules, such rules should be well-designed (clearly defined, simple, transparent, consistent, and flexible), allow effective implementation (by entailing ex ante and ex post compliance and efficient monitoring), and be enforceable (in terms of decision making, amendment, and sanctions).[18]

The use of fiscal rules is, on average, associated with improved fiscal performance (IMF 2009; Schaechter and others 2015). If rules are designed to prevent conflicts with the stabilization function of fiscal policy, they are indeed associated with less procyclical policies (Debrun and others 2008). But fiscal rules are often introduced to lock in earlier consolidation efforts rather than being implemented at the beginning of the fiscal adjustment. The positive association between fiscal rules and fiscal performance may generally reflect changes in countries' attitudes toward fiscal rectitude—determining both the improved fiscal performance and the introduction of rules.

Fiscal institutions are crucial for fiscal policy (Alesina and Perotti 1996a), especially in the presence of ideological fragmentation (de Haan, Jong-A-Pin, and Mierau 2013).[19] Fiscal frameworks not involving formal rules but focused on transparent and credible strategies backed by proper fiscal institutions can also provide a viable approach to supporting fiscal discipline. Recent evidence has shown that countries with stronger budget institutions have more sustainable public finances (Dabla-Norris and others 2010; IMF 2014). Specifically, countries with comprehensive fiscal reporting, forecasting, and risk disclosure seem to be less vulnerable to political biases in fiscal policy. Those with more credible medium-term frameworks, performance budgeting systems, and intergovernmental fiscal arrangements are quicker to announce adjustment plans and better at protecting public investment. And countries with more unified and disciplined budget processes are more effective in implementing budget plans. This book shows that in developing countries, strengthening fiscal institutions such as public financial management systems or linking annual budgets to medium-term budget frameworks could mitigate the political pressures to overspend. This is particularly important in countries that are highly dependent on natural resource revenues.

Finally, independent fiscal councils have been introduced to provide independent information and analysis and to monitor compliance with government's own commitments and legislated fiscal rules. The IMF (2013) asserted that, all else equal, well-designed fiscal councils can promote stronger fiscal discipline.[20] Different analyses point to a number of key features of effective fiscal councils (Debrun and Kinda 2014): strict operational independence from politics, the provision of public assessment of budgetary forecasts, strong presence in the public debate (notably through an effective communication strategy), and an explicit role in monitoring fiscal policy rules. The book provides additional evidence

---

[18] For a discussion of how fiscal rules should be designed, see Kopits and Symansky (1998).

[19] These authors find that strong budgetary institutions, whether they are based on delegation to a strong minister of finance or on fiscal contracts, reduce the deficit bias in European Union countries, especially in the presence of strong ideological fragmentation.

[20] In the context of the European Union's fiscal rules, Larch and Braendle (2016) advocate transferring the stabilization function from national governments to independent fiscal councils.

on the positive impact of fiscal councils in further constraining the influence of politics on fiscal policy.

ORGANIZATION AND MAIN FINDINGS OF THIS BOOK

This book consists of three parts: Part I explores how domestic political factors affect fiscal policy outcomes. It focuses on the impact that elections, ideology, and fragmentation of decision making have on fiscal policy variables such as the public deficit, debt, revenues, or expenditures. Part II examines how institutions, fiscal rules, and fiscal councils can reduce the impact of politics on fiscal policy and improve fiscal results. Part III analyzes the interaction between political factors and institutions in supranational governance frameworks, such as those involving the European Union and the IMF.

Three principal messages can be gleaned from the book: First, politics has a decisive influence on fiscal policy formulation and performance because fiscal policy is itself intrinsically political. Second, fiscal rules and budget institutions help attenuate the effect of politics on fiscal policy but are ineffective at forcing political actors to act against their own will. Third, while supranational rules and institutions exert influence on domestic fiscal policymaking, long-lasting good fiscal behavior requires ownership on the part of national political systems.

The book starts by looking at whether governments stick to their own fiscal policy plans. In Chapter 2, Sanjeev Gupta, João Tovar Jalles, Carlos Mulas-Granados, and Michela Schena analyze the political causes and consequences of fiscal consolidation promise gaps, defined as the distance between planned fiscal adjustments and actual consolidations. The consolidation promise gaps can be sizable (about 0.3 percent of GDP per year, or 1.1 percent of GDP during an average three-year adjustment episode). Three political factors explain these consolidation gaps: First, proximity to elections reduces the promise gap as policymakers seek to show voters that they are capable of delivering on their announced plans. Second, greater political strength—the government's control of parliament and weakness of the opposition—is associated with smaller promise gaps. At the same time, democratic accountability is important for the reduction of promise gaps. The authors find that governments that delivered on their promised fiscal consolidation plans were rewarded by financial markets and not penalized by voters.

Chapter 3, by Christian Ebeke and Dilan Ölçer, analyzes the impact of elections on fiscal policy and offers evidence on the potential role of fiscal rules in reducing electoral budget cycles. Focusing on low-income countries, the authors investigate the behavior of fiscal variables during and after elections. The results indicate that during election years, government consumption significantly increases and leads to larger budget deficits. During the two years following elections, the fiscal adjustment is carried out through increases in trade taxes and cuts to government investment, with no significant reductions in government consumption. The authors find evidence that the presence of both fiscal rules and IMF programs helps dampen the magnitude of the political budget cycle in low-income countries.

In addition to the role of elections and fragmentation, Chapter 4 introduces another political factor—ideology—that influences fiscal policymaking. Mark Hallerberg and Jürgen von Hagen discuss how partisanship can affect tax policy decisions, both during fiscal consolidations and in normal times in advanced economies. They find that economic factors (such as banking crises) affect tax rates, but there is a political dimension to these tax changes: left-wing governments are less likely than right-wing governments to increase the value-added tax rate and more likely to increase the top personal income tax rate as part of a pronounced fiscal consolidation, but there seem to be no partisan effects on tax policy during normal times. The effect of elections on tax policy is negligible, with only a corporate income tax rate increase more likely the year after an election.

The next three chapters explore the effects of politics on different components of public expenditures. In Chapter 5, Sanjeev Gupta, Estelle X. Liu, and Carlos Mulas-Granados provide empirical evidence of the impact of elections on public investment. Looking at a large sample of presidential and parliamentary democracies across developed and developing countries, they find that the growth rate of public investment is higher at the beginning of electoral cycles and decelerates thereafter. This happens because government consumption expenditure is more visible than capital expenditure before elections. The peak in public investment growth occurs 28 months before elections, and each month closer to the next election, the growth rate of public investment declines by 0.7 percentage point. Other political variables, such as cabinet ideology and government fragmentation, have less influence on short-term public investment dynamics but are more relevant in the medium term.[21]

Chapter 6, by Yehenew Endegnanew, Mauricio Soto, and Geneviève Verdier, examines the impact of elections on the government wage bill. By taking advantage of a newly assembled database comprising advanced, emerging, and low-income countries, they find that elections increase the share of the government wage bill to GDP, particularly in nonadvanced economies: at current levels of the wage bill, elections result in an increase of about 0.2 percent of GDP in emerging market economies and low-income countries. In addition, election-year increases in the wage bill tend to be associated more with increases in government employment than with changes in pay, with the exception of emerging economies, where government pay also tends to increase.

The role of political fragility and the interaction between social spending and energy subsidies is discussed by Christian Ebeke and Constant Lonkeng Ngouana in Chapter 7. They present a model in which high energy subsidies and low

[21] In addition to the short-term evidence on electoral investment cycles shown in Chapter 5, Gupta, Liu, and Mulas-Granados (2015) report results on the impact of political fragmentation and cabinet ideology for medium-term public investment booms that span several election cycles.

public social spending can emerge as an equilibrium outcome of a political game between the elite and the middle class when the delivery of the public good is subject to weak domestic institutions. They find that public spending on education and health was, on average, two-thirds percentage point of GDP lower in countries where energy subsidies were 1 percentage point of GDP higher than the average. Moreover, this trade-off is larger in a context of political ineffectiveness, measured by an index of fragmentation and political fragility.

In Chapter 8, Fabian Gunzinger and Jan-Egbert Sturm provide additional evidence that political fragmentation can generate suboptimal fiscal policy outcomes. They quantify the effect of the fragmentation of power on the size of fiscal stimulus packages put in place in response to the Great Recession. On average, more political fragmentation (measured by the degree of legislative control that parliaments exert over governments) reduced the size of a country's fiscal stimulus package by between 1.0 and 2.7 percentage points of GDP. In contrast, in contexts with lower or no fragmentation, government stimulus packages were sizable. Among all the political variables tested in the model, the presence of political fragmentation and constraints (for example, strong parliamentary opposition) was by far the most robust political factor explaining the differences observed in countercyclical fiscal policies to stimulate the economy after deep recessions.

In the final chapter of the first part of the book (Chapter 9), Ernesto Crivelli, Sanjeev Gupta, Carlos Mulas-Granados, and Carolina Correa-Caro study the impact of fragmented politics on public debt. The chapter shows a strong positive association between political fragmentation and public debt changes between two consecutive legislative elections. This effect holds true for all indicators associated with "common pool" and "veto player" theories. Common pool indicators are those that capture the political pressures for additional spending, whereas the veto player indicators help identify the political sources of resistance to reform. This chapter shows that corruption magnifies the negative effects of political fragmentation on public debt accumulation. For example, in countries with high corruption, high political fragmentation (measured by weak majorities in the parliament or a large number of ministries) multiplies the increase in public debt. Finally, the introduction of fiscal councils helps attenuate the negative impact of political fragmentation on public debt dynamics.

Part II of the book focuses on how institutions, fiscal rules, and fiscal councils can reshape politics and have positive effects on fiscal policy outcomes. In Chapter 10, Vitor Gaspar, Laura Jaramillo, and Philippe Wingender illustrate via case studies the nature of the political conditions and institutions that characterized countries as they crossed a specific tax-to-GDP-growth tipping point. The existence of such a tipping point is interpreted as likely to come from the strong association between tax, legal, and administrative capacities.[22] The chapter

[22] Gaspar, Jaramillo, and Wingender (2016) show this relationship statistically in an empirical paper using a contemporary database covering 139 countries from 1965 to 2011 and a historical database for 30 advanced economies from 1800 to 1980.

highlights three key political factors that go together with enhanced tax capacity: constitutive institutions (for example, social pacts between the elite and citizens to develop welfare state policies), inclusive politics (for example, participation of all relevant actors in collective decision making), and credible leadership. The role of constitutive institutions was evident in Spain and Colombia, as an explicit political settlement between political elites and citizens preceded tax capacity building. Both countries recognized that greater levels of taxation were essential to meet the emerging spending pressures associated with the economic, social, and institutional demands prompted by those countries' new constitutions. Inclusive politics facilitated new center-periphery agreements crucial to building new tax collection schemes, as in China and Lagos State of Nigeria. And credible leadership was clearly present across the four case studies, resulting from deliberate decisions by policymakers to implement a shift in the economic model, taking advantage of opportunities offered by economic or political crises.

Together with domestic institutions, strong external commitments can have a positive effect on fiscal discipline. In Chapter 11, João Tovar Jalles, Carlos Mulas-Granados, and José Tavares discuss how exchange rate regimes affect fiscal discipline, taking into account the effect of underlying political conditions. They present a model in which the disciplining effect of the exchange rate regime on fiscal outcomes could be affected by weak politics (defined as policymakers facing a short political horizon and fragile cohesion). Contrary to common perception but in line with similar studies, their results show that being at (or moving toward) fixed exchange rates is harmful for fiscal discipline. This outcome occurs because under fixed exchange rates, the economic cost of fiscal indiscipline and default takes longer to be felt than under alternative regimes, thus allowing policymakers to overspend. Strong politics (with distant elections and lack of fragmentation) helps induce fiscal discipline but is not enough to counter the negative impact of fixed exchange rate regimes. The authors use a synthetic control method to illustrate how the transition from flexible to fully fixed exchange rates under the euro negatively affected fiscal discipline in European countries.

The subsequent three chapters of Part II discuss how fiscal rules can help attenuate the distorting effect of political factors on fiscal policy. Chapter 12, by Till Cordes, Tidiane Kinda, Priscilla Muthoora, and Anke Weber, presents evidence suggesting that expenditure rules are associated with spending control, countercyclical fiscal policy, and improved fiscal discipline. This appears to be related to the properties of expenditure rules given that compliance rates are generally higher than with other types of rules (concerning the budget balance or debt, for example). In particular, compliance with expenditure rules is higher if the expenditure target is directly under the control of the government and if the rule is not a mere political commitment but enshrined in law or in a coalition agreement.

Chapter 13, by Andrea Bonfatti and Lorenzo Forni, demonstrates that subnational governments are able to tame the political budget cycle by using fiscal rules. The authors find that Italian municipalities subject to fiscal rules face more limited political budget cycles than municipalities not subject to rules. They find that the political budget cycle increases real capital spending by about 35 percent, on average, in the years before municipal elections, while subnational fiscal rules manage to reduce this spending by about 66 percent in municipalities where such a rule is applicable.

In Chapter 14, Mar Delgado-Téllez, Victor D. Lledó, and Javier J. Pérez propose a framework with which to study noncompliance with centrally mandated fiscal targets in Spanish regions. Their framework shows that regional fiscal noncompliance increases with the size of growth forecast errors and fiscal adjustment needs, factors not fully under the control of regional governments. But fiscal noncompliance tends to increase during election years. The chapter shows that fiscal rules have a positive impact but are not sufficient to guarantee compliance with fiscal targets at the subnational level. Enhancing fiscal compliance in countries with multilevel governance systems requires a comprehensive assessment of intergovernmental fiscal arrangements that goes beyond strengthening the rules-based framework.

The remaining two chapters of the second part of the book present evidence suggesting that strong budget processes and institutions are crucial for good fiscal performance. In Chapter 15, Sanjeev Gupta, Sami Yläoutinen, Brian Olden, Holger van Eden, Teresa Curristine, Tom Josephs, Eliko Pedastsaar, and Johann Seiwald discuss budget institutions that can support planning and delivery of credible fiscal strategies in the fiscal policymaking process. These institutions are grouped in three categories: institutions that help provide an understanding of the fiscal outlook and future challenges; institutions that are crucial to formulating a credible fiscal strategy; and finally, a third group of institutions that secure the efficient implementation of any fiscal strategy. The resulting framework is applied to low-income countries and the status of their budget institutions is compared with that prevailing in Group of 20 advanced and emerging market economies. The chapter ends with a recommendation to prioritize and sequence reform efforts regardless of surrounding political conditions.

Chapter 16, by Xavier Debrun, Marc Gérard, and Jason Harris, revisits the potential contribution of politically independent fiscal councils to improve fiscal performance. Using a simple theoretical model, these authors illustrate that fiscal councils cannot credibly exert a direct constraint on day-to-day policy choices, but they can exert an indirect influence. By contributing to the broader public debate on fiscal policy—through the provision of unbiased quantitative and qualitative analysis, forecasts, and possibly recommendations—these institutions can reduce informational asymmetries hindering voters' ability to reward good policies and penalize bad ones. The authors explore the empirical relevance of this argument by looking at the media impact of fiscal councils in relation to "real-time" fiscal developments. Evidence shows that fiscal councils' activity and media impact increase in times of budget slippages or relative fiscal activism; unfortunately, however, media impact is only weakly correlated with subsequent policy changes.

Part III of the book revisits how some of the political and institutional factors discussed in Part I and Part II affect fiscal policy in a supranational policy setting. In Chapter 17, Vitor Gaspar compares the early American experience to the ongoing European struggle to a complete Economic and Monetary Union. Following Sargent (2012), the starting point of his chapter is that the United States had to undergo a political transformation between 1789 and 1795 to make it possible to ground public finances in solid fundamentals. Because changing policy outcomes systematically requires changing the rules and incentives of politics, the U.S. experience can be useful for today's Europe in helping align political incentives with macrofiscal stability and financial integration. U.S. history shows that there is a close relationship between the different layers of fiscal policy, finance, and politics. For a program to be successful in Europe, it needs to be viable in all of these layers at the same time. One crucial element of Alexander Hamilton's program was the establishment of U.S. federal bonds as the ultimate safe asset. Similar issues are now being debated in Europe around the concept of European Safe Bonds.[23]

In Chapter 18, Luc Eyraud, Vitor Gaspar, and Tigran Poghosyan continue to explore the political sources of fiscal policy outcomes in today's Europe. This chapter provides evidence of how political factors have been associated with fiscal procyclicality, excessive deficits, distorted budget composition, and poor compliance with fiscal rules in the euro area since its creation. From a conceptual point of view, the chapter extends the analysis of political economy factors and policy distortions to the supranational level; from an empirical point of view, the chapter reviews a series of policy biases, including the relationship between country size and budget execution; and from a normative point of view, the chapter brings a novel perspective on supranational fiscal governance reforms by focusing on how to correct political incentives at the national level instead of insisting on ever more complicated rules and illusive application of rigid sanctions. A crucial factor is to ensure that the existence of supranational rules is not used to dilute the ultimate national responsibility for fiscal policy.

The final chapter of the book explores how supranational institutions such as the IMF can exert influence on national fiscal policies. Chapter 19, by Ernesto Crivelli and Sanjeev Gupta, studies whether revenue conditionality in IMF programs helped overcome domestic political barriers in implementing revenue reforms in a large number of low- and middle-income countries. Their results indicate that such conditionality had a positive impact on tax revenue, with the strongest improvement felt in taxes on goods and services, including the value-added tax. Revenue conditionality matters more for low-income countries, particularly those where revenue ratios are below the group's average. Moreover, the IMF's revenue conditionality was more effective when targeted to a specific tax because a narrow focus for tax reform helps avoid political reaction against widespread tax hikes.

[23] For further explanation and references, see Brunnermeier, James, and Landau (2016).

REFERENCES

Acemoglu, D., and J. A. Robinson. 2013. "Economics versus Politics: Pitfalls of Policy Advice." *Journal of Economic Perspectives* 27 (2): 173–92.

Alesina, A. 1989. "Politics and Business Cycles in Industrial Democracies." *Economic Policy* 8: 57–98.

———, and A. Drazen. 1991. "Why Are Stabilizations Delayed?" *American Economic Review* 81 (5): 1170–88.

Alesina, A., S. Ozler, N. Roubini, and P. Swagel. 1996. "Political Instability and Economic Growth." *Journal of Economic Growth* 1 (2): 189–211.

Alesina, A., and M. Paradisi. 2015. "Political Budget Cycles: Evidence from Italian Cities." Working Paper 20570, National Bureau of Economic Research, Cambridge, Massachusetts.

Alesina, A., and A. Passalacqua. 2015. "The Political Economy of Government Debt." Working Paper 21821, National Bureau of Economic Research, Cambridge, Massachusetts.

Alesina, A., and R. Perotti. 1995. "The Political Economy of Budget Deficits." *IMF Staff Papers* 42 (1): 1–31

———. 1996a. "Budget Deficits and Budget Institutions." Working Paper 5556, National Bureau of Economic Research, Cambridge, Massachusetts.

———. 1996b. "Income Distribution, Political Instability, and Investment." *European Economic Review* 40 (6): 1203–28.

Alesina, A., and H. Rosenthal. 1995. *Partisan Politics, Divided Government, and the Economy*. Cambridge, U.K.: Cambridge University Press.

Alesina, A., and N. Roubini. 1992. "Political Cycles: Evidence from OECD Economies." *Review of Economic Studies* 59 (4): 663–88.

———, and G. Cohen. 1997. *Political Cycles and the Macroeconomy*. Cambridge, Massachusetts: MIT Press.

Alesina, A., and L. Summers. 1993. "Central Bank Independence and Macroeconomic Performance: Some Comparative Evidence." *Journal of Money, Credit and Banking* 25 (2): 151–62.

Alesina, A., and G. Tabellini. 1990. "A Positive Theory of Fiscal Deficits and Government Debt." *Review of Economic Studies* 57 (3): 403–14.

Alt, J. 1985. "Political Parties, World Demand, and Unemployment: Domestic and International Sources of Economic Activity." *American Political Science Review* 79 (4): 1016–40.

———, and D. Lassen. 2006a. "Fiscal Transparency, Political Parties and Debt in OECD Countries." *European Economic Review* 50 (6): 1403–39.

———. 2006b. "Transparency, Political Polarization and Political Budget Cycles in OECD Countries." *American Journal of Political Science* 50 (3): 530–50.

Alt, J. E., and S. S. Rose. 2009. "Context-Conditional Political Budget Cycles." In *The Oxford Handbook of Comparative Politics*, edited by C. Boix and S. C. Stokes. Oxford, U.K.: Oxford University Press.

Álvarez, R. M., G. Garrett, and P. Lange. 1991. "Government Partisanship, Labor Organization and Macroeconomic Performance." *American Political Science Review* 85 (2): 541–56.

Angelopoulos, K., G. Economides, and P. Kammas. 2012. "Does Cabinet Ideology Matter for the Structure of Tax Policies?" *European Journal of Political Economy* 28 (4): 620–35.

Armingeon, K. 2012. "The Politics of Fiscal Responses to the Crisis of 2008–2009." *Governance* 25 (4): 543–65.

Barro, R. J. 1979. "On the Determination of the Public Debt." *Journal of Political Economy* 87 (5): 940–71.

Besley, T., and T. Persson. 2011. *Pillars of Prosperity: The Political Economics of Development Clusters*. Princeton, New Jersey: Princeton University Press.

———. 2013. "Taxation and Development." In *Handbook of Public Economics*, Volume 5, edited by A. J. Auerbach, R. Chetty, M. Feldstein, and E. Saez. Amsterdam: North Holland.

———. 2014a. "The Causes and Consequences of Development Clusters: State Capacity, Peace and Income." *Annual Review of Economics* 6 (1): 927–49.

———. 2014b. "Why Do Developing Countries Tax So Little?" *Journal of Economic Perspectives* 28 (4): 99–120.
Boix, C. 1997. "Political Parties and the Supply Side of the Economy: The Provision of Physical and Human Capital in Advanced Economies, 1960–90." *American Journal of Political Science* 41 (3): 814–45.
———. 2000. "Partisan Governments, the International Economy and Macroeconomic Policies in Advanced Nations, 1960–93." *World Politics* 53 (1): 38–43.
Brandon, T., and Y. Yook. 2012. "Political Uncertainty and Corporate Investment Cycles." *Journal of Finance* 67 (1): 45–83.
Brender, A., and A. Drazen. 2005. "Political Budget Cycles in New Versus Established Democracies." *Journal of Monetary Economics* 52 (7): 1271–95.
Brunnermeier, M. K., H. James, and J.-P. Landau. 2016. *The Euro and the Battle of Ideas.* Princeton, New Jersey: Princeton University Press.
Buchanan, J. M. 1960. *Fiscal Theory and Political Economy.* Chapel Hill, North Carolina: University of North Carolina Press.
———, and R. E. Wagner. 1976. "Revenue Structure, Fiscal Illusion and Budgetary Choice." *Public Choice* 25 (1): 45–61.
Buti, M., and P. van den Noord. 2004. "Fiscal Policy in EMU: Rules, Discretion and Political Incentives." European Economy–Economic Papers 206, European Union, Brussels.
Chang, T., W.-Y. Chen, R. Gupta, and D. K. Nguyen. 2013. "Are Stock Prices Related to the Political Uncertainty Index in OECD Countries? Evidence from the Bootstrap Panel Causality Test." *Economic Systems* 39 (2): 288–300.
Cox, G., and M. McCubbins. 2001. "The Institutional Determinants of Economic Policy Outcomes." In *Presidents and Parliaments,* edited by S. Haggard and M. McCubbins. Cambridge, U.K.: Cambridge University Press.
Dabla-Norris, E., A. Richard, L. F. Zanna, T. Prakash, E. Kvintradze, V. Lledo, I. Yackovlev, and S. Gollwitzer. 2010. "Budget Institutions and Fiscal Performance in Low-Income Countries." Working Paper 10/8, International Monetary Fund, Washington.
Debrun, X., and T. Kinda. 2014. "Strengthening Post-Crisis Fiscal Credibility: Fiscal Councils on the Rise—A New Dataset." Working Paper 14/58, International Monetary Fund, Washington.
Debrun, X., L. Moulin, A. Turrini, J. Ayuso-i-Casals, M. S. Kumar, A. Drazen, and C. Fuest. 2008. "Tied to the Mast? National Fiscal Rules in the European Union." *Economic Policy* 23 (54): 297–362.
de Haan, J., R. Jong-A-Pin, and R. Mierau. 2013. "Do Budgetary Institutions Mitigate the Common Pool Problem? New Empirical Evidence for the EU." *Public Choice* 156 (3): 423–41.
de Wolff, J. 1998. *The Political Economy of Fiscal Decisions: The Strategic Role of Public Debt.* Heidelberg: Physica-Verlag.
Downs, A. 1957. *An Economic Theory of Democracy.* New York: Harper.
Drazen, A., and M. Eslava. 2010. "Electoral Manipulation via Voter-Friendly Spending: Theory and Evidence." *Journal of Development Economics* 92 (1): 39–52.
Franzese, R. J. 2002. "Electoral and Partisan Cycles in Economic Policies and Outcomes." *Annual Review of Political Science* 5: 369–421.
———. 2007. "Fiscal Policy with Multiple Policymakers: Veto Actors and Deadlock; Collective Action and Common Pools; Bargaining and Compromise." In *Veto Players and Policy Change,* edited by H. Magara, 118–61. Tokyo: Waseda University Press.
Frieden, J., and R. Rogowski. 1996. "The Impact of the International Economy on National Policies: An Analytical Overview." In *Internationalization and Domestic Politics,* edited by R. O. Keohane. Cambridge, Massachusetts: Harvard University Press.
Garrett, G. 1998. *Partisan Politics in the Global Economy.* Cambridge, U.K.: Cambridge University Press.
Gaspar, V., L. Jaramillo, and P. Wingender. 2016. "Tax Policy and Growth: Is There a Tipping Point?" Working Paper 16/234, International Monetary Fund, Washington.

Golosov, G. 2015. "Party Systems, Electoral Systems, and Legislative Fragmentation: A Cross-National Empirical Study." *Party Politics* 1–11. http://journals.sagepub.com/doi/pdf/10.1177/1354068815603624/.

Grilli, V., D. Masciandaro, and G. Tabellini. 1991. "Institutions and Policies: Political and Monetary Institutions and Public Financial Policies in the Industrial Countries." *Economic Policy* 6 (13): 341–92.

Gupta, S., E. X. Liu, and C. Mulas-Granados. 2015. "Now or Later? The Political Economy of Public Investment in Democracies." Working Paper 15/175, International Monetary Fund, Washington, DC.

Hall, P. 1986. *Governing the Economy: The Politics of State Intervention in Britain and France*. Oxford, U.K.: Oxford University Press.

Hallerberg, M., R. Strauch, and J. von Hagen. 2007. "The Design of Fiscal Rules and Forms of Governance in European Union Countries." *European Journal of Political Economy* 23 (2): 338–59.

Hallerberg, M., and J. von Hagen. 1997. "Electoral Institutions, Cabinet Negotiations, and Budget Deficits within the European Union." Discussion Paper 1555, Center for Economic and Policy Research, Washington, DC.

Hardin, G. 1968. "The Tragedy of the Commons." *Science* 162 (3859): 1243–48.

Hayek, F. A. 1978. *New Studies in Philosophy, Politics, Economics and the History of Ideas*. Chicago: University of Chicago Press.

———. 1988. *The Fatal Conceit*. London: Routledge.

Hibbs, D. 1977. "Political Parties and Macroeconomic Policies." *American Political Science Review* 71 (4): 1467–87.

———. 1987. *The American Political Economy*. Cambridge, MA: Harvard University Press.

Illera, R. M., and C. Mulas-Granados. 2008. "What Makes Fiscal Consolidations Last? A Survival Analysis of Budget Cuts in Europe (1960–2004)." *Public Choice* 134 (3): 147–61.

International Monetary Fund (IMF). 2009. "Fiscal Rules: Anchoring Expectations for Sustainable Public Finances." July, Washington, DC. https://www.imf.org/external/np/pp/eng/2009/121609.pdf.

———. 2013. "The Functions and Impact of Fiscal Councils." July, Washington, DC. http://www.imf.org/external/pp/longres.aspx?id=4791.

———. 2014. "Budget Institutions in G-20 Countries: An Update." April, Washington, DC. http://www.imf.org/external/np/pp/eng/2014/040714c.pdf.

———. 2016. *World Economic Outlook: Subdued Demand—Symptoms and Remedies*. October, Washington, DC. http://www.imf.org/external/pubs/ft/weo/2016/02/.

Katsimi, M., and V. Sarantides. 2012. "Do Elections Affect the Composition of Fiscal Policy in Developed, Established Democracies?" *Public Choice* 151 (1): 325–62.

Klomp, J., and J. de Haan. 2013a. "Conditional Budget Cycles: A Review of Recent Evidence." *Public Choice* 157 (3): 387–410.

———. 2013b. "Political Budget Cycles and Election Outcomes." *Public Choice* 157 (1): 245–67.

Kopits, G., and S. A. Symansky. 1998. "Fiscal Policy Rules." Occasional Paper 122, International Monetary Fund, Washington, DC.

Kraft, J. 2016. "Social Democratic Austerity: The Conditional Role of Agenda Dynamics and Issue Ownership." *Journal of European Public Policy*. http://dx.doi.org/10.1080/13501763.2016.1231708.

Larch, M., and T. Braendle. 2016. "Independent Fiscal Councils: Neglected Siblings of Independent Central Banks? A European Union Perspective." Unpublished, Brussels.

Laswell, H. 1936. *Politics: Who Gets What, When, and How*. New York: McGraw-Hill.

Lockwood, B. 2005. "Fiscal Decentralization: A Political Economy Perspective." Warwick Economics Research Paper Series 721, University of Warwick, Coventry.

MacIntyre, A. 2001. "Institutions and Investors: The Politics of the Economic Crisis in Southeast Asia." *International Organizations* 55 (1): 81–122.

Mian, A., A. Sufi, and F. Trebbi. 2014. "Resolving Debt Overhang: Political Constraints in the Aftermath of Financial Crises." *American Economic Journal: Macroeconomics* 6 (2): 1–28.

Mierau, J., R. Jong-A-Pin, and J. de Haan. 2007. "Do Political Variables Affect Fiscal Policy Adjustment Decisions? New Empirical Evidence." *Public Choice* 133 (3/4): 297–319.

Milesi-Ferretti, G.-M., R. Perotti, and M. Rostagno. 2002. "Electoral Systems and Public Spending." *Quarterly Journal of Economics* 117 (2): 609–57.
Mulas-Granados, C. 2006. *Economics, Politics and Budgets: The Political Economy of Fiscal Adjustments in Europe*. London: Palgrave Macmillan.
Muller, W. C., and K. Strom. 1999. *Policy, Office or Votes? How Political Parties in Western Europe Make Hard Decisions*. Cambridge, U.K.: Cambridge University Press.
Musgrave, R. A. 1959. *The Theory of Public Finance: A Study in Public Economy*. New York: McGraw-Hill.
Nordhaus, W. D. 1975. "The Political Business Cycle." *Review of Economic Studies* 42 (2): 169–90.
Notermans, T. 2000. *Money, Markets and the State. Social Democratic Policies since 1918.* Cambridge, U.K.: Cambridge University Press.
Pastor, L., and P. Veronesi. 2013. "Political Uncertainty and Risk Premia." *Journal of Financial Economics* 110 (3): 520–45.
Perotti, R. 1998. "The Political Economy of Fiscal Consolidations." *Scandinavian Journal of Economics* 100 (1): 367–94.
———, and Y. Kontopoulos. 2002. "Fragmented Fiscal Policy." *Journal of Public Economics* 86 (2): 191–222.
Persson, T., and L. Svensson. 1989. "Why a Stubborn Conservative Would Run a Deficit: Policy with Time Inconsistent Preferences." *Quarterly Journal of Economics* 104 (2): 325–45.
Persson, T., and G. Tabellini. 2002. "Political Economics and Public Finance." In *Handbook of Public Economics*, edited by John B. Taylor and Michael Woodford. Amsterdam: Elsevier.
———. 2003. *The Economic Effect of Constitutions*. Cambridge, MA: MIT Press.
Rose, S. 2006. "Do Fiscal Rules Dampen the Political Business Cycle?" *Public Choice* 128 (3/4): 407–31.
Roubini, N., and J. D. Sachs. 1989. "Political and Economic Determinants of Budget Deficit in the Industrial Democracies." *European Economic Review* 33 (5): 903–38.
Sargent, T. 2012 "Nobel Lecture: United States Then, Europe Now." *Journal of Political Economy* 120 (1): 1–40.
Schaechter, A., T. Kinda, N. Budina, and A. Weber. 2015. "Fiscal Rules in Response to the Crisis—Toward the 'Next-Generation Rules.' A New Dataset." Working Paper 12/197, International Monetary Fund, Washington, DC.
Schumpeter, J. A. 1991. "The Crisis of the Tax State." In *The Economics and Sociology of Capitalism,* edited by R. Swedberg. Princeton, NJ: Princeton University Press, originally published in German, in 1918.
———, J. A. 1942. *Capitalism, Socialism and Democracy.* New York: Harper & Brothers.
Shi, M., and J. Svensson. 2006. "Political Budget Cycles: Do They Differ across Countries and Why?" *Journal of Public Economics* 90 (8–9): 1367–89.
Solow, R. M. 2004. "Is Fiscal Policy Possible? Is It Desirable?" In *Structural Reform and Macroeconomic Policy*, edited by R. M. Solow, 23–39. London: Palgrave Macmillan.
Spolaore, E. 2004. "Adjustments in Different Government Systems." *Economics and Politics* 16 (2): 117–46.
Starke, P., A. Kaasch, and F. van Hooren. 2014. "Political Parties and Social Policy Responses to Global Economic Crises: Constrained Partisanship in Mature Welfare States." *Journal of Social Policy* 43 (2): 225–46.
Streb, J. M., and G. Torrens. 2013. "Making Rules Credible: Divided Government and Political Budget Cycles." *Public Choice* 156 (3): 703–22.
Tavares, J. 2004. "Does Right or Left Matter? Cabinets, Credibility and Fiscal Adjustments." *Journal of Public Economics* 88 (12): 2447–68.
Ter-Minassian, T. 1997. *Fiscal Federalism*. Washington, DC: International Monetary Fund.
Tsebelis, G. 1995. "Decision Making in Political Systems: Veto Players in Presidentialism, Parliamentarism, Multicameralism, and Multipartyism." *British Journal of Political Science* 25 (3): 289–326.
———. 2000. "Veto Players and Institutional Analysis." *Governance* 13 (4): 441–74.
———. 2002. *Veto Players: How Political Institutions Work*. Princeton, NJ: Princeton University Press.

Tsebelis, G., and E. C. C. Chang. 2004. "Veto Players and the Structure of Budgets in Advanced Industrialized Countries." *European Journal of Political Research* 43 (3): 449–76.

Volverink, B., and J. de Haan. 2001. "Fragmented Government Effects on Fiscal Policy: New Evidence." *Public Choice.* 109 (3/4): 221–41.

von Hagen, J., A. H. Hallett, and R. Strauch. 2001. "Budgetary Consolidation in EMU." Economics Papers 148, European Commission, Brussels.

Weingast, B. R., K. A. Shepsle, and C. Johnsen. 1981. "The Political Economy of Benefits and Costs: A Neoclassical Approach to Distributive Politics." *Journal of Political Economy* 89 (4): 642–64.

PART I

Elections, Ideology, and Political Fragmentation

CHAPTER 2

Governments and Promised Fiscal Consolidations: Do They Mean What They Say?

SANJEEV GUPTA, JOÃO TOVAR JALLES, CARLOS MULAS-GRANADOS, AND MICHELA SCHENA

INTRODUCTION

Several reasons could explain why fiscal outcomes may deviate from plans. First, the macroeconomic scenario may unfold differently from that foreseen in the plan (Frankel 2011). Second, the design of fiscal rules may be such that adherence to them requires fiscal discipline in plans but not in outcomes. Finally, policymakers may find it difficult to implement fiscal plans because of opposition from vested interest groups (Beetsma, Giuliodori, and Wierts 2009; von Hagen 2010). In fact, political factors can be particularly important in explaining fiscal outcomes when elections are approaching or if political fragmentation is large (Perotti 1998; von Hagen, Hallet, and Strauch 2001; Perotti and Kontopoulos 2002; Protrafke 2011).[1]

The difference between budget plans and budget implementation is labeled the promise gap. The size of promise gaps has a bearing on credibility and democratic accountability of elected governments. For example, large and systematic fiscal promise gaps may increase uncertainty for economic agents and lower the credibility of the government, thus increasing long-term interest rates on government bonds (Baldacci and Kumar 2010; Beetsma and others 2015). In addition, when governments do not deliver on their promises, the quality of democracy may suffer (Przeworski and others 1999). In a fully functioning democracy with

The authors are grateful to Vitor Gaspar, Ben Clements, and the participants in the IMF Fiscal Affairs Department seminar for useful comments and suggestions.

[1] In addition to elections and political fragmentation, fiscal consolidations could be influenced by the government's ideology. Although ideology is not relevant for explaining the size of consolidation promise gaps in the sample in this chapter, it has been shown to affect the composition of the budget. A number of scholars (Boix 1997; Franzese 2002; Mulas-Granados 2003, 2006; Tavares 2004; Konishi 2006; Mierau, Jong-A-Pin, and de Haan 2007; Angelopoulos, Malley, and Philippopoulos 2012) have shown that left-wing governments may prefer revenue-based adjustments to ensure financing for the welfare state, whereas right-wing governments may opt for expenditure-based consolidations.

rational, forward-looking voters and politicians, the electorate expects governments to be responsive to their economic and fiscal preferences.

This chapter studies two questions: First, what explains fiscal consolidation promise gaps? Second, what is the reaction of markets and voters to promise gaps incurred by incumbent parties? This chapter holds the view that these two issues are interrelated. Parties in government are motivated by specific policy agendas and by their willingness to remain in office (Müller and Strom 1999).[2] When governments deliver on their promised policies they are likely to be reelected. If they fall short on these promises, they could be penalized by voters unless this deviation benefits the electorate in the short term. At the same time, financial markets monitor these actions, and if they see politically motivated deviations from promised fiscal discipline, they react negatively.

Because these questions are intertwined, the analysis tackles them empirically in two steps. For this purpose, a new database of fiscal consolidations was created that compares narrative budget plans with actual fiscal performance in 17 Organisation for Economic Co-operation and Development (OECD) countries during 1978–2015.[3] We find that fiscal promise gaps were sizable (about 0.3 percent of GDP per year, or 1.1 percent of GDP over a typical three-year adjustment episode). Economic factors and forecast errors are important in explaining the differences between budget plans and fiscal outcomes, but political factors also play a role: greater electoral proximity, stronger political cohesion, and higher accountability were all associated with smaller promise gaps. Finally, governments that delivered on their promised fiscal consolidation plans were rewarded by financial markets and not penalized by voters.

This chapter makes three contributions to the existing literature: first, it updates the narrative database from Devries and others (2011) and Alesina and others (2015); second, it considers simultaneously the role of three political factors (electoral proximity, political strength, and institutional accountability) in explaining consolidation promise gaps; and third, it examines the consequences of promise gaps on market sentiment and government popularity among the electorate.

The remainder of the chapter is organized as follows; the second section briefly discusses the data and the definition of the dependent variable. The third section

[2] According to Müller and Strom (1999) political parties can be guided by two objectives: the pursuit of policy and the pursuit of office. Pure policy seekers pursue the maximum leverage over public policy outcomes; pure office seekers strive to win and retain office as an end in itself or for the perks it affords. Normally, parties in government try to maximize both objectives at the same time, because staying in office guarantees further influence on the policy agenda, and delivering on the policies preferred by citizens typically increases the chances of remaining in office.

[3] For a discussion of alternative ways to identify fiscal consolidations using the narrative and positive approaches, see Afonso and Jalles (2014) and Escolano and others (2014).

explores the economic and political causes of consolidation promise gaps. The fourth section looks into the reaction of markets and the electorate to these gaps. The fifth section inspects the consequences of consolidation promise gaps. The last section concludes and presents policy implications.

DEFINING FISCAL PROMISE GAPS

Identifying Fiscal Consolidation Episodes

The literature on fiscal adjustment episodes is vast and for a long time has relied on the positive approach, by which fiscal consolidations are associated with large changes in the cyclically adjusted primary balance (CAPB).[4] More recently, scholars have identified consolidation episodes following a narrative approach, which relies on approved budget plans and historical accounts of past fiscal policy. Such an approach was first popularized by Romer and Romer (2010) and Devries and others (2011), who subsequently made publicly available a list of fiscal consolidation episodes for 17 advanced economies between 1978 and 2009.[5] More recently, Alesina and others (2015) updated that database for a subset of European countries through 2012. This chapter updates the database for all 17 countries included in Devries and others (2011). It follows the same approach, and relies on historical description surrounding changes in budget deficits every year as recorded in national budget laws, the European Commission's Stability and Convergence Programs, and the OECD's country reviews.[6]

In this sample, 73 episodes of fiscal consolidations are identified. Table 2.1 summarizes these episodes by country. The number of fiscal contractions per country ranges from two in Canada and Finland, to seven in France and the United States. The size of fiscal consolidation episodes varies from 0.04 percent of GDP to 4.74 percent of GDP, with an average size of fiscal adjustment equal to 1.06 percent of GDP. The average duration of the reported fiscal episodes is 3.3 years, with the shortest duration corresponding to 1 year (21 episodes) and the longest duration corresponding to 14 years (Canada).

---

[4] Some caveats surrounding the traditional CAPB approach have been highlighted recently (see Afonso and Jalles 2014). In particular, the CAPB approach could bias empirical estimates toward finding evidence of non-Keynesian effects. Many nonpolicy factors influence the CAPB and can lead to erroneous conclusions regarding fiscal policy changes. For example, a stock price boom raises the CAPB by increasing capital gains tax revenue and tends to coincide with an expansion of private demand (Morris and Schuknecht 2007). Even when the CAPB accurately measures fiscal actions, these actions could include discretionary responses to economic developments.

[5] Note that the narrative approach used by Devries and others (2011) uses historical accounts from OECD and EU annual reports describing what happened to the budget deficit in a particular country and period, but they do not go into the details of policymakers' intentions, discussions, and congressional records. This differs from the approach used in Romer and Romer (2010), who identify exogenous tax policy changes by carefully analyzing U.S. congressional documents.

[6] A description of this update for each country and consolidation year is available in the Annex 2.1.

Table 2.1. Fiscal Consolidation Years, 17 Advanced Economies, 1978–2015

Country	Fiscal Consolidation—Sample Years
Australia	1985–88, 1994–99, 2010–12, 2014–15
Austria	1980–81, 1984, 1996–97, 2001–02, 2011–12, 2015
Belgium	1982–85, 1987, 1990, 1992–94, 1996–97, 2010–15
Canada	1984–97, 2010–15
Denmark	1983–86, 1995, 2012
Finland	1992–97, 2011
France	1979, 1987, 1989, 1991–92, 1995–97, 1999–2000, 2011–15
Germany	1982–84, 1991–95, 1997–2000, 2003–04, 2006–07, 2011–12
Ireland	1982–88, 2009–15
Italy	1991–98, 2004–07, 2010–15
Japan	1997–98, 2003–07
Netherlands	1981–88, 1991–93, 2004–05, 2011–13, 2015
Portugal	1983, 2000, 2002–03, 2005–07, 2010–15
Spain	1983–84, 1989–90, 1992–97, 2009–15
Sweden	1984, 1993–98, 2011, 2015
United Kingdom	1979–82, 1994–99, 2010, 2012, 2014–15
United States	1978, 1980–81, 1985–86, 1988, 1990–98, 2011, 2013–15

Source: Authors' calculations.
Note: See Annex 2.1 for details.

Figure 2.1. Absolute Frequency of Fiscal Consolidation Episodes over Time, 1978–2015

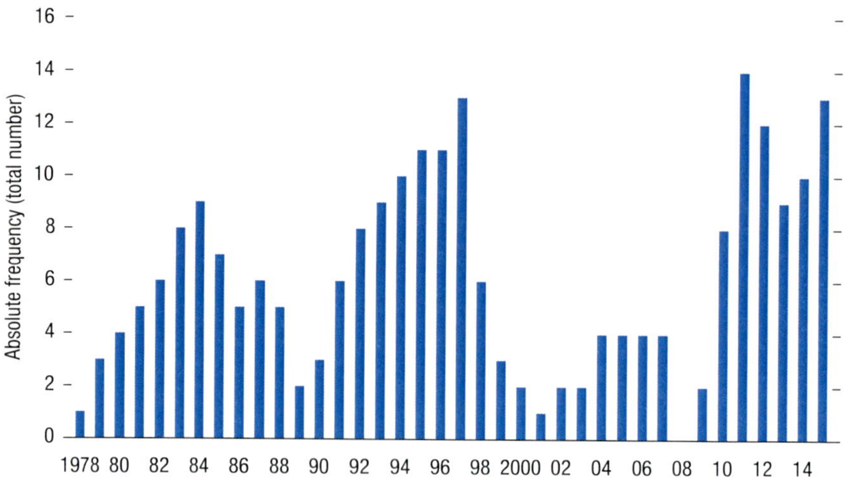

Source: Authors' calculations.

Figures 2.1 and 2.2 show the distribution of fiscal consolidation episodes over time as well as their distribution by size (in percentage of GDP). Most episodes took place in the mid-1980s; the late 1990s (led by European countries' need to qualify for the single currency union); and between 2010 and 2015, in the

Figure 2.2. Relative Frequency of Fiscal Consolidation Episodes, by Size of Consolidation

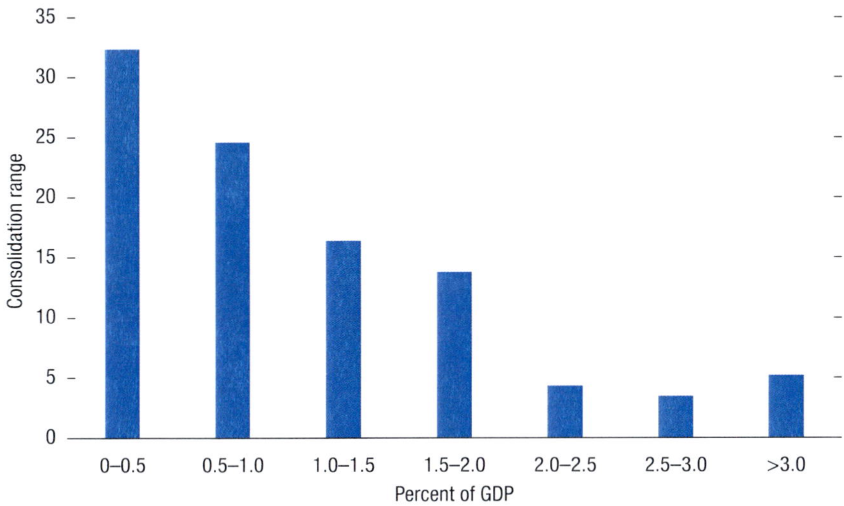

Source: Authors' calculations.

aftermath of the recent financial crisis (following the cross-country coordinated fiscal stimuli that took place). In more than 35 percent of fiscal adjustment episodes, the size was between 0 and 0.5 percent of GDP. In only 5 percent of cases was the adjustment larger than 3 percent of GDP.

Measuring Consolidation Promise Gaps

Consolidation promise gaps (CPGs) are defined as the difference between the size of planned fiscal adjustment (PFA), as measured by the narrative approach, and the size of the realized fiscal adjustment (RFA), as measured by changes in the budget balance (all expressed in percentage of GDP).[7]

$$CPG = PFA - RFA.$$

The promise gap can have either sign. Governments can deliver less fiscal adjustment than initially planned (positive promise gap) or they can implement a larger adjustment than initially foreseen (negative promise gap). Using data at the general government level, Figure 2.3 shows the average size of

[7] For robustness purposes, we also define the dependent variable using changes in the cyclically adjusted budget balance or changes in the primary balance and results are qualitatively similar. These results are available upon request from the authors.

Figure 2.3. Size of Consolidation Promise Gaps (baseline), by Country

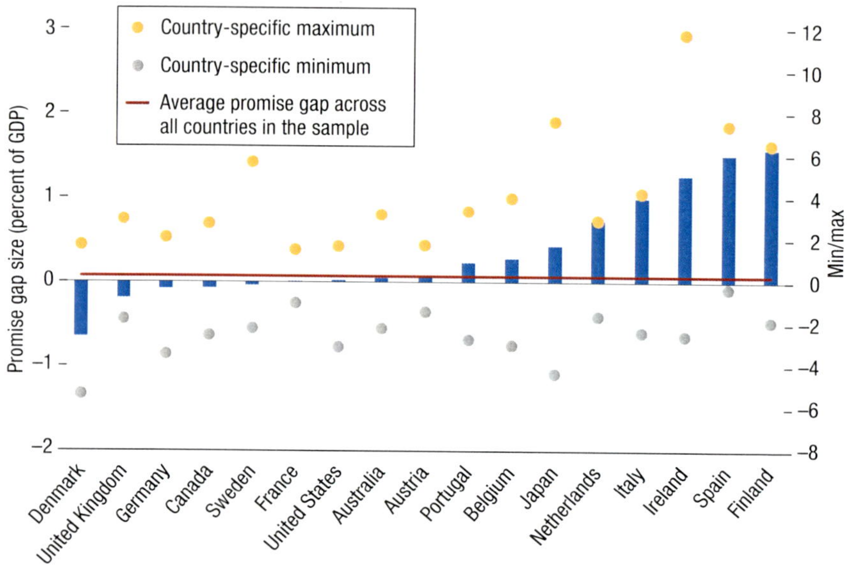

Source: IMF *World Economic Outlook* and authors' calculations.

promise gaps by country.[8] Finland, Spain, Ireland, and Italy have the largest positive promise gaps, while Denmark, the United Kingdom, Germany, Canada, and Sweden managed to deliver, on average, larger fiscal consolidations than initially planned.

Panel 1 of Figure 2.4 shows the promise gap using the primary balance to correct for the effect of interest payments. Panel 2 of Figure 2.4 shows the promise gap using the structural balance, which allows the analysis to take into account the effects stemming from the economic cycle (for example, Finland) or one-off measures (for example, Ireland's 2009 banking sector capitalization) that would otherwise distort the overall picture. Although the ordering of the countries varies, the average promise gap remains the same (0.3 percent of GDP) under all measures.

[8] The use of general government data allows us to compare countries with different degrees of fiscal decentralization. In some countries, like Canada or Spain, regional government finances are sizable and their fiscal accounts are not always correlated with those of the central government.

Figure 2.4. Size of Consolidation Promise Gaps (Alternatives), by Country

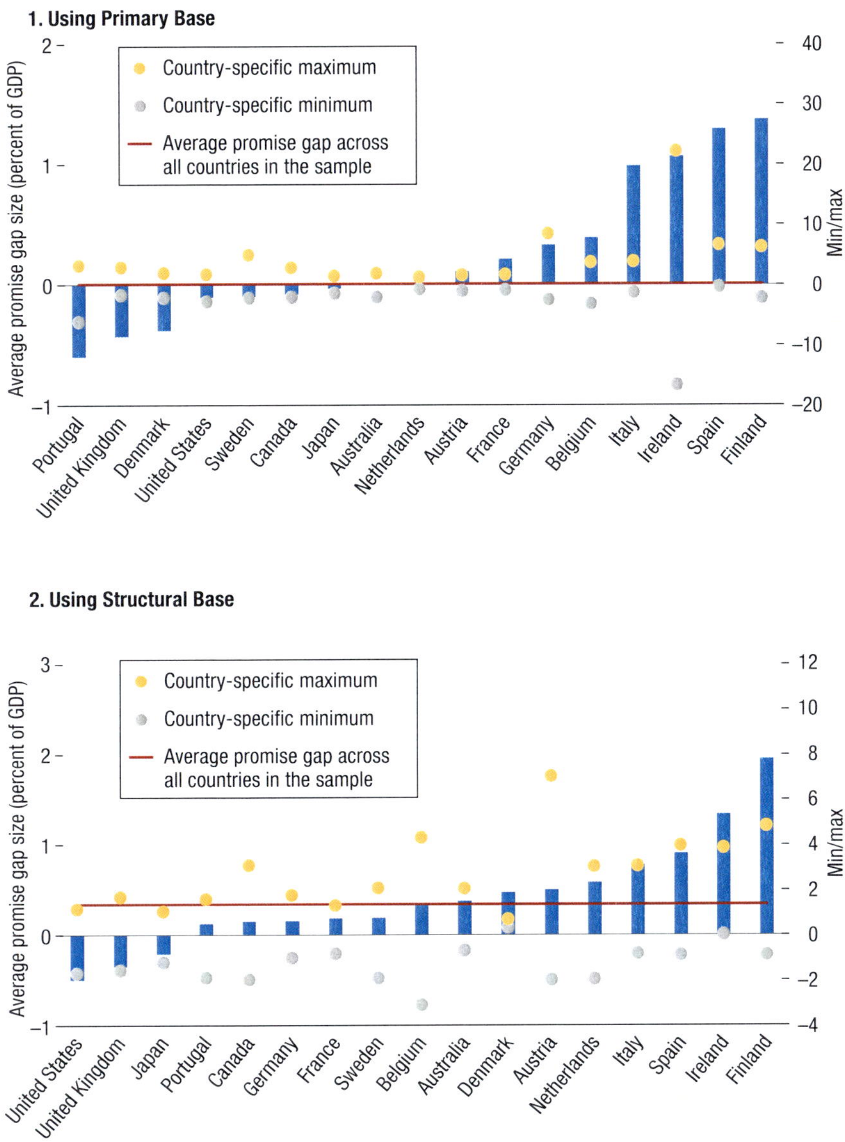

Sources: IMF *Fiscal Monitor* and authors' calculations.

THE POLITICAL AND ECONOMIC DETERMINANTS OF CONSOLIDATION PROMISE GAPS

Economic Factors: Stylized Facts

To explain the size of consolidation promise gaps, the role of initial fiscal conditions, such as the initial level of the debt-to-GDP ratio and the initial level of fiscal sustainability, is examined.[9] The analysis also looks at the size of the output gap and at growth forecast errors.[10,11] Figure 2.5 plots average promise gaps for high and low levels of different variables of interest.

The bar charts show that initially adverse fiscal conditions (high levels of debt and low fiscal sustainability) are subsequently associated with smaller consolidation promise gaps. This outcome is in line with results from Escolano and others (2014), who find that countries under fiscal stress are willing to undertake stronger fiscal adjustments and deliver on their commitments to undertake more sizable consolidations. In addition, Figure 2.6 shows that adverse economic conditions (as evidenced by large output gaps and high real GDP growth forecast errors) are also associated with smaller consolidation promise gaps.

Political Factors: Principal Components Analysis

Several political factors can affect the size of consolidation promise gaps. The existing literature mainly focuses on the possible role of elections and budget institutions (Beetsma, Giuliodori, and Wierts 2009; Beetsma and others 2013; Beetsma and others 2015) and finds that these variables are not very statistically significant. In our view, testing a few political variables can suffer from selection bias. This chapter proposes instead a more comprehensive analysis of political factors that can potentially affect promise gaps. It focuses on three political dimensions (each containing multiple variables) and builds political indicators

[9] The sustainability factor is defined as the difference between the actual primary balance and the debt-stabilizing primary balance (see Escolano and others [2014] for further details). Higher values of the initial sustainability factor imply that countries have primary balances close to (or above) the debt-stabilizing optimum level, and therefore they are not under fiscal stress.

[10] Output gap is calculated as actual minus potential GDP using data from the World Economic Outlook database.

[11] We use the 3-, 9-, 15-, and 21-month GDP forecast errors from the World Economic Outlook database. Forecast errors are defined as the difference between actual real GDP growth and forecasted real GDP growth. A large positive forecast error implies that GDP grew more than predicted. All forecast error variables yield qualitatively similar results; hence, the chapter presents regression estimates using only one, the 9-months ahead variant.

Figure 2.5. Size of Promise Gaps and Economic Conditions

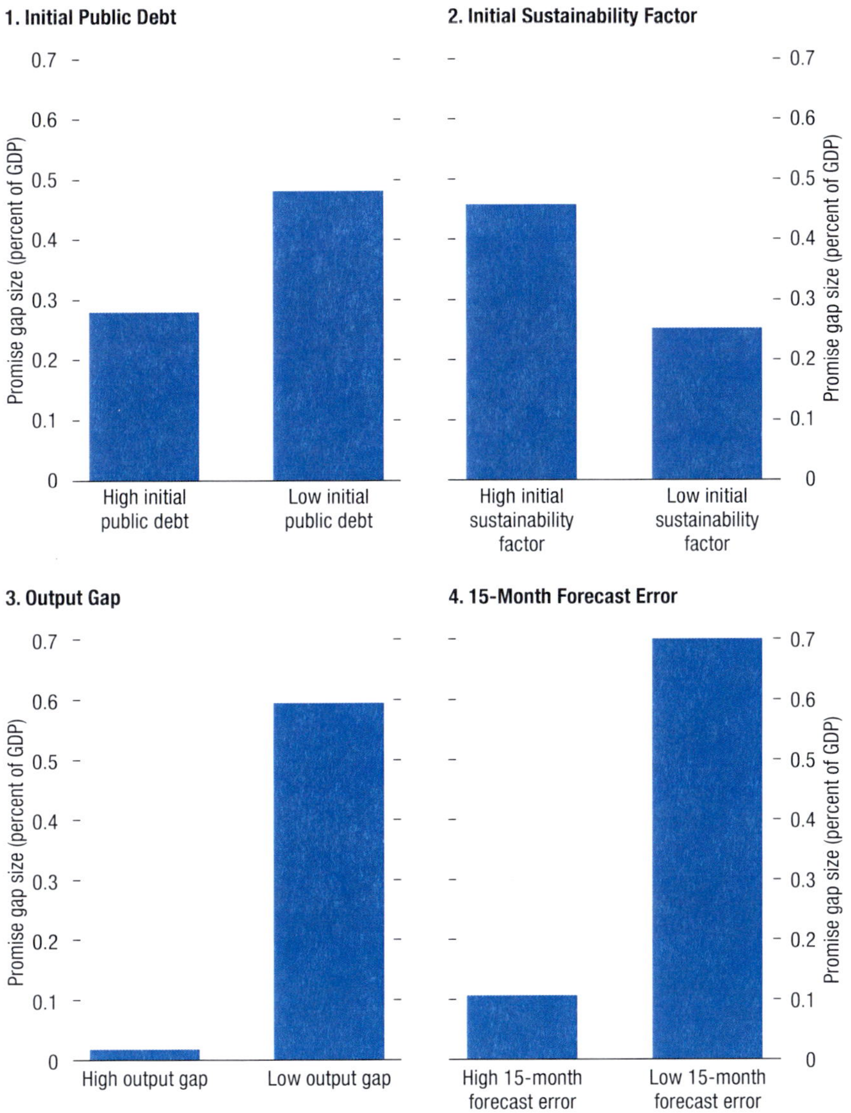

Sources: IMF *World Economic Outlook* and authors' calculations.
Note: "Initial" refers to the year before the start of a given consolidation episode. High and low levels are identified by cases above the 75th percentile of the distribution and below the 25th percentile, respectively.

Figure 2.6. Size of Promise Gaps and Political Conditions

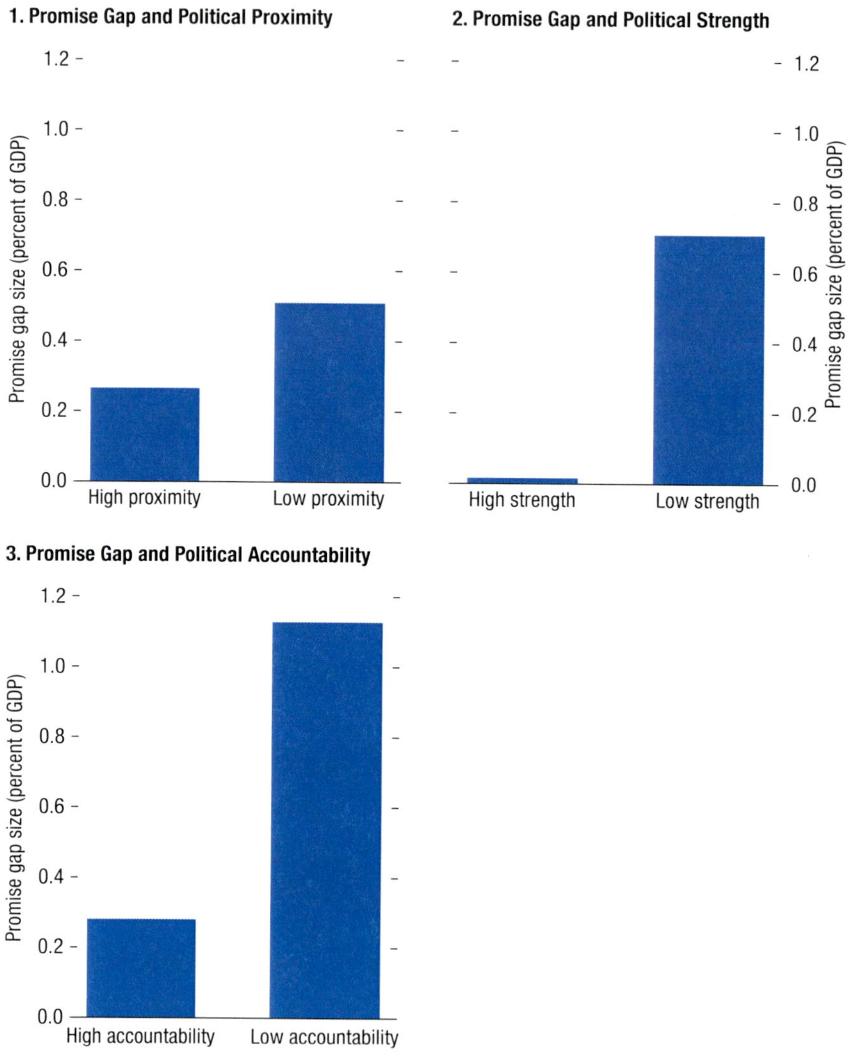

Source: Authors' calculations.

Note: For details on the three political variables (proximity, strength, and accountability), refer to the main text. High and low levels are identified by cases above the 75th percentile of the distribution and below the 25th percentile, respectively.

through principal components analysis (PCA). These three political dimensions are detailed as follows:[12]

- Electoral *proximity*: This dimension takes into account the time that policymakers have until upcoming elections. Politicians facing coming elections have stronger incentives to deliver on their budget promises and report lower consolidation promise gaps. Four variables are used to compute the *proximity* PCA. Higher electoral proximity is associated with more years in office, fewer years left in current term, a party of chief executive with a short tradition in office, and fewer months to the next election.[13] Only the first principal component is retained.[14]
- Political *strength*: This dimension takes into account the number of political actors participating in budgetary decisions who typically exhibit conflicting budgetary demands. These actors could be parties in government—or in opposition—interest groups, or, more generally, veto players. Strong governments are those that operate in less fragmented political environments and are likely to be subject to less stringent spending demands. Therefore, they are typically associated with tighter fiscal discipline and lower promise gaps. Four variables are used to compute the *strength* PCA. More political strength is associated with a high margin of parliamentary majority, low cabinet fragmentation, executive control of all houses, and a weak opposition. Only the first principal component is retained.
- Political *accountability*: This dimension takes into account the institutional context within which fiscal policy decisions are made. When politicians operate under more transparency, better governance, and more mechanisms objectively monitoring their activities, they tend to be more responsive to citizens' demands and more accountable to voters for the promises they make. Politicians operating in institutional contexts with more accountability would be associated with more fiscal discipline and lower promise gaps. Five variables are used to compute the *accountability* PCA. A higher accountability index is associated with more voice and accountability, with more regulatory quality, more government effectiveness, control of corruption, and with the rule of law.[15] Only the first principal component is retained.

---

[12] We also explored the role of government ideology but results were inconclusive because more than two-thirds of consolidation episodes were planned and implemented by centrist governments. Results are available from the authors upon request.

[13] This latter indicator refers to actual months left to next election, after the fact, while the variable "more years left in current term" is observed ex ante. Both are informative.

[14] A likelihood ratio test was used to examine the "sphericity" case, allowing for sampling variability in the correlations. This test comfortably rejects sphericity at the 1 percent level. The first factor explains almost 40 percent of the variance in the standardized data (see Table 2.3).

[15] Government effectiveness captures perceptions of the quality of public services, the quality of the civil service and the degree of its independence from political pressures, the quality of policy

Table 2.2. Summary of Political Composite Variables and Descriptive Statistics

Concept	Variables
Proximity	Years in office
	Years left in current term
	Party of chief executive more time in office
	Months to next election
Strength	Margin of majority
	Cabinet strength
	Executive control of all houses
	Weak opposition
Accountability	Voice and accountability
	Regulatory quality
	Government effectiveness
	Control of corruption
	Rule of law

Source: Authors' calculations.
Note: For each variable, the average is 0 and the standard deviation is 1.

Table 2.3. Factor Loadings and Uniqueness

	Factors			
Variables	Proximity	Strength	Accountability	Uniqueness
Years in office	0.39			0.29
Years left in current term	0.41			0.28
Party of chief executive more time in office	0.37			0.29
Months to next election	0.45			0.28
Margin of majority		0.93		0.12
Cabinet strength		0.90		0.17
Executive control of all houses		0.76		0.42
Weak opposition		0.72		0.47
Voice and accountability			0.87	0.22
Regulatory quality			0.89	0.10
Government effectiveness			0.82	0.13
Control of corruption			0.96	0.07
Rule of law			0.94	0.11
Share Explained	**0.39**	**0.69**	**0.85**	

Source: Authors' calculations.

The *proximity* and *strength* variables are each represented by one factor composed of four underlying variables.[16] *Accountability* is represented by one factor composed of five underlying variables.[17] The resulting principal components indices are described in Table 2.2; Table 2.3 lists the corresponding factor loadings.[18] The

formulation and implementation, and the credibility of the government's commitment to such policies. See Worldwide Governance Indicators at http://info.worldbank.org/governance/wgi/index.aspx#home.

[16] The source for each component variable is the Database on Political Institutions 2015 (Cruz, Keefer, and Scartascini 2015).

[17] The sources for each component variable is the World Bank's World Governance Indicators.

[18] PCA is based on the classical covariance matrix, which is sensitive to outliers. Here we conduct a robust estimation of the covariance matrix. A well-suited method is the minimum covariance

principal components can be interpreted by focusing on the factor loadings and the uniqueness of each variable.[19] With regard to political *proximity*, uniqueness is relatively low for all variables, which implies that the retained factor spans the original variables adequately. As to political *strength*, the factor appears to describe mostly the margin of majority and cabinet strength. In principle, both factors should enter with positive coefficients in the regressions. Finally, with respect to *accountability*, the factor is mainly driven by the role of government effectiveness.

Figure 2.6 plots the average size of consolidation promise gaps for low and high levels of the three principal component indicators along the three dimensions associated with *proximity, strength,* and *accountability*. As expected, political strength and high institutional accountability are associated with lower consolidation promise gaps. Moreover, the higher the electoral proximity, the higher the inherent pressure for the incumbent government to deliver on its promises to maximize the possibilities of being reelected for a new term; that is, the higher the electoral proximity, the lower the consolidation promise gap. The difference between the average size of promise gaps under the high and low values of each principal component seems more important for political *strength* and *accountability* than for *proximity*.

Economic and Political Factors: Panel Regressions

To test the role of the abovementioned economic and political factors simultaneously, panel regression analyses are used. The 229 years of fiscal consolidation in the panel database are used to estimate equation (2.1):

$$CPG_{it} = \delta_i + \beta' IC_{it} + \theta' EC_{it} + \rho' POL_{it} + \epsilon_{it}, \qquad (2.1)$$

where CPG_{it} is the consolidation promise gap in country i and year t, IC_{it} is a vector of initial fiscal conditions (measured by the lagged value of the public-debt-to-GDP ratio),[20] $'EC_{it}$ is a vector of economic conditions (measured by the output gap and the alternative measures of GDP forecast errors), and $'POL_{it}$ is a vector of political variables (where each of the principal components—*proximity, strength,* and *accountability*—are first included, followed by a selection of political variables from each component). β, θ, and ρ are unknown coefficients to be estimated. ϵ_{it} is an independent and identically distributed disturbance term satisfying usual assumptions of zero mean and constant variance. Equation (2.1)

determinant (MCD) that considers all subsets containing h percent of the observations and estimates the variance of the mean on the data of the subset associated with the smallest covariance matrix determinant. Specifically, we implement Rousseeuw and van Driessen's (1999) algorithm. When we computed the same indices with the MCD version, we obtained similar results, suggesting that outliers are not driving the factor analysis.

[19] Uniqueness of a variable is the share of its variance that is not accounted for by all the factors.

[20] We do not include the sustainability factor because it is collinear with initial levels of debt.

is estimated by ordinary least squares with robust standard errors clustered at the country level.

Table 2.4 reports results for economic determinants and confirms that larger initial debt levels, annual improvements in the output gap, and larger forecast errors all lead to smaller consolidation promise gaps. Table 2.5 adds

Table 2.4. Economic Determinants of Consolidation Promise Gaps

	Specification			
Regressors	**(1)**	**(2)**	**(3)**	**(4)**
Lagged Debt	−0.026***			−0.028***
	(0.005)			(0.007)
Change in Output Gap		−0.540***		−0.605***
		(0.070)		(0.092)
Lagged GDP Forecast Error			−0.200	−0.202*
			(0.133)	(0.107)
Constant	1.690***	0.087	−0.332	2.097***
	(0.543)	(0.388)	(0.597)	(0.725)
Observations	228	231	162	162
R^2	0.175	0.287	0.146	0.467

Source: Authors' calculations.

Note: Dependent variable = consolidation promise gaps as defined in the main text. Robust standard errors clustered at the country level are in parentheses. Time and country fixed effects are omitted for reasons of parsimony.

*$p < .1$; ***$p < .001$.

Table 2.5. Economic and Political Determinants of Consolidation Promise Gaps *(Principal components analysis)*

	Specification			
Regressors	**(1)**	**(2)**	**(3)**	**(4)**
Lagged Debt	−0.020***	−0.021***	−0.063**	−0.057*
	(0.007)	(0.007)	(0.029)	(0.032)
Change in Output Gap	−0.557***	−0.545***	−0.497*	−0.536*
	(0.085)	(0.084)	(0.292)	(0.312)
Proximity	−0.072			0.035
	(0.138)			(0.356)
Strength		−0.531*		−0.570
		(0.284)		(1.079)
Accountability			−2.726*	−3.202*
			(1.561)	(1.811)
Constant	1.232**	1.824***	3.911*	4.193*
	(0.573)	(0.651)	(2.054)	(2.345)
Observations	162	162	41	41
R^2	0.404	0.417	0.839	0.841

Source: Authors' calculations.

Note: Dependent variable = consolidation promise gaps as defined in the main text. The time span of this regression covers the period 1978–2009 to perfectly match the Devries and others (2011) data set. Robust standard errors clustered at the country level are in parentheses. Time and country fixed effects are omitted for reasons of parsimony.

*$p < .1$; **$p < .05$; ***$p < .01$.

Table 2.6. Economic and Political Determinants of Consolidation Promise Gaps
(Select individual variables)

	Specification			
Regressors	**(1)**	**(2)**	**(3)**	**(4)**
Lagged Debt	−0.035***	−0.026***	−0.033***	−0.014
	(0.009)	(0.007)	(0.011)	(0.014)
Change in Output Gap	−0.304**	−0.575***	−0.493***	−0.026
	(0.123)	(0.092)	(0.139)	(0.200)
Recent Elections	−0.388***			−0.302
	(0.147)			(0.307)
Margin of Majority		−4.373**		−7.480**
		(2.007)		(3.546)
Government Effectiveness			−3.899***	−4.104**
			(1.310)	(1.942)
Lagged GDP Forecast Error	−0.173	−0.181*	−0.062	0.026
	(0.113)	(0.107)	(0.162)	(0.190)
Constant	4.905***	4.082***	8.413***	12.755***
	(1.248)	(1.158)	(2.305)	(3.020)
Observations	119	162	94	65
R^2	0.375	0.484	0.534	0.501

Source: Authors' calculations.
Note: Dependent variable = consolidation promise gaps as defined in the main text. Robust standard errors clustered at the country level are in parentheses. Time and country fixed effects are omitted for reasons of parsimony.
$^*p < .1$; $^{**}p < .05$; $^{***}p < .01$.

to the economic determinants the three political indicators computed by PCA and illustrates that the most important factors in explaining cross-country differences in consolidation promise gaps are political strength and accountability. Table 2.6 includes a subset of relevant political variables for each PCA one at a time and then jointly and shows that they are all associated with lower promise gaps.[21]

To ensure that the results are not biased by the decision to combine three data sets that may have different approaches to narrating fiscal developments, the empirical analysis is also run on the original Devries and others (2011) database, which shows that even when using a single-source database the main results hold.[22]

[21] From the *Proximity* PCA we take the months to next elections and build a variable that identifies whether an election has taken place recently (that is, in the past year); from the *Strength* PCA we take the margin of majority; and from the *Accountability* PCA we take the indicator of government effectiveness.

[22] In Annex 2.2 we repeat the estimation but constrain the time span to 2009 to match exactly the Devries and others (2011) sample. Results are qualitatively similar and generally marked by more statistical significance throughout.

THE ECONOMIC AND POLITICAL CONSEQUENCES OF CONSOLIDATION PROMISE GAPS

The preceding section shows that political factors such as proximity of elections, lack of political strength, or low systemic accountability can derail planned fiscal consolidations and increase the size of promise gaps. Policymakers in such circumstances may be tempted (or forced by surrounding political conditions) to deviate from initial consolidation plans, provided they can compensate for the negative backlash from markets. To gauge empirical support to this line of reasoning, the reactions of financial markets and the electorate to consolidation promise gaps are analyzed in this section. First, some stylized facts are presented, then the results of regression analysis and impulse-response functions are presented.

The Consequences of Consolidation Promise Gaps: Stylized Facts

If we assume that markets and voters expect governments to deliver on their fiscal promises, the analysis of their reaction to promise gaps can be better understood if the sample is split between episodes in which governments overperformed and managed to deliver more consolidation than initially planned, and episodes in which they underperformed and fell short of their promises. Note that in the sample, the average size of the promise gaps in underperforming episodes was equivalent to 2.8 percent of GDP, while the average size of the promise gap in overperforming episodes was 1.2 percent of GDP.

Figure 2.7 plots the evolution of government popularity[23] and five-year bond spreads (against Germany) from four years before the consolidation episode started to four years after. On the one hand, government popularity seems to be generally unaffected by the sign of consolidation promise gaps. There is a slight decline in popularity in the aftermath of consolidation episodes in which governments fall short of their promises. Taking this evidence with a grain of salt (because it is not strongly significant), it shows that policymakers may be mistaken when they assume that they could obtain a boost in popularity by not delivering on their fiscal consolidation plans. Although it is possible that, in general, voters prefer more public goods and dislike fiscal adjustments, it seems that once a promise to consolidate the budget is made, they do not like it to be broken. On the other hand, markets seem to react more decisively: government bond spreads increase in both subsamples at the start of (and immediately after) the consolidation, but the spike is larger and more long lasting in the case of underperforming fiscal adjustments.

[23] "Government popularity" refers to the average percentage of approval or support of the executive leader (president or prime minister) per year, or for the EU countries, the percentage of respondents who trust the national government (the EU conducts a survey of its member countries and this is the question that is asked).

Figure 2.7. Voters' and Markets' Reactions to Consolidation Promise Gaps

1. Overperformance

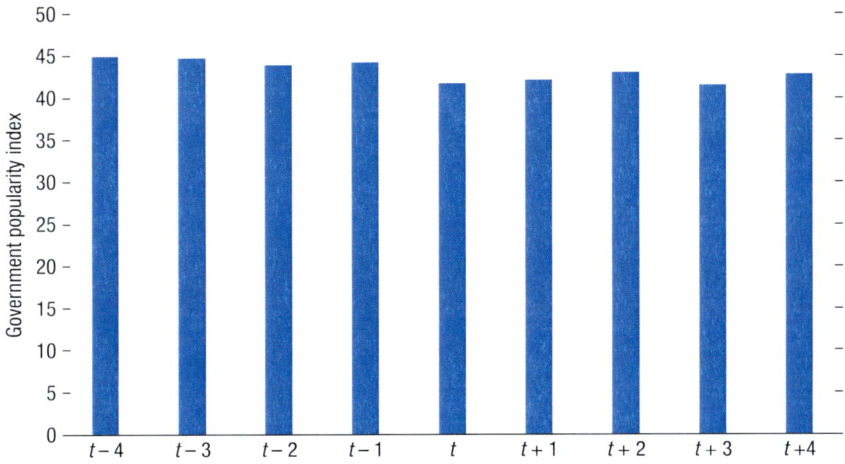

2. Underperformance

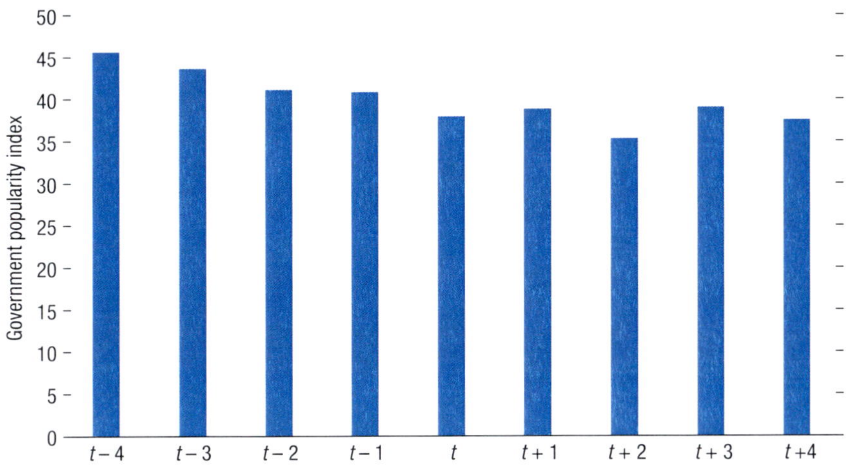

Source: Authors' calculations.
Note: "Overperformance" refers to negative consolidation promise gap; "underperformance" refers to the positive consolidation promise gap. The variable t is the start of the consolidation episode. The horizontal axis is measured in years. "Government popularity index" refers to the average percentage of approval or support of the executive leader (president or prime minister) per year; for the European Union countries, it refers to the percentage of respondents who trust the national government.

Figure 2.7. Voters' and Markets' Reactions to Consolidation Promise Gaps *(continued)*

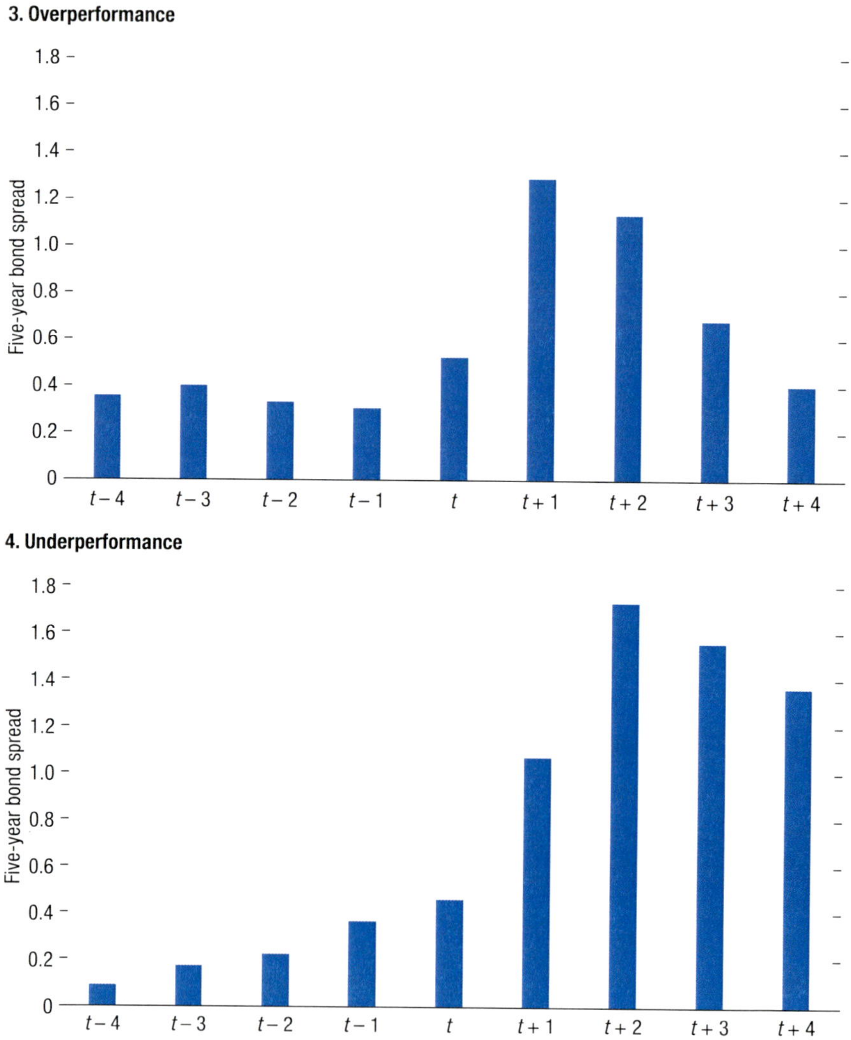

Sources: Bloomberg; and authors' calculations.
Note: "Overperformance" refers to the negative consolidation promise gap; "underperformance" refers to the positive consolidation promise gap. The variable *t* is the start of the consolidation episode. The horizontal axis is measured in years. "Government popularity index" refers to the average percentage of approval or support of the executive leader (president or prime minister) per year; for the European Union countries, it refers to the percentage of respondents who trust the national government.

THE CONSEQUENCES OF CONSOLIDATION PROMISE GAPS: IMPULSE-RESPONSE FUNCTIONS

To estimate the dynamic impact of promised fiscal consolidations over the short and medium term on both a financial market indicator and on government popularity, the analysis follows Jordà's (2005) method to generate impulse-response functions (IRFs).[24] This method consists of estimating IRFs directly from local projections. For each period k, the following regression is estimated:

$$Y_{i,t+k} - Y_{i,t} = \delta_i^k + \alpha_t^k + \sum_{j=1}^{l} \gamma_j^k \Delta Y_{i,t-j} + \beta_k CPG_{i,t} + X'_{i,t}\rho_k + \varepsilon_{i,t}^k, \quad (2.2)$$

with k=1,…,5 and where Y corresponds either to the five-year government bond spreads (relative to Germany) or government popularity; $CPG_{i,t}$ is the consolidation promise gap variable (in country i at time t); $X'_{i,t}$ is the same vector of control variables described in equation (2.2); δ_i^k are country fixed effects added to capture unobserved heterogeneity across countries and time-unvarying factors; α_t^k are time effects; γ_j^k and ρ_k are coefficients to be estimated for the lagged dependent variable and set of controls, respectively; $\varepsilon_{i,t}^k$ is a disturbance term satisfying usual assumptions; and β_k measures the distributional impact of fiscal consolidation episodes for each future period k. The lag length (l) is set at two as selected by the Akaike information criteria, but the findings are strongly robust to different lag structures.[25] Equation (2.2) is estimated using Beck and Katz's (1995) panel-corrected standard error estimator. IRFs are obtained by collecting the estimated β_k with confidence intervals computed using β_k's standard errors.[26]

Alternative ways of estimating dynamic impacts are available, but, as explained here, those are inferior options. The first possible alternative would be to estimate a panel vector autoregression. However, this type of estimation is generally considered a "black box" since all relevant regressors are considered endogenous. Moreover, one has to know the exact order in which they enter the system. Since economic theory rarely provides such an ordering, the Choleski decomposition is often used as a solution of limited value for providing structural information to a vector autoregression (VAR). Moreover, a major limitation

[24] Annex 2.3 presents the results of a static approach to testing the reactions of markets and voters to positive and negative promise gaps.

[25] Results are not shown for reasons of parsimony but are available upon request.

[26] The presence of a lagged dependent variable and country fixed effects could bias the estimation of γ_j^k and β_k in small samples (Nickell 1981). However, in this case, this is not a problem because the finite sample bias is about 0.03 (that is, 1/T, where T is 38).

of the VAR approach is that it has to be estimated to low-order systems. Since all effects of omitted variables are in the residuals, this may lead to large distortions in the IRFs, making them of little use for structural interpretations (see, for example, Hendry 1995). In addition, all measurement errors or misspecifications also induce unexplained information left in the error terms, making interpretation of the IRFs even more difficult (Ericsson, Hendry, and Prestwich 1998). One should bear in mind that because of its limited number of variables and the aggregate nature of the shocks, a VAR model should be viewed as an approximation of a larger structural system. In contrast, the approach used here does not suffer from these identification and size-limitation problems and, in fact, has been suggested by Auerbach and Gorodnichenko (2013), among others, as a sufficiently flexible alternative.

A second alternative for assessing the dynamic impact of fiscal consolidation episodes would be to estimate an autoregressive-distributed-lag model of changes in inequality and consolidation episodes and to compute the IRFs from the estimated coefficients (Romer and Romer 1989; Cerra and Saxena 2008). Note that the IRFs obtained using this method, however, tend to be lag sensitive, thus undermining the overall stability of the IRFs. Moreover, the statistical significance of long-lasting effects can result from one-type-of-shock models, particularly when the dependent variable is very persistent, as with the Gini coefficient (Cai and Den Haan 2009). In contrast, such issues are not experienced in the local projection method because lagged dependent variables enter as control variables and are not used to derive the IRFs. Finally, estimated IRFs' confidence intervals are computed directly using the standard errors of the estimated coefficients without the need for Monte Carlo simulations.

To explore whether the impact of consolidation promise gaps on both markets and the electorate depends on the state of the business cycle, the following alternative regression is estimated:

$$\begin{aligned} Y_{i,t+k} - Y_{i,t} &= \delta_i^k + \alpha_t^k + \sum_{j=1}^{l} \gamma_j^k \Delta Y_{i,t-j} + \beta_k^{bad} Y(z) CPG_{i,t} \\ &\quad + \beta_k^{good} \left(1 - Y(z)\right) CPG_{i,t} + X'_{i,t}\rho_k + \varepsilon_{i,t}^k \end{aligned} \tag{2.3}$$

with $Y(z_{it}) = \dfrac{\exp(-\gamma z_{it})}{1+\exp(-\gamma z_{it})}, \quad \gamma > 0,$

where z is an indicator of the state of the economy (using the real GDP growth rate) normalized to have zero mean and unit variance. The remainder of the variables and parameters are defined as in equation (2.2). This method is equivalent

Figure 2.8. Local Projection Method: Impulse Response Functions

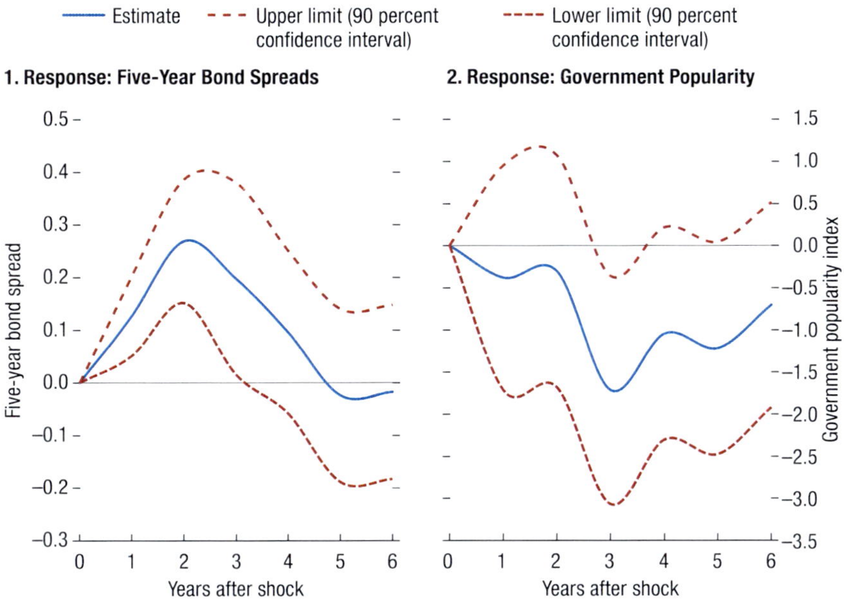

Sources: Bloomberg; and authors' calculations.

to Granger and Teräsvirta's (1993) smooth transition autoregressive model, whose advantage relative to estimating VARs for each regime is that it uses a larger number of observations to estimate the IRFs, thus increasing stability and precision.

Figure 2.8 confirms the previous results obtained by estimating equation (2.2). In the aftermath of a promise gap shock, five-year government spreads increase strongly and are statistically significant at usual levels. In contrast, the reaction of voters is weaker. Government popularity declines gradually, but the IRF is statistically weaker. Figure 2.9 shows the results of estimating equation (2.3). It seems that markets penalize incumbent governments more (by raising government bond spreads) and for a longer period for not delivering on their promises during bad times. As in Figure 2.8, the reaction of voters is not positive, and shows instead a marginally significant decrease in popularity during bad times one year after the promise gap shock.

Figure 2.9. Local Projection Method: Impulse Response Functions Conditioned on the Phase of the Business Cycle

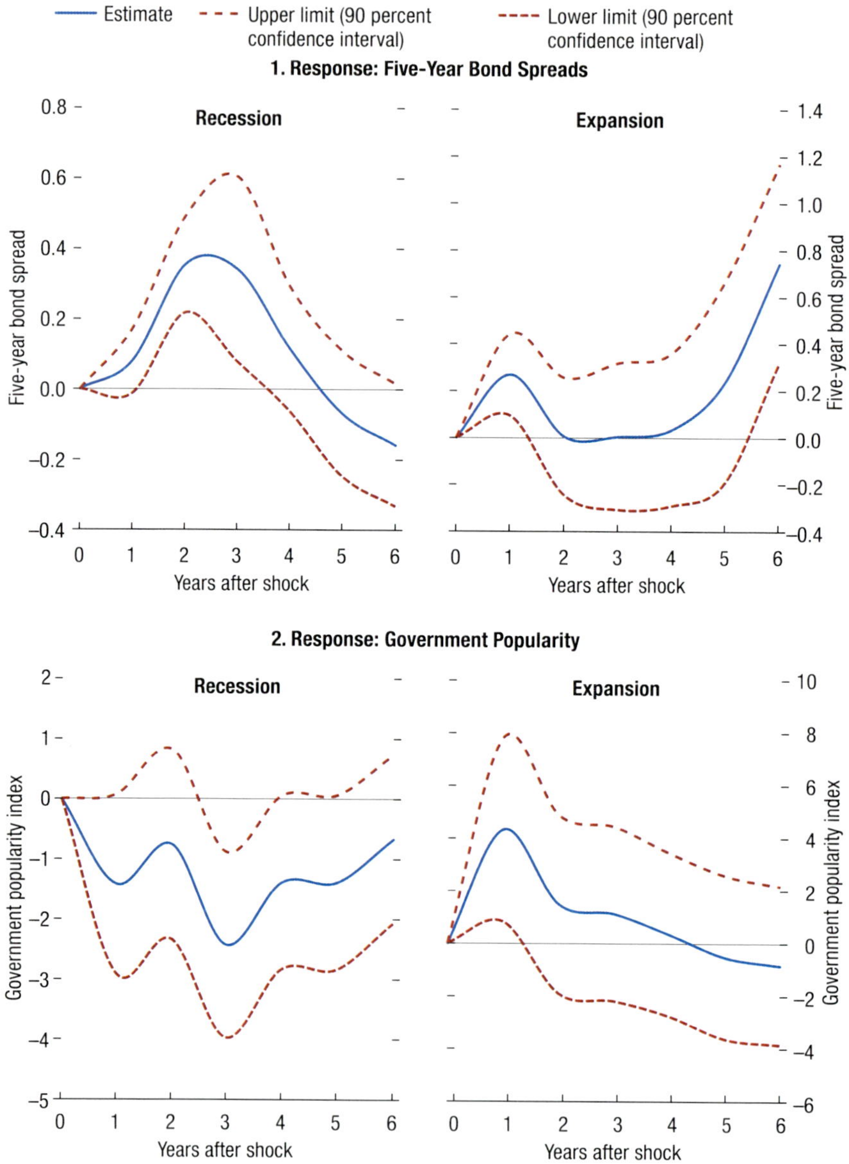

Sources: Bloomberg; and authors' calculations.

CONCLUSIONS AND POLICY IMPLICATIONS

This chapter analyzes the causes and consequences of fiscal consolidation promise gaps, defined as the distance between planned fiscal adjustments and actual consolidations, and finds that these gaps are sizable; both economic and political factors affect them. In particular, smaller initial debt levels, annual improvements in the output gap, and smaller forecast errors result in narrower promise gaps. The role of political factors in explaining consolidation promise gaps is important: newly elected governments, with a large margin of majority and high government effectiveness are more likely to deliver on their planned fiscal adjustments. Finally, evidence is found that financial markets penalize (reward) underperformers (overperformers), but the electorate is less responsive.

These results have important policy implications. First, policymakers should be more cautious in formulating ambitious fiscal consolidations (especially when they are revenue driven). Second, governments can deliver on their promised spending cuts by improving their capacity to deliver public services efficiently. Also, stronger starting conditions (as reflected by lower fiscal imbalances) could lead to lower promise gaps later on. Finally, policymakers should not be tempted to deviate from initial adjustment plans hoping to compensate for a subsequent market backlash with a boost in popularity because voters do not react positively to broken promises.

ANNEX 2.1. DESCRIPTION OF THE SAMPLE SELECTION

The data set on planned fiscal consolidations used in this chapter was constructed combining three sources of data. First we resorted to the Devries and others (2011) data, which cover fiscal consolidation plans in 17 advanced economies between 1978 and 2009. Despite some methodological differences in the selection of planned consolidation episodes, we lengthened the sample through 2013 using the enlarged narrative data set of Alesina and others (2015). These authors focus on 11 countries (Austria, Belgium, Denmark, France, Germany, Ireland, Italy, Portugal, Spain, United Kingdom, and United States) and expand the narrative data set through 2013. Finally, for the remaining countries and years, we used the European Commission's Stability and Convergence Programs (first vintage), complemented with country budget sources to further expand coverage to 2015.[27]

---

[27] By construction, even if a government has sustained a fiscal adjustment over various years (for example, the United Kingdom until 2015), the data would be compiled in tranches, corresponding to the three sources of data used.

Annex Table 2.1.1. Sample Selection

Country	Years	Source
Australia	1978–2009	Devries and others 2011
	2010–2015	Country sources
Austria	1978–2009	Devries and others 2011
	2010–2013	Alesina and others 2015
	2014–2015	Country sources
Canada	1978–2009	Devries and others 2011
	2010–2015	Country sources
Denmark	1978–2009	Devries and others 2011
	2010–2013	Alesina and others 2015
	2014–2015	SCP
Finland	1978–2009	Devries and others 2011
	2010–2015	SCP
Germany	1978–2009	Devries and others 2011
	2010–2013	Alesina and others 2015
	2014–2015	SCP
Ireland	1978–2009	Devries and others 2011
	2010–2013	Alesina and others 2015
	2014–2015	SCP
Italy	1978–2009	Devries and others 2011
	2010–2013	Alesina and others 2015
	2014–2015	SCP
Japan	1978–2009	Devries and others 2011
	2010–2015	Unavailable
Netherlands	1978–2009	Devries and others 2011
	2010–2015	SCP
Portugal	1978–2009	Devries and others 2011
	2010–2013	Alesina and others 2015
	2014–2015	SCP
Spain	1978–2009	Devries and others 2011
	2010–2013	Alesina and others 2015
	2014–2015	SCP
Sweden	1978–2009	Devries and others 2011
	2010–2015	SCP
United Kingdom	1978–2009	Devries and others 2011
	2010–2013	Alesina and others 2015
	2014–2015	Country sources
United States	1978–2009	Devries and others 2011
	2010–2013	Alesina and others 2015
	2014–2015	Country sources

Note: SCP = Stability and Convergence Program.

The following is a description of the data used to expand the database until 2015 using the European Commission's data and country sources. Where one-off items or rounding cause the consolidation size (reported as the primary budget) to differ from the sum of change in revenue and change in expenditure, the difference is divided evenly between the tax size and the expenditure size. These cases are noted with an asterisk (*).

Australia

Australia

Year	Consolidation Size	Tax Size	Expenditure Size	Tax-Based Consolidation	Expenditure-Based Consolidation
2010	1.4	0.15	1.25	0	1
2011	1.9	1.35	0.55	1	0
2012	3.0	1.70	1.30	1	0
2014	1.2	0.40	0.80	0	1
2015	0.5	0.55	−0.05	1	0

Source: Commonwealth of Australia Budget.

Fiscal consolidation in 2010 amounted to 1.4 percent of GDP with expenditure cuts of 1.25 percent of GDP and tax hikes of 0.15 percent of GDP. Fiscal consolidation in 2010 was motivated by deficit reduction. They key objective of Australia's deficit exit strategy was to limit expenditure growth by introducing a 2 percent cap on annual real public spending growth until the budget returned to surplus. On the revenue side, the government raised taxes on tobacco and continued implementation of its tax reform agenda.

Fiscal consolidation in 2011 amounted to 1.9 percent of GDP with expenditure cuts of 0.55 percent of GDP and tax hikes of 1.35 percent of GDP. As in 2010, fiscal consolidation in 2011 was motivated by deficit reduction.

Fiscal consolidation in 2012 amounted to 3.0 percent of GDP with expenditure cuts of 1.3 percent of GDP and tax hikes of 1.7 percent of GDP. As in 2011, fiscal consolidation in 2012 was motivated by deficit reduction.

Fiscal consolidation in 2014 amounted to 1.2 percent of GDP with expenditure cuts of 0.8 percent of GDP and tax hikes of 0.4 percent of GDP. As in 2012, fiscal consolidation in 2014 was motivated by deficit reduction, with the hope of achieving a budget surplus by 2023–24. A one-off government grant to the Reserve Bank of Australia in late 2013 contributed 0.6 percent of GDP to the consolidation in 2014.

Fiscal consolidation in 2015 amounted to 0.5 percent of GDP with an expenditure increase of 0.05 percent of GDP and tax hikes of 0.55 percent of GDP. Fiscal consolidation in 2015 was consistent with the government's medium-term fiscal strategy of returning the budget to surplus, maintaining strong fiscal discipline, strengthening the balance sheet, and redirecting government spending to increase productivity and workforce participation.

Austria

Austria

Year	Consolidation Size	Tax Size	Expenditure Size	Tax-Based Consolidation	Expenditure-Based Consolidation
2015	0.1	0.15	−0.05	1	0

Source: Stability and Convergence Program.

*Fiscal consolidation in 2015 amounted to 0.1 percent of GDP with tax hikes of 0.15 percent of GDP and an expenditure increase of 0.05 percent of GDP. Structural fiscal consolidation was a key policy area for Austria in 2015. The country's tax reform package was projected to tangibly reduce the tax burden, while cuts in expenditure on public administration and subsidies, tax fraud, and tax exemptions should generate adequate financing of the reform.

Belgium

Belgium

Year	Consolidation Size	Tax Size	Expenditure Size	Tax-Based Consolidation	Expenditure-Based Consolidation
2014	0.4	−0.90	1.30	0	1
2015	0.4	−0.65	1.05	0	1

Source: Stability and Convergence Program.

Fiscal consolidation in 2014 amounted to 0.4 percent of GDP with expenditure cuts of 1.3 percent of GDP and tax cuts of 0.9 percent of GDP. Consolidation, which slowed in 2014, was necessary to ensure debt sustainability in Belgium. In particular, the country's high public expenditure offers scope for a larger role for spending cuts in fiscal consolidation, especially in social transfers and public consumption. Belgium faced further problems in 2014 because the tax structure was heavily tilted toward labor income and numerous tax expenditures distorted the system.

*Fiscal consolidation in 2015 amounted to 0.4 percent of GDP with expenditure cuts of 1.05 percent of GDP and tax cuts of 0.65 percent of GDP. As in 2014, consolidation in 2015 was motivated by deficit reduction and debt sustainability.

Canada

Canada

Year	Consolidation Size	Tax Size	Expenditure Size	Tax-Based Consolidation	Expenditure-Based Consolidation
2010	0.4	0.40	0	1	0
2011	0.3	0.05	0.25	0	1
2012	0.2	−0.10	0.30	0	1
2013	0.4	0.20	0.20	0	0
2014	0.8	0.25	0.55	0	1
2015	0.2	0.45	−0.25	1	0

Source: Canada's Economic Action Plan Budget.

Fiscal consolidation in 2010 amounted to 0.4 percent of GDP with tax hikes of 0.4 percent of GDP. Fiscal consolidation in 2010 was motivated by deficit reduction and the objective of eliminating the deficit by 2015 through

Canada's Economic Action Plan. The government aimed to limit tax increases and to restrain growth in spending through targeted measures, including national defense spending, the international assistance envelope, and administrative costs.

*Fiscal consolidation in 2011 amounted to 0.3 percent of GDP with expenditure cuts of 0.25 percent of GDP and tax hikes of 0.05 percent of GDP. As in 2010, fiscal consolidation in 2011 was motivated by deficit reduction and the objective of eliminating the deficit by 2015.

Fiscal consolidation in 2012 amounted to 0.2 percent of GDP with expenditure cuts of 0.3 percent of GDP and tax cuts of 0.1 percent of GDP. As in previous years, fiscal consolidation in 2012 was motivated by deficit reduction and the objective of eliminating the deficit by 2015. The one-year Strategic and Operating Review was launched in 2011 with the aim of improving the efficiency and effectiveness of government operations and programs; it yielded savings of $5.2 billion on an ongoing basis.

Fiscal consolidation in 2013 amounted to 0.4 percent of GDP with expenditure cuts of 0.2 percent of GDP and tax hikes of 0.2 percent of GDP. As in previous years, fiscal consolidation in 2013 was motivated by deficit reduction and the objective of eliminating the deficit by 2015. The government further controlled direct program spending by expanding the use of tele-presence technologies to reduce travel expenses within the government, standardizing information technology, modernizing the production and distribution of government publications, and implementing targeted savings in the operations of the Canada Revenue Agency and Fisheries and Oceans Canada.

*Fiscal consolidation in 2014 amounted to 0.8 percent of GDP with expenditure cuts of 0.55 percent of GDP and tax hikes of 0.25 percent of GDP. As in previous years, fiscal consolidation in 2014 was motivated by deficit reduction and the objective of eliminating the deficit by 2015. The government also introduced measures to improve the integrity of the tax system, closing tax loopholes and strengthening tax compliance to ensure fairness.

*Fiscal consolidation in 2015 amounted to 0.2 percent of GDP with an expenditure increase of 0.25 percent of GDP and tax hikes of 0.45 percent of GDP. As in previous years, fiscal consolidation in 2015 was motivated by deficit reduction. The government fulfilled its promise to balance the budget in 2015.

Denmark

Denmark

Denmark did not show evidence of fiscal consolidation in 2014 or 2015.

Finland

Finland					
Year	Consolidation Size	Tax Size	Expenditure Size	Tax-Based Consolidation	Expenditure-Based Consolidation
2011	1.9	0.75	1.15	0	1

Source: Stability and Convergence Program.

*Fiscal consolidation in 2011 amounted to 1.9 percent of GDP with expenditure cuts of 1.15 percent of GDP and tax hikes of 0.75 percent of GDP. The government applied a system of spending limits, which proved effective during the recession, and also increased value-added taxes, energy taxes, excise duties on sweets and soft drinks, and the waste tax to tighten fiscal policy.

France

France					
Year	Consolidation Size	Tax Size	Expenditure Size	Tax-Based Consolidation	Expenditure-Based Consolidation
2014	0.5	0.05	0.45	0	1
2015	0.1	−0.20	0.30	0	1

Source: Stability and Convergence Program.

*Fiscal consolidation in 2014 amounted to 0.5 percent of GDP with expenditure cuts of 0.45 percent of GDP and tax hikes of 0.05 percent of GDP. The government's plans for fiscal consolidation for 2014–16 have been cut back, and the deficit will not be reduced to the Maastricht ceiling (3 percent of GDP) until 2017. The weakness of consolidation efforts in 2014 was primarily due to low tax receipts, a result of weak economic growth and inflation.

*Fiscal consolidation in 2015 amounted to 0.1 percent of GDP with expenditure cuts of 0.3 percent of GDP and tax cuts of 0.2 percent of GDP. To meet the targets set in the Public Finance Planning Act, the government instituted €4 billion in savings measures. The country continued to reduce expenditure, as well as the rate of aggregate tax social security contributions, until 2017.

Germany

Germany

Germany did not show evidence of fiscal consolidation in 2014 or 2015.

Ireland

Ireland

Year	Consolidation Size	Tax Size	Expenditure Size	Tax-Based Consolidation	Expenditure-Based Consolidation
2014	2.4	0.3	2.1	0	1
2015	1.2	−0.9	2.1	0	1

Source: Stability and Convergence Program.

Fiscal consolidation in 2014 amounted to 2.4 percent of GDP with expenditure cuts of 2.1 percent of GDP and tax hikes of 0.3 percent of GDP. As a result of the European Union–IMF (EU-IMF) financial assistance program and the National Recovery Plan (2011–14), Ireland emerged from the crisis with a declining fiscal deficit and a stronger fiscal framework. Fiscal consolidation was motivated by European Commission requirements to reduce the deficit in public finances to less than 3 percent of GDP by 2015.

*Fiscal consolidation in 2015 amounted to 1.2 percent of GDP with expenditure cuts of 2.1 percent of GDP and tax cuts of 0.9 percent of GDP. As in 2014, fiscal consolidation was motivated by European Commission requirements to reduce the deficit in public finances to less than 3 percent of GDP by 2015.

Italy

Italy

Year	Consolidation Size	Tax Size	Expenditure Size	Tax-Based Consolidation	Expenditure-Based Consolidation
2014	0.4	−0.2	0.6	0	1
2015	0.1	−0.3	0.4	0	1

Source: Stability and Convergence Program.

Fiscal consolidation in 2014 amounted to 0.4 percent of GDP with expenditure cuts of 0.6 percent of GDP and tax cuts of 0.2 percent of GDP. Since 2008, there has been a commitment to keep public finances in order by increasing revenues and decreasing expenditures. However, stimulus measures introduced in 2014 also included some reductions to the Social Contributions and the Regional Tax on Productive Activities.

*Fiscal consolidation in 2015 amounted to 0.1 percent of GDP with expenditure cuts of 0.4 percent of GDP and tax cuts of 0.3 percent of GDP. The government approved a legislative document for delivering more growth-friendly tax measures, including a reformed property tax, new environmental taxes, a reform of tax expenditures, and new actions against tax evasion.

Japan

Although the CAPB in Japan in 2014 and 2015 improved, this episode is not included in the sample because published data are unavailable.

Netherlands

Netherlands					
Year	Consolidation Size	Tax Size	Expenditure Size	Tax-Based Consolidation	Expenditure-Based Consolidation
2011	1.9	0.60	1.30	0	1
2012	0.1	0.00	0.10	0	1
2013	0.8	0.65	0.15	1	0
2015	0.3	−0.60	0.90	0	1

Source: Stability and Convergence Program.

*Fiscal consolidation in 2011 amounted to 1.9 percent of GDP with expenditure cuts of 1.3 percent of GDP and tax hikes of 0.6 percent of GDP. The primary goal of the Dutch consolidation strategy in 2011 was to restore financial sustainability. The government aimed to reach fiscal balance in 2015.

Fiscal consolidation in 2012 amounted to 0.1 percent of GDP with expenditure cuts of 0.1 percent of GDP. As in 2011, the goal of fiscal consolidation in 2012 was to restore financial sustainability. Expenditure cuts were focused on social benefits, the public wage bill, and subsidies.

*Fiscal consolidation in 2013 amounted to 0.8 percent of GDP with expenditure cuts of 0.15 percent of GDP and tax hikes of 0.65 percent of GDP. An additional consolidation package in spring 2012 and already planned measures increased consolidation measures in 2013. This package also contained a number of structural reforms, particularly in housing, pensions, and labor markets.

*Fiscal consolidation in 2015 amounted to 0.3 percent of GDP with expenditure cuts of 0.9 percent of GDP and tax cuts of 0.6 percent of GDP. Fiscal sustainability has achieved a positive outlook. The fiscal framework based on a spending ceiling but allowing automatic stabilizers to work on the revenue side has served the Netherlands well, as public debt shifted to less than 70 percent of GDP.

Portugal

Portugal					
Year	Consolidation Size	Tax Size	Expenditure Size	Tax-Based Consolidation	Expenditure-Based Consolidation
2014	0.9	−0.4	1.3	0	1
2015	1.4	−0.1	1.5	0	1

Source: Stability and Convergence Program.

Fiscal consolidation in 2014 amounted to 0.9 percent of GDP with expenditure cuts of 1.3 percent of GDP and tax cuts of 0.4 percent of GDP. Fiscal consolidation in 2014 resulted in a general government deficit of 4.5 percent of GDP, lower than the 4.8 percent projected in the Draft Budgetary Plan for 2015. Excluding deficit-increasing one-off measures, the general government deficit fell to 3.3 percent of GDP, leading to an improvement of the baseline for 2015.

Fiscal consolidation in 2015 amounted to 1.4 percent of GDP with expenditure cuts of 1.5 percent of GDP and tax cuts of 0.1 percent of GDP. As in 2014, fiscal consolidation in 2015 was motivated by deficit reduction. The Stability Program maintained the headline target of the Draft Budgetary Plan for 2015 of a headline deficit of 2.7 percent of GDP.

Spain

Spain

Year	Consolidation Size	Tax Size	Expenditure Size	Tax-Based Consolidation	Expenditure-Based Consolidation
2014	1.7	0.75	0.95	0	1
2015	1.4	−0.10	1.50	0	1

Source: Stability and Convergence Program.

Fiscal consolidation in 2014 amounted to 1.7 percent of GDP with expenditure cuts of 0.95 percent of GDP and tax hikes of 0.75 percent of GDP. Fiscal consolidation in 2014 was motivated by deficit reduction under the Stability Program, which aimed to bring the fiscal deficit to less than 3 percent of GDP in 2016 and to reach the medium-term objective of a balanced budgetary position in structural terms in 2017.

*Fiscal consolidation in 2015 amounted to 1.4 percent of GDP with expenditure cuts of 1.5 percent of GDP and tax cuts of 0.1 percent of GDP. As in 2014, fiscal consolidation in 2015 was motivated by deficit reduction under the Stability Program, which aimed to bring the fiscal deficit to less than 3 percent of GDP in 2016 and to reach the medium-term objective of a balanced budgetary position in structural terms in 2017.

Sweden

Sweden

Year	Consolidation Size	Tax Size	Expenditure Size	Tax-Based Consolidation	Expenditure-Based Consolidation
2011	0.6	−0.8	1.4	0	1
2015	0.5	0.1	0.4	0	1

Source: Stability and Convergence Program.

Fiscal consolidation in 2011 amounted to 0.6 percent of GDP with expenditure cuts of 1.4 percent of GDP and tax cuts of 0.8 percent of GDP. The rollback of stimulus measures to local governments contributed the most to the consolidation plan in 2011; thus, effective consolidation is solely expenditure based.

Fiscal consolidation in 2015 amounted to 0.5 percent of GDP with expenditure cuts of 0.4 percent of GDP and tax hikes of 0.1 percent of GDP. Fiscal policy supported activity through the operation of automatic stabilizers. The fiscal response to the extended period of weak economic growth, in addition to some permanent personal and corporate income tax cuts and increased expenditures for sickness benefits and asylum seekers, decreased the fiscal balance.

United Kingdom

United Kingdom

Year	Consolidation Size	Tax Size	Expenditure Size	Tax-Based Consolidation	Expenditure-Based Consolidation
2014	1.1	0.05	1.05	0	1
2015	1.3	0.20	1.10	0	1

Source: Budget Report of Her Majesty's Treasury and Autumn Statement 2016.

*Fiscal consolidation in 2014 amounted to 1.1 percent of GDP, primarily with spending cuts of 1.05 percent of GDP and tax hikes of 0.05 percent of GDP. The government's consolidation plans have been central to the reduction in the deficit. Reductions in expenditure were a result of the spending reduction announced in the Autumn Statement 2013 and the reduced costs of public service pensions.

Fiscal consolidation in 2015 amounted to 1.3 percent of GDP, primarily with spending cuts of 1.10 percent of GDP and tax hikes of 0.2 percent of GDP. Consolidation in 2015 was a continuation of the government's long-term plan in 2010 to halve the deficit as a share of GDP. With an aim to achieve a surplus in 2019–20, the government aims to undertake about £37 billion of further consolidation measures.

United States

United States

Year	Consolidation Size	Tax Size	Expenditure Size	Tax-Based Consolidation	Expenditure-Based Consolidation
2014	1.6	1.10	0.50	1	0
2015	0.6	0.95	−0.35	1	0

Source: Budget of the U.S. government.

Fiscal consolidation in 2014 amounted to 1.6 percent of GDP with tax hikes of 1.1 percent of GDP and spending cuts of 0.5 percent of GDP. Policy decisions such as the spending caps in the Budget Control Act of 2011, the increase in tax rates for top earners at the beginning of 2013, and the end of the temporary payroll tax holiday contributed to the government's deficit reduction strategy.

*Fiscal consolidation in 2015 amounted to 0.6 percent of GDP, primarily with tax hikes of 0.95 percent of GDP and an expenditure increase of

0.35 percent of GDP. Arrangements such as the Bipartisan Budget Act of 2015 aided in avoiding a federal shutdown, partly relieved automatic federal spending cuts, and relaxed the federal debt limit. Government purchases, including consumption and gross investment, at the federal, state, and local levels, added to the consolidation.

ANNEX 2.2. ROBUSTNESS OF RESULTS IN A HOMOGENEOUS SAMPLE

Combining three sources of data on narrative fiscal consolidations raises two potential problems. The first one is inherent to the narrative methodology, which is itself subjective. While potential (judgmental) measurement errors could have affected the three different sources of data, this analysis assumes that these would be evenly distributed across the three sources because the three data sources followed almost identical criteria for the selection of episodes. The second potential problem arises from possible structural breaks as a consequence of mixing similar but different data sources between 1978 and 2015. To make sure that the main results are robust, the analyses were replicated in the homogeneous sample of Devries and others (2011), which includes data from 17 advanced economies between 1978 and 2009 (see Annex Tables 2.2.1 and 2.2.2). The analysis was also replicated using a sample of promise gaps calculated in a sample built only with data from the Stability and Convergence Programs submitted by the 28 EU member states to the European Commission between 1998 and 2015 (see Annex Tables 2.2.3 and 2.2.4). As shown below, all the results from these tests on two alternative homogeneous samples confirm the robustness of the main findings.

Annex Table 2.2.1. Economic Determinants of Consolidation Promise Gaps, Devries' Database, 1978–2009

	Specification			
Regressors	**(1)**	**(2)**	**(3)**	**(4)**
Lagged Debt	−0.032***			−0.051***
	(0.007)			(0.012)
Change in Output Gap		−0.611***		−0.619***
		(0.082)		(0.119)
Lagged GDP Forecast Error			−0.404**	−0.331***
			(0.166)	(0.123)
Constant	1.892***	0.181	−0.134	3.479***
	(0.638)	(0.450)	(0.736)	(0.908)
Observations	162	165	96	96
R^2	0.225	0.368	0.428	0.712

Source: Authors' calculations.

Note: Dependent variable = consolidation promise gaps as defined in the main text. Robust standard errors clustered at the country level are in parentheses. Time and country fixed effects are omitted for reasons of parsimony.

$^{**}p < .05$; $^{***}p < .01$.

Annex Table 2.2.2. Economic and Political Determinants of Consolidation Promise Gaps, Devries' Database, 1978–2015

	Specification			
Regressors	**(1)**	**(2)**	**(3)**	**(4)**
Lagged Debt	−0.073***	−0.051***	−0.061**	−0.017
	(0.017)	(0.013)	(0.025)	(0.053)
Change in Output Gap	−0.418**	−0.617***	−0.440	−0.346
	(0.157)	(0.121)	(0.271)	(0.536)
Recent Elections	−0.377*			−1.327
	(0.393)			(1.779)
Margin of Majority		−0.420*		−7.306
		(2.847)		(8.870)
Government Effectiveness			−4.424**	−2.952
			(1.735)	(5.379)
Lagged GDP Forecast Error	−0.268**	−0.329**	−0.436	−0.048
	(0.126)	(0.125)	(0.323)	(0.445)
Constant	7.312***	3.656**	11.722***	18.539**
	(2.478)	(1.504)	(2.890)	(7.286)
Observations	73	96	41	29
R^2	0.636	0.713	0.868	0.798

Source: Authors' calculations.
Note: Dependent variable is consolidation promise gaps as defined in the main text. Robust standard errors clustered at the country level are in parentheses. Time and country fixed effects are omitted for reasons of parsimony.
*$p < .1$; **$p < .05$; ***$p < .01$.

Annex Table 2.2.3. Economic Determinants of Consolidation Promise Gaps, Stability and Convergence Program Database, 1998–2015

	Specification			
Regressors	**(1)**	**(2)**	**(3)**	**(4)**
Lagged Debt	−0.026***			−0.026***
	(0.009)			(0.008)
Change in Output Gap		−0.242***		−0.272***
		(0.052)		(0.053)
Lagged GDP Forecast Error			−0.059	−0.107**
			(0.046)	(0.043)
Constant	1.850***	0.571	0.509	1.906***
	(0.708)	(0.504)	(0.503)	(0.635)
Observations	252	253	224	224
R^2	0.148	0.196	0.122	0.263

Source: Authors' calculations.
Note: Dependent variable is consolidation promise gaps as defined in the main text. Robust standard errors clustered at the country level are in parentheses. Time and country fixed effects are omitted for reasons of parsimony.
*$p < .1$; **$p < .05$; ***$p < .01$.

Annex Table 2.2.4. Economic and Political Determinants of Consolidation Promise Gaps, Stability and Convergence Program Database, 1998–2015

Regressors	Specification (1)	(2)	(3)	(4)
Lagged Debt	−0.026***	−0.026***	−0.035***	−0.033***
	(0.008)	(0.009)	(0.009)	(0.009)
Change in Output Gap	−0.299***	−0.271***	−0.240***	−0.266***
	(0.054)	(0.053)	(0.055)	(0.057)
Recent Elections	−1.071*			−1.289**
	(0.586)			(0.632)
Margin of Majority	−0.110**	−0.107**	−0.091**	−0.092**
	(0.043)	(0.043)	(0.045)	(0.045)
Government Effectiveness		−1.330		−3.654
		(2.353)		(2.775)
Lagged GDP Forecast Error			−1.798**	−1.795**
			(0.898)	(0.889)
Constant	1.922***	2.620*	5.479***	7.453***
	(0.631)	(1.414)	(1.731)	(2.257)
Observations	224	224	188	188
R^2	0.275	0.264	0.314	0.336

Source: Authors' calculations.
Note: Dependent variable = consolidation promise gaps as defined in the main text. Robust standard errors clustered at the country level are in parentheses. Time and country fixed effects are omitted for reasons of parsimony.
*$p < .1$; **$p < .05$; ***$p < .01$.

ANNEX 2.3. THE CONSEQUENCES OF CONSOLIDATION PROMISE GAPS: REGRESSION ANALYSIS

To test the reaction of markets and voters to positive and negative promise gaps, the analysis follows a static approach and estimates equation (2.3.1):

$$Y_{it+1} = \delta_i + \vartheta CPG_{it} + \pi' X_{it} + \epsilon_{it}, \tag{2.3.1}$$

where Y_{it} denotes either five-year government bond spreads (relative to Germany) or government popularity in country i at time t; CPG_{it} is the consolidation promise gap variable (in country i at time t); X_{it} is a vector of control variables (that varies with the dependent variable) and includes real GDP growth, public debt (as a percentage of GDP), changes in unemployment, and 21-month real GDP growth forecast errors to control for the macroeconomic environment and minimize endogeneity concerns due to omitted-variables bias. ϑ, π are unknown parameters to be estimated. ϵ_{it} is an independent and identically distributed disturbance term satisfying usual assumptions. Equation (2.3.1) is estimated by ordinary least squares with robust standard errors clustered at the country level.

Annex Table 2.3.1 reports results for the five-year bond spread reaction to fiscal promise gaps, and confirms that financial markets tend to punish fiscal underperformance. Once governments plan for a fiscal adjustment, markets will

Annex Table 2.3.1. Market Reaction to Consolidation Promise Gaps

Dependent Variable = Five-Year Bond Spreads	Performance					
	Underperformers			Overperformers		
Consolidation Promise Gap	0.283***	0.247*	0.260**	0.030	0.077	0.027
	(0.102)	(0.140)	(0.102)	(0.329)	(0.325)	(0.303)
Real GDP Growth		−0.058			−0.370	
		(0.152)			(0.262)	
Public Debt			0.013			0.039**
			(0.008)			(0.016)
Constant	1.101***	1.192***	−0.002	1.627***	2.138***	−1.970
	(0.243)	(0.343)	(0.750)	(0.522)	(0.628)	(1.557)
Observations	55	55	55	30	30	30
R^2	0.128	0.130	0.166	0.000	0.069	0.180

Source: Authors' calculations.
Note: Dependent variable = five-year government bond spreads relative to Germany. Robust standard errors clustered at the country level are in parentheses. Time and country fixed effects are omitted for reasons of parsimony.
*p < .1; **p < .05; ***p < .01.

Annex Table 2.3.2. Voters' Reaction to Consolidation Promise Gaps

Dependent Variable = Government Popularity	Performance			
	Underperformers		Overperformers	
Consolidation Promise Gap	−1.775**	−0.866	0.438	−1.029
	(0.829)	(1.896)	(1.465)	(2.054)
Lagged GDP Forecast Error	4.295***	3.023	0.815	−4.351*
	(1.235)	(3.533)	(1.483)	(2.424)
Change in Unemployment Rate		−2.489		1.267
		(1.904)		(3.170)
Constant	37.307***	41.289***	50.506***	66.202***
	(5.831)	(10.582)	(4.771)	(6.985)
Observations	66	36	57	35
R^2	0.603	0.681	0.748	0.792

Source: Authors' calculations.
Note: Dependent variable = government popularity as defined in the main text. Robust standard errors clustered at the country level are in parentheses. Time and country fixed effects are omitted for reasons of parsimony.
*p < .1; **p < .05; ***p < .01.

follow closely and react negatively when they are not able to meet the targets. Annex Table 2.3.2 reports the results of using government popularity as the dependent variable. In general, voters do not seem to react strongly to consolidation gaps, regardless of the sign (that is, whether one inspects under- or overperformers).

REFERENCES

Afonso, A., and J. T. Jalles. 2014. "Assessing Fiscal Episodes." *Economic Modelling* 37: 255–70.

Alesina, A., O. Barbiero, C. Favero, F. Giavazzi, and M. Paradisi. 2015. "Austerity in 2009–2013." Working Paper 20827, National Bureau of Economic Research, Cambridge, MA.

Angelopoulos, K., J. Malley, and A. Philippopoulos. 2012. "Optimal Taxation and the Skill Premium." Working Paper 3706, CESifo, Munich.

Auerbach, A. J., and Y. Gorodnichenko. 2013. "Corrigendum: Measuring the Output Responses to Fiscal Policy." *American Economic Journal: Economic Policy* 5 (3): 320–22.
Baldacci, E., and M. Kumar. 2010. "Fiscal Deficits, Public Debt, and Sovereign Bond Yields." Working Paper 10/184, International Monetary Fund, Washington, DC.
Beck, N., and J. Katz. 1995. "What to Do (and Not to Do) with Time-Series Cross-Section Data." *American Political Science Review* 89 (3): 634–47.
Beetsma, R., B. Bluhm, M. Giuliodori, and P. Wierts. 2013. "From Budgetary Forecasts to Ex-Post Fiscal Data: Exploring the Evolution of Fiscal Forecast Errors in the European Union." *Contemporary Economic Policy* 31 (4): 795–813.
Beetsma, R., J. Cimadomo, O. Furtuna, and M. Giuliodori. 2015. "The Confidence Effects of Fiscal Consolidations." Working Paper 1770, European Central Bank, Frankfurt.
Beetsma, R., M. Giuliodori, and P. Wierts. 2009. "Budgeting versus Implementing Fiscal Policy in the EU." Discussion Paper 7285, Centre for Economic Policy Research, London.
Boix, C. 1997. "Political Parties and the Supply Side of the Economy: The Provision of Physical and Human Capital in Advanced Economies, 1960–90." *American Journal of Political Science* 41 (3): 814–45.
Cai, X., and W. Den Haan. 2009. "Predicting Recoveries and the Importance of Using Enough Information." Discussion Paper 7508, Centre for Economic Policy Research, London.
Cerra, V., and S. C. Saxena. 2008. "Growth Dynamics: The Myth of Economic Recovery." *American Economic Review* 98 (1): 439–57.
Cruz, C., P. Keefer, and C. Scartascini. 2015. Database of Political Institutions 2015. Washington, DC: Inter-American Development Bank. https://publications.iadb.org/handle/11319/7408?locale-attribute=en.
Devries, P., J. Guajardo, D. Leigh, and A. Pescatori. 2011. "A New Action-Based Dataset of Fiscal Consolidation." Working Paper 11/128, International Monetary Fund, Washington.
Ericsson, N. R., D. F. Hendry, and K. M. Prestwich. 1998. "The Demand for Broad Money in the United Kingdom, 1878–1993." *Scandinavian Journal of Economics* 100 (1): 289–324.
Escolano, J., L. Jaramillo, C. Mulas-Granados, and G. Terrier. 2014. "How Much Is a Lot? Historical Evidence on the Size of Fiscal Adjustments." Working Paper 14/179, International Monetary Fund, Washington, DC.
Frankel, J. 2011. "A Solution to Fiscal Procyclicality: The Structural Budget Institutions Pioneered by Chile." Working Paper 16945, National Bureau of Economic Research, Cambridge, MA.
Franzese, R. 2002. "Electoral and Partisan Cycles in Economic Policies and Outcomes." *Annual Review of Political Science* 5: 369–421.
Granger, C. W. J., and T. Teräsvirta. 1993. *Modelling Nonlinear Economic Relationships*. Oxford, U.K.: Oxford University Press.
Hendry, D. 1995. *Dynamic Econometrics*. Oxford, U.K.: Oxford University Press.
Jordà, O. 2005. "Estimation and Inference of Impulse Responses by Local Projections." *American Economic Review* 95 (1): 161–82.
Konishi, H. 2006. "Spending Cuts or Tax Increases? The Composition of Fiscal Adjustments as a Signal." *European Economic Review* 50 (6): 1441–69.
Mierau, J., R. Jong-A-Pin, and J. de Haan. 2007. "Do Political Variables Affect Fiscal Policy Adjustment Decisions? New Empirical Evidence." *Public Choice* 133 (3): 297–319.
Morris, R., and L. Schuknecht. 2007. "Structural Balances and Revenue Windfalls." Working Paper 737, European Central Bank, Frankfurt.
Mulas-Granados, C. 2003. "The Trade-Off between Growth & Equality and the Economic Impact of Alternative Fiscal Adjustment Strategies in the EU." European Economy Group Working Paper 20/2003 Brussels.
———. 2006. *Economics, Politics and Budgets: The Political Economy of Fiscal Adjustments in Europe*. London: Palgrave Macmillan.
Müller, W. C., and K. Strom. 1999. *Policy, Office or Votes? How Political Parties in Western Europe Make Hard Decisions*. Cambridge, U.K.: Cambridge University Press.
Nickell, S. 1981. "Biases in Dynamic Models with Fixed Effects." *Econometrica* 49 (6): 1417–26.

Perotti, R. 1998. "The Political Economy of Fiscal Consolidations." *Scandinavian Journal of Economics* 100 (1): 367–94.

———, and Y. Kontopoulos. 2002. "Fragmented Fiscal Policy." *Journal of Public Economics* 86: 191–222.

Potrafke, N. 2011. "Does Government Ideology Influence Budget Composition? Empirical Evidence from OECD Countries." *Economics of Governance* 12 (2): 101–34.

Przeworski, A., S. Stokes, and B. Manin, eds. 1999. "Democracy, Accountability, and Representation." Cambridge, U.K.: Cambridge University Press.

Romer, C. D., and D. H. Romer. 1989. "Does Monetary Policy Matter? A New Test in the Spirit of Friedman and Schwartz." In *NBER Macroeconomics Annual 1989*, edited by O. J. Blanchard and S. Fischer, 121–84. Cambridge, MA: MIT Press.

———. 2010. "The Macroeconomic Effects of Tax Changes: Estimates Based on a New Measure of Fiscal Shocks." *American Economic Review* 100 (3): 763–801.

Rousseeuw, P. J., and K. van Driessen. 1999. "A Fast Algorithm for the Minimum Covariance Determinant Estimator." *Technometrics* 41 (3): 212–23.

Tavares, J. 2004. "Does Right or Left Matter? Cabinets, Credibility and Fiscal Policy." *Journal of Public Economics* 88 (12): 2447–68.

von Hagen, J. 2010. "The Sustainability of Public Finances and Fiscal Policy Coordination in the EMU." CASE Network Studies and Analyses 412, Center for Social and Economic Research, Warsaw.

———, A. H. Hallett, and R. Strauch. 2001. "Budgetary Consolidation in EMU." Economics Paper 148, European Commission, Brussels.

CHAPTER 3

Fiscal Policy over the Election Cycle in Low-Income Countries

CHRISTIAN EBEKE AND DILAN ÖLÇER

INTRODUCTION

A growing literature assesses the detrimental effects of policy volatility on long-term growth and aggregate welfare (Fatás and Mihov 2003, 2012). One source of policy volatility might be related to national elections and the incumbent's incentive to use economic policy instruments for reelection purposes. Reelection-minded incumbents might have an incentive to use fiscal and monetary policy in such a way that during election years, public spending or money aggregates increase to satisfy the median voter despite potential adverse effects on fiscal sustainability and aggregate macroeconomic stability.[1] These cycles appear because of asymmetric information—voters lack full information about the incumbent's competencies.

Empirical studies on the political business cycle from the 1970s until the 1990s focused almost entirely on advanced economies and generally did not find a regular statistically significant evidence of cycles.[2] However, more recent studies have shown the effects of politically driven economic cycles in developing countries on government current expenditures, indirect tax revenues, budget deficits (Brender and Drazen 2005; Shi and Svensson 2006; Block 2002; Schuknecht 2000; Vergne 2009; Drazen and Eslava 2010; Ehrhart 2012), and monetary aggregates (Fouda 1997; Block 2002).

Several limitations and pending issues remain. First, most of these studies did not explicitly focus on low-income countries (LICs) but rather pooled together developing countries. The analysis in this chapter focuses on LICs because they are particularly vulnerable during election cycles. With weaker institutional capacity and poor transparency in budgets, these countries face greater risks that election-related fiscal policies will be conducted. By depleting their fiscal buffers

The authors thank Chris Lane, Christian Mumssen, Catherine Patillo, Noah Ndela Jean-Frederic, Susan Yang, Alejandro Guerson, colleagues in the Low-Income Countries Division of the Strategy, Policy, and Review Department at the IMF, as well as participants at the 6th CESifo Workshop on Political Economy and the lunch seminar at Sciences Po (France).

[1] See Brender and Drazen (2008) for an analysis of whether fiscal outcomes affect incumbents' reelection prospects. They find that fiscal deficits do not improve incumbents' reelection prospects in general. In developed countries, a deficit even punishes the incumbent.

[2] Alesina, Roubini, and Cohen (1997) and Drazen (2001) provide excellent reviews on the empirical results.

during election years, LICs further increase their macroeconomic vulnerability and limit their ability to guard themselves from external shocks. Therefore, it is important to better understand the composition of political budget cycles in these countries and consider ways to mitigate related fiscal policy volatility.

Second, although various studies provide insights into what happens to specific variables during elections, they do not typically focus on the composition of the postelection adjustment. Block (2002) analyzes, in a sample restricted to sub-Saharan Africa, a number of fiscal and monetary variables during and after elections and concludes that government spending shifts toward more visible, current expenditures and away from public investment. However, his analysis has several limitations. The period under study is restricted to 1980 to 1995, although for many countries in sub-Saharan Africa, elections were not competitive before 1990, and even during the first half of the 1990s. Moreover, the analysis is limited to presidential systems to address issues related to endogenously timed elections, yet this restriction induces an important selection bias.[3]

This chapter investigates the behavior of a comprehensive set of fiscal variables during and two years after national elections. It seeks to shed light on the main form of fiscal expansion during the election year and the composition of the fiscal retrenchment (if any) in the subsequent years. This analysis uses a recent data set, National Elections across Democracy and Autocracy (NELDA) (Hyde and Marinov 2012), for the election variable and follows the convention in this literature (for example, Shi and Svensson 2006; Brender and Drazen 2008) by focusing on the highest level of national elections. Therefore, it only includes legislative elections for countries with parliamentary political systems and executive elections for countries with presidential elections.

Third, to the best knowledge of the chapter authors, no empirical work examines the effects of fiscal rules and IMF programs on the likelihood, the size, and the composition of political budget cycles in LICs. Therefore, the chapter explores the efficiency of these two main constraints on the ability of the incumbent to pursue a politically motivated fiscal impulse in election years. It formally tests whether active national fiscal rules and IMF programs in LICs help dampen the magnitude of the political budget cycle by limiting the incumbent's incentives to significantly modify fiscal policy for reelection purposes. Inspired by the pioneering work of Rose (2006) in the case of U.S. states, the analysis tests the extent to which national fiscal rules matter in LICs using the IMF data set on fiscal rules (Schaechter and others 2012). This is an interesting question to investigate given that experts always express doubts about the effectiveness of these rules in the LIC context.[4] The issue of the effect of IMF programs on the

[3] Block (2002) analyzes elections that take place at regular times in presidential systems. However, presidential regimes have endogenously timed elections too, particularly in developing countries (Shi and Svensson 2006). Also, countries with presidential regimes have characteristics that systematically distinguish them from parliamentary regimes (Persson and Tabellini 2003).

[4] The predominant national fiscal rules for LICs are debt rules, possibly reflecting institutional weaknesses that would complicate, for example, the implementation of expenditure rules or cyclically

political budget cycle in LICs is also policy relevant. With several LICs having experienced various waves of IMF programs over the past decades, one important question could be the extent to which IMF program conditions have constrained incumbents' election-year extravagances. The chapter follows the work by Hyde and O'Mahony (2010) but focuses on the dampening role of IMF programs on the political budget cycle in LICs.

Fourth, taking advantage of the NELDA data set on elections compiled by Hyde and Marinov (2012), this analysis is able to address the endogeneity of election timing within countries. Moreover, it also factors in the self-selection bias in the decision to adopt fiscal rules or participate in IMF programs. The econometric models are used to control for several variables that ensure that the election effects are well identified so that any shift in fiscal variables associated with a national election must be interpreted as a discretionary fiscal policy by the incumbent. These control variables include external sources of financing (grants and loans), the real GDP growth rate, the inflation rate, and other covariates.

The results indicate that during election years, government consumption increases, leading to higher fiscal deficits by about 1 percentage point. During the two years following elections, fiscal retrenchment takes the form of increased revenue effort in trade taxes and cuts to government investment. However, this post-election partial fiscal adjustment is not translated into reduced current spending envelopes, or sufficient revenue mobilization efforts to fully offset the deviation allowed during the election year. The chapter also finds that national fiscal rules help mitigate the cycles in government consumption. Results also show that LICs with active IMF programs during a national election experience a much lower political budget cycle compared with years in which there is no IMF program.

The remainder of the chapter is organized as follows: The second section sets up the main empirical framework and presents the baseline results. The third section tests the robustness of the baseline results by factoring in the endogeneity of election timing. The fourth section investigates the role of fiscal rules and IMF programs as mitigating factors. The fifth section concludes.

HOW IS FISCAL POLICY CONDUCTED OVER THE ELECTION CYCLE? PRELIMINARY EVIDENCE

This section presents the general framework and the data used to assess the dynamic of fiscal variables during and after the occurrence of a national election in LICs. Several fiscal outcomes (government consumption, public investment, breakdown of tax revenues, and budget balance as percentage of GDP) are used to assess the magnitude of the shocks on the budget during and after elections. The section also discusses the baseline econometric results.

---

adjusted budget balance rules. However, only four LICs use national fiscal rules. Other LICs operate under supranational rules.

Baseline Specification and Data

This chapter estimates several dynamic panel equations linking a given fiscal outcome with the election dummy while controlling for standard determinants of the given fiscal variable. As has now become standard in the literature on fiscal policy, dynamic equations are specified to control for the inertia characterizing fiscal variables over time. The analysis uses a panel data set that covers 68 LICs over 21 years, 1990–2010; 51 of these LICs have had at least one election.[5] A country is classified as an LIC if it benefits from the IMF Poverty Reduction and Growth Trust as of 2010. The choice of time period is based on available data after the democratic reforms that many countries, particularly in sub-Saharan Africa, implemented in 1990 that made elections more competitive.

The baseline specification is as follows:

$$Y_{i,t} = \alpha_i + \sum_{p=0}^{2} \theta_{p+1}\, ELE_{i,t-p} + \rho Y_{i,t-1} + X'_{i,t}\Gamma + \varepsilon_{i,t}, \tag{3.1}$$

where $Y_{i,t}$ is the fiscal outcome in each country i at year t. $\mathbf{X}_{i,t}$ is the vector of country-level covariates that follow and slightly augment the empirical literature on the determinants of government consumption, tax revenues, and budget deficits in developing countries (Rodrik 1998; Keen and Lockwood 2010; Combes and Saadi-Sedik 2006). More specifically, models control for variables such as real GDP growth rate, inflation rate, trade openness, foreign aid, external debt, natural resource rents, agriculture value added, and fiscal rules. All the fiscal variables, inflation rate, external debt, and foreign aid are drawn from the IMF World Economic Outlook database; real per capita GDP growth series were downloaded from Penn World Table 7.1 data set. Natural resource rents and total population data are drawn from the World Bank World Development Indicators database.[6]

The main variables of interest are the three election dummies $ELE_{i,t}$, $ELE_{i,t-1}$, and $ELE_{i,t-2}$, which take the value 1 in case of a national election and 0 otherwise. From equation (3.1), the three coefficients θ_1, θ_2, and θ_3, measure the percentage point change in the fiscal variable during, one year after, and two years after a national election, respectively.[7] The analysis uses the NELDA data set (Hyde and Marinov 2012) for the election variables and follows the convention in this literature (for example, Shi and Svensson 2006; Brender and Drazen 2008)

---

[5] See Annex Table 3.1.1 for the list of countries. The panel data set is unbalanced because some countries have missing values.

[6] Descriptive statistics for the dependent variables are provided in Annex Table 3.1.2.

[7] When investigating how elections affect government spending, one critique may be that the political budget cycles observed are due to the extra cost of running elections, and not necessarily a strategic allocation that is driven by reelection incentives. This is a fair point, though not a real concern for LICs. These countries are very poor and highly dependent on aid. Most of the expenses related to elections are also borne through aid. Therefore, we investigate the effect of elections on government spending while controlling for aid as a share of GDP. The fact that political budget cycles are observed even when keeping aid constant shows that there is a political incentive even if elections were costly to run.

by focusing on the highest level of national elections. Therefore, only legislative elections for countries with parliamentary political systems and executive elections for countries with presidential elections are included. The binary election indicator, *ELE*, takes the value 1 depending on the year in the election cycle, and 0 otherwise, as described above. There were 191 national elections during the sample period. Annex Table 3.1.1 shows the distribution of national elections across LICs over the period of analysis.

The IMF data set is a comprehensive source of information on budget composition based on data collected by economist desks in the field and officially approved by countries. With regard to government spending, this chapter differentiates between current expenditures (proxied by government final consumption) and public investment to assess the effects of elections on the composition of spending.

A certain granularity for tax expenditures is also accommodated.[8] Instead of using only overall tax revenues as many other papers in this literature do, this analysis decomposes tax revenue into three categories—direct, indirect, and trade taxes.[9] Distinguishing between these types of taxes makes the analysis richer by illustrating which taxes the government will make a particular effort to collect during the different years of the election cycle. Ehrhart (2012) bases her analysis on direct and indirect taxes, but there might be a political economy story behind trade taxes as well. Because trade involves crossing borders, it is potentially easier for the government to vary tax effort on these specific locations on the borders (Stotsky and WoldeMariam 1997).[10] By looking at tax revenue ratios at a more disaggregated level, this chapter provides additional insights into the shift in the composition of tax revenue efforts over the whole election cycle. The focus on LICs is another important difference from existing papers.

Equation (3.1) is a dynamic specification and is used because of the strong inertia characterizing the fiscal variables of interest. Government administrations are constrained by budgets, and the current budget largely determines the next period's appropriations. Although such inertia has been argued to provide some stability and predetermines fiscal spending (Schuknecht 2000), the presence of lagged dependent variables and country-specific effects renders the ordinary least squares estimator biased because the lagged dependent variable is correlated with the error term (Nickell 1981). To deal with this issue, there are two commonly

[8] Nonresource tax revenue mobilization is a major challenge in many LICs. While overall tax revenues equate to more than 50 percent of GDP in some countries in the sample, others barely manage to collect 1 percent of GDP. The mean overall tax revenue in the sample is 14.8 percent of GDP. The largest contribution to revenues comes from indirect taxes, followed by direct taxes, and trade taxes.

[9] Indirect taxes, which are broad-based taxes on goods and services, are paid by most citizens and correspond to 5.6 percent of GDP in the sample. Direct taxes represent taxes on income, profits and capital gains, correspond to 4.4 percent of GDP, and are mostly paid by corporations since personal income taxes are almost nonexistent. Finally, trade taxes, which correspond to 3.8 percent of GDP, are taxes on trade and international transactions paid by corporations.

[10] For the Indian states, Khemani (2004) provides an analysis with subcategories of commodity taxes: sales, excise and trade. Data are not available on this level for the 68 low-income countries that we study in this chapter.

used estimators: the difference–generalized method of moments (GMM) estimator (Arellano and Bond 1991) and the system-GMM estimator (Arellano and Bover 1995; Blundell and Bond 1998). In the difference-GMM estimator, equation (3.1) is taken in first differences (to remove country fixed effects), and the first differentiated variables are instrumented by their lagged values in levels. However, Arellano and Bover (1995) and Blundell and Bond (1998) have shown that when the explanatory variables are persistent over time, the lagged values of variables in levels risk being poor instruments for variables in first differences. To improve the efficiency, they propose the system-GMM estimator, which increases the moment conditions. The equation in levels and the equation in differences are combined in a system and then are estimated with an extended GMM system that allows for the use of lagged differences and lagged levels of the explanatory variables as instruments. Hence, the system-GMM estimator controls for unobserved country-specific effects as well as potential endogeneity of the explanatory variables. The chapter uses Windmeijer's (2005) correction of standard errors for finite sample bias. Two specification tests check the validity of the instruments. The first is the GMM standard Sargan/Hansen test of overidentifying restrictions. The second test examines the hypothesis that there is no second-order serial correlation in the first-differenced residuals. The number of lags of the explanatory variables used as instruments is usually limited to reduce the "overfitting" bias (Roodman 2009).

Baseline Estimates

The chapter first reports the baseline findings for the expenditure side, then for the revenue side, and finally for the fiscal balance.

Composition of Expenditures

Table 3.1 presents the results for the system-GMM estimator for the various fiscal outcomes. Column 1 reports that government consumption increases during an election year, with no significant decrease the two years after an election. The coefficient on ELE_t is significant and shows that, on average, consumption as a share of GDP increases by 0.8 percentage point during the election year. The result for government investment is reported in column 2, which shows that government investment as a share of GDP decreases by almost 0.4 percentage point the year following an election. This result is statistically significant. Although the sign of the coefficients for ELE_{t-2} is also negative, it is not significant.

These results indicate that political budget cycles have an impact on government expenditures in LICs. More specifically, governments in LICs tend to increase consumption expenditures during election years, while investments are unchanged. The postelection adjustment takes the form of decreased government investment. These results confirm previous claims (Vergne 2009) that government spending shifts toward more visible consumption during election years. In addition, the analysis shows that the negative effect on government investment appears with a lag and implies that publicly financed projects, for example, in infrastructure, stagnate the year after an election. From the politicians' point of view, this is strategic, because stagnating investments during election years would probably have a negative impact

Table 3.1. Estimates of the Political Budget Cycle across Selected Fiscal Variables in Low-Income Countries, 1990–2010

	(1)	(2)	(3)	(4)	(5)	(6)	(7)
	G	I	T	TGS	TD	TT	Bal
$Election_t$	0.841***	−0.194	0.209	−0.075	0.102	0.112*	−1.047*
	[0.258]	[0.210]	[0.152]	[0.061]	[0.083]	[0.066]	[0.542]
$Election_{t-1}$	−0.059	−0.371**	0.340*	0.134	0.023	0.173***	0.275
	[0.223]	[0.159]	[0.187]	[0.084]	[0.084]	[0.064]	[0.330]
$Election_{t-2}$	−0.049	−0.081	0.290*	0.026	−0.046	0.212*	−0.262
	[0.197]	[0.208]	[0.159]	[0.101]	[0.061]	[0.114]	[0.322]
Lagged Dependent Variable	0.730***	0.813***	0.893***	1.029***	0.831***	0.976***	0.260***
	[0.103]	[0.089]	[0.168]	[0.057]	[0.105]	[0.064]	[0.094]
Real per Capita GDP Growth	−0.032	0.027	0.041**	0.033***	−0.003	0.016***	0.084***
	[0.034]	[0.023]	[0.020]	[0.006]	[0.010]	[0.006]	[0.031]
Official Development Assistance to GDP	0.073**	0.038**	−0.001	−0.000	−0.002	0.005	−0.019
	[0.037]	[0.015]	[0.014]	[0.003]	[0.003]	[0.003]	[0.018]
External Debt to GDP	−0.002	−0.001	−0.004	−0.000	−0.001	−0.001	−0.005
	[0.003]	[0.001]	[0.004]	[0.001]	[0.001]	[0.001]	[0.003]
Trade Openness	0.028**	0.011**	0.013	0.000	0.008*	0.002	0.014
	[0.012]	[0.005]	[0.012]	[0.002]	[0.004]	[0.001]	[0.010]
ln (100 + inflation rate)	−0.149	0.419	−0.049	0.005	0.046	−0.164*	0.582
	[0.443]	[0.335]	[0.214]	[0.083]	[0.088]	[0.094]	[0.458]
Fiscal Rule $Dummy_{t-1}$	1.625***	0.345	0.179	−0.036	0.281	−0.232**	−0.400
	[0.470]	[0.327]	[0.541]	[0.170]	[0.206]	[0.093]	[1.603]
Natural Resource Rents to GDP			−0.003	−0.005	0.010	−0.003	
			[0.006]	[0.005]	[0.013]	[0.003]	
ln (total population)			0.020	−0.010	0.035	0.004	
			[0.104]	[0.029]	[0.023]	[0.049]	
Intercept	1.999	−2.086	0.760	0.040	−0.556	0.711	−5.941**
	[2.348]	[1.785]	[2.320]	[0.590]	[0.653]	[1.225]	[2.385]
Observations	1,234	1,140	815	679	705	679	970
Number of Countries	60	57	56	52	53	52	61
m1: *p*-value	0.004	0.001	0.003	0.000	0.022	0.000	0.017
m2: *p*-value	0.516	0.416	0.530	0.350	0.294	0.104	0.260
Hansen Overidentification Test: *p*-value	0.829	0.060	0.031	0.839	0.249	0.540	0.114
Number of Instruments	17	17	21	21	21	25	23

Source: Authors' estimates.

Note: All equations are estimated using the two-step system-GMM with Windmeijer (2005) correction of standard errors. Standard errors are in brackets. Bal = overall fiscal balance ratio; G = government consumption ratio; I = public investment ratio; T = total tax revenue ratio; TD = tax revenues on income ratio; TGS = tax revenues on goods and services ratio; TT = trade tax revenues ratio.

$^{*}p < .1$; $^{**}p < .05$; $^{***}p < .01$.

on reelection prospects. Although not studied explicitly in this chapter, this postelection investment stagnation may have serious consequences for economic growth.

Composition of Tax Revenues

Column 3 of Table 3.1 shows that government's overall tax effort improves significantly in the years following an election. A look at the composition of tax revenues reveals a more detailed picture of government resource mobilization efforts over the election cycle. In column 4, where indirect taxes (taxes on goods and services) are reported, the results do not suggest the existence of an election-related cycle. Although the coefficient on the ELE_t variable is negative, it is not statistically significant. The coefficients on ELE_{t-1} and ELE_{t-2} are not significantly different from zero either. These results contrast with findings by Ehrhart (2012), who finds a significant and negative impact of elections on indirect taxes using a broader sample of all developing countries. The results in this chapter suggest the opposite, implying that LICs' tax policies differ from those of other developing countries over the election cycle. The different results compared with existing studies can be explained by at least two factors. First, this analysis decomposes total tax revenues into various components to get better granularity and finds that at least for LICs, the impact of national elections is observed in trade tax revenues during the run to rebuild eroded fiscal buffers. Second, the results provide a more detailed assessment of the impact of elections on government indirect tax revenues because it does not pool taxes on goods and services with trade taxes, an approach that is different from previous papers.[11] The results show that within the broad definition of indirect taxes, it is the trade tax revenue ratio that matters, not taxes on goods and services.

In addition, neither does direct tax effort (on income, profits, and capital gains) vary along the election cycle, as shown in column 5. Column 6 shows the results for tax revenues on international trade. Econometric estimates indicate that governments change efforts in collecting trade taxes during election years. There is a slight (barely statistically significant) increase in the ratio of trade taxes to GDP of about 0.11 percentage point during the election year, an effort that is maintained and strengthened during the two postelection years. This explains why total tax revenues increase one and two years after elections. The results clearly suggest that LICs tend to partially rebuild the eroded policy buffers on the revenue side through increased discretionary tax revenue mobilization on international trade. This finding may occur because trade taxes tend to be relatively easier to collect in LICs, given that these countries tend to find it harder than advanced and emerging economies to mobilize revenue, particularly domestic tax revenue.

Overall Fiscal Balance

The dynamic of the overall fiscal balance throughout the election cycle mirrors the behavior of the expenditure and revenue variables (column 7 of Table 3.1). The overall fiscal deficit ratio increases by about 1 percentage point of GDP during the election year, mainly driven by the observed increase in government current spending.[12] In the postelection years, attempts are certainly made to rebuild the eroded fiscal buffers, but it does not appear large and balanced enough to generate any significant statistical impact. The decline in public investment and the observed tax revenue increases in the postelection years constitute the main

---

[11] However, it remains true that trade taxes also include value-added tax revenues collected at the border.

[12] The magnitude of the deviation in the fiscal balance attributed to elections is similar to previous results by Shi and Svensson (2006).

adjustment package in LICs, but fall short of fully rebuilding the eroded fiscal buffers. The irreversibility of government current expenditures and the ratcheting effect are the main factors behind the protracted pressure exerted by elections on overall fiscal performance throughout the years.

DEALING WITH THE ENDOGENEITY OF ELECTION TIMING

One potential critique of the baseline results discussed above is that the analysis treats the election variables as exogenous relative to fiscal policy, which may not be the case. Timing of both elections and fiscal policies could, for example, be influenced by a number of unobserved variables that are not included in the regressions. There may be a bias if, for example, the timing of the election is strategically chosen by the incumbent politician to coincide with favorable economic conditions. One way to address this potential bias is to distinguish between elections whose timing is predetermined relative to current fiscal policies (Shi and Svensson 2006) and election timing that is not predetermined. Using information provided in the NELDA data set, an election is classified as predetermined if it took place on the date fixed by an established constitution or procedure. Conversely, election timing is considered endogenous if the election was early or late relative to the date it was supposed to be held per established procedure.[13]

New election indicators, $ELEPRE_{i,t}$ and $ELEENDO_{i,t}$, are created to replace $ELE_{i,t}$. The variable $ELEPRE_{i,t}$ equals 1 in country i and year t when an election was held at a predetermined time, and 0 otherwise. The variable $ELEENDO_{i,t}$ equals 1 in country i and year t if an election whose timing was not predetermined took place, and 0 otherwise. The postelection indicators were coded accordingly. Among the 191 elections in the sample, 56.5 percent are classified as predetermined.[14] The baseline regressions are reestimated with the new election indicators. If the baseline results are robust, they should also hold for predetermined elections. The revised model takes the following form:

$$Y_{i,t} = \alpha_i + \sum_{p=0}^{2} \varphi_p \, ELEPRE_{i,t-p} + \sum_{p=0}^{2} \kappa_p \, ELEENDO_{i,t-p} + \rho Y_{i,t-1} + \mathbf{X}'_{i,t}\boldsymbol{\Gamma} + \varepsilon_{i,t}. \quad (3.2)$$

The coefficients of interest are φ_p, which capture the impact of elections after ruling out the effects of elections that occurred on an unpredicted schedule compared with the constitutional calendar.

Table 3.2 presents the econometric results. They are very similar to the previous ones in magnitude and impact on fiscal outcomes. Government current expenditures deviate significantly from their normal levels during election years,

[13] This coding is done using the variable *NELDA6* in the NELDA data set. An established procedure is one contained in the constitution.

[14] Out of the 191 elections, 108 are classified predetermined and 38 endogenous. We were unable to classify 45 elections.

Table 3.2. Addressing the Endogeneity of Election Timing in Low-Income Countries, 1990–2010

	(1)	(2)	(3)	(4)	(5)	(6)	(7)
	G	I	T	TGS	TD	TT	Bal
Predetermined Election$_t$	0.758**	−0.231	0.095	−0.074	0.147	0.098*	−1.278**
	[0.327]	[0.183]	[0.167]	[0.089]	[0.116]	[0.055]	[0.618]
Predetermined Election$_{t-1}$	0.224	−0.398**	0.131	0.053	0.093	0.112*	0.253
	[0.305]	[0.188]	[0.255]	[0.108]	[0.086]	[0.058]	[0.438]
Predetermined Election$_{t-2}$	−0.031	−0.159	0.076	−0.020	−0.057	0.171*	−0.466*
	[0.218]	[0.308]	[0.148]	[0.108]	[0.096]	[0.094]	[0.278]
Observations	1,131	1,043	758	633	657	631	900
Number of Countries	60	57	56	52	53	52	61
m1: *p*-value	0.007	0.002	0.004	0.000	0.009	0.001	0.019
m2: *p*-value	0.653	0.390	0.236	0.269	0.250	0.089	0.210
Hansen Overidentification Test: *p*-value	0.583	0.022	0.031	0.864	0.238	0.705	0.217
Number of Instruments	20	20	24	24	24	28	20

Source: Authors' estimates.

Note: Windmeijer (2005) corrected standard errors are in brackets. All specifications include the exact control variables per Table 3.1. The models also control for the endogenous election dummies (dated at year *t*, *t* − 1, and *t* − 2, respectively) that identify whether the election was early or late relative to the date it was supposed to be held per an established constitution or procedure. The predetermined election dummies identify elections that took place on the date fixed by an established constitution or procedure. All equations are estimated using the two-step system-GMM with Windmeijer (2005) correction of standard errors. Bal = overall fiscal balance ratio; G = government consumption ratio; I = public investment ratio; T = total tax revenue ratio; TD = tax revenues on income ratio; TGS = tax revenues on goods and services ratio; TT = trade tax revenues ratio.

*$p < .10$; **$p < .05$; ***$p < .01$.

leading to an increase in the overall fiscal deficit of about 1.3 percentage points of GDP. The postelection years are characterized by an effort to partially rebuild fiscal buffers, but this comes with a price. Public investment is reduced by about 0.4 percentage point of GDP. The result that governments increase their efforts to mobilize trade tax revenues still holds. Two years after the election, the estimates indicate a reduction of the fiscal deficit by about 0.5 percentage point of GDP.

DOMESTIC AND INTERNATIONAL SCRUTINY

A developing literature has tried to identify the role played by various macroeconomic factors on the magnitude of political budget cycles in developing countries. O'Mahony (2010) examines the role played by openness (globalization). Vergne (2009) and Faye and Niehaus (2012) consider the role of media and financing variables such as natural resource rents and official development assistance. Combes, Ebeke, and Maurel (2013) examined the role of migrant remittances inflows on the magnitude of political budget cycles in developing countries. This section examines two main factors not fully analyzed in the LIC context that could dampen electoral fiscal manipulation. The discussion distinguishes between a domestic institutional constraint on fiscal policy and participation in a program with the IMF.

Do Fiscal Rules Matter?

The political budget cycle may be reduced in the presence of national fiscal rules if the rules prevent the incumbent from fiscal extravagances during national elections. This analysis focuses on national fiscal rules because they are more effective and better enforced than supranational rules in the LIC context.[15]

One main challenge in isolating the impact of fiscal rules is to address the obvious endogeneity (self-selection) of the adoption and stability of these rules. This issue is addressed in the empirical specifications. The literature on the role of fiscal rules on the reduction of political budget cycles is not large. Based on a study on the U.S. states, Rose (2006) shows that balanced budget rules help dampen politically driven cycles in overall spending, taxes, and deficits. Not surprisingly, Rose (2006) finds that the stricter the rules are, the weaker are the cycles. Inspired by this study, this analysis tests whether national fiscal rules act as a domestic scrutiny factor that helps dampen political budget cycles in LICs. However, it is important to be prudent when interpreting the results because only a few LICs use national fiscal rules, and enforcement and compliance are limited.

The econometric model exploits the interaction term between the national election dummy and a dummy for the presence of a fiscal rule to quantify the dampening impact (if any) of the presence of a national fiscal rule during election times. Because the adoption and presence of a fiscal rule are likely to be nonrandom, this issue is addressed by using a dummy variable capturing whether a national fiscal rule has been in place for at least five years. Basically, the strategy consists in interacting the election dummy with the five-year lag of the fiscal rule dummy (*FR*).[16] More formally, the specification is the following:[17]

$$Y_{i,t} = \alpha_i + (\theta_1 + \sigma_1 FR_{i,t-5}) ELE_{i,t} + \sigma_2 FR_{i,t-5} + \rho Y_{i,t-1} + \mathbf{X}'_{i,t}\mathbf{\Gamma} + \varepsilon_{i,t}. \quad (3.3)$$

The magnitude of the effect of the political budget cycle on public consumption in the absence of a national fiscal rule is measured by θ_1. In the presence of a rule, the size of the electoral fiscal manipulation is captured by $\theta_1 + \sigma_1$. The main

[15] However, enforcement of and compliance with supranational fiscal rules has been, at best, mixed in most European Union member states, West African Economic and Monetary Union countries, and in the Central African and Economic Monetary Community region (Schaechter and others 2012).

[16] The reader may wonder whether the proposed identification strategy for assessing the impact of a fiscal rule is the best available. For example, it could be interesting to proceed with an instrumental variable strategy to tackle the potential endogeneity of fiscal rules. However, finding such instrumental variables, which need to be fully exogenous to fiscal outcomes, is very challenging. Another strategy might be to pursue a two-step approach in which a selection equation explaining the decision to have a fiscal rule is estimated and used to control for the self-selection bias in the fiscal equation. However, with such a small number of LICs having national fiscal rules, performing the two-step approach does not seem suitable.

[17] Also, we will disregard the postelection dummies used previously and concentrate the analysis on the election year since the cycles in government consumption are observed during election year and cycles on revenues are less robust. Moreover, we do not need to break down the fiscal rule dummy into subcomponents because national fiscal rules in LICs are primarily dominated by debt rules.

hypothesis is that $\theta_1 > 0$; $\sigma_1 < 0$, suggesting that the amplitude of the political budget cycle is higher when the country lacks a fiscal rule compared with when the country has one.

Estimation results are presented in Table 3.3. Results indicate that for LICs without national fiscal rules (most countries), the size of the effect of the political budget cycle on government consumption is about 1 percent of GDP. This result is not much different from the estimations performed earlier in the chapter. However, once the election dummy is interacted with the national fiscal rule dummy, the coefficient turns negative and statistically significant. The

Table 3.3. Do Fiscal Rules and IMF Programs Dampen the Political Budget Cycle in Low-Income Countries?

	(1)	(2)
	G	G
Election Dummy	1.009***	0.963***
	[0.331]	[0.293]
Election × Lagged Fiscal Rule Dummy	−0.870*	
	[0.511]	
Election × IMF Program Dummy		−0.623*
		[0.342]
Lagged Fiscal Rule Dummy	1.986***	1.621***
	[0.662]	[0.376]
IMF Program Dummy		−0.712
		[0.444]
λ (predicted selection correction factor)		0.621**
		[0.253]
Lagged Dependent Variable	0.695***	0.837***
	[0.089]	[0.041]
Real GDP Growth	−0.017	0.004
	[0.041]	[0.014]
Official Development Assistance to GDP	0.073*	0.045***
	[0.037]	[0.017]
External Debt to GDP	−0.003	−0.001
	[0.003]	[0.003]
Trade Openness	0.032***	0.015***
	[0.011]	[0.005]
ln (100 + inflation rate)	−1.189	−0.442
	[0.976]	[0.344]
Intercept	7.809	3.488*
	[5.321]	[1.896]
Observations	1,234	864
Number of Countries	60	59
Joint Significance of Election Coefficients: *p*-value	0.007	0.002
m1: *p*-value	0.002	0.019
m2: *p*-value	0.341	0.114
Hansen Overidentification Test: *p*-value	0.808	0.132
Number of Instruments	17	18

Source: Authors' estimates.

Note: Windmeijer (2005) corrected standard errors in brackets. All equations are estimated using the two-step system-GMM with Windmeijer (2005) correction of standard errors. In column 2, the model controls for the self-selection bias associated with participation in IMF programs through a two-step approach following Maddala 1983, Vella and Verbeek 1999, and Keen and Lockwood 2010. G = government consumption ratio.

$^{*}p < .10$; $^{**}p < .05$; $^{***}p < .01$.

significance of the coefficient of the interaction term is low, however, suggesting that the strength of the dampening role of national fiscal rules is still low in LICs, possibly because of lack of enforcement, lack of compliance, and limited number of LICs using national numerical fiscal rules. When focusing on the marginal effect of elections in LICs that have adopted national fiscal rules, the coefficient estimates in Table 3.3 suggest that the size of the fiscal deviation during an election year is close to 0.13 percentage point of GDP (1 – 0.87 = 0.13).

IMF Program Engagement

The chapter further tests whether countries engaged in programs with the IMF are less likely to experience a political budget cycle. In other words, do IMF programs act as an international scrutiny mechanism that constrains incumbents from using fiscal policy for electoral motives? There are several reasons why IMF programs may contribute to reducing the magnitude of the political budget cycle in LICs. LICs that enter into IMF agreements are subject to conditionality. One key component of programs' conditionality is the adoption of sustainable macroeconomic policies. As a result, if implemented, conditionality constrains government finances, making it more difficult for governments to engage in expansionary fiscal policies during elections. This issue has been discussed and tested by Hyde and O'Mahony (2010) in the context of a large panel of developing countries (94 countries) mixing LICs with other developing nations. The authors find that IMF scrutiny of the economy and pressure on governments to maintain a sustainable fiscal policy make pre-electoral manipulation of the government balance less likely. This result appears robust to the treatment of the selection bias characterizing the decision to request a program with the IMF. This chapter follows the pioneering work by Hyde and O'Mahony (2010) in the case of a large sample of countries but departs from it in several ways that are outlined below.

One important issue in this literature is the potential endogeneity of IMF programs with respect to both elections and macroeconomic outcomes. Scholars have argued that governments prefer not to be under IMF agreements during elections (Dreher 2004), and research has shown that governments are more likely to enter into IMF agreements after elections (Przeworski and Vreeland 2000). This issue is explored in detail in the first-stage selection equation estimated to purge the endogeneity of IMF programs with respect to both election timing and macroeconomic developments.[18] The chapter therefore tries to robustly investigate the effect of IMF programs on the size of the political budget cycle by

[18] However, the strength of the bias due to the potential link between an IMF arrangement and an election is attenuated by one stylized fact. As discussed by Hyde and O'Mahony (2010), the majority of elections in the developing world are held while countries are already under an IMF agreement. LICs are more likely to have intensive program engagement because of their prolonged balance of payments needs.

focusing only on LICs.[19] It also departs from the previous literature in that the main dependent variable is government consumption, the budget item that was found to be strongly correlated with elections throughout the chapter. As further explained below, the selection bias associated with IMF programs has been carefully accounted for using an improved version of the standard first-stage probit model identifying the correlates of IMF programs that take into account LICs' specific characteristics.

To assess the effect of IMF programs (*IMF*), the following model is specified:

$$Y_{i,t} = \alpha_i + \left(\theta + \gamma_1\, IMF_{i,t}\right) ELE_{i,t} + \gamma_2\, IMF_{i,t} + \gamma_3\, \widehat{\lambda}_{i,t} + \rho Y_{i,t-1} + \mathbf{X}'_{i,t}\boldsymbol{\Gamma} + \varepsilon_{i,t}, \quad (3.4)$$

where $\widehat{\lambda}_{i,t}$ is the selection-correction factor associated with the IMF program dummy. More specifically, the model includes the selection factor in addition to the IMF dummy so that γ_1 can be interpreted with limited risk of selection bias. The magnitude of the effect of the political budget cycle on public consumption in the absence of an IMF program is measured by θ. In the presence of an IMF arrangement, the size of the electoral fiscal manipulation is captured by $\theta + \gamma_1$. The main hypothesis is that $\theta > 0$; $\gamma_1 < 0$, suggesting that the political budget cycle is higher when the country is not currently under an arrangement with the IMF compared with when the country is engaged with the IMF.

The correction of the self-selection associated with the decision to participate in an IMF program proceeds as follow: A pooled probit model on the determinants of IMF programs in LICs over the period 1990–2010 is estimated. Standard determinants of IMF programs include previous levels of external reserves, fiscal balance, trade openness, and inflation rate. Also added to this list are the size of natural resource rents, as well as a dummy variable indicating whether a national election is scheduled in the next year, and the election variable interacted with an indicator of electoral competitiveness. These variables are added to the selection model to capture the extent to which LICs are less likely to request IMF programs in the year before national elections, conditional on the degree of competitiveness in the considered election.[20] Controlling for resource rents, for the electoral

[19] This literature has typically used country samples that mix LICs and middle-income economies, tending to overlook the distinct characteristics of LICs as well as the distinct nature and objectives of IMF engagement in these countries. LICs face a number of challenges that differentiate them from other economies, such as the nature of shocks, access to financing, and long-term challenges (poverty reduction, infrastructure needs, institutional and capacity building, and others) that typically imply that the type of IMF facilities and their goals are quite different from other IMF financial instruments available to emerging market or advanced economies.

[20] The selection equation also helps deal with the potential bias that could arise if IMF lending were significantly higher during months before elections. Dreher and Vaubel (2004) found that that is indeed the case. This analysis rules out this effect by always controlling for official development assistance in the regressions and by explicitly controlling for the electoral calendar and timing in the selection equation. Therefore, the risks that these results are fully driven by IMF lending dynamics before and after elections are limited. Moreover, the direction of this bias would work to lower the estimated effect of the IMF programs, leading to underestimated effects instead of inflated effects.

calendar, and for the degree of electoral competitiveness before the year of an IMF program helps factor in some specifics of the LIC context.

Once the probit is estimated on the group of control variables $Z_{i,t}$, the selection correction factor is computed as follows (see Maddala 1983; Vella and Verbeek 1999; Keen and Lockwood 2010):[21]

$$\widehat{\lambda}_{i,t} = \begin{cases} \dfrac{\varphi\left(Z'_{i,t}\widehat{\phi}\right)}{\Phi\left(Z'_{i,t}\widehat{\phi}\right)}, & \text{IMF}_{i,t} = 1, \\ -\dfrac{\varphi\left(Z'_{i,t}\widehat{\phi}\right)}{1-\Phi\left(Z'_{i,t}\widehat{\phi}\right)}, & \text{IMF}_{i,t} = 0, \end{cases} \tag{3.5}$$

where $\varphi(\cdot)$ and $\Phi(\cdot)$ represent the probability density and cumulative density functions of the standard normal distribution, respectively.

Estimation results are presented in Table 3.3. Results suggest that IMF programs dampen the magnitude of the impact of the political budget cycle on consumption in LICs. In the absence of an IMF program, government consumption deviates by about 1 percentage point of GDP during national elections, whereas the size of the deviation drops to 0.34 percentage point of GDP in the presence of an active IMF program. Results also indicate a positive and significant effect of the selection factor $\left(\widehat{\lambda}_{i,t}\right)$, which suggests that accounting for the selection bias in the estimates was crucial and legitimate. The results indicate that both fiscal rules and IMF programs play important roles in LICs by limiting the propensity of incumbents to allow large deviations in government consumption during election years as a means of maximizing their chance of reelection. Although the results seem appealing, they should be interpreted with caution. Indeed, the coefficients associated with the interaction terms of elections interacted with fiscal rules and IMF programs exhibit low significance, which suggests that the dampening role is at play but is not strong enough to generate more precise estimates.[22]

[21] Results of the probit selection model identifying the determinants of LICs' participation in IMF programs are available in Annex Table 3.1.3.

[22] There are several reasons for these results. First, only four LICs have adopted active national fiscal rules, an issue that certainly contributes to reducing the explanatory power of the fiscal dummy in the model. It could also be that these rules are not sufficiently enforced, exacerbating the credibility problems faced by these institutional arrangements in many LICs. Second, even though the selection equation associated with IMF programs explicitly controls for several covariates, the self-selection bias is always only partially controlled for. In addition, because the majority of elections in LICs are held while countries are already in an IMF agreement, the statistical power of the IMF program dummy in dampening the political cycle is limited.

CONCLUDING REMARKS

This chapter investigates political budget cycles in LICs by analyzing the behavior of the following variables throughout the election cycle: government consumption, government investment, tax revenue composition, and fiscal balance. The analysis finds that during election years, government consumption increases and leads to higher fiscal deficits. During the two years following elections, fiscal adjustment takes the form of increased revenue effort in trade taxes and cuts to government investment. The chapter shows that the size of the political budget cycle is much lower in countries that have adopted national fiscal rules and in those participating in IMF programs during the election period.

The behavior of these variables throughout the election cycle is analyzed because the way governments decide to manipulate fiscal policy may have implications for future economic growth. The results in this chapter show that elections not only incur a macroeconomic cost when they take place, but also trigger a painful fiscal adjustment in which public investment is largely sacrificed and trade put at risk. Although economic growth is not explicitly studied in this chapter, the different policy tools that LICs seem to be using during the political budget cycle suggest a negative effect on economic growth. One reason for this negative effect is the overall volatility in fiscal policy that elections trigger. Another is that trade may be hampered by the increased postelection effort to mobilize trade taxes. Similarly, the decrease in investment may directly hamper growth.

This chapter uses a novel data set on fiscal rules to highlight that such rules may help dampen election-driven cycles in the budget. Although the mere existence of fiscal rules does not mean that they will be enforced, they may be a first step toward tying the hands of politicians or governments who have incentives to influence political budget cycles. The chapter also shows that IMF programs in LICs have contributed to lowering the magnitude of the political budget cycle.

ANNEX 3.1. SUPPLEMENTARY TABLES

Annex Table 3.1.1. Countries in the Sample and Number of National Elections, by Country, 1990–2010

Country	No. of National Elections	Country	No. of National Elections	Country	No. of National Elections
Afghanistan	2	The Gambia	4	Nepal	3
Armenia	5	Georgia	5	Nicaragua	4
Bangladesh	3	Ghana	5	Niger	4
Benin	4	Guinea	4	Nigeria	4
Bolivia	6	Guinea-Bissau	5	Papua New Guinea	4
Burkina Faso	4	Haiti	6	Rwanda	2
Burundi	2	Honduras	5	Senegal	3
Cambodia	3	Kenya	4	Sierra Leone	3
Cameroon	3	Kyrgyz Republic	5	Solomon Islands	1
Central African Republic	4	Lesotho	3	Tajikistan	4
Chad	3	Liberia	2	Tanzania	5
Comoros	5	Madagascar	5	Timor-Leste	1
Democratic Republic of the Congo	1	Malawi	4	Togo	4
Republic of Congo	3	Mali	4	Uganda	3
Côte d'Ivoire	4	Mauritania	5	Uzbekistan	3
Djibouti	3	Moldova	8	Yemen	2
Ethiopia	3	Mozambique	4	Zambia	5

Source: National Elections across Democracy and Autocracy (NELDA) data set (Hyde and Marinov 2012).
Note: Only legislative elections for countries with parliamentary political systems, and executive elections for countries with presidential elections, are included.

Annex Table 3.1.2. Descriptive Statistics, Low-Income Country Sample, 1990–2010

Variable	No. of Observations	Mean	Standard Deviation	Minimum	Maximum
Election Dummy	1,330	0.13	0.34	0	1
Government Consumption Ratio	1,145	15.20	7.52	1.53	62.17
Public Investment Ratio	1,044	7.37	5.69	0.08	59.85
Total Tax Revenue Ratio	832	14.68	6.51	1.27	58.11
Taxes on Goods and Services Ratio	666	5.47	3.19	0.04	16.96
Direct Taxes Ratio	697	4.31	3.07	0.01	23.89
Trade Taxes Ratio	666	3.88	2.87	0	14.12
Overall Fiscal Balance Ratio	1,004	−2.48	6.74	−72.35	61.83
Real per Capita GDP Growth	1,273	1.23	7.68	−71.24	64.20
Official Development Assistance Ratio	1,276	13.22	11.74	−2.56	146.89
External Public and Publicly Guaranteed Debt Ratio	1,226	85.47	110.30	0.58	2,394.86
Trade Openness Ratio	1,179	76.28	37.18	0.19	213.22
ln (100 + inflation)	1,279	5.40	0.65	4.61	10.35
National Fiscal Rule Dummy	1,330	0.02	0.14	0	1
ln (total population)	1,330	15.16	1.92	11.13	18.86
Total Natural Resource Rents Ratio	1,330	4.85	12.29	0	105.73
Reserve Coverage (in months of imports)	1,204	3.50	2.58	0	19.75
Political Globalization (KOF Institute Index)	1,313	46.40	18.46	6.59	90.90
Change in Real per Capita GDP Growth	1,266	0.00	10.00	−60.55	132.33

Source: Authors' calculations from various sources.
Note: All variables expressed as ratios denote nominal values normalized by nominal GDP of each country.

Annex Table 3.1.3. Correlates of Participation in IMF Programs in Low-Income Countries

Dependent Variable: IMF Program Dummy	**LPM**	**Probit**
Period: 1990–2010	**(1)**	**(2)**
International Reserves Coverage (in months of imports)$_{,t-1}$	0.00496	−0.0425**
	[0.0152]	[0.0178]
Fiscal Balance to GDP$_{,t-1}$	0.00286	−0.00296
	[0.00349]	[0.00966]
ln (100 + inflation rate)$_{,t-1}$	−0.0494	0.00539
	[0.0867]	[0.0650]
Official Development Assistance to GDP$_{,t-1}$	0.00882***	0.0417***
	[0.00261]	[0.00547]
ln (population)$_{,t-1}$	−0.0856	0.146***
	[0.313]	[0.0307]
(Election × Competition)$_{,t+1}$	0.0408**	0.163**
	[0.0198]	[0.0665]
Election Dummy$_{,t+1}$	−0.244*	−0.790*
	[0.133]	[0.410]
Political Globalization (KOF Institute Index)$_{,t}$	−0.00115	0.0204***
	[0.00382]	[0.00325]
Change in Real per Capita GDP Growth$_{,t}$	−0.00204**	−0.00654
	[0.000880]	[0.00499]
Intercept	2.085	−3.430***
	[4.483]	[0.532]
Country Fixed Effects	Yes	No
Observations	916	916
R^2	0.043	0.177
Countries	63	63

Source: Authors' estimates.

Note: Robust standard errors in brackets. The variable "Competition" is not included additively because of its mechanical perfect colinearity with the election dummy variable. LPM = linear probability model with country fixed effects.

*$p < .1$; **$p < .05$; ***$p < .01$.

REFERENCES

Alesina, A., N. Roubini, and G. D. Cohen. 1997. *Political Cycles and the Macroeconomy.* Cambridge, MA: MIT Press.

Arellano, M., and S. Bond. 1991. "Some Tests of Specification for Panel Data: Monte Carlo Evidence and an Application to Employment Equations." *Review of Economic Studies* 58 (2): 277–97.

Arellano, M., and O. Bover. 1995. "Another Look at the Instrumental Variable Estimation of Error-Components Models." *Journal of Econometrics* 68 (1): 29–51.

Block, S. A. 2002. "Political Business Cycles, Democratization, and Economic Reform: The Case of Africa." *Journal of Development Economics* 67 (1): 205–28.

Blundell, R., and S. Bond. 1998. "Initial Conditions and Moment Restrictions in Dynamic Panel Data Models." *Journal of Econometrics* 87 (1): 115–43.

Brender, A., and A. Drazen. 2005. "Political Budget Cycles in New versus Established Democracies." *Journal of Monetary Economics* 52 (7): 1271–95.

———. 2008. "How Do Budget Deficits and Economic Growth Affect Reelection Prospects? Evidence from a Large Panel of Countries." *American Economic Review* 98 (5): 2203–20.

Combes, J.-L., C. Ebeke, and M. Maurel. 2013. "The Effect of Remittances Prior to an Election." Working Paper, CERDI Etudes et Documents, 2013-07. https://halshs.archives-ouvertes.fr/halshs-00826999/document/.

Combes, J.-L., and T. Saadi-Sedik. 2006. "How Does Trade Openness Influence Budget Deficits in Developing Countries?" *Journal of Development Studies* 42 (8): 1401–16.
Drazen, A. 2001. "The Political Business Cycle after 25 Years." *NBER Macroeconomics Annual 2000* 15: 75–138.
———, and M. Eslava. 2010. "Electoral Manipulation via Voter-Friendly Spending: Theory and Evidence." *Journal of Development Economics* 92 (1): 39–52.
Dreher, A. 2004. "The Influence of IMF Programs on the Re-election of Debtor Governments." *Economics and Politics* 16 (1): 53–76.
———, and R. Vaubel. 2004. "Do IMF and IBRD Cause Moral Hazard and Political Business Cycles? Evidence from Panel Data." *Open Economies Review* 15 (1): 5–22.
Ehrhart, H. 2012. "Elections and the Structure of Taxation in Developing Countries." *Public Choice* 156 (1): 195–211.
Fatás, A., and I. Mihov. 2003. "The Case for Restricting Fiscal Policy Discretion." *Quarterly Journal of Economics* 118 (4): 1419–47.
———. 2012. "Policy Volatility, Institutions and Economic Growth." *Review of Economics and Statistics* 95 (2): 325–76.
Faye, M., and P. Niehaus. 2012. "Political Aid Cycles." *American Economic Review* 102 (7): 3516–30.
Fouda, S. M. 1997. "Political Monetary Cycles and Independence of the Central Bank in a Monetary Union: An Empirical Test for a BEAC Franc Zone Member Country." *Journal of African Economies* 6 (1): 112–31.
Hyde, S. D., and N. Marinov. 2012. "Which Elections Can Be Lost?" *Political Analysis* 20 (2): 191–210.
Hyde, S. D., and A. O'Mahony. 2010. "International Scrutiny and Pre-Electoral Fiscal Manipulation in Developing Countries." *Journal of Politics* 72 (3): 690–704.
Keen, M., and B. Lockwood. 2010. "The Value-Added Tax: Its Causes and Consequences." *Journal of Development Economics* 92 (2): 138–51.
Khemani, S. 2004. "Political Cycles in a Developing Economy: Effect of Elections in the Indian States." *Journal of Development Economics* 73 (1): 125–54.
Maddala, G. S. 1983. *Limited-Dependent and Qualitative Variables in Econometrics*. Econometric Society Monographs. Cambridge, U.K.: Cambridge University Press.
Nickell, S. 1981. "Biases in Dynamic Models with Fixed Effects." *Econometrica* 49 (6): 1417–26.
O'Mahony, A. 2010. "Engineering Good Times: Fiscal Manipulation in a Global Economy." *British Journal of Political Science* 41 (2): 315–40.
Persson, T., and G. Tabellini. 2003. *The Economic Effects of Constitutions: What Do the Data Say?* Cambridge, MA: MIT Press.
Przeworski, A., and J. R. Vreeland. 2000. "The Effect of IMF Programs on Economic Growth." *Journal of Development Economics* 62 (2): 385–421.
Rodrik, D. 1998. "Why Do More Open Economies Have Bigger Governments?" *Journal of Political Economy* 106 (5): 997–1032.
Roodman, D. 2009. "A Note on the Theme of Too Many Instruments." *Oxford Bulletin of Economics and Statistics* 71 (1): 135–58.
Rose, S. 2006. "Do Fiscal Rules Dampen the Political Business Cycle?" *Public Choice* 128 (3/4): 407–31.
Schaechter, A., T. Kinda, N. Budina, and A. Weber. 2012. "Fiscal Rules in Response to the Crisis—Toward the Next-Generation Rules. A New Dataset." Working Paper 12/187, International Monetary Fund, Washington, DC.
Schuknecht, L. 2000. "Fiscal Policy Cycles and Public Expenditure in Developing Countries." *Public Choice* 102 (1/2): 113–28.
Shi, M., and J. Svensson. 2006. "Political Budget Cycles: Do They Differ across Countries and Why?" *Journal of Public Economics* 90 (8–9): 1367–89.
Stotsky, J. G., and A. WoldeMariam. 1997. "Tax Effort in Sub-Saharan Africa." Working Paper 97/107, International Monetary Fund, Washington, DC.

Vella, F., and M. Verbeek. 1999. "Estimating and Interpreting Models with Endogenous Treatment Effects." *Journal of Business and Economic Statistics* 17 (4): 473–78.

Vergne, C. 2009. "Democracy, Elections and Allocation of Public Expenditures in Developing Countries." *European Journal of Political Economy* 25 (1): 63–77.

Windmeijer, F. 2005. "A Finite Sample Correction for the Variance of Linear Efficient Two-Step GMM Estimators." *Journal of Econometrics* 126 (1): 25–51.

CHAPTER 4

Economic and Political Determinants of Tax Policies in OECD Countries

MARK HALLERBERG AND JÜRGEN VON HAGEN

This chapter explores the economic and political causes of tax policy changes in Organisation for Economic Co-operation and Development (OECD) countries over the period 1990–2015. The analysis considers rate changes of the most important taxes in developed economies, that is, corporate income taxes (CIT), personal income taxes (PIT), and value-added taxes (VAT). The results show that banking crises affect tax rates, but that there is a political dimension to their effects—left-leaning governments are less likely to increase the VAT rate, and more likely to increase the top PIT rate, than right-leaning governments. There is also evidence that the left is more likely to raise the top income tax rate as part of pronounced fiscal consolidation. Perhaps surprisingly, the research finds no evidence of partisan effects during more "normal," noncrisis times. The effects of elections are also generally muted, with only a CIT rate increase more likely the year after an election. Changes in other countries make it more likely that a given government changes its own rates. Increases in both the VAT rate and the top PIT rate are more likely when governments are consolidating their cyclically adjusted budget balances. Among European Union (EU) member states, VAT rate changes are more likely if a given government is in the euro area and in the period after 2011. Small EU member states also are more likely to raise PIT and CIT rates, which is consistent with an argument that pressure to consolidate under the Stability and Growth Pact was higher for small states during the period under study.

INTRODUCTION

Tax policy is one of the core activities of government. It determines how much revenue the government has to finance its activities. It also determines which groups in society contribute how much to this revenue, which means that it

Mark Hallerberg: Hertie School of Governance, Berlin. Jürgen von Hagen: University of Bonn, Indiana University Kelley School of Business, the Center for Economic and Policy Research, and the Portuguese Fiscal Council. The views expressed in this paper do not represent the position of the Portuguese Fiscal Council. The authors thank Paul Hadji-Lazaro for very able research assistance.

redistributes income and wealth. It can encourage or discourage certain economic activities and the choice of their geographical location and, thus, regulate and cause distortions to economic activities. As a result, tax policy is the object of the activities of political parties and interest groups. In democratic societies, it is conducted on the basis of economic considerations and political motivations.

This chapter explores the economic and political causes of changes in tax policies in OECD countries over the period 1990–2015. More specifically, it studies changes in tax rates, which are taken as a main indicator of a government's desired changes in tax policies. The chapter explores the case that development of a given tax base over time is heavily influenced by economic activity and, therefore, by forces and factors other than tax policy. Thus, measures of tax revenues (or changes thereof) are noisier indicators of policy changes than are tax rates. The chapter considers rate changes to the most important taxes in developed economies—CIT, PIT, and VAT. Rates are the principal instruments of tax policy for several reasons. Tax legislation defines tax rates and tax bases, but changes in the definition of the latter are less common and are difficult to observe. Moreover, changes in tax rates usually lead to changes in revenues in the same direction.[1] Furthermore, tax rates affect tax competition across jurisdictions. For example, Devereux and Griffith (1998) find that, while differences in tax rates did not affect American firms' decisions to enter the European market, they did affect where firms located within Europe. Devereux, Lockwood, and Redoano (2008) argue that international competition in the dimension of corporate tax rates is intensified by the absence of capital controls.

During the period investigated in this chapter, several notable developments occurred that might have affected the likelihood of changes in tax policies. First, it was a period of high and increasing international capital mobility and thus one of intensifying international tax competition. Noticing its potentially harmful effects, the OECD launched a program combating harmful tax competition in 1998.[2] A second development was the spread of democracy. The transition to democracy in Central Europe and in some Latin American countries in the sample, such as Chile and Mexico, introduced new voters, and potentially new interests, into the political arena, and these new players may have wanted changes in tax policies. As Gehlbach (2008) notes for Eastern Europe, this should spur more "normal" politics

[1] In broad terms, the share of tax revenue as a percentage of GDP was stable, on average, in the OECD, increasing only from 32 percent in 1990 to 34 percent in 2013. These numbers, however, hide considerable variation across countries both in total revenue and in the combination of taxes in place. The most important tax in most countries is the PIT. The OECD average revenue collection as a percentage of GDP declined somewhat, from about 10 percent in 1990 to about 9 percent in 2013. However, the Slovak Republic collected PIT revenues of just 3 percent of GDP in 2013, while Denmark in that same year collected almost 26 percent of GDP. The overall reliance on VAT was proportionately lower, with increases from about 5.0 percent of GDP to 6.6 percent of GDP, on average, in the OECD and a range from 3.5 percent of GDP in Australia to almost 10.0 percent of GDP in Denmark. Finally, for CIT, on profits (and not including capital gains), Australia collected almost 5 percent of GDP in 2013 while Estonia collected less than 1 percent of GDP. Data from https://stats.oecd.org/Index.aspx?DataSetCode=REV, downloaded September 13, 2016.

[2] See OECD (1998). For a review of the results see Avi-Yonah (2009).

in countries where the ease of collection across different types of taxes (which is the case in OECD countries) is similar. Third, most OECD countries had high and rising levels of public debt during this period, while only a few managed to reduce their debt burdens significantly. As a result of the financial crisis that started in 2008, high debt burdens became a pressing issue, especially toward the end of the sample period. Fourth, the period contains several episodes of financial crises that put pressure on governments in opposite ways. On the one hand, governments wished to respond to incipient crises with fiscal stimulus packages that included tax cuts. On the other hand, governments had debt-sustainability concerns that forced them to consolidate their budgets and reduce their debt, and some of them introduced tax increases for that purpose. These contrasts were particularly prominent in Europe toward the end of the sample period, where the crisis was especially acute and where some countries received IMF- and EU-sponsored programs to stabilize their economies. Fifth, the countries belonging to the EU and in particular to the Economic and Monetary Union introduced new kinds of fiscal rules to keep government budget deficits and debt in check. This chapter explores the impacts of these developments on the tax policies of OECD countries. Furthermore, it asks how political factors such as elections and the ideological orientation of governments shaped these policies.

The chapter is structured as follows: The second section describes the developments of CIT, PIT, and VAT rates over the sample period, that is, the dependent variables. The third section develops the main hypotheses. The fourth section presents the empirical analysis and results. The analysis finds that banking crises affect tax rates, but that there is a political dimension to their effects—left-leaning governments are less likely to increase the VAT rate, and more likely to increase the top PIT rate, than right-leaning governments. Changes in other countries make it more likely that a given government changes its own rates. Increases in both the VAT rate and the top PIT rate are also more likely when governments are consolidating their cyclically adjusted budget balances. Among EU member states, VAT rate changes are more likely if a given government is in the euro area and in the period after 2011. The only political variable that affects the CIT rate is the occurrence of an election, with rate increases more likely the year after an election has been held. The final section concludes.

DESCRIBING TAX POLICIES IN OECD COUNTRIES

The main source of data for tax rates is the OECD tax database. In addition, information is taken from OECD Consumption Tax Trends and from the European Commission and national sources. Because of missing values in the data, an unbalanced panel of 34 OECD countries results.[3]

[3] These are Australia, Austria, Belgium, Canada, Chile, the Czech Republic, Denmark, Estonia, Finland, France, Germany, Greece, Hungary, Iceland, Ireland, Israel, Italy, Japan, the Republic of Korea, Luxembourg, the Netherlands, New Zealand, Mexico, Norway, Poland, Portugal, the Slovak Republic, Slovenia, Spain, Sweden, Switzerland, Turkey, the United Kingdom, and the United States.

The chapter describes tax policies with an indicator variable equal to one for a given country and given year when an increase in the relevant tax rate occurs, zero when there is no change, and negative one when there is a decrease in the tax rate.

Corporate Income Taxes

Figure 4.1 describes the development of CIT rates in the OECD countries during the sample period. A first, important observation comes from Figure 4.1, panel 1, which shows that the unweighted average tax rate declined steadily during the sample period by a total of 15 percentage points, from 40 percent to 25 percent. Governments in OECD countries generally lifted the tax burden on corporate income by a very large margin.

Panel 2 of Figure 4.1 looks at this average trend in more detail by showing the change in CIT rates between 1990 and 2000 and between 2001 and 2015.

Figure 4.1. Corporate Income Taxes in OECD Countries, 1991–2015
(Percent)

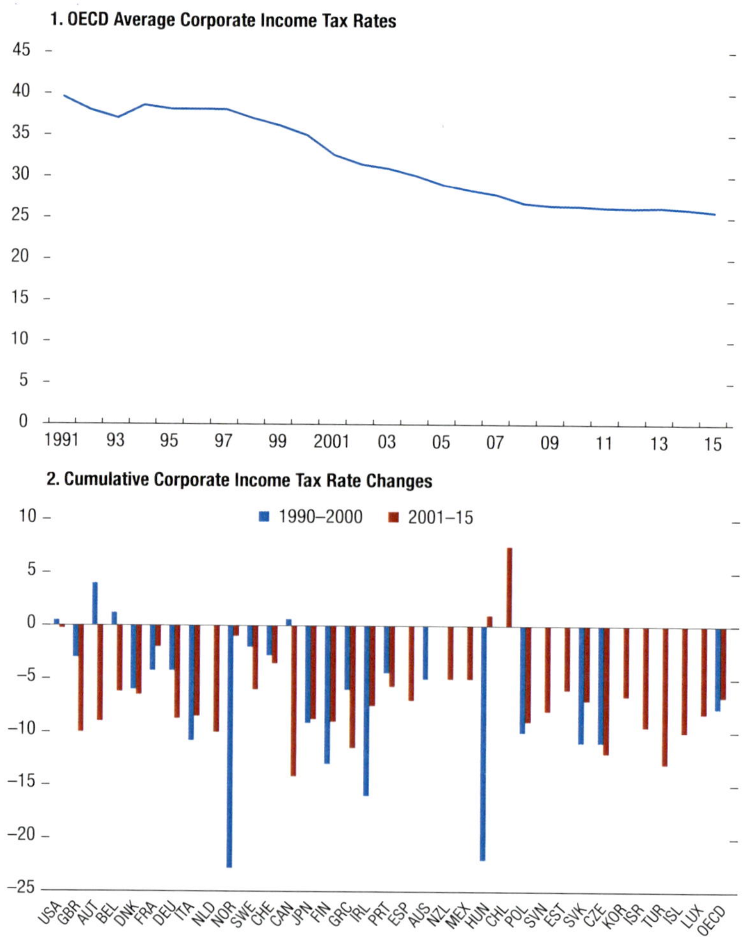

Figure 4.1. Corporate Income Taxes in OECD Countries, 1991–2015 *(continued)*

(Percent)

3. Share of OECD Countries Changing Corporate Income Tax Rates

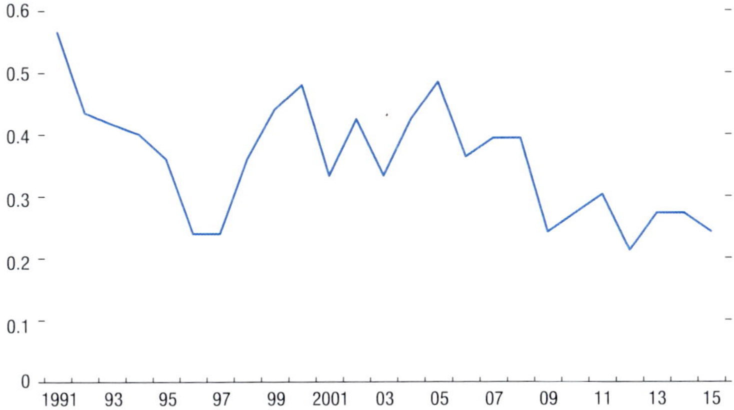

4. Balance of Corporate Income Tax Rate Changes

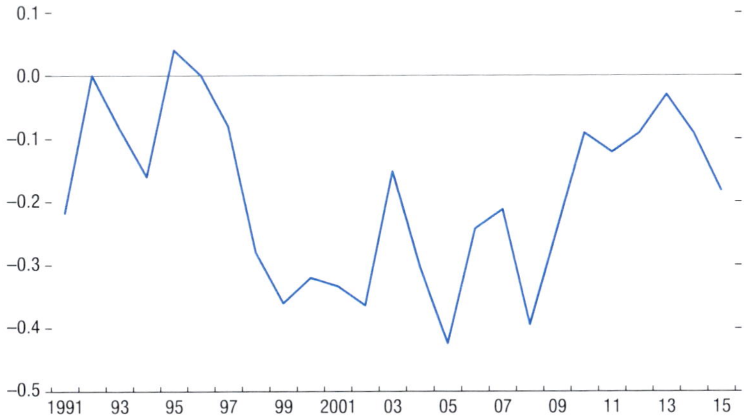

5. Average Frequency of Corporate Income Tax Rate Changes

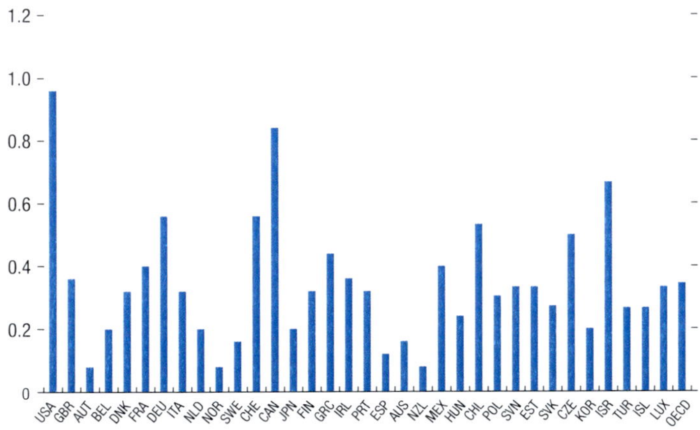

Sources: Authors' calculations based on OECD Tax Revenue Statistics (http://www.oecd.org/ctp/tax-policy/tax-database.htm), June 2016; and OECD Consumption Tax Trends 1999, 2001, 2004, 2006.
Note: OECD = Organisation for Economic Co-operation and Development.

Austria, Belgium, and Canada were the only countries that increased rates in the first period; Hungary and Chile were the only countries that increased rates in the second period. On average, over all countries, the rate cuts were almost equal in both periods, but there are substantial differences between individual countries in both periods.

Panel 3 of Figure 4.1 shows the share of OECD countries that changed CIT rates in each year, that is, the number of countries with rate changes divided by the total number of countries for which data are available for that year. In 1991, 60 percent of all OECD countries implemented rate changes. Rate changes became rarer in the mid-1990s, but toward the end of the decade they became more common again, peaking at 50 percent of countries in 2000. After the mid-2000s, rate changes again became less common among the OECD countries.

Panel 4 of Figure 4.1 shows the balance of rate changes in the OECD, that is, the number of countries with rate increases minus the number of countries with rate decreases divided by the number of countries in the sample in that year. It indicates the dominant policy trend among the OECD countries in each year. This dominant trend was clearly negative in the early 1990s and from 1998 to 2008, suggesting that pressures on CIT rates from tax competition were strong for OECD governments during these years. Only in the wake of the financial crisis that started in late 2008 did this pressure weaken.

Panel 5 of Figure 4.1 shows the average frequency of CIT rate changes for each country during the sample period. This is the number of years in which a rate change occurred divided by the total number of years for which observations are available. The figure shows a large degree of variation in frequency across countries. Canada and the United States changed rates almost every year. In contrast, the frequency in Austria, New Zealand, and Norway was about 10 percent, indicating that tax rate changes occur only once in 10 years, on average. The average OECD frequency was 0.34, corresponding to a tax rate change every three years.

Personal Income Taxes

PITs are progressive in all OECD countries, implying that rates for different income brackets can change in different ways. This analysis represents PIT policy by changes in rates for the top bracket.

Panel 1 of Figure 4.2 shows that the average top PIT rate in the OECD declined from 43 percent to 35 percent during the sample period, with a slight increase after the financial crisis that started in 2008. Panel 2 of Figure 4.2 shows that cumulative PIT rate changes are more heterogeneous across countries than CIT rate changes. Mexico, New Zealand, Sweden, the United Kingdom, and the United States in the 1990s, and Japan and Portugal after 2001, saw noticeable increases in PIT rates, while all other countries had decreases in PIT rates. The share of countries with tax rate changes, shown in panel 3 of Figure 4.2, was generally lower than for CIT rates. Starting at 40 percent in 1990, the top rate oscillated around 20 percent for the rest of that decade. The early 2000s saw an increase in tax policy activism in the OECD. Following the financial crisis of 2008, the share of countries with tax rate changes hovered around 25 percent.

Figure 4.2. Personal Income Taxes in OECD Countries, 1990–2015

(Percent)

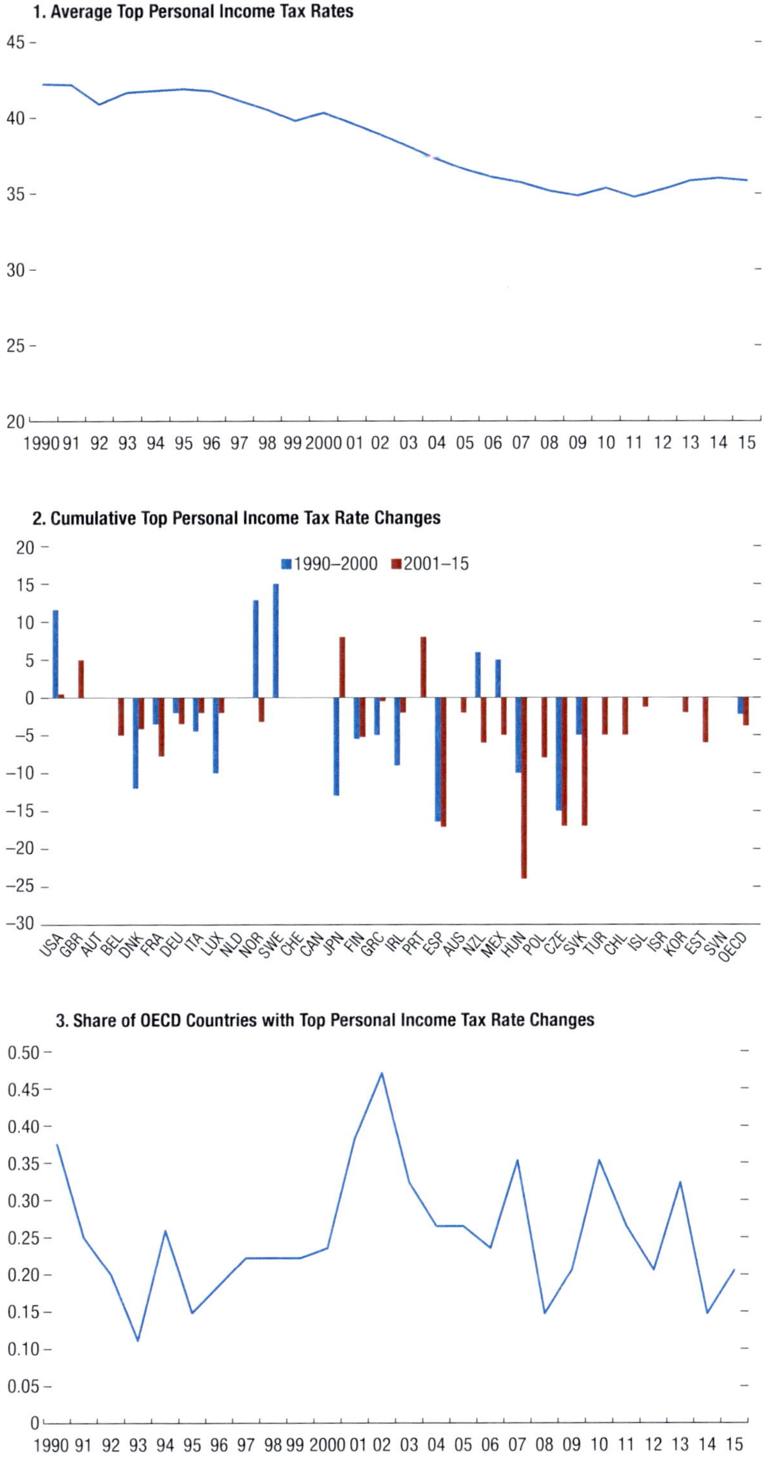

Figure 4.2. Personal Income Taxes in OECD Countries, 1990–2015 ***(continued)***
(Percent)

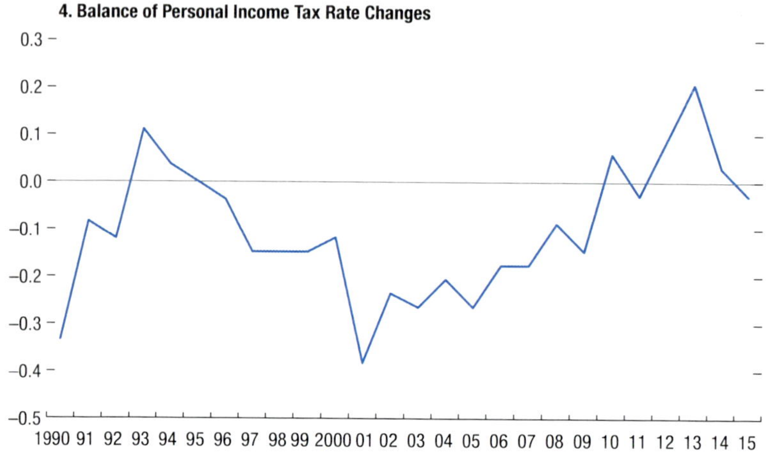

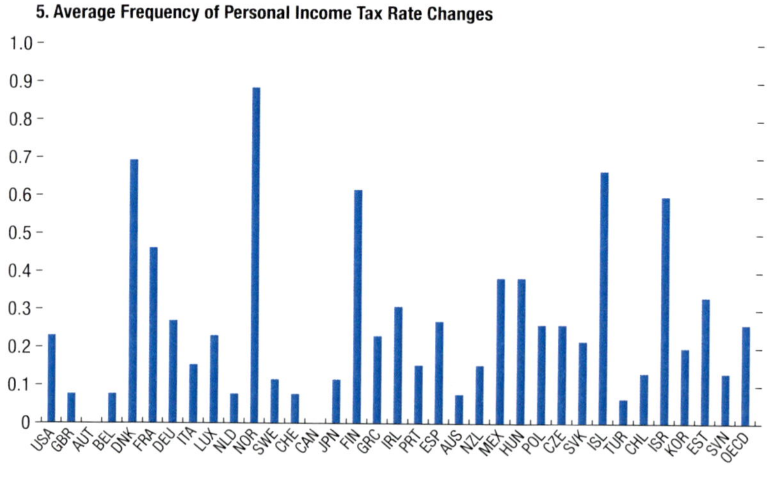

Sources: Authors' calculations based on OECD Tax Revenue Statistics (http://www.oecd.org/ctp/tax-policy/tax-database.htm), June 2016; and OECD Consumption Tax Trends 1999, 2001, 2004, 2006.
Note: OECD = Organisation for Economic Co-operation and Development.

Panel 4 of Figure 4.2 shows the balance of rate changes in the OECD countries. It was positive only in two brief periods—from 1993 to 1995 and from 2009 to 2013, that is, immediately after the financial crisis of 2008. The development over time resembles the balance of CIT rate changes. Considering the frequency of PIT rate changes in individual countries (panel 5 of Figure 4.2), a large degree of heterogeneity again is evident. In contrast to CIT rate changes, Canada and the United States are among the countries with the lowest frequencies, while Denmark, Finland, and Norway have particularly high frequencies.

Value-Added Taxes

Panel 1 of Figure 4.3 shows that the average VAT rate increased in the OECD during the sample period from slightly higher than 16.5 percent to slightly higher than 19 percent. Overall, then, the burden of taxation shifted from incomes to consumption during this period. Because the elasticity of the tax base for corporate and personal income taxes with regard to tax rate changes is probably higher than the elasticity of consumption, this shift may reflect the pressures of international tax competition and the need of growing government sectors to secure a stable revenue base. Panel 2 of Figure 4.3 indicates that the Czech

Figure 4.3. Value-Added Tax Rates in OECD Countries, 1990–2015
(Percent)

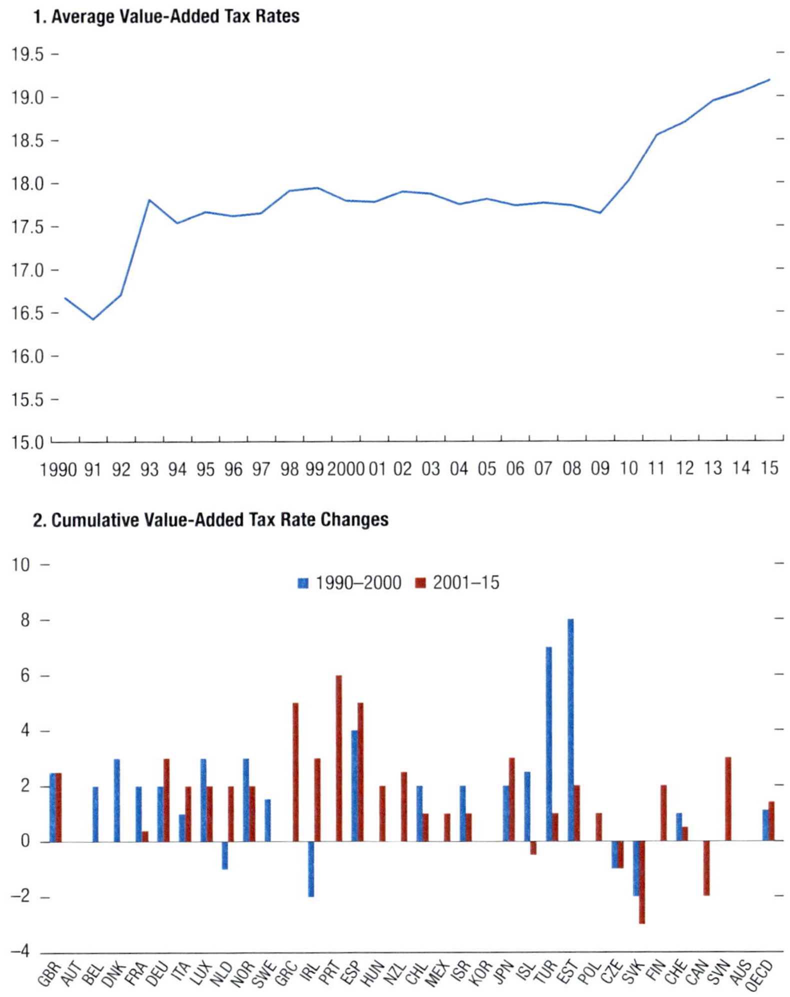

Figure 4.3. Value-Added Tax Rates in OECD Countries, 1990–2015 *(continued)*

(Percent)

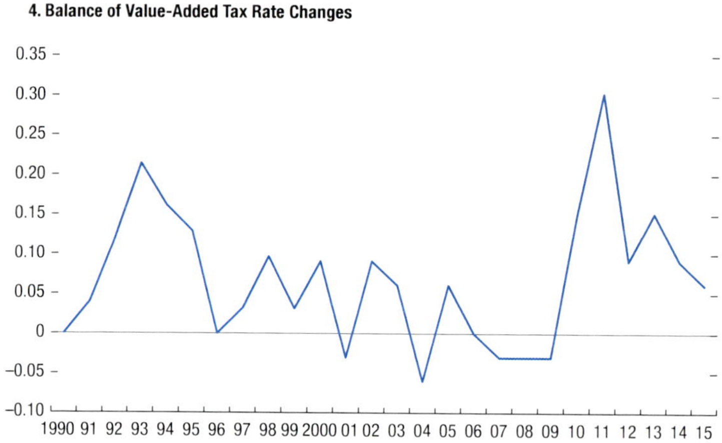

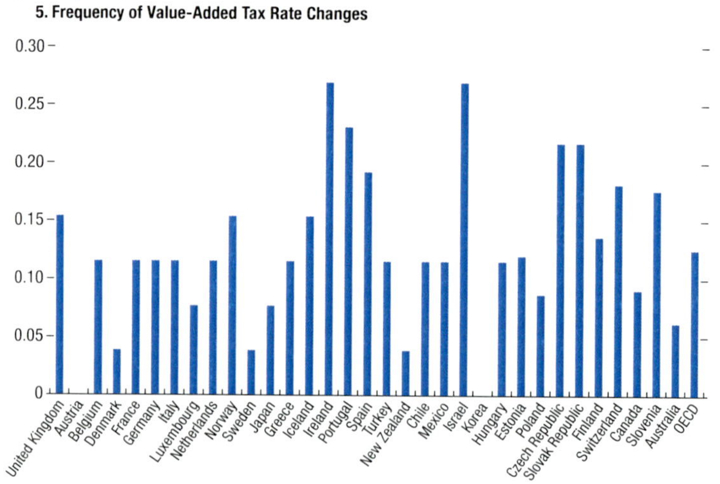

Sources: Authors' calculations based on OECD Tax Revenue Statistics (http://www.oecd.org/ctp/tax-policy/tax-database.htm), June 2016; and OECD Consumption Tax Trends 1999, 2001, 2004, 2006.
Note: OECD = Organisation for Economic Co-operation and Development.

Republic, Ireland, the Netherlands, and the Slovak Republic in the first decade, and Canada, the Czech Republic, Iceland, and the Slovak Republic in the period 2001–15 were the only countries implementing VAT rate cuts. All other countries experienced rate hikes of various sizes. Estonia and Turkey had the largest rate hikes in the 1990s, while Greece and Portugal, which both experienced fiscal crises after 2010, had the largest cumulative rate hikes during 2001–15.

EMPIRICAL HYPOTHESES AND OPERATIONALIZATION

The previous section shows that tax rates and, hence, tax policies, vary substantially across the three types of taxes, across countries, and across time. This section develops some empirical hypotheses derived from standard economic as well as politico-economic considerations explaining the variation. It also indicates which explanatory variables are chosen for the empirical section that follows. The hypotheses are grouped into five categories. The first group is related to "normal" tax policies, linking them to economic developments in a conventional way. It sets the benchmark for the subsequent effects. The second group considers government responses to crisis situations, defined as the incidence of financial crises. The third group represents political factors of partisanship and electoral effects. The fourth group studies the effects of fiscal rules. The final group checks whether EU governments that now operate under the common framework of the Excessive Deficit Procedure (Maastricht Treaty), the Stability and Growth Pact (introduced in 1998), and the Fiscal Compact (introduced as a response to the European debt crisis that started in 2010) behave differently compared with other OECD governments.

Normal Tax Policies

Conventional public finance theory suggests that governments use tax policies for macroeconomic stabilization, cutting rates during recessions and raising rates during expansions. While some of this theory in practice is embedded in progressive tax schedules, one may expect that governments use discretionary changes in tax rates for taxes that are less progressive. Furthermore, unless tax schedules are indexed to the price level, tax policy may respond to increases in inflation to correct for "bracket creep" in progressive taxes. This could lead to pressures to reduce top PIT rates in particular. In this vein, Mahon (2004) finds that higher inflation in previous periods is correlated with tax rate reductions in Latin American countries during the period 1977–95.

This gives the following hypotheses:

H1: Governments are more likely to cut tax rates following periods of low growth and more likely to raise tax rates following periods of high growth.[4]

Empirical operationalization: Lagged real GDP growth.

H2: Governments are more likely to cut PIT rates following years of high inflation.

Empirical operationalization: Lagged inflation rates.

[4] Data for all economic variables are taken from the International Monetary Fund's World Economic Outlook April 2016 database.

Debt sustainability is a second main concern of normal tax policies. To maintain the sustainability of public debt, primary budget surpluses must respond positively to rising public debt (for example, Bohn 1998). Although increases in tax rates may not be required because the adjustment could come through primary spending cuts, rising public debt makes increases in tax rates more likely, while declining public debt relieves pressures for tax rate hikes. This argument is captured empirically by including lagged ratios of government debt to GDP as explanatory variables.

This gives the following hypothesis:

H3: A low debt burden in the previous year makes tax rate cuts more likely, while the reverse is true for a high debt burden.

Empirical operationalization: Lagged government debt as percentage of GDP.

Episodes of persistent and large government deficits and rising public debt may force governments to implement large fiscal consolidations to maintain the sustainability of their debts. When this occurs, governments must decide on the appropriate mix between tax and expenditure adjustments. Based on OECD data from the early 1970s to the mid-1990s, Alesina and Perotti (1997); Perotti, Strauch, and von Hagen (1998); Hughes-Hallett, Strauch, and von Hagen (2002); and Alesina and Ardagna (2010) show that consolidations based on spending cuts are more likely to be successful in the sense that they lead to lasting reductions in deficits and debts.[5] The suggested reason is that governments are likely to give in to political pressures for more spending as soon as larger revenues start flowing in following an increase in tax rates. Perotti, Strauch, and von Hagen (1998) show that successful fiscal consolidations are also associated with increases in revenues from taxes on labor rather than on business.[6] Based on these considerations, one may expect that large and successful fiscal consolidations are associated with PIT rate increases but not with CIT rate increases. Finally, since VAT revenues in practice respond to rate changes faster than most other taxes, large and successful consolidations are expected to involve VAT rate increases.

Following this literature, the analysis identifies episodes of large and successful fiscal consolidations as periods during which the primary structural budget balance increased by at least 1.5 percent of GDP in two consecutive years. The data for the ratio of primary structural balances to GDP are taken from the OECD. The exercise uses a dummy variable for the existence of such episodes as an explanatory variable. Note that this approach implicitly assumes a two-stage decision-making process, with the decision to implement a large consolidation at the first stage and the choice of consolidation strategy and instruments at the second

[5] Alesina, Favero, and Giavazzi (2015) argue that output losses are lower when fiscal consolidations are based primarily on expenditure cuts rather than on tax increases.

[6] Perotti, Strauch, and von Hagen (1998) also show that, in contrast, the large fiscal expansions preceding fiscal consolidations are often associated with declines in the revenue from taxes on labor as well as increases in government transfers and wages.

stage. The analysis takes the decision at the first stage as given and considers the tax policy aspects at the second stage.

This gives the following hypothesis:

H4: Large, successful consolidations are associated with VAT and PIT rate increases.

Empirical operationalization: A dummy variable for episodes of large and successful fiscal consolidations.

Finally, the importance of tax competition among OECD countries is also considered. Tax competition occurs when the tax base is mobile across country borders and responds to international differences in tax rates. One may expect that tax competition is strongest in taxes falling on capital, less strong in taxes falling on labor, and least strong in taxes falling on consumption. The intensity of tax competition in the OECD is measured by including the balance of tax rate changes in the OECD from the previous section. The more countries that cut tax rates in a given year, the stronger the pressure on an individual government to do the same.[7] At the same time, the literature has argued that large countries are less exposed to tax competition than small countries because size translates into market power in international capital markets and investors are more reluctant to leave large markets than small markets in response to increases in tax rates (for example, Haufler and Wooton 1999; Wilson 1999). The analysis includes the natural log of population to account for country size.

This gives the following hypotheses:

H5: A country is more likely to change its tax rate if other countries are changing their tax rates. A tax increase is more likely if others are raising taxes and a tax cut is more likely if others are cutting taxes.

Empirical operationalization: Balance of tax changes in the OECD in a given year.

H6: Small countries are more likely to cut rates.

Empirical operationalization: Natural log of population.

Tax Policy in Crisis Mode

This section turns to tax policies in crisis mode. We consider two types of crises. The first are banking crises, which represent important fiscal shocks, since, when a sizable part of the banking system fails, only the government has the ability to provide liquidity and to deal with insolvency issues. Whatever tools governments choose, the fiscal costs of the crisis are likely to be expensive and call for additional tax revenues (see Honohan and Klingebiel 2000; Amaglobeli and others 2015). Moreover, markets may be skeptical about the ability of governments to repay what they borrow unless they raise tax rates to show their determination to

[7] Because each country has a weight of only 1/34 in this variable, simultaneity is unlikely to affect the estimates of the relevant coefficients.

avoid a fiscal crisis coming out of the banking crisis. Furthermore, Wälti (2016) argues that government reforms to the financial sector are more likely when there is a sudden stop in international financing. Such a scenario may put pressure on government to raise funds domestically and to do so quickly. Alesina and Drazen (1991) argue that the necessary fiscal response to a crisis may be delayed by "wars of attrition" that arise when different groups in society are able to block the required policy changes and shift the burden of adjustment to other groups. As time passes, however, the burden of adjustment becomes larger and, as a result, the likelihood of tax rate changes increases. Consistent with this argument, Hallerberg and Scartascini (forthcoming) find that the governments of Latin American countries that experienced a banking crisis were more likely to increase tax rates, particularly of the VAT.

Following from this research, expectations are that banking crises in OECD countries make tax cuts less likely and tax increases more likely, which leads to the following hypothesis:

H7: Tax cuts are less likely, and tax increases are more likely, during banking crises.

Empirical operationalization: The standard IMF data set for banking crises, which is Laeven and Valencia (2013).[8]

The analysis also examines whether there was anything specific to the 2008–09 financial crisis. Both the European Commission and the G20 urged countries to engage in fiscal expansions if they had the fiscal room to do so in this period. Therefore, in the initial years of the crisis, the effect might be the opposite of what the analysis first posited, that is, there should be a fiscal expansion, which can be paid for through a tax increase.

H8: Tax cuts were more likely in the years 2008–09.

Empirical operationalization: Include a dummy variable for these years.

Countries facing fiscal crises may turn to the IMF for financial assistance, which, if granted, comes with conditions specified by IMF adjustment programs. The incidence of an IMF adjustment program is, therefore, another indicator for a fiscal crisis. Mahon (2004) finds that governments made more tax changes when under a program. The logic is that the IMF expects changes that particularly raise additional revenues. In a more general paper on the effects of IMF conditionality, however, Biglaiser and Rouen (2011) do not find any effects specifically on taxation. To identify the incidence of IMF adjustment programs, the analysis uses the data provided by Dreher (2006), as updated by that author through 2012 and

[8] Note that the Laeven and Valencia (2013) data set ends in 2013. We assume the banking crisis has ended since they coded a crisis in place in 2013 in Belgium, Denmark, France, Germany, Hungary, Italy, Luxembourg, the Netherlands, Sweden, Switzerland, the United Kingdom, and the United States. We assume a crisis continues through 2015 in Austria, Greece, Iceland, Ireland, Portugal, Slovenia, and Spain.

by the current authors through the end of 2015.[9] Based on those data, a dummy variable is defined that equals one when a country falls under an IMF program during a given year and zero otherwise.

This gives the following hypothesis:

H9: Countries under IMF adjustment programs are more likely to increase tax rates.

Empirical operationalization: A dummy variable for the incidence of IMF adjustment programs.

Finally, tax responses to fiscal crises can be part of broader reforms that combine changes on the expenditure and revenue side of the budget with changes in other policy domains such as social insurance or labor market regulation. For example, tax rates may go up because a policy reform extends social insurance coverage to a group in society that was previously excluded. Alternatively, efforts may be made to reduce the distortions that taxation imposes on the economy. Tax rate changes, therefore, could occur in the context of changes in labor market regulation. The analysis uses an IMF data set indicating the incidence of public wage bill and employment reforms in a given country and year to identify periods of reform and define a dummy variable accordingly (IMF 2016).

This gives the following hypothesis:

H10: Tax changes are combined with reforms of the public wage bill and employment.

Empirical operationalization: A dummy variable for whether there was a reform in a given year.

Political Determinants of Tax Policy

How do politics affect tax policies? Political parties run on campaign planks that suggest they will change the tax burden for certain constituencies if they win the election. The standard analysis, which goes back to Hibbs (1977), is that the political right is most likely to favor "capital" while the political left is more likely to support "labor." Looking at the tax burden in Europe, Osterloh and Debus (2012) find that left party control of government is associated with corporate tax increases in 32 European countries from 1980 to 2006; Angelopoulos, Economides, and Kammas (2012) similarly find that left-leaning governments rely more on taxation of capital than on labor taxation in a sample of 16 OECD countries over the period 1970–2000. Looking at revenues rather than tax rate changes, Stein and Caro (2013) find that the left raises overall tax levels as well as income tax levels. They find no partisan effects on VAT revenues. Building on this work and applying it to the data in this analysis, expectations are that the right cuts taxes on income and corporations and raises the VAT, which is regressive

[9] The data set through 2012 is available at http://www.uni-heidelberg.de/fakultaeten/wiso/awi/professuren/intwipol/datasets_en.html. Downloaded June 18, 2016.

and spreads the tax burden to a greater part of the population than pays the top marginal income tax rate. Left-leaning governments are expected to want the reverse policies, that is, they are more likely to cut the VAT but increase the top rate of the PIT and the CIT.

This exercise uses the Database of Political Institutions (DPI) provided by Cruz, Keefer, and Scartascini (2016) to identify the political partisanship of governments. In this data set, governments are either right or left leaning. A government that has a right-leaning orientation is coded as one while left-leaning governments are coded as zero.

This yields the following hypothesis:

H11: Right-leaning governments are more likely to cut CIT and PIT rates and raise VAT rates, while left-leaning governments are more likely to do the reverse.

Empirical operationalization: Partisanship dummy for right-leaning governments.

Based on Latin American evidence, however, Capello (2014) argues that partisan differences dissolve in crisis settings. In such settings, governments have to react in any way they can, and there is simply no room or time to take partisan issues into account. This line of reasoning suggests the relevance of an interaction between crises and partisanship. For taxation, the inclusion of such a term could also be justified based on another argument: A crisis puts strong pressure on governments to raise taxes, and when that happens, they are more likely than under normal circumstances to raise taxes on their opponents. This suggests that right-leaning governments will increase the VAT rate and left-leaning governments will increase PIT and CIT rates during a banking crisis.

This yields the following hypothesis:

H12: In a financial crisis, right-leaning governments are more likely to increase the VAT rate while left-leaning governments are more likely to increase CIT and PIT rates.

Empirical operationalization: A term that interacts the banking crisis dummy with the partisanship dummy.

Political theory considers the effects of political fragmentation on the ability of governments to adjust tax and other policies. The more fragmented a political setting, the more difficult it is for the government to overcome the resistance of organized political interest groups to changes in tax policies. A good measure of political fragmentation is the number of "veto players" in the relevant decision-making process. A veto player is an actor in the policy process who can block changes to the tax policy status quo and whose assent is therefore required to implement such changes. For example, there are three institutional veto players in the United States when passing tax legislation—the two houses of Congress and the president. Tsebelis (2002) contends that the further apart are the most preferred policies of such players from each other, the more difficult it is for any one of them to achieve a change in the status quo. Thus, changes in tax policy are less likely if a U.S. president faces opposing majorities in one or both houses of Congress. Indeed, Basinger and Hallerberg (2004) find that the greater the ideological distance between veto players, the less likely is change in tax systems to occur.[10]

This analysis uses the variable "checks" from the DPI data set (Cruz, Keefer, and Scartascini 2016) to measure fragmentation. This variable counts the number of institutional and party veto players whose assent is required for change in policy, leading to the following hypothesis[11]:

H13: Countries with more institutional veto players have fewer changes in tax rates than countries with fewer institutional veto players.

Empirical operationalization: The variable "checks" from the DPI data set.

Another important political factor that could affect tax policies is the occurrence of elections. Political economy literature argues that governments are likely to cut tax rates and unlikely to increase them before elections, even if the arguments from normal tax policies would call for an increase. Several lines of reasoning support this conjecture. In a simple Keynesian framework of political business cycles, cutting tax rates is an attractive way to try to stimulate the macroeconomy, with many voters benefiting from increased economic growth and voting for the incumbent government (Nordhaus 1975; Hibbs 1977). In a rational-expectations version of political business cycles (Rogoff and Sibert 1988), cutting taxes is a signal to voters that the incumbent government has greater competence in economic policy than its opponents. In a distributional politics version of the argument, tax rate cuts are targeted at the constituencies of the ruling party; any growth effects are secondary. Von Hagen and Brückner (2002), Buti and van den Noord (2003), and von Hagen (2006) find electoral budget cycles in the euro area, especially in the early years of the introduction of the euro. At the same time, the political business cycle literature anticipates tax increases in the year after an election, which would correct for the increased deficits in an electoral year.

This yields the following hypothesis:

H14: Tax rate increases are less likely in years preceding elections and more likely in years following elections.

Empirical operationalization: A dummy for the year of the election and a lagged dummy variable for a legislative election year. Data from DPI.

---

[10] Note that Gehlbach and Malesky (2010) find that increasing the number of veto players can lead to a *greater* probability of policy change. Their rationale is that having more active players makes it harder for a particular special interest to block the given reform. In terms of operationalizing this concept of "veto players," Calvo (2014) finds that one-party control of the legislature or the lack of such control is most relevant in this context. To test whether one-party control affects changes in tax rates, we explored whether the "allhouse" variable from the DPI data set (Cruz, Keefer, and Scartascini 2016), which is coded as one when one party controls the relevant institutions, affects the results, but they do not change with this variable included.

[11] See the DPI codebook for further details. We also consider other ways that fragmentation could affect the probability of changes in tax rates. Governments with majorities in parliament should have an easier time passing legislation. Similarly, governments with larger majorities should also be more likely to make changes. We include variables for both concepts from the DPI data set, namely "allhouse" and "govfrac," as alternative measures of fragmentation. In no cases are these alternatives statistically significant.

Fiscal Rules

Fiscal rules are numerical restrictions on budgetary aggregates such as total government spending, revenues, budget balances, primary or structural balances, or on the ratio of public debt to GDP. Such rules aim to increase fiscal discipline and strengthen the credibility of the government's commitment to stable fiscal policies.[12] Rules restricting budget balances may, however, induce a bias toward higher taxes. On the one hand, they create pressures for tax rate hikes in times of low growth when government spending increases because of automatic stabilizers, such as unemployment insurance benefits or other types of welfare spending.[13] On the other hand, budget balance rules can force governments to increase taxes if they face spending demands from their constituencies that they cannot resist and the additional tax burden falls on other social groups.

To identify countries and periods in the sample in which budget balance rules existed, the fiscal rules data set provided by the IMF is used to construct a dummy variable that is equal to one if a rule existed and zero otherwise.[14]

This leads to the following hypothesis:

H15: Countries with budget balance rules are more likely to increase tax rates than countries that do not have these rules.

Empirical operationalization: A dummy variable is included for countries that have budget balance rules in place.

European Union Effects

An extension of this framework examines EU member states. Although taxation is mostly a competence for the member states and not for the Union, minimum rates are in place for the VAT. Stage III of Economic and Monetary Union introduced a currency union, the euro area, in 11 member states in 1999. Today, the euro area has 19 members. All EU members are today subject to a common economic governance framework, which, however, is stricter for members of the euro area. Within this framework, the European Commission can recommend that a member state be declared as having an "excessive deficit" if the commission perceives that there are serious concerns about the sustainability of that state's public finances. If the European Council of Ministers approves the European Commission's recommendation, that member state is expected to adopt appropriate policies to reduce its deficit, and it can be reprimanded for failing to do so. Reforms of this framework, which were labeled "Six Pack" and "Two Pack," were adopted in 2011–12 with the intention of strengthening this framework after its failure to avert public debt crises in Cyprus, Greece, Ireland, Italy, Portugal, and Spain. Therefore, there are pressures,

---

[12] See Kopits and Symansky (1998) for a general discussion of fiscal rules and Schaechter and others (2012) for an overview of the design and development of fiscal rules in the past 30 years.

[13] Poterba (1995) shows how budget balance rules at the state level have had adverse effects on the dynamics of state taxes in the United States.

[14] The data set is available at http://www.imf.org/external/datamapper/FiscalRules/map/map.htm. Downloaded June 18, 2016.

especially on euro area members, to reduce budget deficits. This pressure may have affected their tax policies and made tax increases more likely.

This yields the following hypotheses:

H16: Euro area member states are more likely to raise tax rates.

Empirical operationalization: A dummy variable for states in the euro area.

H17: EU member states under an "excessive deficit procedure" are more likely to raise tax rates.[15]

Empirical operationalization: A dummy variable for states under an excessive deficit procedure.

H18: After 2011, EU rules on debts and deficits resulted in increased pressures to raise tax rates.

Empirical operationalization: A dummy variable for the post-2011 period for EU states.

There is an additional wrinkle to the analysis. Baerg and Hallerberg (2016) find that the Council of Ministers is more likely to keep the original text and recommendations proposed by the European Commission when it reprimands the fiscal policies of small EU member states. In contrast, large member states, like France and Germany, frequently seem to be able to achieve a weakening of the recommendations that the European Commission proposed. This difference suggests that small states face a more powerful constraint on fiscal policy from the EU than large states. Population is already included as a measure of size in the analysis under hypothesis H6 (tax competition). In the current context, size can be interpreted as a proxy for the political power of the member states under Economic and Monetary Union. In this case, however, the prediction for EU member states with differential application of the Stability and Growth Pact would be the opposite—large states would not face the same pressure to consolidate as small states, so they would cut taxes more and increase them less than small states.

EMPIRICAL ANALYSIS AND RESULTS

To test empirically the hypotheses stated above, a binary time-series cross-section ordered logit model is estimated. The dependent variable of this model can take one of three values in each period: 1 for an increase in the tax rate, 0 for no change in the tax rate, and −1 for a cut in the tax rate. Intuitively, the model estimates the likelihood of the occurrence of each of these events given the values of the explanatory variables. The model thus explains the *direction* but not the *intensity* of the tax policies in the sample.[16] That is, it tells us whether a government is likely to move in a certain direction conditional on the realization

[15] Data from http://ec.europa.eu/economy_finance/economic_governance/sgp/corrective_arm/index_en.htm. Downloaded July 1, 2016.

[16] This empirical model follows the form of the one reported in Hallerberg and Scartascini (2016) but with a somewhat different set of independent variables.

of the explanatory variables, but it does not tell us how far it will move in that direction—how much it will raise or cut a tax rate. This limitation is due to the nature of the data.

Models of this kind are estimated for the three types of taxes under consideration, PIT, CIT, and VAT. Apart from the explanatory variables developed in the previous section, the exercise also includes variables indicating the number of previous changes in the tax rate during the sample period as well as the time since the last change. This approach is based on the consideration that governments may want to avoid frequent tax changes. The time period covered is 1990–2015. The overall sample is all OECD countries. There are, however, restrictions on data sources for some countries, so that an unbalanced panel results. Nevertheless, there are at least 24 and up to 34 countries in any given year in the analysis. Table 4.1 provides a summary of the findings, and the statistical results that include marginal effects and standard errors

Table 4.1. Summary of Findings

Hypothesis	Evidence
H1: Governments cut tax rates following low growth; increase rates after high growth.	Opposite for VAT: more likely to cut rate with high growth and increase with low growth
H2: Governments are more likely to cut PIT rates following years of high inflation.	No support
H3: A low debt burden makes tax rate cuts more likely; high debt burden makes tax rate cuts less likely.	No support
H4: Large, successful consolidations are associated with VAT and PIT rate increases; large fiscal expansions are associated with PIT rate cuts.	Large, successful consolidations associated with VAT and PIT rate increases
H5: A country changes rates in the same direction as changes in other countries.	Supportive evidence, all types of taxes
H6: Small countries are more likely to cut rates.	Opposite for CIT: large countries more likely to cut rate. Also, for the EU sample, large states are also more likely to decrease top PIT rate.
H7: Tax cuts are less likely, and tax increases are more likely during banking crises.	VAT increase less likely, PIT increase more likely
H8: Tax cuts are more likely during 2008–09.	No support
H9: Countries under IMF programs increase tax rates.	No support
H10: Reforms in employment lead to tax changes.	VAT increase more likely
H11: Right-leaning governments cut CIT and PIT rates and raise VAT rates, whereas left-leaning governments do the reverse.	No support
H12: In a financial crisis, right-leaning governments raise VAT, and left-leaning governments raise CIT and PIT rates.	Left less likely to raise VAT, more likely to raise PIT in a crisis
H13: The more institutional veto players there are, the fewer changes in tax rates.	No support
H14: Tax rate increases are less likely in the years before elections and more likely after elections.	CIT rate increases more likely after an election, cuts less likely
H15: Balanced budget rules are more likely to increase tax rates.	No support
H16: Euro area states raise tax rates.	VAT rate increases more likely in euro area states
H17: Excessive deficit procedure raises rates.	No support
H18: There were tax increases after 2011 in EU states.	PIT and CIT cuts less likely; PIT and CIT increases more likely

Source: OECD Tax Revenue Statistics (http://www.oecd.org/ctp/tax-policy/tax-database.htm), June 2016; and OECD Consumption Tax Trends 1999, 2001, 2004, 2006.

Note: CIT = corporate income tax; EU = European Union; OECD = Organisation for Economic Co-operation and Development; PIT = personal income tax; and VAT = value-added tax.

for decreases and increases for the VAT, PIT, and CIT appear in Annex Table 4.1.1 for the full sample and Annex Table 4.1.2 for the EU sample.[17]

Normal Tax Policy

Changes in GDP affect only the VAT rate, with increases in economic growth making a VAT rate cut somewhat more likely (about a 0.3 percentage point increase in the probability for every 1.0 percentage point increase in the growth rate) and a VAT increase less likely (about a 0.8 percentage point decrease in the probability for every 1.0 percentage point increase in the growth rate). Other economic variables, such as the lagged inflation rate or the lagged overall debt burden, do not make it more likely that the three taxes are changed.

There is some clear evidence of tax competition, that is, that the balance of tax rate changes in the OECD affects tax policy in individual countries. This variable is highly significant for all three types of taxes and has the strongest effects for PIT and CIT rates. For example, if half of the OECD countries are increasing their top income tax rate, it is 13.3 percentage points more likely that a country will increase its own rate. If half of the OECD countries cut their top PIT rate, it is 31.0 percentage points more likely that a country will cut its rate. Population size effects only apply for the CIT. Countries with large populations are somewhat more likely to reduce their CIT rates in this period and somewhat less likely to increase this rate.

Tax Policy in Crisis Mode

As a reminder, the main specification includes an interaction term, which means that the marginal effect associated with "banking crisis" is the effect when "Executive Right" is coded zero, that is, when a center or left-leaning government is in power during a banking crisis. The analysis indeed identifies partisan effects during a crisis—a left-leaning or centrist government is about 8.0 percentage points less likely to increase the VAT than a right-leaning government at the $p < 0.05$ level of significance. A left-leaning government is about 2.0 percentage points more likely to cut the VAT in a banking crisis, and about 7.0 percentage points more likely to increase the top PIT rate (albeit both at $p < 0.1$ level of significance only). This finding suggests that partisanship affects tax responses in ways anticipated earlier in the chapter for these two types of taxes during banking crises; there are no significant results for changes in CIT rates.

Turning to large fiscal consolidations, large and successful consolidations are found to be associated with tax changes. Increases in both the VAT rate and the top PIT rate are more likely during large fiscal contractions, meaning that it is about 10 percentage points more likely that there will be a VAT rate increase and about 11 percentage points more likely there will be a top PIT rate increase.

[17] One should note that with the interaction terms included, the interpretation of the marginal effect of "banking crisis" in Annex Tables 4.1.1 and 4.1.2 is whether there is a change in the tax rate when the interaction term is zero, that is, when there is not a right-leaning government in power.

This finding means that the consolidations in the data set are connected with tax increases.[18] Another type of "reform" is also relevant, namely labor market reforms. Reforms of public wage bills and employment, which occur often (though not always) during or after crises, are associated with a 9 percentage point increase in the likelihood of a VAT rate increase.

In contrast, the remaining variables do not seem to have an effect on changes in rates. Being under an IMF program does not spur further changes in these types of taxes. Counter to expectations, the crisis years of 2008 and 2009 also do not have a tangible effect. This outcome suggests that other relevant variables have been identified, such as a banking crisis year and the behavior of other states in the sample, meaning that a simple time dummy is no longer statistically significant.

Political Determinants of Tax Policy

Beyond the clear partisan effect during a crisis, differences between the left and the right in noncrisis years are not found. The results reported in Annex Table 4.1.3 further explore whether partisanship affects the type of tax changes used during a pronounced fiscal consolidation. As found for crisis situations, the left is more likely to raise the top PIT rate and less likely to cut it. Legislative elections in a previous year seem to have an effect only for the CIT, and in the expected direction—governments are about 2.0 percentage points more likely to increase this tax, and about 0.6 percentage point less likely to cut it, after an election. These results, which are replicated for all further specifications in unreported work, also investigate whether there are tax changes the year of an election, and show no evidence that cycles result in changes in tax rates.

The same is the case for the institutional "checks" variable—country-years that have institutions that increase the transaction costs for passing legislation (veto players) do not seem to reduce the chances of changes in tax rates except for one case—more institutional checks make it somewhat more likely that there is a CIT rate cut, and somewhat less likely that there is a CIT rate increase.[19]

Fiscal Rules

The balanced budget amendment does not seem to spur tax rate changes. The substantive effects in all specifications are close to zero, and in none of them is it statistically significant.

---

[18] We also explored a less strict definition of "consolidation" or "expansion," which counted one year below the given cut-off instead of two. In this case, the results for the VAT are as for the stricter version, but expansions are associated with an 8 percentage point increase in the likelihood of a top PIT rate cut and a 4 percentage point lower chance of a PIT increase. This finding suggests that there is an immediate effect of top PIT rate cuts that does not affect the cyclical budget balance over two consecutive budgets. Moreover, for one-year consolidations only, increases in the top PIT rate are not statistically significant at the $p < 0.1$ level.

[19] Strictly speaking, the prediction from the "checks" variable is that there should be a greater probability of no change in the three types of taxes. This corresponds to the case in which the dependent variable is coded zero. While we do not report these results here, for the CIT rate with no change, this variable is significant in the expected direction, with the marginal effect about 4 percentage points.

European Union Effects

Annex Table 4.1.2 reports results on specific EU effects. Only EU states are in this sample. Being a member of the euro area affects the VAT especially, making it more likely that a member state increases it and less likely that it decreases it. The effects of banking crisis conditional on partisanship are also more pronounced—the left is 13 percentage points less likely than the right to increase the VAT rate during a banking crisis. At the same time, the political right is significantly more likely to cut the top PIT rate during a banking crisis. Member states under IMF programs are also more likely to reduce the top PIT rate. There are also clear effects from 2012, that is, the period when the "Two Pack" and "Six Pack" economic governance reforms were in place and where notable problems with debt burdens remained. Both PIT and CIT cuts are less likely and PIT and CIT increases are more likely. Curiously, however, over the period, being identified as having an "excessive deficit" does not make tax changes any more likely. As expected, there is a difference between large and small states, with larger states more likely to cut, and less likely to increase, PIT and CIT rates. This finding is consistent with an argument that small states faced more pressure than large states to consolidate in the EU under the Stability and Growth Pact.

CONCLUSIONS

This chapter reviews changes over the past 25 years in the three main taxes governments use in OECD countries: CIT, PIT, and VAT. Variation has occurred both across countries and across time.

The analysis identifies political reasons that explain some of this variation. Left-leaning governments are more likely to cut VAT rates and to increase PIT rates during a financial crisis. This propensity means that the costs of adjustment are more likely to be borne by the political opponents of the parties in office. Similarly, electoral cycles clearly have an effect, although they appear only for the CIT—rates are more likely to be increased and less likely to be cut in the year following an election.

There are also relevant associations with significant fiscal adjustments. Governments that successfully increase the cyclical budget balance more than 1.5 percent of GDP in two consecutive years also increase both the VAT rate and the top PIT rate. This suggests that the type of tax used in the consolidation, and not just the divide between expenditure- and revenue-driven consolidations, may be a key policy instrument. Looking further at partisan effects, the left is more likely to use increases in PIT rates as part of a fiscal consolidation.

Many of the OECD countries are also in the EU, and the EU's rules have some effect on tax policy as well. Euro area member states throughout the period are more likely to raise their VAT rates. In the period after 2011, which is when the overall fiscal framework was strengthened, it became more likely that there would be tax increases in the other two types of taxes. It is noteworthy that the lagged change in GDP is not included in the model. This suggests additional pressure for tax changes during this period.

The limitations of this study must be acknowledged. The analysis measures only whether a given tax rate was increased or decreased and not the scale of the change. Other types of changes to tax systems also affect the base of a given tax. Future work could explore whether the crisis, partisan, and consolidation effects identified here also affect the scale of changes in rates and changes in other dimensions of tax policy.

ANNEX 4.1. SUPPLEMENTARY TABLES

Annex Table 4.1.1. Ordered Logit, Marginal Effects

	VAT		PIT		CIT	
	(1)	(2)	(3)	(4)	(5)	(6)
Variables	**Decrease**	**Increase**	**Decrease**	**Increase**	**Decrease**	**Increase**
Change in GDP (lag)	0.002*	−0.008**	−0.007	0.003	0.005	−0.002
	(0.001)	(0.003)	(0.006)	(0.003)	(0.008)	(0.003)
Inflation (lag)	−0.002	0.006	0.009	−0.004	0.016	−0.005
	(0.002)	(0.006)	(0.006)	(0.003)	(0.010)	(0.003)
Gross Debt (lag)	−0.000	0.000	−0.000	0.000	0.000	−0.000
	(0.000)	(0.000)	(0.001)	(0.000)	(0.000)	(0.000)
Population (natural lag)	0.002	−0.008	−0.007	0.003	0.019*	−0.006*
	(0.003)	(0.009)	(0.019)	(0.008)	(0.011)	(0.004)
Balance of Tax Changes	−0.161***	0.506***	−0.621***	0.267***	−0.821***	0.273***
	(0.059)	(0.135)	(0.126)	(0.083)	(0.153)	(0.096)
Banking Crisis	0.029**	−0.093***	−0.156	0.067*	0.094	−0.031
	(0.014)	(0.034)	(0.103)	(0.038)	(0.077)	(0.026)
2008 or 2009	0.010	−0.030	0.008	−0.003	−0.054	0.018
	(0.014)	(0.045)	(0.056)	(0.024)	(0.058)	(0.019)
Fiscal Contraction—	−0.030**	0.095***	−0.259***	0.111***	−0.114	0.038
Cyclical Balance > 1.5 × GDP	(0.013)	(0.032)	(0.082)	(0.042)	(0.132)	(0.046)
IMF Program	−0.029	0.090**	0.051	−0.022	0.083	−0.028
	(0.018)	(0.042)	(0.070)	(0.029)	(0.077)	(0.025)
Reforms Public Wage, Employment	−0.001	0.003	−0.025	0.011	0.007	−0.002
	(0.008)	(0.025)	(0.043)	(0.018)	(0.047)	(0.015)
Executive Politically Right	−0.016	0.052	0.162*	−0.070*	−0.102	0.034
	(0.015)	(0.043)	(0.095)	(0.036)	(0.095)	(0.032)
Right × Banking Crisis	0.000	−0.001	0.012	−0.005	0.029*	−0.010*
	(0.002)	(0.007)	(0.016)	(0.007)	(0.015)	(0.006)
Checks and Balances	0.003	−0.010	−0.006	0.003	0.013	−0.004
	(0.005)	(0.017)	(0.025)	(0.010)	(0.033)	(0.011)
Legislative Election	0.012*	−0.039*	−0.031	0.013	−0.055*	0.018**
	(0.007)	(0.022)	(0.026)	(0.011)	(0.030)	(0.009)
Legislative Election (lag)	−0.002	0.005	−0.010	0.004	−0.028	0.009
	(0.009)	(0.029)	(0.043)	(0.018)	(0.039)	(0.012)
Budget Balance Rule	−0.000	0.000	−0.025***	0.011***	−0.029***	0.010***
	(0.003)	(0.008)	(0.005)	(0.002)	(0.006)	(0.002)
Number of Previous Tax Changes	−0.002***	0.006***	0.006	−0.002**	0.016***	−0.005***
	(0.001)	(0.002)	(0.004)	(0.001)	(0.004)	(0.002)
Time Since Last Tax Change	0.002*	−0.008**	−0.007	0.003	0.005	−0.002
	(0.001)	(0.003)	(0.006)	(0.003)	(0.008)	(0.003)
Observations	520	520	576	576	571	571

Source: See the main text under the Hypotheses section.

Note: Coefficients displayed are the marginal effects. Standard errors are in parentheses. CIT = corporate income tax; PIT = personal income tax; and VAT = value-added tax.

*** $p < 0.01$, ** $p < 0.05$, * $p < 0.1$.

Annex Table 4.1.2. European Union Member States

	VAT		PIT		CIT	
	(1)	(2)	(3)	(4)	(5)	(6)
Variables	**Decrease**	**Increase**	**Decrease**	**Increase**	**Decrease**	**Increase**
Euro Area Member State	−0.022**	0.059**	−0.005	0.002	−0.005	0.001
	(0.010)	(0.024)	(0.050)	(0.019)	(0.063)	(0.011)
Excessive Deficit Procedure	−0.006	0.015	−0.026	0.010	−0.074	0.013
	(0.016)	(0.044)	(0.045)	(0.017)	(0.062)	(0.012)
EU Country after 2011	−0.024	0.064**	−0.081	0.031	−0.129	0.023
	(0.016)	(0.028)	(0.091)	(0.034)	(0.093)	(0.018)
Change in GDP (lag)	0.002	−0.006**	0.002	−0.001	0.003	−0.000
	(0.001)	(0.003)	(0.008)	(0.003)	(0.010)	(0.002)
Inflation (lag)	−0.007**	0.018***	0.010	−0.004	0.021*	−0.004*
	(0.003)	(0.006)	(0.010)	(0.004)	(0.012)	(0.002)
Gross Debt (lag)	0.000	−0.001	0.000	−0.000	0.002	−0.000
	(0.000)	(0.000)	(0.001)	(0.000)	(0.001)	(0.000)
Population (natural lag)	0.000	−0.000	0.050**	−0.019**	0.060**	−0.011**
	(0.004)	(0.011)	(0.021)	(0.008)	(0.024)	(0.004)
Balance of Tax Changes	−0.208**	0.556***	−0.679***	0.257**	−0.961***	0.170**
	(0.092)	(0.144)	(0.205)	(0.106)	(0.235)	(0.072)
Banking Crisis	0.052**	−0.139***	−0.102	0.038	0.154	−0.027
	(0.027)	(0.043)	(0.101)	(0.043)	(0.117)	(0.022)
2008 or 2009	−0.010	0.027	−0.043	0.016	−0.163	0.029
	(0.028)	(0.071)	(0.070)	(0.025)	(0.113)	(0.024)
Fiscal Contraction—Cyclical Balance > 1.5 × GDP	−0.044*	0.117***	−0.367***	0.139***	−0.117	0.021
	(0.024)	(0.043)	(0.085)	(0.035)	(0.140)	(0.025)
IMF Program	−0.033	0.089	0.257***	−0.097***	−0.001	0.000
	(0.038)	(0.086)	(0.059)	(0.035)	(0.175)	(0.031)
Reforms Public Wage, Employment	−0.034	0.092**	0.012	−0.005	0.182**	−0.032*
	(0.026)	(0.047)	(0.097)	(0.036)	(0.083)	(0.017)
Executive Politically Right	−0.005	0.014	−0.135**	0.051*	−0.000	0.000
	(0.011)	(0.029)	(0.062)	(0.028)	(0.055)	(0.010)
Right × Banking Crisis	−0.025	0.068*	0.255**	−0.096*	−0.176	0.031
	(0.018)	(0.040)	(0.100)	(0.051)	(0.129)	(0.025)
Checks and Balances	0.005	−0.014**	0.027	−0.010	0.072***	−0.013***
	(0.003)	(0.006)	(0.019)	(0.008)	(0.024)	(0.004)
Legislative Election	−0.003	0.007	−0.019	0.007	−0.011	0.002
	(0.008)	(0.021)	(0.026)	(0.010)	(0.048)	(0.009)
Legislative Election (lag)	0.004	−0.011	−0.047	0.018	−0.145***	0.026***
	(0.008)	(0.023)	(0.044)	(0.017)	(0.047)	(0.010)
Budget Balance Rule	−0.005	0.013	−0.000	0.000	0.069	−0.012
	(0.014)	(0.038)	(0.079)	(0.030)	(0.086)	(0.015)
Number of Previous Tax Changes	−0.001	0.004	−0.043***	0.016***	−0.052***	0.009***
	(0.004)	(0.009)	(0.006)	(0.003)	(0.011)	(0.003)
Time Since Last Tax Change	−0.002*	0.006***	0.014***	−0.005***	0.033***	−0.006***
	(0.001)	(0.002)	(0.003)	(0.002)	(0.007)	(0.002)
Observations	300	300	291	291	299	299

Source: See the main text under the Hypotheses section.
Note: The coefficients displayed are the marginal effects. Standard errors are in parentheses. CIT = corporate income tax; PIT = personal income tax; and VAT = value-added tax.
*$p < .1$; **$p < .05$; ***$p < .01$.

Annex Table 4.1.3. Ordered Logit, Additional Interaction

	VAT		PIT		CIT	
	(1)	(2)	(3)	(4)	(5)	(6)
Variables	**Decrease**	**Increase**	**Decrease**	**Increase**	**Decrease**	**Increase**
Executive Politically Right	−0.004	0.012	0.003	−0.001	−0.034	0.011
	(0.006)	(0.020)	(0.033)	(0.014)	(0.035)	(0.013)
Fiscal Contraction—Cyclical Balance > 1.5 × GDP	−0.023	0.072	−0.308***	0.132***	−0.260	0.086
	(0.015)	(0.046)	(0.084)	(0.044)	(0.166)	(0.058)
Executive Right × Fiscal Contraction	−0.021	0.067	0.156	−0.067	0.464**	−0.153**
	(0.029)	(0.085)	(0.232)	(0.101)	(0.204)	(0.072)
Change in GDP (lag)	0.002*	−0.007**	−0.006	0.002	0.003	−0.001
	(0.001)	(0.003)	(0.007)	(0.003)	(0.008)	(0.003)
Inflation (lag)	−0.002	0.007	0.010*	−0.004	0.014	−0.005
	(0.002)	(0.006)	(0.006)	(0.003)	(0.010)	(0.003)
Gross Debt (lag)	−0.000	0.000	−0.000	0.000	0.000	−0.000
	(0.000)	(0.000)	(0.001)	(0.000)	(0.001)	(0.000)
Population (natural lag)	0.002	−0.006	−0.005	0.002	0.019*	−0.006*
	(0.003)	(0.009)	(0.019)	(0.008)	(0.010)	(0.004)
Balance of Tax Changes	−0.163***	0.513***	−0.621***	0.266***	−0.813***	0.268***
	(0.061)	(0.134)	(0.127)	(0.084)	(0.148)	(0.093)
Banking Crisis	0.021**	−0.066**	−0.072	0.031	0.036	−0.012
	(0.010)	(0.028)	(0.061)	(0.024)	(0.052)	(0.017)
2008 or 2009	0.010	−0.032	0.004	−0.002	−0.047	0.016
	(0.014)	(0.045)	(0.057)	(0.025)	(0.059)	(0.019)
IMF Program	−0.003	0.009	0.098	−0.042	−0.036	0.012
	(0.016)	(0.050)	(0.129)	(0.055)	(0.110)	(0.036)
Reforms Public Wage, Employment	−0.028	0.089**	0.041	−0.018	0.114	−0.038
	(0.019)	(0.044)	(0.065)	(0.027)	(0.079)	(0.025)
Checks and Balances	−0.000	0.000	0.014	−0.006	0.028*	−0.009*
	(0.002)	(0.007)	(0.016)	(0.008)	(0.015)	(0.006)
Legislative Election	0.004	−0.012	−0.012	0.005	0.011	−0.004
	(0.005)	(0.017)	(0.025)	(0.010)	(0.031)	(0.010)
Legislative Election (lag)	0.012*	−0.038*	−0.032	0.014	−0.057**	0.019**
	(0.006)	(0.021)	(0.027)	(0.012)	(0.029)	(0.009)
Budget Balance Rule	−0.001	0.003	−0.008	0.003	−0.030	0.010
	(0.009)	(0.029)	(0.043)	(0.018)	(0.038)	(0.012)
Number of Previous Tax Changes	−0.000	0.001	−0.026***	0.011***	−0.028***	0.009***
	(0.003)	(0.008)	(0.005)	(0.002)	(0.007)	(0.002)
Time Since Last Tax Change	−0.002***	0.006***	0.006*	−0.002**	0.016***	−0.005***
	(0.001)	(0.002)	(0.003)	(0.001)	(0.004)	(0.002)
Observations	520	520	576	576	571	571

Source: See the main text under the Hypotheses section.

Note: This table adds an interactive term for partisanship and fiscal contractions. It also reports the results when the year of the election is included. The coefficients displayed are the marginal effects. Standard errors are in parentheses. CIT = corporate income tax; PIT = personal income tax; and VAT = value-added tax.

*$p < .1$; **$p < .05$; ***$p < .01$.

REFERENCES

Alesina, A., and S. Ardagna. 2010. "Large Changes in Fiscal Policy. Taxes Versus Spending." In *Tax Policy and the Economy,* Volume 24, edited by Jeffrey R. Brown, 35–68. Chicago: University of Chicago Press.

Alesina, A., and A. Drazen. 1991. "Why Are Stabilizations Delayed?" *American Economic Review* 81 (5): 1170–88.

Alesina, A., C. Favero, and F. Giavazzi. 2015. "The Output Effect of Fiscal Consolidation Plans." *Journal of International Economics* 96 (Suppl 1): S19–S42.

Alesina, A., and R. Perotti. 1997. "Fiscal Adjustments in OECD Countries: Composition and Macroeconomic Effects." *IMF Staff Papers* 44 (2): 210–48.

Amaglobeli, D., N. End, M. Jarmuzek, and G. Palomba. 2015. "From Systemic Banking Crises to Fiscal Costs: Risk Factors." Working Paper 15/166, International Monetary Fund, Washington.

Angelopoulos, K., G. Economides, and P. Kammas. 2012. "Does Cabinet Ideology Matter for the Structure of Tax Policies?" *European Journal of Political Economy* 28 (4): 620–35.

Avi-Yonah, R. S. 2009. "The OECD Harmful Tax Competition Report: A Tenth Anniversary Retrospective." *Brookings Journal of International Law* 34 (3): 783–95.

Baerg, N., and M. Hallerberg. 2016. "Explaining Instability in the Stability and Growth Pact: The Contribution of Member State Power and Euroskepticism to the Euro Crisis." *Comparative Political Studies* 49 (7): 968–1009.

Basinger, S., and M. Hallerberg. 2004. "Remodeling the Competition for Capital: How Domestic Politics Erases the Race-to-the-Bottom." *American Political Science Review* 98 (2): 261–76.

Biglaiser, G., and K. DeRouen. 2011. "How Soon Is Now? The Effects of the IMF on Economic Reforms in Latin America." *Review of International Organizations* 6 (2): 189–213.

Bohn, H. 1998. "The Behavior of U.S. Public Debt and Deficits." *Quarterly Journal of Economics* 113 (3): 949–63.

Buti, M., and P. van den Noord. 2003. "Discretionary Fiscal Policy and Elections: The Experience of the Early Years of EMU." Working Paper 351, Economics Department, Organisation for Economic Co-operation and Development, Paris.

Calvo, E. 2014. *Legislator Success in Fragmented Congresses in Argentina: Plurality Cartels, Minority Presidents, and Lawmaking.* Cambridge, U.K.: Cambridge University Press.

Capello, D. 2014. "The Politics of Financial Boom and Crisis: Evidence from Latin America." *Comparative Political Studies* 47 (2): 260–86.

Cruz, C., P. Keefer, and C. Scartascini. 2016. "Database of Political Institutions Codebook, 2015 Update (DPI 2015)." Inter-American Development Bank. Updated version of T. Beck, G. Clarke, A. Groff, P. Keefer, and P. Walsh. 2001. "New Tools in Comparative Political Economy: The Database of Political Institutions." *World Bank Economic Review* 15 (1): 165–76.

Devereux, M., and R. Griffith. 1998. "Taxes and the Location of Production: Evidence from a Panel of US Multinationals." *Journal of Public Economics* 68 (June): 335–67.

Devereux, M. P., B. Lockwood, and M. Redoano. 2008. "Do Countries Compete over Corporate Tax Rates?" *Journal of Public Economics* 92 (5–6): 1210–35.

Dreher, A. 2006. "IMF and Economic Growth: The Effects of Programs, Loans, and Compliance with Conditionality." *World Development* 34 (5): 765–88.

Gehlbach, S. 2008. *Representation through Taxation.* Cambridge, U.K.: Cambridge University Press.

———, and E. J. Malesky. 2010. "The Contribution of Veto Players to Economic Reforms." *Journal of Politics* 72 (4): 957–75.

Hallerberg, M., and C. Scartascini. Forthcoming. "Explaining Changes in Tax Burdens in Latin America: Do Politics Trump Economics?" *European Journal of Political Economy.* doi:10.1016/j.ejpoleco.2016.07.004.

Haufler, A., and I. Wooton. 1999. "Country Size and Tax Competition for Foreign Direct Investment." *Journal of Public Economics* 71 (1): 121–39.

Hibbs, D. 1977. "Political Parties and Macroeconomic Policy." *American Political Science Review* 71 (4): 1467–87.
Honohan, P., and D. Klingebiel. 2000. "Controlling the Fiscal Costs of Banking Crises." Working Paper 2441, World Bank, Washington.
Hughes-Hallett, A., R. R. Strauch, and J. von Hagen. 2002. "Budgetary Consolidation in Europe: Quality, Economic Conditions, and Persistence." *Journal of the Japanese and International Economies* 16 (4): 512–35.
International Monetary Fund. 2016. "Managing Government Compensation and Employment—Institutions, Policies, and Reform Challenges." International Monetary Fund, Washington, DC.
Kopits, G., and S. A. Symansky. 1998. "Fiscal Policy Rules." Occasional Paper 162, International Monetary Fund, Washington.
Laeven, L., and F. Valencia. 2013. "Systemic Banking Crises Database." *IMF Economic Review* 61 (2): 225–70.
Mahon, J. E. 2004. "Causes of Tax Reform in Latin America, 1977–95." *Latin American Research Review* 39 (1): 3–30.
Nordhaus, W. D. 1975. "The Political Business Cycle." *Review of Economic Studies* 42 (2): 169–90.
Organisation for Economic Co-operation and Development (OECD). 1998. *Harmful Tax Competition: An Emerging Global Issue.* Paris: OECD.
Osterloh, S., and M. Debus. 2012. "Partisan Politics in Corporate Taxation." *European Journal of Political Economy* 28 (2): 192–207.
Perotti, R., R. R. Strauch, and J. von Hagen. 1998. *Sustainable Public Finances.* London: Centre for Economic Policy Research.
Poterba, J. M. 1995. "Balanced Budget Rules and Fiscal Policy: Evidence from the States." *National Tax Journal* 48 (3): 329–36.
Rogoff, K., and A. Sibert. 1988. "Elections and Macroeconomic Policy Cycles." *Review of Economic Studies* 55 (1): 1–16.
Schaechter, A., T. Kinda, N. Budina, and A. Weber. 2012. "Fiscal Rules in Response to the Crisis. Towards the Next-Generation Rules. A New Dataset." Working Paper 12/187, International Monetary Fund, Washington.
Stein, E., and L. Caro. 2013. "Ideology and Taxation in Latin America." Working Paper 407, Inter-American Development Bank, Washington, DC.
Tsebelis, G. 2002. *Veto Players: How Political Institutions Work.* Princeton, New Jersey: Princeton University Press.
von Hagen, J. 2006. "Fiscal Rules and Fiscal Performance in the EU and Japan." *Monetary and Economic Studies* 24 (1): 25–60.
———, and M. Brückner. 2002. "Monetary and Fiscal Policy in the European Monetary Union." *Monetary and Economic Studies* 20: S-1Special Edition on Exchange Rate Regimes in the 21st Century, 123–54.
Wälti, S. 2016. "Financial Crisis Begets Financial Reform? The Origin of the Crisis Matters." *European Journal of Political Economy* 40: 1–15.
Wilson, J. D. 1999. "Theories of Tax Competition." *National Tax Journal* 52 (2): 269–304.

CHAPTER 5

Now or Later? The Political Economy of Public Investment in Democracies

SANJEEV GUPTA, ESTELLE X. LIU,
AND CARLOS MULAS-GRANADOS

INTRODUCTION

Public investment is often touted as a way to raise output, both in the short term by promoting aggregate demand and in the long term through enhanced supply potential of the economy (IMF, 2014a; Felice, 2016). However, even when shovel-ready projects are available and budget processes are sufficiently strong for implementing investment programs, public investment may not occur. This may be because public investment is less noticeable (Rogoff, 1990) or may have a lower short-term economic multiplier than certain other types of public spending, including public consumption. When elections approach, policymakers may seek to increase public consumption at the expense of public investment to accelerate the economy faster and increase their probabilities of reelection.

In this chapter, we explore the potential relationship between public investment and electoral cycles. In particular, we seek to answer the following question: does the proximity of elections affect the growth rate of public investment? Our empirical approach relies on a unique database covering 67 advanced, emerging and low-income economies with presidential and parliamentary democracies. Using this data, we try to answer to what extent the growth rate of public investment can be explained by the proximity of elections, after controlling for relevant considerations.

In contrast to previous studies that relied on a linear relationship or binary association, we show that the relationship between the growth rate of public investment and the electoral cycle follows an inverted U-shape. Our results show that the growth rate of public investment is larger at the beginning of the mandate, peaks about 28 months before elections, and then declines fast as elections

---

This chapter is reprinted from the *European Journal of Political Economy*, Vol. 45, Sanjeev Gupta, Estelle X. Liu, and Carlos Mulas-Granados, "Now or Later? The Political Economy of Public Investment in Democracies," ©2016, with permission from Elsevier.

approach.[1] One month closer to the next election the growth rate of public investment declines about 0.7 percentage points. Other political and institutional variables are less important. Our results are robust to a number of tests, in particular to the potential endogeneity of election dates.

The chapter is organized as follows. The second section reviews the relevant literature. The third section presents the data and some stylized facts. The fourth section reports the results of the regression analysis on the baseline model. The fifth section performs various robustness tests. And the sixth section summarizes the main findings and concludes.

LITERATURE REVIEW

Since the concept of political business cycles (PBC) was first proposed by Nordhaus (1975), the literature on the political economy of fiscal policy has mainly focused on the political and institutional factors behind budget deficits. Only a few papers have dealt with the political economy of public investment and capital accumulation.[2] The literature can be grouped into three approaches (Eslava, 2006). The first would be the *opportunistic* approach, according to which electoral incentives influence government's budget balance. The second could be labeled as *ideological*, and would include all the papers that see fiscal deficits as arising from conflicts of interest among different political parties with heterogeneous preferences. The third approach—which focuses on *rules and institutions*—highlights their importance behind fragmentation in the decision-making process, thereby affecting budget composition and damaging public investment. The literature on the political economy of public investment can be grouped along the same lines.

The *opportunistic* or *electoral approach* is summarized by Rogoff (1990) who provided a firm theoretical foundation for electoral shifts leading to changes in the composition of public spending. He showed that electoral incentives may induce the incumbent to shift public spending towards more "visible" government consumption and away from public investment. Government consumption expenditures are more "visible" before elections, while capital expenditures (e.g., infrastructure) are mostly long-term projects that increase voters' utility upon completion. Drazen and Eslava (2010) developed this idea further and predicted that changes in composition of public spending during election periods were the result of incumbents attempting to signal that their preferences were closer

[1] Note also that public investment deceleration is accompanied by an acceleration of current spending. Our results confirm at an aggregate multi-country level what other studies suggested at the single-country level. For example, Klein (2004) examined the political cycles in Israel, and found that in the 1980s and 1990s (a period that includes six general elections) in the period before an election public investment declined and civilian consumption rose significantly. Fiva and Navik (2013) also explored these issues at the municipal level in Norway.

[2] Early references in this field are: Sturm and De Haan (1998), De Haan, Sturm and Sikken (1996), De Haan and Sturm (1994), and Sturm (2001).

to those of voters. Empirical evidence in this regard is mixed.[3] Most multicountry studies at the general government level show that elections tend to shift public spending in favor of current spending and away from public investment (Schuknecht, 2000; Block, 2002; Vergne 2009; Katsimi and Sarantides, 2012).[4] However, the evidence from single country studies (e.g., Canada, Colombia, Portugal, and Norway) suggests that at the local government level opposite forces are at play. Local elections are correlated with a shift toward "visible" investment (which at the subnational level takes the form of local infrastructure) together with targeted public transfer programs (Blais and Nadeau, 1992; Kneebone and McKenzie, 2001; Veiga and Veiga, 2007; Alesina and Paradisi, 2014).

The *ideological* or *partisan approach* tries to link the size and the composition of budget with the sign of partisan preferences. In partisan models, parties of the left are expected to favor a larger government and have less aversion to public deficits than parties of the right (Tufte, 1978; Alesina and Tabellini, 1990; Alt and Lassen, 2006). The greater preference for redistribution of left-wing parties would imply more spending, on social transfers. In addition, their preference for a more activist role of the state in the provision of public physical and human capital would imply higher public investment on infrastructure, health and education. Empirical findings support the effect of partisanship on the composition of public spending (Boix, 1997; Francese, 2002; Brauninger, 2005; Potrafke, 2010; Angelopoulus et al., 2012) and during fiscal adjustments, with left-wing parties opting for revenue-based adjustments and right-wing parties opting for expenditure-based ones (Perotti, 1998; Mulas-Granados, 2003, 2006; Mierau et al., 2007).[5] But there can be exceptions to partisanship. Given that politicians need to be opportunistic to win elections, rational politicians may go against their ideological policy preferences (Persson and Svensson, 1989; Pettersson-Lidbom, 2001).

The *rules* or *institutional* approach encompasses a great variety of issues, such as the role that rules and institutions play in constraining or facilitating public investment decisions. In certain cases, the focus is on the way they shape the political and economic context in which governments operate. These contributions can be grouped in three broad areas:

First, the role of electoral rules and political traditions in generating fragmented party systems and weak governments. Minority governments, divided legislatures, coalitions and multiparty cabinets, with a large number of ministers, and with a weak coordinating role for the Ministry of Finance, are all associated with fiscal profligacy and low productive investment (Hallerberg and Von Hagen, 1997; Von Hagen, Hallett and Strauch, 2001; Perotti and Kontopoulos, 2002; Hallerberg,

---

[3] It should be stressed that PBC models are all based on the assumption of competitive elections, which is more applicable to developed established democracies, rather than to emerging and low-income countries, many of which are "new" democracies.

[4] Drazen and Eslava (2010) and Aidt, Veiga and Veiga (2011) show instead that public investment grows during electoral years.

[5] For further evidence on the existence of partisan effects in public spending and tax policies and on the impact of partisanship on specific categories of public spending, such as social and welfare policies, see Cusack (1997). Regarding the impact of ideology on the composition of fiscal revenues, see Hallerberg and Basinger (1998) and Belke et al. (2007).

Strauch, and Von Hagen, 2007). Institutional frameworks that reinforce and centralize budget commitments help eliminate electoral manipulation of budget cycles (Saporiti and Streb, 2008), and frequent changes in government are associated with lower average public investment (De Haan and Sturm, 1997).

Second, the impact of good governance on the level and composition of public finances. Better governance, more transparency, less corruption, and a smaller amount of veto players are all correlated with better quality of public finances. This is true not only at the national but also at the sub-national level, where transparency helps restrict electoral manipulation of spending (Schneider, 2010; Bove and Efthyvoulou, 2013). In this respect, higher levels of public investment could just be the result of corrupt processes and inefficient public management systems.

Finally, the impact of budget rules and institutions on the sustainability of public finances (IMF, 2014b). While the presence of golden rules has not had a differential impact in sustaining higher levels of public investment, there is some evidence that strong budget institutions have been successful in preserving investment from budget cuts during the crisis (IMF, 2014c).

DATA AND STYLIZED FACTS

This study uses data from 67 democracies during 1975 and 2012, covering countries from all regions and income levels.[6] We focus on elections for a national executive figure or a national legislative body, and restrict the sample to countries and periods where competitive elections have taken place. The sample excludes countries where data on public fixed capital formation are not available. Additional details on sample size and selection criteria can be found in Annex Tables 5.1.1 and 5.1.2).

Data on public gross fixed capital formation comes from three sources: *World Economic Outlook* (*WEO*), World Development Indicators (WDI) and Haver Analytics.[7] Data on fiscal variables are drawn from the *WEO*, including total government expenditure, interest payments and current spending, the primary balance and the debt-to-GDP ratio. All these variables are estimated at the general government level.[8] Data on macroeconomic control variables, including real GDP growth and the rate of inflation were collected from *WEO*.

[6] As fiscal data prior to 1990 are generally regarded with poor quality, we replicate our analysis using data after 1990, and find similar conclusions.

[7] Public investment is equivalent to public gross fixed capital formation in this study. Fiscal data on public investment and current spending are taken from two different sources to maximize data availability. This could however create some inconsistencies between the two components. To minimize them, we recalculated non-interest current expenditure as total government spending minus interest payments and minus public investment to ensure mathematical identity. Our series are robust to alternative matching options.

[8] Previous studies in this area are mainly based on central government data. This is the case of papers that study aggregate fiscal variables (see Brender and Drazen, 2005; Shi and Svensson, 2006) as well as papers that look at the composition of public spending (see, e.g., Schuknecht, 2000; Block, 2002; Brauninger, 2005; Vergne, 2009; Katsimi and Sarantides, 2012). However, the reason why we use general government data on public gross fixed capital formation is because we have a wider sample of countries and this variable is available for a larger number of countries at that level.

Figure 5.1. Growth Rate of Public Investment
(Sample average by year, 1976–2012)

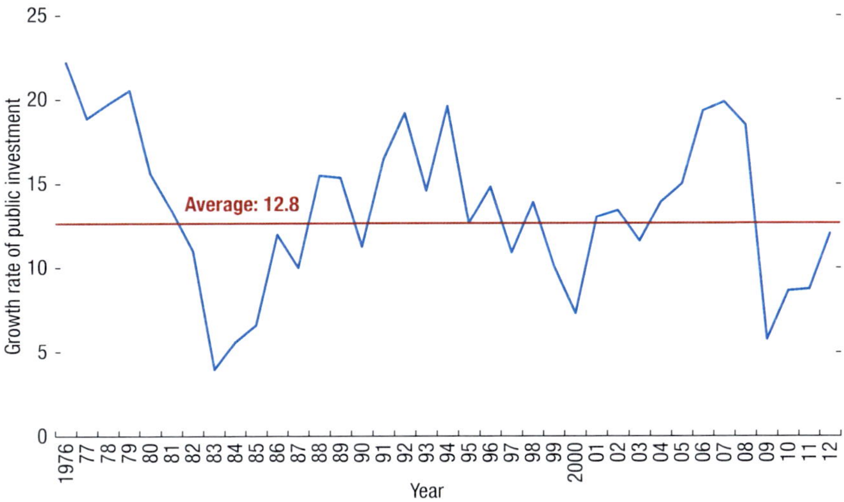

Sources: Haver Analytics; IMF, World Economic Outlook database; World Bank, World Development Indicators; and authors' calculations.
Note: Figure 5.1 illustrates that the average change in public investment varies over time.

These variables help control for the state of the economy that might affect both the political cycle and investment decisions.

We define our dependent variable as the growth rate of nominal public investment.[9] We choose to focus on nominal public investment because in every country budgetary allocation takes place in nominal terms and this is the variable of decision for policymakers. By looking at the change of public investment from one year to the next, scaled by the initial level of investment, our approach allows us to capture the dynamic behavior of the variable and pool together multiple countries and periods with different starting levels of investment.[10] Because this chapter aims at analyzing the impact of months-to-election, which is a time-variant variable, we think that the growth rate of nominal public investment is the best option to capture these dynamics.

On average, the growth rate of public investment in the whole sample is 12.8 percent, but there are important differences by year (Figure 5.1). For example, in 1976, 1994 and 2007 the growth rate of nominal public investment was equal

[9] Our results are robust to alternative definitions of the dependent variable. Following the recommendation of the editor, we also worked with the first differences of nominal public investment divided by GDP in t-1, and with the growth rate of real public investment. See Annex Table 5.5.1 for results using these alternative definitions of the dependent variable. In earlier versions of this chapter, we also used the annual percentage change of the public investment-to-GDP ratio, finding consistent results (these tables are available from the authors upon request.)

[10] Other papers in this field, like Katsimi and Sarantides (2012) and Potrafke (2010) use the first differences of levels of public investment. Our results are also robust to the use of their version of the dependent variable.

Figure 5.2. Growth Rates of Public Consumption and Public Investment
(Over 48 months before elections)

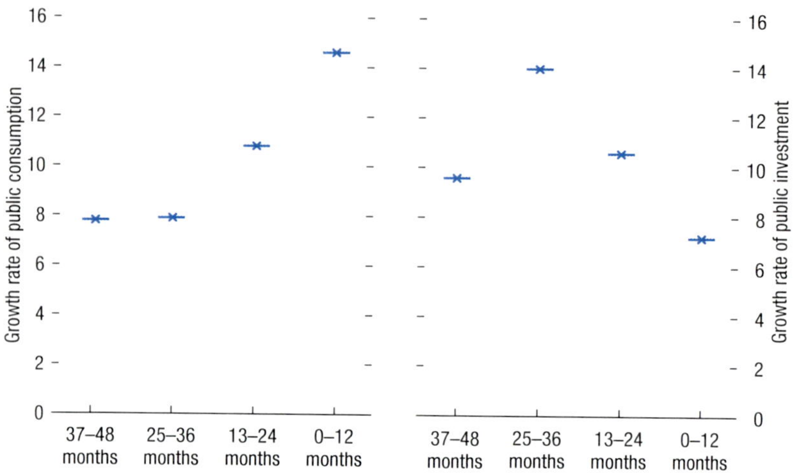

Sources: IMF, World Economic Outlook database; and authors' calculations.
Note: Figure 5.2 shows that as elections approach, the growth rate of public consumption increases and the growth rate of public investment declines.

or above 20 percent, while in 1983, 2000 and 2009 it was around 5 percent or below. In such a heterogeneous sample of 67 countries, these yearly average growth rates combine different cross-country economic and political conditions affecting public investment outcomes.

To analyze the impact of politics on public investment dynamics, our main focus is on election cycles. While previous studies used election year as a dummy variable (e.g., Katsimi and Sarantides, 2012), we created a variable which measures the months remaining to the next election to better capture the impact of election cycles. For example, if an election was held in November 2012, the variable "months to the next election" would take the value 11 in 2011, and value 23 in 2010. Data on election dates by month and year are from the Database of Political Institutions (DPI).[11] For countries with parliamentary systems, we use legislative elections, while for countries with presidential systems, we use executive elections.[12] A majority of the countries in the sample held elections every four years (48-months). As elections approach we observe a reduction in growth rates of public investment, coupled with a slight increase in growth rates of public consumption (Figure 5.2).[13] The observed pattern

[11] DPI is compiled by the Development Research Group of the World Bank.

[12] Note that some election dates might be endogenous. For example, elections might be called earlier than their predetermined date due to adverse economic conditions arising from a slump in investment. We explore this issue further in the fifth section.

[13] The increase in public consumption in percent of GDP does not match exactly the decrease in public investment as a percent of GDP. This provides evidence in favor of the political business cycle

is consistent with previous findings that electoral incentives may induce the incumbent to shift public spending toward more "visible" government consumption and away from public investment goods.

SHORT-TERM CHANGES IN PUBLIC INVESTMENT: THE ROLE OF ELECTIONS

Following previous studies, we analyze the impact of politics on public investment in a dynamic fixed effects model specification.[14]

$$GPI_{i,t} = \alpha_0 + \alpha_1 * Elec_{i,t} + \alpha_2 * Econ_{i,t} + \alpha_3 * Cond_{i,t} + \mu_i + \varepsilon_{i,t}, \quad (5.1)$$

where $GPI_{i,t} = \left(\frac{PI_{i,t} - PI_{i,t-1}}{PI_{i,t-1}} \right) * 100$ is the growth rate of nominal public investment in country i in year t. Note that we include the lagged dependent variable, since public investment dynamics might display a great deal of persistence. Among the set of independent variables, we include $Elec_{i,t}$ as the vector of electoral variables (including the number of months to the next elections, both in linear and quadratic terms), $Econ_{i,t}$ as the vector of economic controls (including the inflation rate, the real GDP growth, the lagged debt-to-GDP ratio and the change in the primary balance), and $Cond_{i,t}$ as the vector of additional social and political conditions (including the initial level of development aid to GDP, the share of people above 65 years of age, the number of government parties, a dummy variable for the ideology of the government, and another dummy to account for the existence of fiscal rules). Finally, equation (5.1) includes μ_i representing country-specific fixed effects and $\varepsilon_{i,t}$ as the error term.[15]

We expect the distance from elections to be positively associated with the growth rate of public investment (the further that distance, or the earlier in the electoral cycle, the higher the growth rate of investment). We also expect that the decline of the growth rate of public investment becomes stronger as we move closer to election date. This is why our baseline model takes into account the nonlinear dynamics of elections by including the months-to-next election variable both in standard and squared terms.

---

hypothesis, according to which governments affect both the size and the composition of the budget to ameliorate GDP and increase their probability of reelection. The simultaneous increase in GDP, which typically follows short-term increases in public spending, affects both the numerator and denominator of both public consumption and public investment ratios. Because the spending multipliers are different for public consumption and investment, the changes in their respective GDP ratios do not exactly match each other.

[14] See for example Schuknecht (2000), Persson and Tabellini (2003), Brender and Drazen (2005), Katsimi and Sarantides (2012).

[15] Summary statistics of the main variables used in table 5.1 for our benchmark results are reported in the Annex Table 5.2.1.

Among economic controls, we expect the lagged dependent variable to have a negative impact on the growth of public investment, since once sufficient resources are allocated for public capital stock accumulation there is typically a lower need for further investment growth. We also expect real GDP and the inflation rate to have a positive impact on nominal public investment, as its values move with prices and growing economic activity generates more resources for capital investment. In addition, we expect initial indebtedness to be a positive sign that financing is available for subsequent investment activity, while positive changes in the primary balance will probably reduce the fiscal space for new investment projects.

Finally, among the set of accompanying conditions, we expect that initial high levels of development aid facilitate investment growth, while aging societies are probably less likely to keep accumulating new infrastructures (Jäger and Schmidt, 2016). In line with the literature presented above, a larger number of government parties and more leftist cabinets should be associated with higher growth rates of investment.[16,17] Controls for the existence of budget rules are included to account for legal limits that may be binding total spending or affecting its composition.[18,19]

We use fixed-effect panel regressions in our benchmark model and complement it with ordinary least squares (OLS) and generalized method of moments (GMM) estimations.[20] The inclusion of a lagged dependent variable introduces a potential bias by not satisfying the exogeneity assumption of the error

[16] The average number of parties in our sample was 2.4. We acknowledge that the number of government parties might not be a precise indicator of political fragmentation. For example, the degree of fragmentation is likely to be lower in a parliament where one party takes the majority, regardless of the number of parties in government. We also used a dummy for coalition governments and results were very similar. In addition, government fragmentation might have different implications in presidential and parliamentary systems. We conducted additional tests, with the existence of a majority government as a control and divided the sample into parliamentary and presidential systems. The results remained robust.

[17] To build this variable (1=left; 0=right) using information from DPI database. Ideology of the government is used for parliamentary system, while ideology of the executive is used for presidential system. However, as there is a high correlation between the government and executive ideology, our results do not change significantly by using either of the two ideology variables as an alternative. When there is a multiparty government, the government's ideology corresponds to the party with the highest number of posts in the cabinet. In our sample left-wing governments held office 56 percent of the time.

[18] Before estimating the model, we test for unit roots in our data. Test results (Annex Table 5.3.1) show that we can reject the null hypothesis of non-stationarity at the 1 percent significance level.

[19] Aside from the above political variables, we also examined the impact of electoral rules, various institutional variables and the existence of fiscal rules. These data come from World Development Indicators (WDI) and the Database of Political Institutions (DPI) of the World Bank and from the fiscal rules database of the IMF. Results were inconclusive and thus not reported.

[20] A fiscal rule imposes a long-lasting constraint on fiscal policy through numerical limits on budgetary aggregates. We include a dummy that takes value 1 if the country has any fiscal rule (expenditure, debt, balanced budget or golden rules), and takes value 0 in the absence of any rule. Recent evidence has shown that the golden rule helped preserve public investment following periods of fiscal contraction (IMF 2014c).

term, and this is why the model is also estimated by using GMM, following Arellano and Bond (1991), Arellano and Bover (1995), and Blundell and Bond (1998).[21]

Additional biases might exist in the benchmark model. First is reverse causality, as fiscal variables may be closely linked to macroeconomic variables, such as real GDP growth. To address this potential issue, we run our regressions using contemporaneous and lagged macroeconomic variables and results were very similar. We also used system GMM with instruments (i.e., sample average debt-to-GDP ratio as instrument for the debt-to-GDP ratio, and sample average real GDP growth as instrument for the real GDP growth) to double check the robustness of the model.[22] Second, with large N and small T panel data, there is potential cross-section dependence. We tested for cross-sectional dependence in the fixed-effects models. The test results strongly reject the null hypothesis of no cross-sectional dependence. Therefore, we use an adjustment proposed by Driscoll and Kraay (1998) to ensure that standard errors are robust to heteroscedasticity.

Table 5.1 summarizes the main model specifications estimated for the sample period.[23] Columns (1)–(6) use country fixed effects with Driscoll-Kraay robust standard errors, while column (7) uses country and time fixed effects.

All models point to a significant impact of elections on the pace of public investment, confirming our hypothesis that distance from elections is associated with higher growth of public investment. The lagged dependent variable is weakly significant, while the rest of the economic controls are strongly significant and with the expected signs. Among the additional social and political variables, only the number of government parties and the ideology of the government are significant.

Overall, the main result of these regression analyses is that when the next election is one month closer, the growth rate of public investment decreases around 0.7 percentage point. The negative coefficients on the squared term of months-to-next election suggest a nonlinear dynamic behavior of public investment before elections. Results are consistent with Rogoff's (1990) hypothesis that

[21] Note that applying Arellano and Bond (1991) or Arellano and Bover (1995)/Blundell and Bond (1998) GMM estimators does not alter our results. Note also that the estimated bias of this formulation is of order 1/T, where T is the time length of the panel, even as the number of countries becomes large (see among others Nickell, 1981; Kiviet, 1995). The average time series length of our panel depends on the fiscal indicator, but in general is around 10 years and the bias is probably not large, but we still use the system GMM as a sensitivity test.

[22] These additional tables are available from authors upon request.

[23] We run our benchmark models on a sample of 4-year (48-month) election cycles in order to better capture the impact of a new government following elections and to avoid outliers and overlapping executive terms. Note that 90 percent of cases have 4-year cycles. Nonetheless, we show in the Annex Table 5.5.2 that our results are robust to using the whole sample or a sample of shorter cycles (36-month).

Table 5.1. Benchmark Results: Impact of Election Cycles

	Growth Rate of Nominal Public Investment						
	(1)	(2)	(3)	(4)	(5)	(6)	(7)
Dependent Variable	Panel Regression with Fixed Effects						Country and Time Fixed Effects
Number of Months before Election	0.638*** [0.281]	0.773*** [0.480]	0.588** [0.286]	0.637** [0.279]	0.641** [0.284]	0.638** [0.280]	0.671*** [0.306]
Number of Months before Election	−0.011** [0.006]	−0.014** [0.009]	−0.010* [0.006]	−0.011** [0.006]	−0.012** [0.007]	−0.011** [0.006]	−0.012*** [0.009]
Lagged Dependent Variable	−0.138* [0.074]	−0.156* [0.076]	−0.137* [0.074]	−0.139* [0.073]	−0.141* [0.072]	−0.138* [0.074]	−0.147*** [0.032]
Inflation Rate	1.149** [0.484]	1.049* [0.530]	1.152** [0.525]	1.143** [0.487]	1.126** [0.485]	1.163** [0.496]	1.190*** [0.260]
Real GDP Growth	2.379*** [0.425]	2.718*** [0.534]	2.343*** [0.453]	2.380*** [0.427]	2.355*** [0.413]	2.379*** [0.424]	2.614*** [0.411]
Lagged Debt/GDP	0.190* [0.099]	0.379** [0.164]	0.212* [0.104]	0.190* [0.098]	0.190* [0.099]	0.189* [0.099]	0.219*** [0.060]

Δ Primary Balance	−1.631***	−1.367***	−1.661***	−1.624***	−1.618***	−1.630***	−1.519***
	[0.357]	[0.405]	[0.379]	[0.358]	[0.353]	[0.356]	[0.359]
Lagged Official Development Aid/GDP		0.378					
		[0.621]					
Old Population Share			−0.921				
			[0.681]				
Number of Government Parties				0.956***			
				[0.305]			
Ideology of Government (Dummy: 1 = left-wing government)					3.493***		
					[0.907]		
Fiscal Rule (Dummy: 1 = existence of any fiscal rule)						1.184	
						[2.840]	
R^2	0.1115	0.1317	0.1116	0.1126	0.1134	0.1116	0.1401
Countries	67	48	66	67	67	67	67
Observations	949	512	937	949	949	949	949
Peak Investment Growth (number of months before election)	**29**	**28**	**29**	**29**	**29**	**29**	**28**

Source: Authors' calculations.

Note: Columns (1)–(6) present regressions with Driscoll-Kraay standard errors. The number of months at which public investment growth peaks is calculated using the coefficients of the standard and square terms of the months-to-election variable. Standard errors in brackets.

*$p < 0.10$, **$p < 0.05$, ***$p < 0.01$

Figure 5.3. Public Investment prior to Elections: Inverted U-Shape

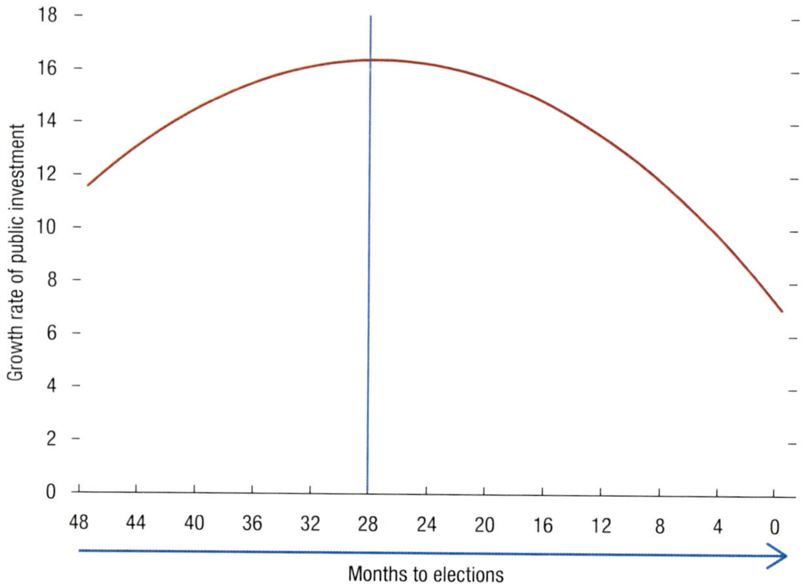

Sources: IMF, World Economic Outlook database; and authors' calculations.
Note: Figure 5.3 shows that as elections approach, the growth rate of public investment ratio declines. This figure is derived from results in Table 5.1, column (7), and includes all the control variables in that estimation.

rents from staying in office and information asymmetry induce incumbents to manipulate fiscal policy towards "visible" public goods.[24]

Figure 5.3 plots the estimated behavior of the pace of public investment over 48 months before elections, using information for 67 countries included in Table 5.1, column (1). Using both coefficients for the standard and squared terms of the electoral variable, we see that the growth rate of public investment to GDP peaks around 28 months before the elections, and then declines sharply as elections approach.

In our view, the nonlinear pattern suggests that governments tend to frontload investment in capital projects at the beginning of their terms, shifting spending towards other items as the next election approaches. This said, we recognize that the observed pattern may be attributable to overlapping of capital project cycles with electoral cycles. The initial phase of the project cycle tends to be time consuming (in terms of project appraisal and selection) and the newly elected governments may require time to start implementing capital projects. However, no project level data are available to test the validity of this hypothesis in a diverse set

[24] Annex Table 5.5.1 provides a simple test for the trade-off between public investment and current expenditure.

of countries, such as those included in the study. The only evidence on 258 rail, bridge, tunnel, and road projects in 20 countries suggests that the average project cycle is different from the standard electoral cycle (Flyvberg, 2009).

ROBUSTNESS OF OUR RESULTS

In this section we test the robustness of our results to country characteristics and the potential endogeneity of election dates.

Country Characteristics

An important concern when working with a heterogeneous sample has to do with the potential presence of group characteristics that cannot be captured using country fixed effects. We therefore perform an additional round of robustness checks to control for the level of development (advanced vs. emerging economies), the age of each democratic country (old vs. new democracies) and corruption.[25] We also look at the relative efficiency of public investment (high vs. low efficiency).[26] Our results are robust to these additional tests, but interesting nuances emerge (Table 5.2).

Overall, in advanced economies, old democracies, and countries with more efficient management systems, public investment growth tends to peak much later during the electoral cycle. Also, the deceleration of public investment is lower in magnitude, implying a milder investment fluctuation due to electoral cycles. The observed pattern could be explained from three complementary perspectives. First, public investment processes are more robust in advanced economies that are mostly old democracies, and the scope for manipulating public investment to enhance reelection possibilities is thus lower than in countries with weaker institutions. Second, in mature democracies there are less information asymmetries and the electorate punishes electoral manipulation of spending by the government. And third, in mature democracies incumbent governments have other means to show their "competencies" to the electorate and do not need to signal them through spending manipulation as predicted by Rogoff (1990).[27]

[25] When corruption indicators from the Database of Political Institutions (DPI) are included in the baseline regressions, they have a positive sign but are statistically insignificant. Corruption indicators are also very correlated with the variables that measure the level of development and the age of democracies. Since the latter generate more robust results, we have reported them in Table 5.2. For interested readers, regression results using corruption indicators are available upon request from the authors.

[26] Data for public investment efficiency is taken from IMF (2015).

[27] Note that in Rogoff's model, the government distorts allocations because it is striving to signal its "competence" in the eyes of voters under asymmetric information. Since voters do not observe public investment and economic growth immediately, the only way for a "competent" incumbent to signal its "competence" is to increase readily identifiable transfers ahead of elections, inducing voters to believe that the government will bring economic growth and revenues to finance those transfers.

Table 5.2. Robustness Check: Country Characteristics and Fixed Elections

	Growth Rate of Nominal Public Investment										
	(1)	(2)	(3)	(4)	(5)	(6)	(7)	(8)	(9)	(10a)	(10b)
Dependent Variable	**Baseline**	**Advanced Economies**	**Emerging Markets**	**Old Democracies**	**New Democracies**	**Higher Public Investment Efficiency**	**Lower Public Investment Efficiency**	**If Last Term in Office**	**Nonendogenous Elections**	**If Fixed Term Election System (Milner 2006)**	**If Fixed Term Election System (Drazen and Eslava 2010)**
Number of Months before Election	0.671***	0.302**	1.087***	0.283**	0.805***	0.513**	0.745**	0.934***	0.727**	0.433*	0.775***
	[0.306]	[0.203]	[0.394]	[0.298]	[0.431]	[0.230]	[0.765]	[0.265]	[0.285]	[0.290]	[0.287]
Number of Months before Election	−0.012***	−0.005**	−0.020**	−0.004**	−0.015***	−0.008*	−0.015**	−0.016***	−0.013**	−0.010*	−0.014**
	[0.009]	[0.004]	[0.008]	[0.004]	[0.009]	[0.005]	[0.015]	[0.005]	[0.006]	[0.006]	[0.006]
Lagged Dependent Variable	−0.147***	−0.088**	−0.109**	−0.115**	−0.144***	−0.111***	−0.159***	−0.094***	−0.096***	−0.128**	−0.133***
	[0.032]	[0.042]	[0.048]	[0.046]	[0.039]	[0.037]	[0.056]	[0.025]	[0.036]	[0.064]	[0.045]
Inflation Rate	1.190***	0.654**	0.527*	0.575*	1.043***	0.639**	1.149**	0.724***	0.596***	0.789**	0.580**
	[0.260]	[0.268]	[0.284]	[0.319]	[0.296]	[0.249]	[0.446]	[0.218]	[0.214]	[0.308]	[0.262]
Real GDP Growth	2.614***	1.636***	2.820***	1.064***	2.647***	2.072***	3.051***	2.030***	2.220***	1.678***	2.838***
	[0.411]	[0.287]	[0.425]	[0.382]	[0.456]	[0.291]	[0.845]	[0.315]	[0.323]	[0.375]	[0.391]
Lagged Debt/GDP	0.219***	0.059	0.226**	0.055	0.314***	0.027	0.394***	0.100**	0.107*	0.018	0.074
	[0.060]	[0.040]	[0.107]	[0.037]	[0.083]	[0.045]	[0.125]	[0.051]	[0.059]	[0.112]	[0.071]
Δ Primary Balance	−1.519***	−2.528***	−1.860***	−2.229***	−1.475***	−2.776***	−1.438**	−1.342***	−1.550***	−2.385***	−0.653**
	[0.359]	[0.364]	[0.495]	[0.406]	[0.430]	[0.367]	[0.664]	[0.289]	[0.295]	[0.472]	[0.329]
R^2	0.14	0.15	0.17	0.14	0.15	0.18	0.14	0.14	0.12	0.22	0.20
Countries	67	22	34	15	52	29	29	67	50	16	38
Observations	949	441	390	324	625	500	313	660	655	207	541
Peak Investment Growth (number of months before election)	**28**	**30**	**27**	**35**	**27**	**32**	**25**	**29**	**28**	**22**	**28**

Source: Authors' calculations.

Note: All models include country and year fixed effects. Standard errors in brackets.

$^*p < 0.10$, $^{**}p < 0.05$, $^{***}p < 0.01$

Potential Endogeneity of Election Dates

Since elections may not be exogenous and can be called earlier in many parliamentary and presidential democracies, we perform tests to ensure the robustness of our results in a subsample of countries with different legal provisions about the timing of their elections. Note, however, that this is not a straightforward exercise because the distinction between electoral systems where the election date is exogenously fixed and systems where early elections may be called is not as clear-cut as it may at first appear. In many countries fixed election periods are set by law and early elections may only be called under "exceptional circumstances," but in fact early elections are the rule rather than the exception. That is, what determines "exceptional circumstances" may in practice be quite different than what appears to be the case from a simple reading of the election laws (Brender and Drazen, 2005).

We conduct robustness tests using various sources of data, mainly to ensure that our conclusions do not have any selection bias. First, using data on elections from the National Elections Across Democracy and Autocracy (NELDA) database we run our baseline model on a sample of countries where governments faced their last term in office (Table 5.2, column (8)) or where elections are not endogenous (Table 5.2, column (9)).[28] In both cases, our baseline results hold. Second, we identify countries where elections are fixed and run the model on these subsamples. For this purpose, we use two main sources of data available in the literature: Milner (2006) identifies 16 countries with "fixed-term elections,"[29] while Brender and Drazen (2005) identify 38 countries with "pre-determined elections" according to both legal and empirical criteria.[30,31] We prefer the second sample, because it has more countries and their selection is more robust. Note that having a legal obligation to hold fixed elections is not a sufficient criterion to be sure that this actually occurs. Many countries have some provision for elections at a date earlier than the end of the legally mandated term of office for the

[28] Non-endogenous elections are those which take place at their expected date (not called earlier or later). Background information to build this variable by the authors is taken from question 6 in NELDA's database, which is formulated as follows: "If regular, were these elections early or late relative to the date they were supposed to be held per established procedure?" In addition, in order to gather information on whether governments faced their last term in office, the authors use question 8 in NELDA's database, which is formulated as follows: "Did the incumbent reach their term limit?"

[29] These countries are Chile, Costa Rica, Cyprus, Estonia, Finland, Latvia, Luxembourg, Mexico, Netherlands, Norway, Poland, Portugal, Slovak Republic, Sweden, Switzerland and United States.

[30] These countries are Argentina, Austria, Belgium, Bolivia, Brazil, Bulgaria, Chile, Colombia, Costa Rica, Czech Republic, Dominican Republic, Ecuador, Estonia, Fiji, Finland, France, Germany, Greece, Guatemala, Honduras, Italy, Israel, Luxembourg, Mali, Mauritius, Netherlands, Nicaragua, Norway, Paraguay, Philippines, Portugal, Poland, Romania, Slovak Republic, Sri Lanka, Switzerland, Trinidad and Tobago, United States, and Uruguay.

[31] For more information about budgetary consequences of fixed term elections, see Dahlberg and Mørk (2011).

executive or the legislature, and whether electoral calendars are actually fixed and elections occur at the legally determined date is an empirical question.[32] Results in Table 5.2, columns (10a) (using Milner data) and column (10b) (using Brender and Drazen data) show that our results hold when using the wider sample of countries with fixed elections.[33]

CONCLUSION AND POLICY IMPLICATIONS

This chapter explores the impact of political and institutional variables on the growth rate in public investment. Using a sample of 67 presidential and parliamentary democracies between 1975 and 2012, the chapter finds that the growth rate of public investment-to-GDP is higher at the beginning of electoral cycles and decelerates as the next election approaches. We estimate that during standard 4-year electoral cycles, the peak in public investment growth occurs around 28 months before elections. Thereafter, changes in public investment decline as elections approach. This holds even when controlling for economic factors and other political variables (i.e., cabinet ideology and government fragmentation). Preliminary evidence on budget rules and institutions suggests that stronger institutions help attenuate the impact of elections on investment, but available information is insufficient to reach definitive conclusions.

Two important policy implications can be drawn from this chapter. First, even when macroeconomic conditions in terms of fiscal space and monetary policy are appropriate and effective "shovel ready" investment projects are available, it may not be possible to expand public investment closer to elections. The incentive for incumbent governments is to increase "visible", more tangible, current spending on tax cuts or transfer programs to shore up political support. Going forward, such spending may be difficult to unwind, thereby creating a deficit bias. It may also impact on the long-term potential of the economy. Second, fiscal consolidation programs would need to explicitly recognize the bias against public investment about two years prior to elections. A strengthening of fiscal frameworks during this period could help in restraining a permanent ratcheting of certain spending items.

---

[32] Using a sample of 68 countries Brender and Drazen (2005) identify 29 countries with pre-determined elections around the world (according to legal criteria). But this number becomes 38 (when a second criterion based on actual frequency of elections is applied).

[33] In the sample using Milner's data, the squared term of the "months-to-next-election" variable is not significant by a small margin. Still the negative relationship between proximity to elections and changes in public investment is significant. Because this is a regression with only 16 countries, it is difficult to make definitive conclusions. By contrast, we view the results using Brender and Drazen's data as more robust.

ANNEX 5.1. SAMPLE AND SELECTION CRITERIA

We select countries and time periods based on the following criteria. First, voters must directly elect the person or persons appearing on the ballot to the national post in question. Second, mass voting must take place. Third, over the sample period, countries should have a multi-party system. Presidential elections which involve an Electoral College such as the United States are included because the Electoral College mechanically implements the outcome of a popular vote. Fourth, each election in the sample should be generally regarded as being sufficiently competitive, meaning that there is a real possibility of change in government. Two major criteria apply in this aspect: a) there were no significant concerns before elections that elections will not be free and fair; b) there were no allegations by Western monitors, if any, of significant voter fraud. For example, although elections in Mexico never resulted in a change of government before 2000, since there were competitive running parties, we included these elections in our sample. Finally, we excluded pre-election years of the first democratic election in each country's history. Using the above criteria, 80 countries were selected. Only for 67 of them, there was consistent data on all variables used in the regression analysis. In this final sample, 44 of these countries were parliamentary democracies, and 23 of them were presidential democracies.

Primary sources of electoral data include the National Elections across Democracy and Autocracy (NELDA) by Hyde and Marinov (2012), the World Economic Yearbook, the *Economist* Intelligence Unit, the CIA World Fact Book and Freedom House.

This methodology differs from most previous studies. Previous studies often focus on old democracies to ensure competitiveness of elections, e.g., Katsimi and Sarantides (2012). A few other studies covered a wide range of countries, but didn't make enough effort to identify competitive elections. For example, Brender and Drazen (2005) studied 102 countries, including 68 democracies with competitive elections using level of democracy from POLITY IV project as the only criteria. Ebeke and Olcer (2013) used a sample of 68 low-income economies, but didn't differentiate competitive elections from the rest.

Annex Table 5.1.1. Parliamentary System: 44 Countries

Country	Starting Year	Country	Starting Year
Advanced Economies		**Emerging Market Economies**	
Australia	1975	Albania	1992
Austria	1975	Bahamas, The	1975
Belgium	1975	Barbados	1975
Canada	1975	Belize	1982
Czech Republic	1993	Bosnia and Herzegovina	2003
Estonia	1992	Botswana	1975
Finland	1975	Bulgaria	2002
France	1975	Cabo Verde	1976
Germany	1975	Croatia	2001
Greece	1987	Fiji	1975
Israel	1975	Guyana	1992
Italy	1975	India	1975
Japan	1975	Macedonia, FYR	1992
Luxembourg	1975	Mauritius	1975
Netherlands	1975	Panama	1979
New Zealand	1975	Poland	1991
Norway	1975	Romania	1990
Portugal	1983	St. Lucia	1980
Slovak Republic	1993	Trinidad and Tobago	1975
Switzerland	1975	Turkey	1981
United Kingdom	1975		
Low-Income Economies			
Bangladesh	1976		
Lesotho	1975		
Moldova	1992		

Source: Authors' calculations.

Annex Table 5.1.2. Presidential System: 23 Countries

Country	Starting Year	Country	Starting Year
Advanced Economies		**Low-Income Economies**	
United States	1975	Bolivia	1975
		Ghana	1992
Emerging Economies		Honduras[1]	1982
Argentina	1975	Malawi	1994
Brazil	1986	Mali	1992
Chile	1989	Mozambique	1990
Colombia	1991	Nicaragua	1975
Costa Rica	1975	Senegal	1990
Dominican Republic	1978		
Ecuador	1975		
Guatemala	1996		
Mexico	1975		
Namibia	1995		
Paraguay	1993		
Peru[2]	1975		
Philippines	1987		
Uruguay	1975		

Source: Authors' calculations.

[1]From 2009 onwards Honduras is counted due to the coup in 2009.

[2]Elections in 1995 and 2000–01 in Peru are not counted.

ANNEX 5.2. DESCRIPTIVE STATISTICS

Annex Table 5.2.1. Descriptive Statistics of Variables Used in Table 5.1

	Observations	Mean	Standard Deviation	Minimum	Maximum
Growth Rate of Public Investment	1,462	12.8	24.2	−88.2	101.0
Months to Election	1,462	23.4	13.6	1.0	48.0
Months to Election	1,462	733.5	687.2	1.0	2,304.0
Inflation Rate	1,460	9.3	18.9	−7.8	333.5
Real GDP Growth	1,462	3.4	3.9	−30.9	23.4
Lagged Public Debt/GDP	931	55.1	32.9	3.7	210.2
Δ Primary Balance	1,157	−0.1	2.9	−34.6	34.3
Old Population Share	1,443	8.9	5.1	2.4	23.0
Number of Government Parties	1,462	2.1	1.8	0.0	16.0
Ideology of Government (1 = left)	1,462	0.4	0.5	0.0	1.0
Fiscal Rule (1 = existence of any fiscal rule)	1,462	0.4	0.5	0.0	1.0
Lagged Official Development Aid/GDP	904	4.8	7.6	−2.5	74.1

Source: Authors' calculations.

ANNEX 5.3. PANEL UNIT ROOT TEST

If our dependent variable is not stationary, we are faced with a spurious relationship when that variable is entered on the right-hand side of the equation. Only a few tests for unit roots are directly applicable to unbalanced data (see Breitung and Pesaran, 2008). Here we rely on the Fisher test to check for the presence of a unit root. We conduct unit-root tests for each panel individually, and then combine the p-values from these tests to produce an overall test. The test assumes that all series in the panel are stationary under the null hypothesis against the alternative that at least one series in the panel is stationary.

Annex Table 5.3.1. Fisher-Type Panel Unit Root Test

Variable	Test Statistics	Probability Value
Growth Rate of Public Investment	569.1	0.00
Δ Primary Balance	408.2	0.00
Inflation Rate	734.6	0.00
Real GDP Growth	589.8	0.00
Lagged Public Debt/GDP	701.1	0.00

Source: Authors' calculations.
Note: The null hypothesis that all panels contain unit roots can be rejected at the levels of the variables.

ANNEX 5.4. THE SHORT-TERM TRADE-OFF BETWEEN CURRENT AND CAPITAL SPENDING

We test here if there is a short-term trade-off between current and capital spending by directly including changes in primary current spending as an additional explanatory variable. Annex Table 5.4.1 presents these results. All models use country and time fixed effects, and control for the change in the primary balance to ensure that the observed change in the composition of public spending are independent of fiscal consolidations and expansions. Results show evidence that there is a significant negative relationship between public investment and current expenditure.[34]

Annex Table 5.4.1. The Tradeoff between Public Investment and Current Expenditure

	Growth Rate of Public Investment	
	(1)	(2)
Dependent Variable		Country and Time Fixed Effects
Number of Months before Election	0.534***	0.621***
	[0.269]	[0.218]
Number of Months before Election	–0.009**	–0.011***
	[0.006]	[0.004]
Lagged Dependent Variable	–0.024	–0.056
	[0.075]	[0.036]
Growth Rate of Public Consumption	–0.021**	–0.021***
	[0.008]	[0.007]
Inflation Rate	0.453**	0.514**
	[0.203]	[0.205]
Real GDP Growth	1.702***	2.153***
	[0.351]	[0.296]
Lagged Debt/GDP	0.058*	0.100*
	[0.067]	[0.053]
R^2	0.10	0.14
Countries	63	64
Observations	777	785
Peak Investment Growth (number of months before election)	**28**	**28**

Source: Authors' calculations.
Note: Standard errors in brackets.
*$p < 0.10$, **$p < 0.05$, ***$p < 0.01$

[34] Katsimi and Sarandides (2012) use the first differences of capital expenditure and current expenditure to total expenditure ratio as a dependent variable to analyze the impact of election year (dummy variable) on expenditure composition in old democracies, and find that capital expenditure is likely to decelerate during elections while current expenditure accelerates. We used a similar methodology in our complete sample of 67 countries and got similar results.

ANNEX 5.5. ROBUSTNESS OF RESULTS TO ALTERNATIVE DEFINITIONS OF THE DEPENDENT VARIABLE AND PANEL TRUNCATION

Finally, following a suggestion by the editor, we tested our results to different definitions of the dependent variable. Annex Table 5.5.1 compares our baseline results using the growth rate of nominal public investment (model 2), with similar regressions using annual change in nominal public investment as a share of GDP in the previous year (model 1), and using the growth rate of real public investment (where we had considerably less observations available due to missing data in the WEO series). In general, the influence of the electoral cycle on public investment is confirmed under the three definitions.

Annex Table 5.5.1. Robustness Using Alternative Definitions of Dependent Variable

	(1)	(2)	(3)
Dependent Variable	**Δ Public Investment/ GDP ($t-1$)**	**Growth Rate of Public Investment (Nominal)**	**Growth Rate of Public Investment (Real)**
Number of Months before Election	0.077***	0.671***	0.066**
	[0.025]	[0.306]	[0.204]
Number of Months before Election	−0.008**	−0.012***	−0.009**
	[0.001]	[0.009]	[0.000]
Lagged Dependent Variable	−0.0487*	−0.147***	−0.093**
	[0.039]	[0.032]	[0.045]
Inflation Rate	0.028**	1.190***	0.044*
	[0.015]	[0.260]	[0.084]
Real GDP Growth	0.245***	2.614***	0.102**
	[0.554]	[0.411]	[0.181]
Lagged Debt/GDP	0.011*	0.219***	0.055**
	[0.204]	[0.060]	[0.212]
Δ Primary Balance	−0.167**	−1.519***	−0.055**
	[0.223]	[0.359]	[0.203]
R^2	0.096	0.1401	0.088
Countries	66	67	44
Observations	902	949	477
Peak Investment Growth (number of months before election)	**27**	**28**	**26**

Source: Authors' calculations.
Note: Standard errors in brackets.
$*p < 0.10$, $**p < 0.05$, $***p < 0.01$

We also tried using slightly different sample selection criteria. In our benchmark selection we truncated our panel and ran our model only on those observations where the electoral cycle was 4-years (48 months) or shorter. The purpose of this choice was twofold: on the one hand, this would help avoid some outliers in which the variable month-to-election could reach up to 120 months, either due to exceptional political circumstances or as a result of missing values in the earlier years of the sample period. On the other hand, these selection criteria would clean the possible noise generated by overlapping cycles, where the last year of one term becomes the first of the next one. By imposing a 48-month limit we were able to extract the full information from the data (as 90 percent of cases have 4-year electoral cycles), while avoiding the noise created by missing values or overlapping dates. Nonetheless, our results are robust to using the whole unrestricted or alternative truncation criteria. Annex Table 5.5.2 reports the results of running our baseline model on the complete (un-truncated) sample (model 1), on the 48-month sample (model 2), and on a shorter 36-month sample (model 3). Because the overwhelming majority of cases have 4-year election cycles, results hold well using other sample selection criteria.

Annex Table 5.5.2. Robustness Using Alternative Definitions of Dependent Variable

	Growth Rate of Public Investment		
	(1)	(2)	(3)
Dependent Variable	**Whole Sample**	**48-Month Sample**	**36-Month Sample**
Number of Months before Election	0.623** [0.245]	0.671*** [0.306]	1.201** [0.485]
Number of Months before Election^2	−0.011** [0.004]	−0.012*** [0.009]	−0.027** [0.012]
Lagged Dependent Variable	−0.168*** [0.032]	−0.147*** [0.032]	−0.177*** [0.035]
Inflation Rate	1.577*** [0.239]	1.190*** [0.260]	2.072*** [0.295]
Real GDP Growth	0.888** [0.408]	2.614*** [0.411]	0.898* [0.482]
Lagged Debt/GDP	0.222*** [0.065]	0.219*** [0.060]	0.231*** [0.074]
Δ Primary Balance	−3.395** [1.444]	−1.519*** [0.359]	−3.569** [1.608]
R^2	0.125	0.1401	0.151
Countries	66	67	66
Observations	1013	949	768
Peak Investment Growth (number of months before election)	**29**	**28**	**22**

Source: Authors' calculations.

Note: Regression are estimated with country and time fixed effects. Standard errors in brackets.

*$p < 0.10$, **$p < 0.05$, ***$p < 0.01$

REFERENCES

Aidt, T., F. Veiga, and L. Veiga, 2011, "Election Results and Opportunistic Policies: A New Test of the Rational Political Business Cycle Model," *Public Choice*, 148, 21–44.

Alesina, A., and G. Tabellini, 1990, "A Positive Theory of Fiscal Deficits and Government Debt," *Review of Economic Studies,* Vol. 57, No. 3, pp. 403–14.

Alesina, A., and M. Paradisi, 2014, "Political Budget Cycles: Evidence from Italian Cities," *NBER Working Paper* No. W20570 (Cambridge: National Bureau of Economic Research).

Alt, J., and D. Lassen, 2006, "Fiscal Transparency, Political Parties, and Debt in OECD Countries," *European Economic Review*, Vol. 50, No. 6, pp. 1403–39.

Angelopolous, K., G. Economides, and P. Kammas, 2012, "Does Cabinet Ideology Matter for the Structure of Tax Policies?" *European Journal of Political Economy*, Vol. 28, No. 4, pp. 620–35.

Arellano, M., and S. Bond, 1991, "Some Test of Specification for Panel Data: Monte Carlo Evidence and an Application to Employment Equations," *Review of Economic Studies*, Vol. 58, No. 2, pp. 277–97.

Arellano, M., and O. Bover, 1995, "Another Look at the Instrumental Variable Estimation of Error-Components Models," *Journal of Econometrics*, Vol. 68, No. 1, pp. 29–51.

Belke, A. F. Baumgartner, F. Schneider, and R. Setzer, 2007, "The Different Extent of Privatization Proceeds in OECD Countries: A Preliminary Explanation Using a Public-Choice Approach," *Public Finance Analysis*, Vol. 63, No. 2, p. 211–43.

Blais, A., and R. Nadeau, 1992, "The Electoral Budget Cycle," *Public Choice*, Vol. 74, No. 3, pp. 389–403.

Block, S., 2002, "Elections, Electoral Competitiveness, and Political Budget Cycles in Developing Countries," Harvard University CID Working Paper No. 78 (Cambridge: Harvard University).

Blundell, R., and S. Bond, 1998, "Initial Conditions and Moment Restrictions in Dynamic Panel Data Models," *Journal of Econometrics*, Vol. 87, No. 1, pp. 115–43.

Boix, C., 1997, "Political Parties and the Supply Side of the Economy: The Provision of Physical and Human Capital in Advance Economies, 1960–90," *American Journal of Political Science*, Vol. 41, No. 3, pp. 814–45.

Bove, V., and G. Efthyvoulou, 2013, "Political Cycles in Public Expenditure: Butter vs. Guns." NEPS Working Papers 7/2013 (Bamberg: National Educational Panel Study).

Brauninger, T., 2005, "A Partisan Model of Government Expenditures," *Public Choice,* Vol. 125, No. 3, 409–29.

Breitung, J., and M. H. Pesaran, 2008, "Unit Roots and Cointegration in Panels," *The Econometrics of Panel Data*, pp. 279–322.

Brender, A. and A. Drazen, 2005, "Political Budget Cycles in New Versus Established Democracies," *Journal of Monetary Economics,* Vol. 52, No. 5, pp. 1271–95.

Bry, G., and C. Boschan, 1971, "Cyclical Analysis of Economic Time Series: Selected Procedures and Computer Programs," NBER Technical Working Paper No. 20 (Cambridge: National Bureau for Economic Research).

Cusack, T., 1997, "Partisan Politics and Public Finance: Changes in Public Spending in the Industrialized Democracies, 1955–1989," *Pubic Choice*, Vol. 91, No. 3–4, pp. 75–95.

Dahlberg, M., & E. Mørk, 2011, "Is There an Election Cycle in Public Employment? Separating Time Effects from Election Year Effects," *CESifo Economic Studies*, 57(3), 480–498.

De Haan, J., and J.E. Sturm, 1994, "Political and Institutional Determinants of Fiscal Policy in the European Community," *Public Choice*, 80, 157–172.

De Haan, J., J.E. Sturm, and B.J. Sikken, 1996, "Government Capital Formation: Explaining the Decline," *Review of World Economics*, 132:1, 55–74.

De Haan, J., and J.E. Sturm, 1997, "Political and Economic Determinants of OECD Budget Deficits and Government Expenditures: A Reinvestigation," *European Journal of Political Economy*, Vol. 13, No. 4, pp. 739–50.

Drazen, A., and M. Eslava, 2010, "Electoral Manipulation via Voter-Friendly Spending: Theory and Evidence," *Journal of Development Economics*, Vol. 92, No. 1, pp. 39–52.

Driscoll, J., and A. Kraay, 1998, "Consistent Covariance Matrix Estimation with Spatially Dependent Panel Data," *The Review of Economics and Statistics*, Vol. 80, No. 4, pp. 549–60.

Ebeke, C. and D. Olcer, 2013, "Fiscal Policy Over the Election Cycle in Low-Income Countries," IMF Working Paper 13/153 (Washington: International Monetary Fund).

Eslava, M., 2006, "The Political Economy of Fiscal Policy: A Survey," IDB Working Paper No. 487 (Washington: Inter-American Development Bank).

European Commission (EC), 2014, "An Investment Plan for Europe." http://ec.europa.eu/priorities/jobs-growth-investment/plan/index_en.htm

Filice, G., 2016, "Size and Composition of Public Investment, Sectoral Composition and Growth". Eur. J. Polit. Econ. 44 (1), 136-158.

Fiva, J.H., and J.G. Navik, 2013, "Do Re-election Probabilities Influence Public Investment?" *Public Choice*, Vol. 157, pp. 305–31.

Flyvberg, B. 2009, "Survival of the Unfittest: Why the Worst Infrastructure Gets Built-and What We Can Do About It," *Oxford Review of Economic Policy*, Vol. 25, No. 3, pp. 344–67.

Francese, R., 2002, "Electoral and Partisan Cycles in Economic Policies and Outcomes," *Annual Review of Political Science*, Vol. 5, pp. 369–421.

Hallerberg, M., and S. Basinger, 1998, "Internationalization and Changes in Tax Policy in OECD Countries: The Importance of Domestic Veto Players," *Comparative Political Studies*, Vol. 31, No. 2, pp. 321–52.

Hallerberg, M., R. Strauch, and J. Von Hagen, 2007, "The Design of Fiscal Rules and Forms of Governance in European Union Countries," *European Journal of Political Economy*, Vol. 23, pp. 338–59.

Hallerberg, M., and J. Von Hagen, 1997, "Electoral Institutions, Cabinet Negotiations, and Budget Deficits within the European Union," CEPR Discussion Papers No. 1555 (Washington: Center for Economic and Policy Research).

Harding, D., and A. Pagan, 2002, "Dissecting the Cycle: A Methodological Investigation," *Journal of Monetary Economics*, Vol. 49, pp. 365–81.

International Monetary Fund (IMF), 2014a, *Fiscal Monitor—Now Is the Time: Fiscal Policies for Sustainable Growth*, April (Washington).

———, 2014b, Budget Institutions in G-20 Countries: An Update, *IMF Board Papers*, (Washington).

———, 2014c, "Is It Time for an Infrastructure Push: The Macroeconomic Effects of Public Investment." *World Economic Outlook* (October Ed.), Chapter 3 (Washington).

———, 2015, "Making Public Investment More Efficient," IMF Policy Papers (Washington). http://www.imf.org/external/np/pp/eng/2015/061115.pdf.

Jäger, P., and T. Schmidt. 2016. "The Political Economy of Public Investment When Population Is Aging: A Panel Cointegration Analysis." *European Journal of Political Economy* 43 (1): 145–58.

Katsimi, M., and V. Sarantides, 2012, "Do Elections Affect the Composition of Fiscal Policy in Developed, Established Democracies?" *Public Choice*, Vol. 151, pp. 325–62.

Kiviet, J., 1995, "On Bias, Inconsistency, and Efficiency of Various Estimators in Dynamic Panel Data Models," *Journal of Econometrics*, Vol. 68, No. 1, pp. 53–78.

Klein, N., 2004, "Political Cycles and Economic Policy in Israel: 1980–1999," *Israel Economic Review*, Vol. 2, No. 1, pp. 55–67.

Kneebone, R., and K. McKenzie, 2001, "Electoral and Partisan Cycles in Fiscal Policy: an Examination of Canadian Provinces," *International Tax and Public Finance*, Vol. 8, No. 5, pp. 753–74.

Mierau, J., R. Jong-A-Pin, and J. De Haan, 2007, "Do Political Variables Affect Fiscal Policy Adjustment Decisions? New Empirical Evidence," *Public Choice*, Vol. 133, No. 3, pp. 297–319.

Milner, H., 2006, "Fixing Canada's Unfixed Election Dates: A Political Season to Reduce the Democratic Deficit", IRPP Policy Papers, Vol. 6, No. 6.

Mulas-Granados, C., 2003, "The Political and Economic Determinants of Budgetary Consolidation in Europe," *European Political Economy Review*, Vol. 1, No. 1.

———, 2006, *Economics, Politics and Budgets: The Political Economy of Fiscal Adjustments in Europe* (London: Palgrave-Macmillan).

Nickell, S., 1981, "Biases in Dynamic Models with Fixed Effects," *Econometrica*, Vol. 49, No. 6, pp. 1417–26.
Nordhaus, W., 1975, "The Political Business Cycle," *The Review of Economic Studies*, Vol. 42, No. 2, pp. 169–90.
Perotti, R., 1998, "The Political Economy of Fiscal Consolidations," *Scandinavian Journal of Economics*, Vol. 100, No. 1, pp. 367–94.
———, and Y. Kontopoulos, 2002, "Fragmented Fiscal Policy," *Journal of Public Economics*, Vol. 86, pp. 191–222.
Persson, T., and L. Svensson, 1989, "Why a Stubborn Conservative Would Run a Deficit: Policy with Time Inconsistent Preferences," *Quarterly Journal of Economics*, 104(2), 325–345.
Persson, T., and G. Tabellini, 2003, *The Economic Effect of Constitutions* (Cambridge: MIT Press).
Pettersson-Lidbom, P., 2001, "An Empirical Investigation of the Strategic Use of Debt," *Journal of Political Economy*, 109(3), 570–583.
Potrafke, N., 2010, "Does Government Ideology Influence Deregulation of Product Markets? Empirical Evidence from OECD Countries," *Public Choice*, Vol. 143, No. 1–2, pp. 135–55.
Rogoff, K., 1990, "Equilibrium Political Budget Cycles," *American Economic Review*, Vol. 80, No. 1, pp. 21–36.
Saporiti, A., and J. Streb, 2008, "Separation of Powers and Political Budget Cycles," *Public Choice*, Vol. 137, No. 1, pp. 329–45.
Schneider, C. J., 2010, "Fighting with One Hand Tied behind the Back: Political Budget Cycles in the West German States," *Public Choice*, Vol. 142, No. 1, pp. 125–50.
Schuknecht, L., 2000, "Fiscal Policy Cycles and Public Expenditure in Developing Countries," *Public Choice*, Vol. 102, No. 1–2, pp. 115–30.
Shi, M., and J. Svensson, 2006, "Political Budget Cycles: Do They Differ across Countries and Why?" *Journal of Public Economics*, Vol. 90, No. 8–9, pp. 1367–89.
Sturm, J.E., 2001, Determinants of Public Capital Spending in Less-Developed Countries, Groningen: CCSO Working Paper 2001/7.
Sturm, J.E. and J. De Haan, 1998, "Public Capital Spending in the Netherlands: Developments and Explanations," *Applied Economics Letters*, Vol. 5, 5–10.
Summers, L.H. 2013. Remarks in Honor of Stanley Fischer. Fourteenth Jacques Polak Annual Research Conference, International Monetary Fund, Washington, November 7–8.
Summers, L.H., 2014, "Why Public Investment Really Is a Free Lunch," *Financial Times*, October 6, 2014. Available at: http://www.ft.com/cms/s/2/9b591f98-4997-11e4-8d68-00144feab7de.html#axzz3cs6Bu2k7.
Teulings, C. and R. Baldwin, eds. 2014. *Secular Stagnation: Facts, Causes and Cures*. (London: Centre for Economic Policy Research).
Tufte, E., 1978, *Political Control of the Economy* (Princeton: Princeton University Press).
Veiga, L., and F. Veiga, 2007, "Political Business Cycles at the Municipal Level," *Public Choice*, Vol. 131, No. 1, pp. 4564.
Vergne, C., 2009, "Democracy, Elections and Allocation of Public Expenditures in Developing Countries," *European Journal of Political Economy*, Vol. 25, No. 1, pp. 63–77.
Von Hagen, J., A.H. Hallett, and R. Straucht, 2001, "Budgetary Consolidation in EMU," *Economics Papers*, Vol. 148 (Brussels: European Commission).

CHAPTER 6

Do Elections Affect the Wage Bill?

YEHENEW ENDEGNANEW, MAURICIO SOTO, AND GENEVIÈVE VERDIER

INTRODUCTION

The electoral cycle can affect fiscal policy when incumbents wish to influence political outcomes. The wage bill—which, at about 25 percent of government expenditure on average, is among the largest items in government budgets—is one important instrument at the disposal of elected officials. Increases in the wage bill generally provide a short-term boost to economic output, which can improve the odds for incumbents at the ballot box. Moreover, the wage bill largely reflects government employment and pay policies, which are crucial to ensuring key government functions are carried out, including education, health, sanitation, and security. Increases in the number of employees can visibly enhance the quantity and quality of these public services, which voters can interpret as a sign of the competence of the incumbent. Finally, in some countries the government is one of the largest employers, and increases in government pay can have a direct impact on the welfare of many households of likely voters.

Politically motivated increases in the wage bill that do not translate into improvements in service delivery could threaten fiscal sustainability, displacing resources from other priority needs or requiring higher taxes. In addition, election-driven changes in employment and compensation practices hinder civil service accountability. Furthermore, political meddling makes institutional development more difficult. In some countries, this interference can encourage the continuation of clientelistic practices that are often a barrier to development, equity, and stability.

Using a new data set on government wages and employment, this chapter analyzes the impact of elections on the government wage bill and makes three important contributions to the literature. First, the focus on the government wage bill allows the impact on an area that is particularly visible to voters to be isolated. Second, by taking advantage of a newly assembled data set, the fiscal and political cycle can be examined in more than 150 countries during 1990–2014, including 49 low-income countries (LICs). To the authors' knowledge, this is the widest sample of countries used for this type of analysis to date.[1] Third, the data on

[1] Past research has relied on smaller sample sizes that include very few observations of LICs. Klomp and de Haan (2013) include 30 advanced, 28 emerging, and 7 LICs; Brender and Drazen (2005) include 31 advanced, 30 emerging, and 7 LICs; Shi and Svensson (2006) use 27 advanced, 38

government employment provide an opportunity to examine whether changes in the wage bill in the political cycle correspond to changes in employment or to changes in pay policies—the actual policy levers driving the wage bill. This analysis fills a gap in the literature related to the scarcity of high-quality data on government employment.

This analysis indicates that elections do increase the government wage bill as a share of GDP, particularly in emerging market economies and LICs. The results are both economically and statistically significant: at current levels of the wage bill, elections result in an increase of the ratio of the wage bill to GDP of about 0.2 percentage point in emerging market economies and LICs. In addition, election-year increases in the wage bill tend to be associated more with increases in government employment than with changes in pay, with the exception of emerging economies, where government pay also tends to increase.

The remainder of this chapter is organized as follows. The second section provides a brief literature review. The third section discusses the data used in this chapter and presents descriptive statistics. The fourth section examines the main factors explaining differences in the wage bill and employment across countries and over time. The fifth section analyzes the impact of elections on the wage bill. The sixth section decomposes this impact by employment and pay. The final section concludes.

LITERATURE REVIEW

The interaction between the electoral cycle and macroeconomic policy has been studied extensively.[2] The general consensus is that the political cycle is more likely to affect fiscal than monetary policy, with changes in the latter being largely accommodative of fiscal impulses. This finding occurs partly because fiscal policy can have real effects on the economy even when anticipated. In particular, the proximity of elections introduces incentives for incumbents to conduct fiscal expansions to stimulate the economy and improve their chances of winning. Even outgoing governments have incentives for fiscal expansion if it ties the hands of the incoming government, requiring unpopular tax increases or expenditure cuts that can raise the probability of a return to power in the

---

emerging, and 20 LICs; Cahuc and Carcillo (2012) include 29 advanced and 5 emerging; Eckardt and Mills (2014) use 6 advanced, 19 emerging, and 3 LICs; and Schuknecht (2000) uses 24 developing economies (a group that includes both emerging and LICs).

[2] Nordhaus (1975) develops a formal model illustrating the interaction between elections and monetary policy. Assuming inflation expectations depend on recent changes in prices (that is, myopic voters), policymakers can maximize their probability of reelection by conducting expansionary monetary policy to stimulate the economy before the election and reversing course after voters have cast their ballots. Research has since extended this work to integrate forward-looking voters, rational expectations, and fiscal policy and to conduct empirical tests (Drazen [2001] and Dubois [2016] provide surveys of this literature).

next round of elections (Mulas-Granados 2006). The empirical literature is generally supportive of the electoral-cycle hypothesis on government expenditure (Klomp and de Haan 2013), with the impact being more marked in less developed economies and newer democracies (Shi and Svensson 2006; Brender and Drazen 2005).

This chapter focuses on the impact of elections on the government compensation of employees—the wage bill. This expenditure item can be particularly attractive to policymakers wishing to stimulate the economy just before an election for various reasons. First, the wage bill can have a rapid impact on output. Although theoretical models generally assume that the multiplier for government consumption (the wage bill plus goods and services expenditure) is smaller than that for government investment, no clear evidence verifies that this is the case, at least in advanced economies. In fact, empirical studies often find that the multiplier for consumption can be higher than that for investment (Batini and others 2014), which suggests that, at least in the short term, policymakers can get more bang for their buck by increasing the wage bill. Second, relative to other forms of expenditure—for example, capital spending—increases in the wage bill can be rolled out more easily because they do not require procurement processes commonly required in other forms of government consumption (goods and services purchases) or public investment. Moreover, wage increases and hiring practices are often at the discretion of the executive branch. Third, under an opportunistic political cycle, one could expect public expenditure to increase in areas most visible to voters (Rogoff 1990; Akhmedov and Zhuravskaya 2004). Voters may favorably respond to boosts in government employment in the delivery of services that affect them directly, such as education, health, sanitation, and security. In addition, as the principal employer in some countries, governments can have a direct impact on the welfare of many households through increases in public compensation. Finally, governments may be beholden to powerful constituencies (for example, public sector unions) that hold sway during political campaigns.

A number of studies focus more specifically on the wage bill. Using a sample of 24 developing economies in 1973–92, Schuknecht (2000) finds the political fiscal cycle is largely related to expansion of public expenditure during elections, although the impact on the wage bill is not statistically significant. Eckardt and Mills (2014) find that the government wage bill tends to be more procyclical and responsive to elections than total government expenditure, and the impact appears more pronounced in emerging economies. Cahuc and Carcillo (2012) find that episodes of fiscal drift (when the shares of public wage bills and deficits in GDP rise together) are more frequent during election years using a sample of Organisation for Economic Co-operation and Development countries between 1995 and 2009. In addition, Dahlberg and Mörk (2011), using data from Sweden and Finland, find a significant election year effect in local government employment. Drazen and Eslava (2010) also find that the wage bill in local governments in Colombia appears to increase before elections. However, these studies focus on small samples over a limited time horizon.

Moreover, little evidence is provided regarding the role of employment in driving the government wage bill.

DATA

This chapter uses data for 1990–2014 from different sources. For government compensation of employees and employment, it uses the newly developed IMF Harmonized Government Wage and Employment Data (IMF 2016a).[3] For the political cycle, this chapter uses the 2015 Database of Political Institutions (Cruz, Keefer, and Scartascini 2016). Demographic data come from the United Nation's World Population Prospects (United Nations 2015) and economic growth from the World Economic Outlook Database (IMF 2016b). Descriptive statistics are presented in Table 6.1. The main variables used in the analysis include the following:

- *Wage bill.* The wage bill is estimated as the general government compensation of employees as a percentage of GDP. The pooled sample covers 1990–2014 and includes 156 countries (34 advanced, 73 emerging, and 49 LICs) with an average of 21 years of data (Table 6.1). The wage bill ranges between 3.8 percent (10th percentile) and 12.9 percent (90th percentile) of GDP, with a sample mean of 8.2 percent of GDP.
- *Government employment.* The indicator for government employment corresponds to general government employment as a share of the population ages 15 to 64 (an estimate of the working-age population). Data are more scarce for government employment: the pooled sample includes 116 countries (33 advanced, 54 emerging, and 29 LICs) with an average of 12 years of data. Government employment is between 3.9 percent (10th percentile) and 15.8 percent (90th percentile) of the working-age population. The sample mean government employment is 9.5 percent of the working-age population.
- *Elections.* The indicator variable for election years takes the value of one in the calendar years of executive elections for presidential regimes or legislative elections for parliamentary regimes, and zero in other years. Data are available for 165 countries (35 advanced, 75 emerging, and 55 LICs) in the pooled sample 1990–2014. On average, elections represent 20 percent of the observations, being more frequent in the advanced economies (26 percent of the time) than in the emerging economies (19 percent) and LICs (17 percent).

[3] For compensation of employees, the IMF data set compiles data from sources including the IMF's World Economic Outlook and Government Finance Statistics, the Organisation for Economic Co-operation and Development's General Government Accounts, and EUROSTAT's Annual Government Finance Statistics and AMECO. For general government employment, the IMF data set assembles data from the International Labour Organization's LABORSTA data (public sector employment and employment of general government sector) and ILOSTAT (employment by institutional sector), and data from individual countries.

Table 6.1. Descriptive Statistics of the Pooled Sample, 1990–2014

	Pooled Data (1990–2014)			
	All	Advanced Economies	Emerging Market Economies	Low-Income Countries
Government Wage Bill (percent of GDP)				
Mean	8.2	10.7	7.9	6.4
Median	7.8	10.7	7.8	5.5
10th Percentile	3.8	6.9	4.2	3.1
90th Percentile	12.9	14.2	11.8	10.9
Government Employment (percent of working-age population)				
Mean	9.5	12.3	8.3	4.5
Median	8.9	10.9	7.3	4.1
10th Percentile	3.9	7.3	4.5	1.0
90th Percentile	15.8	22.5	13.4	9.9
Elections				
Mean Election Indicator (1 = elections, 0 = otherwise)	0.20	0.26	0.19	0.17
Mean Parliamentary System Indicator (1 = parliamentary, 0 = otherwise)	0.44	0.86	0.39	0.23
Demographics				
Population				
Mean	29.1	26.4	38.3	18.3
Median	7.9	7.5	6.0	9.2
10th Percentile	0.6	0.4	0.3	1.6
90th Percentile	62.7	62.2	72.5	40.3
Percent of Population, Ages 0–14 Years				
Mean	31.9	18.5	30.6	42.1
Median	32.8	18.2	30.8	43.5
10th Percentile	16.9	14.6	18.8	34.7
90th Percentile	45.5	22.6	41.3	47.4
Percent of Population, Ages 65 Years and Older				
Mean	7.2	14.4	6.6	3.4
Median	4.9	14.7	5.3	3.1
10th Percentile	2.7	10.5	3.1	2.5
90th Percentile	15.4	18.1	13.2	4.6
Real Economic Growth				
Mean	4.1	2.6	4.6	4.4
Median	4.0	2.6	4.5	4.8
10th Percentile	(3.3)	(1.5)	(3.5)	(4.5)
90th Percentile	12.5	7.1	13.8	15.0
Nonwage Expenditure (percent of GDP)				
Mean	23.1	31.5	21.9	18.1
Median	22.1	31.8	20.6	16.5
10th Percentile	11.9	23.7	12.3	10.1
90th Percentile	36.2	40.3	33.5	27.7
Public Debt (percent of GDP)				
Mean	63.1	57.1	51.4	83.1
Median	49.8	53.0	42.9	59.7
10th Percentile	17.0	14.4	13.3	27.5
90th Percentile	114.3	100.4	90.2	150.7

(continued)

Table 6.1. Descriptive Statistics of the Pooled Sample, 1990–2014 ***(continued)***

	Pooled Data (1990–2014)			
	All	Advanced Economies	Emerging Market Economies	Low-Income Countries
Observations				
Government Wage Bill (percent of GDP)	3,235	798	1,508	929
Government Employment (percent of working-age population)	1,438	601	671	166
Elections and Demographics	4,122	874	1,873	1,375
Economic Growth	3,724	784	1,699	1,241
Nonwage Expenditure	2,997	746	1,349	902
Public Debt	3,993	849	1,819	1,325
Countries				
Government Wage Bill (percent of GDP)	156	34	73	49
Government Employment (percent of working-age population)	116	33	54	29
Elections and Demographics	165	35	75	55
Economic Growth	165	35	75	55
Nonwage Expenditure	154	34	71	49
Public Debt	160	34	73	53
Average Number of Years				
Government Wage Bill (percent of GDP)	21	23	21	19
Government Employment (percent of working-age population)	12	18	12	6
Elections and Demographics	25	25	25	25
Economic Growth	23	22	23	23
Nonwage Expenditure	19	22	19	18
Public Debt	25	25	25	25

Source: Authors' calculations using IMF Harmonized Government Wage and Employment Data.

- *Demographics.* In the pooled sample, the population is 29.1 million on average and 7.9 million at the median. The average share of the population younger than age 15 is 31.9 percent and the average share of the population age 65 and older is 7.2 percent. Higher-income economies tend to have older age structures—on average, advanced economies have smaller shares of children and larger shares of elderly in their populations.
- *Economic growth.* The average annual real GDP growth is 4.1 percent (median 4 percent) in the pooled sample. On average, growth declines with the level of development, implying some degree of convergence—low-income economies grow on average by 4.4 percent per year compared with 2.6 percent per year in advanced economies.
- *Nonwage government expenditure.* On average, the sample government expenditure in items other than the wage bill is 23.1 percent of GDP, ranging from 18.1 percent of GDP in the LICs, to 21.9 percent of GDP in the emerging economies, and 31.5 percent of GDP in the advanced economies.

- *Public debt.* The average gross public debt is 63.1 percent of GDP in the pooled sample. On average, government indebtedness is higher in the LICs (83.1 percent of GDP) than in the advanced and emerging economies (57.1 percent and 51.4 percent of GDP, respectively).

CROSS-COUNTRY VARIATION IN GOVERNMENT WAGE BILL: STYLIZED FACTS

Figure 6.1 illustrates the evolution of the share of the government wage bill in GDP using a balanced panel (that is, maintaining a constant number of countries over time) starting in 1990 for advanced and emerging economies and in 2000 for LICs. This figure indicates that government compensation of employees is substantially higher in advanced than in emerging economies and LICs. The average ratio of the wage bill to GDP seems relatively stable or declining in advanced economies, albeit with a noticeable increase in 2009 that coincides with the financial crisis. In emerging economies, the wage bill has been trending up since 2007. In LICs, the wage bill has been steadily rising since the early 2000s.

A linear regression is useful for describing the factors that explain the variation across countries and over time in the government wage bill. The specification assumes the following form:

$$WB_{it} = \alpha + \beta \boldsymbol{X}_{it} + \varepsilon_{it},$$

where *WB* is the share of the wage bill in GDP and $\boldsymbol{X}$ is a vector of control variables that includes the level of income, the size and age distribution of the

Figure 6.1. Compensation of General Government Employees
(Percent of GDP)

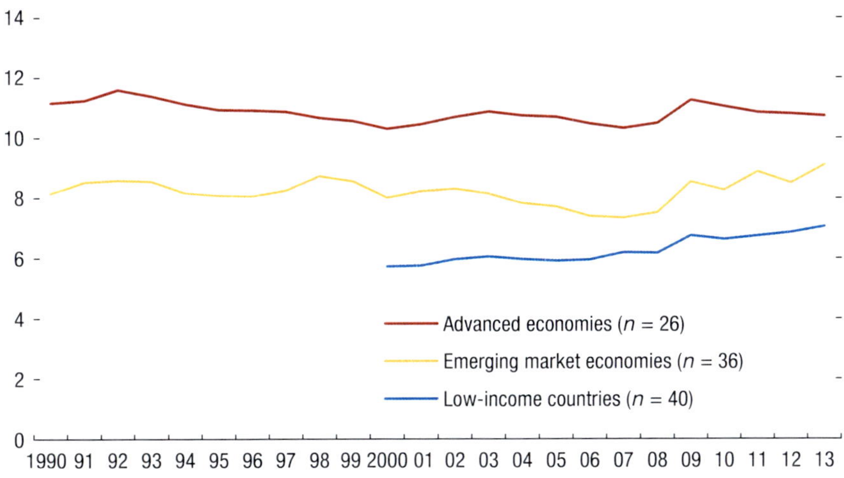

Source: Authors' calculations using IMF Harmonized Government Wage and Employment Data.

population, the level of government expenditure other than compensation of employees, the level of public debt, and time trends.

In the pooled sample, these variables explain about 39 percent of the variation in the wage bill. The results are summarized in Figure 6.2. Relative to LICs, emerging and advanced economies have higher wage bills (statistically significant for advanced economies). This finding is consistent with Wagner's law—as economies develop, governments tend to expand to respond to higher demand from the population for the provision of public goods, which tend to be superior goods (Bird 1971; Shiavo-Campo and Sundaram 2001). In

Figure 6.2. Factors Associated with the Variation in the Ratio of the Government Wage Bill to GDP
(Percentage points of GDP)

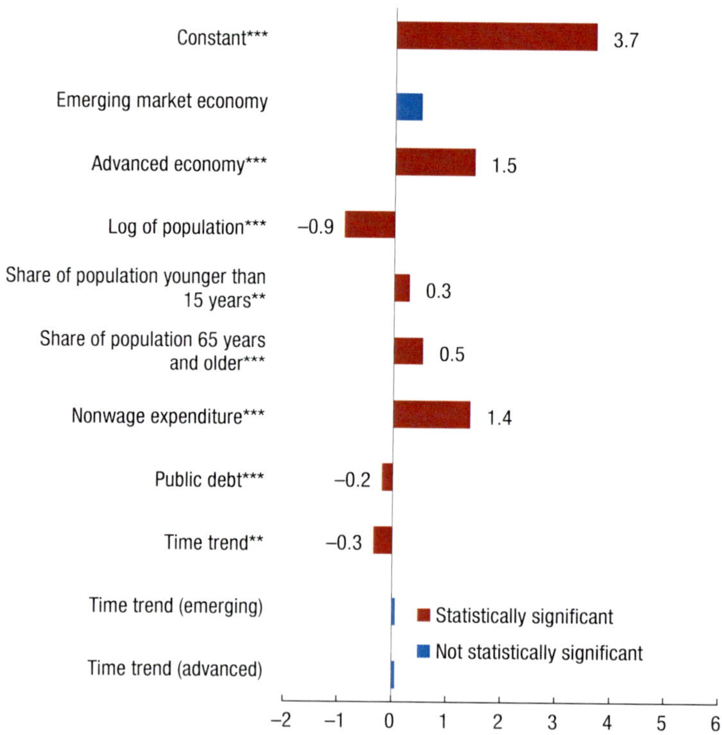

Source: Authors' calculations using IMF Harmonized Government Wage and Employment Data.
Note: Figure depicts coefficients of an ordinary least squares regression on the share of government compensation of employees in GDP. Sample size is 2,813 country-years and adjusted R-squared is 0.39. For the dependent variables population, share of population younger than 15 years, share of population 65 years and older, nonwage expenditure, and public debt, the figure shows the impact of a one standard deviation increase in these variables. For the time trend, the figure shows the 10-year trend.
$^{**}p < .05$; $^{***}p < .01$.

addition, as economies develop, the evolving nature of economic activity might facilitate tax collection (for example, the growing share of wages and salaries), providing more resources to finance public activities (Tanzi and Schuknecht 2000).

Demographic factors explain part of the variation in the government compensation of employees. The negative and statistically significant coefficient for population indicates scale effects in the government wage bill—all else equal, a one standard deviation increase in the size of the population is associated with a reduction in the wage bill of 0.9 percentage point of GDP. The age profile of a country also affects the wage bill. A larger share of children in the population can create pressure to increase the government wage bill and employment associated with education (a one standard deviation increase in the share of children increases the wage bill by 0.3 percentage point of GDP). In addition, a one standard deviation increase in the share of the elderly is associated with an increase in the wage bill of 0.5 percentage point of GDP, possibly reflecting pressures related to health care provision.

Fiscal considerations also affect the wage bill. A one standard deviation increase in nonwage expenditure increases the wage bill by 1.4 percentage points. This finding likely reflects country preferences on the size of government. In contrast, increases in public debt are negatively correlated with the wage bill—a one standard deviation increase in public debt reduces the wage bill by 0.2 percentage point of GDP, suggesting that concerns about fiscal sustainability might be associated with wage bill containment.

Finally, the time trend coefficients imply that the wage bill has been declining gradually over time (by about 0.3 percentage point every decade, all else equal).

IMPACT OF ELECTIONS ON THE GOVERNMENT WAGE BILL

Incumbents have an interest in using fiscal policy to influence voters' choices. This influence could be achieved by increasing civil service wages and boosting government hiring before elections, which would increase household incomes for public servants and potentially improve service delivery. Assuming voters put sufficient weight on these outcomes in their political choices, increases in the wage bill could tilt the ballot box in favor of incumbents. Following the literature, the chapter evaluates this hypothesis by examining changes in the ratio of the wage bill to GDP in years with and without elections.

Table 6.2 presents evidence of a link between changes in the wage bill and elections. The data give credence to the presence of a political cycle in the wage bill—the wage bill increases more strongly in election years than in years without elections, particularly in LICs. The average increase during election years is higher than in years without elections by about 0.08 percentage point in the whole sample and 0.19 percentage points in LICs. The results are similar at the median, albeit of smaller magnitude.

Table 6.2. Changes in Government Wage Bill, by Election Year, 1990–2014

	Change in Wage Bill to GDP			
	All	Advanced Economies	Emerging Market Economies	Low-Income Countries
Mean				
All	0.06	−0.02	0.07	0.11
No Election	0.04	−0.03	0.05	0.07
Election	0.12	0.01	0.12	0.27
Difference (Election – No Election)	0.08	0.05	0.06	0.19
Median				
All	0.00	−0.05	0.00	0.08
No Election	0.00	−0.05	−0.01	0.07
Election	0.05	−0.04	0.06	0.20
Difference (Election – No Election)	0.05	0.00	0.08	0.13
Observations				
All	3,074	764	1,433	877
No Election	2,442	557	1,170	715
Election	632	207	263	162

Source: Authors' calculations using IMF Harmonized Government Wage and Employment Data.

To assess the impact of elections on the wage bill while controlling for other factors, a regression is estimated that includes macroeconomic and structural controls:

$$\Delta WB_{it} = (\alpha + f_i) + \beta \boldsymbol{X}_{it} + \varepsilon_{it},$$

where f_i represents country fixed effects, ΔWB is the change in the wage bill as a percentage of GDP, and $\boldsymbol{X}$ is a vector with the key explanatory variable being an indicator variable for election years, including a differential for advanced economies (an interaction between election year and advanced economy indicators). The analysis uses four different specifications. The first three correspond to ordinary least squares regressions using the level of development (an indicator variable for advanced economies), demographics (annual population growth and changes in the shares of children and elderly in the population), and annual GDP growth. The fourth specification is a fixed-effects regression that adds controls for country-specific characteristics and year effects.

Regression analyses confirm the impact of elections on changes in the ratio of the government wage bill to GDP while controlling for other factors (Table 6.3).[4] Elections increase the government wage bill in relation to GDP by 0.11–0.19 percentage point (statistically significant under all specifications). At the current level of wages to GDP, this is equivalent to about a 2 percent increase in the wage bill in

[4] Similar regressions using the share of government employment in the working-age population suggest a positive impact of elections of 0.06–0.08 percentage point of the working-age population, although this coefficient is only statistically significant in one specification.

Table 6.3. Regression Analysis: Impact of Elections on Changes in the Government Wage Bill

	OLS						Fixed Effects	
	Coefficient	*P*-value	Coefficient	*P*-value	Coefficient	*P*-value	Coefficient	*P*-value
Dependent Variable: Change in Government Wage Bill to GDP								
Constant	0.082***	0.00	0.061**	0.01	–0.003*	0.06	0.010***	0.00
Advanced Economy	–0.104***	0.00	–0.096***	0.00	–0.020	0.58		
Election			0.112**	0.01	0.186***	0.00	0.167***	0.00
Election × Advanced Economy			–0.064	0.29	–0.174***	0.01	–0.160***	0.01
Growth of Population					0.943	0.49	5.033*	0.05
Change in Share of Population, Ages 0–14 Years					0.065	0.26	0.147**	0.03
Change in Share of Population, Ages 65+ Years					0.035	0.70	0.186	0.21
Growth of Real GDP (*t* – 2)					0.866***	0.00	0.915***	0.00
Change in Nonwage Expenditure (*t* – 2)					–0.006	0.12	–0.009	0.11
Change in Public Debt (*t* – 2)					–0.003*	0.06	–0.001	0.71
Year Effects	No		No		No		Yes	
R-squared	0.00		0.00		0.03		0.11	
Observations	3,074		3,074		2,456		2,456	

Source: Authors' calculations using IMF Harmonized Government Wage and Employment Data.
Note: OLS = ordinary least squares.
$^{*}p < .1$; $^{**}p < .05$; $^{***}p < .01$.

low-income and emerging economies and a 1 percent increase in advanced economies. The negative coefficient in the interaction between elections and advanced economies indicates that the impact is much less marked in advanced economies.

The growth of the population has a positive effect on the wage bill, and the effect is particularly significant in the fixed-effects specification. Although larger countries tend to have lower wage bills because of scale effects (the analysis in levels presented in the previous sections), short-term positive shocks to population growth increase wage bill expenditures, likely as a result of short-term responses to maintain adequate service delivery.

The positive coefficient on the (lagged) growth of real GDP implies that positive short-term shocks to GDP translate into a higher wage bill as a percentage of GDP. Note that the correlation between the growth rates of these two variables is 0.56, suggesting procyclicality—when real GDP increases, the wage bill tends to increase in real terms.

The coefficients on the fiscal variables suggest that increases in other types of spending are not statistically significant. With regard to (lagged) public debt, the coefficients indicate that a positive shock to public debt tends to reduce the wage bill, although this result is not statistically significant in the fixed-effects specification.

One important question is whether the election effects on the wage bill are persistent—if the impact of elections is offset by reductions in the wage bill in

Table 6.4. Regression Analysis: Impact of Elections on Changes in the Government Wage Bill, by Year Relative to Election Year

Coefficients of Election Dummy	Fixed Effects
Election Year	0.17***
One Year after Election	−0.05
Two Years after Election	0.04
One Year before Election	−0.01
Two Years before Election	−0.05

Source: Authors' calculations using IMF Harmonized Government Wage and Employment Data.
Note: Table displays coefficient for year dummies relative to election years, using a fixed-effects specification similar to that in the last column of Table 6.3.
$^{**}p < .05$; $^{***}p < .01$.

postelection years, then the political cycle would not materially affect the long-term path of the wage bill. Repeating the exercise using years just preceding or following election years as explanatory variables yields coefficients that are not statistically different from zero (Table 6.4). This outcome suggests that the wage bill is not ramped up in anticipation of elections and that the additional spending is not reduced even after the votes have been counted.

The results are robust to different specifications. A regression using the wage bill as a share of total government expenditure as a dependent variable provides comparable results. The coefficient for elections is 0.75 percentage point of expenditure, which implies an increase in the wage bill as a percentage of GDP of about 0.2 percentage point.

DRIVERS OF WAGE BILL INCREASES DURING ELECTIONS

This section examines whether increases in the wage bill associated with elections are due to increases in employment or to increases in pay. The ratio of the wage bill to GDP can be expressed as the product of the number of government workers as a share of the working-age population and average government pay as a share of GDP per working-age population:

$$\frac{\textit{government wage bill}}{\textit{GDP}} = \frac{\textit{government employment}}{\textit{population}_{\textit{age 15–64 years}}} \times \frac{\textit{average government pay,}}{\dfrac{\textit{GDP}}{\textit{population}_{\textit{age 15–64 years}}}}$$

where average government pay is defined as $\dfrac{\textit{government wage bill}}{\textit{government employment}}$.

Table 6.5. Decomposition of Changes in the Ratio of the Wage Bill to GDP

	All	Advanced Economies	Emerging Market Economies	Low-Income Countries
Impact of Election on Government Wage Bill to GDP	0.09**	0.05	0.17**	0.05
Due to Government Employment	0.06	0.05	0.05	0.17*
Due to Government Pay	0.03	0.00	0.12	−0.11
Observations	970	457	437	76

Source: Authors' calculations using IMF Harmonized Government Wage and Employment Data.
Note: Table displays coefficient for year dummies relative to election years, using a fixed-effects specification similar to that in the last column of Table 6.3.
*$p < .1$; **$p < .05$.

Using this identity, the change in the wage bill is decomposed into the increase due to an expansion of employment and the increase due to a rise in average pay.

To examine the impact of elections, a fixed-effects regression is used for each component. The decomposition in election years is compared with that in non-election years (Table 6.5). The sample is restricted to country-years with nonmissing data for both the ratio of the wage bill to GDP and the ratio of employment to the working-age population. The results for the wage bill are similar to those in the full sample presented in Table 6.3—the wage bill to GDP increases by 0.09 in election years, and this result is statistically significant. The decomposition suggests that about two-thirds of the impact is due to changes in employment and one-third due to increases in wages.

In *advanced economies*, the annual change in the wage bill in election years is 0.05 percentage point of GDP, but this is not statistically significant. The decomposition indicates that the impact of elections in the wage bill is largely due to increases in the ratio of government employment to working-age population, while government pay does not seem to be affected by elections.

In *emerging economies*, the average annual change in the wage bill is positive and significant (0.17 percentage point per year). In these countries, only one-third of the impact is due to employment, and the remainder is due to changes in government pay.

In *LICs*, the wage bill increases by 0.05 percentage point of GDP in election years. In these countries, election year increases seem more associated with increases in employment (associated with a 0.17 percentage point of GDP increase in the wage bill, statistically significant) than with changes in government pay (which seems to decline in election years, but the result is not statistically significant).

CONCLUSION

Substantial evidence suggests that electoral cycles can affect fiscal policy, but less is known about whether governments use the public wage bill to affect political outcomes. This chapter sheds new light on this question by taking advantage of a newly assembled data set covering 25 years of public wage bill data in more than 150 countries, including 49 LICs. The data set also provides information on public employment, which is used in this analysis to separate the contribution of average pay from that of employment in election-cycle-induced changes in the public wage bill.

The chapter finds evidence that the wage bill is subject to a political cycle. Positive changes in the wage bill are associated with election years, particularly in emerging economies and LICs. The impact of elections is robust as well as economically and statistically significant, increasing the share of public wages in GDP by 0.11–0.19 percentage point. This finding is the equivalent of an approximately 2 percent increase in the wage bill in emerging economies and LICs and a 1 percent increase in advanced economies at current levels of public wages to GDP. The analysis finds some evidence that elections have a positive impact on public employment, though the result is not robust across specifications. Taking advantage of the data on government employment, the analysis finds that overall, election-year increases in the wage bill tend to be associated more with increases in government employment than with changes in pay, with the exception of emerging economies, where government pay also tends to increase.

This work has important implications for public policy. Efforts to ensure fiscal sustainability should emphasize the need to strengthen wage bill oversight and depoliticize government pay and employment policies. One attractive option for delinking pay raises from the election cycle is to rely on independent agencies for advice on wage increases, typically taking into account private sector developments and fiscal affordability (as is done, for example, in Australia and Japan). For employment, it is crucial to control hiring to ensure that it reflects genuine service delivery needs. This effort should be supported by periodic functional reviews to help identify potential overlap in functions across different government entities.

REFERENCES

Akhmedov, A., and E. Zhuravskaya. 2004. "Opportunistic Political Cycles: Test in a Young Democracy Setting." *Quarterly Journal of Economics* 119 (4): 1301–38. http://qje.oxfordjournals.org/content/119/4/1301.short.

Batini, N., L. Eyraud, L. Forni, and A. Weber. 2014. "Fiscal Multipliers: Size, Determinants, and Use in Macroeconomic Projections." Technical Notes and Manuals, International Monetary Fund, Washington. https://www.imf.org/external/pubs/ft/tnm/2014/tnm1404.pdf.

Bird, R. M. 1971. "Wagner's Law of Expanding State Activity." *Public Finance* 26 (1): 1–26.

Brender, A., and A. Drazen. 2005. "Political Budget Cycles in New versus Established Democracies." *Journal of Monetary Economics* 52 (7): 1271–95. http://www.sciencedirect.com/science/article/pii/S0304393205000887.

Cahuc, P., and S. Carcillo. 2012. "Can Public Sector Wage Bills Be Reduced?" Working Paper 1788, National Bureau of Economic Research, Cambridge, MA. http://bit.ly/2cwZcQr.

Cruz, C., P. Keefer, and C. Scartascini. 2016. "Database of Political Institutions Codebook, 2015 Update (DPI2015)." Inter-American Development Bank. Updated version of T. Beck, G. Clarke, A. Groff, P. Keefer, and P. Walsh. 2001. "New Tools in Comparative Political Economy: The Database of Political Institutions." *World Bank Economic Review* 15 (1): 165–76.

Dahlberg, M., and E. Mörk. 2011. "Is There an Election Cycle in Public Employment? Separating Time Effects from Election Year Effects." *CESifo Economic Studies* 57 (3): 480–98. http://bit.ly/2cD4Dwb.

Drazen, A. 2001. "The Political Business Cycle after 25 Years." In *NBER Macroeconomics Annual 2000*, edited by B. Bernanke and K. Rogoff, 75–117. Cambridge, MA: MIT Press.

———, and M. Eslava. 2010. "Electoral Manipulation Via Voter-Friendly Spending: Theory and Evidence." *Journal of Development Economics* 92 (1): 39–52.

Dubois, E. 2016. "Political Business Cycles 40 Years after Nordhaus." *Public Choice* 166 (1): 235–59. http://link.springer.com/article/10.1007/s11127-016-0313-z.

Eckardt, S., and Z. Mills. 2014. "What Goes Up Must Come Down: Cyclicality in Public Wage Bill Spending." Working Paper 6760, World Bank, Washington. http://bit.ly/2cCXvzW.

International Monetary Fund (IMF). 2016a. "Managing Government Compensation and Employment—Institutions, Policies, and Reform Challenges." Policy Paper, IMF, Washington, DC. https://www.imf.org/external/np/pp/eng/2016/040816a.pdf.

———. 2016b. World Economic Outlook Database. Washington. https://www.imf.org/external/pubs/ft/weo/2016/01/weodata/index.aspx.

Klomp, J., and J. de Haan. 2013. "Political Budget Cycles and Election Outcomes." *Public Choice* 157 (1): 245–67. http://link.springer.com/article/10.1007/s11127-012-9943-y.

Mulas-Granados, C. 2006. *Economics, Politics and Budgets: The Political Economy of Fiscal Consolidations in Europe*. Basingstoke: Palgrave Macmillan.

Nordhaus, W. 1975. "The Political Business Cycle." *Review of Economic Studies* 42 (April): 169–90.

Rogoff, K. 1990. "Equilibrium Political Budget Cycles." *American Economic Review* 80 (1): 21–36. http://scholar.harvard.edu/files/rogoff/files/51_aer90.pdf.

Schiavo-Campo, S., and P. Sundaram. 2001. *To Serve and to Preserve: Improving Public Administration in the Competitive World*. Manila: Asian Development Bank.

Schuknecht, L. 2000. "Fiscal Policy Cycles and Public Expenditure in Developing Countries." *Public Choice* 102 (1): 115–30. http://link.springer.com/article/10.1023/A:1005026806998.

Shi, M., and J. Svensson. 2006. "Political Budget Cycles: Do They Differ across Countries and Why?" *Journal of Public Economics* 90 (8–9): 1367–89. http://bit.ly/2cvbax6.

Tanzi, V., and L. Schuknecht. 2000. *Public Spending in the 20th Century: A Global Perspective*. Cambridge, U.K.: Cambridge University Press.

United Nations. 2015. "World Population Prospects: The 2015 Revision, Methodology of the United Nations Population Estimates and Projections." Department of Economic and Social Affairs, Population Division, New York. https://esa.un.org/unpd/wpp/.

CHAPTER 7

Energy Subsidies and Public Social Spending: Theory and Evidence

CHRISTIAN EBEKE AND CONSTANT LONKENG NGOUANA

INTRODUCTION

Many studies have stressed the fiscal cost and environmental impact of energy subsidies (see, for example, IEA 2011; IMF 2013a; Parry and others 2014; and World Bank 2010, among others).[1] A comprehensive assessment by Clements and others (2013) suggests that pretax energy subsidies amounted to 0.7 percent of global GDP in 2011.[2] The figures are even more striking when the negative externalities from energy consumption are factored in (posttax energy subsidies were estimated to be about 2.9 percent of global GDP in 2011, equivalent to 8.5 percent of total government revenues; see Clements and others 2013). In addition, generalized energy subsidies have important distributional effects—there is wide micro-based evidence that they mostly benefit the wealthy, given their higher energy consumption.[3] High energy subsidies, at least until the recent past, have been a major policy challenge, especially when energy prices were high and on the rise.

From a political economy standpoint, many governments have argued that energy subsidies help shelter the purchasing power of the poor from high energy costs. At the same time, under limited budgetary resources, energy subsidies may come at the cost of lower spending elsewhere in the budget, including priority social expenditures. A natural question is, therefore, why the poor would support energy subsidies, a form of redistribution that disproportionately benefits

[1] See also IEA and others (2010), a joint report on the scope of energy subsidies (with suggestions for phasing them out) for the 2010 G20 summit meeting in Toronto.

[2] Pretax energy subsidies (obtained as the difference between a benchmark price of energy and the price paid by consumers) are generally higher among net oil exporters. These subsidies absorbed about 22 percent of government revenues in the Middle East and North Africa region in 2011 (see IMF 2013b).

[3] In a review of the evidence on the welfare impact of energy subsidy reform across 20 countries from Africa, Asia, the Middle East, and Latin America, Arze del Granado, Coady, and Gillingham (2012) find that the top income quintile captures six times more in subsidies than the bottom, in absolute terms. These distributional effects vary substantially across products, with the subsidies on gasoline being the most regressive. Also, IEA (2011) finds that the poorest 20 percent of households receive only about one-tenth of natural gas and electricity subsidies.

upper-income groups. Or put differently, under which conditions could high energy subsidies and low public social spending occur as an equilibrium outcome of a political game determining the composition of public spending?[4] It could be argued that the elite exploit imperfect information to make "sneaky" transfers to their constituency (see Coate and Morris 1995). This explanation, however, seems hard to reconcile with long-lived energy subsidies, especially if they indeed crowd out categories of public spending that are relevant to the poor.

Against this backdrop, this chapter develops a simple political game between the elite and the middle class to examine the conflicting allocation of public resources between energy subsidies and public social spending. The analysis shows that high energy subsidies and low social spending may indeed emerge in equilibrium when the delivery of the public good is subject to important bottlenecks, reflecting weak domestic institutions or political ineffectiveness. Intuitively, the poor support that equilibrium because energy subsidies provide a small but certain benefit to consumption, whereas the delivery of the public good is subject to significant leakages (for example, through corruption). The elite, internalizing this, set a subsidy rate that is suboptimally high, crowding out public social spending, especially when fiscal space is narrow.[5]

This chapter empirically tests the above predictions of this conceptual framework, using a large cross-section of low- and middle-income countries. A key empirical challenge to identifying the crowding-out effect of energy subsidies on public social spending is that the two aggregates may be jointly determined in the budget process. A simple ordinary least squares (OLS) estimation would therefore deliver biased estimates. To address this simultaneity bias and other potential sources of endogeneity, the procedure instruments subsidies in a given country by the level of subsidies in neighboring countries. In addition, it takes into account political constraints on the executive to capture how easily politicians can implement subsidy policies.

The instrumental variable estimation results suggest that energy subsidies indeed crowd out public social spending. More specifically, the analysis finds that a 1 percentage point increase in energy subsidies relative to GDP leads, on average, to a reduction of public spending in education and health by two-thirds percentage point of GDP. The estimations also point to important nonlinearities: the crowding out is stronger in the presence of weak domestic institutions or in an environment of political ineffectiveness.

This analysis is related to the existing literature along three dimensions. On the theoretical front, very little work has modeled the impact of energy subsidies on the economy. Chapter 14 of Acemoglu (2014) surveys a number of general

[4] IMF (2014) provides empirical evidence that public support for redistributive policies has grown in recent decades, partly because of rising inequality. Energy subsidies, however, disproportionately benefit upper-income groups and would not reduce inequality, which adds to the puzzle.

[5] The rich favor the high-energy-subsidies equilibrium because it provides large private savings on their energy bill (using public resources) and therefore more personal resources are left for non-energy consumption.

theories as to why inefficient forms of redistribution may occur in a political equilibrium. Energy subsidies, however, warrant separate treatment, given their peculiar features—they are "generalized," highly regressive, and have become widespread over the recent past (see Annex Figures 7.1.1 and 7.1.2). This chapter models energy subsidies explicitly and examines how they conflict with the provision of public social services in an economy, contingent on the quality of its institutions. Plante (2014) uses an open economy dynamic general equilibrium model in which oil is used as an input into the production function of firms, and finds that fuel subsidies reduce aggregate welfare, mainly by distorting the relative price of nontradable to tradable goods. Also, Strand (2013) develops a political economy model in which two interest groups value two different types of fuel (gasoline versus kerosene). He then characterizes the conditions under which positive subsidies emerge in equilibrium for each type of fuel, in autocracies and in young democracies.

With regard to domestic institutions in public finances, Abed and Gupta (2002) present a number of analyses of the impact of governance and corruption on the composition of government expenditures (and on economic performance). Mauro (1998) finds in a cross-section of countries that corruption reduces government spending on education. The conceptual framework in this chapter complements those results by providing a channel through which weak domestic institutions affect public social spending.[6]

Regarding the empirical strategy, the use of subsidies in neighboring countries in identifying the causal relationship between energy subsidies and social spending (both policy choices) builds on the literature on spatial spillovers in fiscal choices. For example, Keen and Lockwood (2010) find that the adoption of the value-added tax (VAT) in a given country depends on the fraction of neighboring countries that have already adopted it. Fatás and Mihov (2013) examine how domestic institutions (constraints on the executive, in particular) affect policy volatility and hence economic growth.

The remainder of the chapter is organized as follows: The second section presents the political game and its main implications. The third section tests the predictions of the model, with emphasis on the identification strategy. The fourth section concludes and draws policy implications, with reference to recent developments in international oil prices.

THE POLITICAL GAME

Economic Environment

The analysis considers an economy populated by two types of agents: the rich with income y_r, and the relatively poor with income y_p; $y_p < y_r$. The rich can be thought of as representing the elite and the relatively poor as representing

[6] Baqir (2002) also finds that democratization is a significant predictor of government spending on education and health in a large panel of countries.

the middle class.[7] Each agent derives utility from a private good, c (aggregate of energy consumption, c_e, and non-energy consumption, c_n) and from a public good, k. The economy is endowed with a resource rent, z, and income is subject to proportional taxation at a fixed rate, $\overline{\tau}$. The common pool of resources is used to subsidize energy and undertake social spending. A peculiar feature of social expenditures—potentially valued differently by the rich and the poor—is that their delivery is subject to bottlenecks (the economy incurred a deadweight loss, ζ, for each dollar of public social spending), reflecting weak domestic institutions.

The Game and Its Equilibrium

Setup and Timing of Events

The model developed here is relatively simple but provides a convenient way to examine the interplay between energy subsidies and public social spending. The utility function of agent i is given by equation (7.1):[8]

$$u_i(c_i,k) = ln(c_i) + v_i(k),\ v_i' > 0,\ v_i'' < 0, \tag{7.1}$$

where the private good c is a Cobb-Douglas aggregate of the energy and non-energy goods:[9]

$$c_i = c_{i,e}^{\theta} c_{i,n}^{1-\theta}, \quad 0 < \theta < 1. \tag{7.2}$$

Consider the following timing of events: At the beginning of the game, nature chooses the level of bottlenecks, ζ, in the economy.[10] This choice is observed by both the rich and the poor. The game then proceeds as follows: (1) the rich decide on the subsidy rate, δ; (2) the poor choose how much to spend on the public good, k (public social spending); and (3) the rich and the poor each decide how much of the subsidized private good (energy, c_e) and of the nonsubsidized private good (non-energy, c_n) to consume. This game structure reflects the fact that the rich benefit the most from energy subsidies (as shown below and consistent with empirical evidence) and would therefore push for them, whereas the poor are ex

---

[7] Throughout the chapter, the subscript r denotes rich agents (or members of the elite) and p denotes poor agents (part of the middle class).

[8] It is important to stress that the results do not depend heavily on the specification of the utility function—the adopted functional forms aim at developing the main intuitions of the model through the lens of closed-form solutions. For instance, we briefly discuss below the implications of adopting a functional form that is nonseparable in c and k.

[9] The model assumes that the share of the energy good (and of the non-energy good) is the same in the consumption basket of the rich and the poor. Solving the model with different consumption shares across the two groups of agents is straightforward.

[10] This is equivalent to assuming that the quality of domestic institutions is exogenous. In reality, however, public social spending would improve the human capital of the poor and perhaps their participation in the electoral process in a democracy. This model is quasi-static in that sense.

ante likely to favor social expenditures, given the high cost of market-provided services.[11]

Solving the Game (Backward Induction)

The political game can be solved backward as follows:

Third Stage of the Game: Each Agent Decides on the Consumption of Private Goods

For a given subsidy rate δ, and a given provision of the public good *k*, each agent decides the amount of the private good to consume. Showing that the Cobb-Douglas specification combined with the log utility on the aggregate private good induces each agent to devote a constant share of his or her disposable income to energy and non-energy consumption is straightforward.

The corresponding shares are θ for energy and 1 – θ for non-energy consumption:

$$(1-\delta)\, p_w c_{i,e} = \theta y_i \left(1-\overline{\tau}\right) \tag{7.3a}$$

$$c_{i,n} = (1-\theta)\, y_i \left(1-\overline{\tau}\right), \tag{7.3b}$$

where δ is the subsidy rate—the agent only pays a fraction 1 – δ of the international energy price, p_w, normalized so that the price of the non-energy good equals unity.[12] Equation (7.3) sheds some light on two interesting features of the model specification. First, the constant consumption shares imply that energy consumption increases with the subsidy rate for given disposable income and international energy price. Second, the rich benefit the most from energy subsidies (to an extent that increases with the relative income, y_r/y_p, of the rich), consistent with micro evidence.[13]

Second Stage of the Game: The Poor Choose the Amount of Social Spending

Taking the subsidy rate δ as given, the poor choose the amount of public social spending. It is assumed that only a fraction, 1 – ζ, of social expenditures actually contributes to social infrastructure because of various bottlenecks, reflecting weak domestic institutions. Relatively bad institutions would translate into a high value of ζ. There are several practical interpretations of ζ. It can be viewed as the

[11] The timing of the game may be thought of as reflecting that the middle class forms the majority of the population, prompting the elite to internalize their "move" (see backward induction below). This timing is common in the political economy literature (see, for example, the seminal paper by Acemoglu and Robinson [2001], and Acemoglu [2014, Chapter 13]).

[12] The amount of energy subsidy is a combination of the subsidy rate and the amount of energy that agents consume in equilibrium.

[13] This holds partly because the demand for energy of the rich is more elastic to the price of energy (and therefore to the subsidy) than that of the poor. In fact, the demand for the energy good, *e*, by agent *i* is written as $c_{i,e} = \theta\left(1-\overline{\tau}\right) y_i / (1-\delta)\, p_w \Rightarrow \left(\partial c_{r,e} / \partial\delta\right) / \left(\partial c_{p,e} / \partial\delta\right) = y_r / y_p$.

share of budgeted social expenditures that are diverted away from their intended purpose (for example, through corruption). ζ may also reflect efficiency losses in the delivery of social spending. $1 - \zeta$ could also be thought of as the perceived return to social infrastructure such as education.[14] The amount of subsidies and public social spending (the latter adjusted for the deadweight loss incurred in the delivery of the public good) is naturally constrained by the available resources:[15]

$$\delta p_w\left(\lambda c_{p,e}+(1-\lambda)c_{r,e}\right)+\frac{k}{1-\zeta}\leq z+\bar{\tau}y, \tag{7.4}$$

where λ is the fraction of rich people in the population and $y = \lambda y_r + (1 - \lambda)y_p$ is aggregate income. Given equation (7.3), equation (7.4) boils down to

$$\frac{\delta\theta}{1-\delta}(1-\bar{\tau})y+\frac{k}{1-\zeta}\leq z+\bar{\tau}y. \tag{7.5}$$

The poor maximize $u_p(c_p, k) = ln(c_p) + v_p(k)$, subject to equation (7.5), the economy's budget constraint. After some simple algebraic manipulations, and taking into account the results from the third stage of the game, equation (7.6) results:

$$ln\left(c_p\right)=\alpha_p-\theta ln(1-\delta), \tag{7.6}$$

where the constant α_p is a nonlinear combination of parameters, including the consumption share of energy, disposable income, and the exogenous price of energy.[16] Interestingly, the utility of the poor increases with the subsidy rate δ, a condition that we do not impose ex ante. An expression similar to equation (7.6) holds for the rich. We can already anticipate that the optimal choice of the public good by the poor will reflect the interplay between the utility derived from energy subsidies and that provided by the public good.

The Lagrangian of a poor agent's maximization problem is written as follows:

$$\mathcal{L}(k,\mu_p)=\left[\alpha_p-\theta ln(1-\delta)+v_p(k)+\mu_p\left(z+\bar{\tau}y-\frac{\delta\theta}{1-\delta}(1-\bar{\tau})y+\frac{k}{1-\zeta}\right)\right].$$

The optimal choice of k is dictated by the two following conditions, in addition to the nonnegativity constraint on μ_p and the budget constraint:

$$\text{(i):}\quad v_p'(k)=\frac{u_p}{1-\zeta}\Rightarrow\mu_p=(1-\zeta)v_p'$$

$$\text{(ii):}\quad \mu_p\left(z+\bar{\tau}y-\frac{\delta\theta}{1-\delta}(1-\bar{\tau})y+\frac{k}{1-\zeta}\right)=0.$$

---

[14] The model may also be set up in a way that z captures the probability that the politician will actually deliver on the public good's promise.

[15] Note that the non-energy good, n, does not enter the common pool budget constraint, given that it is entirely privately paid for by agents.

[16] $\alpha_p = ln\left((1-\bar{\tau})y_p p_w\right)+\theta ln(\theta)+(1-\theta)ln(1-\theta)$.

The first condition implies that $\mu_p > 0$, given that $v'_p > 0$ and $\zeta < 1$. Condition (ii) therefore yields the following optimal choice for k, denoted k^*:

$$k^* = (1-\zeta)\left(z + \overline{\tau}y - \frac{\delta}{1-\delta}\theta(1-\overline{\tau})y\right). \tag{7.7}$$

The optimal social spending choice has some interesting features. The first term in the second set of brackets represents the common pool of resources in the economy and could be thought of as mirroring the available fiscal space. The second term captures the cost of energy subsidies.

Given that ζ, $\overline{\tau}$, $\delta < 1$, one has

$$\frac{\partial k^*}{\partial \delta} = -\frac{(1-\zeta)}{(1-\delta)^2}\theta(1-\overline{\tau})y < 0. \tag{7.8}$$

A higher subsidy rate lowers the amount of resources available for public social spending. This was expected given that the total amount of subsidies increases with the subsidy rate, and subsidies and social spending are the only uses of the common pool of resources in the model. Notwithstanding this negative marginal effect of subsidies on social expenditures, equation (7.7) suggests that a sizable resource endowment, or more generally, a large fiscal space, would limit the impact of energy subsidies on public social spending. This implication of the model is tested in the empirical section of the chapter.

Equation (7.7) implies that the amount of public social spending (chosen by the poor) decreases with the extent of leakages in the delivery of the public good:[17]

$$\frac{\partial k^*}{\partial \zeta} < 0.$$

The above derivative is partial in the sense that it does not capture the indirect impact of ζ on k^*, through δ. In fact, the chapter shows below that the choice of δ by the elite in the first stage of the game also depends on ζ, the bottlenecks that hamper delivery of the public good.

First Stage of the Game: The Elite Set the Subsidy Rate

Taking into account the above choices, the utility function of the rich is

$$\alpha_r - \theta ln(1-\delta) + v_r\left(k^*(\delta,\zeta)\right),$$

where the constant α_r is the counterpart of α_p (see the second stage of the game above). We write $k^*(\delta, \zeta)$ to emphasize that the optimal level of the public good depends on the subsidy rate (and on the quality of domestic institutions), as

[17] Equation (7.7) suggests that this condition holds as long as the entire pool of common resources is not devoted to energy subsidies in equilibrium (which is highly likely).

shown above. The first-order condition (with respect to δ) for an interior solution is

$$\frac{\theta}{(1-\delta)}+\frac{\partial k^{*}}{\partial\delta}v_{r}'\left(k^{*}\right)=0.$$

Using equation (7.8), and after some algebraic manipulations, the optimal choice of δ is given by

$$\delta^{*}=1-(1-\zeta)(1-\overline{\tau})yv_{r}'\left(k^{*}\right). \tag{7.9}$$

It follows that

$$\frac{\partial\delta^{*}}{\partial\zeta}=(1-\overline{\tau})yv_{r}'\left(k^{*}\right)>0.$$

The bottlenecks in the delivery of the public good lower its benefit, leading to a second-best outcome of higher energy subsidies and lower public social spending. Equation (7.9) also suggests that the rich would choose a lower subsidy rate if the public good provides good quality services at the margin (that is, if $v_{r}'\left(k^{*}\right)$ is high).

Although we assume an exogenous tax rate, $\overline{\tau}$, the model provides some useful insights into the role of taxation: if the social contract were designed such that energy subsidies were contingent on a higher income tax rate (or a more progressive tax system), the process would intuitively converge toward a "higher equilibrium" of low energy subsidies (see equation (7.9)) and high priority social spending (see equations (7.7) and (7.8)).

In summary, the transmission mechanism in the model is one whereby weak domestic institutions (and to some extent low-quality public services) induce the rich to choose a high subsidy rate. This in turn crowds out public spending, especially under narrow fiscal space. Intuitively, the poor support that equilibrium because energy subsidies provide a small but certain benefit to consumption, whereas delivery of the desirable public good is subject to significant leakages. These predictions of the model are tested in the empirical section.

The model has been kept simple to develop the intuition through the lens of closed-form solutions. The model could be extended along several dimensions. First, we assume that agents' utility is separable in public and private goods. In reality, however, they could be either strong complements or substitutes. Second, domestic institutions are assumed to be exogenous in this model. However, a large body of the political economy literature documents perverse effects of the natural resources endowment on domestic institutions. This model could therefore be extended to account for that interplay (for example, by setting $\zeta = \zeta(z)$, an increasing function of z). Third, for tractability and transparency, the model assumes that income is the main source of heterogeneity between the rich and the poor. Each type of agent may, however, have different intrinsic preferences between the energy and the non-energy goods. The model developed in this chapter can be extended to account for that particular feature, for example, by allowing the share of the energy good (and of the non-energy good) to be different across the consumption baskets of the rich and the poor.

EMPIRICAL ANALYSIS

Data Description and Stylized Facts

Data Description: Energy Subsidies and Social Spending

The data on energy subsidies are drawn from Clements, Gupta, and Nozaki (2013) and are computed based on the "price gap" approach (see Koplow 2009). The measure of energy subsidies includes subsidies on a wide range of products (petroleum products, gas, coal, and electricity) for a panel of low- and middle-income countries.[18] Consumer subsidies arise when the prices paid by consumers, including both firms (intermediate consumption) and households (final consumption), are below a benchmark price, while producer subsidies arise when prices received by suppliers are above this benchmark. The benchmark price for calculating subsidies on an energy product that is internationally traded is based on the international price. When the energy product is mostly nontraded (such as electricity), the appropriate benchmark price is the cost-recovery price for the domestic producer, augmented by distribution costs and a normal return to capital. The advantage of the "price gap" approach is that it helps capture subsidies that are implicit, such as those provided by countries that supply petroleum products to their populations at prices below those prevailing on international markets. More formally, energy subsidies are computed as follows:

$$s_{i,t}^{e} = \sum_{e=1}^{m} (p_{w,t}^{e} - p_{i,t}^{e}) c_{i,t}^{e}, \qquad (7.10)$$

where e denotes the energy product potentially subsidized (petroleum products, gas, coal, or electricity), $c_{i,t}^{e}$ is the total domestic consumption of product e in country i in year t, p_w is the benchmark price (in local currency), and p is the domestic price.[19]

Estimates of pretax energy subsidies based on this approach do suffer from some limitations. First, subsidies calculated here mostly reflect consumer subsidies because producer prices are not available for a large number of countries. Second, consumption and price data often come from different sources that are not necessarily comparable across countries. Third, benchmark prices by product (especially products that are traded internationally) rely on the assumption of similar transportation and distribution margins across countries. Such

---

[18] The list of countries covered by the analysis is presented in Annex Table 7.1.1.

[19] Given that pretax subsidies are positively defined, by definition, s_i^e is censored and takes the value 0 whenever the price gap is negative.

measurement errors in the data have implications, explored later in the text, for the choice of the econometric specification.

We obtain data on social spending from the World Bank's World Development Indicators (2013) database. Despite some data limitations for earlier years (especially during the 1980s and the 1990s), substantial efforts have been made to record public social spending for the past decade for a large number of countries. In that vein, Clements, Gupta, and Nozaki (2013) provide a comprehensive data set on public spending on education and health covering 140 countries. Their series, however, end in 2009. Because the recent period (post-2008) during which energy subsidies have risen substantially (on the back of rising international oil prices) is key to this analysis, the World Development Indicators series is used. For the purpose of this analysis, a narrow but relatively easy-to-capture concept of public social spending is adopted, defined as the sum of public expenditure in education and health (expressed as a percentage of GDP for cross-country comparability).[20] Many other control variables used in the estimations (see specification below) are also from the World Development Indicators (2013) database.

Given that we are interested in the effect of energy subsidies on social spending, which is conditional on the quality of institutions and political environment of each country, the subsidies variable is interacted with several time-varying indicators of the quality of domestic institutions and the fragility of the political environment.

The first variable interacted with energy subsidies is a synthetic index of governance quality that aggregates six dimensions of governance reported in the World Bank's World Governance Indicators data set: voice and accountability, political stability and absence of violence, government effectiveness, regulatory quality, rule of law, and control of corruption. To build the governance indicators used in the econometric estimations, all the original governance-quality indicators are transformed using the following formula:

$$G_{i,t} = \frac{max\left(x_{i,t}\right) - x_{i,t}}{max\left(x_{i,t}\right) - min\left(x_{i,t}\right)}, \tag{7.11}$$

where x represents an indicator of governance quality and $min(x)$ and $max(x)$ represent the minimum and the maximum of that indicator, respectively. This transformation ensures that G takes values between 0 and 1. G increases with deterioration of the quality of governance. To aggregate the six indicators into a normalized index, principal component analysis is used. The aggregate index of governance is the first principal component of the vector of the six indicators of governance already constructed.

The second set of indicators interacted with energy subsidies focuses on the extent of political fragility. For this, the analysis relies on indicators assembled by the Center for Systemic Peace. The first indicator measures the degree of state

[20] Clements, Gupta, and Nozaki (2013) adopt a similar definition.

Figure 7.1. Change in Subsidies and Social Spending across Regions between 2002–06 and 2007–11

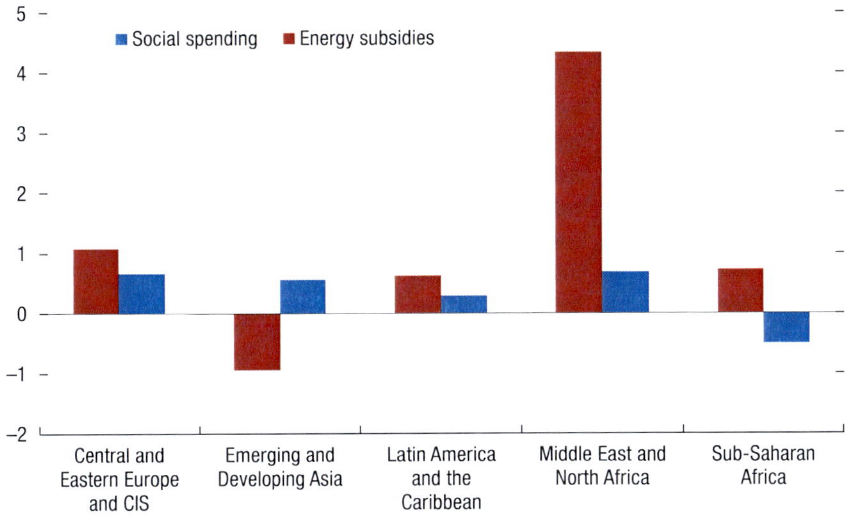

Sources: Clements, Gupta, and Nozaki 2013; World Development Indicators 2013; and authors' calculations.
Note: CIS = Commonwealth of Independent States.

fragility. The fragility index scores each country on both effectiveness and legitimacy in four performance dimensions: security, political, economic, and social. Each of the indicators is rated on a four-point fragility scale: 0 for "no fragility," 1 for "low fragility," 2 for "medium fragility," and 3 for "high fragility," with the exception of the economic effectiveness indicator, which is rated on a five-point scale (including 4 for "extreme fragility"). The state fragility index, then, combines scores on the eight indicators and ranges from 0 for "no fragility" to 25 for "extreme fragility."

Finally, to better isolate the effect of the political environment on the subsidies–social spending trade-off, the component "political ineffectiveness" is extracted from the broad state fragility index discussed above and the model is reestimated.

Stylized Facts

We start with a panel data set covering 109 low- and middle-income countries over 2000–11, the period for which energy subsidies data are available, from Clements, Gupta, and Nozaki (2013).[21] The estimate of energy subsidies for each country is normalized by its GDP in current prices.

Figure 7.1 provides some insights into the question examined in the chapter. It portrays the evolution of energy subsidies and social spending between two episodes

[21] The countries covered in the sample are listed in Annex Table 7.1.1.

Figure 7.2. Energy Subsidies and Social Spending across Countries: What Has Happened?

(2007–11 average vs. 2002–06 average)

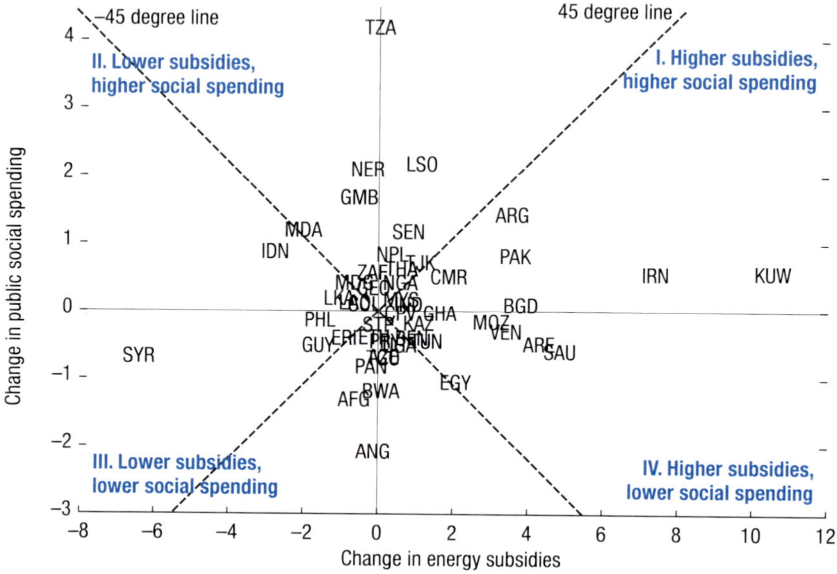

Sources: Clements, Gupta, and Nozaki 2013; World Development Indicators 2013; and authors' calculations.
Note: Data labels in the figure use International Organization for Standardization (ISO) country codes.

(2002–06 and 2007–11) across different regions of the globe. (Annex Figure 7.1.1 and Annex Figure 7.1.2 illustrate the intensification of energy subsidies between 2006 and 2011 around the globe and in the Middle East and North Africa region, respectively.)[22] Although subsidies decreased in emerging and developing Asia between the two subperiods, they increased in sub-Saharan Africa. Strikingly, social spending moved in opposite directions across (and in) both regions, pointing to a potential trade-off between energy subsidies and social spending. In contrast, social spending did not decline in the resource-rich Middle East and North Africa (MENA) region, despite the sharp increase in energy subsidies in the region, suggesting that countries' endowment or resource space may condition the extent of crowding out.

Figure 7.2 provides a more disaggregated picture (at the country level) and paints a quite similar story: (1) energy subsidies rose around the globe between the two identified subperiods (most countries in the sample are to the right of

[22] We consider averages over subperiods rather than yearly time series for robustness. In fact, changes in subsidies and social spending from one year to another could be arbitrary. The 2006–07 cutoff is chosen to reflect the dynamics in energy prices, but the point made here holds for alternative cutoff dates (and hence subperiods).

the vertical axis), but the evolution of social spending was uneven (countries are almost equally split below and above the horizontal axis); (2) some resource-rich countries were somewhat able to afford higher subsidies without cutting public social spending (at face value), and when social spending did decrease in resource-rich countries, the decline was much lower than the increase in subsidies (above the negative 45-degree line); and (3) in general, where social spending did increase, the increase was lower than the increase in subsidies (below the 45-degree line). Consequently, only a handful of countries went through the virtuous circle of lower energy subsidies and higher public social spending (second quadrant) during the two identified subperiods.

Note that the patterns discussed above are based on a panel data structure, whereas the econometric analysis focuses on the cross-section dimension of the data for reasons discussed below. Nonetheless, these patterns provide useful insights into the link between subsidies and social spending. The main advantage of Figures 7.1 and 7.2 is that they illustrate how subsidies and social spending changed over the two subperiods for groups of countries (Figure 7.1) and for individual countries (Figure 7.2). Presenting similar evidence in a pure cross-section setting requires controlling for other relevant countries' characteristics, including demographics. This is done more systematically in the econometric analysis below; the discussion also elaborates on the choice of estimation method.

Econometric Analysis

Model Specification

We propose an empirical strategy to investigate the potential impact of energy subsidies on public social spending. Identifying the causal link between these two aggregates is complicated by a number of factors discussed below. We consider the following cross-section estimation:

$$\left(\frac{Social}{Y}\right)_i = \alpha + (\beta_1 + \beta_2 F_i)\left(\frac{Subsidies}{Y}\right)_i + \beta_3 F_i + \boldsymbol{X}_i' \Gamma + \varepsilon_i, \qquad (7.12)$$

where *Social* is the sum of public spending on education and health, and *Subsidies* is total pretax energy subsidies as defined above (both series expressed as percentages of GDP). The vector $\boldsymbol{X}$ comprises a battery of controls that have been identified as relevant determinants of public social spending in the literature (see, for example, Baqir 2002; Clements, Gupta, and Nozaki 2013; IMF 2003; Mauro 1998 to name only a few). These controls include countries' demographic characteristics (dependency ratio and urbanization) and macroeconomic aggregates such as initial real per capita income, government size, the degree of trade openness, and macroeconomic volatility (measured as the standard deviation of the annual growth rate of real GDP).[23] Importantly, and related to the

[23] It is worth emphasizing the need to control for government size in the model. In fact, all categories of spending may also decline regardless of what happens to energy subsidies (for example, if tax

conceptual framework, the vector $\boldsymbol{X}$ also contains measures of the quality of domestic institutions.

We also assess the extent to which the crowding out, if any, depends on relevant countries' economic and political characteristics embodied in F_i, namely the quality of domestic institutions and political effectiveness.[24] It is therefore useful to consider special cases in thinking about equation (7.12). When $F_i = 0$ (linear case), the crowding-out coefficient is given by β_1. If $F_i \neq 0$ (nonlinear case), the crowding out depends on the level of the variable F_i and is given by $\beta_1 + \beta_2 F_i$.

Why Adopt a Cross-Sectional Specification?

Although it is tempting to use panel estimations to exploit the full structure of the data set (time and cross-section dimensions), such an approach may not be desirable in this context for a number of technical reasons. First, the subsidy variable is likely to be contaminated with measurement errors, despite its careful derivation. These measurement errors may lead to an attenuation bias in the presence of country fixed effects. This issue is even more relevant here because most within-country variations (year to year) in the subsidies variable do not always represent a shift in the subsidy regime, but in some cases may reflect changes in the benchmark price if domestic prices are sticky across countries in the short term. We therefore run the risk of identifying the impact of shocks to energy prices on social spending rather than the crowding-out effect of subsidies on social spending, the focus of this analysis.

Second, the measure of energy subsidies used here captures implicit subsidies not necessarily reflected in the budgets. Using yearly data could be misleading, potentially leading to a stronger attenuation bias, because the estimates of the crowding-out coefficient would be biased downward (in absolute terms). This occurs because year-to-year changes in implicit subsidies are not necessarily "financed" by cutting public social spending, but might instead lead to "losses" incurred by state-owned enterprises (SOEs), financed via arrears accumulation by SOEs or public debt at large. Using within-country averages over the period of analysis would limit this bias because subsidies would eventually lead to fiscal retrenchment: SOEs cannot run losses indefinitely (without bailout from the central government) nor can debt be built up indefinitely without adjustment.

Third, the short time period (2000–11) and the strong inertia characterizing the dependent variable (public social spending) and some of its determinants (such as demographics, institutions, and natural resources dependency, which change only slowly over time) limit the information content of the time dimension of the data. This feature of the variables of interest, coupled with the short time dimension, exposes the risk that fixed effects absorb almost all the variations in the data in panel estimations.

---

revenues fall). We therefore control for government size (spending-to-GDP ratio, excluding subsidies) to make sure we isolate the marginal effect of subsidies on public social spending. We focus on social spending for political economy reasons, as highlighted in the introduction.

[24] All the variables are averages over the sample period (2000–11).

The country-specific averages of the energy-subsidies-to-GDP ratios mostly reflect what could be referred to as "subsidy regimes" or "pricing regimes," meaning the extent to which some countries tend to subsidize energy products more than others.[25] The between-country variation is an appealing dimension of the data. Using cross-sectional estimates implies assessing questions such as do countries more prone to subsidizing energy products also have less social spending?

Identification Strategy: Addressing the Endogeneity of Subsidies

One of the main challenges associated with cross-sectional studies is how to properly control for unobservable factors to limit the risks of endogeneity bias. One could easily control for a pair of fixed effects (country and time) to obtain clean parameter estimates of the effects of subsidies in panel data estimations. The limits associated with the panel specification in the context of this analysis are discussed above.

The sources of endogeneity associated with energy subsidies may vary. First, because subsidies and social spending may be jointly determined, OLS estimates of β_1 and β_2 (see equation (7.12)) would suffer from a simultaneity bias. Second, the fact that cross-sectional estimations cannot control for unobservable factors that may jointly affect the subsidy regime and the level of public social spending is yet another potential source of bias.

Against this backdrop, this chapter proposes an identification strategy based on the level of subsidies in neighboring countries. The set of instruments is also enriched to include the extent of political constraints on the executive as an "exogenous" source of variation in the level of energy subsidies across countries, conditional on a battery of covariates. Two main conditions should govern the relevance of these instruments: First, they should be strongly correlated with the subsidies-to-GDP ratio in the observed country. In other words, the instruments, even after controlling for other covariates, should be significant in the first-stage equations modeling the cross-country variation in energy subsidies. The strength of the instruments is gauged using the F-stat and Shea R^2 associated with the first-stage regressions. Second, the instruments should be correlated with the outcome of interest (here, the ratio of public social spending to GDP) only through their impact on the subsidies variable or through any other variable that is already controlled for in the econometric specifications. This criterion of orthogonality is tested using the Sargan overidentification test.

Another critical question is whether these instruments are economically relevant. What is the story behind their selection? The first instrumental variable records the average level of subsidies (as a percentage of GDP) in neighboring countries. The identification strategy in this analysis is based on the intuition that countries are more likely to subsidize energy products if other countries in their neighborhood are doing the same. The procedure also tests whether this could

---

[25] The authors are grateful to David Coady for bringing this useful interpretation to our attention.

be more likely if the country of interest is a net commodity exporter, because pressures to share the pie would be higher.[26] Various factors can justify the effects of neighboring subsidy regimes on countries' behavior. One main argument is related to political economy. In the absence of informational asymmetries (we assume that citizens are aware of the policies adopted in neighboring countries over a 12-year horizon, the horizon over which the sample data are averaged), the hypothesis is that citizens are more likely to ask for energy subsidies if neighboring countries subsidize, and even more so if the home country is an oil producer. These types of spatial spillovers in fiscal choices have been used to model fiscal policy choices in developing countries in the literature (see, for example, Keen and Lockwood 2010 on VAT adoption).

The instrumental variable is constructed as the weighted average of energy-subsidies-to-GDP ratios over all neighboring countries, using the worldwide gravity database assembled by the CEPII.[27] More specifically, for each country i in the sample, the energy subsidy intensity in neighboring countries ($ESINC_i$) is evaluated as

$$ESINC_i = \frac{1}{n}\sum_{j=1}^{n} s_j \times d_{i,j}, \tag{7.13}$$

where s_j is the subsidy-to-GDP ratio in country j and

$$d_{i,j} = \begin{cases} 1 \text{ if countries } i \text{ and } j \text{ are neighbors} \\ 0 \quad\quad\quad \text{otherwise} \end{cases}. \tag{7.14}$$

Because the instrument is built using neighboring countries' data, it seems relatively exogenous to the level of public social spending in each country. It could be argued that the subsidy intensity in neighboring countries (the main instrument) simply captures common shocks affecting countries. Because a wide range of variables, including trade openness, are also controlled for, the latter risk is limited. The risk would be more severe if the analysis were using yearly panel data, given that a common oil shock may trigger, at least in the short term, synchronized fiscal policy responses, including decisions to partially or fully subsidize. By looking at averages of subsidy-to-GDP ratios, we are measuring to some extent subsidies or pricing regimes across countries, devoting attention to the structural component of these regimes, instead of year-over-year shifts in implicit subsidies.

The second instrument is the degree of political constraints on the executive. The assumption is that political constraints on the policy discretion of the executive are likely to limit his or her ability to develop and implement energy subsidy policies. The idea that political constraints limit fiscal policy discretion

[26] To anticipate the estimation results a bit, the extent of energy subsidies in neighboring countries alone accounts for one-quarter of the total variation in energy subsidies across countries and for up to half of the variation among net oil exporters.

[27] The database is available at http://cepii.fr/CEPII/fr/bdd_modele/presentation.asp?id=6.

has been established empirically (for example, Fatás and Mihov 2013; Ebeke and Öçer 2013). A potential issue with this instrument, however, is that if it is correlated with energy subsidies, it may also be correlated with other expenditure categories, including public social spending. The instrument would then violate the fundamental exclusion restriction. This risk, however, is limited because the econometric specification controls for overall government size (net of subsidies), in both the first- and second-stage regressions. Moreover, public social spending is a more traditional budgetary expense than energy subsidies, and the constraints on the executive would, arguably, be more binding for the latter.

When the econometric specification involves interaction terms (subsidies crossed with some conditional variables) as is the case here, the instrumental variable approach is amended to account for the additional endogenous variables generated by the interaction terms—we therefore instrument not only the subsidy-to-GDP ratio, but also its interaction terms. The matrix of instruments thus includes the additive term of the two instruments discussed above, including their respective interaction terms with each conditional variable.

Estimation Results

Baseline Estimations (Linear Model)

Equipped with the above framework, the model is estimated using two-stage least squares with robust standard errors. Table 7.1 presents the results of the instrumental variable estimations. The second-stage estimates are reported in panel 1 of the table and the first-stage estimates are displayed in panel 2. The table displays the results of the linear effect of subsidies on public social spending, followed by nonlinear effects, conditional on relevant country characteristics, including the quality of domestic institutions and the extent of political effectiveness. The average crowding-out effect of energy subsidies on public social spending is estimated (see column (1)) to be about two-thirds (less than unity). In addition, all the significant coefficients have the expected signs. In particular, government size independently affects the level of social spending positively. The results are unchanged when government size is replaced with total tax revenues.[28]

The first-stage regressions, which use subsidies in neighboring countries and political constraints on the executive as instruments for subsidies, show the significance of the instrumental variables, indicating a strong association, even in the presence of the full set of controls. The Hansen test of overidentification also suggests that the instruments are not strongly uncorrelated, with the residuals of the structural model at the 10 percent significance threshold. Although this level of significance may appear weak, allowing for interaction terms significantly improves the outcome of the test (see columns (2)–(4)). We can therefore

[28] Government size and tax revenues could not be included simultaneously in the regressions because of their high correlation.

Table 7.1. Energy Subsidies and Public Social Spending: The Role of Governance and Political Effectiveness

	(1)	(2)	(3)	(4)
	Panel A: Dependent Variable = Public Social Spending-to-GDP (second stage)			
Energy Subsidies to GDP	−0.661***	0.155	−0.0243	−0.237
	(0.248)	(0.713)	(−0.104)	(−0.870)
Energy Subsidies to GDP × Weak Governance		−2.502**		
		(−2.236)		
Energy Subsidies to GDP × State Fragility			−0.0887**	
			(−2.072)	
Energy Subsidies to GDP × Political Ineffectiveness				−0.965**
				(−2.561)
Weak Governance		−1.215		
		(−0.710)		
State Fragility			−0.0235	
			(−0.284)	
Political Ineffectiveness				0.161
				(0.445)
Log Initial per Capita Income	0.663	2.957	2.251	2.205
	(2.329)	(1.406)	(0.970)	(1.094)
Oil Rents to GDP		−0.000989***	−0.000967***	−0.00103***
		(−4.324)	(−4.047)	(−4.542)
Public Debt to GDP	0.002	−0.00696*	−0.00468	−0.00738*
	(0.005)	(−1.664)	(−1.114)	(−1.700)
Government Total Expenditures to GDP	0.193***	0.264***	0.258***	0.270***
	(0.028)	(9.115)	(9.101)	(9.339)
Age-Dependency Ratio	0.039	0.155***	0.156***	0.145***
	(0.047)	(3.671)	(3.492)	(3.246)
Urbanization Rate	0.016	0.0229*	0.0170	0.0226*
	(0.016)	(1.779)	(1.276)	(1.690)
Trade Openness	0.011*	0.0158***	0.0164***	0.0164***
	(0.007)	(2.811)	(2.919)	(2.738)
Output Volatility	−0.196***	0.0122	−0.0457	−0.00849
	(0.070)	(0.186)	(−0.716)	(−0.125)
Military Expenditures to GDP		−0.316***	−0.302***	−0.339***
		(−4.205)	(−4.152)	(−4.449)
	Panel B: Dependent Variable = Energy Subsidies-to-GDP (first stage)			
Energy Subsidy Intensity in Neighboring Countries	0.075***	0.076**	0.086**	0.087**
	(0.024)	(0.037)	(0.038)	(0.041)
Subsidies in Neighbors × Oil Rents to GDP		0.003**	0.003***	0.003**
		(0.001)	(0.001)	(0.001)
Subsidies in Neighbors × Weak Governance		0.305**		
		(0.143)		
Subsidies in Neighbors × State Fragility			0.015***	
			(0.006)	
Subsidies in Neighbors × Political Ineffectiveness				0.063**
				(0.031)
Constraints on the Executive	−0.296***	−0.171	−0.224**	−0.208*
	(0.087)	(0.108)	(0.100)	(0.106)
Observations	108	104	104	104
R^2	0.328	0.588	0.573	0.556
Joint Significance of Subsidies Coefficients: *p*-value		0.028	0.078	0.020
F-stat of First Stage	18.359	8.895	9.307	9.523
Hansen Overidentification Test: *p*-value	0.044	0.408	0.173	0.257

Source: Authors' calculations.

Note: All first-stage specifications include the full set of control variables as they appear in the second stage. Standard errors appear in parentheses.

*$p < .1$; **$p < .05$; ***$p < .01$.

conclude that public social spending tends to be lower on average in countries with higher energy subsidies (all expressed as percentages of GDP).

Is the crowding out exacerbated by weak governance and political ineffectiveness? One central implication of this theoretical model (see "The Political Game" section) is that the quality of domestic institutions shapes the extent of the crowding-out effect of energy subsidies on public social spending. That prediction is tested here by assessing whether the crowding out is stronger in countries exhibiting high levels of institutional and political vulnerability. To do this, the baseline specification is modified to include a battery of interaction terms characterizing the institutional and political environment. The estimated interaction terms are negative (as expected) and significant. This outcome suggests that the marginal effect of energy subsidies on public social spending is larger when governance is weak or in an environment characterized by political ineffectiveness.

CONCLUSION AND POLICY IMPLICATIONS

This chapter examines, both conceptually and empirically, the impact of energy subsidies on public social spending. It first shows that high energy subsidies and low public social spending can emerge as the equilibrium outcome of a political game between the elite and the middle class when the delivery of the public good is subject to leakages, reflecting weak domestic institutions or political ineffectiveness. The chapter then proposes an empirical strategy to test this supposition and other predictions of our model using a large cross-section of low- and middle-income countries. The chapter documents a negative statistical association between energy subsidies and public social spending before conducting a more systematic examination of a potential causal relationship between these two aggregates. Because energy subsidies and public social spending may be jointly determined in the budget process, OLS estimates would suffer from a simultaneity bias. To address this concern and other potential sources of endogeneity in the cross-section estimations, an identification strategy is adopted whereby subsidies in a given country are instrumented by the level of subsidies in neighboring countries and political constraints on the executive. The instrumental variable estimations indeed suggest a causal relationship between energy subsidies and public social spending. More specifically, the analysis finds that public spending on education and health were, on average, two-thirds percentage point of GDP lower in countries where energy subsidies were 1 percentage point of GDP higher. Moreover, the crowding out is stronger when governance is weak and in an environment of political ineffectiveness.

The findings have important policy implications. On the one hand, they suggest that non-resource-rich countries with narrow fiscal space would have to move expeditiously with subsidy reform to relax the constraints weighing on public social spending. On the other hand, resource-rich economies will find it challenging to keep energy subsidies, in view of mounting social spending pressures, including from the youth, given the volatile nature of commodity prices. The recent sharp drop in global oil prices seems to validate this point. In fact, in line with the conceptual framework and empirical findings, resource-rich countries were somewhat able to afford high energy subsidies with relatively limited crowding out of public social spending thanks to their large fiscal space at a time when oil prices were relatively high. Those subsidy regimes will clearly be harder to sustain at much-depressed oil prices, as existing fiscal buffers get eroded. On the positive side, reforming energy subsidies is likely to pose fewer political headaches at low international oil prices. The recent sharp drop in global oil prices, therefore, represents a golden opportunity for governments, resource-rich and non-resource-rich alike, to durably reform energy subsidies. In that vein, depoliticizing domestic energy pricing by, for instance, adopting an automatic pricing mechanism (see Coady and others 2012), seems to be a good transition toward fully deregulated energy prices.

ANNEX 7.1. SUPPLEMENTARY TABLES AND FIGURES

Annex Table 7.1.1. List of Countries in the Sample

Albania	Ecuador	Malawi	Syria
Algeria	Egypt	Malaysia	Tajikistan
Angola	El Salvador	Mali	Tanzania
Argentina	Equatorial Guinea	Mauritania	Thailand
Armenia	Eritrea	Mauritius	Togo
Azerbaijan	Fiji	Mexico	Trinidad and Tobago
Bahrain	Gabon	Moldova	Tunisia
Belarus	The Gambia	Morocco	Turkey
Benin	Georgia	Mozambique	Uganda
Bhutan	Ghana	Namibia	Ukraine
Bolivia	Guatemala	Nepal	United Arab Emirates
Botswana	Guinea	Nicaragua	Uruguay
Brazil	Guinea-Bissau	Niger	Venezuela
Bulgaria	Guyana	Oman	Vietnam
Burkina Faso	Hungary	Pakistan	Yemen
Burundi	India	Panama	Zambia
Cambodia	Indonesia	Paraguay	
Cameroon	Iran	Peru	
Cabo Verde	Jordan	Philippines	
Central African Republic	Kazakhstan	Poland	
Chad	Kenya	Qatar	
Chile	Kuwait	Republic of Congo	
China	Kyrgyz Rep.	Romania	
Colombia	Lao P.D.R.	Russia	
Comoros	Latvia	Rwanda	
Costa Rica	Lebanon	Saudi Arabia	
Croatia	Lesotho	Senegal	
Côte d'Ivoire	Liberia	Sierra Leone	
Democratic Republic of the Congo	Libya	Solomon Islands	
Djibouti	Lithuania	South Africa	
Dominican Republic	Madagascar	Swaziland	

Annex Figure 7.1.1. Energy Subsidies Intensity around the Globe (2006 vs. 2011)
(Percent of GDP)

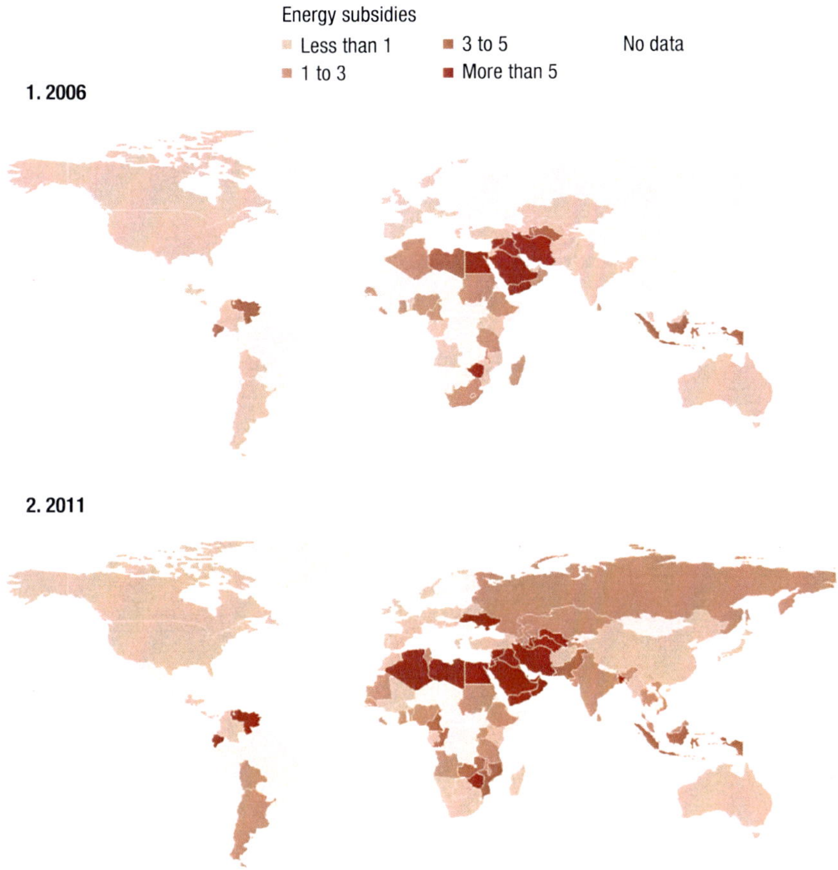

Source: Clements and others 2013.

Annex Figure 7.1.2. Energy Subsidies Intensity: Zoom on the MENA Region (2006 vs. 2011)

(Percent of GDP)

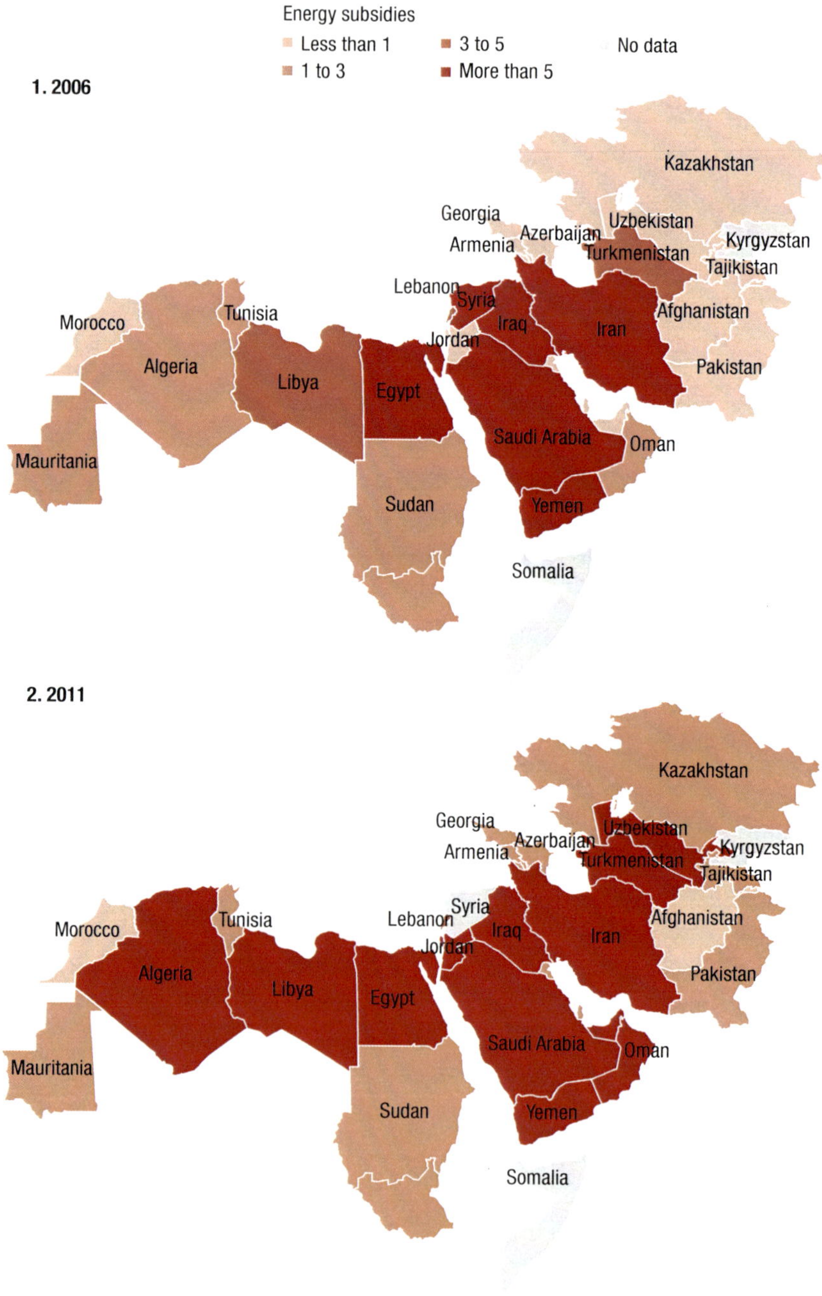

Source: Clements and others 2013.

REFERENCES

Abed, G. T., and S. Gupta. 2002. *Governance, Corruption, and Economic Performance.* Washington, DC: International Monetary Fund.

Acemoglu, D. 2014. Political Economy Lecture Notes. MIT, Cambridge, MA.

———, and J. A. Robinson. 2001. "A Theory of Political Transitions." *American Economic Review* 91 (4): 938–63.

Arze del Granado, F. J., D. Coady, and R. Gillingham. 2012. "The Unequal Benefits of Fuel Subsidies: A Review of Evidence for Developing Countries." *World Development* 40 (11): 2234–48.

Baqir, R. 2002. "Social Sector Spending in a Panel of Countries." Working Paper 02/35, International Monetary Fund, Washington, DC.

Clements, B., D. Coady, S. Fabrizio, S. Gupta, T. Alleyne, and C. Sdralevich. 2013. *Energy Subsidy Reform: Lessons and Implications.* Washington, DC: International Monetary Fund.

Clements, B., S. Gupta, and M. Nozaki. 2013. "What Happens to Social Spending in IMF-Supported Programmes?" *Applied Economics* 45: 4022–33.

Coady, D., J. Arze del Granado, L. Eyraud, H. Jin, V. Thakoor, A. Tuladhar, and L. Nemeth. 2012. "Automatic Fuel Pricing Mechanisms with Price Smoothing: Design, Implementation, and Fiscal Implications." Technical Notes and Manuals 12/03, International Monetary Fund, Washington, DC.

Coate, S., and S. Morris. 1995. "On the Form of Transfers to Special Interests." *Journal of Political Economy* 103 (6): 1210–35.

Ebeke, C., and D. Öçer. 2013. "Fiscal Policy over the Election Cycle in Low-Income Countries." Working Paper 13/53, International Monetary Fund, Washington, DC.

Fatás, A., and I. Mihov. 2013. "Policy Volatility, Institutions, and Economic Growth." *Review of Economics and Statistics* 95 (2): 362–76.

International Energy Agency (IEA). 2011. "Development in Energy Subsidies." In *World Energy Outlook.* Paris: IEA.

IEA, Organization of the Petroleum Exporting Countries, Organisation for Economic Co-operation and Development, and World Bank. 2010. *Analysis of the Scope of Energy Subsidies and Suggestions for the G-20 Initiative.* Joint report submitted to the G-20 Summit Meeting, Toronto, Ontario, Canada, June 26–27.

International Monetary Fund (IMF). 2003. "Fiscal Adjustment in IMF-Supported Programs." Independent Evaluation Office, Washington, DC.

———. 2013a. "Energy Subsidy Reform: Lessons and Implications." Board Paper, IMF, Washington.

———. 2013b. *Regional Economic Outlook, Middle-East and Central Asia.* World Economic and Financial Surveys. Washington, DC: International Monetary Fund.

———. 2014. "Fiscal Policy and Inequality." Policy Paper, IMF, Washington, DC.

Keen, M., and B. Lockwood. 2010. "The Value Added Tax: Its Causes and Consequences." *Journal of Development Economics* 92 (2): 138–51.

Koplow, D. 2009. "Measuring Energy Subsidies Using the Price-Gap Approach: What Does It Leave Out?" International Institute for Sustainable Development, Winnipeg.

Mauro, P. 1998. "Corruption and the Composition of Government Expenditure." *Journal of Public Economics* 69 (2): 263–79.

Parry, I., D. Heine, E. Lis, and S. Li. 2014. *Getting Energy Prices Right: From Principle to Practice.* Washington, DC: International Monetary Fund.

Plante, M. 2014. "The Long-Run Macroeconomic Impacts of Fuel Subsidies." *Journal of Development Economics* 107 (March): 129–43.

Strand, J. 2013. "Political Economy Aspects of Fuel Subsidies: A Conceptual Framework." Policy Research Working Paper 6392, World Bank, Washington, DC.

World Bank. 2010. "Subsidies in the Energy Sector: An Overview." Background Paper for the World Bank Group Energy Sector Strategy, Washington, DC.

———. 2013. World Development Indicators Database. World Bank, Washington, DC.

CHAPTER 8

It's Politics, Stupid! Political Constraints Determine Governments' Reactions to the Great Recession

FABIAN GUNZINGER AND JAN-EGBERT STURM[1]

INTRODUCTION

After the collapse of Lehman Brothers in September 2008, the world economy was hit by an economic crisis of a scale not seen since the Great Depression; during the winter half-year 2008/2009 world trade collapsed by almost 20 percent while world industrial production shrank by about 12 percent. The Great Recession, as the shock came to be known, did—at least in terms of its size—come as a surprise to virtually everyone. Governments around the world were surprised too, yet many reacted quickly by introducing fiscal stimulus packages.

However, the size of these packages varied considerably across countries. The UNCTAD Trade and Development Report (UNCTAD 2009) highlights that countries such as Kazakhstan, Saudi Arabia and Singapore had scheduled to implement discretionary packages amounting to 11.1, 9.2 and 8 percent of GDP, respectively. On the other end of the spectrum, the packages scheduled by the

This chapter is reprinted from *Kyklos*, Vol. 69, Fabian Gunzinger and Jan-Egbert Sturm, "It's Politics, Stupid! Political Constraints Determine Governments' Reactions to the Great Recession," ©2016, with permission from Wiley.

[1] Fabian Gunzinger: Department of Economics, University of Oxford, United Kingdom, fabian.gunzinger@economics.ox.ac.uk; Jan-Egbert Sturm: KOF Swiss Economic Institute, ETH Zurich, Leonhardstrasse 21, 8092 Zurich, Switzerland and CESifo, Munich, Germany, sturm@kof.ethz.ch, phone: +41 44 632 5001, fax: +41 44 632 1150 (corresponding author). We thank Stefan Boes, Konstantin Büchel, Christian Busch, Malin Hu, Marie Proprawe, Nora Strecker, Lukas Voellmy, James R. Vreeland and participants of the 11th Carroll Round at Georgetown University (Washington, D.C., 21 April 2012), the Beyond Basic Questions Workshop (Lucerne, 13-15 June 2013), the Silvaplana Workshop in Political Economy (Pontresina, 20-24 July 2013), the ECB Public Finance Workshop (Frankfurt, 16 October 2013), the Economics Seminar at the University of Reading (10 February 2014), the 2014 Workshop on Political Economy at the Catholic University of Milan (12-13 May 2014), the Symposium on The Future of Political Economy (Freiburg, 29-31 May 2014), the International Political Economy Society (IPES) meeting (Washington, D.C., 14-15 November 2014), as well as anonymous referees and the editors for helpful suggestions and comments. All remaining errors are ours.

governments in Italy and Switzerland were 0.3 and 0.5 percent of their respective GDP levels.[2]

What explains these differences? Policy-oriented organizations and recent academic research have so far concentrated on three factors: "need," the size of the shortfall in aggregate demand that discretionary spending aims to compensate for; "fiscal space," the government's fiscal ability to spend in time of need; and "effectiveness," the fraction of the fiscal spending that translates into aggregate demand.[3]

In contrast, the role of domestic political factors is often neglected. Given that fiscal policy is enacted within a political environment, this environment should be expected to influence the outcome. In this paper we attempt to address this shortcoming by explicitly taking politics into account. We do this by estimating the effect of political constraints on the size of stimulus packages that were enacted in the wake of the crisis. We approximate the degree of political constraints by looking at whether a country's executive party had control over the majority of legislative branches that are relevant for policy making. If it did, we consider it to have been free of political constraints as it had unilateral law-making power and was not required to cooperate with the opposition in order to enact fiscal stimulus measures.

We find that the effect of political constraints on the size of fiscal stimulus packages that governments have enacted in reaction to the shock of 2008–09 is large, statistically significant and robust to alternative dependent variables, alternative model specifications and changes in the sample. Our results suggest that on average, governments without political constraints have implemented stimulus packages that were—depending on the fiscal stimulus measure used—about 1 to 2.7 percentage points of GDP larger in size than packages enacted by governments that faced political constraints, and thus did have to cooperate with the opposition.

What our results do not and cannot show is whether these stimulus packages were appropriate responses to the crisis in the sense that they were effective in supporting economic recovery. For that we would have to analyse the consequences of different fiscal measures on the business cycle. There is a substantial, at times ideologically driven, literature on these questions,[4] but our concern here is a different one: we are interested in the drivers behind the size of these stimulus packages, not in their effectiveness.

---

[2] For an overview of stimulus sizes for all countries, see Annex Table 8.1.6.

[3] See, for instance, OECD (2009), IMF (2009a), Aizenman and Jinjarak (2011) and Ilzetzki et al. (2013). Aizenman and Jinjarak (2011) directly test for, and confirm, their importance for the size of stimulus packages, while the findings of Ilzetzki et al. (2013) suggest that more fiscal space and less trade openness makes stimulus more effective. For a more elaborate discussion on the link between fiscal space, or "fiscal leeway," and fiscal policy, see Blanchard et al. (2010).

[4] See, for instance, Auerbach and Gorodnichenko (2012), Chodorow-Reich et al. (2012), Cogan and Taylor (2009), Conley and Dupor (2013), Feyrer and Sacerdote (2011), Furceri and Sousa (2011).

The remainder of this paper is organized as follows. The second section discusses our conceptual framework. In the third section a selective overview of the related literature is given. Whereas the data and the empirical model are introduced in the fourth section, the fifth section presents the empirical results. The sixth section offers some concluding remarks.

CONCEPTUAL FRAMEWORK

Why should political constraints have an impact on a government's response to an economic shock? A vast literature on economic voting finds that if voters are satisfied with the economic performance prior to an election, they re-elect the incumbent government while if they are not, they do not.[5] Bartels (2011) looks at the electoral consequences of economic stimulus packages during the Great Recession and finds that

> voters consistently punish . . . incumbent governments for bad economic conditions, with little apparent regard for the ideology of the government or global economic conditions at the time of the election. [There is also] some evidence of electoral responses to specific fiscal policy choices, most notably, a boost in incumbent governments' electoral support associated with spending on economic stimulus programs. (p. 1)

These findings have strong implications for political incentives. If incumbent governments expect to be punished for bad economic performance and to be rewarded for enacting stimulus packages in the wake of economic downturns, then we should expect them to enact stimulus packages of a size they deem optimal given need, fiscal space and the effectiveness of such packages. For the same reason, we would expect opposition parties to try to block, delay or reduce the size of such packages. In addition to political calculus, any type of fiscal stimulus will have distributional consequences that the opposition may oppose based on ideological differences. Hence, in countries where the opposition has the political means to influence legislation, we should, everything else being equal, expect stimulus packages to be smaller, at least initially.

What about autocratic regimes? To the extent that the legitimacy of the political regime depends on its delivery of economic progress, the same logic for enacting fiscal stimulus packages applies. Olson (2000) argues that a stable and durable autocratic regime has a strong interest to provide prosperity-enhancing public goods to protect the economic system from which it extracts taxes. When faced with a shortfall in aggregate demand, the goal of such a regime is the preservation of its rent, creating the incentive to introduce fiscal stimulus measures. What is different, of course, is the absence of an opposition that can delay or negotiate down the size of such packages or attempt to change its composition. All else equal, we therefore expect packages of non-democracies, like those in democracies

[5] For major contributions see Lewis-Beck (1988) and Duch and Stevenson (2008). For summaries of the literature see Lewis-Beck and Paldam (2000) and Hibbs (2006).

that do not face political constraints, to be larger than those of democracies that do face such constraints.

The above reasoning rests on the premise that voters hold the government responsible for poor economic conditions, and reward it for enacting stimulus packages as a reaction to crises, regardless of whether the government faces political constraints or not. If this assumption is relaxed, then alternative interpretations for the negative relationship between the size of stimulus packages and political constraints emerge.

Suppose that voters realise that politically constrained governments should not be (fully) blamed for poor economic conditions. In such a case, constrained governments might spend less political capital and effort on enacting the stimulus package they deem optimal, because they know that they will not be blamed (as much) for a poor economic recovery. The observed outcome would remain the same: we would expect stimulus packages to be smaller in the presence of political constraints.

A further explanation for the negative relationship is that political constraints might prevent governments from enacting stimulus packages that are larger than what is socially optimal. If unconstrained governments are faced with an exogenous economic shock that reduces their re-election chances, this might shorten their time-horizon substantially. As a result, such governments might try to enact stimulus packages that are larger than what is socially optimal as a high-risk strategy to secure re-election. Political constraints could prevent this kind of behaviour. Not only would they make the implementation of oversized packages more difficult, but also the political burden of facing poor economic conditions would, as argued above, be shared with the opposition and so the time-horizon of such governments would not be shortened as much.

All of these explanations have in common that they lead to a negative relationship between stimulus size and political constraints and, given the data at hand, we cannot empirically discriminate between them. Nevertheless, they all underline the main message of this paper: political constraints matter.

RELATED LITERATURE

There are three strands of the literature on the interaction between politics and economics that are related to our argument.

First, there is research that highlights the importance of politics for both fiscal and monetary policy outcomes: Porteba (1994) finds that one-party governments can and do react faster to unexpected fiscal deficit shocks than their divided-government counterparts. Weise (2012) concludes that the political environment in the United States in the 1970s was a main determinant of the Federal Reserve's too moderate anti-inflationary policy, and that a change in the political environment was also behind the Federal Reserve's switch to a more aggressive policy after 1979. Spolaore (2004) argues that cabinet systems in which there is a single decision maker adjust faster to shocks than systems with multiple decision makers.

A second strand highlights political economy considerations as a major drawback for discretionary fiscal policy. Blinder (1997) outlines the merits of moving a greater number of policy decisions away from the realm of politics into the realm of technocracy, so as to make them the result of a deliberative and objective process rather than the outgrowth of political considerations. Blanchard et al. (2010) mention the limits that political constraints impose on the de facto usefulness of discretionary fiscal policy. Cecchetti (2002) argues that when it comes to fiscal policy, political considerations tend to collide with economic prescriptions, while Romer (2012) mentions political-economy aspects to be important in understanding fiscal policy responses to the crisis.

Finally, Armingeon (2012) directly investigates the importance of politics in government's reaction to the Great Recession. He finds that a unified government was a necessary condition for deviating from what he calls the default reaction to the crisis: a moderate fiscal expansion. In particular, in his qualitative and categorical analysis, he finds that it was only unified governments that enacted large fiscal stimulus packages. While these findings indicate that politics has played a role in determining the size of fiscal stimulus packages, they provide limited information on the size and strength of this relationship. It is this literature to which our paper contributes most directly.

EMPIRICAL MODEL AND DATA DESCRIPTION

Our estimation relies on a simple OLS framework, with stimulus package size as the dependent variable, political constraints as the main explanatory variable, and a set of control variables to capture need, fiscal space, and effectiveness. This section discusses the precise definition, measurement and data sources for each of these variables.

Size of Stimulus Packages

To measure the size of the fiscal stimulus we rely on two different sources and construct four different variables. All four of these variables have in common that they concentrate on fiscal policy measures initiated or carried out in the crisis year 2009.[6] We consider the bankruptcy of Lehman Brothers in autumn 2008 and the subsequent collapse in world trade as a largely exogenous shock and do not want to mix this up with events, like the euro crisis, happening after an initial recovery in the second half of 2009 and early 2010.

[6] We consciously decide against differentiating between expenditure increases and bank bailouts. The reason is that the underlying political calculus for incumbent and opposition parties should be the same: if bailing out banks helps alleviate the economic shock (or prevent an even larger one), incumbents should want to do it, while the opposition should want to prevent or at least delay it. As such, the expenditures on bank bailouts are simply part of the overall fiscal package. However, taking those countries out in which substantial bank bailouts have occurred does not change our results.

Our first variable is directly taken from Table 1.8 in UNCTAD (2009). This table was compiled by the UNCTAD secretariat using a number of different sources.[7] The variable corresponds to discretionary measures on public spending or revenues in response to the financial crisis, excluding so-called automatic stabilizers and scheduled to be implemented across a one- to three-year window. Hence, it covers discretionary "promises" of governments in selected countries as percentage of GDP over a somewhat varying implementation horizon. There are a few caveats when using this data: time horizons of these stimulus packages differ substantially and the exact definition of what is part of a stimulus package is likely to be country- and source-dependent to some extent.[8] Furthermore, this particular data set only allows us to use a sample of 44 OECD and emerging market countries. Both data quality and coverage have led us to also look for other data sources.

The second variable is taken from Appendix Table 5 in Horton et al. (2009). It compares primary deficit forecasts for 2009 as published by the IMF in its July 2009 Update (IMF 2009b) and its October 2007 release of the *World Economic Outlook* (IMF 2007). We view this as a measure for the forecasted change in fiscal policy induced by the Great Recession and not related to changing interest payments of the government. The difference with the UNCTAD measure is twofold. First, it includes both discretionary measures as well as changes caused by automatic stabilizers.[9] Second, it has a fixed time horizon: it reflects "promises" for the year 2009. These differences notwithstanding, in both cases, we are looking at forecasts, i.e., "promises," and not at actual realizations.

But there might be a difference between the political promises for spending made during the crisis year and the spending that was actually implemented. To take this into account, our two remaining variables focus on actual realizations. Focusing on actual spending also has the advantage that it avoids issues surrounding the definition of stimulus packages, which, as discussed above, are likely to differ between countries. To construct our variables we use information released in the April 2013 IMF *World Economic Outlook* (IMF 2013) and take actual changes in *primary* fiscal deficits between 2008 and 2009. To increase the sample size, we also look at actual changes in (total) fiscal deficits during the crisis year.

Table 8.1 summarizes our four main dependent variables. Overall, the size of the fiscal stimulus is substantial with averages ranging from close to 2.5 to

[7] For six countries where UNCTAD does not provide data, we use data from OECD (2009). The relevant countries are the Czech Republic, Denmark, Finland, Luxembourg, New Zealand and Slovak Republic.

[8] Note, however, a country's method for measuring its stimulus package is unlikely to be correlated with the size of that package. The consistency of our results is therefore not compromised.

[9] Conceptually, we prefer a measure that only takes discretionary aspects into account. However, we do have to realize that it is far from obvious to disentangle cyclical and structural movements in fiscal data. Cyclically adjusted data are well-known to be heavily revised—up to the size of the actual measure (see, e.g., Orphanides [2001], Orphanides and Van Norden [2002] and Jong-a-Pin et al. [2012])—making it problematic to link it to real-time decisions. Furthermore, the sample of countries for which such data is available is very limited. As it is likely that the extent of automatic stabilizers in an economy is related to the size of the public sector, we include the latter as an explanatory variable in all of our models.

Table 8.1. Descriptive Statistics and Correlation Matrix for the Dependent Variables

		Descriptive statistics					Source
		Obs.	Average	Standard Deviation	Minimum	Maximum	
Promised Stimulus 2008–12	Discretionary measures	44	2.44	3.39	−8.3	8.0	UNCTAD
Promised Stimulus 2008–09	Change forecasted primary deficit	40	4.97	3.29	−0.7	14.9	IMF 2009b/2007
Realized Stimulus in 2009	Change primary deficit 2009 (% 2007-GDP)	108	4.16	4.31	−3.4	21.6	IMF 2013
	(only democracies)	77	3.58	3.36	−3.4	15.7	IMF 2013
Realized Stimulus in 2009	Change deficit 2009 (% 2007-GDP)	151	4.00	4.48	−4.1	25.3	IMF 2013
	(only democracies)	100	3.52	3.50	−4.1	17.5	IMF 2013

		correlation \ obs.					
Variable description		(1)	(2)	(3)	(4)	(5)	(6)
(1) Promised Stimulus 2008–12	Discretionary measures		36	40	36	44	39
(2) Promised Stimulus 2008–09	Change forecasted primary deficit	−0.01		37	34	40	36
(3) Realized Stimulus in 2009	Change primary deficit 2009 (% 2007-GDP)	0.14	0.75		77	108	77
(4)	(only democracies)	−0.01	0.79	1.00		77	77
(5) Realized Stimulus in 2009	Change deficit 2009 (% 2007-GDP)	0.03	0.74	0.98	0.96		100
(6)	(only democracies)	−0.11	0.77	0.96	0.96	1.00	
	Correlation with the political constraints dummy:	−0.31	−0.29	−0.16	−0.18	−0.10	−0.11

almost 5 percent of (pre-crisis) GDP. Although it covers up to three years, the UNCTAD variable contains the lowest values. A likely explanation for this is that by construction, it is the only variable that does not include the effect of automatic stabilizers. The table also reveals that, on average, democracies have enacted smaller fiscal stimulus measures than autocracies.[10] Finally, with standard deviations between 3.3 and 4.5 percent of GDP, it is also safe to say that there is wide variation in the size of stimulus packages initiated during the Great Recession.

Political Constraints

Political constraints are captured by a binary variable that equals one if during the Great Recession (i.e., during the winter of 2008/2009) a country's executive party did not have a majority in the legislative branches that have law-making power. Conversely, the variable is equal to zero if throughout that same period, the party of the executive did have a majority in these branches and could therefore unilaterally enact law. All political variables—including this one—are taken from the 2012 version of the Database of Political Institutions (Beck et al. 2001). This particular variable is based on the variable ALLHOUSE.[11,12]

Given the exogenous character of the shock we are analyzing, we are convinced that we can treat our political constraint dummy as exogenous. Nonetheless, in Annex 8.1, we present robustness exercises where we investigate possible endogeneity issues. The results support our view.

While the constraints dummy likely captures the most direct dimensions of political constraints, there are more subtle constraints that, by virtue of being a dummy variable, it cannot capture. Consider, as an example, the events in the United States in early 2011. At the time the American Recovery and Reinvestment Act was enacted and signed into law by the Democratic president Barack Obama, the Democratic Party also controlled both the Senate and the House of Representatives. So, according to the definition of our constraints dummy, the Democrats were free of political constraints. And yet, there is evidence to suggest that both the Democratic Party's internal disputes as well as public pressure prevented the stimulus package from being even larger than the

[10] In defining democracies, we use the classification of Cheibub et al. (2010). Accordingly, the basic conditions for a regime to be coded as democratic are that i) the executive and legislative are elected and ii) multiple parties are allowed for and exist. A two-group mean-comparison test reveals that the averages of democracies and non-democracies are significantly different from each other.

[11] During the year 2009, the only election that potentially led to a change in this variable relative to 2008 was the legislative election in June 2009 in Argentina. We, however, take values as relevant for the winter 2008/2009, which always equal those for 2008.

[12] Henisz (2000; 2002) constructed political constraint variables that indicate whether the executive party is the largest party in the upper and lower house. As being the largest party does not necessarily imply having a majority, the correlations between the ALLHOUSE variable and those from Henisz are merely around 0.3. Given that in our line of argumentation having a majority is indispensable, we stick to using the ALLHOUSE variable.

actual $787 billion. Alter (2011) and Wallace-Wells (2001) report, for instance, that Christina Romer and Larry Summers, the President's key economic advisers at the time, both believed that to close the entire output gap, the stimulus package would need to be above the politically incendiary 1 trillion dollar mark. So, as in the case of our stimulus measures, it is important to realize that while the variable captures an important part of what we aim to measure, it cannot account for all the country-specific subtleties.

Need for Fiscal Stimulus

The need for discretionary measures depends on both the expected size and type of the shock and the expected degree to which automatic stabilizers will alleviate it.

To proxy the size of the shock, we use the realised drop in exports during the winter half-year 2008/2009 relative to the winter half-year 2007/2008, measured as a percentage of 2007 GDP levels. For this we resort to the monthly export figures published in the IMF Direction of Trade Statistics. The timing of when stimulus measures were announced and implemented makes it very unlikely that they had a substantial impact on the size of this export shock, so that we can treat the variable as exogenous.

To proxy the role of automatic stabilizers we follow Gali (1994) and use the pre-crisis level of government expenditure as a percentage of GDP, as measured for 2007 and published by the IMF in April 2013 (IMF 2013). We thus assume that a larger public sector is more stabilizing than a smaller one. Depending on the dependent variable, we expect either a positive or a negative effect of this variable: for a given output gap, a higher level of government expenditure should reduce the size of discretionary measures, while it should increase the change in the deficit (i.e., in the total fiscal stimulus). The change in the deficit should increase because for a given size of the discretionary stimulus, higher government expenditures automatically alleviate the negative consequences of the shock, independent of the political decision-making process.

Fiscal Space

To capture a government's fiscal space, we use two variables: the gross public debt-to-GDP ratio as measured for 2007, and the deficit-to-GDP ratio for 2007. Both are taken from the IMF *World Economic Outlook* published in April 2013 (IMF 2013). The differences across countries, particularly in pre-crisis deficit levels, are substantial. These reflect, among other things, differences in natural resources. In particular, those countries that export substantial amounts of oil or gas tend to have much smaller deficits or even substantial surpluses.[13]

[13] We have also looked into using oil and gas reserves as published by British Petroleum. However, that would reduce our sample substantially.

Effectiveness of Fiscal Stimulus

To take the effectiveness of any fiscal stimulus into account, we include a broad measure of economic globalization as part of the KOF Globalization Index. We refer to figures for the year 2007. Small open economies have fewer opportunities to stimulate their own economy because a larger part of a given measure evaporates away to the rest of the world. At the same time, they also benefit more from measures undertaken by large trading partners. Both of these mechanisms reduce incentives to undertake large fiscal stimulus measures.

Table 8.2 shows the descriptive statistics for the above-mentioned right-hand-side variables as well as for all variables used in our robustness exercises and discussed in Annex 8.1.[14] Regarding our main variable of interest, about half of the countries in our sample face political constraint, in the sense that the executive and legislative bodies are controlled by different parties. Quite a number of the countries in our sample are non-democratic. When focusing on democracies only, around 70 percent of the governments were not able to enact law unilaterally and were thereby politically constrained during the crisis period. The constraints dummy is not highly correlated with any of the control variables, so that including these variables into the model will most likely only have the effect of increasing the precision by which we can estimate the effect of the constraints dummy. There is also hardly any correlation among the control variables themselves, with the natural exception being the dummies for European Union (EU) and euro area membership, where the correlation coefficient is 0.71. Apart from that, the second highest correlation coefficient is between narrow money growth and official reserves and equals 0.56. Furthermore, our economic globalization measure and our measure of government size have a high absolute correlation of 0.45; more globalized economies, which often are European, also tend to have higher government expenditure shares.[15]

EMPIRICAL RESULTS

Table 8.3 presents our main results. Columns (1), (2), (3) and (5) report results for each of the four dependent variables using the full sample for which data is available.[16] Columns (4) and (6) of the table restrict the sample of our two realised deficit measures to only democratic countries.

---

[14] We try to avoid issues of reverse causality by using pre-crisis data—data that is not yet influenced by the economic shock following the collapse of Lehman Brothers in September 2008.

[15] This is in line with the findings of Rodrik (1998). He makes the point that more open economies are more likely to have larger government sectors as a form of insurance against the volatility created by openness.

[16] The last row in Table 8.1 reports correlation coefficients between the political constraint dummy and these dependent variables. All of these are negative and mostly statistically significant indicating that also in a parsimonious regression that only includes political constraints and a constant, political constraints reduce the size of the stimulus measures. The coefficient estimates of such bivariate regressions (not shown) are comparable to those presented in Table 8.3.

Table 8.2. Descriptive Statistics and Correlation Matrix for the Main Explanatory Variables

	Descriptive Statistics					
	Obs.	Average	Standard Deviation	Minimum	Maximum	Source
Political Constraint Dummy	151	0.54	0.50	0.0	1.0	DPI2012
Government Expenditures in 2007	151	30.25	10.38	7.6	52.6	IMF, WEO April 2013
Change in 2009 Growth Forecast in April 2009 r.t. April 2008	148	–0.47	1.23	–5.0	4.1	IMF, WEO April 2009/October 2008
Change of Exports in Winter 2008/09 (%20 07-GDP)	143	–4.03	5.31	–44.2	2.6	IMF, DOTS 2013
Percent Change Local Currency to USD between 2008:Q2 and 2008:Q4	140	12.43	11.68	–8.0	63.5	IMF
Growth Official Reserves (in USD) between 2008:Q2 and 2008:Q4	142	–4.65	18.27	–48.1	94.9	IMF
Government Debt in 2007 (percent of GDP)	145	49.22	50.17	1.3	494.9	IMF, WEO April 2013
Government Deficit in 2007 (percent of GDP)	151	–0.48	6.91	–57.1	15.7	IMF, WEO April 2013
Lending Rate in Winter 2008/09	116	13.46	7.95	1.0	52.6	IMF
Central Bank Independence, Legal Measure	88	0.62	0.20	0.2	0.9	Crowe and Meade (2008)
Central Bank Governor Irregular Turnover Rate	124	0.12	0.10	0.0	0.6	KOF
Change in the Lending Rate between August and December 2008	116	0.46	2.33	–8.1	8.2	IMF
Growth Rate of M1 between August and December 2008	78	5.14	10.25	–18.4	31.7	Datastream, central banks
KOF Economic Globalization in 2007	131	63.82	16.95	23.9	96.4	KOF
KOF Political Globalization in 2007	150	69.45	19.64	23.4	98.0	KOF
G20 Dummy	151	0.12	0.33	0.0	1.0	G20
Dummy for EU Membership	151	0.18	0.38	0.0	1.0	EU
Dummy for EMU/Euro Area Membership	151	0.10	0.30	0.0	1.0	ECB
Under an IMF Program	151	0.54	0.50	0.0	1.0	ECB

(continued)

Table 8.2. Descriptive Statistics and Correlation Matrix for the Main Explanatory Variables *(continued)*

Variable Description	Correlation\Observations (1)	(2)	(3)	(4)	(5)	(6)	(7)	(8)	(9)	(10)	(11)	(12)	(13)	(14)	(15)	(16)	(17)	(18)	(19)
(1) Political Constraint Dummy		151	148	143	140	142	145	151	116	88	124	116	78	131	150	151	151	151	151
(2) Government Expenditures in 2007	0.10		148	143	140	142	145	151	116	88	124	116	78	131	150	151	151	151	151
(3) Change in 2009 Growth Forecast in April 2009 r.t. April 2008	0.04	−0.13		140	138	139	142	148	114	86	121	114	77	129	147	148	148	148	148
(4) Change of Exports in Winter 2008/09 (%20 07-GDP)	−0.10	−0.01	−0.27		134	134	138	143	111	86	119	111	77	127	143	143	143	143	143
(5) Percent Change Local Currency to USD between 2008:Q2 and 2008:Q4	0.24	0.24	−0.17	0.02		138	135	140	109	85	122	109	76	125	140	140	140	140	140
(6) Growth Official Reserves (in USD) between 2008:Q2 and 2008:Q4	−0.06	0.00	0.05	−0.11	−0.23		136	142	110	87	122	110	78	125	141	142	142	142	142
(7) Government Debt in 2007 (percent of GDP)	0.01	0.04	0.25	−0.45	−0.18	0.12		145	110	87	119	110	76	127	144	145	145	145	145
(8) Government Deficit in 2007 (percent of GDP)	−0.12	0.17	−0.07	0.34	−0.15	−0.14	0.21		116	88	124	116	78	131	150	151	151	151	151
(9) Lending Rate in Winter 2008/09	0.08	−0.11	−0.01	0.19	−0.01	0.13	−0.05	0.11		66	100	116	59	101	116	116	116	116	116
(10) Central Bank Independence, Legal Measure	0.28	0.22	−0.19	0.00	0.10	0.16	−0.17	0.03	0.16		86	66	68	86	88	88	88	88	88
(11) Central Bank Governor Irregular Turnover Rate	0.16	−0.15	−0.03	0.20	−0.01	0.02	−0.11	0.03	0.35	0.26		100	75	115	124	124	124	124	124
(12) Change in the Lending Rate between August and December 2008	0.09	−0.06	0.00	0.03	0.20	−0.17	−0.12	−0.02	0.28	0.20	0.31		59	101	116	116	116	116	116
(13) Growth Rate of M1 between August and December 2008	−0.07	−0.07	0.23	0.06	−0.03	0.56	0.21	0.20	0.28	−0.04	0.23	−0.11		74	77	78	78	78	78
(14) KOF Economic Globalization in 2007	0.24	0.48	−0.31	−0.37	0.31	−0.09	−0.11	−0.26	−0.23	0.27	−0.10	0.02	−0.35		131	131	131	131	131
(15) KOF Political Globalization in 2007	0.10	0.20	−0.21	0.12	0.38	−0.20	−0.10	0.14	−0.03	0.17	0.09	0.14	−0.19	0.27		150	150	150	150
(16) G20 Dummy	−0.03	0.12	−0.10	0.13	0.21	−0.05	0.05	0.06	−0.04	−0.10	0.01	0.04	0.05	0.00	0.38		151	151	151
(17) Dummy for EU Membership	0.25	0.54	−0.26	−0.13	0.32	−0.19	−0.05	0.04	−0.22	0.45	−0.09	0.03	−0.45	0.62	0.44	0.04		151	151
(18) Dummy for EMU/Euro Area Membership	0.13	0.44	−0.15	−0.05	0.17	−0.16	0.05	0.03	−0.19	0.40	−0.05	−0.10	−0.24	0.45	0.34	0.08	0.71		151
(19) Under an IMF Program	0.11	−0.14	0.07	0.00	−0.05	0.05	0.12	0.02	0.24	0.11	0.00	0.03	0.12	−0.31	−0.10	−0.21	−0.18	−0.19	

Table 8.3. Main Results

Variables	(1) Promised Discretionary Measures 2008–12	(2) Promised Stimulus 2008–09	(3) Realized Change Primary Deficit 2009	(4) Realized Change Primary Deficit 2009: Democracies	(5) Realized Change Deficit 2009	(6) Realized Change Deficit 2009: Democracies
Political Constraint	−0.971	−2.629**	−2.712***	−2.413**	−1.613**	−1.730*
	(−1.354)	(−2.259)	(−3.397)	(−2.223)	(−2.357)	(−1.770)
Government Expenditures in 2007 (percent of GDP)	−0.0483	−0.00225	0.0567	0.0848**	0.0527	0.0864**
	(−0.716)	(−0.0418)	(1.325)	(2.050)	(1.440)	(2.426)
Change of Exports in Winter 2008/09 (%2007-GDP)	−0.106	0.188	−0.212	−0.215	−0.154	−0.135
	(−0.596)	(0.740)	(−1.402)	(−1.366)	(−1.196)	(−0.935)
Government Debt in 2007 (percent of GDP)	−0.00356	0.000598	−0.00845	−0.0242*	−0.00451	−0.0182
	(−0.379)	(0.0350)	(−0.619)	(−1.846)	(−0.355)	(−1.445)
Government Deficit in 2007 (percent of GDP)	−0.165	−0.284***	−0.428***	−0.206*	−0.419***	−0.229*
	(−1.278)	(−3.615)	(−2.643)	(−1.882)	(−2.695)	(−1.736)
KOF Economic Globalization in 2007	−0.0803	0.0684	−0.0150	−0.0285	−0.00534	−0.0247
	(−1.082)	(1.136)	(−0.398)	(−0.812)	(−0.169)	(−0.815)
Under an IMF Program	−6.272**	−1.147	−1.216	−1.816*	−0.733	−0.888
	(−2.462)	(−1.127)	(−1.237)	(−1.948)	(−1.065)	(−1.251)
Constant	10.82***	2.561	4.658**	5.163**	3.353**	4.259*
	(3.464)	(0.770)	(2.433)	(2.236)	(2.113)	(1.981)
Observations	43	40	94	71	123	88
Adjusted R^2	0.389	0.200	0.343	0.253	0.287	0.168
Mean Dependent Variable	2.444	4.973	4.111	3.594	3.896	3.535
Standard Deviation Dependent Variable	3.432	3.292	4.318	3.289	3.998	3.090

Notes: t-statistics in parentheses. Huber-White robust standard errors are used.
$^{***}p < 0.01$, $^{**}p < 0.05$, $^{*}p < 0.1$.

The political constraints variable has a strong impact on the size of each of these fiscal stimulus measures, although it is only marginally significant when using our first measure of promises.[17] Depending upon the dependent variable the results suggest that, on average, political constraints decrease the size of the fiscal

[17] When removing the IMF dummy from the first column the political constraint variable turns significant with an estimated coefficient of about −1.8. More in general, we have checked for outlying observations and, besides some countries that were under an IMF program, did not encounter such.

Figure 8.1. Differences in Average Size of Stimulus Packages across Politically Constrained and Unconstrained Countries
(Percent of GDP)

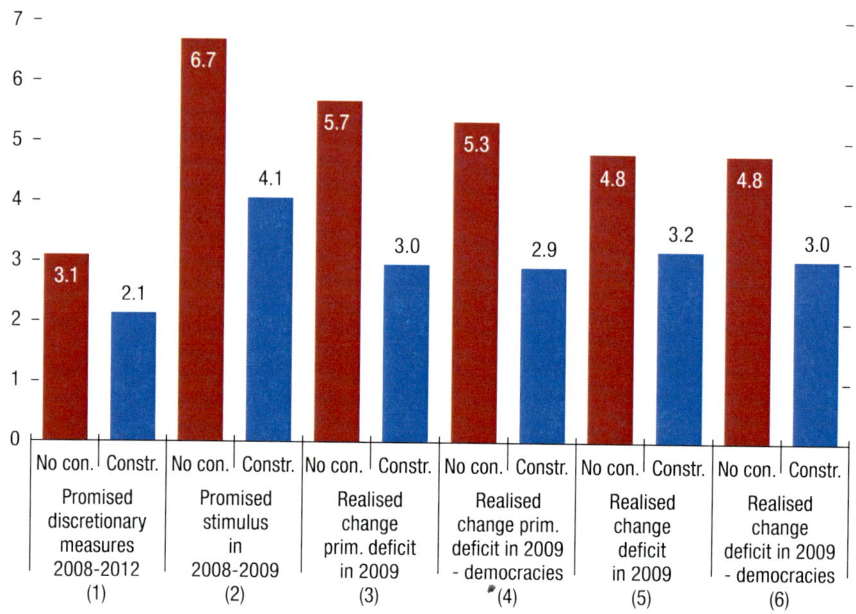

Note: This figure is based upon the results presented in Table 8.3. The numbers at the bottom of the graph refer to the columns in Table 8.3.

stimulus by between 1 and 2.7 percentage points of GDP. The next-to-last row of the table reports the average size of the stimulus packages within each sample. The average stimulus packages range from 2.4 to 5.0 percent of GDP. Relative to that, the average impact of such political constraints amounts to between 25 and 80 percent of this average size. Figure 8.1 visualises these results. It compares the average sizes of our different stimulus measures for governments that do face political constraints and for those that do not. Whereas unconstrained governments did initiate stimulus packages of on average around 5 percent of GDP, this is roughly reduced to 3 percent for those that were politically constrained. Compared to the remaining variables in the model, the political constraint variable is by far the most robust and has a high explanatory power. When removing the political constraint variable the adjusted R-squared drops by 0.09 points.[18]

Removing individual countries from our analysis or reducing the sample size by taking other specific groups of countries out (like oil-producing countries) does not affect our conclusions.

[18] Only the initial deficit share explains more of the variation in the dependent variable; its removal leads to a reduction of 0.19 point of the adjusted R-squared.

Of the other variables, only the initial government deficit turns out to be significant with the expected sign as often as our political constraints dummy; countries with high deficits enacted smaller stimulus packages, on average. The initial debt level has the expected negative sign, but is not statistically significant in most specifications. Nevertheless, fiscal space indeed appears to have been an important factor when explaining the size of the fiscal stimulus measures.

Perhaps surprisingly, "need" does not appear to have been that important. The effect of the change in exports during the winter half-year 2008/2009 mostly has the expected negative sign—a stronger drop has led to larger stimulus measures—but it is not significant.[19]

The initial size of the government sector, as measured by government expenditures as a share of GDP, turns significantly positive when focusing on realised changes in primary deficits. In line with the argument that government size largely reflects the importance of automatic stabilizers, and that larger automatic stabilizers reduce the need for discretionary stimulus in a crisis, the measure has a (insignificant) negative effect on the size of discretionary stimulus packages in column (1).[20]

Our measure of the effectiveness of the stimulus packages, the degree of globalization of a country, mostly has the expected negative sign, albeit never significant. The correlation with our measure of government size might be causing a multicollinearity problem. However, also without the government expenditures as a share of GDP included, the KOF Economic Globalization Index is never significant (and the political constraints coefficient is hardly affected by this).[21]

Being under an IMF program reduces at least the promises made by the government. Regarding actual realization it is less often significant. Nevertheless, these results indicate that this kind of international pressure does have an effect on the fiscal policy stance.

These results could be sensitive to both alternative specifications of factors we do include into our model and to the inclusion of different variables. Furthermore, the underlying sample of countries might have consequences. In Annex 8.1 we discuss a number of alternatives and present a large battery of robustness checks. In a nutshell: changing the set of explanatory variables, the sample of countries, or removing (potentially) extreme observations does not alter our conclusion. We always find very similar results to those presented in Table 8.3.

These robustness checks do provide some indication regarding the channel through which the effect is likely to emerge. When including a dummy for the occurrence of executive elections before June 2009 and interacting that with

[19] Our growth forecast comparison for the year 2009 usually did not lead to an expected significant negative coefficient and is therefore not included in this baseline regression.

[20] Although government expenditures are mathematically used in the construction of the government deficit variable, in our sample these two variables are hardly correlated (see Table 8.2). As therefore to be expected, the conclusions do not change if we include each of them separately.

[21] Removing the KOF Economic Globalization Index does, however, increase the level of significance of the government size measure somewhat. This has no effect on our main variable of interest, political constraints.

our political constraint variable, we find that in an environment without political constraints the realised primary deficit (and thus the fiscal stimulus) turns out to be about 2.4 percentage points larger than without upcoming elections. Conversely, in a country where the government faces political constraints, the occurrence of an executive election leads to a reduction of the fiscal stimulus by about 1 percentage point of GDP. This suggests that especially, but not only, during election times, political constraints tie the hands of the incumbent government. Hence, political budget cycles are more likely to occur in countries in which the executive party has control over the legislative branches. Note, though, that these interaction results should not be overemphasized (and are therefore not included in Table 8.3), as they rest upon only a handful of observations.[22]

Overall the conclusion of all our robustness tests is that our results are highly robust to changing the dependent variable, the use of alternative sets of explanatory variables and changing the sample of countries.

CONCLUDING REMARKS

In this paper, we use a simple framework to assess the impact of political constraints on the size of fiscal stimulus packages. We find that on average, political constraints reduce the size of fiscal stimulus packages by about 1 to 2.7 percentage points of GDP—an effect that is large, statistically significant and robust to alternative specifications. The results are thus in line with the widespread perception that political realities limit the de facto usefulness of discretionary fiscal policies as a tool to ameliorate negative economic shocks. To our knowledge it is, however, the first paper that quantifies that effect. Whether this implies that fiscal packages have been too small under a politically constrained government, or too large under a politically unconstrained one cannot be answered by the data at hand. For this a thorough analysis of the effectiveness of different fiscal stimulus programmes is needed. Whereas the United States, as an example of a country having an unconstrained government in our set-up, appears to have successfully implemented large fiscal stimulus measures during 2009, a politically constrained country like Switzerland has also fared well while implementing hardly any fiscal stimulus. Already this anecdotal evidence makes clear that analysing how to most successfully bring an economy back on its feet is not going to be an easy task.

The result that political constraints matter is important because in trying to make sense of policy decisions, we naturally focus on what we deem important. The accuracy of growth forecasts and, even more so, the role of fiscal space are omnipresent in policy discussions since the outset of the crisis. What our findings suggest is that discussing how legislative procedures can be designed to allow for optimal reactions to an economic crisis would be important as well.

---

[22] This is in line with the findings of Streb et al. (2009) who find that political business cycles are smaller in countries where the government faces effective checks and balances, which they proxy by incomplete control of the legislative body and adherence to the law.

ANNEX 8.1. ALTERNATIVE SPECIFICATIONS AND ROBUSTNESS CHECKS

Our main results could be sensitive to alternative specifications of factors we do include into our model, the inclusion of different explanatory variables and to changes in the underlying sample. In this annex, we briefly discuss a number of alternatives and present robustness exercises along these lines. In doing so, we concentrate on the dependent variable measuring the realised change in primary deficits for the year 2009. The results using other dependent variables are very much in line with those shown below. Overall, the important message from the robustness exercises is that the results confirm our hypothesis and show that the effect of political constraints is large, statistically significant and robust along different dimensions.

Using Forecasts to Capture the Size of the Economic Shock

Auerbach and Gorodnichenko (2012) find that the size of fiscal multipliers varies considerably over the business cycle: 0 to 0.5 in expansions, and 1 to 1.5 during recessions. This suggests that also the size of the demand shortfall could matter for the effectiveness of fiscal stimulus. An alternative to the change in export variable, we can capture the size of the economic shock based on changes in growth forecasts for the year 2009. To do so, we compare IMF projections in April 2008 (IMF 2008a) with those in October 2008 (IMF 2008b), i.e., after the collapse of Lehman Brothers, for the year 2009. This measure should capture the economic shock as perceived in the early days after the collapse of Lehman Brothers, but only little, if anything, of the stimulus measures that were enacted in reaction to it.[23]

By considering both the export and forecast measure we also, in an admittedly crude way, correct for two different types of shocks; the change in exports clearly reflects a trade shock, while the change in the growth forecast captures other types of shocks as well. To also capture a balance-of-payments crisis we take into account both the percentage change of the exchange rate vis-à-vis the US dollar and the growth in official reserves between the second and fourth quarters of 2008.[24]

Monetary Policy

Besides fiscal policy, monetary policy is another way in which the public sector can try to stimulate its economy. Hence, in those countries where—given the severity of the crisis, fiscal space and effectiveness of fiscal policy—monetary policy has reacted more strongly, the pressure on fiscal policy to act might be

[23] As is common practice in forecasting, the short-term fiscal policy assumptions used by the IMF are largely based on officially announced budgets. Hence, most if not all fiscal stimulus measures are not included in this measure, thereby alleviating the reverse causality problem.

[24] Ideally we would have also liked to take an explicit measure for real estate crises on board. However, data availability prevents us from doing so. This is therefore indirectly taken care of via our change-in-growth-forecast variable.

lower. Using both the change in policy rates, approximated by the change in the lending rate, from the beginning of the third quarter of 2008 to the start of 2009 and the growth rate of M1 during the same period, we try to capture this dimension of the overall policy reaction to the crisis.

Government Lending Rate

Although monetary policy turned expansionary around the globe and thereby also reduced refinancing costs of governments, substantial differences in interest rates still existed during the winter of 2008/2009. To reflect such cross-country differences, we include the average lending rate during the winter half-year of 2008/2009 as published by the IMF in its International Financial Statistics.[25]

Central Bank Independence

From a political-institutional point of view, the probability that the money printing press might ultimately be used to deal with high public debt levels could alleviate worries of the current government regarding the unsustainability of future higher debt levels and reduce fiscal constraints. Thus, countries in which the central bank is politically less independent from the government might be willing to increase deficits substantially more than other countries. To take this into account, we use two different indicators for central bank independence, both of which are available for a relatively large number of countries. The first one measures legal independence and goes back to the work of Cukierman (1992) and Cukierman et al. (1992). It is based on how a central bank works internally (how is the central bank governor appointed and is an explicit policy target defined) and how its relationship with the government is arranged (how are disputes settled and are there rules limiting the amount of lending to the government). Crowe and Meade (2008) have updated this *de jure* indicator of central bank independence to reflect the year 2003. Especially for emerging and developing countries such a legal measure might, however, deviate substantially from actual practice. For that reason, we follow the literature and also construct a *de facto* measure of central bank independence based on the frequency of *irregular* central bank governor turnovers.[26,27]

[25] We have also experimented with the long-term government bond yields, Treasury bill rates, money market rates and discount rates, as published by the IMF in its International Financial Statistics. These series are in general highly correlated. As, in contrast to these other interest rates, lending rates are available for most of the countries in our sample, we prefer using those. The results do not change qualitatively.

[26] Based on the work of Sturm and De Haan (2001) and Dreher et al. (2008; 2010), the KOF Swiss Economic Institute published annually a database containing information on the term in office of central bank governors for almost all countries in the world starting from the year 1970. We use the 2013 vintage and calculate the average irregular turnover rate during the period 1990–2008.

[27] We also experimented with the use of a central bank governor turnover rate that includes changes occurring after the regular term in office did end. The qualitative results are unaffected by this.

International Policy Environment

Countries more sensitive to international political pressure or that are strongly integrated in international policy coordination activities might put greater effort into stimulating their own, and thereby also foreign, economies.

After the collapse of Lehman Brothers, the general fear of an overall meltdown generated a substantial amount of political pressure on governments to act in a timely and substantial manner. As indicated by the Leader's Statement after the London Summit, the G20 very much pushed for strong coordinated actions on the side of its partners (G20 Information Centre 2009). To take this into account, we experiment with both a G20 dummy and a variable measuring the degree to which a country is politically integrated with the rest of the world, which we proxy with the political globalization measure from the KOF Globalization Index.

Whereas international pressure might have induced countries to spend more than they otherwise would have, one could also argue that an international political constraint like the Maastricht Treaty or the Stability and Growth Pact (SGP), which force member countries of the Economic and Monetary Union to focus on certain deficit and debt targets, had exactly the opposite effect. By using EU and EMU dummies, we check whether this international political constraint had an influence on the size of average fiscal stimulus measures in the euro area.

Hence, whereas international policy coordination (via the G20) might have reduced the free-rider problem during the Great Recession, the existence of other international arrangements like the SGP could have had the opposite effect. The involvement of the IMF in domestic (fiscal) policy also belongs to this latter category. In case a country was already under a program of the IMF at the start of the Great Recession, this is likely to have limited its fiscal space.

Annex Table 8.1.1 presents the results in the case in which each of these alternative variables is added to the specification listed in Table 8.3. None of these variables turns out to be significant and most importantly, the results regarding our main explanatory variable, political constraints, does not qualitatively change.

In a next step we add political-institutional variables. Including these variables only makes sense when we look at democracies. Hence, we will now restrict our attention to that particular subset.

Political System

Our main explanatory variable, the degree of political constraints, will generally be determined by institutional choices and a complex political game, both of which seem unlikely to be systematically related to the size of fiscal stimulus packages. There is a considerable body of literature in political science that shows that the two most important factors influencing the probability of one party controlling both executive and legislative bodies are the decision between presidential and parliamentary system and the choice of the voting system.[28]

---

[28] See, for instance, Lijphart (1990; 1999).

Annex Table 8.1.1. Robustness Tests for Extended Versions of the Baseline Model Using the Realized Change in Primary Deficits as Dependent Variable

Variables	(1) Change Growth Forecast for 2009	(2) Percent Change Exchange Rate	(3) Growth Official Reserves	(4) Lending Rate in Winter 2008/09	(5) CBI, Legal Measure	(6) irr. CB Government Turnover Rate	(7) Change in Lending Rate	(8) Growth Rate of M1	(9) KOF Political Globalization	(10) G20 Dummy	(11) EU Dummy	(12) Euro area Dummy
Political Constraint	−2.844***	−2.555***	−2.589***	−2.119**	−2.915***	−2.178***	−2.059**	−2.367***	−2.696***	−2.711***	−2.621***	−2.767***
	(−3.523)	(−3.306)	(−3.068)	(−2.257)	(−3.222)	(−2.989)	(−2.180)	(−3.134)	(−3.457)	(−3.371)	(−3.245)	(−3.458)
Government Expenditures in 2007 (percent of GDP)	0.0534	0.0636	0.0556	0.0626	0.0195	0.0671	0.0648	0.0226	0.0662	0.0564	0.0664	0.0447
	(1.239)	(1.640)	(1.628)	(1.035)	(0.513)	(1.551)	(1.076)	(0.624)	(1.436)	(1.274)	(1.313)	(1.014)
Change of Exports in Winter 2008/09 (%2007–GDP)	−0.189	−0.0704	−0.0688	−0.315*	−0.0423	−0.0868	−0.358*	0.100	−0.199	−0.213	−0.219	−0.217
	(−1.301)	(−0.643)	(−0.653)	(−1.800)	(−0.330)	(−0.764)	(−1.903)	(0.978)	(−1.324)	(−1.373)	(−1.368)	(−1.444)
Government Debt in 2007 (percent of GDP)	−0.00872	−0.0177*	−0.0188*	−0.0120	−0.00728	−0.0150	−0.0103	0.00679	−0.00841	−0.00851	−0.00898	−0.00994
	(−0.654)	(−1.683)	(−1.762)	(−0.675)	(−0.499)	(−1.346)	(−0.551)	(0.609)	(−0.600)	(−0.622)	(−0.651)	(−0.719)
Government Deficit in 2007 (percent of GDP)	−0.414***	−0.368**	−0.356**	−0.287*	−0.503***	−0.391***	−0.287*	−0.451***	−0.421***	−0.428**	−0.421**	−0.427**
	(−2.668)	(−2.544)	(−2.513)	(−1.987)	(−4.117)	(−5.204)	(−1.867)	(−3.414)	(−2.689)	(−2.599)	(−2.544)	(−2.600)
KOF Economic Globalization in 2007	0.00279	0.00778	0.00488	−0.0566	0.00176	−0.0247	−0.0537	0.0384	−0.00462	−0.0149	−0.00836	−0.0216
	(0.0735)	(0.233)	(0.151)	(−1.262)	(0.0546)	(−0.693)	(−1.226)	(1.303)	(−0.122)	(−0.387)	(−0.211)	(−0.560)
Under an IMF Program	−1.006	−1.686**	−1.987**	−1.412	−1.517*	−1.362	−1.620	−0.806	−1.430	−1.207	−1.221	−1.148
	(−1.020)	(−2.085)	(−2.544)	(−0.992)	(−1.709)	(−1.549)	(−1.197)	(−0.805)	(−1.543)	(−1.161)	(−1.256)	(−1.162)
Constant	4.057**	4.335**	4.296**	7.456***	3.945**	5.715***	6.133***	2.064	6.569***	4.650**	4.022	5.395**
	(2.097)	(2.507)	(2.456)	(3.206)	(2.014)	(2.949)	(2.811)	(1.178)	(2.724)	(2.358)	(1.660)	(2.521)
Additional Variable (see column header)	0.518	−0.0451	0.0153	−0.0709	2.012	−3.469	−0.0990	−0.0266	−0.0369	0.0388	−0.620	1.076
	(1.352)	(−1.276)	(0.561)	(−1.240)	(1.405)	(−1.013)	(−0.638)	(−0.569)	(−1.299)	(0.0593)	(−0.529)	(1.375)
Observations	94	92	90	68	69	84	68	65	94	94	94	94
Adjusted R^2	0.354	0.369	0.366	0.240	0.443	0.314	0.228	0.477	0.356	0.335	0.337	0.341
Mean Dependent Variable	4.111	3.835	3.766	4.113	3.945	3.820	4.113	3.823	4.111	4.111	4.111	4.111
Standard Deviation Dependent Variable	4.318	3.888	3.903	4.293	3.935	3.482	4.293	3.450	4.318	4.318	4.318	4.318

Note: t-statistics in parentheses. Huber–White robust standard errors are used. Dependent variable: Change in primary deficit in 2009 (% 2007–GDP). CBI = ???
***$p < 0.01$, **$p < 0.05$, *$p < 0.1$.

In a presidential system, such as the United States, where there are separate elections for both executive and legislative bodies, the probability of one party controlling both bodies is smaller than in a parliamentary system, such as the United Kingdom, where winning a majority in the House of Commons allows a party to appoint the prime minister.

At the same time, a plurality voting system, as is being used in the United Kingdom, makes it more likely for a single party to win a majority than in the case of a proportional system, such as in Germany. Within any given system, whether one party rules both bodies further depends on a host of factors such as election dates and the political climate, all of which are unlikely to be systematically correlated with any factor determining the size of fiscal stimulus packages.[29] By including dummies for plurality and parliamentary systems we control for what might be more underlying causes of differences in fiscal policy.

Political Orientation of Government

There is a substantial literature on whether a government's political orientation has an effect on its fiscal policy.[30] Partisan theory suggests that left-wing governments implement more expansionary policies and intervene more heavily in the economy in general (Dreher and Sturm 2012). We therefore control for partisan composition of the government by including a dummy that equals one in the case in which the executive is considered to be from a left-wing party.

Minority Governments

Edin and Ohlsson (1991) argue that minority governments have more difficulties than majority (coalition) governments to reduce deficits and debt levels. In a similar vein, Falcó-Gimeno and Jurado (2011) argue that minority governments have to negotiate with the opposition over the budget. Furthermore, Brück and Stephan (2006) find that minority governments tend to make overly optimistic budget forecasts. We include a minority government dummy and a variable measuring the fraction of seats held by the government to capture such potential effects.

---

[29] While the political fate of individual political parties is clearly tied to economic variables, this seems unlikely to be the case for the political constraints the ruling party faces. To see this, consider an exemplary case where dire economic conditions lead an incumbent party to lose both its legislative and executive powers to an opposition party. This change in political power would leave the value of the constraints dummy unchanged. However, in the case in which only legislative elections were held, it would have only lost its legislative powers, causing our constraints dummy to switch from zero to one. This stylized example illustrates that rather than depending directly on economic conditions, the political constraints variable depends on a complex mix of different factors ranging from institutional choices to economic and political conditions at the time of elections.

[30] See, for instance, Alesina et al. (1998), Alt and Lassen (2006), Andrikopoulos et al. (2004), Angelopoulos et al. (2012), Cusack (1997; 1999), Herwartz and Theilen (2014) and Persson and Svensson (1989).

Coalition Governments and Fragmentation

Game theory suggests that cooperation is more difficult when the number of players is large. In this view, coalition governments will find it more difficult to close budget deficits after adverse shocks, since parties in the coalition will veto spending cuts or tax increases that impinge on the interests of their respective constituencies. Roubini and Sachs (1989a; 1989b) find that broad coalition governments experience higher deficits than one-party governments. Subsequent research by Edin and Ohlsson (1991) and De Haan and Sturm (1994; 1997) found less support for this hypothesis. We nonetheless include a coalition dummy control for this in our setting. Perotti and Kontopoulos (2002) subsequently broadened this approach somewhat by arguing that this overlooks what they call size fragmentation. One possible source of fragmentation of fiscal policy making is the number of decision makers. The larger the number of decision makers, the less each will internalize the costs that a certain policy will impose on others. It can be argued that the relevant group here is each political party in government. Indeed, Perotti and Kontopoulos (2002) find evidence that the higher the number of parties in government, the looser fiscal policy is. Although De Haan et al. (1999) do not find that coalition governments generally have more difficulty in keeping their budgets in line after an adverse economic shock, they also report that more fractionalized governments experience larger government debt growth. To capture possible effects of government fragmentation, we include a variable measuring the probability that two members of government do not belong to the same party. In a similar vein, we also take into account how fractionalized the opposition is by taking on board the probability that two members of the opposition are not of the same party.[31]

Political Budget Cycles

The final political-institutional variable that we include reflects the findings of the political budget cycles (PBC) literature and is closely linked to our motivation for why political constraints are relevant in democracies. PBC research examines the existence and determinants of election cycles in public spending, taxes and government budget deficits. Older theoretical PBC models emphasize the incumbent's intention to secure re-election by maximizing his expected vote share at the next election (Nordhaus, 1975). It is assumed that the electorate is backward looking and the government is evaluated on the basis of its past track record. As a result, these models imply that governments, regardless of ideological orientation, adopt expansionary fiscal policies before elections in order to stimulate the economy.[32] More recent PBC models emphasize the role of temporary information

---

[31] The high correlation between our minority government dummy and the fraction of seats held by the government and that between the coalition dummy and the probability of government members not being of the same party is expected; in both cases, the first variable is a dummy version of the second.

[32] For recent empirical contributions that find a political business cycle, see, for instance, Aidt et al. (2011), Benito et al. (2013).

Annex Table 8.1.2. Robustness Tests with Additional Political Variables, One at a Time, while Using the Realised Change in Primary Deficits as Dependent Variable

	(1)	(2)	(3)	(4)	(5)	(6)	(7)	(8)	(9)	(10)	(11)	(12)
Variables	**Plurality System**	**Parliamentary System**	**Left-Wing Executive**	**Minority Government**	**Fraction Seats Held by Government**	**Coalition Government**	**P(Government Member Not Same Party)**	**P(Opposition Member Not Same Party)**	**Executive Election**	**Executive Election**	**Legislative Election**	**Legislative Election**
Political Constraint	−2.410**	−2.465**	−2.414**	−2.495**	−2.661**	−2.430*	−2.531**	−2.571**	−2.413**	−2.221*	−2.414**	−2.179*
	(−2.249)	(−2.302)	(−2.195)	(−2.243)	(−2.493)	(−1.944)	(−2.175)	(−2.264)	(−2.209)	(−1.967)	(−2.262)	(−1.791)
Government Expenditures in 2007 (percent of GDP)	0.0850**	0.0991**	0.0845*	0.0886**	0.0564	0.0842*	0.0644	0.0469	0.0848*	0.0791*	0.0752**	0.0778**
	(2.007)	(2.315)	(1.972)	(2.142)	(1.451)	(1.802)	(1.497)	(1.282)	(1.958)	(1.819)	(1.999)	(2.054)
Change of Exports in Winter 2008/09 (%2007-GDP)	−0.216	−0.235	−0.214	−0.227	−0.211	−0.214	−0.230	−0.200	−0.215	−0.229	−0.247	−0.253
	(−1.314)	(−1.510)	(−1.399)	(−1.412)	(−1.353)	(−1.373)	(−1.339)	(−1.205)	(−1.349)	(−1.435)	(−1.518)	(−1.559)
Government Debt in 2007 (percent of GDP)	−0.0241*	−0.0230*	−0.0242*	−0.0245*	−0.0188	−0.0242*	−0.0198	−0.0153	−0.0242*	−0.0227	−0.0277**	−0.0295**
	(−1.828)	(−1.765)	(−1.843)	(−1.864)	(−1.468)	(−1.832)	(−1.498)	(−1.159)	(−1.785)	(−1.670)	(−2.171)	(−2.396)
Government Deficit in 2007 (percent of GDP)	−0.206*	−0.209*	−0.206*	−0.211*	−0.215*	−0.205*	−0.216*	−0.216*	−0.206*	−0.200*	−0.186*	−0.192*
	(−1.789)	(−1.879)	(−1.878)	(−1.961)	(−1.878)	(−1.846)	(−1.869)	(−1.925)	(−1.846)	(−1.780)	(−1.781)	(−1.730)
KOF Economic Globalization in 2007	−0.0284	−0.0231	−0.0284	−0.0299	−0.00412	−0.0282	−0.0119	0.00370	−0.0285	−0.0276	−0.0283	−0.0314
	(−0.815)	(−0.694)	(−0.804)	(−0.850)	(−0.119)	(−0.761)	(−0.304)	(0.107)	(−0.782)	(−0.749)	(−0.846)	(−0.912)
Under an IMF Program	−1.813*	−1.957**	−1.814*	−1.938**	−1.470	−1.810*	−1.579	−1.382	−1.816*	−1.836*	−1.739*	−1.734*
	(−1.885)	(−2.020)	(−1.935)	(−2.000)	(−1.553)	(−1.841)	(−1.575)	(−1.517)	(−1.924)	(−1.937)	(−1.954)	(−1.903)
Constant	5.126**	4.779**	5.181**	5.091**	3.549	5.154**	4.524*	3.654	5.163**	5.043**	5.233**	5.247**
	(2.211)	(2.189)	(2.121)	(2.198)	(1.244)	(2.197)	(1.886)	(1.497)	(2.210)	(2.119)	(2.274)	(2.241)
Additional Political Variable (see column header)	0.0248	−0.935	−0.0312	0.691	1.123	0.0390	−0.428	0.158	0.00391	2.430***	1.330*	2.127
	(0.0326)	(−1.007)	(−0.0454)	(0.772)	(0.434)	(0.0401)	(−0.277)	(0.109)	(0.00395)	(2.844)	(1.758)	(1.417)
Additional Political Variable × Political Constraint Dummy										−3.352***		−1.128
										(−2.948)		(−0.655)
Observations	71	71	71	71	70	71	70	69	71	71	71	71
Adjusted R^2	0.241	0.257	0.241	0.246	0.263	0.241	0.262	0.246	0.241	0.240	0.269	0.261
Mean Dependent Variable	3.594	3.594	3.594	3.594	3.520	3.594	3.520	3.437	3.594	3.594	3.594	3.594
Standard Deviation Dependent Variable	3.289	3.289	3.289	3.289	3.254	3.289	3.254	3.202	3.289	3.289	3.289	3.289

See first part of Table 8.2; authors' calculations.

Note: t-statistics in parentheses. Huber-White robust standard errors are used. Dependent variable: Change in primary deficit in 2009 (% 2007-GDP).

$^{***}p < 0.01$, $^{**}p < 0.05$, $^{*}p < 0.1$.

asymmetries regarding the politicians' level of competence in explaining electoral cycles in fiscal policy. In these models, signalling is the driving force behind the PBC (see, e.g., Rogoff and Sibert, 1988; Tabellini and Persson, 2003; and Shi and Svensson, 2006). Pina and Venes (2011) and Jong-a-Pin et al. (2012) show that in OECD countries, there is evidence of electoral effects in revisions of official revenue and spending statistics. To capture possible effects from political business cycles, we include dummies for both executive and legislative elections that took place in the period between October 2008 and June 2009.

Adding these additional political-institutional variables to our regressions is not affecting our conclusion. The political constraint variable remains significant and its coefficient of a similar order of magnitude. With only two exceptions, none of the additional political-institutional variables turns out to be significant in explaining our stimulus measure. These exceptions relate to elections and further strengthen our results. In case of executive elections in an environment without political constraints, the actual change in the primary deficit is significantly larger than when the same elections take place in a politically constrained environment. In the latter case, the overall reduction is more than 3 percentage points of GDP larger than without any elections (but still facing political constraints). The occurrence of legislative elections also seems to stimulate running a larger deficit. Albeit statistically not significant, this again appears to be largely due to elections in countries without political constraints.[33]

Changes in (Primary) Deficits over a Longer Time Horizon

Our empirical analysis is set up such that all control variables are measured before the start of the crisis and the crisis is treated as an exogenous shock. By at the same time focusing on the year 2009, which circumvents interference of other events (like the euro crisis and the Fukushima catastrophe), non-conventional policy reactions (like monetary Quantitative Easing programmes in certain countries), or the euro area debt crisis, we try to get as close as possible to a causal interpretation of our results. Nevertheless, one could argue that political constraints cause policymakers to react slower, but not necessarily less. By 2010, many countries, however, already had moved into recovery mode and first stimulus measures were put to a halt. Hence, it could well be argued that policy reactions by that time would already have been "behind the curve." To have some first suggestive evidence on whether policy action was merely postponed, we have extended our dependent variables measuring realised changes in (primary) deficits to not only capture the change during 2009, but also that including the year 2010. Annex Table 8.1.3 summarizes the results. Whereas the sign of our political constraint

---

[33] We have not only estimated models in which the election variables are interacted with the political constraint variable, but have also done this for our baseline variables and all other political-institutional variables checked in this annex. Whereas the interaction effects are basically never significant, the coefficient on our political constraints variable remains negative and almost always highly significant. Our qualitative conclusions are not affected by including such interaction effects.

Annex Table 8.1.3. Changing the Time Horizon of the Realized Changes in (Primary) Deficits, While Using the Realized Change in Primary Deficits as Dependent Variable

	(1)	(2)	(3)	(4)	(5)	(6)	(7)	(8)
Variables	**Realized Change Primary Deficit 2009**	**Realized Change Primary Deficit 2009–10**	**Realized Change Primary Deficit 2009: Democracies**	**Realized Change Primary Deficit 2009–10: Democracies**	**Realized Change Deficit 2009**	**Realized Change Deficit 2009–10**	**Realized Change Deficit 2009: Democracies**	**Realized Change Deficit 2009–10: Democracies**
Political Constraint	−2.712***	−1.325	−2.413**	−1.206	−1.613**	−0.747	−1.730*	−0.848
	(−3.397)	(−1.445)	(−2.223)	(−1.059)	(−2.357)	(−0.918)	(−1.770)	(−0.857)
Government Expenditures in 2007 (percent of GDP)	0.0567	0.0420	0.0848**	0.0612	0.0527	0.0386	0.0864**	0.0590
	(1.325)	(0.836)	(2.050)	(1.243)	(1.440)	(0.801)	(2.426)	(1.362)
Change of Exports in Winter 2008/09 (%2007-GDP)	−0.212	−0.0782	−0.215	−0.187	−0.154	0.0749	−0.135	−0.150
	(−1.402)	(−0.452)	(−1.366)	(−0.956)	(−1.196)	(0.481)	(−0.935)	(−0.885)
Government Debt in 2007 (percent of GDP)	−0.00845	−0.0108	−0.0242*	−0.0161	−0.00451	−0.00616	−0.0182	−0.0152
	(−0.619)	(−0.849)	(−1.846)	(−1.183)	(−0.355)	(−0.474)	(−1.445)	(−1.299)
Government Deficit in 2007 (percent of GDP)	−0.428***	−0.316***	−0.206*	−0.190***	−0.419***	−0.335***	−0.229*	−0.227***
	(−2.643)	(−3.196)	(−1.882)	(−3.463)	(−2.695)	(−3.633)	(−1.736)	(−3.621)
KOF Economic Globalization in 2007	−0.0150	−0.0324	−0.0285	−0.0269	−0.00534	−0.00615	−0.0247	−0.0207
	(−0.398)	(−0.841)	(−0.812)	(−0.492)	(−0.169)	(−0.190)	(−0.815)	(−0.477)
Under an IMF Program	−1.216	−2.013**	−1.816*	−2.703***	−0.733	−1.357	−0.888	−1.892**
	(−1.237)	(−2.072)	(−1.948)	(−3.345)	(−1.065)	(−1.635)	(−1.251)	(−2.373)
Constant	4.658**	5.779***	5.163**	4.645	3.353**	3.846**	4.259*	4.083
	(2.433)	(2.879)	(2.236)	(1.483)	(2.113)	(2.450)	(1.981)	(1.663)
Observations	94	94	71	71	123	123	88	88
Adjusted R^2	0.343	0.133	0.253	0.103	0.287	0.083	0.168	0.091
Mean Dependent Variable	4.111	3.590	3.594	3.375	3.896	3.297	3.535	3.326
Standard Deviation Dependent Variable	4.318	4.185	3.289	3.805	3.998	4.267	3.090	3.738

Note: t-statistics in parentheses. Huber-White robust standard errors are used.
***$p < 0.01$, **$p < 0.05$, *$p < 0.1$.

variable remains negative, its impact declines and is no longer statistically significant.

Changing the Sample of Countries

Given that we use what is arguably an unexpected exogenous shock hitting all countries around the world, we are working in a cross-section framework. This limits our degrees of freedom and we therefore concentrate most of our analysis on those samples that are as large as possible. Nevertheless, differences across different country groups might exist. To check the robustness of our results in this sense, Annex Table 8.1.4 varies the underlying sample in different ways.

The first two columns repeat the main results from Annex Table 8.1.3. Whereas in the main text we rely on the definition of Cheibub et al. (2010) to distinguish between democracies and autocracies, column (3) uses a different split. Parts of our reasoning assume competitive elections. As an alternative, we therefore include in column (3) only those countries in which multiple parties did win seats.[34] Although this increases the number of observations slightly, it does not affect our conclusions. The subsequent columns (4) to (11) distinguish between OECD, non-OECD, G20, non-G20, EU, non-EU and euro area and non–euro area members. In all of these subsamples our political constraint variable remains significantly negative.

Checking for Outlying Observations

Perhaps some extreme and thereby potentially outlying observations might drive our results. Particularly noteworthy are the three negative stimulus packages of Hungary, Ireland and Iceland in the UNCTAD (2009) data. As reported by UNCTAD (2009), these countries did all commit large financial resources to rescue their financial sectors while, at the same time, imposing restrictive fiscal policies such as tax increases and cuts in public expenditures of more than 7 percent of GDP. The extraordinary conditions in these countries might have an influence on our results. Column (2) of Annex Table 8.1.5, however, shows that dropping these observations has no real impact on our regression results.

Countries with (in an absolute sense) large values of either the dependent variable or any of the control variables might also have a substantive influence on our regression results. For that reason, we exclude in each of the remaining columns in Annex Table 8.1.5 the upper and lower 10 percent of the distribution regarding either the dependent variables, or in turn each of the control variables. Each time discarding around 20 percent of our (potentially influential) observations does not change our results in any qualitatively meaningful way. The political constraint variable remains highly significant and negative.

---

[34] The data are taken from the Database of Political Institutions and imply that the variables LIEC and EIEC of that database take on values larger than 5.

Annex Table 8.1.4. Robustness Tests with Changing the Underlying Set of Countries, While Using the Realized Change in Primary Deficits as Dependent Variable

	(1)	(2)	(3)	(4)	(5)	(6)	(7)	(8)	(9)	(10)	(11)
Variables	**Full Sample**	**Democracies**	**Multiparty Systems**	**OECD Countries**	**Non-OECD Countries**	**G20 Countries**	**Non-G20 Countries**	**EU Member States**	**Non-EU Member States**	**Euro Area Members**	**Non-Euro Area Members**
Political Constraint	−2.712***	−2.413**	−2.254***	−3.364***	−2.159**	−2.929**	−2.708***	−1.965*	−2.308**	−3.337**	−2.665***
	(−3.397)	(−2.223)	(−2.904)	(−4.740)	(−2.176)	(−3.248)	(−2.778)	(−1.983)	(−2.487)	(−2.495)	(−3.056)
Government Expenditures in 2007 (percent of GDP)	0.0567	0.0848**	0.0614	−0.00213	0.0729	0.0715	0.0555	−0.0259	0.0704	−0.105	0.0480
	(1.325)	(2.050)	(1.441)	(−0.0331)	(1.146)	(0.912)	(1.198)	(−0.313)	(1.137)	(−0.825)	(1.008)
Change of Exports in Winter 2008/09 (%2007-GDP)	−0.212	−0.215	−0.236	0.00201	−0.233	0.134	−0.220	0.0240	−0.291	−0.0381	−0.250
	(−1.402)	(−1.366)	(−1.468)	(0.0174)	(−1.106)	(0.574)	(−1.374)	(0.219)	(−1.304)	(−0.312)	(−1.446)
Government Debt in 2007 (percent of GDP)	−0.00845	−0.0242*	−0.00559	0.0100	−0.0124	0.00562	−0.0119	0.0265	−0.0168	0.0257	−0.0121
	(−0.619)	(−1.846)	(−0.368)	(0.897)	(−0.664)	(0.537)	(−0.698)	(1.383)	(−1.083)	(1.292)	(−0.830)
Government Deficit in 2007 (percent of GDP)	−0.428***	−0.206*	−0.338**	−0.296***	−0.489*	−0.554*	−0.426**	−0.183	−0.408**	−0.454*	−0.427**
	(−2.643)	(−1.882)	(−2.304)	(−6.265)	(−1.890)	(−1.895)	(−2.476)	(−1.241)	(−2.146)	(−2.069)	(−2.476)
KOF Economic Globalization in 2007	−0.0150	−0.0285	−0.00625	0.0687	−0.0244	−0.0104	−0.0153	0.0523	−0.00726	0.0381	−0.0266
	(−0.398)	(−0.812)	(−0.152)	(1.314)	(−0.521)	(−0.155)	(−0.365)	(0.923)	(−0.164)	(0.438)	(−0.643)
Under an IMF Program	−1.216	−1.816*	−0.780	−0.515	−1.443		−1.192	−4.076***	−0.812		−1.192
	(−1.237)	(−1.948)	(−0.678)	(−0.322)	(−1.294)		(−1.165)	(−4.924)	(−0.765)		(−1.230)
Constant	4.658**	5.163**	3.018	0.844	4.702	3.979	4.830**	1.648	3.749	7.347	5.549**
	(2.433)	(2.236)	(1.393)	(0.283)	(1.620)	(1.159)	(2.207)	(0.343)	(1.305)	(0.726)	(2.502)
Observations	94	71	84	29	65	15	79	26	68	14	80
Adjusted R^2	0.343	0.253	0.259	0.336	0.339	0.469	0.321	0.375	0.358	−0.198	0.346
Mean Dependent Variable	4.111	3.594	3.787	4.370	3.996	4.194	4.096	3.969	4.166	4.924	3.969
Standard Deviation Dependent Variable	4.318	3.289	3.890	1.818	5.060	2.368	4.607	2.191	4.907	1.437	4.634

Note: *t*-statistics in parentheses. Huber-White robust standard errors are used. Dependent variable: Change in primary deficit in 2009 (% 2007-GDP). Only democratic countries are included in the sample. OECD = Organisation for Economic Co-operation and Development.

$^{***}p < 0.01$, $^{**}p < 0.05$, $^{*}p < 0.1$.

Annex Table 8.1.5. Robustness Tests by Removing Potentially Influential Observations, While Using the Realized Change in Primary Deficits as Dependent Variable

	(1)	(2)	(3)	(4)	(5)	(6)	(7)	(8)
Variables	**Full Sample**	**Excluding Hungary, Iceland, and Ireland**	**Excluding Tails of Change in Primary Deficit**	**Excluding Tails of Government Expenditure Shares**	**Excluding Tails of Change in Growth**	**Excluding Tails of Change in Export Shares**	**Excluding Tails of Government Debt Shares**	**Excluding Tails of Government Deficit Shares**
Political Constraint	−2.712***	−2.731***	−1.262**	−2.026**	−3.396***	−3.075***	−1.971**	−2.158**
	(−3.397)	(−3.406)	(−2.371)	(−2.460)	(−3.660)	(−3.244)	(−2.401)	(−2.127)
Government Expenditures in 2007 (percent of GDP)	0.0567	0.0572	0.0510*	0.134***	0.0421	0.0683	0.0555	0.0346
	(1.325)	(1.275)	(1.902)	(2.740)	(1.113)	(1.448)	(1.341)	(0.772)
Change of Exports in Winter 2008/09 (%2007-GDP)	−0.212	−0.231	−0.0258	−0.487***	−0.134	−0.357**	−0.124	−0.184
	(−1.402)	(−1.417)	(−0.362)	(−2.751)	(−1.092)	(−2.091)	(−1.094)	(−1.388)
Government Debt in 2007 (percent of GDP)	−0.00845	−0.00800	0.000485	−0.00553	−0.0176	−0.0187	−0.0459**	−0.00404
	(−0.619)	(−0.584)	(0.0611)	(−0.432)	(−1.638)	(−1.593)	(−2.555)	(−0.356)
Government Deficit in 2007 (percent of GDP)	−0.428***	−0.418**	−0.262***	−0.551***	−0.340**	−0.359**	−0.228**	−0.442**
	(−2.643)	(−2.497)	(−4.999)	(−3.836)	(−2.433)	(−2.183)	(−2.165)	(−2.411)
KOF Economic Globalization in 2007	−0.0150	−0.0162	0.00346	−0.0709**	0.0112	−0.0232	0.00726	−0.0176
	(−0.398)	(−0.421)	(0.134)	(−2.132)	(0.261)	(−0.572)	(0.201)	(−0.457)
Under an IMF Program	−1.216	−1.178	−0.713	0.0309	−1.394	−1.287	−2.257**	−1.379
	(−1.237)	(−1.012)	(−1.137)	(0.0278)	(−1.517)	(−1.386)	(−2.573)	(−1.570)
Constant	4.658**	4.613**	2.734*	4.368*	4.488**	5.136**	4.792**	5.086**
	(2.433)	(2.214)	(1.889)	(1.966)	(2.092)	(2.577)	(2.382)	(2.408)
Observations	94	91	77	74	72	77	76	77
Adjusted R^2	0.343	0.339	0.234	0.455	0.431	0.409	0.287	0.151
Mean Dependent Variable	4.111	4.127	3.730	3.987	4.198	4.152	3.894	3.730
Standard Deviation Dependent Variable	4.318	4.365	2.231	4.242	3.979	4.191	3.508	3.201

Note: t-statistics in parentheses. Huber-White robust standard errors are used. In columns (3) to (8), the upper and lower 10 percent of the observations regarding the respective variable are removed from the sample.
Dependent variable: Change in primary deficit in 2009 (% 2007-GDP).
***$p < 0.01$, **$p < 0.05$, *$p < 0.1$.

Annex Table 8.1.6. List of Countries and Values for the Main Dependent Variables

Countries	Promised Discretionary Measures 2008–12	Promised Stimulus 2008–09	Realized Change Primary Deficit 2009	Realized Change Deficit 2009	Political Constraint	Democracy	Countries	Promised Discretionary Measures 2008–12	Promised Stimulus 2008–09	Realized Change Primary Deficit 2009	Realized Change Deficit 2009	Political Constraint	Democracy
Albania			2.70	2.25	1	1	Liberia			0.54	0.45	1	1
Algeria			13.94	14.16	0	0	Lithuania			4.29	3.87	1	1
Angola			2.52		0	0	Luxembourg	3.6		3.93	3.22	1	1
Argentina	6.4	2.3	3.15	2.48	0	1	Madagascar			2.15		1	1
Armenia			5.01	4.85	1	1	Malawi			0.66		1	1
Australia	5.4	5.2	3.37	3.27	1	1	Malaysia	2.8	2.2	2.14	2.60	0	0
Austria	1.2	3.7	3.02	2.93	1	1	Maldives			10.25	8.75	1	1
Azerbaijan			13.83		1	0	Malta			–0.70		0	1
Bangladesh			–0.50	–0.84	0	0	Mauritius			0.88		0	1
Barbados			0.63	0.32	0	1	Mexico	1.6	2.0	3.48		1	1
Belarus			–1.23	–1.48	1	0	Moldova			5.10		0	1
Belgium	1.4	4.2	4.49	4.64	1	1	Mongolia			0.71		1	1
Belize			1.58	1.84	0	1	Morocco			2.62	2.73	0	0
Bhutan			0.80		1	1	Mozambique			3.63		0	0
Bolivia			3.33		1	1	Namibia			4.33	3.82	0	0
Botswana			3.53	3.43	0	0	Nepal			2.71	2.53	1	1
Brazil	5.6	1.9	1.94	1.75	1	1	Netherlands	2.5	5.9	5.91	6.04	1	1
Bulgaria		2.9	3.78	3.38	1	1	New Zealand	4.3	4.4	3.04	3.23	1	1
Burkina Faso			1.37	1.26	0	0	Nicaragua			0.85	0.65	1	1
Burundi			3.18	3.32	0	1	Niger			7.14		1	1
Cambodia			4.63	4.61	0	0	Nigeria		14.9	15.92	15.74	0	1
Cameroon			2.38		0	0	Norway	1.2	8.1	8.99	8.22	1	1
Canada	4.1	4.7	4.22	3.43	1	1	Pakistan		0.0	–0.87	–2.32	1	1
Cabo Verde			6.19	6.15	1	1	Panama			1.68	1.87	1	1
Chad			13.36	13.03	0	0	Papua New Guinea			12.43	12.13	1	1
Chile	2.8	8.0	8.33	8.18	0	1	Paraguay			2.22		1	1

(continued)

Annex Table 8.1.6. List of Countries and Values for the Main Dependent Variables *(continued)*

Countries	Promised Discretionary Measures 2008–12	Promised Stimulus 2008–09	Realized Change Primary Deficit 2009	Realized Change Deficit 2009	Political Constraint	Democracy	Countries	Promised Discretionary Measures 2008–12	Promised Stimulus 2008–09	Realized Change Primary Deficit 2009	Realized Change Deficit 2009	Political Constraint	Democracy
China	6.2	3.4	2.58		0	0	Peru	3.2		4.38	4.61	1	1
Comoros			−3.16		1	1	Philippines	3.1	1.0	2.74	2.70	1	1
Costa Rica			3.57	3.71	1	1	Poland	1.2	1.2	4.12	3.56	1	1
Croatia			2.67	2.50	0	1	Portugal	0.8	4.6	6.27	6.32	0	1
Cyprus			6.95	7.24	1	1	Republic of Congo			19.29	20.59	1	0
Czech Republic	3.0		3.44	3.18	1	1	Romania			2.24	1.86	1	1
Côte d'Ivoire			1.05	1.24	1	0	Russia	5.4	6.6	10.81	10.67	0	0
Denmark	2.5	5.7	5.91	5.68	1	1	Rwanda			0.63	0.68	0	0
Djibouti			6.13		0	0	Samoa			2.60		0	0
Dominican Republic			0.70	0.33	1	1	Senegal			0.28	0.17	0	1
Ecuador			4.17		1	1	Sierra Leone			−0.88	−0.65	1	1
Egypt			0.02	0.43	0	0	Singapore	8.0		7.27	7.35	0	0
El Salvador			2.67		1	1	Slovak Republic	1.1		5.50	5.29	1	1
Equatorial Guinea			25.29		0	0	Slovenia			4.99	4.90	1	1
Eritrea			−1.32		0	0	Solomon Islands			−1.97		1	1
Estonia			−0.55	−0.52	1	1	South Africa	7.4	3.0	5.48	5.31	0	0
Ethiopia			−1.64		0	0	Spain	3.9	10.1	6.28	6.15	1	1
FYR Macedonia			1.72		1	1	Sri Lanka			3.78	1.58	1	1
Finland	3.1	5.7	6.86	6.51	1	1	St. Lucia			2.22	2.32	0	1
France	1.5	5.0	4.04	4.57	0	1	Suriname			4.19	3.51	1	1
Gabon			5.32		0	0	Swaziland			5.77		0	0
Georgia			4.19		0	1	Sweden	3.3	6.9	3.11	3.17	1	1
Germany	3.6	4.4	2.88	3.02	1	1	Switzerland	0.5		1.31	1.30	1	1
Ghana			−1.41		0	1	Syria			0.12		0	0
Greece	0.8	3.0	5.56	5.57	0	1	Taiwan	2.1		2.98		1	1
Grenada			0.76	0.40	0	1	Tajikistan			1.06		0	0
Guatemala			1.65	1.54	1	1	Tanzania			4.25		0	0

Guinea			6.27	6.70	0	0	Thailand	3.4		3.20	3.34	1	1
Guinea-Bissau			–4.08	–3.43	1	1	The Bahamas			1.93	1.80	0	1
Guyana			0.12	0.11	0	0	The Gambia			1.58	1.45	0	0
Haiti			2.10		1	0	Timor-Leste			17.48		1	1
Honduras			3.06	2.97	1	1	Togo			2.12	1.91	0	0
Hungary	–7.7	–0.7	0.68	0.26	1	1	Trinidad and Tobago			15.40	15.07	0	1
Iceland	–7.3	6.1	8.14	6.04	1	1	Tunisia			0.62	0.64	0	0
India	1.8	4.3	2.49	1.93	1	1	Turkey	1.1	6.5	3.29	3.13	0	1
Indonesia	2.0	0.7	1.99		1	1	Turkmenistan			1.83		0	0
Iraq			9.71	9.46	1	0	Uganda			0.08	–0.05	0	0
Ireland	–8.3	10.8	5.21	4.64	1	1	Ukraine		2.7	2.86	2.25	1	1
Israel			3.02	3.03	1	1	United Arab Emirates			21.72	21.56	0	0
Italy	0.3	3.4	2.51	3.18	1	1	United Kingdom	1.9	9.5	5.98	6.12	0	1
Jamaica			4.42	–1.71	0	1	United States	5.5	11.5	6.35	6.61	0	1
Japan	4.7	7.2	5.66	5.47	0	1	Uruguay			0.30	0.10	0	1
Jordan			4.95	4.84	0	0	Uzbekistan			6.56	6.57	1	0
Kenya			1.67	1.43	1	1	Vanuatu			0.83		1	1
Korea	6.2	5.9	1.62	1.97	1	1	Venezuela			5.61	9.25	0	1
Kyrgyz Republic			2.14		1	1	Vietnam			7.49	7.23	0	0
Lao P.D.R.			4.67	4.87	0	0	Yemen			5.15	5.18	0	0
Latvia			–1.16	–1.59	1	1	Zambia			2.08		1	0
Lebanon			–0.01		1	0	Zimbabwe			1.06		0	0
Lesotho			13.29	13.28	0	0							

REFERENCES

Aidt, Toke S., Francisco Jose Veiga and Linda Goncalves Veiga. (2011). Election Results and Opportunistic Policies: A New Test of the Rational Political Business Cycle Model, Public Choice. 148(1–2): 21–44.

Aizenman, Joshua and Yothin Jinjarak. (2011). The Fiscal Stimulus of 2009-10: Trade Openness, Fiscal Space and Exchange Rate Adjustment, National Bureau of Economic Research Working Papers 17427.

Alesina, Alberto, Roberto Perotti and José Tavares. (1998). The Political Economy of Fiscal Adjustments, *Brookings Papers on Economic Activity*. 29(1): 197–266.

Alt, James E. and David Dreyer Lassen. (2006). Fiscal Transparency, Political Parties, and Debt in OECD Countries, *European Economic Review*. 50: 1403–1439.

Alter, Jonathan. (2011). *The Promise: President Obama, Year One*. London: Simon & Schuster.

Andrikopoulos, Andreas, Ioannis Loizides and Kyprianos Prodromidis. (2004). Fiscal Policy and Political Business Cycles in the EU, *European Journal of Political Economy*. 20(1): 125–152.

Angelopoulos, Konstantinos, George Economides and Pantelis Kammas. (2012). Does Cabinet Ideology Matter for the Structure of Tax Policies?, *European Journal of Political Economy*. 28(4): 620–635.

Armingeon, Klaus. (2012). The Politics of Fiscal Responses to the Crisis of 2008–2009, *Governance*. 25(4): 543–565.

Auerbach, Alan J. and Yuriy Gorodnichenko. (2012). Measuring the Output Responses to Fiscal Policy, *American Economic Journal: Economic Policy*. 4(2): 1–27.

Bartels, Larry. (2011). Ideology and Retrospection in Electoral Responses to the Great Recession. URL: http://www.princeton.edu/~bartels/stimulus.pdf.

Beck, Thorsten, George Clarke, Alberto Groff, Philip Keefer and Patrick Walsh. (2001). New Tools in Comparative Political Economy: The Database of Political Institutions, *World Bank Economic Review*. 15(1): 165–176.

Benito, Bernardino, Francisco Bastida and Cristina Vicente. (2013). Creating Room for Manoeuvre: a Strategy to Generate Political Budget Cycles under Fiscal Rules, Kyklos. 66(4): 467–496.

Blanchard, Olivier, Giovanni Dell'Ariccia and Paolo Mauro. (2010). Rethinking Macroeconomic Policy. *Journal of Money, Credit and Banking*. 42(1): 199–215.

Blinder, Alan S. (1997). Is Government Too Political?, *Foreign Affairs*. 76(6): 115–126.

Brück, Tilman and Andreas Stephan. (2006). Do Eurozone Countries Cheat with their Budget Deficit Forecasts?, Kyklos. 59(1): 3–15.

Cecchetti, Stephen G. (2002). The Problem with Fiscal Policy. URL: www.arts.ualberta.ca/econweb/ landon/cpi18.pdf.

Cheibub, José Antonio, Jennifer Gandhi and James Raymond Vreeland. (2010). Democracy and Dictatorship Revisited, Public Choice. 143(1/2): 67–101.

Chodorow-Reich, Gabriel, Laura Feiveson, Zachary Liscow, and William Gui Woolston. (2012). Does State Fiscal Relief during Recessions Increase Employment? Evidence from the American Recovery and Reinvestment Act, *American Economic Journal: Economic Policy*. 4(3): 118–45.

Cogan, John F. and John B. Taylor. (2011). What the Government Purchases Multiplier Actually Multiplied in the 2009 Stimulus Package, NBER Working Paper 16505.

Conley, Timothy G. and Bill Dupor. (2013). The American Recovery and Reinvestment Act: Solely a government jobs program?, *Journal of Monetary Economics*. 60(5): 535–549.

Crowe, Christopher and Ellen E. Meade. (2008). Central Bank Independence and Transparency: Evolution and Effectiveness, European Journal of Political Economy. 24(4): 763–777.

Cukierman, Alex. (1992). *Central Bank Strategy, Credibility, and Independence*. Cambridge, MA: MIT Press.

Cukierman, Alex, Steven B. Webb and Bilin Neyapti. (1992). Measuring the Independence of Central Banks and its Effects on Policy Outcomes, *World Bank Economic Review*. 6: 353–398.

Cusack, Thomas R. (1997). Partisan Politics and Public Finance: Changes in Public Spending in the Industrialized Democracies 1955–1989, *Public Choice.* 91(3/4): 375–395.

———. (1999). Partisan Politics and Fiscal Policy, *Comparative Political Studies.* 32(4): 464–486.

De Haan, Jakob and Jan-Egbert Sturm. (1994). Political and Institutional Determinants of Fiscal Policy in the European Community, Public Choice. 80: 157172.

———. (1997). Political and Economic Determinants of OECD Budget Deficits and Government Expenditures: A Reinvestigation, *European Journal of Political Economy.* 13: 739–750.

De Haan, Jakob, Jan-Egbert Sturm and Geert Beekhuis. (1999). The Weak Government Thesis: Some New Evidence, *Public Choice.* 101(3/4): 163–167.

Dreher, Axel and Jan-Egbert Sturm. (2012). Do the IMF and the World Bank Influence Voting in the UN General Assembly?, Public Choice. 141: 363–397.

Dreher, Axel, Jan-Egbert Sturm and Jakob De Haan. (2008). Does High Inflation Cause Central Bankers to Lose their Job? Evidence Based on a New Data Set, *European Journal of Political Economy.* 24(4): 778–787.

———. (2010). When is a Central Bank Governor Replaced? Evidence Based on a New Data Set, *Journal of Macroeconomics.* 32: 766–781.

Duch, Raymond M. and Randolph T. Stevenson. (2008). *The Economic Vote: How Political and Economic Institutions Condition Election Results.* Cambridge: Cambridge University Press.

Edin, Per-Anders and Henry Ohlsson. (1991). Political Determinants of Budget Deficits: Coalition Effects Versus Minority Effects, *European Economic Review.* 35: 1597–1603.

Falcó-Gimeno, Albert and Ignacio Jurado. (2011). Minority Governments and Budget Deficits: The Role of the Opposition, European Journal of Political Economy. 27(3): 554–565.

Feyrer, James and Bruce Sacerdote. (2011). Did the Stimulus Stimulate? Real Time Estimates of the Effects of the American Recovery and Reinvestment Act, NBER Working Papers 16759, National Bureau of Economic Research.

Furceri, Davide and Ricardo M. Sousa. (2011). The Impact of Government Spending on the Private Sector: Crowding-out versus Crowding-in Effects, Kyklos. 64(4): 516–533.

G20 Information Centre. (2009) London Summit – Leader's Statement. URL: http://www.g20.utoronto.ca/2009/2009communique0402.pdf.

Gali, Jordi. (1994). Government Size and Macroeconomic Stability, *European Economic Review.* 38(1): 117–132.

Henisz, Witold J. (2000). The Institutional Environment for Economic Growth, *Economics & Politics.* 12(1): 1–31.

———. (2002). The Institutional Environment for Infrastructure Investment, Industrial and Corporate Change. 11(2): 355–389.

Herwartz, Helmut and Bernd Theilen. (2014). Partisan Influence on Social Spending Under Market Integration, Fiscal Pressure and Institutional Change, *European Journal of Political Economy.* 34: 409–424.

Hibbs, Douglas. (2006). Voting and the Macroeconomy, in: Barry R. Weingast and Donald Wittman (eds.), The Oxford Handbook of Political Economy. Oxford: Oxford University Press: 565–586.

Horton, Mark, Manmohan Kumar and Paolo Mauro. (2009). The State of Public Finances: A Cross-Country Fiscal Monitor, IMF Staff Position Note SPN/09/21.

Ilzetzki, Ethan, Enrique G. Mendoza and Carlos A. Végh. (2013). How Big (Small?) are Fiscal Multipliers?, *Journal of Monetary Economics.* 60(2): 239–254.

International Monetary Fund (IMF). (2007). World Economic Outlook Database, October 2007 Edition. URL: http://www.imf.org/ external/pubs/ft/weo/2007/02/weodata/index.aspx.

———. (2008a). World Economic Outlook Database, April 2008 Edition. URL: http://www.imf.org/ external/pubs/ft/weo/2008/01/weodata/index.aspx.

———. (2008b). World Economic Outlook Database October 2008 Edition. URL: http://www.imf.org/ external/pubs/ft/weo/2008/02/weodata/index.aspx.

———. (2009a). The Size of the Fiscal Expansion: An Analysis for the Largest Countries. URL: http:// www.imf.org/external/np/pp/eng/2009/020109.pdf.

———. (2009b). *World Economic Outlook; Crisis and Recovery.* URL: http://www.imf.org/external/pubs/ft/weo/2009/01/.

———. (2013). World Economic Outlook Database, April 2013 Edition. URL: http://www.imf.org/ external/pubs/ft/weo/2013/01/weodata/index.aspx.

Jong-a-Pin, Richard M., Jan-Egbert Sturm and Jakob De Haan. (2012). Using Real-Time Data to Test for Political Budget Cycles, KOF Working Papers No. 313.

Lewis-Beck, Michael. S. (1988). *Economics and Elections: The Major Western Democracies.* Michigan: University of Michigan Press.

Lewis-Beck, Michael S. and Martin Paldam. (2000). Economic Voting: An Introduction, *Electoral Studies.* 19(2/3): 113–121.

Lijphart, Arend. (1990). The Political Consequences of Electoral Laws, 1945–85, *The American Political Science Review.* 84(2): 481–496.

———. (1999). *Patterns of Democracy: Government Forms and Performance in Thirty-Six Countries.* Yale: Yale University Press.

Nordhaus, William D. (1975). The Political Business Cycle, *The Review of Economic Studies.* 42(2): 169–190.

OECD. (2009). *Economic Outlook, Interim Report March 2009.* URL: http://www.oecdbookshop.org/oecd/display.asp?lang=EN&sf1=identifiers&st1=5ksm2rb4ff44.

Olson, Mancur. (2000). *Power and Prosperity. Outgrowing Communist and Capitalist Dictatorships.* New York: Basic Books.

Orphanides, Athanasios. (2001). Monetary Policy Rules Based on Real-Time Data, *American Economic Review.* 91(4): 964-985.

Orphanides, Athanasios and Simon van Norden. (2002). The Unreliability of Output Gap Estimates in Real Time, *Review of Economics and Statistics.* 84: 569–583.

Perotti, Roberto and Yianos Kontopoulos. (2002). Fragmented Fiscal Policy, *Journal of Public Economics.* 86: 191–222.

Persson, Torsten and Lars E. O. Svensson. (1989). Why a Stubborn Conservative would Run a Deficit: Policy with Time-Inconsistent Preferences, *The Quarterly Journal of Economics.* 104(2): 325–345.

Pina, Álvaro M. and Nuno M. Venes. (2011). The Political Economy of EDP Fiscal Forecasts: An Empirical Assessment, European *Journal of Political Economy.* 27(3): 534–546.

Porteba, James M. (1994). State Responses to Fiscal Crises: The Effects of Budgetary Institutions and Politics, *Journal of Political Economy.* 102(4): 799–821.

Rodrik, Dani. (1998). Why do More Open Economies Have Bigger Governments?, *Journal of Political Economy.* 106(5): 997–1032.

Rogoff, Kenneth and Anne Sibert. (1988). Elections and Macroeconomic Policy Cycles, *The Review of Economic Studies.* 55: 1–16.

Romer, David. (2012). What Have We Learned about Fiscal Policy from the Crisis?, in: Olivier J. Blanchard, David Romer, Michael Spence and Joseph E. Stiglitz (eds.), In the Wake of the Crisis: Leading Economists Reassess Economic Policy. Cambridge (Mass.): The MIT Press: 57–66.

Roubini, Nouriel and Jeffrey Sachs. (1989a). Government Spending and Budget Deficits in the Industrial Countries, *Economic Policy.* 8: 99–132.

———. (1989b). Political and Economic Determinants of Budget Deficits in the Industrial Economies, *European Economic Review.* 33: 903–938.

Shi, Min, and Jakob Svensson. (2006). Political Budget Cycles: Do They Differ across Countries and Why?, *Journal of Public Economics.* 90(8/9): 1367–1389.

Spolaore, Enrico. (2004). Adjustments in Different Government Systems, Economics & Politics. 16(2): 117–146.

Streb, Jorge M., Daniel Lema and Gustavo Torrens. (2009). Checks and Balances on Political Budget Cycles: Cross-Country Evidence, Kyklos. 62(3): 426–447.

Sturm, Jan-Egbert and Jakob De Haan. (2001). Inflation in Developing Countries: Does Central Bank Independence Matter? New Evidence Based on a New Data Set, CESifo Working Paper 511.

Tabellini, Guido and Torsten Persson. (2003). Do Electoral Cycles Differ Across Political Systems?, IGIER Working Paper No. 232.

UNCTAD. (2009). Trade And Development Report 2009. URL: http://unctad.org/en/Docs/tdr2009_en.pdf.

Wallace-Wells, Benjamin. (2001). What's Left on the Left. Paul Krugman's Lonely Crusade. *New York Magazine*. URL: http://nymag.com/news/politics/paul-krugman-2011-5/.

Weise, Charles L. (2012). Political Pressures on Monetary Policy During the US Great Inflation, *American Economic Journal: Macroeconomics*. 4(2): 33–64.

CHAPTER 9

Fragmented Politics and Public Debt

ERNESTO CRIVELLI, SANJEEV GUPTA, CARLOS MULAS-GRANADOS, AND CAROLINA CORREA-CARO

INTRODUCTION

Rising public-debt-to-GDP ratios can be attributed to either large fiscal deficits or weak economic activity. Standard economic wisdom advocates following a countercyclical fiscal policy during recessions and letting public debt grow, and lowering it during economic expansions (Barro 1979; Lucas and Stokey 1983). However, data since the 1970s show that debt reductions in good times rarely compensate for debt accumulation in bad times.[1] Perhaps other factors are at play, possibly of a political nature (Alesina and Passalacqua 2015)—the incentives to overspend tend to increase with the number of political actors involved in budget decisions.

This chapter uses data for 92 advanced and emerging market and developing economies during 1975–2015 to study the relationship between the key indicators of political fragmentation and changes in public debt.[2] More precisely, the questions addressed are the following: Is higher political fragmentation associated with debt increases? Does the presence of veto players make it more difficult to lower debt?

Some scholars have focused on explaining political factors behind large cross-country differences in debt levels, while others have focused on short-term variations in debt ratios in a small sample of countries. One weakness with both approaches is that they do not align debt and political dynamics, which typically

The authors are grateful to Suman Basu, Era Dabla-Norris, Vitor Gaspar, Fabien Gonguet, Laura Jaramillo, Joao Jalles, Javier Kapsoli, Constant Lonkeng, Sanaa Nadeem, Tigran Poghosyan, John Ralyea, Christiane Roehler, Manrique Saenz, and participants at a FAD seminar for many helpful suggestions.

[1] According to Escolano and Gaspar (2016), this debt accumulation bias is a relatively recent development, starting after the 1970s. Before that, debt spikes were typically followed by similar periods of debt decline. In their words, "Over the past two and a quarter centuries, the path of government debt ratios in the United Kingdom and the United States were characterized by occasional large increases prompted by national emergencies such as wars and large economic crises followed by long periods of sustained reductions in debt ratios" (Escolano and Gaspar 2016, 6).

[2] Comprising emerging and low-income economies. Annex 9.1 lists the countries.

change every four to five years with the change of government. This analysis adopts instead a unique approach in two dimensions: first, the time frames are legislative periods (the span between two consecutive elections); and second, a large panel data set with ample variation across space and time is used. The advantage of following this approach is that it allows the effects that divided governments, fragmented legislatures, and ruling coalitions have on debt dynamics during their entire tenure to be encapsulated.

The analysis also focuses on the quality of institutions given that earlier studies have found corruption to be positively associated with the accumulation of public debt. Political fragmentation can thus have a distinctive impact on public debt dynamics in societies in which corruption is perceived to be high.

This analysis finds strong evidence that political fragmentation plays a prominent role in explaining public debt dynamics. The results are consistent with the hypotheses underlying both *common pool* and *veto players* theories. In addition, the chapter shows that the prevalence of corruption magnifies the effect of political fragmentation. The impact of political fragmentation on debt dynamics appears to be asymmetric, with larger and more significant effects during periods of debt decrease.

The chapter is structured as follows: The next section reviews the relevant literature and discusses the two principal theories in this area. The third section presents the empirical model and the data, and the fourth section discusses the main results. The fifth section explores the differential impact of political fragmentation on public debt dynamics based on the level of perceived corruption and the overall prevailing level of public debt. The final section summarizes and concludes.

LITERATURE REVIEW

Earlier literature (Barro 1979; Lucas and Stokey 1983; Aiyagari and others 2002) focused on explaining how the observed pattern of debt accumulation differs from the normative prescription. The school of public choice has argued that "fiscal illusion" and Keynesian policies were behind excessive deficits and resulting debt accumulation (Buchanan and Wagner 1977). Voters suffer from fiscal illusion in that they do not understand the notion of the intertemporal budget constraint and overestimate the benefits of current spending relative to the costs of future taxation. Keynesian policies prescribe spending and deficits during recessions, but the political process creates an asymmetry during expansions, not allowing for spending cuts and higher taxes, ultimately leading to an increase in the size of government and persistent deficits (Alesina and Passalacqua 2015).

Another strand of recent research focuses on the role of rational actors—voters, lobbyists, politicians, and bureaucrats—in causing fiscal outcomes to deviate from the optimal level. Political economy models that assume rational voters show that politicians may exploit only temporarily a certain degree of information asymmetry. Empirically, political budget cycles explain only a small departure from optimal policy around election times, especially in new democracies (Persson and Tabellini 2002; Brender and Drazen 2005; Drazen and Eslava 2010; Alesina and Paradisi 2014).

In contrast, the literature that studies public debt dynamics irrespective of the electoral calendar focuses on how the number of political actors may affect spending, deficits, and debt accumulation. Two main theories have been advanced to explain suboptimal behavior: common pool and veto players.

Common Pool

Weingast, Shepsle, and Johnsen (1981) argue that representative legislatures often pass budgets that give priority to local projects in districts they represent. Often referred to as pork-barrel spending, it is an increasing function of the number of electoral districts. Presented as the law of $1/n$, where total public revenue is a *common pool*, 1, available to n representatives (policymakers or districts), which they overuse proportionally to n in distributing benefits. The deviations of fiscal policy from the optimal—which would maximize social welfare—will be greater when the number of actors who represent subsets of the national purse (that is, spending ministers and parties in government) increases. A larger number of actors who thus fail to fully internalize the costs of raising additional revenue will lead to higher-than-optimal levels of spending and deficit financing (Wehner 2010).

Veto Players

A government system with a large number of veto players and sharp ideological differences among them on policy options enhances policy stability—that is, it is difficult to change the status quo (Tsebelis 1995, 2000, 2002). The status quo then becomes the preferred policy choice of those involved. Changes will only materialize once a certain number of institutional or partisan actors agree. This stasis makes it difficult to adapt policy to changing circumstances. As the number of veto players increases, fiscal adjustment becomes slower, leading to suboptimal public debt accumulation (Roubini and Sachs 1989; Alesina and Drazen 1991; Spolaore 2004). Similarly, as the ideological distance between the government players increases, the likelihood of any policy change from the status quo decreases (Franzese 2005; Tsebelis and Chang 2004). The presence of a large number of veto players and sharp ideological polarization among them reduces the chances of agreeing on policy changes and stabilizing the magnitude of excessive public debt (Cox and McCubbins 2001; MacIntyre 2001; Mian, Sufi, and Trebbi 2014). In contrast to the common pool, the veto players model explains the changes in public debt rather than the actual level of public debt.

EMPIRICAL MODEL AND DATA

The econometric approach followed here relates cross-country variation in public debt to multiple aspects of political fragmentation, including common pool considerations and the influence of veto players (Franzese 2002, 2005; Battaglini 2011). Unlike in previous empirical models that test the impact of alternative political outcomes on annual changes in public debt (Kagan 2015), this analysis focuses, in addition, on the period between elections for a national legislative body, thus restricting the sample to countries and periods in which competitive elections have taken place. The exercise thus tests the impact of political fragmentation on changes in public debt that occurred in years between legislative elections. The reason for focusing on multiyear legislatures (which typically last four or five years between two consecutive elections) is that debt creation is ultimately a decision of parliaments. In countries where there is a debt ceiling (for example, the United States), Congress has to explicitly approve any new debt limit. In other countries, debt issuance is decided by the executive but is usually the result of parliaments not passing revenue-raising measures or approving excessive spending.

First, debt episodes (the change in government debt) between two legislative election periods are defined, using data from the World Bank's Database of Political Indicators (DPI), which provides years in which those elections were held.[3]

Second, cross-country variations in public debt as a function of political fragmentation are modeled, controlling for the structure of the economy:

$$\Delta D_{it} = \beta_0 + \beta_1 PF_{it} + \zeta' X_{it} + \varepsilon_{it}, \tag{9.1}$$

where ΔD_{it} denotes the change in public debt, expressed relative to GDP, in country i = 1,. . .,N at period t = 1,. . .,L, as defined above; PF denotes political fragmentation variables; and $\boldsymbol{X}$ is a vector of controls. For the baseline results, equation (9.1) is estimated using ordinary least squares. The analysis covers 806 episodes of changes in public debt between legislative elections for 92 advanced and emerging market and developing economies for the period 1975–2015.

A concern in this literature is the existence of reverse causality. It is possible that at least some of the correlations uncovered in this chapter are instead generated by (1) an omitted driving variable (such as an economic crisis or stagnant growth) causing political fragmentation, an increase in public debt, and high levels of unemployment that make it difficult to reduce public debt without significant social cost; or (2) reverse causation whereby the need for fiscal consolidation engenders political polarization and fragmentation. By focusing on multiyear debt episodes, the econometric approach used in this chapter greatly reduces the likelihood of reversed causality. In addition, for robustness, an instrumental variable approach is subsequently used in estimating equation (9.1) using annual changes in public debt, with instruments based on lagged values of the political fragmentation variables (one electoral period back in time), and also including country fixed effects.

Data on gross general government debt, expressed relative to GDP, are drawn from the IMF's historical public debt database.[4] Figure 9.1 shows the evolution of public debt over time and across advanced and emerging market and developing economies in the sample. Figure 9.1 indicates large accumulations of public debt in the 1970s and 1980s in both advanced and emerging market and developing

[3] Results are broadly similar for electoral periods that exclude instances of early or repeated elections.
[4] Originally compiled in Mauro and others (2013) and updated using the IMF's World Economic Outlook and International Financial Statistics data.

Figure 9.1. Change in Public Debt
(Annual averages, percent)

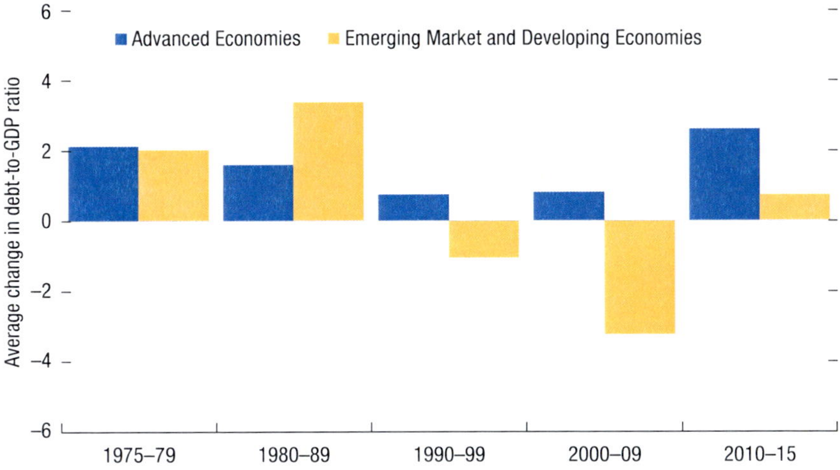

Sources: IMF, World Economic Outlook and International Financial Statistics databases; and Mauro and others 2013.

economies, with debt accumulating at a pace of more than 2 percent of GDP on a yearly basis over that period. Alesina and Passalacqua (2015) discuss alternative hypotheses of political distortions behind this sharp increase in public debt among advanced economies during a peace period.[5] This debt accumulation was followed by fiscal consolidation in the 1990s and a large part of the early 2000s that generally slowed or reduced debt accumulation. The financial crisis of 2008–09 again triggered accumulation of government debt, in particular among advanced economies.[6]

Data on political fragmentation relating to the common pool considerations are also drawn from DPI. Four alternative indicators from this database are considered to test the hypothesis. First, government terms characterized by larger parliamentary majorities are expected to react faster to the need for fiscal adjustment. To account for this, an indicator for *margin of majority* is included, which is defined as the fraction of parliamentary seats held by the government as a share of total seats. Second, the extreme situation is represented by the case in which the government party has an absolute majority (more than 50 percent of the seats) in the houses that have lawmaking powers, which is tested using a dummy variable *control of parliament* that takes the value one if this is the case and zero otherwise.[7] Alternatively, a third indicator for *executive polarization* is tested,

[5] Easterly (2014) suggests that in the early 1970s, many countries did not internalize a secular growth downturn requiring a reduction of government spending to keep the size of government constant, which ultimately led to an accumulation of debt.

[6] Descriptive statistics in Figures 9.1 and 9.2 do not differ significantly once countries that have received debt relief under the Heavily Indebted Poor Countries (HIPC) initiative are excluded.

[7] In addition, a fifth indicator for the *number of opposition parties* has been considered.

which measures the ideological distance between the executive's party (left, right, or center orientation) and the other three largest parties' orientation.[8] Finally, an additional predictor of political fragmentation is cabinet fragmentation within the executive branch of government. To account for this, the analysis follows Perotti and Kontopoulos (2002) in considering an indicator for the *size of the cabinet*, measured by the number of ministries, from Seki and Williams (2014).

Data on political fragmentation relating to the veto players theory are drawn from several sources. The actual *number of veto players* in a given country considers "individual or collective decision-makers whose agreement is required for the change of the status quo" (Tsebelis 1995, 289). Similarly, the analysis includes *checks and balances*, from DPI, which measures the number of political players influencing the government's decision making. In addition, the number of working days lost due to strike[9] from the International Labour Organization's Social Dialogue Database are considered as a proxy for social tensions, making policy changes more difficult to pass, and thus translating into larger public debt accumulation or slower debt reductions. The analysis also considers popular support, from the International Country Risk Guide, measuring the level of support for government (and its leaders), which facilitates the implementation of reforms. Finally, the *old-age dependency ratio* from the World Bank's World Development Indicators (WDI) is included. This indicator is defined as the ratio of older dependents—people older than 64—to the working-age population (those ages 15–64), to account for possible rigidities in the speed of public debt adjustment, related to a growing share of age-specific public spending on health and pensions.

Figure 9.2 illustrates the impact of selected political fragmentation indicators on debt dynamics, suggesting that indeed larger fragmentation, related to both the common pool and the veto players theories, is generally associated with higher increases in public debt (or smaller reductions). Among advanced economies, the increase in public debt on average over legislative periods has been about 3 percentage points of GDP higher in countries with below-average margins of majority in the parliament. Among emerging and developing countries, public debt has decreased about 1 percentage point of GDP faster in countries with above-average majority in the parliament, or in countries where political polarization is low. Similar magnitudes are found when considering the number of ministries.[10] For the selected indicators for the veto players theory, the increase in public debt has been about 2 percentage points higher in advanced economies facing a large number of days of strike while the decrease has been about 1 percentage point lower in emerging and developing

---

[8] The variable takes the value zero if the legislative index of political competitiveness or the executive index of political competitiveness—both from DPI—are less than 6 (elections are not competitive) and if the chief executive's party has an absolute majority in the legislature.

[9] This indicator counts the days of strike in major economic sectors. If two or more economic sectors conduct strikes in a given day, then the indicator adds these sectors together, which may result in more than 365 days of strike in a given year.

[10] The groups (low/high) for the number of ministries and the number of veto players are computed using the average, plus or minus one standard deviation.

Figure 9.2. Indicators of Political Fragmentation and Changes in Public Debt
(Average change in public debt over periods, percent)

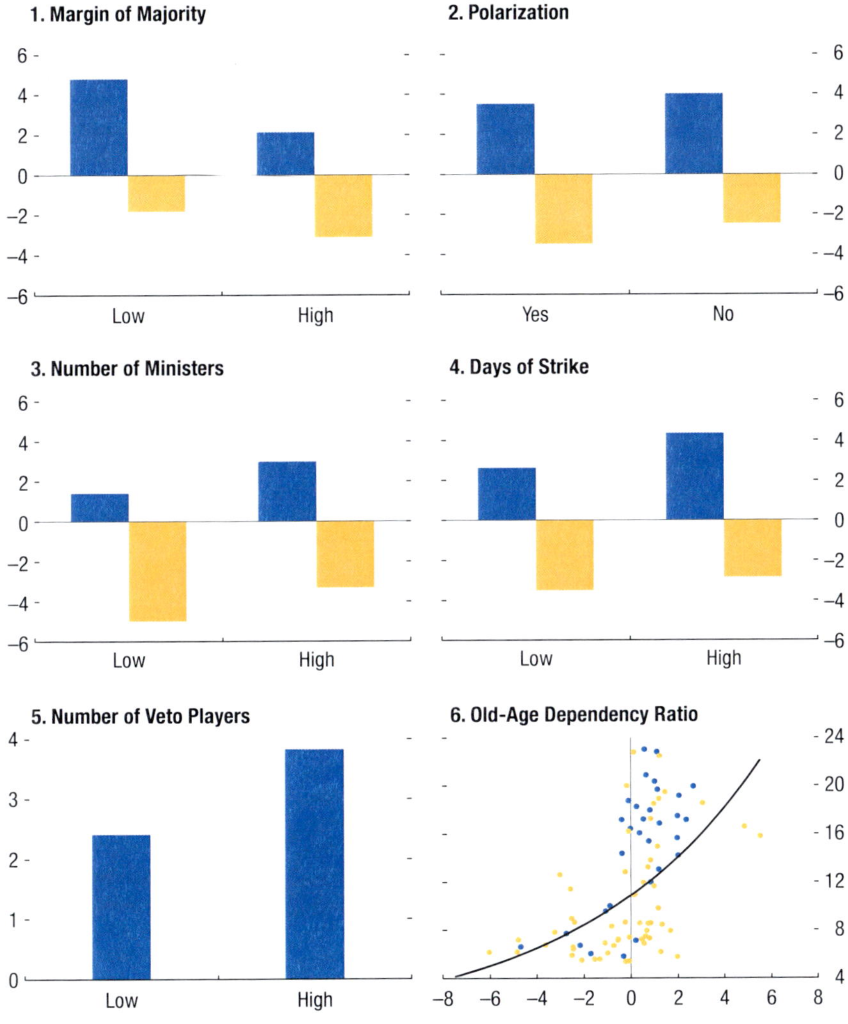

Sources: Escolano and others 2014; International Labour Organization; World Bank, World Development Indicators; and authors' calculations.

countries. Also, the number of veto players leads to faster accumulation of public debt (about 1½ percentage points of GDP) among advanced economies, the only group for which this indicator is available. Finally, for both advanced and emerging market and developing economies, a clear positive correlation emerges between the average accumulation of public debt (horizontal axis) and the average old-age dependency ratio (vertical axis). The analysis also looks at the role of the traditional control variables, such as changes in tax revenue and government spending, that affect

Table 9.1. Descriptive Statistics

Variable	Average	Minimum	Maximum	Standard Deviation
Debt to GDP (percent)	50.20	0.97	289.55	37.47
Advanced Economies	50.96	1.60	283.96	36.51
Emerging Market and Developing Economies	49.56	0.97	289.55	38.25
Change in Debt to GDP	0.15	−117.25	118.91	10.64
Advanced Economies	1.00	−84.97	93.43	6.10
Emerging Market and Developing Economies	−0.57	−117.25	118.91	13.30
Margin of Majority	0.68	0.03	1	0.21
Control of Parliament	0.52	0	1	0.50
Polarization	0.52	0	2	0.83
Number of Ministries	26.04	1	101	13.08
Number of Opposition Parties	3.16	0	168	11.27
Number of Veto Players	2.29	1	6	1.23
Checks and Balances	2.93	1	18	1.81
Popular Support	2.26	0	3.91	0.57
Days of Strike	381.33	0	12,765	869.98
Old-Age Dependency Ratio	12.22	3.74	41.90	6.82
Legislative Election	0.23	0	1	0.42
Executive Election	0.09	0	1	0.29
Change in Natural Resource Rents	0.04	−20.57	34.55	2.39
Inflation	0.40	−0.31	156.06	4.41
Change in Nominal Exchange Rate	0.85	−1.00	2,626.77	39.36
Trade Openness	65.56	1.33	809.22	50.94
Per Capita GDP (log)	10.89	5.80	17.37	2.38
Social Spending to GDP (percent)	25.33	0	55.51	14.62
Control of Corruption (percentile rank)	53.53	0	100	30.15
Quality of Bureaucracy	2.15	0	4	1.17
Change in Unemployment Rate	0.01	−12	17	1.14

Source: Authors' calculations.

government debt dynamics.[11] Data are drawn from the World Bank's WDI and the IMF's *World Economic Outlook*. The data include per capita GDP in constant U.S. dollars (and the change in per capita GDP); the share of agriculture in value added; the degree of trade openness, measured as the sum of the shares of imports and exports in GDP; consumer price index inflation (and the change in consumer price index inflation); the change in natural resources rents;[12] the change in the nominal exchange rate; the change in the unemployment rate; and the share of social spending in GDP.

Finally, the quality of institutions is also controlled for using the International Country Risk Guide corruption index, as well as institutional strength and quality of the bureaucracy indicators. The final sample size varies depending on the specification. Table 9.1 provides descriptive statistics. The list of countries included in the sample is provided in Annex 9.1.

[11] For a review, see, for example, Crivelli and Gupta (2016), Baunsgaard and Keen (2010), Baldacci and others (2008), and Rodrik (1998).

[12] This variable from the World Bank's World Development Indicators captures the sum of natural resource rents from oil, gas, coal (hard and soft), minerals, and forests, expressed as a percentage of GDP.

MAIN RESULTS

This section reports the results of estimating equation (9.1) for all episodes of changes in public debt between legislative elections during 1975–2015. Table 9.2 provides the basic results using ordinary least squares for political fragmentation related to the common pool theory; variables capturing the veto players theory are presented in Table 9.3. For robustness and ease of comparison with earlier literature, results based on annual changes in public debt, using an instrumental variable estimation approach, are presented in Annex 9.2 (Annex Tables 9.2.1

Table 9.2. Common Pool Theory: Legislative Periods

	(1)	(2)	(3)	(4)	(5)
Margin of Majority	−8.160**				
	(1.231)				
Control of Parliament		−6.300***			
		(2.077)			
Polarization			−1.071		
			(1.581)		
Number of Ministries				0.146***	
				(0.054)	
Number of Opposition Parties					0.025
					(0.036)
R^2	0.286	0.303	0.303	0.542	0.286
F-statistic	7.74	8.25	8.22	10.61	7.61
P-value	0.000	0.000	0.000	0.000	0.000
Observations	359	360	344	238	360
Number of Countries	61	61	59	32	61

Source: Authors' calculations.
Note: Dependent variable = change in debt-to-GDP ratio. All control variables are included in all regressions. Robust standard errors are in parentheses.
$^*p < .1$; $^{**}p < .05$; $^{***}p < .01$.

Table 9.3. Veto Players Theory: Legislative Periods

	(1)	(2)	(3)	(4)	(5)
Number of Veto Players	1.451*				
	(0.896)				
Days of Strike		0.002**			
		(0.0006)			
Checks and Balances			1.057**		
			(0.482)		
Popular Support				−5.964***	
				(2.221)	
Old-Age Dependency Ratio					0.397**
					(0.184)
R^2	0.447	0.253	0.112	0.400	0.274
F-statistic	7.13	7.02	3.38	10.42	8.59
P-value	0.000	0.000	0.000	0.000	0.000
Observations	99	202	763	257	348
Number of Countries	16	57	61	61	60

Source: Authors' calculations.
Note: Dependent variable = change in debt-to-GDP ratio. All control variables are included in all regressions. Robust standard errors are in parentheses.
$^*p < .1$; $^{**}p < .05$; $^{***}p < .01$.

and 9.2.2). For brevity, the full set of control variables is only shown in the annex tables and omitted in tables in the main text. These control variables are generally significant in explaining changes in public debt and present the expected sign.

The regressions reveal that the effect of political fragmentation on changes in public debt is generally significant and can be large. The estimated coefficients from the common pool theory indicators (Table 9.2) suggest, for instance, that less fragmentation in the parliament facilitates fiscal consolidation. For each additional 10 percentage points of parliamentary majority, there is an average public debt reduction of about three-quarters of a percentage point of GDP, with full control of the parliament leading to a reduction in public debt of 6 percentage points of GDP. In contrast, a more polarized political system (measured by the lack of majority and divergent political preferences) can induce larger debt accumulation: the estimated coefficient suggests that the maximum level of polarization creates an average differential in public debt increase of about 2 percentage points of GDP vis-à-vis minimum polarization, even though the estimated coefficient is not statistically significant. Finally, a more fragmented government, measured by the number of ministries, creates scope for faster debt accumulation as the size of the cabinet increases (although the estimated effect seems relatively small).

The indicators on the veto players theory (Table 9.3) are significantly correlated with changes in public debt during legislative periods, and the magnitude of their effect is strong. According to the estimated coefficients, each additional veto player generates an average increase in public debt during a legislative period of about 1.5 percentage points of GDP. Also, each additional 100 days of strike[13] explain an increase in public debt of about 0.2 percentage point of GDP. In addition, each additional political actor influencing government decision making (an increase in the variable "checks and balances" by one-half standard deviation) leads to a faster accumulation of public debt by 1 percentage point of GDP. Interestingly, a decrease in popular support for the government (by 1 standard deviation) also leads to faster debt accumulation by about 3½ percentage points of GDP during a legislative period.

Finally, each 10 percentage point increase in the old-age dependency ratio contributes to an average increase in public debt of 4 percentage points of GDP.

ROBUSTNESS TESTS

The previous section showed that political fragmentation can have a sizable impact on public debt dynamics. It also showed that these results are robust to alternative definitions of the period under analysis (that is, public debt changes during multi-year periods between legislative elections and during annual changes in debt). This section assesses the robustness of the results to alternative specifications. It first looks at the sensitivity of the results to the simultaneous inclusion of both the common pool and veto players variables. It then explores the potentially differential

[13] Note that the average number of strike days in the most recent legislature period under study was 100 days, including all sectors in the economy, as reported by the International Labour Organization.

Table 9.4. Common Pool and Veto Player Variables

	(1)
Change in Debt$_{t-1}$	0.145***
	(0.036)
Margin of Majority	−4.775**
	(2.477)
Number of Ministries	0.037**
	(0.020)
Days of Strike	−0.001
	(0.001)
Checks and Balances	0.198*
	(0.124)
Old-Age Dependency Ratio	0.154**
	(0.043)
Time Fixed Effects	Yes
R^2	0.517
F-statistic	2.99
P-value	0.000
Observations	706
Number of Countries	35

Source: Authors' calculations.
Note: Dependent variable is change in debt-to-GDP ratio. All control variables are included in all regressions. Instrumental variables approach with instruments is based on lagged values of the dependent variable, including country fixed effects. Robust standard errors are in parentheses.
$^*p < .1$; $^{**}p < .05$; $^{***}p < .01$.

impact of political fragmentation on public debt dynamics based on the level of perceived corruption and the prevailing level of public debt.[14] Further robustness tests consist of isolating periods of debt increase and decrease, separately, and looking at the role of independent fiscal institutions in mitigating the impact of fragmentation. To address potential endogeneity concerns, all results presented in this section use an instrumental variable estimation approach, as discussed above.

Other checks were performed on the results of the previous section. In particular, to control for countries that have received debt relief under the Heavily Indebted Poor Countries (HIPC) initiative, HIPC countries were excluded from the sample. Also, given the importance of nominal GDP in driving public debt levels (especially in developing countries), the analysis considers the level of public debt, rather than the public-debt-to-GDP ratio, and controls for the change in GDP in the regressions. Relatedly, because increases in public-debt-to-GDP ratios capture many other factors beyond fiscal profligacy (including, for example, increases due to stock-flow adjustments), an alternative measure was considered using the general government's primary balance. The results for these additional checks are qualitatively identical to those presented above and thus have been omitted to preserve space.

The first robustness test consists in exploring the relative importance of the different fragmentation hypotheses more closely. Table 9.4 reports the results of

[14] In addition to controlling for the level of GDP per capita in all regressions, a further test consisted in exploring the potentially differential effect based on the level of development of the country, by splitting the sample into OECD versus non-OECD countries. The results were inconclusive and have been omitted to preserve space.

including both the common pool and veto players variables in the regression. For this exercise, only variables that are not highly correlated within each group are included.[15] Results are qualitatively similar to those presented in the previous section, and the estimated coefficients are similar in magnitude, which further reinforces the importance of considering both aspects of political fragmentation.

The next robustness test consists in assessing whether the effect of political fragmentation on public debt dynamics is influenced by the level of corruption. Earlier evidence has shown that the level of corruption can be positively associated with the level of public debt (IMF 2016; Cooray and Schneider 2013), either through a direct increase in public spending (Kaufmann 2010; Tanzi and Davoodi 2002), or indirectly by affecting its composition (Gupta, De Mello, and Sharan 2001; Mauro 1998), and by reducing the ability of a government to raise tax revenues (IMF 2016; Schneider, Buehn, and Montenegro 2010; Kaufmann 2010).

This analysis splits the sample on the basis of the World Bank corruption indicator, which reflects perceptions of the extent to which public power is exercised for private gain. Table 9.5 presents the results for countries belonging to the upper 50th percentile of perceived level of control of corruption (that is, those with the lowest level of corruption); Annex Table 9.2.3 presents results for countries in the lower 50th percentile (high corruption).

A simple comparison of the results of indicators for the common pool theory shows that in countries with low perceived corruption (Table 9.5), less political fragmentation—as measured by a larger margin of majority or control of parliament—is negatively and significantly associated with changes in public debt. The opposite can be observed in countries with high perceived corruption (Annex Table 9.2.3), where a higher margin of majority or even the full control of parliament are not necessarily associated with reductions in public debt. Interestingly, a more fragmented government, measured by the number of ministries, is associated with much faster debt accumulation in countries with high perceived corruption: the estimated coefficient is some 40 times higher in countries with high perceived corruption as compared with countries with low perceived corruption and is highly significant.

The indicators on the veto players theory show a similar pattern. The estimated coefficients for the number of days of strike and the old-age dependency ratio are larger and more significant in Annex Table 9.2.3, implying a stronger link between political fragmentation and accumulation of public debt in countries with high corruption. Interestingly, higher popular support is associated with slower debt accumulation in countries with low perceived corruption but faster debt accumulation in countries with high perceived corruption (although this last coefficient is not statistically significant). The only exception is checks and balances, which is positively associated with increases in public debt only in countries with low perceived corruption.

---

[15] We also exclude variables with only a limited number of observations, such as the number of veto players, which is only available for advanced economies.

Table 9.5. Low Perceived Corruption

	Common Pool Theory					Veto Players Theory				
	(1)	(2)	(3)	(4)	(5)	(6)	(7)	(8)	(9)	(10)
Change in Debt$_{t-1}$	0.059	0.068	0.070	0.090	0.001	0.353***	0.170***	0.026	0.119***	0.029
	(0.102)	(0.096)	(0.096)	(0.177)	(0.021)	(0.047)	(0.026)	(0.022)	(0.046)	(0.020)
Margin of Majority	−4.266**									
	(2.142)									
Control of Parliament		−1.560**								
		(0.780)								
Polarization			0.223							
			(0.430)							
Number of Ministries				0.020						
				(0.019)						
Number of Opposition Parties					0.042					
					(0.068)					
Number of Veto Players						0.370*				
						(0.222)				
Days of Strike						0.001				
							(0.002)			
Checks and Balances								0.477**		
								(0.208)		
Popular Support									−0.713*	
									(0.515)	
Old-Age Dependency Ratio										0.052
										(0.124)
Time Fixed Effects	Yes	Yes	Yes	Yes	Yes	Yes	Yes	Yes	Yes	Yes
R^2	0.170	0.170	0.200	0.372	0.196	0.519	0.239	0.207	0.391	0.196
F-statistic	2.32	2.59	2.38	1.52	2.84	1.80	3.58	2.34	1.43	3.27
P-value	0.000	0.000	0.000	0.000	0.000	0.000	0.000	0.000	0.000	0.000
Observations	1,513	1,611	1,551	1,258	1,561	439	1,215	1,605	533	1,849
Number of Countries	90	91	89	41	92	20	58	91	81	83

Source: Authors' calculations.

Note: Dependent variable = annual change in debt-to-GDP ratio. Instrumental variables approach with instruments is based on lagged values of the dependent variable, including country fixed effects. All control variables are included in all regressions. Robust standard errors are in parentheses.

$*p < .1$; $**p < .05$; $***p < .01$.

A further robustness test consists in assessing the differential impact of political fragmentation on public debt dynamics while separately considering periods of decreasing public debt (Table 9.6) and periods of increasing public debt (Annex Table 9.2.4). A comparison of the results shows an apparent asymmetry. For periods in which public debt decreased, the results are largely as presented earlier, that is, more political fragmentation—through both common pool and veto players theory—is associated with slower reduction in public debt; less political fragmentation—as, for example, measured by a higher margin of majority or attaining control of parliament—is associated with faster debt reduction. However, most of the estimated coefficients are statistically insignificant for the common pool theory, meaning these results do not necessarily hold in periods in which public debt increased.

Results for indicators on the veto players theory are similar for periods of both debt increase and decrease, except that as in the previous case, the estimated coefficients are smaller for periods of debt increase. Only the indicator for popular support behaves differently, and it is negatively and significantly correlated with periods of debt increase only, suggesting that weaker popular support can lead to faster debt accumulation.

An additional robustness check is performed by analyzing the differential impact of political fragmentation on public debt dynamics once initial conditions are accounted for. For this purpose, a debt-to-GDP threshold is defined using the sample average of 50 percent. This level of public debt is used as a threshold above which the economy becomes vulnerable to shocks, and with further increases in public debt potentially affecting economic growth more significantly.[16] The underlying hypothesis is that countries with a debt-to-GDP ratio above 50 percent face a hard constraint that may prevent political fragmentation from affecting debt dynamics. The results for countries that are below the defined threshold are almost identical to those presented in the main results section and are not repeated here to preserve space. When focusing on periods for which countries are above the defined threshold, however, the results become much weaker (Annex Table 9.2.5), which confirms the underlying hypothesis. Only the interactive coefficient for higher fragmentation measured as the number of ministries is positively and significantly correlated with changes in public debt. Among the veto players indicators, only the interactive coefficient for popular support is significant but positively correlated with public debt changes, suggesting that weaker popular support at high debt levels leads to lower debt accumulation rates. In sum, higher political fragmentation has little impact on further increasing public debt once a high level of public debt has been accumulated. Interestingly, however, the opposite is also true, that is, less political fragmentation does not appear to be effective in accelerating public debt consolidation once that level of high public debt has been accumulated.

[16] Although below the 60 percent threshold included as a criterion (upper limit) in the European Union's Stability and Growth Pact (and also used in Reinhart and Rogoff [2010]), the 50 percent threshold is likely more relevant for developing countries. Results using a 60 percent threshold, however, do not differ significantly.

Table 9.6. Debt Decreases

	Common Pool Theory					Veto Players Theory				
	(1)	(2)	(3)	(4)	(5)	(6)	(7)	(8)	(9)	(10)
Change in Debt$_{t-1}$	0.007	0.010	0.008	0.160***	−0.060**	0.129**	0.070*	−0.038*	0.202***	0.009
	(0.092)	(0.084)	(0.084)	(0.021)	(0.020)	(0.069)	(0.027)	(0.021)	(0.046)	(0.084)
Margin of Majority	−4.778***									
	(1.735)									
Control of Parliament		−2.579***								
		(0.644)								
Polarization			1.494***							
			(0.358)							
Number of Ministries				0.034*						
				(0.018)						
Number of Opposition Parties						0.052*				
					(0.039)					
Number of Veto Players						0.466*				
						(0.275)				
Days of Strike								0.001		
							(0.001)			
Checks and Balances								0.412*		
								(0.228)		
Popular Support									0.116	
									(0.885)	
Old-Age Dependency Ratio										0.272***
										(0.048)
Time Fixed Effects	Yes	Yes	Yes	Yes	Yes	Yes	Yes	Yes	Yes	Yes
R^2	0.123	0.129	0.122	0.419	0.172	0.391	0.117	0.174	0.235	0.153
F-statistic	4.00	4.07	3.79	2.45	3.89	3.69	5.69	3.75	1.47	3.73
P-value	0.000	0.000	0.000	0.000	0.000	0.000	0.000	0.000	0.000	0.000
Observations	1,109	1,080	1,051	619	1,122	165	659	1,066	415	1,172
Number of Countries	90	92	89	41	92	20	59	91	81	92

Source: Authors' calculations.

Note: Dependent variable = annual change in debt-to-GDP ratio. Instrumental variables approach with instruments is based on lagged values of the dependent variable, including country fixed effects. All control variables are included in all regressions. Robust standard errors are in parentheses.

$^*p < .1$; $^{**}p < .05$; $^{***}p < .01$.

A final robustness check consists in analyzing how the existence of independent fiscal institutions affects the impact of fragmentation on public debt dynamics. A small but growing literature has argued that independent fiscal institutions, such as fiscal councils, could improve policymakers' incentives to opt for sound fiscal policies even in the presence of political fragmentation (IMF 2013). First, by fostering transparency over the political cycle, a fiscal council can improve democratic accountability and discourage opportunistic shifts in fiscal policy (for example, preelection spending sprees). Second, through independent analysis, assessments, and forecasts, such bodies can raise public awareness of the consequences of unsustainable policy paths resulting from the presence of veto players, or contribute to a stability culture that directly addresses fiscal illusion linked to the common pool problem. Hence, a fiscal council can raise the reputational and electoral costs of unsound fiscal policies associated with political fragmentation. Third and finally, a fiscal council can provide direct inputs to the budget process—for example, forecasts or assessments of structural positions—thereby closing technical loopholes that allow governments to circumvent numerical fiscal rules.

Using the IMF Fiscal Council Dataset,[17] a dummy variable is defined that takes the value one if the fiscal council in a given country has a score that is above the sample average and takes the value zero otherwise (or in the absence of a fiscal council). Annex Tables 9.2.6 and 9.2.7 present the results for strong and weak fiscal councils, respectively. The results suggest that the impact of fragmentation on the accumulation of public debt is stronger and more significant in countries without fiscal councils or in countries where fiscal councils are weaker than the average.[18]

CONCLUDING REMARKS AND POLICY IMPLICATIONS

This chapter focuses on the political determinants behind public debt dynamics. Using an empirical approach, it tests the role of traditional indicators of political fragmentation in explaining changes in public debt. The analysis both looks at annual data and introduces a selection of periods between consecutive legislative elections that is novel to the literature.

---

[17] See http://www.imf.org/external/np/fad/council. The IMF Fiscal Council Dataset describes key features of 39 institutions identified as fiscal councils as of 2014 across the IMF membership. The data set includes general information such as the name and acronym of the council and its date of creation, the main features of the council's remit, their specific tasks and instruments to influence the conduct of fiscal policy, as well as key institutional characteristics such as the existence of formal guarantees of independence, accountability requirements, and human resources. Debrun and Kinda (2014) provide the list and definition of variables included in the Fiscal Council Dataset. They also describe the variety of sources used to assemble the data.

[18] The establishment of fiscal councils is usually preceded by the adoption of fiscal rules, in many instances to ensure that these rules are followed. As such, the identified impact could be driven by the existence of fiscal rules. We also considered the potential impact of fiscal rules in mitigating the impact of political fragmentation. Results are qualitatively similar but significance generally weakens, potentially suggesting that fiscal rules can indeed mitigate the impact of political fragmentation and help the development of sound fiscal frameworks.

The results show that political fragmentation plays a prominent role in explaining public debt dynamics. The main theoretical hypotheses are confirmed—both common pool theory and veto players theory indicators show a positive association between political fragmentation and changes in public debt. In addition, we show that corruption magnifies these effects: in societies perceived to be corrupt, high political fragmentation has a sizable impact on debt increases. In contrast, low political fragmentation is not effective at reducing public debt in the presence of high corruption

Finally, the impact of political fragmentation on debt dynamics appears to be somewhat asymmetric, with larger and more significant effects of fragmentation in periods of debt decline. This finding only applies, however, to normal times, that is, when public debt is relatively low (less than 50 percent of GDP). For countries with high levels of public debt, political fragmentation cannot explain further increases in public debt. In addition, low political fragmentation appears to be ineffective in reducing public debt above that threshold.

The findings of this chapter are relevant for policymakers. An environment of political fragmentation is likely to be associated with excessive spending, deficits, and debt, regardless of whether such a policy stance is good or bad for the economy. This points to the need to strengthen fiscal institutions (fiscal rules and fiscal councils, in particular) to limit the impact that political fragmentation has on government spending. The use of a binding medium-term budget or fiscal framework could be considered, which sets, for instance, binding expenditure ceilings for a number of years, thereby constraining the ability of political players to influence fiscal policy. It points to the need for greater transparency in the decision-making process so that the public can better understand how fiscal and economic decisions are made in the short term and what their implications are in the long term.

ANNEX 9.1. COUNTRIES IN THE SAMPLE

Advanced economies: Australia, Austria, Belgium, Canada, Cyprus, Czech Republic, Denmark, Estonia, Finland, France, Germany, Greece, Iceland, Ireland, Israel, Italy, Korea, Luxembourg, Netherlands, New Zealand, Norway, Portugal, Singapore, Slovak Republic, Slovenia, Spain, Sweden, Switzerland, United Kingdom, United States.

Developing countries:[19] Albania, Argentina, Armenia, Bolivia,* Brazil, Bulgaria, Burkina Faso,* Cambodia, Cameroon, Chad,* Chile, China, Colombia, Republic of Congo,* Croatia, Côte d'Ivoire,* Ethiopia,* Georgia, Ghana,* Haiti,* Honduras,* Hungary, India, Indonesia, Islamic Republic of Iran, Jordan, Kazakhstan, Kenya, Lao P.D.R., Latvia, Lithuania, Madagascar,* Mali,* Mexico, Moldova, Morocco, Mozambique,* Myanmar, Nepal, Nicaragua,* Nigeria, Pakistan, Peru, Philippines, Poland, Romania, Saudi Arabia, Senegal,* Sudan,* Tanzania,* Thailand, Turkey, Uganda,* Ukraine, Uzbekistan, Vietnam, Yemen, Zambia.*

[19] Countries denoted with an asterisk are those that have benefited from the Highly Indebted Poor Countries initiative.

ANNEX 9.2. OTHER RESULTS

Annex Table 9.2.1. Common Pool Theory: Annual Data

	(1)	(2)	(3)	(4)	(5)
Change in Debt$_{t-1}$	0.122***	0.115***	0.115***	0.166***	0.116***
	(0.027)	(0.026)	(0.027)	(0.029)	(0.027)
Margin of Majority	−5.871**				
	(2.659)				
Control of Parliament		−1.730**			
		(0.816)			
Polarization			0.092		
			(0.413)		
Number of Ministries				0.032**	
				(0.015)	
Number of Opposition Parties					0.002
					(0.035)
Legislative Election	0.037	0.014	0.012	0.337	0.061
	(0.514)	(0.522)	(0.546)	(0.440)	(0.520)
Executive Election	0.947	0.837	0.610	1.302*	0.971
	(0.799)	(0.805)	(0.851)	(0.789)	(0.805)
Change in Oil Rents	−0.291**	−0.281*	−0.266*	1.029**	−0.276*
	(0.152)	(0.155)	(0.158)	(0.413)	(0.154)
Change in Unemployment Rate	0.199	0.144	0.239	−0.029	0.235
	(0.191)	(0.184)	(0.202)	(0.199)	(0.190)
Share of Social Spending	0.114	0.158**	0.188**	0.056**	0.122
	(0.082)	(0.083)	(0.087)	(0.025)	(0.084)
Quality of Bureaucracy	−0.428	−0.532	−0.247	−0.400	−0.458
	(0.894)	(0.896)	(0.897)	(0.458)	(0.921)
Corruption	−0.373	−0.374	−0.407	−0.389*	−0.333
	(0.473)	(0.481)	(0.483)	(0.250)	(0.480)
Inflation	−0.281***	−0.294***	−0.287***	−0.065	−0.277***
	(0.058)	(0.056)	(0.057)	(0.051)	(0.058)
Change in Inflation	0.135***	0.161***	0.147***	0.659***	0.150***
	(0.060)	(0.057)	(0.059)	(0.087)	(0.060)
Change in Nominal Exchange Rate	0.116***	0.117***	0.123***	0.113***	0.113***
	(0.014)	(0.015)	(0.015)	(0.015)	(0.015)
Trade Openness	0.006	−0.013	−0.010	0.003	−0.013
	(0.017)	(0.017)	(0.018)	(0.004)	(0.017)
Per Capita GDP	0.071***	0.072***	0.086***	0.015	0.081***
	(0.025)	(0.026)	(0.027)	(0.111)	(0.026)
Change in per Capita GDP	−0.679***	−0.700***	−0.759***	−0.948***	−0.679***
	(0.086)	(0.084)	(0.089)	(0.103)	(0.086)
Constant	−75.256***	−77.952***	−95.313***	−0.568	−87.781***
	(28.977)	(29.329)	(30.228)	(2.103)	(29.152)
Time Fixed Effects	Yes	Yes	Yes	Yes	Yes
R^2	0.297	0.290	0.296	0.493	0.283
F-statistic	1.83	1.88	1.84	2.11	1.76
P-value	0.000	0.000	0.000	0.000	0.000
Observations	1,153	1,205	1,147	750	1,193
Number of Countries	61	61	59	32	61

Source: Authors' calculations.
Note: Dependent variable = change in debt-to-GDP ratio. Instrumental variables approach with instruments is based on lagged values of the dependent variable, including country fixed effects. Robust standard errors are in parentheses.
$^*p < .1$; $^{**}p < .05$; $^{***}p < .01$.

Annex Table 9.2.2. Veto Players Theory: Annual Data

	(1)	(2)	(3)	(4)	(5)
Change in Debt$_{t-1}$	0.316***	0.213***	0.160***	0.215***	0.162***
	(0.065)	(0.027)	(0.028)	(0.037)	(0.028)
Number of Veto Players	0.837***				
	(0.306)				
Days of Strike		0.0005*			
		(0.0003)			
Checks and Balances			0.619***		
			(0.225)		
Popular Support				−0.932*	
				(0.533)	
Old-Age Dependency Ratio					0.112***
					(0.040)
Legislative Election	−0.052	0.855	−0.018	−0.364	0.397
	(0.475)	(0.611)	(0.501)	(0.578)	(0.570)
Executive Election	1.194	0.452	0.540	1.931**	0.744
	(1.240)	(1.038)	(0.796)	(0.827)	(0.852)
Change in Oil Rents	−1.227	0.193	−0.361**	−0.419***	−0.378**
	(1.081)	(0.337)	(0.161)	(0.138)	(0.169)
Change in Unemployment Rate	0.966***	0.874***	0.164	0.449**	0.321*
	(0.292)	(0.267)	(0.182)	(0.221)	(0.202)
Share of Social Spending	0.034	0.057	0.089	0.024	0.175
	(0.157)	(0.421)	(0.085)	(0.113)	(0.137)
Quality of Bureaucracy	−2.561	1.165***	−0.186	1.342***	0.896**
	(1.870)	(0.407)	(0.865)	(0.542)	(0.411)
Corruption	0.064	−0.995***	−0.266	−1.200	−1.078***
	(0.465)	(0.307)	(0.452)	(0.869)	(0.310)
Inflation	−0.333*	−0.260***	−0.207***	−0.098	−0.263***
	(0.195)	(0.057)	(0.057)	(0.097)	(0.051)
Change in Inflation	0.048***	0.017*	0.097*	0.015	0.195***
	(0.017)	(0.010)	(0.061)	(0.090)	(0.068)
Change in Nominal Exchange Rate	0.007	0.028***	0.137***	−0.435	0.139***
	(0.016)	(0.064)	(0.017)	(2.960)	(0.019)
Trade Openness	0.014	0.008*	−0.006	0.015	−0.001
	(0.038)	(0.005)	(0.016)	(0.024)	(0.004)
Per Capita GDP	0.058	0.099	0.064***	0.093***	−0.002
	(5.504)	(0.131)	(0.025)	(0.036)	(0.119)
Change in per Capita GDP	−0.586***	−0.645***	−0.708***	−0.406***	−0.549***
	(0.186)	(0.094)	(0.082)	(0.093)	(0.089)
Constant	4.109	−4.641	−72.019***	−134.25***	1.064
	(57.826)	(8.466)	(28.100)	(42.839)	(1.886)
Time Fixed Effects	Yes	Yes	Yes	Yes	Yes
R^2	0.675	0.546	0.316	0.377	0.466
F-statistic	1.06	1.25	1.86	1.26	1.38
P-value	0.000	0.000	0.000	0.000	0.000
Observations	210	1,063	1,149	655	1,119
Number of Countries	16	57	61	61	60

Source: Authors' calculations.

Note: Dependent variable = change in debt-to-GDP ratio. Instrumental variables approach with instruments is based on lagged values of the dependent variable, including country fixed effects. Robust standard errors are in parentheses.

$^{*}p < .1$; $^{**}p < .05$; $^{***}p < .01$.

Annex Table 9.2.3. High Perceived Corruption

	Common Pool Theory					Veto Players Theory			
	(1)	(2)	(3)	(4)	(5)	(6)	(7)	(8)	(9)
Change in Debt$_{t-1}$	−0.003	−0.012	0.082**	0.006	−0.024	0.009	−0.083	0.102**	−0.019
	(0.042)	(0.095)	(0.040)	(0.060)	(0.095)	(0.095)	(0.040)	(0.054)	(0.039)
Margin of Majority	2.805								
	(3.471)								
Control of Parliament		−1.328							
		(1.837)							
Polarization			1.348						
			(1.168)						
Number of Ministries				0.748**					
				(0.415)					
Number of Opposition Parties					−0.0697				
					(0.0565)				
Days of Strike							0.011*		
						(0.006)			
Checks and Balances							0.128		
							(0.370)		
Popular Support								0.202	
								(0.438)	
Old-Age Dependency Ratio									0.434***
									(0.127)
Time Fixed Effects	Yes	Yes	Yes	Yes	Yes	Yes	Yes	Yes	Yes
R^2	0.380	0.271	0.262	0.903	0.256	0.552	0.287	0.357	0.227
F-statistic	1.81	2.10	2.09	1.29	1.93	1.16	2.00	2.05	1.64
P-value	0.000	0.000	0.000	0.000	0.000	0.000	0.000	0.000	0.000
Observations	545	591	586	76	589	104	558	259	611
Number of Countries	50	51	50	7	51	22	51	41	51

Source: Authors' calculations.

Note: Dependent variable = change in debt-to-GDP ratio. Instrumental variables approach with instruments is based on lagged values of the dependent variable, including country fixed effects. All control variables are included in all regressions. Robust standard errors are in parentheses.

$^*p < .1$; $^{**}p < .05$; $^{***}p < .01$.

Annex Table 9.2.4. Debt Increases

	Common Pool Theory					Veto Players Theory				
	(1)	(2)	(3)	(4)	(5)	(6)	(7)	(8)	(9)	(10)
Change in Debt$_{t-1}$	0.012	0.065*	0.085***	0.207**	0.078***	0.222***	0.189**	0.076**	0.057*	0.091***
	(0.089)	(0.027)	(0.028)	(0.042)	(0.030)	(0.063)	(0.084)	(0.028)	(0.038)	(0.027)
Margin of Majority	−2.593*									
	(1.862)									
Control of Parliament		0.750								
		(0.704)								
Polarization			−0.010							
			(0.418)							
Number of Ministries				−0.029						
				(0.026)						
Number of Opposition Parties					−0.070					
					(0.064)					
Number of Veto Players						0.206*				
						(0.014)				
Days of Strike								−0.001		
								(0.001)		
Checks and Balances								−0.132		
								(0.197)		
Popular Support									−0.656*	
									(0.422)	
Old-Age Dependency Ratio										0.245**
										(0.113)
Time Fixed Effects	Yes	Yes	Yes	Yes	Yes	Yes	Yes	Yes	Yes	Yes
R^2	0.224	0.202	0.195	0.315	0.213	0.409	0.230	0.230	0.327	0.187
F-statistic	11.43	8.77	6.80	25.09	10.69	4.51	5.14	3.36	2.16	5.12
P-value	0.000	0.000	0.000	0.000	0.000	0.000	0.000	0.000	0.000	0.000
Observations	1,052	1,125	1,086	727	1,085	313	658	1,097	483	1,288
Number of Countries	91	92	90	42	92	20	60	92	82	92

Source: Authors' calculations.

Note: Dependent variable = annual change in debt-to-GDP ratio. Instrumental variables approach with instruments is based on lagged values of the dependent variable, including country fixed effects. All control variables are included in all regressions. Robust standard errors are in parentheses.

*$p < .1$; **$p < .05$; ***$p < .01$.

Annex Table 9.2.5. High Level of Public Debt

	Common Pool Theory					Veto Players Theory				
	(1)	(2)	(3)	(4)	(5)	(6)	(7)	(8)	(9)	(10)
Change in Debt$_{t-1}$	0.122***	−0.022	0.113***	0.113***	0.050*	0.310***	0.296***	0.155***	0.009	0.115***
	(0.027)	(0.029)	(0.027)	(0.030)	(0.027)	(0.066)	(0.047)	(0.028)	(0.061)	(0.028)
Margin of Majority	−0.027									
	(1.081)									
Control of Parliament		−0.814								
		(1.436)								
Polarization			0.506							
			(0.489)							
Number of Ministries				0.041**						
				(0.019)						
Number of Opposition Parties					0.188					
					(0.126)					
Number of Veto Players						0.152				
						(0.300)				
Days of Strike								−0.001		
								(0.002)		
Checks and Balances								0.209		
								(0.148)		
Popular Support									0.812**	
									(0.398)	
Old-Age Dependency Ratio										0.040
										(0.041)
Time Fixed Effects	Yes	Yes	Yes	Yes	Yes	Yes	Yes	Yes	Yes	Yes
R^2	0.259	0.256	0.257	0.364	0.258	0.705	0.260	0.334	0.258	0.217
Observations	1,153	1,032	1,147	750	1,003	210	583	1,149	478	1,156
Number of Countries	61	72	59	32	72	16	41	68	61	61

Source: Authors' calculations.

Note: Dependent variable = annual change in debt-to-GDP ratio. Coefficients represent the differential impact (the interactive term) for public-debt-to-GDP ratio above 50 percent. Instrumental variables approach with instruments is based on lagged values of the dependent variable, including country fixed effects. All control variables are included in all regressions. Robust standard errors are in parentheses.

*$p < .1$; **$p < .05$; ***$p < .01$.

Annex Table 9.2.6. Strong Fiscal Council

	Common Pool Theory					Veto Players Theory				
	(1)	(2)	(3)	(4)	(5)	(6)	(7)	(8)	(9)	(10)
Change in Debt$_{t-1}$	0.160***	0.179***	0.179***	0.180***	0.138***	0.430***	0.151***	0.137***	0.181*	0.177***
	(0.053)	(0.056)	(0.055)	(0.073)	(0.036)	(0.080)	(0.063)	(0.035)	(0.086)	(0.056)
Margin of Majority	−1.729*									
	(1.366)									
Control of Parliament		−0.676**								
		(0.389)								
Polarization			0.138							
			(0.247)							
Number of Ministries				0.034						
				(0.45)						
Number of Opposition Parties					−0.032					
					(0.063)					
Number of Veto Players						0.127				
						(0.225)				
Days of Strike							0.0002			
							(0.0003)			
Checks and Balances								0.103		
								(0.123)		
Popular Support									−0.851**	
									(0.457)	
Old-Age Dependency Ratio										0.004
										(0.032)
Time Fixed Effects	Yes	Yes	Yes	Yes	Yes	Yes	Yes	Yes	Yes	Yes
R^2	0.457	0.462	0.455	0.563	0.526	0.727	0.488	0.528	0.625	0.456
F-statistic	11.78	11.23	10.92	6.41	3.15	12.06	8.10	2.99	1.70	11.61
P-value	0.000	0.000	0.000	0.000	0.000	0.000	0.000	0.000	0.000	0.000
Observations	589	600	589	420	501	124	426	500	120	588
Number of Countries	16	16	16	11	16	5	14	16	15	16

Source: Authors' calculations.

Note: Dependent variable = change in debt-to-GDP ratio. Instrumental variables approach with instruments is based on lagged values of the dependent variable, including country fixed effects. All control variables are included in all regressions. Robust standard errors are in parentheses.

$^*p < .1$; $^{**}p < .05$; $^{***}p < .01$.

Annex Table 9.2.7. Weak or No Fiscal Council

	Common Pool Theory					Veto Players Theory				
	(1)	(2)	(3)	(4)	(5)	(6)	(7)	(8)	(9)	(10)
Change in Debt$_{t-1}$	0.017	0.004	0.014	0.190***	0.033	0.305***	0.211**	0.046*	0.233***	0.033
	(0.023)	(0.022)	(0.082)	(0.028)	(0.080)	(0.057)	(0.092)	(0.023)	(0.035)	(0.077)
Margin of Majority	−2.059									
	(3.447)									
Control of Parliament		−1.617*								
		(0.965)								
Polarization			−0.062							
			(0.598)							
Number of Ministries				0.048*						
				(0.033)						
Number of Opposition Parties					−0.002					
					(0.018)					
Number of Veto Players						0.503*				
						(0.319)				
Days of Strike							0.0004*			
							(0.0002)			
Checks and Balances								0.429*		
								(0.290)		
Popular Support									−0.387	
									(0.585)	
Old-Age Dependency Ratio										0.122***
										(0.033)
Time Fixed Effects	Yes	Yes	Yes	Yes	Yes	Yes	Yes	Yes	Yes	Yes
R^2	0.180	0.151	0.151	0.380	0.135	0.524	0.240	0.158	0.356	0.145
F-statistic	1.99	1.68	1.59	1.31	1.70	1.95	1.73	1.64	1.20	1.42
P-value	0.000	0.000	0.000	0.000	0.000	0.000	0.000	0.000	0.000	0.000
Observations	1,570	1,703	1,644	951	1,861	323	1,046	1,762	733	1,875
Number of Countries	75	76	74	30	76	15	49	76	67	76

Source: Authors' calculations.

Note: Dependent variable = change in debt-to-GDP ratio. Instrumental variables approach with instruments is based on lagged values of the dependent variable, including country fixed effects. All control variables are included in all regressions. Robust standard errors are in parentheses.

*$p < .1$; **$p < .05$; ***$p < .01$.

REFERENCES

Aiyagari, S., A. Marcet, T. J. Sargent, and J. Seppala. 2002. "Optimal Taxation without State-Contingent Debt." *Journal of Political Economy* 110 (6): 1220–54.
Alesina, A., and A. Drazen. 1991. "Why Are Stabilizations Delayed?" *American Economic Review* 81 (5): 1170–88.
Alesina, A., and M. Paradisi. 2014. "Political Budget Cycles: Evidence from Italian Cities." Working Paper 20570, National Bureau of Economic Research, Cambridge, Massachusetts.
Alesina, A., and A. Passalacqua. 2015. "The Political Economy of Government Debt." Working Paper 21821, National Bureau of Economic Research, Cambridge, Massachusetts.
Baldacci, E., B. Clements, S. Gupta, and Q. Cui. 2008. "Social Spending, Human Capital, and Growth in Developing Countries." *World Development* 36 (8): 1317–41.
Barro, R. J. 1979. "On the Determination of the Public Debt." *Journal of Political Economy* 87 (5): 940–71.
Battaglini, M. 2011. "The Political Economy of Public Debt." *Annual Review of Economics* 3 (September): 161–89.
Baunsgaard, T., and M. Keen. 2010. "Tax Revenue and (or?) Trade Liberalization." *Journal of Public Economics* 94 (9–10): 563–77.
Brender, A., and A. Drazen. 2005. "Political Budget Cycles in New Versus Established Democracies." *Journal of Monetary Economics* 52 (7): 1271–95.
Buchanan, J. M., and R. E. Wagner. 1977. *Democracy in Deficit: The Political Legacy of Lord Keynes*. Indianapolis, Indiana: Liberty Fund, Inc.
Cooray, A., and F. Schneider. 2013. "How Does Corruption Affect Public Debt? An Empirical Analysis." WP 1322, Department of Economics, Johannes Kepler University of Linz.
Cox, G., and M. McCubbins. 2001. "The Institutional Determinants of Economic Policy Outcomes." In *Presidents and Parliaments*, edited by S. Haggard and M. McCubbins. Cambridge, U.K.: Cambridge University Press.
Crivelli, E., and S. Gupta. 2016. "Does Conditionality in IMF Programs Promote Revenue Reform?" *International Tax and Public Finance* 23 (3): 550–79.
Debrun, X., and T. Kinda. 2014. "Strengthening Post-Crisis Fiscal Credibility—Fiscal Councils on the Rise. A New Dataset." Working Paper 14/58, International Monetary Fund, Washington.
Drazen, A., and M. Eslava. 2010. "Electoral Manipulation via Voter-Friendly Spending: Theory and Evidence." *Journal of Development Economics* 92 (1): 39–52.
Easterly, W. 2014. *The Tyranny of Experts*. New York: Basic Books.
Escolano, J., and V. Gaspar. 2016. "Optimal Debt Policy under Asymmetric Uncertainty." Working Paper 16/178, International Monetary Fund, Washington.
Escolano, J., L. Jaramillo, C. Mulas-Granados, and G. Terrier. 2014. "How Much Is a Lot? Historical Evidence on the Size of Fiscal Adjustments." Working Paper 14/179, International Monetary Fund, Washington.
Franzese, R. 2002. "Electoral and Partisan Cycles in Economic Policies and Outcomes." *Annual Review of Political Science* 5: 369–421.
———. 2005. "Empirical Strategies for Various Manifestations of Multilevel Data." *Political Analysis* 13 (4): 430–46.
Gupta, S., L. De Mello, and R. Sharan. 2001. "Corruption and Military Spending." *European Journal of Political Economy* 17 (4): 749–77.
International Monetary Fund (IMF). 2013. "The Functions and Impact of Fiscal Councils." Staff Discussion Note 16/5, May, Washington, DC. https://www.imf.org/external/np/pp/eng/2013/071613.pdf.
———. 2016. "Corruption: Cost and Strategies." Staff Discussion Note 16/5, Washington, DC. http://www.imf.org/external/pubs/cat/longres.aspx?sk=43888.
Kagan, E. 2015. "Testing Competing Interpretations of Public Debt: An Empirical Analysis of the Veto Player and Common Pool Theory in a Transnational Context." Paper presented at the Achievements and Challenges for the Emerging Economies of Central Europe Economics and Business Conference, London, June 22–24.

Kaufmann, D. 2010. "Can Corruption Adversely Affect Public Finances in Industrialized Countries?" Brookings Institution, Washington, DC. http://www.brookings.edu/research/opinions/2010/04/19-corruption-kaufmann.

Lucas, R. E., and N. L. Stokey. 1983. "Optimal Fiscal and Monetary Policy in an Economy without Capital." *Journal of Monetary Economics* 12 (1): 55–93.

MacIntyre, A. 2001. "Institutions and Investors: The Politics of the Economic Crisis in Southeast Asia." *International Organizations* 55 (1): 81–122.

Mauro, P. 1998. "Corruption and the Composition of Government Expenditure." *Journal of Public Economics* 69 (2): 263–79.

———, R. Romeu, A. Binder, and A. Zaman. 2013. "A Modern History of Fiscal Prudence and Profligacy." Working Paper 13/05, International Monetary Fund, Washington.

Mian, A., A. Sufi, and F. Trebbi. 2014. "Resolving Debt Overhang: Political Constraints in the Aftermath of Financial Crises." *American Economic Journal: Macroeconomics* 6 (2): 1–28.

Perotti, R., and Y. Kontopoulos. 2002. "Fragmented Fiscal Policy." *Journal of Public Economics* 86 (2): 191–222.

Persson, T., and G. Tabellini. 2002. "Political Economics and Public Finance." In *Handbook of Public Economics*, edited by J. B. Taylor and M. Woodford. Amsterdam: Elsevier.

Reinhart, C., and K. Rogoff. 2010. "Growth in a Time of Debt." *American Economic Review: Papers and Proceedings* 100 (May): 573–78.

Rodrik, D. 1998. "Why Do More Open Economies Have Bigger Governments?" *Journal of Political Economy* 106 (5): 997–1032.

Roubini, N., and J. D. Sachs. 1989. "Political and Economic Determinants of Budget Deficit in the Industrial Democracies." *European Economic Review* 33 (5): 903–38.

Schneider, F., A. Buehn, and C. Montenegro. 2010. "Shadow Economies All over the World: New Estimates for 162 Countries from 1999–2007." Policy Research Working Paper 5356, World Bank, Washington.

Seki, K., and L. K. Williams. 2014. "Updating the Party Government Data Set." *Electoral Studies* 34: 270–79.

Spolaore, E. 2004. "Adjustments in Different Government Systems." *Economics and Politics* 16 (2): 117–46.

Tanzi, V., and H. Davoodi. 2002. "Corruption, Public Investment, and Growth." In *Governance, Corruption, and Economic Performance*, edited by G. Abed and S. Gupta, 280–99. Washington: International Monetary Fund.

Tsebelis, G. 1995. "Decision Making in Political Systems: Veto Players in Presidentialism, Parliamentarism, Multicameralism, and Multipartyism." *British Journal of Political Science* 25 (3): 289–326.

———. 2000. "Veto Players and Institutional Analysis." *Governance* 13 (4): 441–74.

———. 2002. *Veto Players: How Political Institutions Work*. Princeton, NJ: Princeton University Press.

———, and E. C. C. Chang. 2004. "Veto Players and the Structure of Budgets in Advanced Industrialized Countries." *European Journal of Political Research* 43 (3): 449–76.

Wehner, J. 2010. "Cabinet Structure and Fiscal Policy Outcomes." *European Journal of Political Research* 49 (5): 631–53.

Weingast, B. R., K. A. Shepsle, and C. Johnsen. 1981. "The Political Economy of Benefits and Costs: A Neoclassical Approach to Distributive Politics." *Journal of Political Economy* 89 (4): 642–64.

PART II

Institutions, Rules, and Fiscal Councils

CHAPTER 10

Political Institutions, State Building, and Tax Capacity: Crossing the Tipping Point

VITOR GASPAR, LAURA JARAMILLO, AND PHILIPPE WINGENDER

INTRODUCTION

The building of tax capacity is closely linked to the process of economic development and growth. There is a long intellectual history behind this conception of the role of taxes and the state. Joseph Schumpeter, in his famous paper "The Crisis of the Tax State" (Schumpeter 1918), links state and tax so closely that he stresses that his qualification "tax" in "tax state" can be regarded as almost redundant. He emphasizes that taxes are not only associated with the historical origin of the state, they are also active in shaping it. In his view, the organic development of taxation was associated with the organic development of other dimensions of the state. For Schumpeter, the analysis of the consequences of taxation requires a long-term perspective that allows for structural and self-reinforcing evolutionary dynamics to play out in full. Those dynamics are not only economic but also social and political. Besley and Persson (2011, 2013, 2014a, 2014b) are interpreted as bringing a similar perspective to contemporary research.

A recent study (Gaspar, Jaramillo, and Wingender 2016) argues that there is a minimum tax-to-GDP threshold associated with higher sustained growth. The authors investigate the existence of a tipping point in tax revenue levels. Tipping points are characterized by sharp changes occurring around some threshold. The work shows that once the tax-to-GDP level reaches about 12¾ percent, real GDP per capita increases sharply and in a sustained manner over the following decade. The effect of the tax tipping point on real GDP per capita after 10 years is on the order of 7.5 percent, that is, the average country that crossed from taxes as 12.5 percent of GDP to taxes as 13 percent of GDP was likely to be 7.5 percent larger than an otherwise similar country that remained below the threshold.

Of particular note is that the tipping point occurs for both developing economies in a contemporary data set, as well as for advanced economies in a historical data set spanning a much longer period starting in the early nineteenth century. These results raise the possibility that tax thresholds and tipping points are an inherent feature of the development of modern economies and the state and institutions that facilitate their emergence.

Far from demonstrating the effect of a single variable, tax tipping points indicate the presence of much deeper and broader changes in institutions and state capacity to sustain such effects on economic growth. This raises an important question: What political conditions and institutions facilitate the shift to greater state and tax capacity?

Using case studies, this chapter attempts to illustrate the nature of political conditions and institutions that accompanied countries as they crossed the tax-to-GDP threshold. It illustrates that improvements in taxation have been a part of a deeper process of state capacity building in these countries. Countries were chosen on the basis of their levels of development at both the time of their crossing the tax-to-GDP threshold and their subsequent economic development. Care was also taken to select a group that provides different insights, both from a regional and a historical perspective. The chapter therefore focuses on the following cases: (1) Spain crossed the 12¾ percent tax-to-GDP threshold in 1983; (2) China last crossed the tax threshold in 2001; (3) Colombia saw its tax-to-GDP level exceed the threshold for the first time in 2001; and finally (4) Lagos State in Nigeria saw a substantial increase in tax capacity, although at the national level, Nigeria is still below the 12¾ percent tax-to-GDP threshold.

The case studies illustrate the enabling political conditions that supported the building of state and tax capacity. In particular, the chapter highlights three important political ingredients: constitutive institutions, inclusive politics, and credible leadership. Constitutive institutions are evident in Spain and Colombia, where an explicit political settlement between political elites and citizens embodied in the enactment of new constitutions preceded tax capacity building. Both of these countries recognized that greater levels of taxation were essential to meet the emerging spending pressures associated with the economic, social, and institutional demands prompted by their new constitutions. Inclusive politics facilitated new center-periphery agreements crucial to building new tax collection schemes, as discussed in the cases of China and Lagos State.

Credible leadership was also clearly apparent. Across the four case studies, policymakers made a deliberate decision to implement a shift in the economic model, taking advantage of opportunities offered by economic or political crises. In Spain, the transition to democracy created the opportunity to build broader coalitions around the issue of building tax capacity. In Colombia, the economic crisis of the late 1990s helped foster the political consensus needed to implement several fiscal reforms. Efforts to mobilize internal tax revenues in Lagos State can be linked to its political rivalry with the federal government following the transition from military rule. In China, the main driver for greater tax capacity was the collapse of state-owned enterprise (SOE) revenues associated with the transition out of a patrimonial state toward a market-oriented economy.

This chapter does not try to present a general theory about the institutions and politics behind state capacity. Rather, the goal is to illustrate with a few case studies the political conditions that have supported broader changes in state and tax capacity. The aim is for these cases to serve as useful input for the process of developing a more general theory that integrates politics, institutions, and tax capacity.

POLITICAL INSTITUTIONS ENABLING STATE AND TAX CAPACITY BUILDING

What political conditions and institutions facilitate the shift to greater state and tax capacity? This question remains unanswered and is subject to considerable debate. The literature is vast, but most scholars point to a number of institutional features that can be grouped in three sets of political conditions that underpin state and tax capacity building (Figure 10.1):

- *Constitutive institutions*: According to Fritz and Menocal (2007), at the core of constitutive institutions is the political settlement that binds together state and society, ruling elites and citizens, public service providers and taxpayers. This political settlement (typically an explicit agreement) provides the necessary legitimacy for those who govern over those who are ruled. It is a key element in creating a social pact and the sense of shared public realm that leads to an effective state capable of collecting taxes and delivering public goods. To be considered legitimate, a political settlement must be acceptable to the majority of actors who need to be brought on board a state-building process, especially in postconflict settings, democratic transitions (Haggard and Kaufman 1995), and deeply divided societies (Hesselbein, Golooba-Mutebi, and Putzel 2006). Key constitutive institutions include a written constitution, free competitive elections, security and justice mechanisms, and a functioning meritocratic civil service.
- *Inclusive politics*: For Acemoglu (2005, 2016) and Acemoglu and Robinson (2016), the presence of inclusive political institutions is a key determinant of state capacity building. Inclusive politics comprises two main components: pluralism and centralization. Pluralism implies broad distribution of political

Figure 10.1. Complementarities in State Capacity

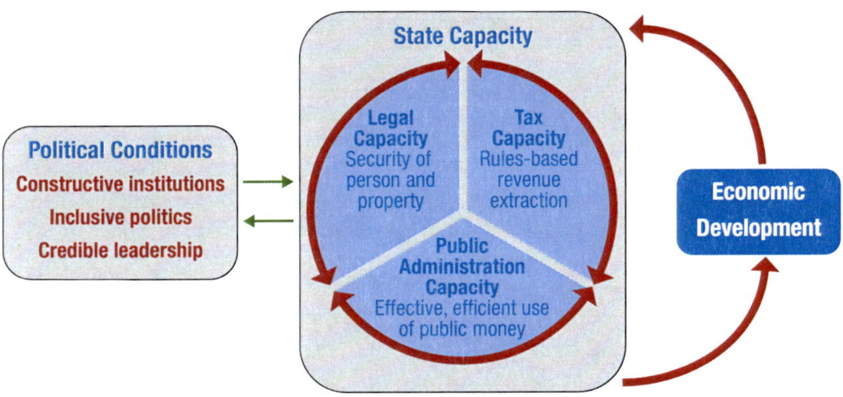

Source: Authors' compilation.

power and participation, constraints and checks on politicians, and the rule of law. Centralization requires the Weberian monopoly of legitimate violence over a territory and the ability of the state to regulate economic activity, impose taxes, and provide public goods. Various tensions between the center and the periphery often arise in state-building situations. According to Dobbins and others (2007), the center should be strengthened until it develops a good degree of control over general resources before engaging in horizontal redistribution among regions. At the same time, inclusive politics means that excessive centralization should be avoided by growing local capacity that works in synergy with the center (Brinkerhoff and Johnson 2008).

- *Credible leadership:* The 2008 Commission on Growth and Development Report, under the chairmanship of Nobel laureate Michael Spence, attempted to draw lessons about strategies and policies that produce high levels of sustained growth in developing countries. A crucial ingredient identified by the commission was a "capable, credible, and committed government" (Commission on Growth and Development 2008, 3). By this it meant a system of governance and leadership with the flexibility to adjust policy and institutional structures to changing circumstances and opportunities, but doing so in a manner that is credible and commands broad support. Underscoring the role of leadership, Brady and Spence (2009) draw on the evidence from high-growth countries studied by the Commission on Growth and Development (2008). They identify two key stages in successful economic leadership. The first stage is the process by which the political leadership chooses an appropriate economic model and builds a political consensus to support the model. The process of choosing a new model is often associated with opportunities offered at times of economic or political crisis.[1] The second stage is concerned with ensuring enough political stability for the economic plan to work. This implies that leaders have the capacity to adapt growth strategies—and to retain support for such changes—as circumstances change. Jones and Olken (2005) support this hypothesis. They study the effects of leadership on growth by looking at 57 cases in post–World War II economies in which an exogenous change in the country's leader occurred (sudden death, resignation, and so forth). They find that the change of national leader is related to economic growth.

These political conditions are key ingredients for enabling the building of state and tax capacity. This chapter follows Besley and Persson (2011, 2013, 2014a, 2014b) and argues that state capacity is shaped by the interaction between tax capacity, legal capacity, and public administration capacity. Tax capacity not only

[1] Several authors have argued the connection between crisis and reforms. In their seminal paper, Alesina and Drazen (1991) show in their model that a change to the status quo is more likely when the economy is in crisis. Weyland (2002) studies the circumstances under which the Washington Consensus reforms in the 1990s were implemented in Argentina, Brazil, Peru, and Venezuela, confirming the hypothesis put forth earlier by Kahneman and Tversky (1979) that in times of crisis, reforms are more likely to happen.

provides a stable and elastic source of revenue for the government to finance government activities, but a government with a larger stake in the economy through a developed tax system has stronger motives to play a productive role in the economy. Public administration capacity refers to the government's effective and efficient use of public money. This competence directly affects the ability of governments to implement policy and deliver public services, which in turn influences citizens' trust in government. Legal capacity refers to the government's ability to secure private property rights.

The chapter further argues that the strength of tax capacity depends crucially on social norms of compliance. Kiser and Levi (2015) emphasize that the more effective and trustworthy a government is, the more legitimacy it is likely to attain and the more it will be able to elicit compliance without excessive monitoring or punitive action. Similarly, as proposed by Levi (1988), the government can achieve a high degree of quasi-voluntary compliance with the taxation system when citizens comply with taxation out of a combination of strategic and normative considerations. Strategic considerations refer to the calculation of the probability of being caught and the punishment involved. Normative considerations refer to a sense of fairness: the citizen believes that sufficient public goods are being provided in return for tax payments, and that others are also paying their fair share. A variety of other authors have also argued that creating a culture of compliance is central to raising revenue. For example, Gordon (1989) refers to individual morality, Posner (2000) to tax-compliance norms, and Torgler (2007) to tax morale. Social norms of compliance are, in turn, closely associated with a higher demand by citizens for accountable and transparent government, as argued by Moore (2007); Bräutigam, Fjeldstad, and Moore (2008); and Ross (2004). These relationships are illustrated in Figure 10.2. In a similar vein, studies have found strong correlations between taxation and democratization (Ross 2004), public goods provision (Timmons 2005), and quality of governance (Moore 2004).

Figure 10.2. Tax Capacity, Social Norms, and Accountability

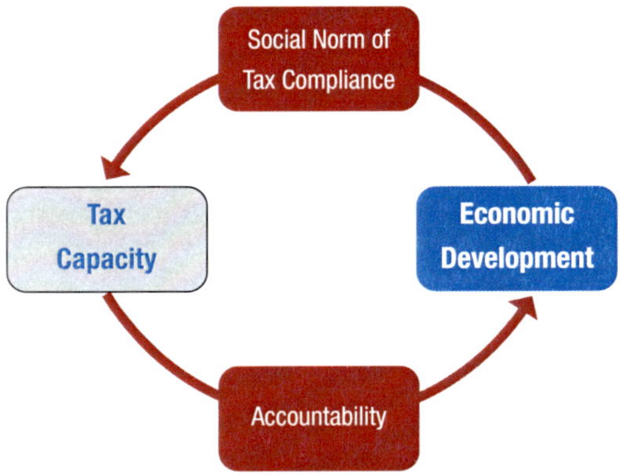

Source: Authors' compilation.

STATE CAPACITY AND GROWTH AFTER CROSSING THE TAX TIPPING POINT

To provide a more granular perspective on the findings of Gaspar, Jaramillo, and Wingender (2016) described above, this section contrasts the growth and institutional performance of individual countries before and after they crossed the tax threshold.

Using the contemporary data set of the aforementioned paper, which assembles a panel for 139 countries from 1965 to 2011, 59 developing countries are found to have crossed the tax threshold of 12.88 percent of GDP without reversal (see Annex Table 10.1.1). Among these episodes, the median year for crossing the tax threshold is 2002, without clustering around any specific time periods. Figure 10.3 shows cumulative real GDP per capita growth 10 years before and 10 years after crossing the 12.88 percent of GDP tax threshold. Only 19 episodes are displayed, out of the 60 identified, based on the availability of 20 years of consecutive data around the time the tax threshold was crossed. Of these 19 cases, two-thirds saw higher ensuing cumulative real GDP per capita growth, by an average of 12 percent.

Figure 10.3. Cumulative Real GDP Per Capita Growth Before and After Countries Cross the Tax-to-GDP Threshold
(Percent)

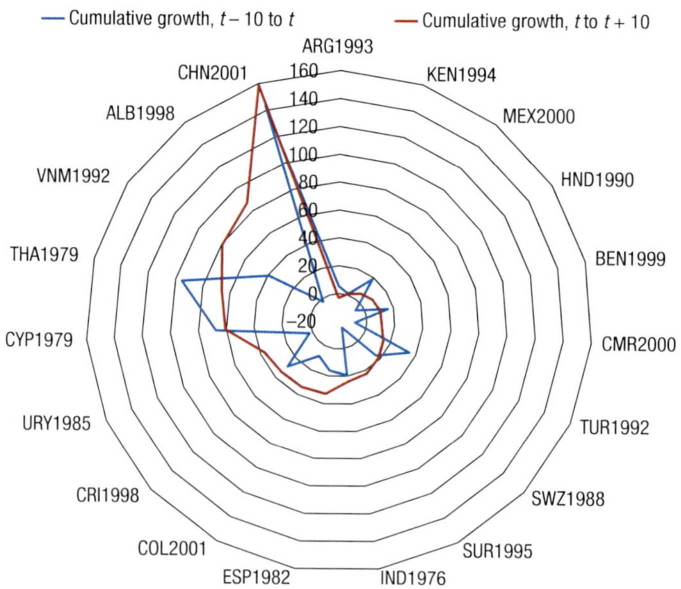

Source: Gaspar, Jaramillo, and Wingender 2016.
Note: The graph includes only 19 episodes (out of 60) for which 20 years of consecutive data are available. Cumulative growth, $t - 10$ to t, indicates countries' cumulative GDP growth in the 10 years before crossing the tax-to-GDP threshold. Cumulative growth, t to $t + 10$ shows cumulative GDP growth in the 10 years after crossing the tax-to-GDP threshold. The four-digit numbers after the country abbreviations indicate the calendar year in which each country crossed the tax-to-GDP threshold. ALB = Albania; ARG = Argentina; BEN = Benin; CMR = Cameroon; COL = Colombia; CRI = Costa Rica; CYP = Cyprus; ESP = Spain; HND = Honduras; IND = India; KEN = Kenya; MEX = Mexico; SUR = Suriname; SWZ = Switzerland; THA = Thailand; TUR = Turkey; URY = Uruguay; VNM = Vietnam.

Figure 10.4. Cumulative Real GDP Per Capita Growth Before and After Countries Cross the Tax-to-GDP Threshold
(Percent)

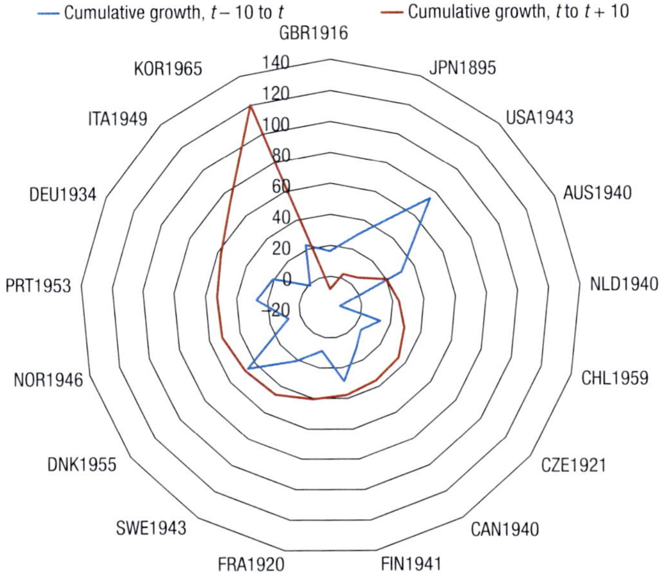

Source: Gaspar, Jaramillo, and Wingender 2016.
Note: Cumulative growth, $t-10$ to t indicates countries' cumulative GDP growth in the 10 years prior to crossing the tax to GDP threshold. Cumulative growth, t to $t+10$ shows cumulative GDP growth in the ten years following the crossing of the tax to GDP threshold. The four-digit numbers following the country abbreviations indicate the calendar year in which each country crossed the tax to GDP threshold.

Using the historical data set of Gaspar, Jaramillo and Wingender (2016), consisting of a panel of 30 advanced countries between 1800 and 1980, 17 countries are found to have crossed the tax threshold of 12.65 percent of GDP without reversal (see Annex Table 10.1.1). Interestingly, several of the countries crossed the threshold around World War II. In most cases, 10-year cumulative real GDP per capita growth was considerably higher after the country crossed the tax threshold, by an average of 19 percent (Figure 10.4). Exceptions are Australia, Japan, the United Kingdom, and the United States. However, if the Great Depression is excluded for the United Kingdom and the peak of the war buildup is excluded for the United States, one would also see higher real GDP per capita growth after these two countries crossed the tax threshold.

Looking beyond cumulative real GDP per capita growth, improvements are found in other indicators of state capacity after countries crossed the tax-to-GDP threshold. Using the contemporary data set, Figure 10.5 shows that countries saw lower volatility in tax revenues after crossing the threshold. This finding suggests that the increase in tax capacity was associated with greater stability of revenue, which in turn would support less volatility of government spending. Figure 10.6 shows that for many countries, the prevalence of corruption declined after crossing the tax threshold. This finding is consistent with the expectation of greater

Figure 10.5. Volatility of Tax Revenue

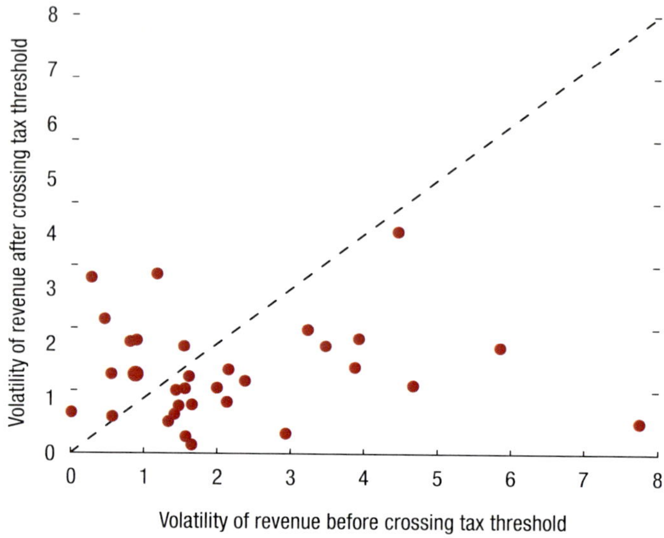

Source: Authors' estimates.
Note: Volatility was calculated as the standard deviation of tax to GDP, taking into account the underlying

Figure 10.6. Corruption Index

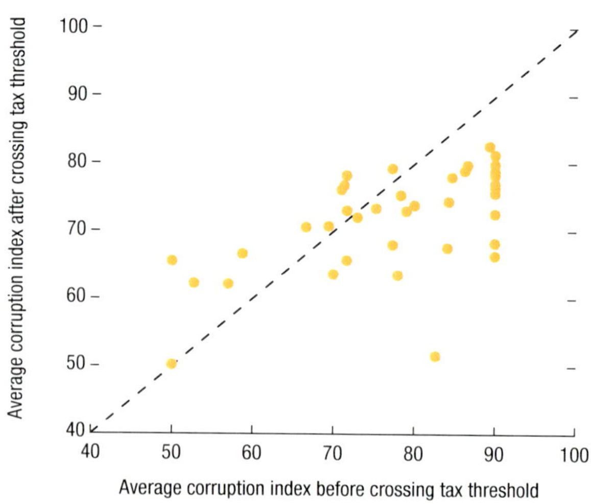

Sources: Heritage Foundation Index of Economic Freedom; and authors' estimates.
Note: The average corruption index ranges from 0 to 100, based on the Heritage Foundation Index of Economic Freedom. The index on corruption from the Heritage Foundation was transformed so that a higher index indicates higher corruption.

transparency and accountability demanded by citizens when tax compliance increases. Countries also saw an improvement in legal capacity indicators that are expected to be supportive of sustained economic development, in particular, protection of property rights (Figure 10.7) and regulatory quality (Figure 10.8).

Figure 10.7. Protection of Property Rights

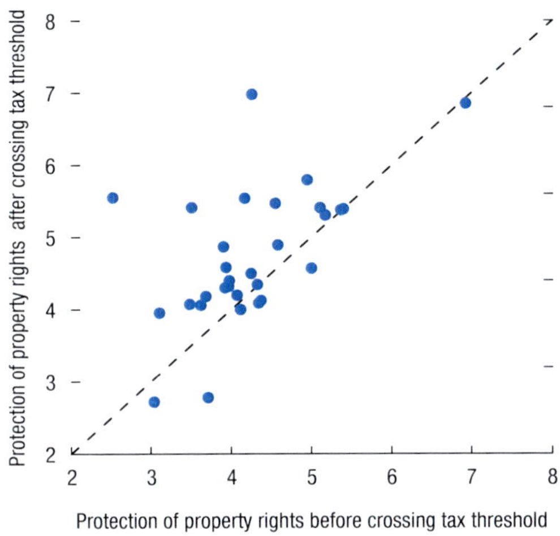

Sources: The Fraser Institute Economic Freedom Indicators; and authors' estimates.
Note: Indicator is defined as "Property rights, including over financial assets, are poorly defined and not protected by law (= 1) or are clearly defined and well protected by law (= 7)."

Figure 10.8. Regulatory Quality

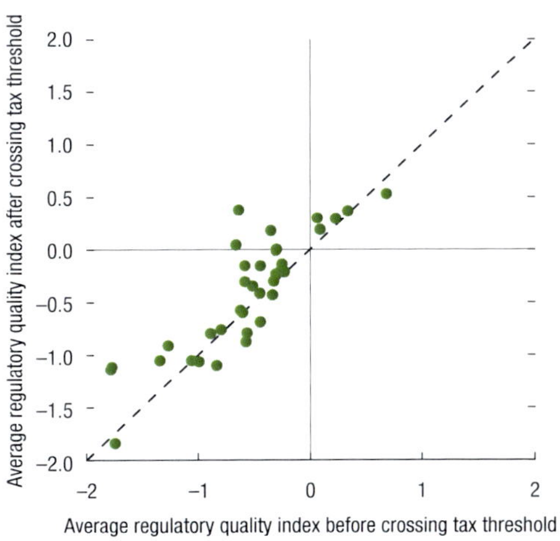

Sources: World Bank, World Governance Indicators; and authors' estimates.
Note: Indicator reflects perceptions of the ability of the government to formulate and implement sound policies and regulations that permit and promote private sector development.

CASE STUDIES

This chapter attempts via case studies to illustrate the nature of political conditions that accompanied countries as they crossed the tax-to-GDP threshold. The discussion that follows illustrates that improvements in taxation have been part of a deeper process of state capacity building in these countries. Note that the aim of this chapter is not to offer a general model that would encompass these cases. Rather, the goal is to provide an overview of the political context that fostered implementation of reforms to increase tax capacity in four selected cases. For each case, the discussion covers the political conditions that have accompanied state and tax capacity building, noting the role of constitutive institutions, inclusive politics, and credible leadership. The discussion then turns to growth performance around the time the country crossed the threshold. Where available, the associated changes in the social norms of tax compliance are documented. The case studies also discuss the behavior of other indicators that suggest that tax capacity moved in conjunction with improvements in other aspects of state capacity, in particular, legal and public administration capacity.

Four cases are reviewed: Spain (crossed in 1983), China (2001), Colombia (2001), and Lagos State in Nigeria, which saw a substantial increase in tax capacity, although at the national level, Nigeria is still below the 12¾ percent tax-to-GDP threshold.[2] Countries were chosen on the basis of their levels of development at the time of their crossing of the tax-to-GDP threshold and their subsequent experience in economic development to this day. Care was also taken to select a group that provides different insights from both a regional and a historical perspective. It is important to note that for each of these cases, the tax reforms discussed below do not imply that further improvements in the tax system were not needed. Indeed, most countries subsequently implemented additional tax policy and administration reforms to improve fairness, increase efficiency, and reduce administrative complexity.

Across all four case studies, constitutive institutions, inclusive politics, and credible leadership played a role in the process of state and tax capacity building. First, important constitutive institutions were in place in Spain and Colombia, where explicit political settlements between political elites and citizens preceded state and tax capacity building. In Spain, the transition to democracy and the new Constitution of 1978 paved the way to economic modernization and welfare state development. Similarly, in Colombia, the Constitution of 1991 facilitated a new distribution of power between the center and the subnational governments, increased checks and balances within the political system, and mandated more public services. In both cases, it was recognized that greater levels of taxation were essential to meeting the emerging spending pressures associated with the economic, social, and institutional demands prompted by the new constitutions. Second, inclusive politics facilitated new center-periphery agreements that were crucial to building new tax collection schemes, as discussed for China and Lagos State.

[2] Discussion of the political economy of state building in countries with natural resources is beyond the scope of this chapter. See Collier (2010) for a comprehensive analysis of this issue.

Credible leadership was also clearly present across the four case studies. In all cases, policymakers made a deliberate decision to implement a shift in the economic model, taking advantage of opportunities offered by economic or political crisis. In Spain, transition to democracy created the opportunity to build broader coalitions around the issue of building tax capacity. In Colombia, the economic crisis of the late 1990s helped foster the political consensus needed to implement several fiscal reforms. Efforts to mobilize internal tax revenues in Lagos State can be linked to its political rivalry with the federal government following the transition from military rule. In China, the main driver for greater tax capacity was the collapse in SOE revenues associated with the transition out of a patrimonial state toward a market-oriented economy. The case studies also illustrate that in all these episodes, policymakers needed to build broader coalitions to ensure enough political stability for the economic plan to work.

SPAIN

Political Context of Reforms to Increase Tax Capacity

The improvement in tax revenue performance observed in Spain during the early 1980s reflected the social and political consensus that emerged after the death of General Francisco Franco in 1975. A political transition to democracy was necessary in the context of intense social conflict and a deep economic crisis—including high inflation and unemployment rates and significant balance of payments and public sector deficits. In the face of these challenges, a wide public consensus emerged that the country needed to greatly improve its basic public services, welfare programs, and public infrastructure, and at the same time modernize its economic institutions, a consensus embodied in the Constitution of 1978. It was also recognized that a significant increase in public spending had to be financed through greater levels of taxation. Spain's reform efforts during this period were further encouraged by its ambition to join the European Economic Community (EEC), the application for which was made in 1977.

The Unión de Centro Democrático (UCD) government, elected in 1977 with 34.4 percent of the vote, managed to build a national political consensus in 1977–79, during which all political parties signed the Moncloa Pacts. Early in its time in office, the UCD government presented an economic program that included economic adjustment measures together with fiscal structural and financial system reforms. However, when negotiations with social organizations stalled, the government decided to seek an agreement across all political parties in Parliament. Enrique Fuentes Quintana, Vice President for Economic Affairs, convinced political parties to negotiate and to use his Economic Reparation and Reform Program as a basis. These agreements were called the Moncloa Pacts. Success of the Moncloa Pacts was based on the subordination of collective negotiations to price stability and the use of progressive taxation and public expenditure policies as instruments of income distribution (Comin 2007).

The Moncloa Pacts provided the blueprint for fundamental tax system reform. The tax system under the Franco regime exercised a low and regressive tax burden, with widespread tax evasion. The Moncloa Pacts addressed both tax policy and tax administration. On tax policy, they included four main elements: (1) a personal income tax, with a comprehensive tax base and progressive tax schedule, to replace the existing income tax; (2) a permanent personal net wealth tax, properly harmonized with the personal income tax, applicable on real wealth bases and with a progressive tax schedule; (3) a corporate income tax, without the exemptions that had been frequent in the previous corporate income tax; and (4) the introduction of a value-added tax (VAT) to align indirect taxation with the EEC's system.

The UCD government took the first steps toward strengthening tax compliance, but did not fully advance the reforms outlined in the Moncloa Pacts. Early on, the government managed to pass Law 50/1977 of Urgent Tax Reform Measures. A personal net wealth tax was introduced in 1978. The main objective of the new wealth tax was not to increase revenues but rather to obtain information on all sources of income to adequately apply the new personal income tax to be introduced in 1979. Conscious of pervasive tax evasion, the government coupled the introduction of the net wealth tax with a tax amnesty provision to motivate taxpayers to reveal hidden sources of income. Other measures implemented during this period included the abolition of bank secrecy and the introduction of criminal sanctions for fiscal offences (Sánchez Maldonado and Gómez Sala 2007). However, little progress was made in modernizing the tax administration.

Reforms stalled following the approval of the Constitution of 1978. Party differences became significant in the context of the 1979 elections. Disagreements among social and business groups with regard to details of fiscal reform eroded the previous consensus. The various UCD governments that followed did not reach the majority in Parliament needed for passage of reform, which prevented implementation of the tax reforms set out in the Pacts. Moreover, fragmentation within the UCD itself further weakened the government.

Sufficient political clout to implement the tax reforms outlined in the Moncloa Pacts was not achieved until the early 1980s. The momentum for tax reform gained support with the Socialist Party's ample win in the 1982 elections (with 48.1 percent of the vote), as well as Spain's preparations for joining the EEC in 1986. The VAT was introduced through Law 30/1985, a condition for entering the EEC. The government took decisive steps to reorganize the tax administration. It substantially increased human resources and invested in information systems. Measures were put in place to fight tax fraud. It introduced the New Tax Management Procedure, which increased the use of self-assessment for collecting the main taxes, and established a unique taxpayer's personal identification code. Territorial deconcentration was a further important change in the organizational reform of the tax administration (see Onrubia 2007).[3]

[3] Decentralization of the public sector brought about by the 1978 Constitution required that both spending competencies and public revenues be transferred from the central to the regional governments.

Performance of Growth and State-Capacity Indicators

Beginning in 1983, cumulative growth of real GDP per capita was greater than that observed in earlier years and remained relatively higher until the global financial crisis (Figure 10.9).[4]

During this period, the increase in tax revenues can be attributed both to changes in the tax system and to greater compliance rates. The change in the overall social norms of tax compliance can be illustrated using the response to the question "Is it justifiable to cheat on taxes if you have a chance?" from the World Values Survey (Martinez-Vazquez 2007). The social norm of compliance is measured by those that answer "it is never justifiable to cheat on taxes." The sharp increase in this measure for Spain from 1981 to 1994, shown in Figure 10.10, suggests that there was a significant improvement in citizens' willingness to voluntarily comply with taxation. Furthermore, available government data confirm the

Figure 10.9. Spain: Taxation and Cumulative Growth of Real GDP per Capita over Ensuing 10 Years
(Percent)

Sources: IMF, World Economic Outlook database; Organisation for Economic Co-operation and Development Tax Statistics; and authors' estimates.
Note: Tax-to-GDP figures do not include social security contributions. The red dashed line indicates the tax threshold of 12 3/4 percent of GDP.

[4]Other indicators of state capacity (such as regulatory quality, corruption, and protection of property rights) are only available starting in the mid-1980s; therefore, we are not able to show changes in these indicators around the time that Spain crossed the tax-to-GDP threshold in 1983.

Figure 10.10. Spain: Social Norms of Tax Compliance

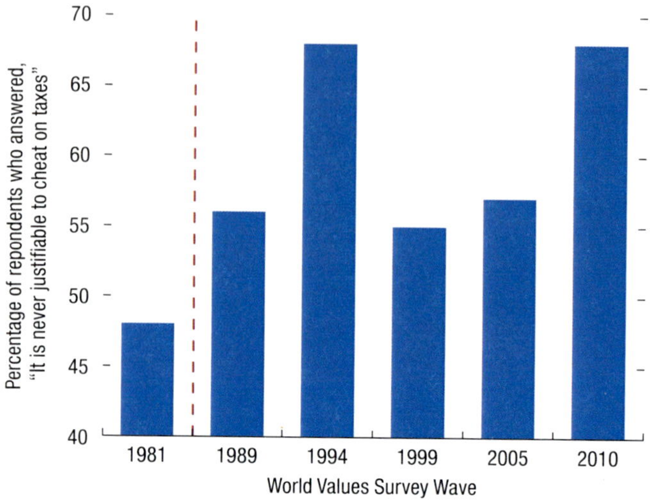

Source: World Values Survey. 1981–2014 Longitudinal Aggregate v.20150418. World Values Survey Association (www.worldvaluessurvey.org).
Note: The red dashed line indicates the time period in which Spain crossed the tax threshold of 12 3/4 percent of GDP.

Table 10.1. Spain: Personal Income Tax Compliance, 1979–86

	1979	1980	1981	1982	1983	1984	1985	1986
Filing (percent of potential tax returns)	52.2	56.9	56.2	56.1	59.4	58.7	61.0	64.1
Tax Base Reporting								
Share of True Taxable Income	42.9	47.8	48.9	49.6	50.8	50.5	52.0	55.1
Share of True Labor Taxable Income	54.0	62.1	63.4	64.8	66.6	66.7	68.9	71.3
Share of True Nonlabor Taxable Income	22.3	23.3	24.6	25.2	23.4	24.6	26.2	30.4

Source: Onrubio 2007.

improvement in tax compliance over the period. In 1990, the Commission for the Study and Prevention of Tax Evasion quantified personal income tax compliance during the period 1979–87 to illustrate the extent of tax evasion and avoidance. Table 10.1 shows notable improvement in tax filing as well as income reporting in the early 1980s.

CHINA

Tax is the foundation of state governance. It plays an important role in social and economic life.

Mr. Jun Wang, Commissioner, State Administration of Taxation of the People's Republic of China, March 2016

Political Context of Reforms to Increase Tax Capacity

In the late 1970s, China embarked on a path toward a market-oriented economy. While maintaining the overall framework of predominant public ownership, China adopted a policy of opening up trade and investment with the rest of the world and restructured its domestic economy. The government gradually relaxed mandatory planning, decentralized economic decision making, and allowed market forces to influence an increasing number of prices. For example, more investment was channeled from capital goods to consumer goods production. The government raised the prices for agricultural products by more than 20 percent in 1979 and significantly increased grain imports. Steps were taken to decentralize foreign trade and give more fiscal autonomy to provincial governments. Preferential policies were conferred on special economic zones to attract foreign investment. Importantly, reforms were launched to provide incentives to state-owned enterprises (SOEs) to increase production (see Bell and others 1993; Coase and Wang 2013).

China initiated its reform process in the wake of a major political transition. Following the death of Mao Zedong in 1976, the ultra-left faction (referred to as the "Gang of Four") was ousted from power by a coalition of moderate forces consisting of senior veterans of the Communist Party and younger cadres that had emerged during the period of the Cultural Revolution (Bell and others 1993). The party was initially led by Mao's designated successor, Hua Guofeng. During this time, the economy was partially recentralized and the planning apparatus strengthened. An ambitious 10-year development plan was launched, focused on investment in heavy industry and strong reliance on imports of capital equipment. However, the plan was soon abandoned because the surge in capital imports resulted in serious balance of payments problems.

By late 1978, reformist views gained dominance within the party, spearheaded by Deng Xiaoping. At the Third Plenum of the Central Committee of the Communist Party in December 1978, the leadership resolved to focus the party's work on reforming those aspects of the economic system that had impeded economic development. There was, however, no unanimity in views on the pace and nature of reform, particularly the role of the market versus planning. Conservatives favored retaining a central role for planning in a reformed economic system, whereas the more radical elements envisaged a greatly diminished and reformed role for planning (Bell and others 1993). Despite periodic shifts in policy emphasis, the more radical views prevailed. In 1992, a decisive ideological change occurred when the party called for the establishment of a socialist market economy.

As part of its reform efforts, the Chinese authorities sought to increase their tax capacity rather than rely solely on the profits from SOEs. Before 1978, state enterprises were required to turn all of their profits over to the state, which was the main source of government revenue (Lin 2009). Tax reform efforts began in 1979. State enterprises were allowed to keep part of their profits to expand production and to issue bonuses and awards to workers. In 1983, SOEs became subject to income taxes instead of contributing their profits. However, widespread evasion prompted the government to shift to a "contract responsibility system." Rather than trying to monitor each company's sales and profits, the government instead signed a contract with each SOE specifying its tax liability for the next several years. In some of these contracts, tax payments were set ex ante, usually based on the previous year's profits plus an increment. Other contracts consisted of a base payment with a supplementary tax imposed on profits earned above a set level. In 1989, the government launched a new tax reform under which SOEs were required to submit a portion of their profits to the government after paying corporate income taxes.

The sharp decline in the tax-to-GDP ratio during the early 1990s exposed the weaknesses in China's tax administration. Some studies estimated that up to 30 percent of SOEs, 60 percent of joint ventures, 80 percent of private enterprises, and 100 percent of individual street vendors failed to comply with their tax obligations in the mid-1990s (Brondolo and Zhang 2016). China's impending accession to the World Trade Organization—application for which took place in December 1995—increased the urgency for tax reform.

The sharp drop in revenues limited the ability of the central government to conduct macroeconomic or redistributive policies (Ahmad 2011), which prompted the Chinese government to undertake comprehensive reform of the tax system. The 1994 tax reform included four main elements:

- *Simplification and standardization of the tax structure.* The government lowered the income tax rate from 55 percent to a universal rate of 33 percent. A new VAT was enacted at 17 percent on most goods and services, and a reduced rate of 13 percent on agricultural products and inputs, energy, and minerals.
- *Change in revenue sharing between the central and local governments.* In the previous system, local governments collected taxes and then remitted a negotiated amount to the central government. The reform divided taxes into three distinct categories: central, local, and shared. The central government was assigned all revenue from consumption (excise) taxes, customs duties, and import-related VAT and consumption taxes. Shared taxes included domestic VAT, enterprise income tax, and personal income tax. All remaining taxes, including the business turnover tax on services, social security contributions, and stamp duties on real estate transactions, were allocated to local governments. In general, harder-to-collect taxes were assigned to local governments, which presumably had an information advantage over the national government (Wang 1997).
- *Centralization of the tax administration.* The central government established its own revenue collection agency, the State Administration of Taxation (SAT). The SAT was charged with collecting central and shared taxes, while the local tax system was to collect local taxes. This reform was crucial for enforcement. Local governments could no longer game the tax-sharing mechanism by strategically lowering their tax effort or reclassifying revenues to reduce remittances to the center (Wang 1997).
- *Curbing the ability of local governments to grant tax breaks.* In the previous system, local governments had discretion to grant reduced tax rates and tax exemptions. They had often used this discretion to channel budgetary funds into extrabudgetary funds, thereby reducing the revenues shared with the center. The reform required local governments to obtain approval by the State Council for any tax exemption.

To strengthen tax administration, the Tax Collection Law was enacted in 1992. The law set out the procedures for each tax administration function, vested the tax authorities with powers to enforce the tax laws, and defined the rights and obligations of taxpayers. In 1994, the government launched the Golden Tax Project to establish a computerized database of the records of both taxpayers and tax collectors (central and local).

To garner political support for the reform and persuade provinces to relinquish tax space to the SAT, the center agreed to three main concessions. The first concession by the center was to agree to a lump-sum transfer to each province to ensure that revenue after 1993 would not be lower than that in 1993. Of course, local governments also wanted a share in the revenues from the new taxes, especially the VAT. Therefore, the second concession by the center was to increase the central compensation to provinces by 30 percent of the average growth rate of VAT and consumption tax collections. A third concession was to allow a two-year "transitional period" in which tax breaks authorized by local governments in years before the reform would continue to be effective, and lower corporate income tax rates would be applicable to some enterprises with low profitability (Wang 1997). The first concession was geared toward obtaining political support from the richer provinces. The second concession was a lure for all the provinces. The last concession was geared toward obtaining political support from the poorer provinces, which collectively were large in number.

Performance of Growth and State-Capacity Indicators

China last crossed the 12¾ percent of GDP tax threshold in 2001. Tax to GDP had risen above the threshold in the 1980s, but as the result of great reliance on revenues from large, capital-intensive SOEs. By the early 1990s, tax to GDP had dropped below the threshold. Brondolo and Zhang (2016) attribute the decline in the tax-to-GDP ratio to a number of structural factors, including (1) less reliance on revenues from SOEs, not fully compensated for by taxation of non-SOEs; (2) a relative shift in value added from goods to services, with the former having higher effective tax rates than the latter; and (3) an increase in the trade surplus, which reduced the tax base because exports are excluded from the VAT base. It is important to stress that the drop in the contribution from SOEs has a deep structural interpretation. State dependence on revenues from state property or entrepreneurial activities is, from the viewpoint of the development of the tax state, a characteristic of an earlier stage of development. From this viewpoint, it is only after shifting away from overreliance on SOE taxation that China built tax capacity on a sustained basis.

As illustrated in Figure 10.11, cumulative growth of real GDP per capita over the 10 years since 2001 was considerably higher than that observed in earlier years. Furthermore, several indicators related to legal capacity and accountability improved noticeably after crossing the threshold, including protection of property rights, regulatory quality, and corruption (Figure 10.12). However, the World Values Survey does not show improvements in the social norms of compliance—the willingness to pay taxes remained basically unchanged.

Figure 10.11. China: Taxation and Cumulative Growth of Real GDP per Capita over Ensuing 10 Years
(Percent)

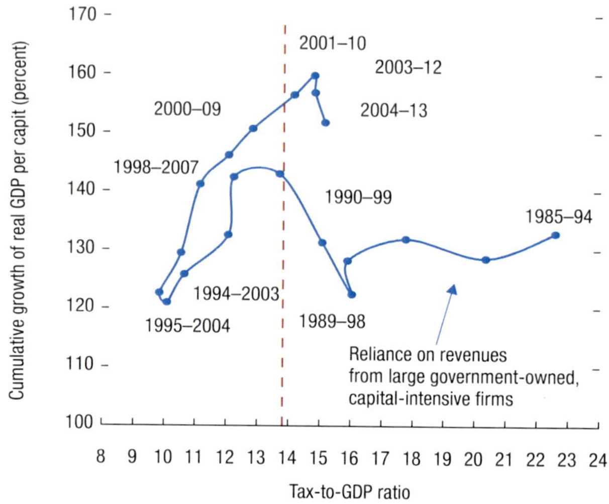

Sources: IMF, World Economic Outlook database; National Bureau of Statistics of China, *China Statistical Yearbook 2014*; and authors' estimates.
Note: The red dashed line indicates the tax threshold of 12 3/4 percent of GDP.

Figure 10.12. China: Social Norms of Compliance and Other Institutional Indicators

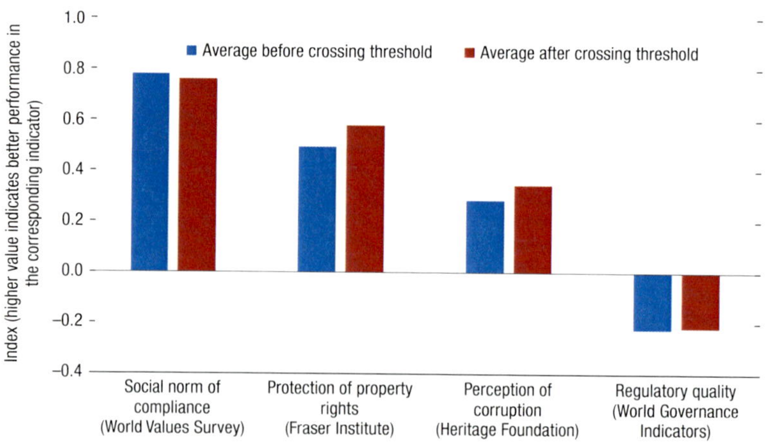

Sources: The Fraser Institute Economic Freedom Indicators; Heritage Foundation Index of Economic Freedom; World Bank, World Governance Indicators; World Values Survey 1981–2014 Longitudinal Aggregate v.20150418. World Values Survey Association (www.worldvaluessurvey.org); and authors' estimates.
Note: All indicators were rescaled to range between 0 and 1. Social norm of compliance corresponds to the share of survey respondents who answer that "it is never justifiable to cheat on taxes"; a high value of the protection of property rights indicates that they are clearly defined and well protected by law; a high value of the perception of corruption index indicates a low perception of corruption; and a high value of the regulatory quality index indicates that the government is perceived to have strong ability to formulate and implement sound policies and regulations.

COLOMBIA

> *Strengthening our tax, budget, and planning institutions is an essential part of progress towards development. Achieving this requires substantial improvements in all our institutions and in politics.*
>
> Mr. Guillermo Perry Rubio, Minister of Finance and Public Credit 1994–96, February 2014

Political Context of Reforms to Increase Tax Capacity

The increase in tax capacity in Colombia can be seen as a response to the new political, economic, and social demands that emerged from the 1991 Constitution. The 1991 Constitution sought to increase state presence by devolving fiscal and political power to subnational governments. This entailed giving subnational governments an increasing proportion of central government revenues. The constitution extended the coverage of basic social services and strengthened the judiciary. The new constitution also increased checks and balances within the political system. The president lost some capacity as an agenda-setter relative to the previous period, while Congress and the Constitutional Court gained relative power (Cárdenas, Junguito, and Pachón 2006).

These reforms gave rise to significant spending pressures. Furthermore, independence of the central bank, approved as part of the constitution, restricted its capacity to finance the government. The country was simultaneously embarking on a series of economic liberalization policies. Increased spending linked to the new constitution was coupled with other expenditure pressures, particularly those related to the financial imbalance in the pension system and increased resource demands from the defense sector. Higher tax revenue was therefore crucial to finance the sharp increase in spending and offset the decline in revenue from the reduction in trade tariffs.

Several structural economic and fiscal reforms were implemented in the early 1990s. Cesar Gaviria, a candidate of the Liberal Party, was elected president with 48.2 percent of the vote. The government had a majority coalition in Congress, thus facilitating the enactment of difficult reforms. Structural reforms to liberalize the economy included the reduction of trade barriers, privatization, labor market reform, and opening of the capital account. In 1990, tax changes were introduced mainly with the aim of encouraging savings and deepening capital markets through the repatriation of capital, among other measures. The authorities reduced the corporate tax rate, introduced a much lower tax rate on income from repatriated capital, and exempted stock market income from taxation. As spending pressures continued to mount, tax reform was introduced in 1992–93 with the objective of lowering the fiscal deficit. The VAT rate was increased to 14 percent and the base broadened. An income tax surcharge was introduced to fund national security expenditure. Public enterprises, public funds, and financial cooperatives became subject to taxation. Tax administration reforms included implementation of audit plans, introduction of computerized audit management, improvement of the monitoring and recovery of tax arrears, and introduction of stiffer sanctions for tax evasion and contraband (IMF 2001).

The ensuing administration of Ernesto Samper intended to advance structural tax reform but lacked political backing. Samper, from the Liberal Party, began his presidency with a majority coalition in Congress but suffered a deep political crisis following allegations of illicit campaign contributions. The Administration proposed a tax reform in 1995 to eliminate VAT and income tax exemptions and strengthen tax administration. However, the government was unable to garner support, even from its own party members in Congress. Weak party discipline was further fueled by the willingness of individual members of Congress to protect the narrow tax interests of their campaign finance contributors (Salazar 2013). To increase revenues, the government ended up relying mostly on the increase in the general VAT rate to 16 percent.

Further reform was achieved in the late 1990s, with political support facilitated by the need to respond quickly to the economic and financial crisis. Andres Pastrana took office as president in 1998, but without a congressional majority. He won 51.9 percent of the vote in the run-off election as the candidate for the Great Alliance for Change party, a multiparty coalition made up of heterogeneous political groups. However, soon after elections, Colombia faced a deep crisis. Following the Asian and Russian financial crises, Colombia's exchange rate came under pressure, the economy entered recession, Colombia lost its investment-grade rating, there was a mortgage crisis, and several banks had to be intervened. The magnitude of the economic and financial crisis, however, helped foster the political consensus needed to implement several fiscal reforms (Olivera, Pachón, and Perry 2006). A temporary financial transactions tax was created to finance financial sector rescue operations. The 1998 tax reform increased the VAT tax base, eliminated some exemptions, and mandated the subscription of public bonds in proportion to net wealth. The 2000 tax reform made permanent the financial transactions tax and increased some VAT bases. The reform also contributed to a reduction in tax evasion and strengthening of tax administration by introducing heavier penalties and supporting improvements in collections through electronic filing (see González and Calderón 2002).

Performance of Growth and State-Capacity Indicators

After crossing the tax threshold in 2001, Colombia saw cumulative real GDP per capita growth over the ensuing 10 years that was higher than observed in earlier years (Figure 10.13). The increase in tax revenues was accompanied by an improvement in several indicators associated with willingness to pay taxes, legal capacity, and accountability (Figure 10.14). The social norm of compliance, as measured by the World Values Survey, increased noticeably after Colombia crossed the threshold, suggesting that the increase in collections was linked in part to greater voluntary tax compliance. Corruption was perceived to be less prevalent, which suggests that higher taxation prompted greater demand for government transparency and accountability. Measures of protection of property rights and regulatory quality also improved, suggesting that the increase in taxation was accompanied by strengthening of the country's legal capacity.

Figure 10.13. Colombia: Taxation and Cumulative Growth of Real GDP per Capita over Ensuing 10 Years
(Percent)

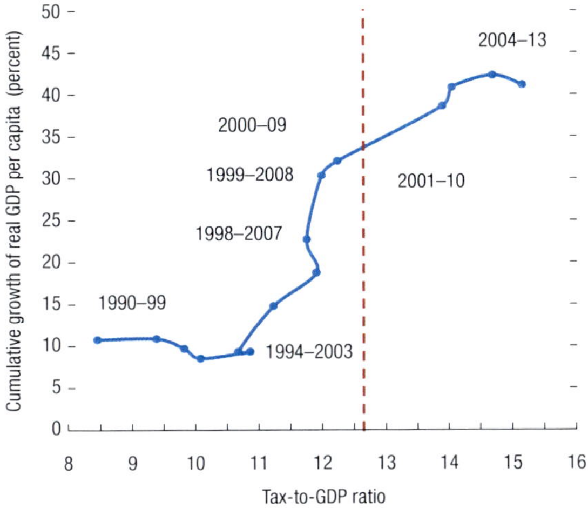

Sources: IMF, World Economic Outlook database; Organisation for Economic Co-operation and Development Tax Statistics; and authors' estimates.
Note: Tax-to-GDP figures do not include social security contributions. The red dashed line indicates the tax threshold of 12 3/4 percent of GDP.

Figure 10.14. Colombia: Social Norms of Compliance and Other Institutional Indicators

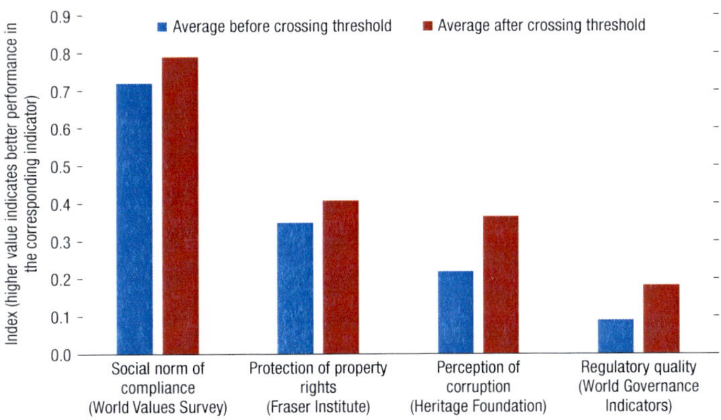

Sources: The Fraser Institute Economic Freedom Indicators; Heritage Foundation Index of Economic Freedom; World Bank, World Governance Indicators; World Values Survey 1981–2014 Longitudinal Aggregate v.20150418. World Values Survey Association (www.worldvaluessurvey.org); and authors' estimates.
Note: All indicators were rescaled to range between 0 and 1. Social norm of compliance corresponds to the share of survey respondents who answer that "it is never justifiable to cheat on taxes"; a high value of the protection of property rights indicates that they are clearly defined and well protected by law; a high value of the perception of corruption index indicates a low perception of corruption; and a high value of the regulatory quality index indicates that the government is perceived to have strong ability to formulate and implement sound policies and regulations.

LAGOS STATE, NIGERIA

> *As we improved tax administration and revenues grew, the citizenry became more interested in government's developmental programs, literally insisting on seeing the benefits of their contribution.*
>
> Mr. Ade Ipaye, Special Adviser for Taxation and Revenue in Lagos State 2007–11, May 2016.

Political Context of Reforms to Increase Tax Capacity

Despite strong growth since the 1990s, Nigeria faces large weaknesses in its economic and human development. Nigeria's real GDP per capita has doubled since 1995. However, when compared with countries with similar income levels, Nigeria lags behind across many human development indicators, such as life expectancy, infant mortality, and educational attainment. A central driver of Nigeria's growth has been the oil sector (Akinlo 2012), which makes the country vulnerable to oil price volatility and calls into question whether growth rates can be sustained. Indeed, after the sharp decline in oil prices since 2014, the Nigerian economy fell into recession in 2016. This situation is not uncommon for resource-rich countries. On average, countries that have an abundance of natural resources often show a record of relatively poor economic performance compared with non-resource-rich countries, as shown by Torvik (2009); Arezki, Gylfason, and Sy (2011); and IMF (2015). Furthermore, Collier and Goderis (2007) find that although in the short term an increase in commodity export prices raises growth, in the long term, growth is substantially reduced.

Heavy reliance by the government on oil revenue has prevented Nigeria from building its own tax capacity. Non-oil tax revenues averaged about 4 percent of GDP between 2005 and 2015, which puts it among the countries with the lowest tax collections in the world. This rate is also well below the levels of taxation in countries with similar income levels. Unsurprisingly, the weak tax capacity is associated with weak indicators of legal and public administration capacity.

Despite very weak tax capacity at the national level, the experience of Lagos State illustrates that it is possible to improve tax capacity and voluntary tax compliance, which in turn can foster greater legal and public administration capacity. Since the early 2000s, the Lagos State government has succeeded in boosting tax revenues to develop basic infrastructure, expand public services, and improve law enforcement.

Efforts to improve tax capacity in Lagos State can be traced back to the early 2000s. Nigeria began a transition away from military rule following the death of General Sani Abacha in 1998. National and state elections were held in 1999. Bola Tinubu was elected governor of Lagos State as the candidate of the Alliance for Democracy, the opposition party to the Nigerian President's People's Democratic Party (PDP). Governor Tinubu was reelected in 2003, again as a candidate from the opposition party to the president. His successor, Babatunde

Fashola, elected in 2007 and reelected in 2011, was also from the opposition party to the PDP-controlled national government. As prominent opposition leaders, Lagos State politicians were eager to demonstrate that they could deliver more benefits to their constituents than the PDP. Building tax capacity was crucial for their objectives, given that resource allocations (including revenue sharing of oil receipts) received by Lagos State were insufficient to meet their spending needs. For example, according to De Gramont (2015), in 2002, the state government's personnel costs alone exceeded its statutory allocation from the federal government.

Governor Tinubu made taxation an early priority. In the late 1990s, the Lagos State government lacked basic tax capacity. Taxes were paid in cash to revenue officials who gave out handwritten receipts. The state finance ministry was not able to clearly track payments made into state bank accounts. State revenue staff were ill-equipped to effectively audit businesses. Tax evasion was pervasive. During Tinubu's first term, tax collection was shifted from cash transactions toward electronic payments through banks. Taxes could now be paid directly into government coffers at a number of bank branches. Greater attention was also placed on enforcement.

Tax administration in Lagos State reached a turning point in 2005. Political rivalry added further impetus to the ongoing reform process aimed at increasing internal revenues when, in 2004, President Obasanjo cut off federal funding for local governments in Lagos State because of a dispute over the creation of new local governments. As a first step, management of the existing internal revenue board was replaced by a new team and it was given greater autonomy. The revenue board was then transformed into a new agency, the Lagos State Internal Revenue Service (LIRS). LIRS came into full force in 2007. It was able to pay higher salaries and use greater flexibility in hiring and internal management than the ordinary civil service. As a result, it was able to attract better-qualified staff and offer better training (Asaolu, Dopemu, and Monday 2015).

Governor Fashola continued to make taxation a central focus of his administration. LIRS increased its monitoring capacity. In-house audit capacity was increased. A self-assessment filing system for individuals was introduced. Efforts were made to bring informal-sector workers into the tax net through payment of a flat tax. Meanwhile, infrastructure construction and public service reforms accelerated to clearly display to citizens the benefits of their tax contributions.

As part of the reform process, significant efforts were made to increase voluntary tax compliance. Since 2007, regular tax stakeholder conferences have been convened with representatives from the private sector, labor unions, civil society groups, and informal-sector associations to discuss tax payment and their expectations from the government. Public works projects in Lagos display large signs urging people to pay their taxes. LIRS has enlisted public figures to record messages about the importance of tax payment and runs a tax essay competition for youth.

Figure 10.15. Lagos State: Tax Revenue, by Source, 1998–2011

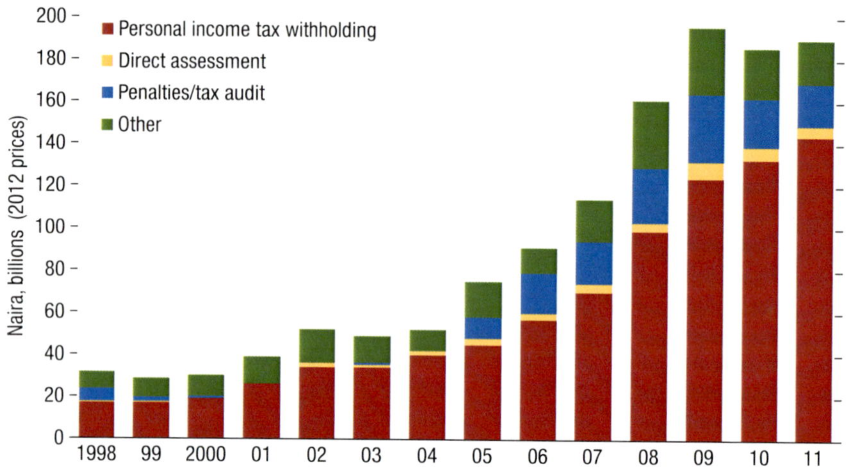

Source: De Gramont 2015.

Public perceptions that the state government has been doing its job well appear to have influenced individuals' readiness to pay taxes. De Gramont (2015) reports a 2010 survey in which 74 percent of respondents said they were somewhat or very satisfied with the state government's use of tax revenues. Bodea and Lebas (2014) report that residents of Lagos expressed the highest support among all residents of urban centers in Nigeria for the statement that "citizens should always pay their taxes."

The impact of these tax system reforms has been remarkable. Between 1999 and 2010, internal tax revenues increased almost eightfold, as shown in Figure 10.15. Both revenues and tax audit penalties increased markedly after the 2005 tax administration overhaul. As a result of these efforts, in 2014, about 70 percent of Lagos State government revenue was derived from internally generated tax revenue.

CONCLUSIONS

This chapter complements a recent study (Gaspar, Jaramillo, and Wingender 2016) on the determinants of economic growth and development of state capacity. While the previous study uncovered a robust and significant statistical threshold effect of the level of taxes on subsequent growth, the current chapter attempts to document the political environment that supported broader changes in state capacity that accompanied the crossing of the tax threshold in the four cases analyzed.

This chapter's goal is not to present general theory about the institutions and politics behind state capacity. Rather, the aim is to illustrate with a few case studies the political conditions that have supported broader changes in state and tax capacity. We hope that the insights into these cases can serve as useful input for the development of a more general theory that integrates politics, institutions, and tax capacity.

Across all four case studies, constitutive institutions, inclusive politics, and credible leadership played a role in the process of state and tax capacity building. Constitutive institutions were in place in Spain and Colombia, where explicit political settlements between political elites and citizens preceded state and tax capacity building. Inclusive politics facilitated new center-periphery agreements that became central elements of the building of tax capacity, as discussed for China and Lagos State. Credible leadership was also clearly apparent across the four case studies. In all cases, policymakers made a deliberate decision to implement a shift in the economic model, taking advantage of opportunities offered by economic or political crisis.

This chapter also makes the case that improvements in tax-to-GDP levels can only be sustained when accompanied by changes in social norms of tax compliance. Greater tax compliance then entails greater demand by citizens for an effective, trustworthy, and equitable government. Spain and Colombia saw sustained increases in taxpayers' compliance norms after crossing the 12¾ percent tax-to-GDP threshold. This finding suggests that the improvement in tax collections was not only due to stricter tax enforcement but was also the result of greater voluntary compliance. The case studies also show lower perceptions of corruption, suggesting that higher taxation generated greater demand for government transparency and accountability. In China and Colombia, stronger tax capacity was also accompanied by improved legal capacity, such as the protection of property rights and regulatory quality. The Nigeria case study illustrates that sustained economic and human development does not follow if growth is not accompanied by the building of state and tax capacity.

As in the quote that serves as the epigraph to the section on Nigeria, the evidence collected here is suggestive of the importance of a double-sided accountability social contract. As tax administration and tax capacity improve, social norms of behavior change, leading to quasi-voluntary compliance on the part of taxpayers. Tax revenues become more important and elastic, allowing government revenues to become more stable. Public governance improves as citizens demand (and the administration delivers) accountability. As the process deepens, public administration increasingly focuses on the public good and acquires the capacity to deliver. It is from such deep social, institutional, and political dynamics that we find the explanation for a tipping point in tax-to-GDP levels that significantly accelerates the growth and development process.

ANNEX 10.1.1 YEAR IN WHICH COUNTRIES CROSSED THE TAX-TO-GDP THRESHOLD WITHOUT REVERSAL

Annex Table 10.1.1. Year in Which Countries Crossed the Tax-to-GDP Threshold without Reversal

Contemporary Data Set (12.88 percent of GDP threshold)				Historical Data Set (12.65 percent of GDP threshold)	
Albania	1998	Liberia	2006	Australia	1940
Argentina	1993	Malawi	2004	Canada	1940
Armenia	1997	Maldives	2011	Chile	1959
Bahamas, The	2006	Mexico	2000	Czechoslovakia	1921
Benin	1999	Mali	2002	Denmark	1955
Bolivia	2004	Mozambique	2009	Finland	1941
Burkina Faso	2011	Nepal	2010	France	1920
Cabo Verde	1992	Nicaragua	2010	Germany	1934
Cameroon	2000	Papua New Guinea	1978	Italy	1949
Chad	2010	Peru	2003	Japan	1895
China	2001	Philippines	2005	Korea	1965
Colombia	2001	Portugal	1976	Netherlands	1940
Costa Rica	1998	Solomon Islands	2003	Norway	1946
Cyprus	1979	Spain	1982	Portugal	1953
Dominica	1977	Sri Lanka	2010	Sweden	1943
Dominican Republic	2004	South Africa	1973	United Kingdom	1916
El Salvador	2010	Suriname	1995	United States	1943
Ethiopia	2010	Swaziland	1988		
Gambia, The	2006	São Tomé and Príncipe	2004		
Georgia	2004	Tajikistan	2002		
Ghana	2010	Thailand	1979		
Greece	1966	Togo	2003		
Guinea	2005	Tonga	1993		
Honduras	1990	Turkey	1992		
India	1976	Uruguay	1985		
Kenya	1994	Vanuatu	1984		
Kiribati	1987	Vietnam	1992		
Kyrgyz Republic	2002	Zambia	2010		
Lao P.D.R.	2009	Zimbabwe	2010		
Lebanon	2002				

Source: Gaspar, Jaramillo, and Wingender 2016.

REFERENCES

Acemoglu, D. 2005. "Politics and Economics in Weak and Strong States." *Journal of Monetary Economics* 52 (7): 1199–226.

———. 2016. "Political Economy of State Building." Public Lecture at the World Bank, Washington, DC, April 4. http://pubdocs.worldbank.org/en/991631459795243817/DEC-Lecture-Daron-Acemoglu-Presentation.pdf.

———, and J. Robinson. 2016. "Paths to Inclusive Political Institutions." Unpublished report. http://economics.mit.edu/files/11338.

Ahmad, E. 2011. "Should China Revisit the 1994 Fiscal Reform?" Asia Research Centre Working Paper 52, London School of Economics, London.

Akinlo, A. E. 2012. "How Important Is Oil in Nigeria's Economic Growth?" *Journal of Sustainable Development* 5 (4): 165–79.

Alesina, A., and A. Drazen. 1991. "Why Are Stabilizations Delayed?" *American Economic Review* 81 (5): 1170–88.

Arezki, R., T. Gylfason, and A. Sy. 2011. *Beyond the Curse: Policies to Harness the Power of Natural Resources*. Washington, DC: International Monetary Fund.

Asaolu, T. O., S. O. Dopemu, and J. U. Monday. 2015. "Impact of Tax Reforms on Revenue Generation in Lagos State: A Time Series Approach." *Research Journal of Finance and Accounting* 6 (8): 85–96.

Bell, M. W., H. E. Khor, K. Kochhar, J. Ma, S. N'guiamba, and R. Lall. 1993. "China at the Threshold of a Market Economy." Occasional Paper 107, International Monetary Fund, Washington, DC.

Besley, T., and T. Persson. 2011. *Pillars of Prosperity: The Political Economics of Development Clusters*. Princeton, NJ: Princeton University Press.

———. 2013. "Taxation and Development." In *Handbook of Public Economics*, Vol. 5, edited by A. J. Auerbach, R. Chetty, M. Feldstein, and E. Saez. Amsterdam: North Holland.

———. 2014a. "Why Do Developing Countries Tax So Little?" *Journal of Economic Perspectives* 28 (4): 99–120.

———. 2014b. "The Causes and Consequences of Development Clusters: State Capacity, Peace and Income." *Annual Review of Economics* 6: 927–49.

Bodea, C., and A. Lebas. 2014. "The Origins of Voluntary Compliance: Attitudes Toward Taxation in Urban Nigeria." *British Journal of Political Science* 46 (1): 215–38.

Brady, D., and M. Spence. 2009. "Leadership and Politics: A Perspective from the Growth Commission." *Oxford Review of Economic Policy* 25 (2): 205–18.

Bräutigam, D., O.-H. Fjeldstad, and M. Moore. 2008. *Capacity and Consent: Taxation and State Building in Developing Countries*. Cambridge, U.K.: Cambridge University Press.

Brinkerhoff, D. W., and R. W. Johnson. 2008. "Good Enough Governance in Fragile States: The Role of Center-Periphery Relations and Local Government." Paper presented at the 4th International Specialised Conference, "International Aid and Public Administration," Ankara, Turkey, June 23–27.

Brondolo, J., and Z. Zhang. 2016. "Tax Administration Reform in China: Achievements, Challenges, and Reform Priorities." Working Paper 16/68, International Monetary Fund, Washington, DC.

Cárdenas, M., R. Junguito, and M. Pachón. 2006. "Political Institutions and Policy Outcomes in Colombia: The Effects of the 1991 Constitution." Research Network Working Paper R-508, Inter-American Development Bank, Washington, DC.

Coase, R., and N. Wang. 2013. "How China Became Capitalist." Cato Policy Report, Cato Institute, Washington, DC.

Collier, P. 2010. "The Political Economy of Natural Resources." *Social Research* 77 (4): 1105–32.

———, and B. Goderis. 2007. "Commodity Prices, Growth, and the Natural Resource Curse: Reconciling a Conundrum." Working Paper Series, Centre for the Study of African Economies, University of Oxford, Oxford, U.K.

Comín, F. 2007. "Reaching a Political Consensus: The Moncloa Pacts, Joining the European Union and the Rest of the Journey." In *Fiscal Reform in Spain: Accomplishments and Challenges*, edited by J. Martinez-Vazquez and J. F. Sanz-Sanz. Cheltenham, U.K.: Edward Elgar Publishing.

Commission on Growth and Development. 2008. *The Growth Report: Strategies for Sustained Growth and Inclusive Development*. Washington, DC: World Bank.

De Gramont, D. 2015. "Governing Lagos: Unlocking the Politics of Reform." Carnegie Endowment for International Peace, Washington, DC. http://carnegieendowment.org/2015/01/12/governing-lagos-unlocking-politics-of-reform-pub-57671

Dobbins, J., S. G. Jones, K. Crane, and B. Cole De Grasse. 2007. *Beginner's Guide to Nation-Building*. Santa Monica: RAND.

Fritz, V., and A. R. Menocal. 2007. "Understanding State-Building from a Political Economy Perspective." Overseas Development Institute, London.

Gaspar, V., L. Jaramillo, and P. Wingender. 2016. "Tax Capacity and Growth: Is There a Tipping Point?" Working Paper 16/234, International Monetary Fund, Washington, DC.

González, F. A., and V. Calderón. 2002. "Las reformas tributarias en colombia durante el siglo XX (II)." Reformas Tributarias Boletines de Divulgación, Departamento Nacional de Planeación. https://colaboracion.dnp.gov.co/CDT/Estudios%20Econmicos/Las%20reformas%20tributarias%20en%20Colombia%20durante%20el%20siglo%20XX%20(II).pdf.

Gordon, J. 1989. "Individual Morality and Reputation Costs as Deterrents to Tax Evasion." *European Economic Review* 33 (4): 797–805.

Haggard, S., and R. Kaufman, eds. 1995. *The Political Economy of Democratic Transitions.* Princeton, NJ: Princeton University Press.

Hesselbein, G., F. Golooba-Mutebi, and J. Putzel. 2006. "Economic and Political Foundations of State-Making in Africa: Understanding State Reconstruction." Working Paper 2, Crisis States Research Center, London.

International Monetary Fund (IMF). 2001. "Colombia: Selected Issues and Statistical Appendix." Country Report No. 01/68, IMF, Washington, DC.

———. 2015. *Fiscal Monitor: The Commodities Roller Coaster—A Fiscal Framework for Uncertain Times.*

Jones, B. F., and B. A. Olken. 2005. "Do Leaders Matter? National Leadership and Growth Since World War II." *Quarterly Journal of Economics* 120: 835–64.

Kahneman, D., and A. Tversky. 1979. "Prospect Theory: An Analysis of Decision Under Risk." *Econometrica* 47 (2): 263–91.

Kiser, E., and M. Levi. 2015. "Interpreting the Comparative History of Fiscal Regimes." In *Fiscal Regimes and the Political Economy of Premodern States*, edited by A. Monson and W. Sheidel. Cambridge, U.K.: Cambridge University Press.

Levi, M. 1988. *Of Rule and Revenue.* Berkeley: University of California Press.

Lin, S. 2009. "The Rise and Fall of China's Government Revenue." East Asia Institute Working Paper 150, National University of Singapore.

Martinez-Vazquez, J. 2007. "The Spanish Tax Reform: Overview and Lessons." In *Fiscal Reform in Spain: Accomplishments and Challenges*, edited by J. Martinez-Vazquez and J. F. Sanz-Sanz. Cheltenham, U.K.: Edward Elgar Publishing.

Moore, M. 2004. "Revenues, State Formation, and the Quality of Governance in Developing Countries." *International Political Science Review* 25 (3): 297–319.

———. 2007. "How Does Taxation Affect the Quality of Governance?" *Tax Notes International* 47 (1): 79.

Olivera, M., M. Pachón, and G. Perry. 2006. "Political Economy of Fiscal Reform: Colombia, 1986–2006." Working Paper 181, Inter-American Development Bank, Washington, DC.

Onrubia, J. 2007. "The Reform of the Tax Administration in Spain." In *Fiscal Reform in Spain: Accomplishments and Challenges*, edited by J. Martinez-Vazquez and J. F. Sanz-Sanz. Cheltenham, U.K.: Edward Elgar Publishing.

Posner, P. 2000. "Law and Social Norms: The Case of Tax Compliance." *Virginia Law Review* 86 (8): 1781–819.

Ross, M. L. 2004. "Does Taxation Lead to Representation?" *British Journal of Political Science* 34 (2): 229–49.

Salazar, N. 2013. "Political Economy of Tax Reforms: The Case of Colombia." Woodrow Wilson Center Update on the Americas, Washington, DC.

Sánchez Maldonado, J., and J. S. Gómez Sala. 2007. "The Reform of Indirect Taxation in Spain: VAT and Excise." In *Fiscal Reform in Spain: Accomplishments and Challenges*, edited by J. Martinez-Vazquez and J. F. Sanz-Sanz. Cheltenham, U.K.: Edward Elgar Publishing.

Schumpeter, J. A. 1918. Die Krise des Steuerstaates. *Zeitfragen aus dem Gebiete der Soziologie* 4: 3–74. (Reprinted as J. A. Schumpeter. 1991. "The Crisis of the Tax State." In *The Economics and Sociology of Capitalism*, edited by R. Swedberg, 99–140. Princeton, NJ: Princeton University Press.)

Timmons, J. F. 2005. "The Fiscal Contract: States, Taxes, and Public Services." *World Politics* 57: 530–67.

Torgler, B. 2007. *Tax Compliance and Tax Morale: A Theoretical and Empirical Analysis.* Cheltenham, U.K.: Edward Elgar.

Torvik, R. 2009. "Why Do Some Resource-Abundant Countries Succeed While Others Do Not?" *Oxford Review of Economic Policy* 25 (2): 241–56.
Wang, S. 1997. "China's 1994 Fiscal Reform: An Initial Assessment." *Asian Survey* 37 (9): 801–17.
Weyland, K. 2002. *The Politics of Market Reform in Fragile Democracies: Argentina, Brazil, Peru, and Venezuela*. Princeton, NJ: Princeton University Press.

CHAPTER 11

Fiscal Discipline and Exchange Rates: Does Politics Matter?

JOÃO TOVAR JALLES, CARLOS MULAS-GRANADOS, AND JOSÉ TAVARES

INTRODUCTION

The issue of what type of exchange rate regime is better for fiscal discipline has a long history in macroeconomics. Traditionally, the view that fixed exchange rate regimes could be associated with increased fiscal discipline was widely accepted. However, more recent theoretical models, together with mixed empirical evidence, have paved the way to an alternative policy view according to which flexible exchange rate regimes are also compatible with healthy public finances.[1] In parallel, many countries have moved from fixed to flexible exchange rates in the past two decades.[2] On the economic front, two opposing views are at stake: the first considers a fixed peg to be a provider of credible discipline and associates fixed exchange rates with enhanced fiscal restraint; the second defends the notion that flexible rates induce better fiscal performance instead because they expose the costly economic consequences of fiscal profligacy and do not allow policymakers to hide the deterioration of fiscal balances behind a loss of domestic reserves.

The empirical evidence that examines the relationship between fiscal discipline and exchange rate regimes is mixed. Gavin and Perotti (1997) uncover

J. Jalles and C. Mulas-Granados are with the International Monetary Fund. J. Tavares is with the Nova School of Business and Economics in Lisbon and the Center for Economic Policy Research in London. The authors are grateful to Vitor Gaspar, Sanjeev Gupta, and Ben Clements for useful comments and suggestions. Participants at the FAD Seminar Series also contributed with valuable discussions. The authors also thank Jaime Marques Pereira, Michela Schena, and Carolina Correa-Caro for excellent research assistance. The opinions expressed herein are those of the authors and do not necessarily reflect those of the authors' employers.

[1] For instance, the 1990s witnessed a series of crises in emerging market economies, as well as European countries under the Exchange Rate Mechanism, that suggested financial openness, monetary independence, and pegs were incompatible.

[2] As reviewed in Bordo (2003), exchange rate regime choice evolved considerably over the past century. In the early twentieth century, adopting the gold standard—and, thus, a hard peg—seemed the obvious policy choice, followed by most advanced economies. Today the policy choice is the opposite, though equally "obvious." All advanced economies, with the exception of euro area countries among themselves, have adopted flexible exchange rates. Developing countries, with some exceptions, seem more or less constrained to follow the prevailing policy view, and mimic, if not follow, advanced economies' actions.

an association between fixed exchange rate regimes and public deficits in Latin American economies, but they do not find similar evidence for advanced, industrialized economies. Fatás and Rose (2001) find that, while adherence to a common currency area is not associated with increased fiscal discipline, adoption of a currency board is. Tornell and Velasco (1995, 1998) and Sun (2003) present evidence of the effects of fixed exchange rate regimes on fiscal discipline. Their analysis is limited to a specific set of countries, notably the Communauté financière d'Afrique (CFA) zone in Africa and the pegged currency union in the Caribbean. In sum, there are divergent empirical results as to the relationship between exchange rate regimes and fiscal discipline.

This chapter posits that these mixed findings stem from the literature neglecting the importance of the political context in which fiscal policy decisions are made. On the political front, this analysis proposes that two dimensions affecting fiscal policy decisions must be taken into account: first, the electoral calendar, a timing dimension that directly affects the policymaker's horizon; and second, the degree of cohesion or political fragmentation that policymakers enjoy—or not—within the government coalition structures or the legislature. In other words, considering the underlying political conditions, both electoral timing and political cohesion, under which fiscal policy choices are made is crucial to properly understanding how alternative exchange rate regimes interact with fiscal outcomes. This chapter examines the question of how politics affects the interaction between currency regime and fiscal discipline using the broadest possible sample yet available.

Determining whether fixed or flexible exchange rates are better for enhanced fiscal discipline in the presence of different political conditions is important for several reasons. First, the exchange rate regime may affect the incentives to use deficits with electoral motives (Tanzi and Schuknecht 1997) or limit the sustainability of fiscal adjustments (Lane and Perotti 2003; Lambertini and Tavares 2005). Second, if flexible exchange rates are associated with closer public scrutiny of policymakers and this in turn encourages fiscal discipline, shifting to a flexible regime may be a "low-cost" institutional fix to the absence of fiscal discipline. This idea is particularly important in countries where credible economic and political institutions do not exist or are incapable of monitoring fiscal authorities. A flexible exchange rate regime can in these cases be seen as a substitute, albeit an imperfect one, for the harder task of building better institutions. Third, as the experience of the euro area during the sovereign debt crises illustrates how hard and credible pegs, even in advanced economies, are not necessarily associated with fiscal restraint. Here too, one of the determinants of the fiscal stance may be the quality of institutions that are charged with ensuring accountability and transparency at the national level. Finally, many of the developing countries adopting fixed pegs are small open economies, vulnerable to considerable exogenous shocks, so that determining how internal politics affects the relationship between fixing the exchange rate and fiscal performance becomes a key issue.[3]

[3] Duttagupta and Tolosa (2006) explore the sample of small economies in the Caribbean, while Tornell and Velasco (1995) present evidence for the CFA franc community in Africa.

The results in this chapter show that, in general, fixed exchange rate regimes are associated with less fiscal discipline. When political conditions are taken into account, strong political environments help improve fiscal discipline, and more so under flexible exchange rate regimes. In other words, policymakers not facing immediate elections and who can operate without political fragmentation are associated with better fiscal performance, especially when under a flexible exchange rate regime.

The remainder of the chapter is organized as follows: The second section reviews the literature. The third section presents a generic model illustrating the mechanisms by which political conditions (as measured by political *Horizon* and *Cohesion*) affect the relationship between exchange rate regimes and fiscal discipline. The fourth section describes the data and presents the main results. The fifth section provides several robustness exercises. The sixth section discusses fiscal discipline in the euro area using synthetic control analysis. The final section summarizes the main findings and concludes.

LITERATURE REVIEW: EXCHANGE RATE REGIMES AND FISCAL DISCIPLINE

The Traditional Argument

The traditional argument holds that fixed exchange rates encourage fiscal discipline. This argument is steeped in a long tradition, going back at least a century,[4] according to which adhering to a specie standard, or a stable currency, would be associated with sound money and predictable policies that would keep inflation under control and lead to fiscal restraint. The idea is that lax fiscal policies could eventually lead to a collapse of the peg, which is a very costly scenario (Giavazzi and Pagano 1988; Frankel, Goldstein, and Masson 1991). This traditional argument emphasizes how anticipation of the harsh economic impact of defaulting from a fixed exchange rate regime disciplines policymakers today and leads to sound fiscal policy.

In most theoretical setups, the fiscal and monetary policymakers care for both government expenditure and the usual trade-off is in place, whereby larger government transfers today or tomorrow translate into higher inflation either today or tomorrow. In a sense, what makes default inevitable in some instances of fixed rates and fiscal laxity is that the central bank eventually abandons the peg to avoid hyperinflation, a deeper output decline, or both. In other words, the monetary authority has access only to a limited commitment technology, where the limitation concerns time.[5]

[4] See Bordo (2003) for a review of exchange rate regime adoption.

[5] Limited commitment can be interpreted as a response to the need to keep the government solvent, an optimal response given the cost of commitment, or both. The likelihood of this happening relates to fiscal dominance.

The Dynamic Approach

Several authors have challenged the traditional argument and suggest, instead, that a fixed exchange rate regime may actually induce fiscal indiscipline (Tornell and Velasco 1995, 1998; Sun 2003; Duttagupta and Tolosa 2006). In the presence of impatient policymakers who heavily discount the future, the fact that the economic cost of fiscal indiscipline and default takes time to occur leads policymakers to spend more today.[6]

Whereas the traditional argument did not consider the relevance of time and how policymakers discount the future, Tornell and Velasco (1995, 1998) show that if the economic costs of fiscal indiscipline were sufficiently delayed, a fixed exchange rate regime would not limit the policymaker's tendency to overspend. In their setup, policymakers completely discount the future and thus, under fixed exchange rates, run reserves down through higher current spending. In contrast, flexible exchange rates would bring immediate economic punishment to fiscal laxity through currency depreciation and higher inflation.[7]

Sun (2003) develops a dynamic model integrating the traditional argument and Tornell and Velasco's (1995, 1998) dynamic counterargument, showing how each one overemphasizes part of a larger story. According to Sun, the economic costs of fiscal indiscipline exist under both exchange rate regimes. While in the short term fixed exchange rates shelter policymakers from the consequences of lax fiscal policies, a higher future punishment, or a more balanced consideration of the future can induce fiscal discipline under fixed rates. However, given the temporally uneven structure of incentives under fixed exchange rate regimes, there is greater incentive for lower expenditures under flexible exchange rate regimes.[8]

Political Economy Dimensions: *Horizon* and *Cohesion*

In this chapter's view, existing models focus on the economic costs of fiscal indiscipline, while not carefully spelling out the political dimension. In particular, when these models discuss the policymakers' time horizon, they refer to how long it takes them to face economic disaster as a result of a fiscal crisis that would force their countries to abandon the currency peg. This chapter postulates that, in this time horizon, policymakers also take into account the distance to elections and the amount of time that they have been in government. This is because we consider politicians to be office seekers rather than policy seekers, and their prime objective is to

---

[6] For this intertemporal choice to be available to the policymaker, it is important that the policymaker either has sufficient reserves or access to credit. Otherwise, deficits would immediately lead to a currency depreciation.

[7] Tornell and Velasco (1995, 1998) do not explicitly consider the trade-off between present and future punishment in fixed and flexible regimes; they completely discount the future in the former case and do not explicitly consider the future in the latter.

[8] Duttagupta and Tolosa (2006) suggest a comparative model of fiscal policy for countries that either go it alone or are integrated in a currency union.

maximize their probabilities of staying in power.[9] In addition, policymakers are forced to take into consideration the degree of political fragmentation they face when designing budget measures to be approved by parliament. In this context, this chapter proposes the introduction of an explicit electoral component in the policymaker's time horizon defined by Tornell and Velasco (1995, 1998) and Sun (2003). In addition, the chapter also proposes the inclusion of a new political dimension, that is, this degree of political cohesion. The two components of the revised theoretical framework can be summarized as follows:

- Political *Horizon*: The time policymakers have before forthcoming elections—or regime change in autocratic regimes. Politicians facing longer horizons have fewer incentives to overspend and thus associate with more fiscal discipline.
- Political *Cohesion*: The number of political actors participating in budgetary decisions who exhibit conflicting budgetary demands. These actors could be parties in government, or in opposition, in interest groups, or, more generally, veto players. Politicians who operate in more cohesive political environments are likely to be subject to less strident spending demands and be associated with tighter fiscal discipline.

In this framework, strong politics—a long horizon for the policymaker and high cohesion of the political body—add credibility to a flexible exchange rate system, leading to fiscal discipline. The next section spells out these hypotheses formally in an illustrative model.

THEORETICAL FRAMEWORK

Consider an economy in which there are two periods and three economic agents: a monetary authority, which decides the exchange rate, and two political players with authority over public spending.

The central bank cares about the nominal exchange rate, E_1, which it desires to be close to a target exchange rate, E^*, in both periods. It also cares for output, Y, which it wishes to be as close as possible to a target level, Y^*. This target level can be interpreted as potential output or some other desired reference level of output. The expression for the central bank's loss function would be

$$L = \frac{1}{2} \times \left[\left(Y_1 - Y^* \right)^2 + a_M \times \left(E_1 - E^* \right)^2 \right] + \beta_M \times \frac{1}{2} \times \left[\left(Y_2 - Y^* \right)^2 + a_M \times \left(E_2 - E^* \right)^2 \right], \tag{11.1}$$

[9] In political science, political parties are often seen as primarily office-seeking or policy-seeking parties. Office-seeking parties maximize their control over political office benefits, while policy-seeking parties maximize their impact on public policy (for further analysis on this issue, see Muller and Strom 1999).

where β_M is the discount factor of the central banker, and a_M weighs the losses stemming from deviations in the exchange rate relative to losses from deviations in output. The term $a_M > 1$, so that, given the central bank's nature, deviations in the exchange rate are weighted more heavily than deviations in output. Output levels Y_1 and Y_2 are the weighted sum of the output of the two political constituencies, where the weights γ_1 and γ_2 sum to 1, and accommodate a possible differentiated response of the central bank to the two political players.[10] The central bank's loss function becomes

$$L = \frac{1}{2} \times \left[\left(\left(\gamma_1 \times Y_{1,1} + \gamma_2 \times Y_{2,1} \right) - Y^* \right)^2 + a_M \times \left(E_1 - E^* \right)^2 \right]$$
$$+ \beta_M \times \frac{1}{2} \times \left[\left(\left(\gamma_1 \times Y_{1,2} + \gamma_2 \times Y_{2,2} \right) - Y^* \right)^2 + a_M \times \left(E_2 - E^* \right)^2 \right], \quad (11.2)$$

where 1 stands for constituency and 2 stands for period, in $Y_{1,1}$ and $Y_{1,2}$.

The fiscal players care only about their constituency's output, and the higher it is the better for them. Consequently, the loss function of constituency 1 is represented by:

$$L_{F_i} = -\ln Y_{i,1} - \beta_F \times \ln Y_{i,2}, \quad (11.3)$$

where $Y_{i,1}$ and $Y_{i,2}$ have been defined before, and β_F is the policymakers' discount factor, which may be different from β_M. The parameter β_F is a proxy for political horizon, so that its value is smaller the shorter the policymakers' time horizon due to the proximity of elections or higher likelihood of turnover due to a longer stay in power.

Output in periods 1 and 2 positively depends on the exchange rate, respectively, E_1 and E_2. The policymakers vie for transfers to their constituencies, TRF_1, and TRF_2, which increase output. However, these transfers have to be paid for in period 2, so that $D = TRF_1 + TRF_2$. Debt is fully repaid in period 2, and the debt burden is shared by the two constituencies according to weights α_1 and $\alpha_2 = 1 - \alpha_1$, each greater than 0 and smaller than 1. Thus, output in periods 1 and 2 can be summarized as

$$\begin{cases} Y_{1,1} = Y^* + E_1 + TRF_1 \\ Y_{2,1} = Y^* + E_1 + TRF_2 \end{cases} \quad (11.4)$$

$$\begin{cases} Y_{1,2} = Y^* + E_2 - \alpha_1 \times D \\ Y_{2,2} = Y^* + E_2 - \alpha_2 \times D. \end{cases} \quad (11.5)$$

[10] Note that the central bank cares about both keeping the exchange rate stable and avoiding steep drops in output. Because higher borrowing levels by fiscal authorities would have a greater output cost, the central bank would react to debt increases by gradually accommodating them through currency depreciation.

In period 0, before the start of the game, the monetary authority sets a fixed exchange rate E_1. We do not endogenize this choice of the exchange rate in period 0. In period 1, the two political players engage in a fiscal game whereby each decides the degree of transfers to their own constituencies. The deterrent to spending "too much" in period 1 is the fact that transfers, which increase utility in period 1, also increase debt that has to be fully repaid in period 2 and thus decreases utility in period 2. The extent to which each fiscal policymaker engages in transfers today depends on the amount of future debt that it will have to be repaid in the future. In period 2, because the central bank cares for output as well as for the exchange rate, it will default on the exchange rate. But the extent to which the central bank will accommodate fiscal profligacy depends on a_M, and the policymakers take that factor into consideration.

Two key political economy parameters affect the degree of indebtedness. The first is the political *Horizon*, that is, the extent to which the fiscal policymakers value the future. The horizon is related to electoral and other incentives that may make the policymaker less responsive to the future consequences of indebtedness. When the political horizon is longer, policymakers value the decrease in utility tomorrow due to debt repayment relatively more than the current increase in utility, driven by transfers. The second factor affecting indebtedness is the degree of political *Cohesion*, which is a function of the share of debt to be repaid by each fiscal actor in period 2. When each political actor is responsible for 50 percent of debt repayment, the political system is more cohesive, and both policymakers behave responsibly in fiscal terms.

The model is now solved by backward induction. First, we determine the rate of devaluation chosen in period 2 by the central banker for each level of indebtedness. In other words, in period 2, the central bank decides how much debt it will accommodate through devaluation. The central bank's reaction function to debt accumulation is the following:

$$E_2 = \frac{a_M \times E^* + D \times (\alpha_1 \times \gamma_1 + \alpha_2 \times \gamma_2)}{1 + a_M}. \quad (11.6)$$

As expected, the higher the debt incurred in period 1 by the policymakers, the higher the exchange rate depreciation by the central bank in period 2. Also as expected, the combination of parameters associated with D shows that the accommodation is less than one for one, given that $a_M > 1$, and $(\alpha_1 \times \gamma_1 + \alpha_2 \times \gamma_2)$ is generally smaller than 1. The higher a_M, that is, the more averse the central bank is to exchange rate deviations, the less it accommodates debt. Furthermore, as a_M increases to infinity, E_2 tends to E^* and there is no debt accommodation whatsoever. This is the case of a fully credible and unchangeable fixed exchange rate.

Working backward, in period 1, the policymakers take into consideration the expected future behavior of the central bank and each constituency's share of the debt burden to decide the extent of the transfers to mobilize. Total transfers—and thus debt, one period later—are given by the intersection of two fiscal reaction functions where each constituency's level of transfers depends on the others', as below:

$$TRF_1 = -\frac{Y^* + a_M \times \left(E^* + Y^*\right)}{2\times\left(\alpha_2 \times \gamma_2 - \alpha_1 \times \left(a_M - \gamma_1 + 1\right)\right)} - \beta_F \times \frac{\left(E_1 + Y^*\right)}{2} - \frac{TRF_2}{2} \quad (11.7)$$

$$TRF_2 = -\frac{Y^* + a_M \times \left(E^* + Y^*\right)}{2\times\left(\alpha_1 \times \gamma_1 - \alpha_2 \times \left(a_M - \gamma_2 + 1\right)\right)} - \beta_F \times \frac{\left(E_1 + Y^*\right)}{2} - \frac{TRF_1}{2}. \quad (11.8)$$

A one-monetary-unit increase in transfers to a specific constituency leads to a decrease in transfers by the other player by less than one unit, so that an equilibrium exists. Figures 11.1 and 11.2 illustrate the two main political economy propositions that can be derived from this model. Other things being equal,

- *Proposition 1*: A decrease in the discount factor, β_F, of the fiscal policymakers so that they act under a longer political *Horizon*, leads to lower indebtedness (Figure 11.1).
- *Proposition 2*: An increase in political *Cohesion*, expressed by a more even distribution of the debt burden between political constituencies, leads to a decrease in public debt (Figure 11.2).

Figure 11.1. Political *Horizon* and Indebtedness

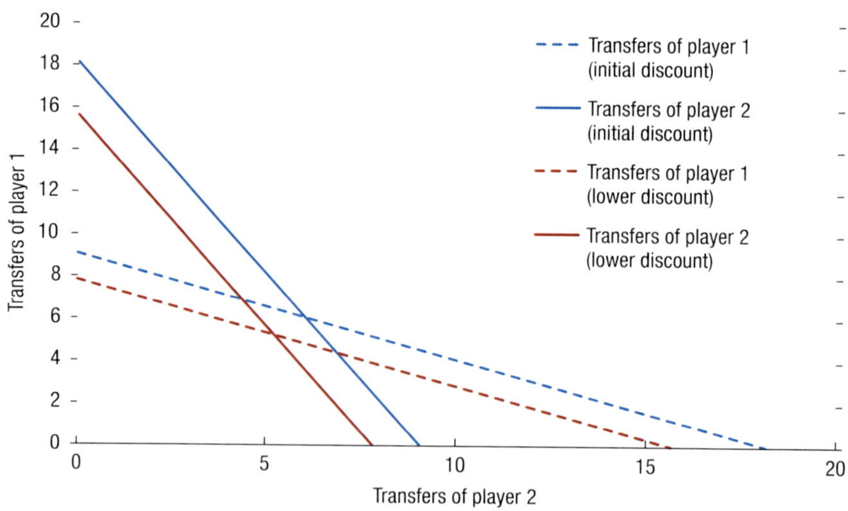

Source: Authors' calculations.
Note: A lower discount of the future (that is, higher political *Horizon*) leads to lower indebtedness (that is, more fiscal discipline).

Figure 11.2. Political *Cohesion* and Indebtedness

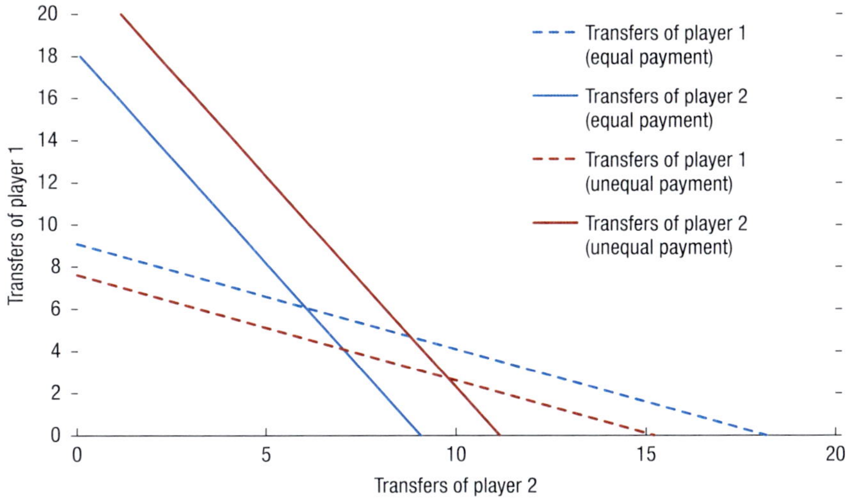

Source: Authors' calculations.
Note: A higher level of burden sharing (that is, higher political *Cohesion*) leads to lower indebtedness (that is, more fiscal discipline).

EMPIRICAL ANALYSIS

Data Description

To test the propositions above, an unbalanced panel of 79 countries, including 31 advanced countries and 48 emerging and low-income economies, between the years 1975 and 2012, is used to estimate the following specification:

$$FD_{it} = \alpha_i + \delta_t + \phi ER_{it} + \theta POL_{it} + \mathbf{X}'_{it}\beta + \lambda(ER_{it} \times POL_{it}) + \varepsilon_{it}, \quad (11.9)$$

where FD_{it} is the proxy for fiscal discipline, given by the primary balance, measured as a percentage of GDP;[11] ER_{it} is a dummy variable taking the value one when a country is under a fixed exchange rate regime and zero if under a flexible exchange rate regime;[12] $\mathbf{X}'_{it}$ is a vector of control variables expected to affect the fiscal policy stance and comprises the real GDP growth rate, trade openness (exports plus imports as share of GDP), terms of trade, log of total reserves in

[11] From the IMF's International Financial Statistics.

[12] We use the classification of exchange rate regimes provided by Reinhart and Rogoff (2004) and generate a dummy variable that takes the value one (fixed exchange rate) if the country/year observation has any value between 1 and 8 in Reinhart and Rogoff's classification, and takes the value zero otherwise—original Reinhart and Rogoff values of 9 to 15. We also test the robustness of the results by generating another dummy variable that uses Coarse's classification from the IMF.

Table 11.1. Summary of Political Composite Variables and Descriptive Statistics

Concept	Variables
Horizon	Years in office
	Years left in current term
	Party of chief executive more time in office
	Months to next election
Cohesion	Margin of majority
	Cabinet strength
	Executive control of all houses
	Weak opposition

Source: Authors' calculations.
Note: The average and standard deviation of the respective principal component are normalized to 0 and 1, respectively.

U.S. dollars, private credit as a percentage of GDP, and the consumer price inflation rate.[13] The parameters α_i, δ_t are country and time effects that capture unobserved heterogeneity across countries and time-unvarying factors. The term ε_{it} is a white noise identically and independently distributed disturbance term satisfying standard assumptions of zero mean and constant variance. Finally, POL_{it} accounts for political factors and is constructed using principal component analysis, to obtain the common factor(s) of each block of variables comprising two components termed *Horizon* and *Cohesion*. These are defined as follows:

- Political *Horizon*: A longer political horizon is associated with fewer years in office, more years left in current term, the chief executive's party with a long time in office, and more months to next election.[14] Only the first principal component is retained.[15]
- Political *Cohesion*: Stronger political cohesion is associated with a high margin of the parliamentary majority supporting the cabinet, low cabinet fragmentation, executive control of all houses, and a weak opposition. Only the first principal component is retained.

Horizon and *Cohesion* variables are each represented by one factor composed of four underlying variables.[16] The resulting principal components indices are described in Table 11.1, while Table 11.2 lists the corresponding factor loadings.[17] The principal components can be interpreted by focusing on the factor loadings

[13] This is in line with Duttagupta and Tolosa (2006).

[14] This latter indicator refers to actual months left to next election, after the fact, while the variable "more years left in current term" is observed ex ante. Both are informative.

[15] A likelihood ratio test was used to examine the "sphericity" case, allowing for sampling variability in the correlations. This test comfortably rejects sphericity at the 1 percent level. The first factor explains almost 40 percent of the variance in the standardized data (see Table 11.2).

[16] The source for each component variable is the Database on Political Institutions (Cruz, Keefer, and Scartascini 2016).

[17] Principal component analysis is based on the classical covariance matrix, which is sensitive to outliers. Here we conduct a robust estimation of the covariance matrix. A well-suited method is the minimum covariance determinant (MCD) that considers all subsets containing *h* percent of the observations and estimates the variance of the mean on the data of the subset associated with the smallest covariance matrix determinant. Specifically, we implement Rousseeuw and van Driessen's (1999) algorithm. When we compute the same indices with the MCD version, we obtain similar results, suggesting that outliers are not driving the factor analysis.

Table 11.2. Factor Loadings and Uniqueness

	Factors		
Variables	***Horizon***	***Cohesion***	**Uniqueness**
Years in Office	0.39		0.29
Years Left in Current Term	0.41		0.28
Party of Chief Executive More Time in Office	0.37		0.29
Months to Next Election	0.45		0.28
Margin of Majority		0.93	0.12
Cabinet Strength		0.90	0.17
Executive Control of All Houses		0.76	0.42
Weak Opposition		0.72	0.47
Percent Explained	0.39	0.69	

Source: Authors' calculations.

Figure 11.3. Primary Balance, Exchange Rates, and Political Conditions

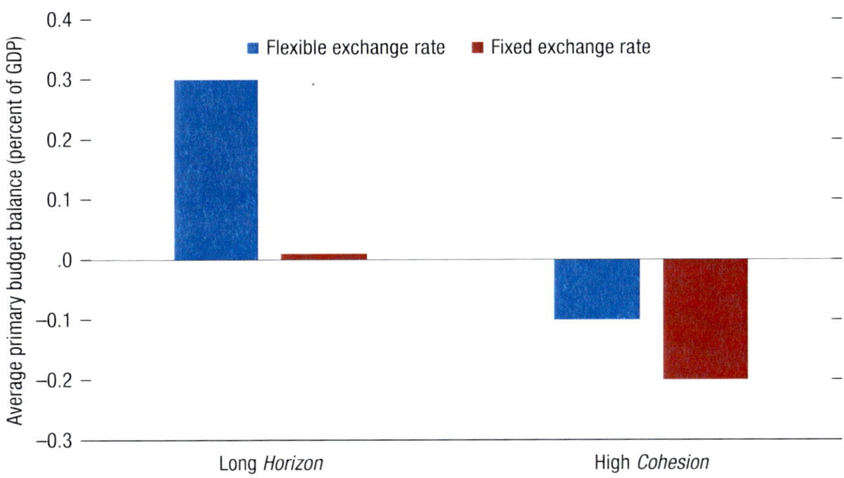

Source: Authors' calculations.

and the uniqueness of each variable.[18] With regard to political *Horizon*, uniqueness is relatively low for all variables, which implies that the retained factor spans the original variables adequately. As to political *Cohesion*, the factor appears to describe mostly the margin of majority and cabinet strength. In principle, both factors should enter with positive coefficients in the regressions.

A first look at the data shows that it is in line with the findings of Tornell and Velasco (1995) and Sun (2003) so that fiscal discipline is lower under fixed exchange rate regimes than under flexible ones (Figure 11.3). Also, stylized facts seem to

[18] Uniqueness of a variable is the share of its variance that is not accounted for by all the factors.

confirm the propositions of the theoretical model presented above: in contexts of long political *Horizon*, the average primary surplus is only 0.01 percent of GDP under fixed exchange rate regimes, and it reaches 0.3 percent of GDP under flexible exchange rates. These differences are smaller in contexts of high political *Cohesion*. In such cases, the average primary deficit is –0.2 percent of GDP under fixed exchange rates and at –0.1 percent of GDP.

Baseline Panel Results

First, equation (11.9) is estimated using ordinary least squares with heteroskedastic and serial correlation robust standard errors clustered at the country level. Alternative estimators are also used that correct for the standard econometric pitfalls, including possible reverse causality between exchange rate regimes and the fiscal stance, and omitted variable bias simultaneously affecting both the choice of the exchange rate regime and the fiscal stance. To correct for serial correlation and possible cross-sectional heteroskedasticity, feasible generalized least squares regressions are run using estimated cross-section residual variances as weights, thus attaining a more efficient estimate than under ordinary least squares.

Second, having in mind potential cross-sectional dependencies, the main regression in equation (11.9) is run with Driscoll-Kraay (1998) robust standard errors. This nonparametric technique assumes the error structure to be heteroskedastic, autocorrelated up to some lag, and possibly correlated between the groups.

Third, as a closer inspection of the data suggests, influential outliers potentially play a role in cross-section analysis. It is important to consider the extent to which outliers drive the results, particularly in such a heterogeneous sample as this one, which includes emerging market and low-income economies characterized by spells of exchange rate volatility. The analysis uses the method of moments that fits the efficient high breakdown estimator proposed by Yohai (1987).[19] The model described by equation (11.9) is a reduced form; therefore, it does not legitimize causal statements or even immediate quantification of the effect of exchange rate regimes and politics on fiscal discipline. Because causality can run in both directions, some of the right-hand-side regressors may be correlated with the error term. The fixed-effects approach is complemented with a panel instrumental variable–generalized least squares approach. As instruments, the main variables used are those proposed by Acemoglu and others (2003) and Fatás and Mihov (2013). The first instrument—labeled *constraints*—captures potential veto points on the decisions of the executive. A variation of this measure of constraints is a variable constructed by Henisz (2000) called political

[19] In the first stage, it takes the S estimator, a high breakdown value method introduced in Rousseeuw and Yohai (1984) applied to the residual scale. It then derives starting values for the coefficient vectors, and on the second stage applies the Huber-type bi-square M-estimator using iteratively reweighted least squares to obtain the final coefficient estimates.

constraints (labeled *polcon*). This variable differs from our measure in two ways: (1) Henisz (2000) adjusts for the ideological alignment across political institutions; and (2) he argues that each additional constraint has a diminishing marginal effect on policy outcomes, therefore, the link between the overall measure and the veto points should be nonlinear. In addition, dummies are used to control for the presence of rules on expenditure, taxes, and debt.

The first set of results concerns the estimation of equation (11.9) to empirically test Propositions 1 and 2 from the theoretical section. The procedure starts by independently analyzing the variables that measure the exchange rate regime, political *Horizon* and political *Cohesion*. Table 11.3 shows the estimates of the coefficient associated with the fixed exchange rate regime to be always negative and almost always statistically significant at conventional levels. These results are in line with the latest findings in the empirical literature: being in or moving to a fixed exchange rate regime is associated with less fiscal discipline. This confirms our theoretical propositions 1 and 2. A longer political *Horizon* and more political *Cohesion* are both associated with a higher primary balance and more fiscal discipline. The remaining controls are mostly statistically significant and with the expected sign: higher GDP growth, higher inflation, higher reserves,

Table 11.3. Baseline, Fixed Effects Regressions

	Specification						
	(1)	(2)	(3)	(4)	(5)	(6)	(7)
Fixed Exchange Rates	−0.432**	−0.412**	−0.366*	−0.388*	−0.406*	−0.472**	−0.370
	(0.180)	(0.192)	(0.219)	(0.230)	(0.215)	(0.226)	(0.234)
Growth	0.087***	0.098***	0.116***	0.100***	0.116***	0.135***	0.145***
	(0.019)	(0.020)	(0.021)	(0.024)	(0.020)	(0.022)	(0.023)
Trade Openness	0.017***	0.015***	0.021***	0.019***	0.021***	0.012*	0.012*
	(0.005)	(0.005)	(0.006)	(0.006)	(0.006)	(0.006)	(0.007)
Terms of Trade	0.017***	0.018***	0.020***	0.028***	0.016***	0.016***	0.018***
	(0.003)	(0.003)	(0.004)	(0.004)	(0.004)	(0.005)	(0.005)
Reserves	0.438***	0.410***	0.451***	0.398***	0.271***	0.217**	0.226**
	(0.093)	(0.093)	(0.108)	(0.101)	(0.099)	(0.102)	(0.107)
Inflation		0.034***			0.024**	0.030***	0.027***
		(0.011)			(0.011)	(0.010)	(0.010)
Financial Openness			0.017*				
			(0.009)				
Credit				0.045***			
				(0.013)			
Horizon					0.346***		0.310***
					(0.096)		(0.116)
Cohesion						0.241*	0.241
						(0.142)	(0.164)
Observations	2,404	2,216	1,888	1,779	1,808	1,560	1,456
R^2	0.442	0.456	0.476	0.471	0.486	0.478	0.478

Source: Authors' calculations.

Note: The estimation with country and time effects is omitted for reasons of parsimony. Robust standard errors are clustered at the country level in parentheses. The constant term is estimated but omitted.

*$p < .1$; **$p < .05$; ***$p < .01$.

Table 11.4. Interaction Terms, Fixed Effects Regressions

	Specification					
	(1)	(2)	(3)	(4)	(5)	(6)
Fixed Exchange Rates	−0.637***	−0.826***	−0.720***	−0.547**	−0.696***	−0.589**
	(0.208)	(0.236)	(0.263)	(0.214)	(0.262)	(0.267)
Growth	0.111***	0.126***	0.135***	0.117***	0.135***	0.145***
	(0.020)	(0.022)	(0.023)	(0.020)	(0.022)	(0.023)
Trade Openness	0.025***	0.014**	0.016**	0.022***	0.011*	0.012*
	(0.006)	(0.006)	(0.007)	(0.006)	(0.006)	(0.007)
Terms of Trade	0.016***	0.017***	0.019***	0.016***	0.016***	0.018***
	(0.003)	(0.005)	(0.005)	(0.004)	(0.005)	(0.005)
Reserves	0.260***	0.208**	0.214**	0.273***	0.207**	0.224**
	(0.095)	(0.098)	(0.103)	(0.099)	(0.102)	(0.107)
Horizon	0.534***		0.451***	0.519***		0.433***
	(0.114)		(0.144)	(0.117)		(0.148)
Horizon × Fixed Exchange Rates	−0.435***		−0.308	−0.417**		−0.278
	(0.167)		(0.225)	(0.171)		(0.233)
Cohesion		0.370**	0.288		0.364**	0.296
		(0.169)	(0.181)		(0.175)	(0.181)
Cohesion × Fixed Exchange Rates		−0.397*	−0.178		−0.343	−0.146
		(0.231)	(0.287)		(0.259)	(0.294)
Inflation				0.024**	0.029***	0.027***
				(0.010)	(0.010)	(0.010)
Observations	1,904	1,655	1,534	1,808	1,560	1,456
R^2	0.485	0.470	0.472	0.488	0.478	0.479

Source: Authors' calculations.
Note: The estimation with country and time effects is omitted for reasons of parsimony. Robust standard errors are clustered at the country level in parentheses. The constant term is estimated but omitted.
*$p < .1$; **$p < .05$; ***$p < .01$.

better terms of trade, and trade and financial openness are all associated with higher fiscal discipline.[20]

Table 11.4 includes two interaction terms between the dummy variable for fixed exchange rate regimes and the two variables measuring political *Horizon* and *Cohesion*. Again, the analysis delivers a statistically significant and negative estimate of the coefficient on fixed exchange rate regimes and positive coefficients for both political indicators. Interestingly, the interaction terms between the key variables are negative, suggesting that the positive effect of politics (longer *Horizon* or higher *Cohesion*) on the degree of fiscal discipline are particularly relevant for flexible exchange rate regimes. In other words, it is in flexible exchange rate settings that politics seems to matter most.

Note that these results shed light on the questions that motivate this chapter. In line with the model's prediction, both exchange rates and politics matter for fiscal discipline. In line with the model's prediction, flexible (not fixed) exchange rates, and strong politics (long *Horizon* and high *Cohesion*) are associated with better fiscal positions. The exchange rate regime seems to be quantitatively

[20] For reasons of parsimony, the remainder of the chapter refrains from commenting on the controls.

more important than the underlying political conditions. When considered together, strong politics attenuates the damaging effects of fixed rates on fiscal discipline but is insufficient to reverse fiscal profligacy. Moreover, the positive effects of longer political horizon and more political cohesion on fiscal performance are amplified under flexible exchange rate regimes.

ROBUSTNESS CHECKS

Sensitivity to Alternative Estimators, Outliers, and Endogeneity

To test the robustness of the baseline results, a series of robustness checks are performed. First, equation (11.9) is reestimated using feasible generalized least squares and Driscoll-Kraay cross-sectional dependence robust standard errors, as well as the method of moments estimator to check for outliers. Results in Table 11.5 show again that fixed exchange rates are associated with less fiscal discipline, while a longer *Horizon* and higher *Cohesion*[21] are associated with better fiscal performance. The interaction terms between the key variables are also negative and significant. Second, the regressions are estimated using instrumental variables to address endogeneity concerns. Results are reported in Table 11.6 and confirm the baseline set of findings.

Sensitivity to Alternative Definitions of Fiscal Stance

The robustness of the results to a different definition of the dependent variable is also tested by identifying fiscal discipline with strong improvements in the fiscal stance, associated with fiscal consolidations. The dependent variable is now a dummy taking the value one during years of fiscal consolidation. The literature addressing the identification of fiscal adjustment episodes is vast and has relied on changes in the cyclically adjusted primary balance (CAPB) as a share of GDP. Some caveats surrounding this approach have been highlighted recently.[22] To maximize country coverage, this analysis relies on Alesina and Ardagna's (1998) method of identifying fiscal adjustments as years where the CAPB is at least 2 percent of GDP in one year, or at least 1.5 percentage points on average in the past two years.

[21] Results for *Cohesion* are available from the authors upon request.

[22] In particular, the CAPB approach could bias empirical estimates toward finding evidence of non-Keynesian effects (see, for example, Afonso and Jalles 2014). Many nonpolicy factors influence the CAPB and can lead to erroneous conclusions regarding fiscal policy changes. For example, a stock price boom raises the CAPB by increasing capital gains tax revenue and tends to coincide with an expansion in private demand (Morris and Schuknecht 2007). Even when the CAPB accurately measures fiscal actions, these actions include discretionary responses to economic developments.

Table 11.5. Sensitivity to Alternative Estimators

	Specification								
	Feasible Generalized Least Squares			Driscoll-Kraay			Outlier-Robust		
	(1)	(2)	(3)	(4)	(5)	(6)	(7)	(8)	(9)
Fixed Exchange Rates	−0.579***	−0.635***	−0.686***	−0.662***	−0.812***	−0.956***	−0.540***	−0.476*	−0.601**
	(0.164)	(0.181)	(0.181)	(0.240)	(0.267)	(0.277)	(0.207)	(0.269)	(0.259)
Growth	0.119***	0.124***	0.125***	0.187***	0.202***	0.203***	0.160***	0.182***	0.192***
	(0.011)	(0.012)	(0.012)	(0.041)	(0.048)	(0.048)	(0.031)	(0.032)	(0.030)
Trade Openness	0.026***	0.026***	0.026***	0.007	0.013	0.014	0.007***	0.009***	0.010***
	(0.004)	(0.005)	(0.005)	(0.006)	(0.008)	(0.008)	(0.002)	(0.002)	(0.002)
Terms of Trade	0.008***	0.008**	0.008**	0.013***	0.012**	0.012**	0.004	0.010*	0.010*
	(0.003)	(0.004)	(0.004)	(0.004)	(0.005)	(0.005)	(0.003)	(0.006)	(0.005)
Reserves	−0.026	−0.004	−0.005	0.189	0.124	0.125	0.379***	0.420***	0.407***
	(0.067)	(0.073)	(0.073)	(0.191)	(0.204)	(0.205)	(0.044)	(0.055)	(0.056)
Inflation	0.041***	0.037***	0.036***	0.041***	0.029***	0.029***	0.038***	0.042***	0.476***
	(0.015)	(0.012)	(0.012)	(0.009)	(0.009)	(0.008)	(0.004)	(0.004)	(0.056)
Horizon		0.215***	0.315***		0.344***	0.521***		0.013	0.285
		(0.059)	(0.072)		(0.106)	(0.129)		(0.158)	(0.185)
Horizon × Fixed Exchange Rates			−0.247**			−0.423***			−0.631**
			(0.111)			(0.157)			(0.266)
Observations	2,214	1,807	1,807	2,216	1,808	1,808	2,216	1,808	1,808

Source: Authors' calculations.

Note: Estimation is made by either FGLS, Driscoll-Kraay cross-sectional dependence-robust standard errors, or method of moments–estimator for outliers. The estimation with country and time effects is omitted for reasons of parsimony. Robust standard errors are clustered at the country level in parentheses. The constant term is estimated but omitted.

*$p < .1$; **$p < .05$; ***$p < .01$.

Table 11.6. Endogeneity: Instrumental Variables

	Specification				
	(1)	(2)	(3)	(4)	(5)
Fixed Exchange Rates	−0.730***	−0.743***	−0.888***	−0.754***	−0.873***
	(0.203)	(0.217)	(0.227)	(0.225)	(0.303)
Growth	0.208***	0.214***	0.214***	0.247***	0.247***
	(0.019)	(0.020)	(0.020)	(0.022)	(0.022)
Trade Openness	0.008*	0.010**	0.011**	0.002	0.002
	(0.005)	(0.005)	(0.005)	(0.005)	(0.005)
Terms of Trade	0.014***	0.011***	0.011***	0.012**	0.012**
	(0.003)	(0.004)	(0.004)	(0.005)	(0.005)
Reserves	0.088	0.064	0.066	0.231***	0.229***
	(0.073)	(0.078)	(0.077)	(0.087)	(0.087)
Inflation	0.035*	0.029	0.029	0.036*	0.036*
	(0.019)	(0.019)	(0.019)	(0.018)	(0.018)
Horizon		0.365***	0.536***		
		(0.111)	(0.136)		
Horizon × Fixed Exchange Rates			−0.431**		
			(0.200)		
Cohesion				0.133	0.190
				(0.196)	(0.218)
Cohesion × Fixed Exchange Rates					−0.175
					(0.297)
Observations	1,872	1,634	1,634	1,396	1,396

Source: Authors' calculations.

Note: The estimation is by instrumental variable. Country and time effects are omitted for reasons of parsimony. Robust standard errors are clustered at the country level in parentheses. Instruments include constraints on the executive and political constraints (see text for more details). The constant term is estimated but omitted.

*$p < .1$; **$p < .05$; ***$p < .01$.

Because we now have a dependent variable expressed in binary terms, we use a logistic regression to estimate equation (11.1). More precisely, we estimate the following model:

$$\text{Prob}(\text{FD}=1|\text{ER,X}) = \Phi(\lambda_i + \varphi ER + \theta POL + \mathbf{X}'\beta), \tag{11.10}$$

where φ, θ, β are vectors of the parameters to be estimated and $\Phi(.)$ is the logistic function.[23]

Given that the analysis relies on panel data, the structural model can be written as follows:

$$\begin{aligned} FD_{it}^{*} &= \lambda_i + \varphi ER + \theta POL + \mathbf{X}_{it}{}'\beta + \varepsilon_{it}, \\ FD_{it} &= 1 \text{ if } \text{FD}_{\text{it}}^{*} > 0, \text{ and 0 otherwise.} \end{aligned} \tag{11.11}$$

[23] Because probit models do not lend themselves well to the fixed-effects treatment because of the incidental parameter problem (Wooldridge 2002, 484), we estimate a logit model with fixed effects.

with $i = 1, \ldots, 78$; $t = 1980, \ldots, 2013$; λ_i captures the unobserved individual effects; and ε_{it} is the error term.

We take the analysis one step further and also assume that a fiscal adjustment is successful if the improvement in the CAPB for two consecutive years is at least η-times the standard deviation of the CAPB in the full panel (Afonso and Jalles 2012):

$$\begin{cases} 1, if \sum_{i=0}^{1} \Delta b_{t+i} > \eta\sigma \\ 0, otherwise \end{cases}. \tag{11.12}$$

This analysis uses a threshold value of $\eta = 1$.

The results suggest that fixed exchange rate regimes decrease the likelihood of a given government engaging in a fiscal consolidation (see Table 11.7).[24] More important, the likelihood is even smaller if the sample is restricted to successful fiscal episodes, as shown by the higher magnitude—in absolute value—of the estimated coefficients in columns (6)–(10) of Table 11.7. The *Horizon* of the policymakers is never relevant, in line with results in Alesina, Perotti, and Tavares (1998), who find that engaging in fiscal adjustments does not increase the likelihood of cabinet turnover. In this setting, political *Cohesion* becomes statistically irrelevant, and the interaction term between *Cohesion* and exchange rate regime also loses statistical significance.[25]

Sensitivity to Alternative Indicators of Exchange Rate Regime

The robustness of the empirical exercise to a different measure of the exchange rate regime is also tested. Instead of building the dummy variable using a normative classification of exchange rate systems from Reinhart and Rogoff (2004), a positive approach is used. Now, the new dummy variable ER_{it}^{new} takes value one, denoting a fixed exchange rate regime, if the five-year rolling volatility of the real effective exchange rate is smaller than one-third of the five-year rolling average

[24] As a robustness check to Alesina and Ardagna's (1998) method, Giavazzi and Pagano's (1996) method was also used. They propose using the cumulative changes in the CAPB that are at least 5, 4, and 3 percentage points of GDP in, respectively, 4, 3, or 2 years, or 3 percentage points in one year. Results, available upon request, did not qualitatively change.

[25] An alternative dependent variable was also tried by using fiscal discipline defined in nominal levels (instead of percentage of GDP) and in real per capita terms. Results, available in Annex Table 11.1.1, confirm the findings.

Table 11.7. Discretionary Fiscal Consolidations as Proxy for Fiscal Discipline: Logit Estimations

	Specification									
	All Fiscal Consolidations					Successful Fiscal Consolidations				
	(1)	(2)	(3)	(4)	(5)	(6)	(7)	(8)	(9)	(10)
Fixed Exchange Rates	−0.405***	−0.587***	−0.526***	−0.482***	−0.607*	−1.173**	−1.720***	−1.631**	−1.797***	−3.353*
	(0.149)	(0.165)	(0.181)	(0.176)	(0.314)	(0.556)	(0.646)	(0.665)	(0.649)	(1.877)
Growth	0.002	−0.002	−0.003	−0.033	−0.033	0.292***	0.467***	0.463***	0.285**	0.293**
	(0.022)	(0.024)	(0.024)	(0.024)	(0.024)	(0.102)	(0.119)	(0.120)	(0.135)	(0.137)
Trade Openness	0.005*	0.004	0.004	0.009***	0.009***	−0.037**	−0.066***	−0.065***	−0.068*	−0.067*
	(0.003)	(0.003)	(0.003)	(0.003)	(0.003)	(0.018)	(0.023)	(0.024)	(0.039)	(0.039)
Terms of Trade	−0.005	−0.006	−0.006	−0.002	−0.002	−0.086**	−0.152***	−0.151***	−0.081*	−0.080*
	(0.004)	(0.005)	(0.005)	(0.006)	(0.006)	(0.034)	(0.031)	(0.031)	(0.048)	(0.048)
Reserves	0.148**	0.086	0.089	0.097	0.093	−0.629*	−1.103***	−1.078***	−0.204	−0.226
	(0.072)	(0.078)	(0.078)	(0.087)	(0.088)	(0.346)	(0.403)	(0.395)	(0.459)	(0.471)
Horizon		0.098	0.028				0.046	0.219		
		(0.100)	(0.134)				(0.277)	(0.527)		
Horizon × Fixed Exchange Rates			0.149					0.239		
			(0.181)					(0.584)		
Cohesion				0.782***	0.737***				0.723	0.017
				(0.189)	(0.207)				(0.888)	(1.607)
Cohesion × Fixed Exchange Rates					−0.155					−1.553
					(0.342)					(1.777)
Observations	985	857	857	764	764	136	134	134	100	100

Source: Authors' calculations.

Note: This is a logit estimation. The binary type dependent variable is identified in the second row. The constant term is estimated but omitted. Robust standard errors are clustered at the country level in parentheses.

$^*p < .1$; $^{**}p < .05$; $^{***}p < .01$.

Table 11.8. Robustness to Alternative Definition of Exchange Rate Regime

	Specification			
	(1)	(2)	(3)	(4)
Fixed Exchange Rates—New	−0.515	−0.515	−0.952***	−0.907**
	(0.356)	(0.356)	(0.356)	(0.358)
Growth	0.233***	0.233***	0.217***	0.214***
	(0.033)	(0.033)	(0.034)	(0.034)
Trade Openness	−0.005	−0.005	−0.008	−0.009
	(0.007)	(0.007)	(0.008)	(0.008)
Terms of Trade	0.023***	0.023***	0.033***	0.035***
	(0.007)	(0.007)	(0.009)	(0.009)
Reserves	0.226	0.223	0.335**	0.349***
	(0.137)	(0.138)	(0.133)	(0.133)
Horizon	0.301**	0.312**		
	(0.135)	(0.139)		
Horizon × Fixed Exchange Rates—New		−0.230		
		(0.369)		
Cohesion			0.992***	1.044***
			(0.259)	(0.261)
Cohesion × Fixed Exchange Rates—New				−0.852*
				(0.440)
Observations	1,033	1,033	976	976
R^2	0.560	0.561	0.561	0.562

Source: Authors' calculations.
Note: The estimation with country and time effects is omitted for reasons of parsimony. Robust standard errors are clustered at the country level in parentheses. The constant term is estimated but omitted.
*$p < .1$; **$p < .05$; ***$p < .01$.

volatility.[26] Results shown in Table 11.8 suggest that the new definition of fixed exchange regimes (*Fixed ER*-new) still yields negative and, when *Cohesion* is controlled for, statistically significant, coefficients when explaining the degree of fiscal discipline.

CASE STUDY: FISCAL DISCIPLINE AND FIXED EXCHANGE RATES IN THE EURO AREA

The introduction of a single currency in the European Union between 1999 and 2002 was a unique policy experience.[27] An initial set of 11 countries made a voluntary and simultaneous transition from flexible to fully fixed exchange rates after

[26] Volatility is measured by the standard deviation. Note that changing the threshold slightly above or below one-third does not change the results.

[27] In 1999, 11 European Union member states joined the final stage of monetary union and fixed their bilateral exchange rates. The euro was introduced then as a virtual currency, while national currencies remained in circulation for three more years. In 2002, the euro was substituted for national currencies in circulation. The Euro-11 countries are Austria, Belgium, Finland, France, Germany, Luxembourg, Ireland, Italy, Netherlands, Portugal, and Spain.

joining the euro area. This experience is relevant to the analysis in this chapter for two reasons: First, because all euro area countries adhered to the euro at the same time and as part of a common move, the endogeneity of exchange rate regime choice is partially controlled for. In addition, it is normally in well-established democracies that politics seems to matter most for fiscal policy, which points to a case such as the euro area's as worthy of attention.

To understand the effect of this decision on fiscal discipline, a case study analysis is performed using the synthetic control methodology (SCM) on the Euro-11 countries. The SCM is a formal data-driven procedure used to quantify the effect of an event—in this case, the introduction of a fully fixed exchange rate in the euro area—on an outcome variable, here, the primary budget balance. The method relies on the creation of an artificial counterfactual that mimics the primary budget balance before the introduction of the single currency using data on a set of variables from the years before the event, and then comparing the actual outcomes with the counterfactual for the years after the event.[28] The counterfactual—the synthetic unit—is constructed as a weighted average of the primary budget balance in countries with characteristics similar to those of the country under consideration but subsequently unaffected by the event.[29] Country weights are chosen to minimize the distance between the country under consideration and its counterfactual in terms of the primary balance variable and its predictors (Abadie, Diamond, and Hainmueller 2010). The effect of an event is obtained as the difference between the outcome variable for the country in question and the weighted average of the outcome variable for the synthetic control group.

Figure 11.4 plots a number of important results from the SCM exercise that confirm the theoretical predictions and the main empirical results of this chapter. Panel 1 in Figure 11.4 shows that, in the aftermath of moving to fixed exchange rates, the Euro-11 maintained a lower primary balance than in the synthetic counterfactual. In addition, Figure 11.4 shows results for four countries with extreme scores on the political *Horizon* and *Cohesion* variables vis-à-vis the principal component's average value. Countries with high relative scores in at least one of the two political dimensions, such as Austria (higher-than-average horizon) or Portugal (higher-than-average cohesion), display a narrower distance from their synthetic counterfactuals, even if they experienced less fiscal discipline after joining the euro area. In contrast, countries with lower-than-average scores in both political dimensions, such as Belgium, saw their distance to the counterfactual increase. Finally, countries with higher-than-average scores on both political horizon and cohesion (Spain) managed to improve fiscal discipline significantly above their synthetic counterfactual, proving that

[28] See Annex 11.2 for more details.

[29] The control countries included in the synthetic unit are, in this case, OECD member countries other than those under analysis (that is, the Euro-11). We also exclude transition economies. See Annex 11.2.

Figure 11.4. Synthetic Control Analysis, Euro-11

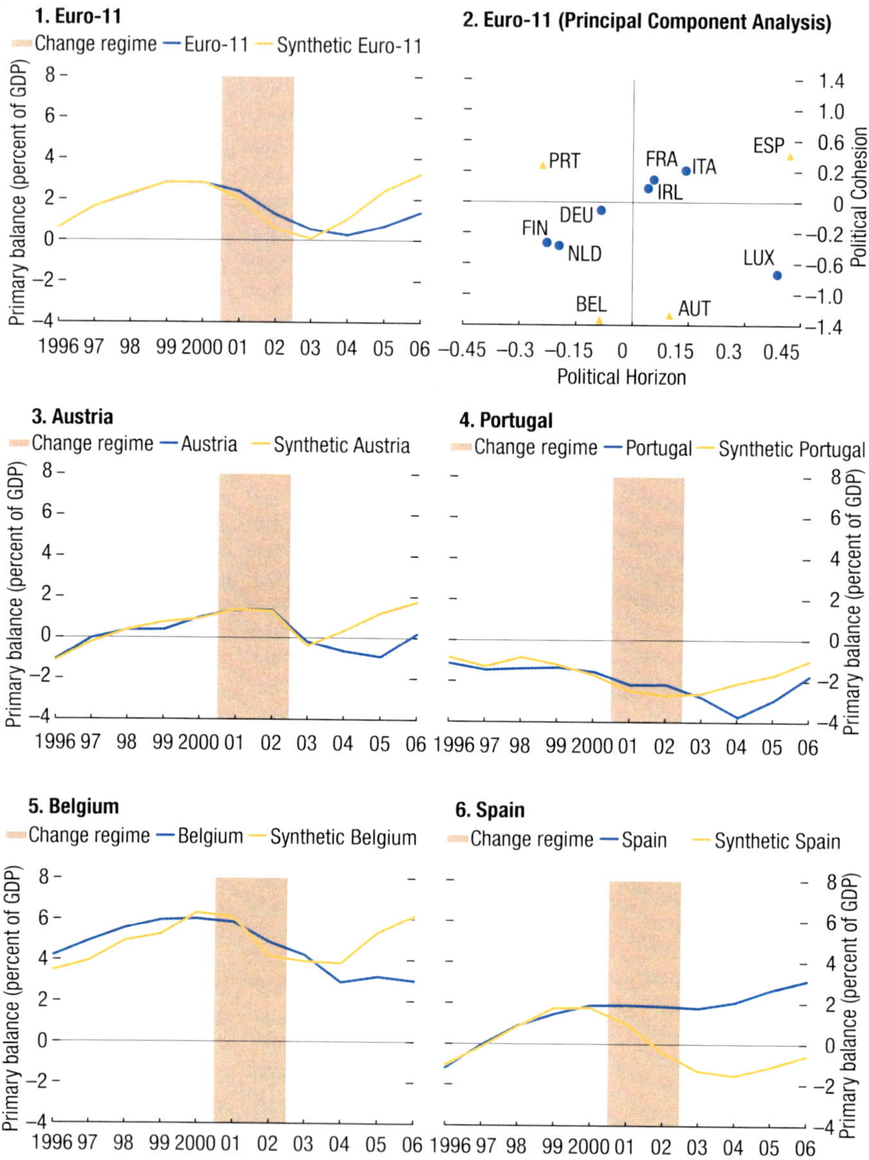

Source: Authors' calculations.

Note: Austria (panel 3) is a country with above-average political *Horizon* and below-average *Cohesion*. Portugal (panel 4) is a country with below-average political *Horizon* and above-average political *Cohesion*. Belgium (panel 5) is a country with below-average political *Horizon* and below-average political *Cohesion*. Spain (panel 6) is a country with above-average political *Horizon* and above-average political *Cohesion*. Euro- 11 = European Union 11 (Austria, Belgium, Finland, France, Germany, Ireland, Italy, Luxembourg, Netherlands, Portugal, and Spain). Data labels in panel 2 use International Organization for Standardization country codes.

strong politics partially compensates for the negative fiscal effect of moving to fixed exchange rates.[30]

CONCLUSION

This chapter presents both theoretical and empirical evidence showing that, contrary to the traditional argument, flexible exchange rate regimes are associated with more fiscal discipline. The fiscal implications of exchange rate regime choice do not occur in a vacuum, but within a specific political context. By bringing politics into the picture, this chapter contributes to the literature by carefully uncovering how the exchange rate regime interacts with the political context to affect fiscal policy outcomes. The results draw on the longest and widest cross-section of country experiences available. The analysis finds that strong political environments characterized by long *Horizon* and high *Cohesion* among policymakers (that is, where elections are not imminent and where there is little political fragmentation) are associated with better fiscal performance.[31]

These results offer important policy lessons from the point of view of fiscal policymaking. First, if policymakers operate in weak political contexts, flexible exchange rates are the preferred option because they are best suited to secure enhanced fiscal discipline. Second, the virtuous effect of flexible exchange rates on fiscal discipline is strengthened by strong political environments, characterized by long political *Horizon* and high political *Cohesion*. Third, in mixed political contexts, policymakers face a difficult choice because moving to a fixed exchange rate regime may negatively affect fiscal performance in a way that political institutions are unable to attenuate.

[30] For Spain, we replicated the analysis using the structural balance concept to control for the potential effect on the primary balance stemming from the real estate bubble that increased fiscal revenues considerably during the late 1990s. Results remain unchanged: although Spain could have adjusted further, it still performed better after the introduction of the euro.

[31] In a recent paper making use of a laboratory experiment, Battaglini, Nunnari, and Palfrey (2016) find evidence that more inclusive requirements for fiscal decision making and more vulnerability to shocks (which can be equated to longer horizons) are associated with lower debt accumulation.

ANNEX 11.1. ROBUSTNESS

Table 11.1.1. Robustness to Alternative Measures of Fiscal Discipline

	Specification									
	Nominal Primary Balance					Real Primary Balance per Capita				
Dependent Variable	(1)	(2)	(3)	(4)	(5)	(6)	(7)	(8)	(9)	(10)
Fixed Exchange Rates	−0.926***	−0.385	−0.424	−0.618*	−0.233	−0.881***	−0.369	−0.411	−0.603*	−0.206
	(0.316)	(0.301)	(0.338)	(0.393)	(0.369)	(0.313)	(0.298)	(0.335)	(0.389)	(0.366)
Growth	−0.006	0.030	0.030	0.042	0.041	−0.005	0.030	0.030	0.043	0.042
	(0.034)	(0.029)	(0.029)	(0.036)	(0.036)	(0.034)	(0.029)	(0.029)	(0.035)	(0.036)
Trade Openness	−0.034***	−0.022***	−0.022***	−0.039***	−0.038***	−0.034***	−0.022***	−0.022***	−0.039***	−0.038***
	(0.007)	(0.006)	(0.006)	(0.010)	(0.010)	(0.007)	(0.006)	(0.006)	(0.010)	(0.010)
Terms of Trade	−0.006	−0.002	−0.002	−0.008	−0.008	−0.006	−0.002	−0.002	−0.008	−0.008
	(0.006)	(0.004)	(0.004)	(0.006)	(0.006)	(0.006)	(0.004)	(0.004)	(0.006)	(0.006)
Reserves	0.625***	0.460***	0.462***	0.832***	0.840***	0.592***	0.427***	0.429***	0.813***	0.821***
	(0.138)	(0.114)	(0.114)	(0.152)	(0.152)	(0.137)	(0.113)	(0.113)	(0.150)	(0.151)
Horizon		−0.154	−0.121				−0.149	−0.114		
		(0.104)	(0.140)				(0.104)	(0.139)		
Horizon × Fixed Exchange Rates			−0.088					−0.093		
			(0.202)					(0.201)		
Cohesion				0.909***	0.746**				0.943***	0.775**
				(0.291)	(0.307)				(0.288)	(0.304)
Cohesion × Fixed Exchange Rates					0.566					0.584
					(0.387)					(0.383)
Observations	1,121	896	896	800	800	1,121	896	896	800	800
R^2	0.740	0.762	0.762	0.737	0.738	0.741	0.756	0.756	0.736	0.737

Source: Authors' calculations.

Note: The estimation with country and time effects is omitted for reasons of parsimony. Robust standard errors are clustered at the country level in parentheses. The constant term is estimated but omitted.

$^*p < .1$; $^{**}p < .05$; $^{***}p < .01$.

ANNEX 11.2. SYNTHETIC CONTROL METHODOLOGY

Step 1: We choose the country cases (Euro-11) and the potential comparator countries; we also choose the explanatory variables.

The group of country cases (Euro-11) is made up of European countries that belong to the OECD and that joined the euro area in 1999 (Annex Figure 11.2.1). The countries under analysis are Austria, Belgium, Finland, France, Germany, Ireland, Italy, Luxembourg, Netherlands, Portugal, and Spain.

The group of comparator countries is made up of European countries that belong to the OECD but did not join the euro area in 1999. Also from that group we exclude transition economies (because of lack of comparable data before the mid-1990s). The countries ultimately in the control group are Denmark, Greece, Iceland, Israel, Norway, Sweden, Switzerland, Turkey, and United Kingdom.

The outcome variable is the primary budget balance (as a percentage of GDP). As predictor variables to match the behavior of the primary balance, we choose the primary balance in 1981, 1993, and 2000; total reserves minus gold (in million U.S. dollars); real GDP growth (percent); terms of trade (U.S. dollars; index); trade openness (percent in U.S. dollars); change in nominal exchange rate; and change in debt-to-GDP ratio. All variables take three-year moving average values to smooth the fluctuations.

The year of the event is 2001 (last year before actual circulation of the single currency).

Annex Figure 11.2.1.

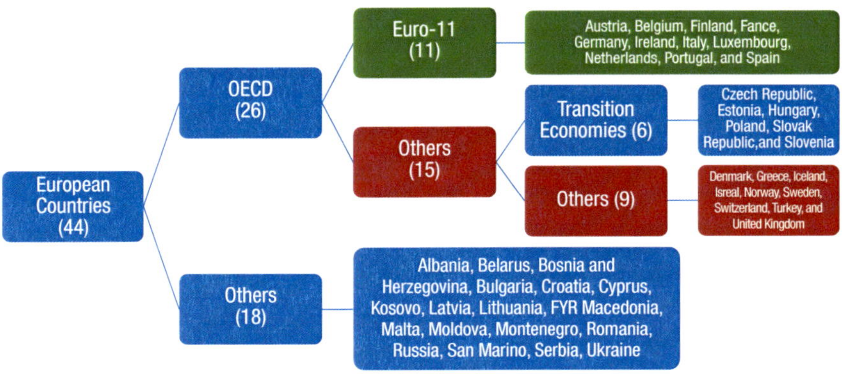

Source: Authors' calculations.
Note: The green boxes signify country cases; the red boxes signify the donor pool. OECD = Organisation for Economic Co-operation; Euro-11 = European Union 11 (Austria, Belgium, Finland, France, Germany, Ireland, Italy, Luxembourg, Netherlands, Portugal, and Spain).

Step 2: Given the group of comparator countries and the outcome and predictor variables, we calculate the synthetic series.

Given country and variable selection, the procedure calculates weights of the predictor variables and comparator countries to reproduce as closely as possible the values of the outcome variable *pre-event*. Not all comparator countries have to receive a positive weight to create the synthetic comparator. The procedure is based on an iterative optimization algorithm as follows:

- Start from some initial vector of weights of the predictor variables V, choose the vector $\boldsymbol{W}^*$ of country weights to minimize a distance $\| X_1 - X_0 W \|$ where X_1 and X_0 are matrices of predictor variables for the unit of interest and its comparator units, respectively, subject to weight constraints (weights have to be between 0 and 1). In particular, $\boldsymbol{W}^*$ minimizes

$$\| X_1 - X_0 W_V \| = \sqrt{(X_1 - X_0 W)' V (X_1 - X_0 W)}. \qquad (11.2.1)$$

- Once the country weights are chosen, the variable weight V^* is chosen among all positive definite and diagonal matrices such that the mean square prediction error of the outcome variable is minimized over *pre-event* periods. In particular,

$$V^* = arg\,\min_{V \in \mathcal{V}} \left(Z_1 - Z_0 W^*(V) \right)' \left(Z_1 - Z_0 W^*(V) \right), \qquad (11.2.2)$$

  where Z_1 and Z_0 are matrices of the outcome variable for the unit of interest and its comparator units, respectively. The resulting V^* is used as input to equation (11.2.1) for the next round of optimization.

- This iterative process continues until V^* and W^* converge. In summary, the synthetic series is constructed by solving a nested optimization problem that minimizes equation (11.2.2) for given $W^*(V)$ given by equation (11.2.1) (Abadie, Diamond, and Hainmueller 2010).
- Using the weights thus obtained, we then use the synthetic comparator to create a counterfactual path of the outcome variable *post-event*.

Step 3: Compare actual post-event outcome variable series with the synthetic comparator.

The difference between the two series is the estimated impact of the event (assuming that all other factors potentially affecting the variable of interest have been controlled for successfully).

REFERENCES

Abadie, A., A. Diamond, and J. Hainmueller. 2010. "Synthetic Control Methods for Comparative Case Studies: Estimating the Effect of California's Tobacco Control Program." *Journal of the American Statistical Association* 105 (490): 493–505.

Acemoglu, D., S. Johnson, J. Robinson, and Y. Thaicharoen. 2003. "Institutional Causes, Macroeconomic Symptoms: Volatility, Crises and Growth." *Journal of Monetary Economics* 50: 49–123.

Afonso, A., and J. T. Jalles. 2012. "Measuring the Success of Fiscal Consolidations." *Applied Financial Economics* 22 (13): 1053–61.

———. 2014. "Assessing Fiscal Episodes." *Economic Modelling* 37: 255–70.

Alesina, A., and S. Ardagna. 1998. "Tales of Fiscal Contractions." *Economic Policy* 27: 487–545.

Alesina, A., R. Perotti, and J. Tavares. 1998. "The Political Economy of Fiscal Adjustments." *Brookings Papers in Political Economy* 1: 197–266.

Battaglini, M., S. Nunnari, and T. R. Palfrey. 2016. "The Political Economy of Public Debt: A Laboratory Study." Discussion Paper 11357, Centre for Economic Policy Research, London.

Bordo, M. 2003. "Exchange Rate Regime Choice in Historical Perspective." NBER Working Paper 9654, National Bureau of Economic Research, Cambridge, Massachusetts.

Cruz, C., P. Keefer, and C. Scartascini. 2016. "Database of Political Institutions Codebook, 2015 Update (DPI 2015)." Inter-American Development Bank. Updated version of T. Beck, G. Clarke, A. Groff, P. Keefer, and P. Walsh. 2001. "New Tools in Comparative Political Economy: The Database of Political Institutions." *World Bank Economic Review* 15 (1): 165–76.

Driscoll, J. C., and A. C. Kraay. 1998. "Consistent Covariance Matrix Estimation with Spatially Dependent Panel Data." *Review of Economics and Statistics* 80: 549–60.

Duttagupta, R., and G. Tolosa. 2006. "Fiscal Discipline and Exchange Rate Regimes: Evidence from the Caribbean." Working Paper 06/119, International Monetary Fund, Washington, DC.

Fatás, A., and I. Mihov. 2013. "Policy Volatility, Institutions and Economic Growth." *Review of Economics and Statistics* 95 (2): 362–76.

Fatás, A., and A. K. Rose. 2001. "Do Monetary Handcuffs Restrain Leviathan? Fiscal Policy in Extreme Exchange Rate Regimes." *IMF Staff Papers* 47: 40–61.

Frankel, J., M. Goldstein, and P. Masson. 1991. "Characteristics of a Successful Exchange Rate System." Occasional Paper 82, International Monetary Fund, Washington, DC.

Gavin, M., and R. Perotti. 1997. "Fiscal Policy in Latin America." In *NBER Macroeconomics Annual 1997*, edited by B. S. Bernanke and J. Rotemberg. Cambridge, MA: MIT Press.

Giavazzi, F., and M. Pagano. 1988. "The Advantage of Tying One's Hands: EMS Discipline and Central Bank Credibility." *European Economic Review* 32 (5): 1075–77.

———. 1996. "Non-Keynesian Effects of Fiscal Policy Changes: International Evidence and the Swedish Experience." *Swedish Economic Policy Review* 3 (1): 67–103.

Greene, W. H. 2012. *Econometric Analysis*, 7th edition. Upper Saddle River, NJ: Prentice Hall.

Henisz, W. J. 2000. "The Institutional Environment for Economic Growth." *Economics and Politics* 12 (1): 1–31.

Lambertini, L., and J. Tavares. 2005. "Exchange Rates and Fiscal Adjustments: Evidence from the OECD and Implications for the EMU." *BEJM Contributions in Macroeconomics* 5 (1): Article 11.

Lane, P., and R. Perotti. 2003. "The Importance of Composition of Fiscal Policy: Evidence from Different Exchange Rate Regimes." *Journal of Public Economics* 87 (9–10): 2253–79.

Morris, R., and L. Schuknecht. 2007. "Structural Balances and Asset Windfalls: The Role of Asset Prices Revisited." Working Paper 737, European Central Bank, Frankfurt.

Muller, W. C., and K. Strom, eds. 1999. *Policy, Office or Votes? How Political Parties in Western Europe Make Hard Decisions*. Cambridge, U.K.: Cambridge University Press.

Reinhart, C. M., and K. S. Rogoff. 2004. "The Modern History of Exchange Rate Arrangements: A Reinterpretation." *Quarterly Journal of Economics* 119 (1): 1–48.

Rousseeuw, P. J., and K. van Driessen. 1999. "A Fast Algorithm for the Minimum Covariance Determinant Estimator." *Technometrics* 41 (3): 212–23.

Rousseeuw, P. J., and V. Yohai. 1984. "Robust Regression by Means of S Estimators." In *Robust and Nonlinear Time Series Analysis*, edited by J. Franke, W. Härdle, and R. D. Martin, 256–74, Lecture Notes in Statistics 26. New York: Springer Verlag.

Sun, Y. 2003. "Do Fixed Exchange Rates Induce More Fiscal Discipline?" Working Paper 03/78, International Monetary Fund, Washington, DC.

Tanzi, V., and L. Schuknecht. 1997. "Reconsidering the Fiscal Role of Government: The International Perspective." *American Economic Review* 87 (2): 164–72.

Tornell, A., and A. Velasco. 1995. "Fiscal Discipline and the Choice of Exchange Rate Regime." *European Economic Review* 39 (3–4): 759–70.

———. 1998. "Fiscal Discipline and the Choice of a Nominal Anchor in Stabilization." *Journal of International Economics* 46 (1): 30.

Wooldridge, J. M. 2002. *Econometric Analysis of Cross Section and Panel Data*. Cambridge, MA: MIT Press.

Yohai, V. J. 1987. "High Breakdown-Point and High Efficiency Robust Estimates for Regression." *Annals of Statistics* 15 (2): 642–56.

CHAPTER 12

Expenditure Rules: Effective Tools for Sound Fiscal Policy?

Till Cordes, Tidiane Kinda, Priscilla Muthoora, and Anke Weber

INTRODUCTION

Discussions about the role of fiscal institutions in promoting sound public finances are increasingly at the forefront of the policy debate. This renewed focus on fiscal institutions comes against the backdrop of a marked deterioration in public finances across most advanced economies since the global financial crisis of 2008. However, it also reflects the need to address the root causes of an apparent deficit and debt bias—even before the crisis, the average debt ratio had reached its highest level since World War II, driven by a ubiquitous increase in the share of government spending in GDP (Cottarelli 2012; IMF 2014).

The previous chapters in this book provide new evidence suggesting that the interaction of politics with fiscal policy influences the timing, level, composition, and financing of spending, contributing in large measure to the observed deficit and debt bias. Fiscal institutions may help contain political pressures on tax and spending decisions by constraining the behavior of governments and opening their policy choices to scrutiny by financial markets and the public (Schuknecht 2004). Notably, procedural rules can be laid down to guide the preparation of annual budgets; numerical fiscal rules can be used to impose limits on the level or growth of key budgetary aggregates; and independent institutions can be mandated to prepare macroeconomic forecasts, analyze the effects of proposed government plans, make policy recommendations, or assess compliance with fiscal targets.

Numerical fiscal rules, particularly expenditure rules, have received increasing attention because of a number of these features.[1] Expenditure rules are directly

The authors thank Nate Arnold, Nina Budina, Xavier Debrun, Julio Escolano, Johannes Eugster, Nan Geng, Sanjeev Gupta, Michael Gorbanyov, Martine Guerguil, Carlos Mulas-Granados, Joana Pereira, Marta Ruiz-Arranz, Svetlana Vtyurina, and participants at the FAD seminar series for helpful comments and discussions. The authors are also grateful to Andrea Schaechter for her encouragements and initial guidance. The main results of this paper were published in the IMF's April 2014 *Fiscal Monitor* and in an IMF working paper in 2015. Ethan Alt and Nathalie Carcenac provided excellent research assistance.

[1] In the European Union, for example, national expenditure rules have been reinforced through inclusion in the "Six-Pack" of an expenditure benchmark to reinforce the preventive arm of the Stability and Growth Pact. Under the expenditure benchmark rule, public spending is not allowed to increase faster than medium-term potential GDP growth unless it is matched by adequate revenues.

aimed at addressing the spending pressures often at the origin of excessive deficits. They are most closely related to the formulation of the annual budget, setting legally binding appropriations that in turn contribute to the rules' enforceability. By the same token, expenditure rules can be used to guard against political failure in coalition governments. According to Hallerberg, Strauch, and von Hagen (2007) and Hallerberg, Strauch, and Yläoutinen (2010), countries with ideologically dispersed coalitions will not be as willing to delegate power to a finance minister representing only one of the parties in government. Instead, coalition governments are more likely to opt for multiyear expenditure targets, which they can credibly fix in their coalition agreement for their electoral period. In practice, several advanced economies where coalition governments tend to dominate the political landscape (Belgium, the Netherlands, Luxembourg, Sweden, and Finland, for example) indeed set expenditure targets in their coalition agreements. Expenditure rules fully accommodate revenue shortfalls resulting from adverse economic shocks, allowing for a stabilizing role for fiscal policy. Importantly, and unlike deficit caps, expenditure rules also help create buffers in good times, when revenue windfalls can make spending pressures difficult to resist. Thus, expenditure rules can mitigate the effect of economic and political cycles. Finally, expenditure rules are also transparent and generally easy to monitor because the requirements for timely data reporting, accounting, and forecasting are more easily met than for other budgetary aggregates (Ayuso-i-Casals 2012).

A lingering concern, however, remains about the effect of expenditure rules on the composition of spending. By reducing incentives for spending overruns, expenditure rules can lead to stricter prioritization and greater efficiency in spending. But the interaction of political economy considerations with a binding constraint on total spending may result in the crowding out of productive but electorally unappealing projects (Debrun 2014).

This chapter draws on the 2013 vintage of the fiscal rules database developed by Schaechter and others (2012) to analyze compliance with fiscal rules. It also investigates the effect of expenditure rules on the level and composition of public spending in advanced and emerging economies using a sample of 29 economies with expenditure rules between 1985 and 2013.

The chapter's findings suggest that expenditure rules are associated with spending control, countercyclical fiscal policy, and improved fiscal discipline. Fiscal performance is better in countries where an expenditure rule exists. This outcome appears to be related to the properties of expenditure rules because compliance rates are generally higher than with other types of rules (on the budget balance or debt, for example). In particular, compliance with expenditure rules is higher if the expenditure target is directly under the control of the government and if the rule is not a mere political commitment but enshrined in law or in a coalition agreement.

Evidence of adverse side effects is mixed. The introduction of expenditure rules is associated with a decrease in public investment only in emerging economies. A possible explanation is that any adverse effects on public investment could have been mitigated in advanced economies by well-designed budgetary frameworks and procedures.

Instead, the empirical analysis points to two positive side effects. First, expenditure rules reduce the volatility of expenditure, thus imparting a degree of predictability to fiscal policy and making it less destabilizing. Importantly, the evidence suggests that expenditure rules have been effective in mitigating political cycles. In economies with expenditure rules, the holding of legislative or executive elections is not associated with higher primary spending relative to nonelection years. Second, expenditure rules are associated with higher public investment efficiency. However, these results need to be interpreted with care given the relatively small sample size.

The rest of the chapter is structured as follows. The second section provides stylized facts on expenditure rules. In particular, it analyzes who uses expenditure rules and the key characteristics of expenditure rules that are (or were) in place. The third section discusses why countries adopt and abandon expenditure rules. The fourth section analyzes whether expenditure rules have been effective in practice, shedding light on compliance with expenditure targets, investigating the behavior of primary balances around the introduction of the rules, and looking at the response of public investment spending and efficiency following their introduction. The final section concludes.

WHAT TYPE OF EXPENDITURE RULES ARE IN PLACE AND WHAT ARE THEIR DESIGN FEATURES?

In this chapter, expenditure rules are defined to include both specific numerical targets fixed in legislation and expenditure ceilings for which the targets can be revised, but only on a low-frequency basis (for example, as part of the electoral cycle), as long as they are binding for a minimum of three years.[2]

In practice, expenditure rules typically take the form of a cap on nominal or real spending growth over the medium term (Figure 12.1). Ceilings on real spending growth are relatively more frequent in advanced economies, possibly reflecting better capacity to estimate outlays in real terms.

Expenditure rules are often used in connection with other national rules. The combination of expenditure rules and budget balance rules is particularly common in advanced economies, whereas in emerging economies, they are often used in connection with debt rules (Figure 12.2).[3] A possible explanation is that not all types of fiscal rules are equally apt to support sustainability, economic stabilization, and possibly size-of-government objectives, even when their design features are fine tuned. Using a combination of fiscal rules can help address the gaps. For example, an expenditure rule combined with a debt rule would assist policymakers with short- to medium-term operational decisions while allowing for some countercyclicality and provide a link to debt sustainability.

Expenditure rules are more commonly established through statutory norms in emerging economies than in advanced economies. In advanced economies, expenditure rules tend to be more closely integrated into the medium-term

---

[2] Using the same definition, a total of 33 expenditure rules were identified as being in place in 29 countries for some or all of the years during the period 1985–2013. Out of the 33, 10 had been dropped by 2013 and two were adopted in 2013. Annex 12.3 provides an overview of each expenditure rule.

[3] In the EU-27 countries, the supranational Maastricht budget balance and debt rules also apply.

Figure 12.1. Types of Expenditure Rules in 2013
(Number of countries)

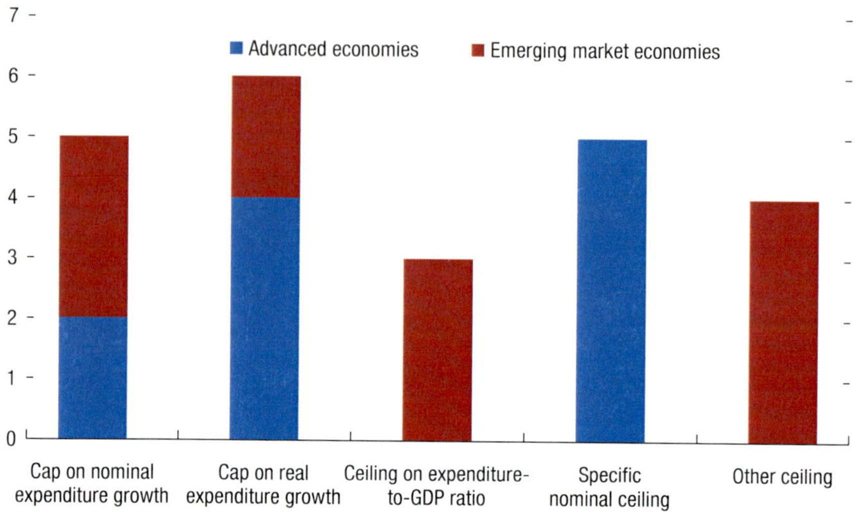

Source: FAD Fiscal Rules database.

Figure 12.2. Combination of Expenditure Rules with Other National Rules in 2013
(Number of countries)

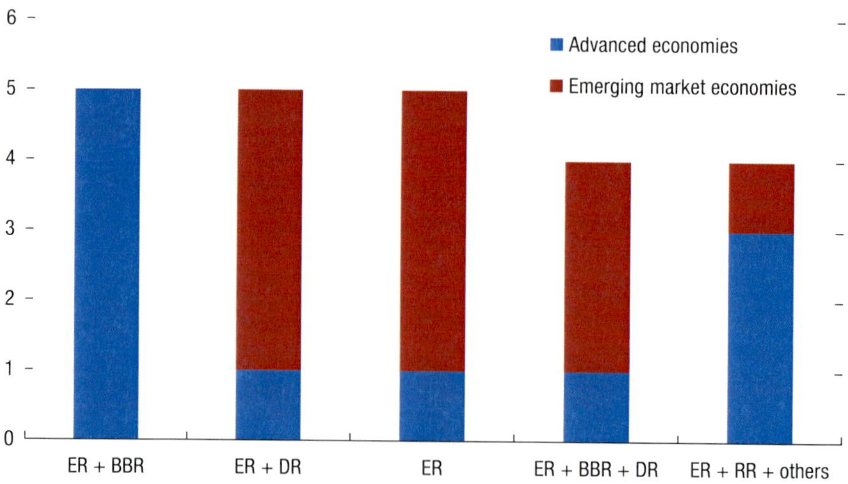

Sources: FAD Fiscal Rules database; and authors' calculations.
Note: BBR = budget balance rule; DR = debt rule; ER = expenditure rules; RR = revenue rule.

Figure 12.3. Legal Basis of Fiscal Rules in 2013
(Percent)

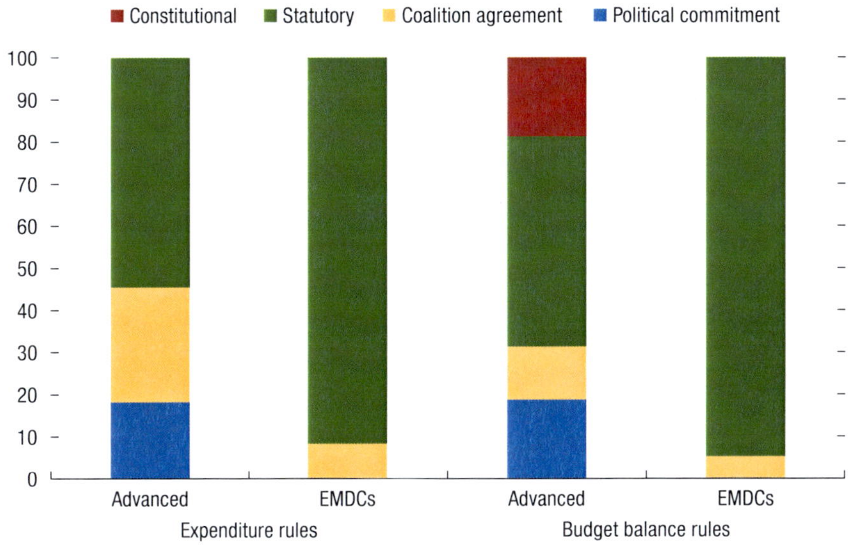

Source: FAD Fiscal Rules database.
Note: EMDCs = emerging market and developing countries.

Table 12.1. Economic Coverage of Aggregate

Item Most Frequently Excluded	Countries Where Exclusions Apply
Interest Payments	Finland, France, Japan, Spain
Cyclically Sensitive Expenditure	Finland, Poland, Spain, United States
Capital Expenditure	Croatia, Ecuador, Peru
Security-Related Spending	Israel, Peru

Source: FAD Fiscal Rules database.

expenditure frameworks, which are sometimes part of coalition agreements (Figure 12.3). Belgium, Finland, Luxembourg, the Netherlands, and Sweden, for example, set expenditure targets in their coalition agreements.

The majority of expenditure rules cover the central government. Of the 23 countries that had expenditure rules in place in 2013, 15 had one at the central government level and 8 at the general government level.[4] The greater prevalence of rules at the central government level may reflect autonomy and coordination issues with subnational governments.

With regard to economic coverage, a number of items are frequently excluded (Table 12.1). Fiscal sustainability considerations argue for more comprehensive

[4] The expenditure rule in Sweden covers the central government and the pension system.

coverage, but other competing objectives (such as improving the composition of spending) and controllability arguments are put forward to exclude certain items. Broad coverage aims at managing total revenue and expenditure and makes the target more transparent and easier to monitor. Nevertheless, it is sometimes seen as desirable to exclude, for example, capital expenditure since it is generally expected to positively contribute to long-term growth. However, this exclusion can cause problems because it weakens the link with gross debt. Moreover, not all capital expenditure is necessarily productive and, depending on country circumstances, other items such as health care and education expenditure may raise potential growth even more. Excluding interest payments and cyclically sensitive expenditure from target variables is also often discussed since they are not under the control of governments in the short run and require short-term adjustments in other expenditure categories, with capital spending often the easiest to cut. An argument for including cyclically sensitive expenditure is that most cyclical sensitivity is on the revenue side.

Design features vary across countries. In advanced economies, expenditure rules are often used in connection with medium-term expenditure frameworks and compliance is monitored by an independent fiscal body, a so-called fiscal council, whereas in emerging economies, formal enforcement mechanisms are more frequent (Figure 12.4).[5] Well-defined escape clauses are relatively rare in connection

Figure 12.4. Design Features of Expenditure Rules in 2013
(Number of countries)

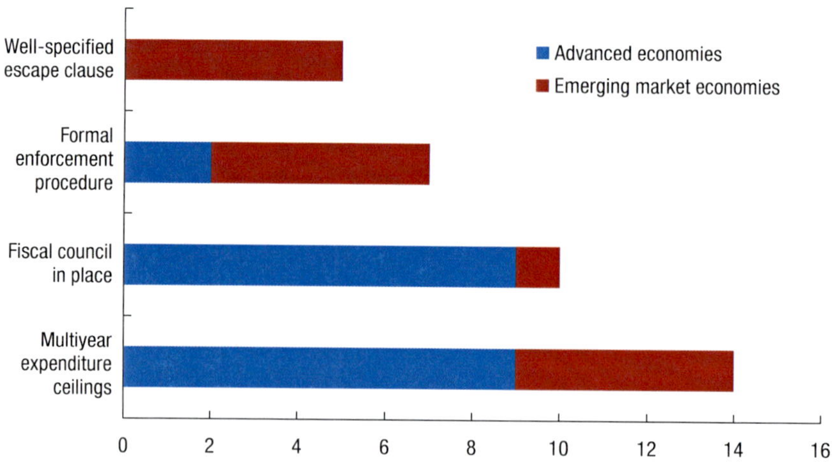

Sources: FAD Fiscal Rules database; and authors' calculations.

[5] These include formal sanctions, which are often part of fiscal responsibility laws and automatic correction mechanisms.

with expenditure rules. Contingencies tend to be handled by leaving a margin between the budget envelope and the expenditure ceiling (Ayuso-i-Casals 2012).

WHY DO COUNTRIES ADOPT AND ABANDON EXPENDITURE RULES?

From 1985 to 2012, 27 economies introduced 31 different expenditure rules. The adoption of these rules may have been motivated by various reasons. First, governments may adopt expenditure rules to help them achieve other supranational fiscal rules. Second, coalition governments can use these rules to bind them to certain fiscal targets for the electoral period. Finally, especially in recent years, economies have adopted expenditure targets in bad economic times to rein in spending. Out of the 31 expenditure rules that have been introduced since 1985, 10 had already been abandoned by 2013, either because the country had never complied with the rule or because fiscal consolidation was so successful that the government did not want to be restricted by the rule in good economic times.

Although expenditure rules are typically used in connection with other fiscal rules, they are most often not adopted at the same time as these other rules (Figure 12.5). Only 6 of the 31 expenditure rules were introduced together with other rules. For instance, Argentina, Brazil, and Peru included expenditure rules in their fiscal responsibility laws as part of a wider set of reforms in 1999 and 2000. However, for 20 of the 31 cases, other fiscal rules were already in place when the expenditure rule was introduced. In particular, many European Union countries adopted national expenditure rules to help them achieve the Maastricht

Figure 12.5. Adoption of Expenditure Rules
(Percent)

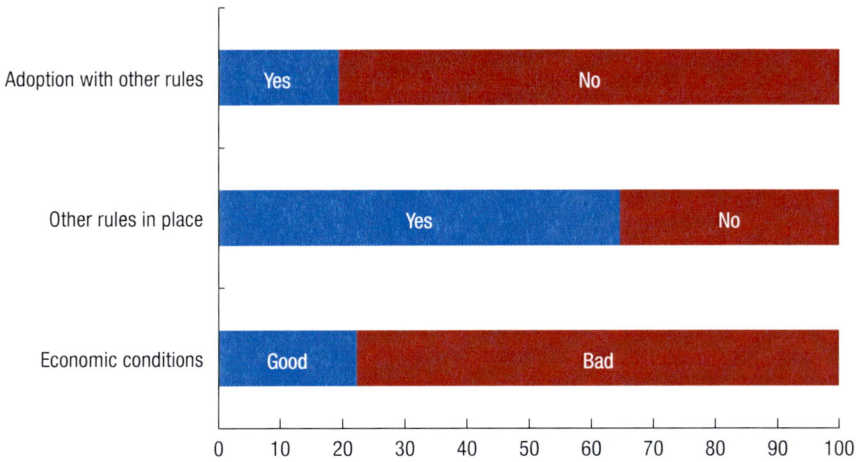

Source: FAD Fiscal Rules database.

deficit and debt limits. Belgium, Denmark, Luxembourg, and the Netherlands introduced national expenditure rules in response to these new supranational fiscal rules after 1992. Sweden and Finland followed a couple of years later after becoming members of the European Union in 1995. The variation in European countries' adoption of national expenditure rules can partly be explained by the different structure of governments. Minority governments, such as in Sweden in the 1990s, have also introduced expenditure rules to agree on fiscal targets for their electoral period with the opposition in parliament.

Most of the expenditure rules were adopted in bad economic times. In all but six cases, the implementation of the expenditure rule was preceded by a negative change in the output gap. More than one-third of the expenditure rules were introduced since 2009, in response to the financial crisis. Earlier findings suggest that expenditure rules were mainly adopted following prior consolidation to lock in fiscal adjustment (IMF 2009). However, taking into account recent adoptions of fiscal rules in response to the crisis, less than a third of all expenditure rules were introduced after fiscal consolidation, defined as an improvement in the budget balance compared with the previous two or three years.

About a third (10 of the 31) of expenditure rules have already been given up for various political and economic reasons. In 6 of the 10 cases, the country did not comply with the rule in the year before giving it up. Once a rule has lost its credibility, countries might not see any benefit in upholding it. In Argentina, Iceland, and Kosovo, the rule was never observed, and all three countries abandoned their prevailing rule when they faced global market turmoil in 2008–09. Bulgaria and Japan also had problems complying with their rules during the financial crisis and decided to implement new expenditure rules. Political changes were more important in other countries. In Australia, the first political commitment to an expenditure rule was only made for the life of parliament. Following an early election in 1988, the new parliament did not specify a new rule.

In some countries, there was a perception that expenditure rules had fulfilled their purpose. Following successful consolidations in Belgium, Canada, and the United States in the 1990s, these countries saw no need to continue to follow their national expenditure rules. Especially in the United States, spending pressures increased during an economic boom at the end of the 1990s. More and more spending was made outside of the expenditure ceilings via an emergency spending category (CBO 2003). The ceilings were raised on an ad hoc basis several times in the two years preceding abandonment of the rule in 2002.

WHAT IS THE EVIDENCE?

Combining the 2013 vintage of the fiscal rules data set with indicators on budgetary outturns from various sources (IMF databases, quantitative and qualitative ex post budgetary assessments from fiscal councils) can help shed light on who complied with expenditure rules and when, on behavior of primary balances around the introduction of the rules, and on associated changes in public investment spending and efficiency. The results reported below need to be interpreted with caution, given that establishing causation between institutions and policy outcomes is a perennial challenge. For instance, it could be that expenditure rules are primarily adopted by countries with an intrinsically strong commitment to fiscal discipline, good public expenditure management practices, or good institutions, generally ex ante. In addition, the relatively small sample suggests that results could be affected by outliers.

Compliance

Previous studies on the impact of expenditure rules on fiscal performance do not analyze whether countries actually comply with the rules they have adopted (Debrun and others 2008; Wierts 2008; Turrini 2008; Holm-Hadulla, Hauptmeier, and Rother 2010; Nerlich and Reuter 2013). This section provides a compliance assessment for almost all countries with expenditure rules, covering 95 percent of the 217 country-years since 1985. Compliance is measured as a dummy variable (that is, it does not control for near misses) and is established using both quantitative and qualitative data from various sources such as the World Economic Outlook database, country budgets, and assessments by fiscal councils.[6] Two points are worth highlighting: First, the assessment of compliance does not control for whether the rule was effectively binding. Put differently, it does not distinguish cases where the rule was met because countries really tried hard.[7] Second, and related, the compliance rates may be exaggerated if countries abandon rules once they become binding. A couple of instances when this occurred are discussed below. Overall, the analysis shows that countries comply more often with expenditure rules than with other fiscal rules. In addition, the section points to two rule characteristics that are associated with higher compliance rates: First, countries comply more often if the expenditure target is directly under the government's control. Second, compliance with expenditure rules is higher if the rule is enshrined in law or in a coalition agreement.

Comparing Expenditure Rules with Other Fiscal Rules

Countries have complied with expenditure rules more than two-thirds of the time. Figure 12.6 shows that expenditure rules have a better compliance record than budget balance and debt rules. The only exception is the high performance of emerging market economies with debt rules. However, this can be explained by European emerging economies' very high compliance rates with the supranational Maastricht debt rule that was not effectively binding for most of these countries. In addition, the high rate of compliance with debt rules can be explained by the favorable impact of financial repression, which translated into persistent negative interest-growth differentials, on debt dynamics (Escolano, Shabunina, and Woo 2011). The higher rate of compliance with expenditure rules is consistent with the fact that these rules are easy to monitor and that they immediately map into

[6] Details on compliance scores are available from the authors upon request.

[7] The question of fiscal rules and incentives for better fiscal performance is taken up in the next section.

Figure 12.6. Compliance with Fiscal Rules, 1985–2012

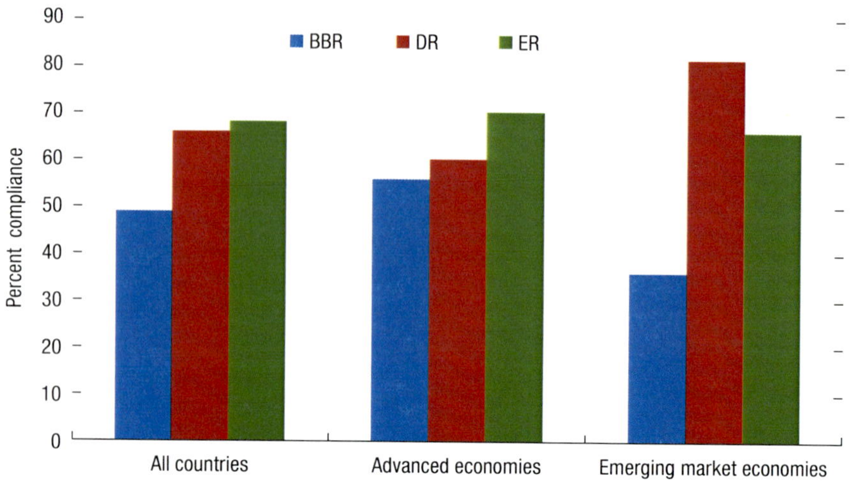

Sources: FAD Fiscal Rules database; and authors' calculations.
Note: The *y*-axis measures the average compliance rate with budget balance rules (BBR), expenditure rules (ER), and debt rules (DR) in all years in which an assessment could be made. BBRs and DRs include both national and supranational rules.

an enforceable mechanism—the annual budget itself. Besides, expenditure rules are most directly connected to instruments that policymakers effectively control. By contrast, the budget balance, and even more so public debt, is more exposed to shocks, both positive and negative, that are out of the government's control.

One of the desirable features of expenditure rules compared with other rules is that they are binding not only in bad but also in good economic times. The compliance rate in good economic times, defined as years with a negative change in the output gap, is at 72 percent—almost the same as in bad economic times at 68 percent. In contrast to other fiscal rules, countries also have incentives to break an expenditure rule in periods of high economic growth with increasing spending pressures. For instance, Iceland never managed to comply with its expenditure rule during its economic boom in the 2000s. The financial and economic crisis of 2009 would have been the first time that Iceland complied with its rule. In the United States, spending pressures also undermined the expenditure rule in good economic times. Belgium and Canada gave up their expenditure rules during periods of relatively high economic growth.

Which Rule Characteristics Are Associated with High Compliance Rates?

Although compliance with expenditure rules is high overall, there is still a large variance between different countries' performance. Although correlations between certain rule characteristics and compliance should be interpreted with caution, two design features in particular are associated with higher compliance

Figure 12.7. Compliance and Type of Rule
(Percent)

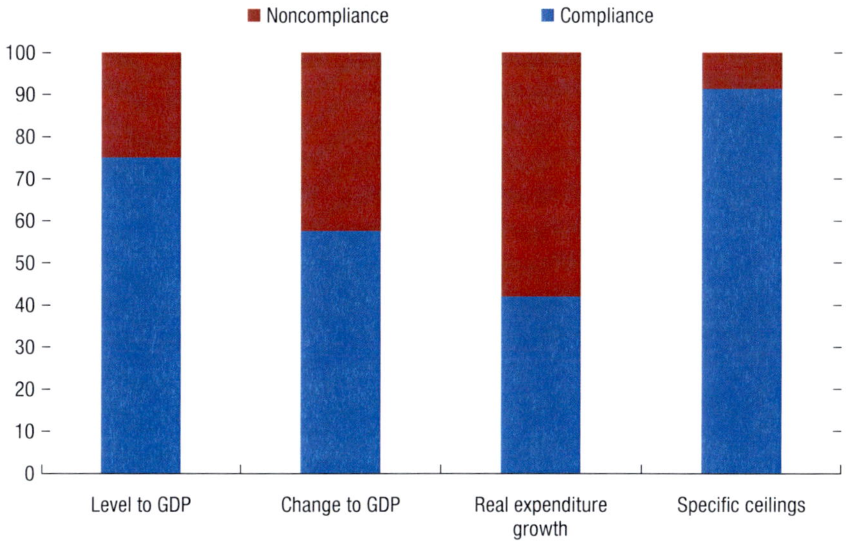

Sources: FAD Fiscal Rules database; and authors' calculations.

rates. First, compliance is higher if the government directly controls the expenditure target. Figure 12.7 shows the compliance rates for different types of expenditure targets. Specific ceilings have the best performance record. For these rules, governments specify nominal targets for each individual year, which gives a clear guideline for the budget process. Although some countries, such as Finland and the Netherlands, first set these targets in real terms, they convert them in the budget process to nominal terms (Ljungman 2008). The government controls these nominal expenditures directly. In contrast, the government does not have full control over expenditure targets if they are defined in relation to GDP or inflation. Evidence suggests that expenditure targets specified in levels of GDP have also had high compliance records. In many cases, however, this outcome occurs because targets were often set at very high levels so that they did not lead to a binding expenditure constraint. Once this target became binding, the lack of control over GDP or inflation became apparent. Botswana, for instance, exceeded its 40 percent expenditure-to-GDP target by more than 5 percentage points because of declining demand for diamonds (IMF 2012).

Nominal expenditure growth rules have a poor performance record compared with GDP and real expenditure growth rules for two reasons. First, the government can aim to comply with the rule, but fail because of unexpected economic shocks. For instance, Iceland targeted transfer payment growth that varied strongly, from 5.9 percent in 2003 to –7.3 percent in 2004 (Gunnarsson 2011). One alternative is to use past macroeconomic indicators, as did Lithuania, which decided to use the average of revenue growth over the past five years as a benchmark instead of yearly changes, which provides a clear ex ante benchmark that does not vary too strongly. The government may also lose control over expenditure targets if these targets include local government spending. In Denmark, for instance, the rule was often broken because local governments overspent, thus breaking the overall rule for the general government (this situation has since been remedied by the adoption of binding expenditure ceilings that include the bulk of local government spending).

Second, the government has a lower incentive to comply with rules specified in relation to other macroeconomic factors because independent institutions, legislators, or the general public cannot hold the government directly accountable for noncompliance. In several countries, the rule was so vaguely specified that even independent institutions had problems checking compliance. For instance, in Luxembourg, the central bank tried to assess the compliance record, but had to make several assumptions to do so (Banque Centrale du Luxembourg 2005). In contrast, in countries with specific nominal ceilings, it is relatively easy for independent institutions to control compliance. For instance, the Swedish Fiscal Council and the U.S. Congressional Budget Office increased visibility of the rule and provided an independent assessment of compliance with the nominal ceiling.

In addition to the type of expenditure target, Figure 12.8 shows a correlation between the legal basis of the rule and average compliance rates. Political commitments have the poorest performance record. In contrast to coalition agreements and statutory rules, political commitments do not have any binding character.

Figure 12.8. Compliance and Legal Basis
(Percent)

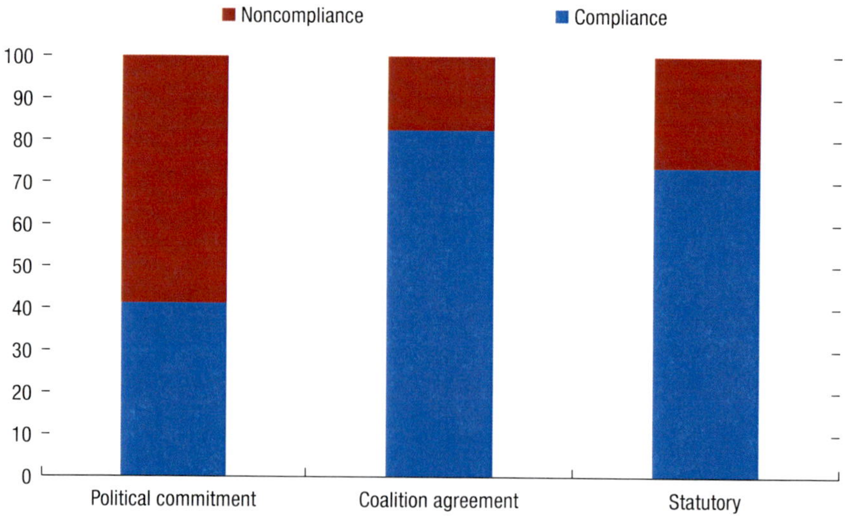

Sources: FAD Fiscal Rules database: and authors' calculations.

Performance in the six countries with coalition agreements is at least as good as in countries with statutory rules, with a high mean compliance rate of more than 80 percent in countries with coalition agreements. Coalition agreements set expenditure caps only for the lifetime of a coalition. By contrast, political commitments and statutory rules often cap expenditures beyond an electoral period. In several instances, new governments decided to abandon the rule, to not comply with it, or to make ad hoc changes in quantitative targets. For example, the 2007 expenditure targets in Israel were increased in an ad hoc manner once the new government was formed. In the United States, the legislature increased spending ceilings on an ad hoc basis for 2001 and 2002. Statutory laws cannot prevent these cases of noncompliance if the specific target and the coverage of the rule are not specified in the law.

Expenditure Rules and Long-Term Sustainability

Have expenditure rules been associated with better fiscal performance? A number of studies focusing on European countries have shown that the presence of expenditure rules could help mitigate spending and procyclical bias (Debrun and others 2008; Wierts 2008; Holm-Hadulla, Hauptmeier, and Rother 2010). Covering a larger sample of advanced and developing economies, new empirical analysis described here extends previous studies on expenditure rules and fiscal performance. It focuses on whether the rule has strengthened long-term sustainability, as reflected in a higher primary balance or lower primary spending after taking into account standard determinants of these variables. The underlying econometric model is attributable to Bohn (1998) and explains the primary balance or primary expenditure by its lagged term (to allow for persistence), lagged gross debt (to capture the long-term solvency constraint), and the output gap (to control for the cyclicality of fiscal policy). The regression model also takes into account the simultaneous existence of an expenditure rule and other rules (budget balance and debt rules). To reduce the selection bias that may be inherent when analyzing countries with expenditure rules exclusively, the econometric analysis relies on a broader and representative sample of 57 advanced and developing economies. In addition to countries with expenditure rules, this broader sample also includes comparable countries that have not introduced expenditure rules during the period of analysis (1985–2012).[8]

The results illustrate that countries with expenditure rules in addition to other rules exhibit, on average, higher primary balances (Table 12.2).[9] Similarly, countries with expenditure rules also exhibit lower primary spending. The results are robust to the use of an alternative indicator for the presence of expenditure rules: the expenditure rule index. In addition to reporting whether a country has an expenditure rule in place, this index also captures the comprehensiveness of the rule. For instance, countries where the expenditure rule covers the general government

---

[8] Annex Table 12.1.1 in Annex 12.1 provides the list of countries included in the regressions in Table 12.2.

[9] As mentioned above, the empirical analysis is subject to a caveat that applies to any empirical study of the impact of institutions on policies: reverse causality. In the absence of convincing instruments, we cannot exclude the possibility that the presence of fiscal rules reflects deep social preferences that would be the true cause of strong outcomes.

Table 12.2. Expenditure Rules and Fiscal Performance

	Dependent Variable							
	Primary Balance in Percent of GDP				Primary Expenditure in Percent of GDP			
	(1)	(2)	(3)	(4)	(5)	(6)	(7)	(8)
Lag Dependent	0.791	0.791	0.796	0.795	0.903	0.902	0.903	0.902
	(28.43)***	(28.23)***	(29.39)***	(29.50)***	(44.46)***	(44.41)***	(41.64)***	(41.19)***
Lag Debt	0.013	0.013	0.013	0.013	−0.011	−0.012	−0.011	−0.012
	(3.47)***	(3.59)***	(3.31)***	(3.41)***	(3.03)***	(3.12)***	(2.84)***	(2.93)***
Output Gap	0.063	0.061	0.064	0.061	−0.021	−0.019	−0.021	−0.019
	(2.36)**	(2.28)**	(2.46)**	(2.39)**	(0.73)	(0.66)	(0.77)	(0.7)
ER Dummy	0.822		0.792		−0.643		−0.646	
	(2.75)***		(2.55)**		(2.07)**		(1.95)*	
ER Index		0.271		0.265		−0.213		−0.214
		(2.50)**		(2.34)**		(1.87)*		(1.73)*
Other Rules	0.781	0.64	0.761	0.628	−0.539	−0.434	−0.536	−0.43
	(3.35)***	(3.14)***	(3.53)***	(3.14)***	(2.17)**	(1.98)**	(2.34)**	(2.03)**
LEGELEC			−0.3	−0.307			0.052	0.058
			(2.08)**	(2.13)**			(0.34)	(0.38)
EXELEC			0.08	0.084			−0.254	−0.256
			(0.34)	(0.36)			(1.03)	(1.04)
Observations	1,085	1,085	1,078	1,078	1,085	1,085	1,078	1,078
Country	57	57	57	57	57	57	57	57

Source: FAD's Fiscal Rules database; IMF World Economic Outlook database; and World Bank's Political Institutions database.
Note: The least squared dummy variable is corrected. Bootstrapped *t*-statistics are in parentheses. LEGELEC and EXELEC are dummy variables that take a value of 1 in years when legislative or executive elections were held. ER = expenditure rule.
$^{*}p < .1$; $^{**}p < .05$; $^{***}p < .01$.

instead of the central government will have a higher index.[10] Moreover, the introduction of dummy variables to capture political pressure in election years suggests that expenditure rules can help preserve good fiscal performance. In particular, the estimated coefficients suggest that neither legislative nor executive elections have a significant effect on primary spending. Legislative elections, however, appear to worsen primary balances, probably through lower revenues. These results suggest two preliminary conclusions. First, expenditure rules appear to be effective at containing politically motivated spending pressures. Second, there is only partial evidence of electoral budget cycles, on the revenue side, once fiscal rules are controlled for.

Event studies, which normalize the implementation date of each country's expenditure rule to year t and use a simple measure of fiscal impulse to gauge the cyclical stance of fiscal policy, illustrate that fiscal policy tended to be countercyclical in the years following the introduction of an expenditure rule (Figure 12.9). For emerging

[10]The expenditure rule index captures the comprehensiveness of expenditure rules by aggregating their key features such as coverage, legal basis, and formal enforcement procedure. See Schaechter and others (2012) for details on the methodology for constructing a similar fiscal rules index.

Figure 12.9. Fiscal Impulse
(Percent of GDP)

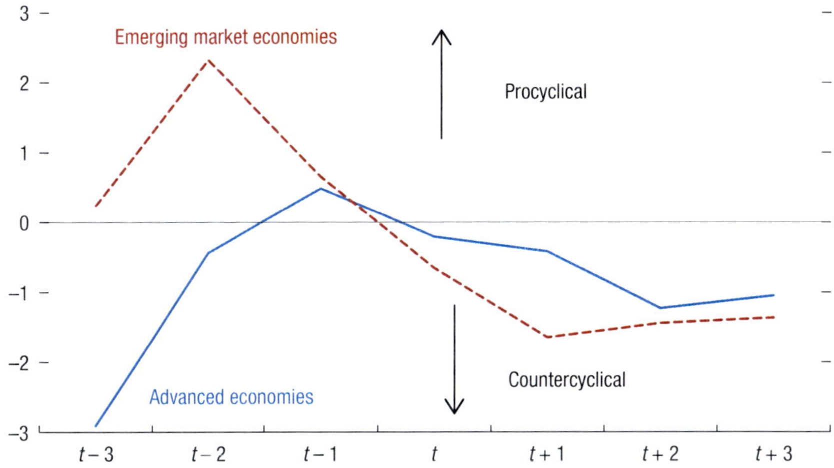

Sources: FAD Fiscal Rules database; and authors' calculations.
Note: Procyclical fiscal impulses are measured by the improvement in the primary balance during good times. A higher value in the figure corresponds to a more procyclical policy. A negative value corresponds to countercyclical policy. The variable *t* indicates the year the rule was implemented.

markets, this sharply contrasts with the years preceding the introduction of a rule, when fiscal policy was procyclical on average. These results confirm, for a broader sample of advanced and emerging economies, existing findings for European economies (Wierts 2008; Holm-Hadulla, Hauptmeier, and Rother 2010). The cyclicality indicator in Figure 12.9 averages fiscal impulses, with procyclical impulses entering with a positive value and countercyclical impulses with a negative value. Specifically, procyclical impulses enter the indicator as improvements in the primary balance during bad times (when growth is below potential) and the negative of deteriorations in the primary balance during good times (when growth is above potential).

Other Implications of Expenditure Rules

Expenditure Rules and Public Investment

Even the best-designed fiscal rules can have undesirable side effects. The most common relates to the risk that policymakers seek to achieve compliance by compressing certain high-quality discretionary items, such as public investment (see Blanchard and Giavazzi 2004). Although this may be an argument for excluding public investment from expenditure rules, there are potential drawbacks to limiting the rule's coverage because it weakens the link with debt sustainability and opens the door to reclassification of spending items.[11]

[11] Including through the creation of new expenditure categories.

Figure 12.10. Expenditure Rules and Spending Composition

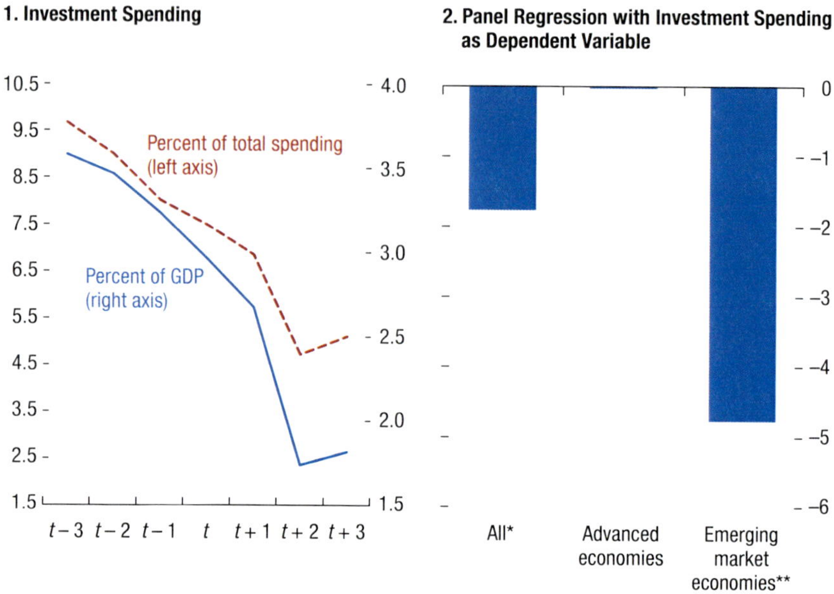

Sources: FAD Fiscal Rules database; and authors' calculations.
Note: Panel 1 shows an average across economies with expenditure rules in place. The variable *t* is for the first year the rule was implemented. Panel 2 shows coefficients from regressions of the investment share of spending on an expenditure rule dummy and other control variables, which include political variables from the World Bank database.
$^{*}p < .1$; $^{**}p < .05$.

Expenditure rules are associated with a significant decrease in investment in emerging economies only. Event studies similar to those described above show that, on average, investment spending falls across countries following the implementation of an expenditure rule (panel 1 of Figure 12.10). However, the result only passes the test of a panel regression for emerging economies (panel 2 of Figure 12.10).[12] The presence of well-designed medium-term budgetary frameworks, which may be more common in advanced economies, could be a mitigating factor and ensure that capital spending is not cut merely to comply with expenditure ceilings in the short term.

Implications for Government Size and Efficiency

The primary objective of expenditure rules is to enhance fiscal sustainability, but there may be other side effects. These potential repercussions include a reduction in the size of government—which might in fact be the intended objective, particularly in some advanced economies—but also a reduction in the volatility of government expenditure, as result of a more medium-term orientation of the

[12] Details of the panel regression can be found in Annex 12.2.

Figure 12.11. Expenditure Rules, Efficiency, and Government Size

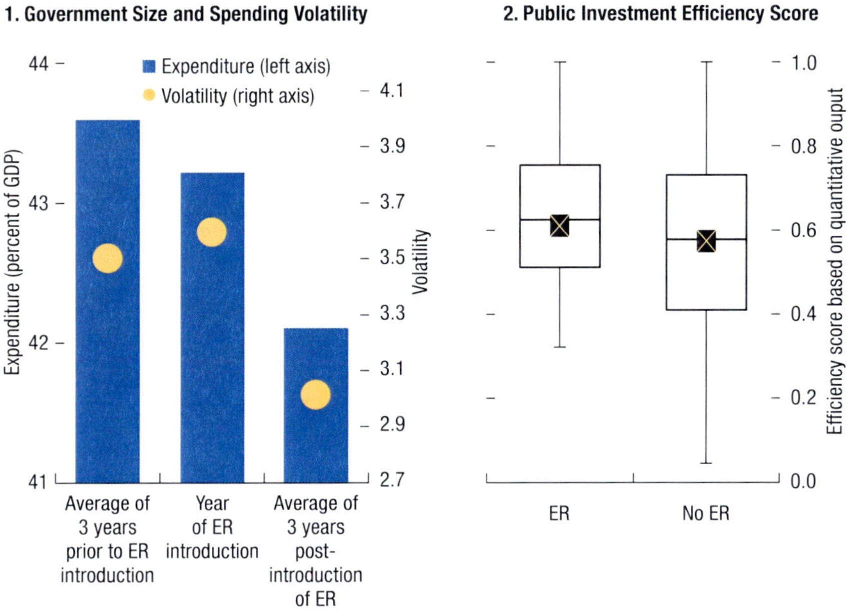

Sources: Dabla-Norris and others 2012; FAD Fiscal Rules database; and authors' calculations.
Note: In panel 1, volatility is calculated as the absolute value of the percentage change in the deviation of expenditure from its trend, as calculated by the Hodrick-Prescott filter. In panel 2, the public investment efficiency score refers to the efficiency scores based on quantitative output estimated using frontier analysis in IMF 2015, which covers 132 economies across income groups. ER = expenditure rule.

budget under expenditure rules. Lower volatility improves the predictability (and credibility) of policy and directly contributes to macroeconomic stability. Finally, expenditure rules may promote greater efficiency.

The data provide some evidence of possible implications for government size and efficiency. Event studies illustrate that the introduction of expenditure rules is indeed followed by smaller governments in both advanced and emerging economies (panel 1 of Figure 12.11).[13]

The volatility of government spending is also found to decline after the introduction of an expenditure rule.[14] The distribution of public investment efficiency

[13] Given that most expenditure rules were implemented in the context of and perhaps part of the response to "bad" times (see Figure 12.5), those patterns may not only be due to the introduction of an expenditure rule. They could also reflect that over the course of the recovery, the share of government spending in GDP typically falls and volatility declines. Nonetheless, introducing an expenditure rule following a rise in spending during recessions can ensure that the expenditure-to-GDP ratio does not stay at an elevated level because of political pressures during the recovery.

[14] Following Grigoli and others (2012), spending volatility is calculated as the absolute value of the percentage change in the deviation of expenditure from its trend as calculated by the Hodrick-Prescott filter.

scores[15] has a higher average level and less dispersion in countries with expenditure rules (panel 2 of Figure 12.11). This outcome could be due to investment projects being prioritized more carefully relative to when there is no binding constraint on investment. However, this result needs to be interpreted with caution given the small share of countries (about 20 percent) with expenditure rules in the sample.

Expenditure Rules and Medium-Term Budgetary Frameworks

Finally, one last desirable side effect of expenditure rules is that they could encourage or foster desirable and complementary public financial management (PFM) reforms, including the introduction of a genuine medium-term budgetary framework (MTBF), and the strengthening of budget procedures, such as the adoption of top-down budgeting (Ayuso-i-Casals 2012). The data indeed suggest that the majority of countries strengthened their medium-term fiscal frameworks either when the expenditure rule was introduced or afterward (Figure 12.12).

Figure 12.12. Expenditure Rules and Medium-Term Fiscal Frameworks
(Number of countries)

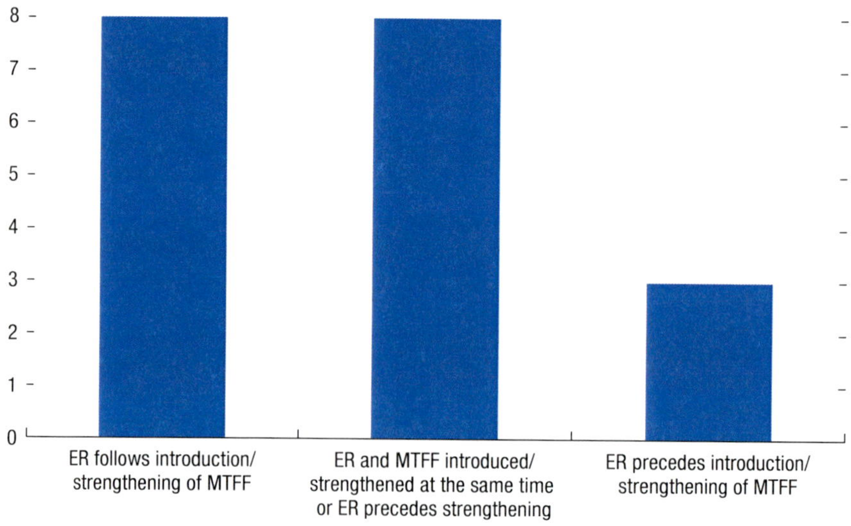

Sources: Grigoli and others 2012; and FAD Fiscal Rules database.
Note: Strengthening the medium-term fiscal framework (MTFF) implies that a country moved from an MTFF to a medium-term budget framework (MTBF) or from an MTBF to a medium-term performance framework. ER = expenditure rule.

[15] The scores are obtained from frontier method estimates based on physical output (IMF 2015). Specifically, an output-oriented data envelopment analysis is used to gauge the efficiency in transforming public investment into physical infrastructure. The data coverage is for 132 countries from 2000 onward.

CONCLUSIONS

This chapter examines the effectiveness of expenditure rules using the fiscal rules data set developed by Schaechter and others (2012). Overall, its findings lend support to the view that expenditure rules can foster better spending behavior if sound PFM systems are in place. Specifically, the analysis shows the following:

- The compliance rate for expenditure rules is greater than that for budget balance rules, particularly if the expenditure rule is directly under the control of the government and the rule is enshrined in law or in a coalition agreement.
- The presence of expenditure rules is associated with stronger fiscal performance, that is, a higher primary balance—after taking into account conventional determinants—and countercyclical policies.
- Expenditure rules are associated with lower levels of public investment in emerging market economies, where weaker PFM systems may be less effective at preventing policymakers from deferring high-quality discretionary spending for the sake of complying with the rule.

These results need to be interpreted with caution given the relatively limited experience with expenditure rules (33 rules during 1985–2013). Moreover, in most cases, expenditure rules are generally used in conjunction with budget balance or debt rules, or both. While these combinations are needed to link the rule to debt sustainability, such simultaneity complicates identification of their impact.

ANNEX 12.1. ECONOMY LIST FOR REGRESSIONS ON EXPENDITURE RULES AND FISCAL PERFORMANCE

Annex Table 12.1.1. Economies Included in Regressions

Advanced Economies		Emerging Market and Developing Economies	
Australia	Italy	Argentina	Malaysia
Austria	Japan	Brazil	Mexico
Belgium	Korea	Bulgaria	Moldova
Canada	Netherlands	Chile	Nicaragua
Cyprus	New Zealand	China	Peru
Czech Republic	Norway	Colombia	Philippines
Denmark	Portugal	Egypt	Poland
Estonia	Singapore	Haiti	Romania
Finland	Slovak Republic	Honduras	Russia
France	Slovenia	Hungary	South Africa
Germany	Spain	India	Thailand
Greece	Sweden	Indonesia	Turkey
Hong Kong SAR	Switzerland	Latvia	Ukraine
Ireland	United Kingdom	Lithuania	
Israel	United States		

Source: IMF, World Economic Outlook database.

ANNEX 12.2. ADDITIONAL REGRESSION RESULTS

Annex Table 12.2.1. Fixed Effects Panel Regressions 1980–2010, Capital Spending as a Share of Total Spending as the Dependent Variable[1]
(Percent of GDP)

	All Economies	Advanced Economies	Emerging Market Economies
Expenditure Rule Dummy	−1.8	−0.01	−4.9
	(1.0)*	(0.8)	(2.3)**
EXELEC	0.6	0.2	1.3
	(1.4)	(1.4)	(2.9)
LEGELEC	−0.1	0.4	−1.0
	(0.9)	(0.7)	(2.5)
Constant	8.4	2.7	17.4
	(0.6)***	(0.6)***	(1.4)***
R^2 (overall)	0.02	0.00	0.01
Observations	490	274	176
Number of Countries	25	13	11
Expenditure Rule Dummy	−1.8	−0.01	−4.9

Sources: FAD Fiscal Rules database; IMF, World Economic Outlook database; and World Bank database of Political Institutions.

Note: LEGELEC = 1 if there was a legislative election in this year. EXELEC = 1 if there was an executive election in this year. Robust standard errors are in parentheses.

[1] A Hausman (1978) test was conducted to check whether a fixed-effects model is preferable to a random-effects model. The hypothesis that the individual-level effects are adequately captured by a random effects model can be rejected at the 1 percent level of significance.

*$p < .1$; **$p < .05$; ***$p < .01$.

ANNEX 12.3. EXPENDITURE RULES DETAILS

Annex Table 12.3.1. Expenditure Rules Details

Country	Statutory Base	Coverage	Target/Constraint	Description	Time Frame	Escape Clause	Independent Body Monitors Implementation	FRL
Argentina	L	GG	Change to GDP	Primary expenditure cannot grow more than nominal GDP or, at most, stay constant in periods of negative nominal GDP growth.	2000–08	No	Yes	Yes
Australia	L	CG	Real expenditure growth rate	Real growth in spending is constrained to 2 percent a year once the economy recovers and grows above trend. Once the budget returns to surplus, and while the economy is growing at or above trend, the government will maintain expenditure restraint by retaining a 2 percent annual cap on real spending growth, on average, until surpluses are at least 1 percent of GDP.	2009–	No	No	Yes
Australia	PC	CG	Change to GDP	Government expenditure cannot be raised as a proportion of GDP in 1985–86 and over the life of the parliament.	1986–88	No	No	No
Belgium	CA	CG	Real expenditure growth rate	Real growth of primary expenditure of CG ought to be equal or be less than 0 percent.	1993–97	No	Yes	No
Botswana	L	CG	Level to GDP	The ceiling on the expenditure-to-GDP ratio is 40 percent. Also, 30 percent of total expenditures should be directed toward development spending, which includes all capital spending and the recurrent spending for health and education.	2003–	No	No	No
Brazil	L	GG	Level to GDP	(1) Personnel expenditure is limited to 50 percent of net current revenue for the federal government, and 60 percent for states and municipalities; (2) permanent spending mandates cannot be created without permanent revenue increases or spending cuts; (3) the government sets numerical multiyear targets for expenditures (for the current year and indicative targets for the next two years).	2001–	Yes	No	Yes
Bulgaria	L	GG	Level to GDP	The ceiling on the expenditure-to-GDP ratio is 40 percent.	2012–	No	No	No
Bulgaria	PC	GG	Level to GDP	The ceiling on the expenditure-to-GDP ratio is 40 percent.	2006–09	No	No	No
Canada	L	CG	Specific ceiling	Federal spending control act sets clear nominal expenditure limits from FY91/92 to FY95/96.	1992–96	No	Yes	No

(continued)

Annex Table 12.3.1. Expenditure Rules Details ***(continued)***

Country	Statutory Base	Coverage	Target/Constraint	Description	Time Frame	Escape Clause	Independent Body Monitors Implementation	FRL
Croatia	L	GG	Change to GDP	The temporary rule calls for general government expenditure cuts of 1 percent of GDP a year until at least a primary balance of zero is achieved in nominal terms.	2012–	Yes	Yes	Yes
Denmark	PC	GG	Real expenditure growth rate	Real growth in public expenditures cannot exceed potential GDP growth, which is a (rough) measure of structural development in the tax base. If growth in expenditures increases beyond potential GDP growth, it must be financed by specific discretionary measures, which increase revenues.	2012–	No	No	No
Denmark	PC	GG	Level to GDP	Public consumption as a share of cyclically adjusted GDP should be reduced to 26.5 percent by 2015.	2009–11	No	No	No
Denmark	PC	GG	Real expenditure growth rate	Target of public consumption as a percentage of cyclically adjusted GDP and real growth in public consumption.	2007–08	No	No	No
Denmark	PC	GG	Real expenditure growth rate	Real public consumption growth capped at 0.5 percent per year, 1.0 percent during 2002–05.	1994–2006	No	No	No
Ecuador	L	GG	Other	Permanent expenditure cannot be higher than permanent revenue, though both are unclearly defined.	2011–	No	No	Yes
Finland	CA	CG	Specific ceiling	Annual limits to government expenditure for the 4-year terms of office of the government. Limits are set in real terms for primary noncyclical expenditures (about 75 percent of total central government spending, about 37 percent of total general government spending).	2003–	No	No	No
France	L (2011–); PC (1998–2010)	CG	Real expenditure growth rate	Targeted increase of expenditure in real terms, or targeted increase of expenditure excluding interest payments and pensions in nominal terms. The stricter provision applies.	1998–	No	Yes	No
Hungary	L	GG	Real expenditure growth rate	Cap real expenditure growth.	2010–11	No	Yes	Yes
Iceland	PC	CG	Real expenditure growth rate	The real expenditure growth limit of the central government (2 percent for public consumption and 2.5 percent for transfers).	2004–08	No	No	No

Israel	L	CG	Real expenditure growth rate	The provision for limiting real growth of the central government fiscal expenditure is 1.7 percent from 2007. For the biannual budget, adopted July 2009, the rules were relaxed to allow a real growth of expenditure of 3 percent for 2009. The Deficit Reduction and Budgetary Expenditure Limitation Laws (2010) make spending growth a function of public debt—rising, as the gap falls between actual debt and the objective of reducing it to 60 percent of GDP; and rising with trend GDP—measured as a 10-year moving average—and with projected inflation. This formula caps real spending growth in 2011 at 2.6 percent.	2005–	No	Yes (since 2009)	No
Japan	PC	CG	Specific ceiling	The "overall expenditure limit" (the amount of the general account expenditure, excluding debt repayment and interest payment) should not exceed that of the previous fiscal year. Reconstruction-related expenditures shall be managed separately from other expenditures, accompanied with their financial resources (cutting other expenditures, nontax revenues including sales of government's assets, and tax revenues by special taxes for reconstruction).	2011–	No	No	No
Japan	PC	CG	Specific ceiling	In 2006, the government set numerical targets (cabinet decision) by spending category (for example, public investment, social security, and so on). The 2006 targets were intended to be valid through FY11/12 and indeed were valid for FY07/08 and FY08/09 budgets. But the targets were abandoned for FY09/10 due to the financial crisis.	2007–09	No	No	No
Kosovo	PC	GG	Real expenditure growth rate	Ceiling on current expenditure growth of 0.5 percent per year in real terms.	2006–08	No	No	No
Lithuania	L	GG	Other	If the GG budgets recorded a deficit on average over the past 5 years, the annual growth of the budget appropriations may not exceed one half of (or 0.5 times) the average growth rate of the budget revenue of those 5 years.	2009–	No	No	No
Luxembourg	CA	CG	Change to GDP	In the course of the legislative period (per coalition agreement), public expenditure growth is maintained at a rate compatible with the medium-term economic growth prospects, which are quantified. Since 2010, the target is to bring expenditure growth back to the medium-term growth prospects, once the countercyclical response to the crisis has been phased out.	1995–	No	No	No

(continued)

Annex Table 12.3.1. Expenditure Rules Details ***(continued)***

Country	Statutory Base	Coverage	Target/Constraint	Description	Time Frame	Escape Clause	Independent Body Monitors Implementation	FRL
Mongolia	L	CG	Change to GDP	The expenditure growth cannot exceed the growth of nonmineral GDP from 2013.	2013–	Yes	No	Yes
Namibia	CA	CG	Level to GDP	Public expenditure levels below 30 percent of GDP.	2011–	No	No	No
Netherlands	CA	GG	Specific ceiling	The real expenditure ceilings are fixed for total expenditure (covering CG, health care, and social security; covers about 90 percent of GG expenditure) and sectoral expenditure for each year of government's four-year office term. Coverage of expenditure was changed in recent years: from 2007–10 interest payments were excluded; since 2009, expenditure is defined in net terms, that is, gross expenditure minus nontax revenues, from 2009–10 expenditure excluded unemployment and social assistance benefits. If overruns are forecast, the Minister of Finance proposes corrective action.	1994–	No	No	No
Peru	L	CG	Real expenditure growth rate	The real growth current expenditure ceiling was 2 percent (2000–02), 3 percent (2003–08), and 4 percent since 2009. Since April 2012, infrastructure maintenance is excluded from the expenditure cap and current expenditures associated with some social programs and equipment for military and police forces.	2000–	Yes	No	Yes
Poland	L	CG	Real expenditure growth rate	The overall increase in CG discretionary spending and all newly enacted spending cannot exceed 1 pps in real terms, based on CPI inflation (defined in the Public Finance Act as a temporary rule but envisaged to be replaced by a permanent rule once the excessive deficit procedure has been abrogated).	2011–	No	No	No
Romania	L	GG	Change to GDP	The total GG expenditure growth should not exceed projected nominal GDP for next three years until budget balance is in surplus. Moreover, personnel expenditure limits are binding for two years as set out in MTBF.	2010–	Yes	Yes	Yes
Russia	L	CG	Other	The rule sets a ceiling on expenditures (oil revenue at the "base" oil price, plus all nonoil revenues, plus a net borrowing limit of 1 percent of GDP). Oil revenues above the "base" oil price need to be saved in the Reserve Fund until it reaches 7 percent of GDP (though there are some allowable exceptions to this under the law).	2013–	Yes	Yes	Yes
Spain	L	CG	Change to GDP	The nominal expenditure growth for central and local governments shall not exceed Spain's nominal medium-term GDP growth. Interest and nondiscretional expenditure on unemployment benefits are excluded.	2011–	No	No	Yes

Sweden	L (2010–); CA (1997–2009)	CG +SS	Specific ceiling	The nominal expenditure ceiling for CG and the pension system is set for a 3-year period with the outer year added annually. Ceilings cannot be adjusted except when there are technical issues. A budgetary margin is used as a buffer. Interest expenditure is excluded from the ceiling.	1997–	No	Yes (since 2007)	No
United States	L	CG	Specific ceiling	In August 2011, Congress enacted discretionary spending caps, saving about $900 billion over the next decade. As a result of the failure to adopt a medium-term comprehensive deficit reduction plan, additional spending cuts (the so-called sequester) came into effect in March 2013. These additional cuts, if not repealed by Congress, will produce savings of US$1.2 trillion over a decade, with one-half of the savings coming from defense spending and the other half from domestic programs (excluding Social Security, Medicaid, parts of Medicare, and certain other entitlement programs).	2011–	No	Yes	No
United States	L	CG	Specific ceiling	The annual appropriations limit adopted under the Budget Enforcement Act of 1990 for discretionary spending was allowed to lapse at the end of FY02/03.	1991–2002	No	Yes	No

Source: FAD Fiscal Rules database 2013.

Notes: CA = coalition agreement; CG = central government; CPI = consumer price index; FRL = Fiscal Responsibility Law; GG = general government; L = legal; PC = political commitment; pps = percentage points; SS = social security.

REFERENCES

Ayuso-i-Casals, J. 2012. "National Expenditure Rules: Why, How and When." *Economic Papers* 473, European Commission, Brussels.

Banque Centrale du Luxembourg. 2005. "La situation économique et financière." *BCL Bulletin* 2005/3, Luxembourg City, Luxembourg.

Blanchard, O. J., and F. Giavazzi. 2004. "Improving the SGP through a Proper Accounting of Public Investment." Discussion Paper 4220, Centre for Economic Policy Research, London.

Bohn, H. 1998. "The Behavior of U.S. Public Debt and Deficits." *Quarterly Journal of Economics* 113 (3): 949–63.

Congressional Budget Office (CBO). 2003. "An Analysis of the President's Budgetary Proposal for Fiscal Year 2004." CBO, Washington, DC. http://www.cbo.gov/sites/default/files/cbofiles/ftpdocs/41xx/doc4129/03-31-analysispresidentbudget-final.pdf.

Cottarelli, C. 2012. "Beyond the Austerity Debate: The Deficit Bias in the Post–Bretton Woods Era." iMF Direct Blog Post, May 21. https://blog-imfdirect.imf.org/2012/05/21/beyond-the-austerity-debate-the-deficit-bias-in-the-post-bretton-woods-era/.

Dabla-Norris, E. J., A. Brumby, Z. M. Kyobe, and C. Papageorgiou. 2012. "Investing in Public Investment: An Index of Public Investment Efficiency." *Journal of Economic Growth* 17 (3): 235–66.

Debrun, X. 2014. "How Expenditure Rules Can Help Get Public Spending Right." Public Financial Management Blog Post, June 30. http://blog-pfm.imf.org/pfmblog/2014/06/how-expenditure-rules-can-help-public-spending-right.html.

———, L. Moulin, A. Turrini, J. Ayuso-i-Casals, and M. S. Kumar. 2008. "Tied to the Mast? The Role of National Fiscal Rules in the European Union." *Economic Policy* 23 (54): 297–362.

Escolano, J., A. Shabunina, and J. Woo. 2011. "The Puzzle of Persistently Negative Interest Rate–Growth Differentials: Financial Repression or Income Catch-Up?" Working Paper 11/260, International Monetary Fund, Washington, DC.

Grigoli, F., Z. Mills, M. Verhoeven, and R. Vlaicu. 2012. "MTEFs and Fiscal Performance." Policy Research Paper 6186, World Bank, Washington, DC.

Gunnarsson, G. 2011. "Reforming Iceland's Fiscal Framework." Unpublished paper, Banca d'Italtia, Rome, Italy. https://www.bancaditalia.it/pubblicazioni/altri-atti-convegni/2011-rules-institution/Gunnarsson.pdf?language_id=1.

Hallerberg, M., R. Strauch, and J. von Hagen. 2007. "The Design of Fiscal Rules and Forms of Governance in European Union Countries." *European Journal of Political Economy* 23 (2): 338–59.

Hallerberg, M., R. Strauch, and S. Yläoutinen. 2010. "Political Power, Fiscal Institutions and Budgetary Outcomes in Central and Eastern Europe." *Journal of Public Policy* 30 (1): 45–62.

Hausman, J. 1978. "Specification Tests in Econometrics." *Econometrica* 46 (6): 1251–71.

Holm-Hadulla, F., S. Hauptmeier, and P. Rother. 2010. "The Impact of Numerical Expenditure Rules on Budgetary Discipline over the Cycle." Working Paper Series 1169, European Central Bank, Brussels.

International Monetary Fund (IMF). 2009. "Fiscal Rules—Anchoring Expectations for Sustainable Public Finances." IMF, Washington, DC. https://www.imf.org/external/np/pp/eng/2009/121609.pdf.

———. 2012. "Botswana: 2012 Article IV Consultation." Washington, DC.

———. 2014. *Fiscal Monitor—Public Expenditure Reforms: Making Difficult Choices.* Washington, DC, October.

———. 2015. "Making Public Investment More Efficient." Policy Paper, IMF, Washington, DC.

Ljungman, G. 2008. "Expenditure Ceilings: A Survey." Working Paper 08/282, IMF, Washington, DC.

Nerlich, C., and W. H. Reuter. 2013. "The Design of National Fiscal Frameworks and Their Budgetary Impact." Working Paper 1588, European Central Bank, Frankfurt.

Schaechter, A., T. Kinda, N. Budina, and A. Weber. 2012. "Fiscal Rules in Response to the Crisis—Toward the 'Next-Generation' Rules. A New Dataset." Working Paper 12/187, IMF, Washington, DC.

Schuknecht, L. 2004. "EU Fiscal Rules: Issues and Lessons from Political Economy." Working Paper 421, European Central Bank, Frankfurt.

Turrini, A. 2008. "Fiscal Policy and the Cycle in the Euro Area: The Role of Government Revenue and Expenditure." European Economy Economic Papers 323, Directorate-General for Economic and Financial Affairs, European Commission, Brussels.

Wierts, P. 2008. "How Do Expenditure Rules Affect Fiscal Behaviour?" Working Paper 166, De Nederlandsche Bank, Amsterdam.

CHAPTER 13

Fiscal Rules to Tame the Political Budget Cycle: Evidence from Italian Municipalities

ANDREA BONFATTI AND LORENZO FORNI

INTRODUCTION

This chapter presents evidence suggesting that fiscal rules can help moderate the political budget cycle. The term "political budget cycle" generally refers to increases in government spending or in the deficit, or decreases in taxes, in an election year or preelection years, which are perceived to have been motivated by the incumbent's desire for reelection. Fiscal rules can limit the political budget cycle because they reduce the politician's incentives to be profligate as a way to be reelected by increasing the cost of preelection profligacy if elected.

The focus of the chapter is on Italian municipalities during the early 2000s when they were subject to the Domestic Stability Pact (DSP), a subnational fiscal rule introduced in 1999. The effect of the rule on the political budget cycle is identified by using the fact that municipalities with fewer than 5,000 inhabitants are exempt from the rule. This analysis estimates that the political budget cycle increases real capital spending by about 35 percent, on average, in the three years before municipal elections and that the subnational fiscal rule reduces this figure by about two-thirds.

A number of recent papers have used Italian administrative municipal data to address an array of political economy issues. Cioffi, Messina, and Tommasino (2012) provide evidence of the political budget cycle in capital and overall spending, while Alesina and Paradisi (2014) on the revenue side exploit the introduction of a new real estate tax in 2011. Gagliarducci and Nannicini (2013) study the effect of wages on the performance of mayors. Alesina, Troiano, and Cassidy (2015) show that younger politicians behave more strategically than older ones. Particularly relevant for the purposes of this chapter is the paper by Grembi, Nannicini, and Troiano (2016), which shows that the relaxation of the DSP for smaller municipalities in 2001 triggered a significant deficit bias.[1]

The authors thank seminar participants at the IMF and the University of Padua.

[1] Acconcia, Corsetti, and Simonelli (2014) use data on investment expenditure of Italian municipalities to estimate the fiscal multiplier at the local level.

This chapter is also related to three other branches of literature. By assessing how fiscal rules can limit the political budget cycle, this contribution naturally fits into the broad political budget cycles literature. See, among many, Rogoff and Sibert (1988); Rogoff (1990); Alesina, Cohen, and Roubini (1997); Persson and Tabellini (2000); Brender and Drazen (2005); Shi and Svensson (2006); and Brender and Drazen (2008). A number of contributions have empirically assessed the political budget cycle. For a recent one on the political cycle in capital expenditures, see Gupta, Mulas-Granados, and Liu (2015). Also related to the work in this chapter is the literature assessing the political budget cycle at the subnational level. For example, Coelho, Veiga, and Veiga (2006) and Veiga and Veiga (2007) provide evidence of the political cycle at the municipal level in Portugal; Foremny and Riedel (2014) in Germany; Drazen and Eslava (2010) in Colombia; and Brollo and Nannicini (2012) in Brazil. Finally, this chapter is also connected to the growing literature on national and subnational fiscal rules (for example, Beetsma and Debrun 2004, 2007; Debrun and others 2008). In this strand of literature, the recent contribution by Grembi, Nannicini, and Troiano (2016) is the first to propose a quasi-experimental design to control for omitted and unobservable factors that may affect previous results and to better establish the causal effect of the introduction of the rule.

This chapter contributes to these different strands of the literature in several ways. First, it provides further evidence on the existence of a political budget cycle at the local level in Italy and quantifies its effects. Second, it provides new evidence that the central government has enforced the DSP, which reduces concerns regarding the endogeneity of the rule, although it still leaves open the possibility that omitted and unobservable factors might affect how municipalities have reacted to the imposition of the rule. The regression discontinuity analysis addresses this issue, focusing on the behavior of municipalities around the 5,000-inhabitant threshold. Finally, and most important, it provides novel evidence that the imposition of the rule has reduced the political budget cycle. To the authors' knowledge, this is the first work that provides robust evidence that fiscal rules can limit the political budget cycle. Even when the introduction of a fiscal rule proves effective, in the sense that it helps contain the deficit, it is very difficult to assess whether it is welfare improving. In contrast, a rule that mitigates the political budget cycle, at least in this respect, is welfare improving.

INSTITUTIONAL SETUP AND THE DOMESTIC FISCAL RULE

The DSP was introduced in 1999 to include subnational authorities (regions, provinces, and municipalities) in the effort to achieve the fiscal targets set at the European level. The operational target of the rule for municipalities (about 8,000 in Italy) has changed over the years and was defined as limits to the growth of spending in 2005 and 2006 and with reference to the overall balance before 2005 and from 2007 onward. The penalties established for not complying with the DSP included limits on hiring, on spending, and on borrowing for investments

(Chiades and Mengotto 2015). Important to this analysis, since 2001, smaller municipalities (those with fewer than 5,000 residents) have been exempted from the DSP. The exemption aimed to provide some relief to small municipalities in the presence of economies of scale in managing the municipal government. In 2015 the DSP was discontinued and replaced with a budget balance rule for all local authorities.

With regard to governance and elections, the decision-making bodies at the municipal level are the mayor (*sindaco*); the executive committee (*giunta comunale*), which is appointed and headed by the mayor; and the municipal council (*consiglio comunale*), endowed with legislative powers. For municipalities with fewer than 15,000 inhabitants, a simple plurality electoral system applies whereby each candidate is supported by a single list.[2] In municipalities with population greater than 15,000, mayoral candidates may be supported by more than one list, and a runoff election takes place if none of the candidates wins an absolute majority of votes in the first round. Since 1993, municipal elections have been held every four years. Since 2000, mayors have served for five years unless particular circumstances (such as the death of the mayor, the appointment to other public or private positions not compatible with the mayor's service, or criminal charges) trigger earlier resignation. Elections usually occur during May and June.

THE DATA

This analysis focuses on the political cycle in capital spending. In 2007, the operational target for the fiscal rule was changed from a spending limit to a budget balance definition; therefore, this analysis focuses on the period before 2007. In addition, information from before 2004 was not available to run this analysis, so the data consist mainly of Italian municipalities' budget information from 2004 to 2006. This information has been combined with data on elections at the municipal level, and with information on the mayor (age, education, gender, political party).[3] Annex Table 13.1.1 reports the variables and sources. A summary of the data set is reported in Table 13.1.

Even within the window of 2004–06, the fiscal rule target changed. In 2004, the rule stated that the difference between current spending and current revenues could not be higher in real terms than it was in 2003. In 2005, current and capital spending was to have been lower than the average over 2001–03, increased by 10 percent. In 2006, current spending was to have been lower by 6.5 percent than it was in 2004 (by 8.1 percent for municipalities with per capita spending over the period 2002–04 greater than their population class average), while capital spending was not to have exceeded the 2004 value, increased by 8.1 percent. Even

[2] An electoral list is a group of persons, either affiliated to a political party or formally independent (*lista civica*), supporting a candidate mayor and eligible to become members of the municipal council.

[3] When a special commissioner is appointed to run a municipality, information on the mayor's characteristics is missing. In these cases, and when information on expenditures or revenues from financial reports is not available, we keep the municipality in the sample, using an unbalanced panel.

Table 13.1. Summary Statistics (2004–06)

Variable	Observations	Mean	Standard Deviation	Median	Minimum	Maximum
		Municipalities				
Capital Spending	20,057	564	879	336	0	27,965
Current Spending	20,057	791	471	688	28	21,725
Total Spending	20,057	1,356	1,209	1,050	178	40,984
Total Transfers	20,057	705	915	461	20	33,049
Total Revenues	20,057	1,602	1,789	1,231	398	109,039
Long-Term Borrowing	20,057	128	256	62	0	11,466
Total Outstanding Debt	20,041	1,124	5,705	821	−1,317	652,402
Taxable Income	20,084	11,813	3,128	12,065	3,066	31,525
Population (units)	20,084	7,405	42,655	2,458	32	2,705,603
Population Ages 15–64 years (percent)	20,084	64.53	4.45	65.28	32.17	81.58
Preelection Years (1/0)	20,084	0.51	0.5	1	0	1
		Mayors				
Female (1/0)	19,674	0.10	0.29	0	0	1
Age	19,670	51	9.64	51	22	86
Education (years)	19,161	14	3.07	13	5	20
Party Affiliated (1/0)	19,674	0.36	0.48	0	0	1
Mandate (first = 1)	20,084	0.81	0.39	1	0	1

Source: Authors' calculations.
Notes: Variables are in real per capita terms (2010 euro).

though the rule for 2004 did not include investment spending, it was expected that capital spending would be included in the rule starting in 2005.[4] Therefore, given existing lags in investment implementation, municipalities anticipated that investment projects begun in 2004 could lead to payments in 2005.

Based on these data, total spending by municipalities in ordinary-statute regions[5] represented almost 5 percent of GDP in 2004 (the starting year for this analysis). Capital spending represented about 38 percent of total spending. In real terms, municipalities spent about €600 per capita annually on investment. Regarding financing, transfers from the regions and the central government over the period represented about 40 percent of overall revenues; own revenues covered the rest. The main taxes financing municipalities were real estate taxes on home property (*imposta comunale sugli immobili*), which provided about 43 percent of municipal tax revenues, and a surcharge on the personal income tax (*imposta sul reddito delle persone fisiche*), which amounted to about 6 percent of municipal tax revenues.[6]

[4] For example, the Budget Law of 2003 (Law 289, December 27, 2002, Art. 29 Comma 11) included a provision stating that the rule for 2005 would have included capital spending, and the Economic and Financial Planning Document for 2004–07, issued in July 2003, mentioned the same point.

[5] We exclude regions with special autonomy (*regioni a statuto speciale*) because they were allowed to set their own fiscal rules for municipal governments.

[6] Municipalities can borrow, but only for investment purposes.

IDENTIFICATION STRATEGY

The models originally proposed to explain the political budget cycle help provide an understanding of the mechanism through which a fiscal rule can limit the cycle. The first models in this literature (Nordhaus 1975; Lindbeck 1976) were based on the premise that voters are myopic and that politicians are able to repeatedly fool them by tweaking policies before elections. Later models (for example, Rogoff and Sibert 1988; Rogoff 1990) assume that voters are rational but do not have full information about incumbents' competence. Voters want to elect the most competent politicians and form rational expectations regarding the incumbent's abilities based on observable current fiscal policy outcomes. A competent administrator is able to provide a given level of public goods at a lower level of taxes than an incompetent one can. The incumbent can signal his or her competence by increasing spending or showcasing new infrastructure projects without at the same time increasing taxes. Before the election, therefore, incumbents will attempt to signal their competence (and thereby increase their chances of reelection) by engaging in expansionary fiscal policy. This leads to a preelection increase in the government deficit even though competent politicians may be in office. However, even competent politicians that want to signal their higher competence might be reluctant to use all the available fiscal space because they are likely to remain in office and have to live with the consequences of this choice. Fiscal rules, such as the DSP, might increase the ex post cost of a preelection fiscal expansion.

To identify this effect in the context of this chapter, in the spirit of Grembi and others (2016), the analysis relies on the fact that the DSP does not apply to municipalities with fewer than 5,000 inhabitants. The identification scheme therefore compares municipalities with more than 5,000 inhabitants (subject to the DSP) with those with fewer than 5,000 inhabitants (not subject to the DSP) around election years. The analysis shows that indeed municipalities below the threshold, controlling for other characteristics, display a larger increase in capital spending in preelection years compared with those with more than 5,000 inhabitants, that is, they are subject to a stronger political budget cycle.

For a homogeneous sample, the baseline analysis focuses on municipalities with fewer than 15,000 inhabitants. The cutoff is established at 15,000 because a different electoral system applies to larger municipalities.[7] An ample literature has shown how different electoral systems can affect fiscal outcomes (for example, Persson and Tabellini 2000; Milesi-Ferretti, Perotti, and Rostagno 2002; with specific reference to the Italian context, see Ferraresi, Rizzo, and Zanardi 2015); therefore, care must be taken in pooling municipalities with different electoral

[7] A relevant issue in analyzing capital spending at the municipal level is that, in recent years, municipalities have outsourced some capital spending to private companies, usually partially or totally owned by the municipality itself. This practice has sometimes been instrumental in circumventing the fiscal rule. Unfortunately, information on these companies is extremely scant. One advantage in focusing on small municipalities (with fewer than 15,000 inhabitants) is that they have outsourced capital spending much less often than larger municipalities (Chiades and Mengotto 2015).

Figure 13.1. Log of Capital Spending per Capita, by Electoral Year and Size of Municipality, 2004–06

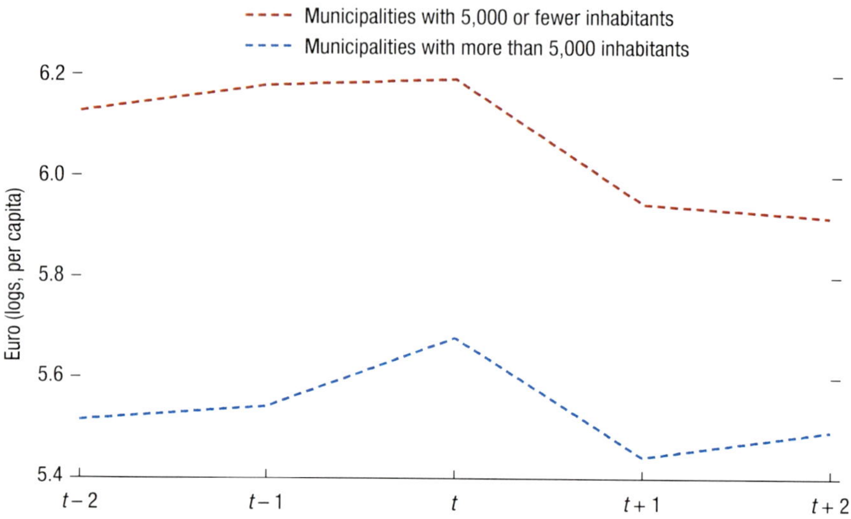

Source: Authors' calculations.
Note: The variable *t* indicates year.

systems because it can lead to bias in the estimates. By limiting the analysis to municipalities with fewer than 15,000 inhabitants, the analysis loses about 600 municipalities from a sample of about 8,000.

Figure 13.1 plots the average level of per capita capital spending (in logarithms) around elections for smaller and larger municipalities. Smaller municipalities are those with fewer than 5,000 inhabitants. Larger ones are those with 5,000–15,000 inhabitants. On the horizontal axis, *t* represents the election year. The figure shows the average level of per capita capital spending in the two years before and after elections. It clearly shows the political budget cycle, with capital spending higher and increasing in election years and in the two years before compared with the two years after elections. The presence of a political budget cycle in capital spending is confirmed by a regression analysis (not reported) in which the log of per capita capital spending is regressed on a dummy equal to one in the election year and in the two preceding years (the political budget cycle variable), a measure of revenues (either total per capita real transfers or total per capita real revenues), a number of mayors' characteristics (gender, age, education measured in years of schooling, affiliation with a national political party and its ideological stance), other time-varying municipality characteristics (proportion of people ages 15–64 years, taxable per capita income), and municipalities' fixed effects and time effects to capture common shocks.[8]

[8] See Bonfatti and Forni (2016) for a more detailed discussion of this point.

Next, the chapter shows evidence that the DSP has been enforced. In fact, for the DSP to have an effect on the political budget cycle, it is essential that a cost be associated with either overspending or breaching the fiscal rule. The literature to date shows no clear evidence of whether the DSP has generally been enforced. Grembi, Nannicini, Troiano (2016), for example, use budget data to estimate whether municipalities have respected the rule and then check whether penalties were subsequently enforced over the period 1999–2004. They find "suggestive evidence that the DSP penalties were enforced" (Grembi, Nannicini, Troiano 2016, 6), because there is a correlation between noncompliance (as estimated by the authors) and subsequent punishment.

For the years 2004–06 the Interior Ministry has provided the list of municipalities that did not comply with the DSP, allowing a direct test to be made of whether the DSP has been enforced. As discussed, municipalities breaching the DSP face limits on hiring, on spending, and on borrowing for investments in the following year. Figures 13.2 and 13.3 indeed show that hiring and long-term borrowing (accrual definition) are noticeably lower for the noncomplying municipalities in the year following a breach of the DSP as compared with complying municipalities. For current spending (Figure 13.4) the evidence is consistent, although less striking. The DSP required that purchases of goods and services be brought to a level not greater than in the last year in which the pact was respected. Overall, the evidence suggests that breaching the rule carried penalties as measured by fiscal aggregates.

Figure 13.2. Average Hiring of Municipalities, per 1,000 Inhabitants, by DSP Compliance in Previous Year, 2005–07

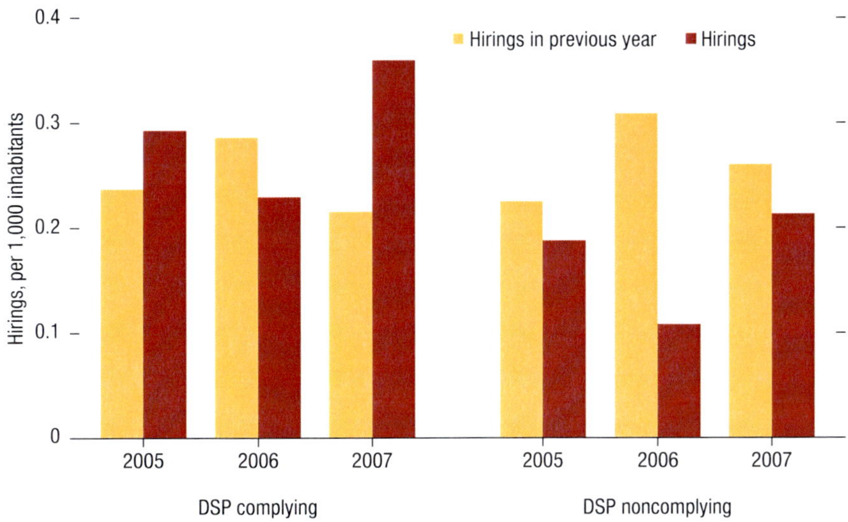

Source: Authors' calculations.
Note: DSP = Domestic Stability Pact.

Figure 13.3. Mean per Capita Long-Term Borrowing (Accrual Basis) of Municipalities, by DSP Compliance in Previous Year, 2005–07

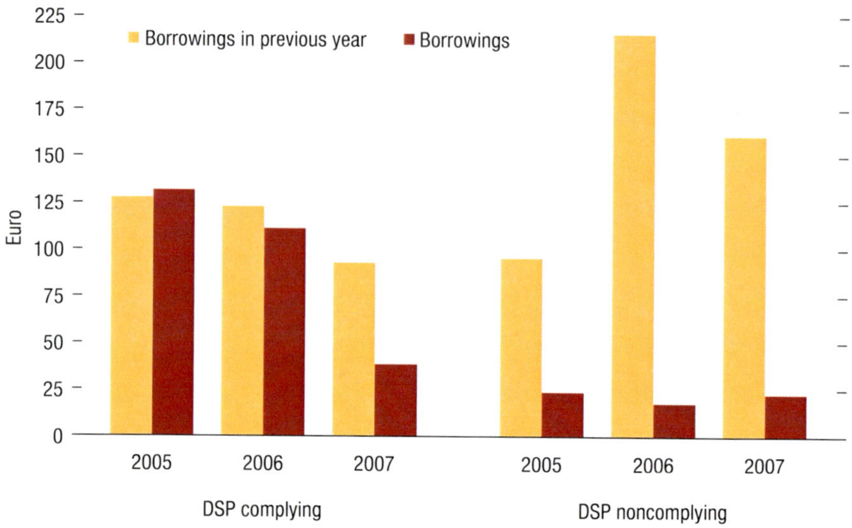

Source: Authors' calculations.
Note: DSP = Domestic Stability Pact.

Figure 13.4. Mean per Capita Purchase of Goods and Services (Cash Basis) of Municipalities, by DSP Compliance in Previous Year, 2005–07

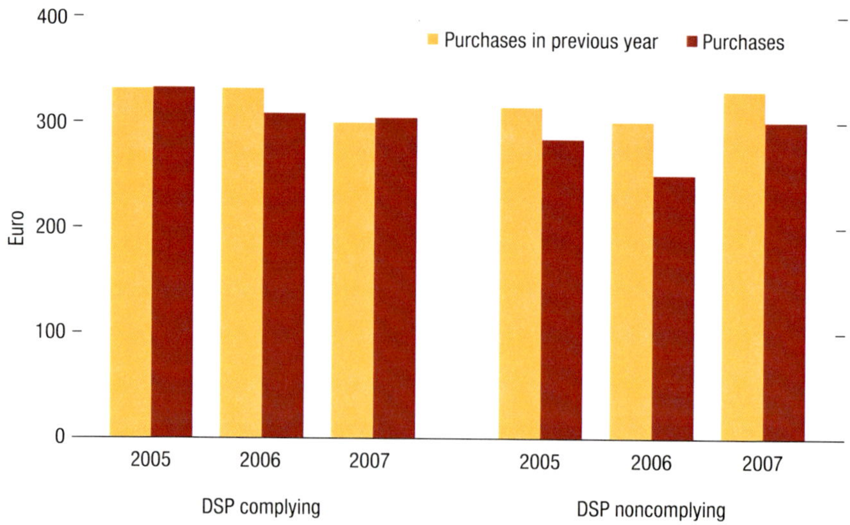

Source: Authors' calculations.
Note: DSP = Domestic Stability Pact.

REGRESSION DISCONTINUITY ANALYSIS

To assess whether the political budget cycle is more muted in larger municipalities (subject to the rule) than smaller ones (not subject to the rule) a regression discontinuity (RD) analysis around the 5,000-inhabitant threshold is performed. Specifically, a difference-in-differences approach is combined with an RD design to get estimates of the difference in capital spending between pre- and postelection years just below and above the 5,000-inhabitant threshold. Around the 5,000-inhabitant threshold, the treatment of being subject to the fiscal constraints of the DSP should be as good as randomly assigned. The treatment changes deterministically at the threshold, while other characteristics should not, setting up a sharp identification scheme. To assess the validity of the exogeneity of the threshold, a McCrary (2008) density test is run around the 5,000-inhabitant threshold in 2006. Figure 13.5 shows no evidence of any statistically significant jump in the population distribution at the threshold, as would be the case if mayors managed to keep the population at less than 5,000 inhabitants to avoid the DSP rules, suggesting that the nonmanipulation assumption is not violated.

Next, Figure 13.6 plots the log difference at the individual municipality level of pre- and postelection years per capita capital spending against municipality population size to see whether a discontinuity occurs around the 5,000-inhabitant threshold. The log difference of pre- and postelection years per capita capital

Figure 13.5. Checking Continuity of the Population Distribution around the 5,000-Inhabitant Threshold

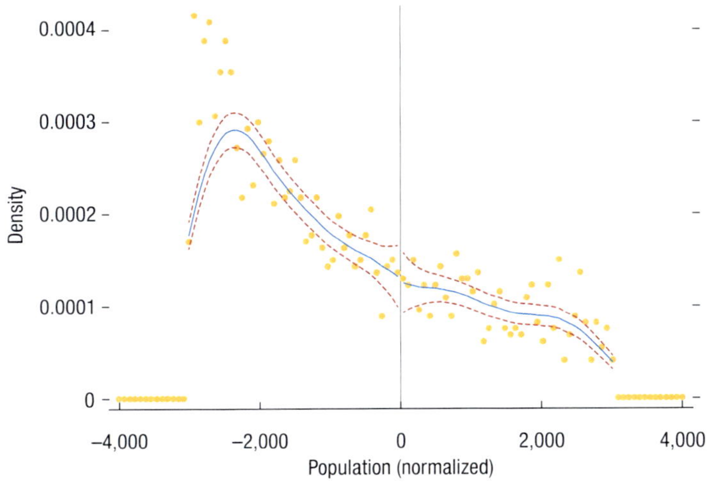

Source: Authors' calculations.
Note: Distribution of binned normalized population around the 5,000-inhabitant threshold in 2006 (population window 2,000–8,000). Bins are computed as normalized average frequencies over equally spaced population intervals. The blue line is a kernel estimate, and the dashed red lines are 95 percent confidence intervals (McCrary 2008). The discontinuity estimate (log difference in height) is –0.02 (standard error = 0.20).

Figure 13.6. Difference in Pre- and Postelection Log of Capital Spending per Capita

(Percentage change)

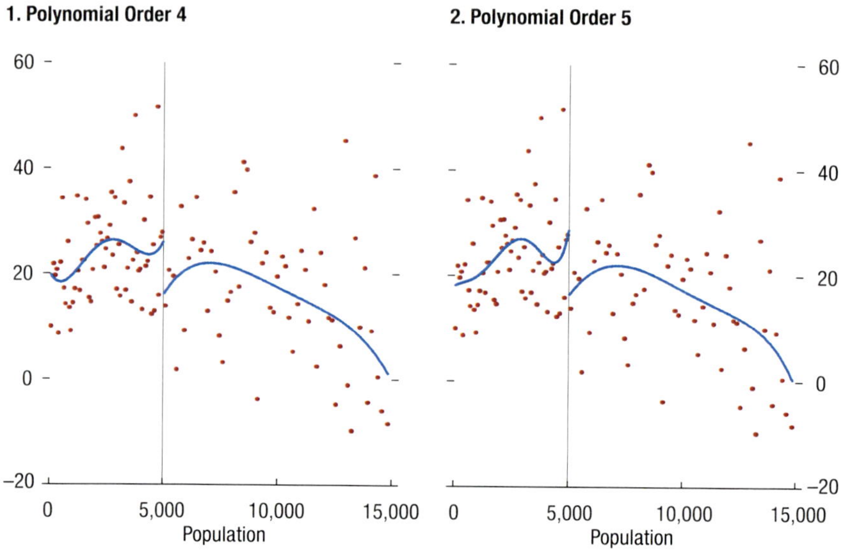

Source: Authors' calculations.

Note: Domestic Stability Pact–complying municipalities only. Mimicking variance evenly spaced number of bins using polynomial regression (Calonico, Cattaneo, and Titiunik 2014). Variables are in real per capita terms (2010 euro).

spending uses the election year and the two previous years as "pre" election and the two years after elections as "post" election. The log difference is used as a measure of the intensity of the political budget cycle. In addition, two polynomials are fit in population size (of order four in the left panel and of order five in the right panel), one for the observations below and one for those above the 5,000-inhabitant threshold. The fitted lines suggest that indeed the political budget cycle is higher to the left of the 5,000-inhabitant threshold than to the right, where the DSP rule is active. However, the dispersion of the observations is high and, moreover, by taking the pre- and postelection difference in capital spending, many observations are lost.

To confirm this result more formally, an RD analysis is run.[9] The baseline RD specification for per capita capital spending y_{it} is the following:

$$y_{it} = \sum_{k=0}^{p}(\delta_k P_{it}^{*k}) + Z_{it}\sum_{k=0}^{p}(\gamma_k P_{it}^{*k}) + W_{it}\left[\sum_{k=0}^{p}(\alpha_k P_{it}^{*k}) + Z_{it}\sum_{k=0}^{p}(\varphi_k P_{it}^{*k})\right]$$
$$+ \beta' X_{it} + \mu_i + \lambda_t + \epsilon_{it}, \tag{13.1}$$

[9] Robustness checks were performed using polynomials of different orders and windows of varying widths around the 5,000-inhabitant threshold. Results are generally robust but lose significance when the order of the polynomial is less than three or the population window is greater than 3,000 inhabitants.

which includes polynomials of order p in the normalized variable $P_{it}^{*} = P_{it} - P_{c}$, where P_c is the 5,000-inhabitant threshold, its interactions with the treatment indicator Z_{it}, equal to one for municipalities subject to the DSP and zero otherwise

$$Z_{it} = \begin{cases} 1 & if\ P_{it}^{*} > 0 \\ 0 & if\ P_{it}^{*} \leq 0, \end{cases}$$

and the electoral dummy W_{it}, equal to one in preelection years (t = −2, −1, 0), where t = 0 is the year of elections, and zero in postelection years (t = 1, 2). Additional covariates X_{it} include mayor's characteristics (gender, age, education, party affiliation, ideological stance), total per capita transfers received by municipalities, the proportion of people ages 15–64 years, and taxable per capita income, while μ_i and λ_t are municipality fixed effects and year effects, respectively.[10]

Table 13.2 reports the estimates at the 5,000-inhabitant threshold of the political budget cycle effect (the α_0 coefficient of the election dummy W_{it}) and the fiscal rule effect on the political budget cycle (the coefficient φ_0 of the interaction between the election dummy and the treatment indicator Z_{it}) from fifth-degree polynomial regressions over the 0–15,000-inhabitant and 4,000–6,000-inhabitant windows. The local estimates confirm the existence of budget cycle: capital spending is 36 percent higher in preelection years, while the fiscal rule proves

Table 13.2. Political Budget Cycle in Log of Capital Spending of Municipalities at the DSP Threshold; RD-FE Estimates (2004–06)

	Population 0–15,000		Population 4,000–6,000	
	(1)	(2)	(3)	(4)
>5,000 Inhabitants	0.070	0.051	0.383*	0.272
	(0.112)	(0.105)	(0.203)	(0.205)
Preelection Years	0.365***	0.348***	0.525***	0.473***
	(0.090)	(0.085)	(0.186)	(0.182)
Preelection Years × >5,000 Inhabitants	−0.238**	−0.182*	−0.721***	−0.631**
	(0.114)	(0.109)	(0.276)	(0.289)
R^2	0.062	0.176	0.107	0.188
Municipalities	5,155	5,010	620	604
Observations	14,848	14,149	1,700	1,627

Source: Authors' calculations.
Note: Variables are in real per capita terms (2010 euro). All specifications include a fifth-degree population polynomial, its interactions with the electoral and population dummies, and time and municipality fixed effects. Other covariates include the mayor's characteristics (gender, age, education, party affiliation, and political leaning) and municipality-level variables (per capita total transfers received, proportion of population ages 15–64 years, and per capita taxable income). Clustered standard errors at the municipality level are in parentheses. DSP = Domestic Stability Pact; RD-FE = regression discontinuity–fixed effects.
*p < .1; **p < .05; ***p < .01.

[10] For other works using municipality fixed effects in RD analysis, see, for example, Petterson-Lidbom (2008) and Ferraresi, Rizzo, and Zanardi (2015).

Figure 13.7. Checking Continuity of Covariates around the 5,000-Inhabitant Threshold for Population below 15,000 (2004–06)

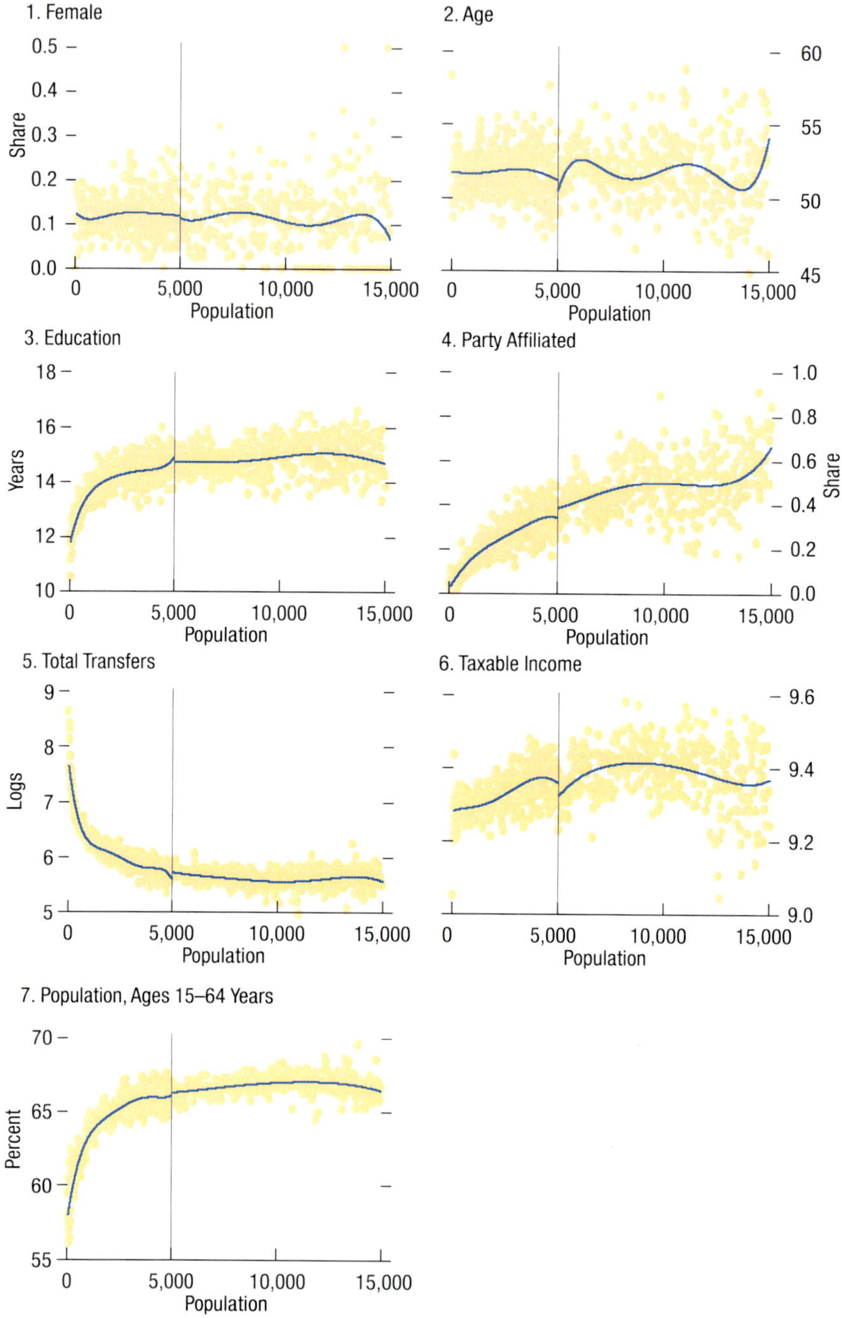

Source: Authors' calculations.
Note: Bins picked to match the variance of the variables (Calonico, Cattaneo, and Titiunik 2014). Fifth-degree population polynomials are fitted on both sides of the threshold. Variables are in real per capita terms (2010 euro).

effective in mitigating the cycle, reducing election expenditure by more than 60 percent (column (1)). If the sample is restricted to the 4,000–6,000-inhabitant window (column (3)), the reduction in capital spending in preelection years for larger municipalities more than offsets the average increase in expenditure in preelection periods. The inclusion of additional covariates (columns (2) and (4)), while confirming the baseline results, reduces the magnitude and significance of the estimated effects.

The analysis then checks whether the control variables, that is, the predetermined characteristics of mayors and of municipalities, are balanced on either side of the DSP threshold. Figure 13.7 shows scatter plots of mayors' and municipalities' characteristics averaged over evenly spaced population bins around the DSP cutoff. From visual inspection of the fifth-order fitted polynomials around the threshold, no evident discontinuities can be detected.

Finally, the issue of the mayor's wage must be addressed. By law, mayors earn more as the population size of the municipality grows (Table 13.3). Gagliarducci and Nannicini (2013) find that the change in wage for Italian municipalities above the 5,000-inhabitant threshold selects more educated and competent mayors into the job, although there is no evidence that they are less prone to the political budget cycle. The mayor's wage, which sharply increases at the 5,000-inhabitant threshold, introduces incentives that can potentially confound the estimated effect of the fiscal rule. To investigate whether the higher wage induces mayors seeking reelection to be more fiscally disciplined, polynomial regressions are run, with a 1,000 bandwidth, at other population thresholds where the mayor's wage increases, namely 1,000, 3,000, and 10,000 inhabitants. The rationale is that if the mayor's wage really matters for the political budget cycle, some effect should also be found at these other thresholds. The results reported in Table 13.4 do not support this hypothesis: no significant effects are found. In particular, no effects are found at the 3,000-inhabitant threshold, which entails a 50 percent wage increase. This latter result is consistent with those of Gagliarducci and Nannicini (2013).

Table 13.3. Legislative Thresholds of Municipalities

Population	Wage of Mayor	Wage of Executive Committee Members (%)	Size of Executive Committee	Size of City Council
≤1,000	1,291	15	4	12
1,000–3,000	1,446	20	4	12
3,000–5,000	2,169	20	4	16
5,000–10,000	2,789	50	4	16
10,000–15,000	3,099	55	6	20

Source: Grembi, Nannicini, and Troiano (2016, 8).

Note: "Wage of mayor" is the monthly gross amount in 2000 (current euro); "wage of executive committee members" is expressed as a percentage of the mayor's wage; "size of executive committee" is the maximum allowed number of executives appointed by the mayor; and "size of city council" is the number of seats in the city council.

Table 13.4. Political Budget Cycle in Log Capital Spending of Municipalities at Population Thresholds Relevant for Mayor's Wage; RD-FE Estimates (2004–06)

	Population 1,000		Population 3,000		Population 5,000		Population 10,000	
	(1)	(2)	(3)	(4)	(5)	(6)	(7)	(8)
>Threshold	0.106	−0.134	0.018	−0.041	0.383*	0.272	−0.158	−0.152
	(0.190)	(0.175)	(0.171)	(0.182)	(0.203)	(0.205)	(0.247)	(0.225)
Preelection Years	0.095	0.063	0.208	0.147	0.525***	0.473***	−0.219	−0.061
	(0.133)	(0.117)	(0.152)	(0.159)	(0.186)	(0.182)	(0.278)	(0.251)
Preelection Years × >Threshold	0.054	0.071	−0.115	0.072	−0.721***	−0.631**	0.278	0.196
	(0.207)	(0.201)	(0.200)	(0.192)	(0.276)	(0.289)	(0.409)	(0.378)
Other Covariates	No	Yes	No	Yes	No	Yes	No	Yes
R^2	0.047	0.192	0.110	0.196	0.107	0.188	0.129	0.176
Municipalities	2,485	2,411	1,183	1,146	620	604	214	211
Observations	7,130	6,797	3,317	3,145	1,700	1,627	559	539

Source: Authors' calculations.

Note: Variables are in real per capita terms (2010 euro). All specifications include a fifth-degree population polynomial, its interactions with the electoral and population dummies, and time and municipality fixed effects. Other covariates include the mayor's characteristics (gender, age, education, party affiliation, and political leaning) and municipality-level variables (per capita total transfers received, proportion of population ages 15–64 years, and per capita taxable income). Clustered standard errors at municipality level are in parentheses. DSP = Domestic Stability Pact; RD-FE = regression discontinuity–fixed effects.

*$p < .1$; **$p < .05$; ***$p < .01$.

CONCLUSIONS

This chapter uses data on Italian municipalities during the early 2000s to present evidence suggesting that fiscal rules can moderate the political budget cycle. The analysis uses the discontinuity in the application of the rule at 5,000 inhabitants to identify the effect of the rule on the political budget cycle. It finds that the political budget cycle increases real capital spending by about 35 percent, on average, in the years before municipal elections and that the subnational fiscal rule reduces these figures by about two-thirds as compared with municipalities not subject to the rule. It also provides evidence that the fiscal rule has been enforced by the central government, at least over the period 2004–06 for which data are available on the municipalities that have breached the DSP. To the authors' knowledge, this is the first analysis to provide robust evidence that fiscal rules can limit the political budget cycle. To this extent, it adds to the small and growing literature attempting to establish the impact of fiscal rules on budget outcomes. In contrast to other papers showing that fiscal rules can have an effect on budget deficits, however, these results have more direct welfare implications. Results showing that fiscal rules can help contain the budget deficit suggest that those rules are enforced, but without implying that they are welfare improving. On the contrary, the political budget cycle is inherently inefficient because it distorts spending and revenues for electoral and political purposes. In this regard, the results in this chapter point to a possible partial welfare-improving role for fiscal rules. In practice, assessing the welfare implications of fiscal rules remains difficult. In the specific Italian case analyzed in this chapter, it is generally accepted that the rule has contributed to reducing local authorities' deficits—but mainly by compressing capital spending. An assessment of the overall welfare effects of the rule, therefore, would have to include not only the benefits from reductions in deficits during the political budget cycle, but also the costs of the decline in capital spending.

ANNEX 13.1. DATA SET DESCRIPTION

Annex Table 13.1.1. Data Set Description

Variable	Description	Source
Capital Spending in Real per Capita Terms (cash definition)	Sum of all cash capital expenditures by municipalities; the largest outlays refer to the construction of buildings, roads, local transport, and purchases of furniture, and other equipment. Nominal values are deflated by using the national consumption price index (all items, base 2010).	Certificati di Conto Consuntivo, Ministero dell'Interno (http://finanzalocale.interno.it)
Current Spending in Real per Capita Terms (cash definition)	Sum of all cash current expenditures by municipalities; the largest outlays refer to personnel and purchases of goods and services. Nominal values are deflated by using the national consumption price index (all items, base 2010).	Certificati di Conto Consuntivo, Ministero dell'Interno (http://finanzalocale.interno.it)
Total Spending in Real per Capita Terms (cash definition)	Sum of all cash current and capital expenditures by municipalities, as defined above. Nominal values are deflated by using the national consumption price index (all items, base 2010).	Certificati di Conto Consuntivo, Ministero dell'Interno (http://finanzalocale.interno.it)
Long-term Borrowing in Real per Capita Terms (accrual definition)	Sum of annual revenues from loans and bonds issued to fund investment projects. Nominal values are deflated by using the national consumption price index (all items, base 2010).	Certificati di Conto Consuntivo, Ministero dell'Interno (http://finanzalocale.interno.it)
Preelection years	Dummy is equal to one in the three years before municipal elections, including the election year.	Archivio Storico delle Elezioni, Ministero dell'Interno (http://elezionistorico.interno.it)
Taxable Income in Real per Capita Terms	Sum of total incomes at municipality level as available from personal income tax returns.	Ministero dell'Economia e delle Finanze
Share of Population, Ages 15–64 Years	Computed as the ratio of population, ages 15–64 years, to total population.	Demo, Istituto Nazionale di Statistica (http://demo.istat.it)
Age of Mayor	The age dummy is equal to one if the mayor is older than the median.	Anagrafe degli Amministratori Locali e Regionali, Ministero dell'Interno (http://amministratori.interno.it)
Education of Mayor	Education is measured in years of schooling by converting International Standard Classification of Education (ISCED) levels. Dummies for three education categories are obtained by aggregating ISCED levels as follows: low (0–2), middle (3–4), and high (5–8).	Anagrafe degli Amministratori Locali e Regionali, Ministero dell'Interno (http://amministratori.interno.it)
Party Affiliation of Mayor	Dummy is equal to one if the list or coalition supporting the winning candidate for mayor at municipal elections is not a *lista civica*; that is, a list not affiliated with a national or regional party.	Anagrafe degli Amministratori Locali e Regionali, Ministero dell'Interno (http://amministratori.interno.it)

REFERENCES

Acconcia, A., G. Corsetti, and S. Simonelli. 2014. "Mafia and Public Spending: Evidence on the Fiscal Multiplier from a Quasi-Experiment." *American Economic Review* 104 (7): 2185–209.

Alesina, A., G. D. Cohen, and N. Roubini. 1997. *Political Cycles and the Macroeconomy*. Cambridge, MA: MIT Press.

Alesina, A., and M. Paradisi. 2014. "Political Budget Cycles: Evidence from Italian Cities." Working Paper 20570, National Bureau of Economic Research, Cambridge, MA.

Alesina, A., U. Troiano, and T. Cassidy. 2015. "Old and Young Politicians." Working Paper 20977, National Bureau of Economic Research, Cambridge, MA.

Beetsma, R. M. W. J., and X. Debrun. 2004. "Reconciling Stability and Growth: Smart Pacts and Structural Reforms." *IMF Staff Papers* 51 (3): 431–56.

———. 2007. "The New Stability and Growth Pact: A First Assessment." *European Economic Review* 51 (2): 453–77.

Bonfatti, A., and L. Forni. 2016. "Do Fiscal Rules Reduce the Political Budget Cycle? Evidence from Italian Municipalities." Marco Fanno Working Paper 208, Department of Economics and Management, University of Padua, Padova, Italy.

Brender, A., and A. Drazen. 2005. "Political Budget Cycles in New versus Established Democracies." *Journal of Monetary Economics* 52 (7): 1271–95.

———. 2008. "How Do Budget Deficits and Economic Growth Affect Reelection Prospects? Evidence from a Large Panel of Countries." *American Economic Review* 98 (5): 2203–20.

Brollo, F., and T. Nannicini. 2012. "Tying Your Enemy's Hands in Close Races: The Politics of Federal Transfers in Brazil." *American Political Science Review* 106 (4): 742–61.

Calonico, S., M. D. Cattaneo, and R. Titiunik. 2014. "Robust Data-Driven Inference in Regression-Discontinuity Design." *Stata Journal* 14 (4): 909–46.

Chiades, P., and V. Mengotto. 2015. "Il calo degli investimenti nei Comuni tra Patto di stabilità interno e carenza di risorse" ("The decline in municipal investments between Domestic Stability Pact and lack of financial resources"). *Economia Pubblica* 42 (2): 5–44.

Cioffi, M., G. Messina, and P. Tommasino. 2012. "Parties, Institutions and Political Budget Cycles at the Municipal Level." Temi di discussione (Economic Working Papers) 885, Bank of Italy.

Coelho, C., F. J. Veiga, and L. G. Veiga. 2006. "Political Business Cycles in Local Employment: Evidence from Portugal." *Economics Letters* 93 (1): 82–87.

Debrun, X., L. Moulin, A. Turrini, J. Ayuso-i-Casals, and M. S. Kumar. 2008. "Tied to the Mast? National Fiscal Rules in the European Union." *Economic Policy* 23: 297–362.

Drazen, A., and M. Eslava. 2010. "Electoral Manipulation via Voter Friendly Spending: Theory and Evidence." *Journal of Development Economics* 92 (1): 39–52.

Ferraresi, M., L. Rizzo, and A. Zanardi. 2015. "Policy Outcomes of Single and Double-Ballot Elections." *International Tax and Public Finance* 22 (6): 977–98.

Foremny, D., and N. Riedel. 2014. "Business Taxes and the Electoral Cycle." *Journal of Public Economics* 115: 48–61.

Gagliarducci, S., and T. Nannicini. 2013. "Do Better Paid Politicians Perform Better? Disentangling Incentives from Selection." *Journal of the European Economic Association* 11 (2): 369–98.

Grembi, V., T. Nannicini, and U. Troiano. 2016. "Do Fiscal Rules Matter?" *American Economic Journal: Applied Economics* 8 (3): 1–30.

Gupta, S., C. Mulas-Granados, and E. Liu. 2015. "Now or Later? The Political Economy of Public Investment in Democracies." Working Paper 155, International Monetary Fund, Washington, DC.

Lindbeck, A. 1976. "Stabilization Policies in Open Economies with Endogenous Politicians." *American Economic Review Papers and Proceedings* 66 (2): 1–19.

McCrary, J. 2008. "Manipulation of the Running Variable in the Regression Discontinuity Design: A Density Test." *Journal of Econometrics* 142 (2): 698–714.

Milesi-Ferretti, G. M., R. Perotti, and M. Rostagno. 2002. "Electoral Systems and Public Spending." *Quarterly Journal of Economics* 117 (2): 609–57.

Nordhaus, W. 1975. “The Political Business Cycle.” *Review of Economic Studies* 42 (2): 169–90.
Persson, T., and G. Tabellini. 2000. *Political Economics: Explaining Economic Policy*. Cambridge, MA: MIT Press.
Petterson-Lidbom, P. 2008. “Do Parties Matter for Economic Outcomes? A Regression-Discontinuity Approach.” *Journal of the European Economic Association* 6 (5): 1037–56.
Rogoff, K. 1990. “Equilibrium Political Budget Cycles.” *American Economic Review* 80 (1): 21–36.
———, and A. Sibert. 1988. “Elections and Macroeconomic Policy Cycles.” *Review of Economic Studies* 55 (1): 1–16.
Shi, M., and J. Svensson. 2006. “Political Budget Cycles: Do They Differ across Countries and Why?” *Journal of Public Economics* 90 (8–9): 1367–89.
Veiga, L., and F. Veiga. 2007. “Political Business Cycles at the Municipal Level.” *Public Choice* 131 (1): 45–64.

CHAPTER 14

On the Determinants of Fiscal Noncompliance: An Empirical Analysis of Spanish Regions

MAR DELGADO-TÉLLEZ, VICTOR D. LLEDÓ, AND JAVIER J. PÉREZ

INTRODUCTION

The process of fiscal consolidation in Europe in the aftermath of the global and euro sovereign debt crisis has brought to the forefront the challenges of enforcing fiscal discipline in federal or decentralized countries. The literature on fiscal federalism has attributed this challenge to the presence of soft budget constraints at the subnational level,[1] that is, the inability of subnational governments (SNGs') to keep fiscal deficit outcomes within targets set as part of fiscal consolidation strategies at the general government level. Soft budget constraints have been shown to originate from the inability of central governments (CGs) to credibly commit to not bailing out SNGs and, as a result, to not constrain SNGs fiscal outcomes (Vigneault 2007). Soft budgets have been shown to be driven by political motives, including reelection and government formation and stability (Sato 2007). They are aggravated by flawed intergovernmental fiscal institutions, including large vertical fiscal imbalances, weak fiscal rules, and limited market discipline (Rodden, Eskelund, and Litvack 2003; Ter-Minassian 2015). Flawed institutions act by raising expectations among voters and creditors that the CG must be accountable in the event SNGs are not able to fulfill their spending mandates or debt obligations.[2] Soft budget constraints have been typically assessed by exploring the determinants of fiscal outturns using fiscal reaction functions.[3]

A small but growing empirical literature on the implementation of fiscal consolidations offers a different perspective. Rather than searching for reasons why fiscal outcomes cannot be constrained and targets enforced, it questions whether fiscal targets or the forecasts on which such targets are based are set appropriately

[1] See Ter-Minassian (2015) for a review of this vast literature.

[2] Attempts to address some of the flaws in the context of the European Union (EU), in particular strengthening fiscal rules without addressing others (for example, vertical fiscal imbalances), have been shown to be ineffective (Foremny 2014; Kotia and Lledó 2016).

[3] See Argimón and Hernández de Cos (2012) for a review of this empirical literature.

in the first place.[4] A number of papers have shown that official forecasts tend to be optimistic among advanced economies (Auerbach 1999; Leal and others 2008; Jonung and Larch 2006; Frankel and Schreger 2013). Optimistic fiscal forecasts have been attributed to difficulties in forecasting downturns and booms in real time (Beetsma and others 2013). Another set of factors is related to strategic considerations, which have been shown to be salient in the EU among countries seeking to comply with the Maastricht convergence process (Strauch and von Hagen 2009) and ex ante deficit rules under the Stability and Growth Pact (SGP) (Bruck and Stephan 2006; Beetsma, Giuliodori, and Wierts 2009).

This chapter contributes to both literatures by seeking to provide a better understanding of the determinants of fiscal noncompliance at the subnational level. Fiscal noncompliance is defined as SNG budget balance outturns below corresponding targets. The focus is to understand whether fiscal noncompliance is the result of soft budgets or of technical and institutional factors that result in unrealistic fiscal targets. An emerging empirical literature has begun to look at the determinants of compliance in rules-based frameworks (Cordes and others 2015; Reuter 2015). However, this literature has mostly focused on national policies and has not discussed the institutional and political considerations behind fiscal noncompliance.

This chapter proposes a conceptual framework that tries to distinguish the impact of a soft budget constraint from that of fiscal forecasting and target setting on fiscal noncompliance. The framework looks at both the capacity and the incentives to comply. It distinguishes between events when SNGs have the capacity but not the incentives to comply with fiscal targets from events when SNGs have the incentives but not the capacity for fiscal compliance. Fiscal noncompliance is defined as voluntary under the former and involuntary under the latter. The discussion argues that voluntary fiscal noncompliance is triggered by factors conducive to soft budget constraints, whereas involuntary fiscal noncompliance is the result of factors conducive to unrealistic or ambitious fiscal targets.

Political economy channels and politics take a front seat in this framework. The framework shows that both voluntary and involuntary fiscal noncompliance occur mainly through political economy channels that jointly influence CGs' and SNGs' decisions to, respectively, enforce and comply with fiscal targets. Channels conducive to voluntary fiscal noncompliance act mainly by increasing CGs' political costs of enforcing and decreasing SNGs' costs of noncomplying with fiscal targets. Channels conducive to involuntary fiscal noncompliance are those that increase CGs' political cost of ensuring fiscal targets at the general government level are met, leading the CG to shift the burden of meeting these targets to SNGs. Such costs are determined by the impact such decisions have on the electoral, government formation, and other political objectives government

[4] Reuter (2015) shows that the introduction of numerical fiscal limits enforced through fiscal rules, even if not complied with, tilts fiscal policy outturns toward those numerical limits. So, in fact, compliance seems to matter less than whether the chosen numerical limit was set to an optimal or appropriate level.

officials and their parties have at the central and subnational levels, which is ultimately framed by politics and political institutions at the supranational, national, and regional levels.

An empirical model is constructed to test this framework. From among a set of economic, institutional, and political factors, the model identifies the ones most relevant to an understanding of voluntary and involuntary fiscal noncompliance. The empirical model is estimated using data from Spain's Autonomous Communities. Spain's Autonomous Communities (hereafter also referred to as regions, regional governments, or simply RGs) makes for an interesting case study for a number of reasons. RGs have gained significant political and fiscal autonomy over the past four decades through a process of decentralization (Hernández de Cos and Pérez 2013). During this period, regional governments have become accountable for delivering more than two-thirds of social services, mostly in the health and education sectors (Lledó 2015). The Spanish decentralization has been asymmetric, with revenue and expenditure decentralization occurring at different paces depending on the region, leading to both temporal and cross-sectional variations in both fiscal and political autonomy indicators. Spain's RGs have been subject to nominal budget balance targets for the past two decades. Their record in meeting these targets, as discussed below, has also varied significantly. And so has the rules-based framework used to monitor and enforce compliance with those targets. In addition to fiscal rules, regions have been subject to market-imposed discipline, given that most RGs' debt is regularly scrutinized by rating agencies. In this respect, Spain is one of the major subsovereign bond issuers worldwide, presenting a significant heterogeneity across regions in issuing practices and amounts (Canuto and Liu 2013; Pérez and Prieto 2015).

The postcrisis period in Spain has been marked by widespread noncompliance. Regions as a group have missed their targets systematically every year since 2010, accounting for the bulk of the fiscal noncompliance at the general government level and constituting one of the main risks to Spain's ongoing fiscal consolidation process (AIReF 2016). Critical to this analysis, fiscal noncompliance, while widespread, varied significantly across regions in both frequency and margins.

The existing empirical literature has studied fiscal discipline among Spanish regions by assessing the determinants of fiscal deficit and public debt outturns (for example, Argimón and Hernández de Cos 2012; Hernández de Cos and Pérez 2013). This literature has typically looked at economic, institutional, and political factors affecting the size of fiscal outturns irrespective of the targets aimed at constraining them. Critical factors promoting fiscal discipline included greater tax autonomy, higher market-financing costs and credit ratings, and the electoral calendar, but fiscal rules and other political factors are excluded. Fiscal indiscipline appears to have a strong inertial component, with the size of regions' fiscal deficits in one year largely influenced by the size in the previous year. A related literature has also looked at the determinants of the CG's budgetary deviations of the CG (Leal and Perez 2011). To the authors' knowledge, Leal and López Laborda (2015) and Lago-Peñas, Fernández-Leiceaga, and Vaquero (2016) are the only empirical analyses examining the regional determinants of compliance with fiscal deficit targets among Spanish regions.

The rest of this chapter is organized as follows. The next section proposes a conceptual framework to identify economic, institutional, and political determinants of fiscal noncompliance in multilevel governance systems. The third section reviews key institutional elements in Spain's multilevel governance system, with a focus on how fiscal targets are set, monitored, and enforced. Informed by the framework and Spain's institutional features, the fourth section proposes alternative hypotheses, details the empirical methodology used to test these hypotheses, and discusses the empirical results. The final section concludes with some policy considerations.

FISCAL NONCOMPLIANCE IN MULTILEVEL GOVERNMENTS: A CONCEPTUAL FRAMEWORK

Defining Fiscal Noncompliance

The proposed framework defines fiscal noncompliance as the outcome when a government is unable to meet numerical fiscal targets or ceilings. The fiscal target or ceiling could be the numerical limit of a fiscal rule. A government unable or unwilling to meet a fiscal target or ceiling is defined as noncompliant.

Fiscal noncompliance can be voluntary or involuntary. Fiscal noncompliance is voluntary when the noncompliant government has the capacity but not the incentives to comply with a fiscal target. Fiscal noncompliance is involuntary when the noncompliant government has the incentives but not the capacity to comply with a fiscal target. A government has the capacity to meet the target if it has sufficient fiscal resources or fiscal instruments to garner the necessary resources to meet the target—hereafter termed fiscal capacity. A government has the incentives to meet the target when the costs of noncomplying with the target outweigh the noncompliance benefits.

The Fiscal Noncompliance Problem

The fiscal noncompliance problem can be characterized as a sequential game between a central and a regional government (panel 1 of Figure 14.1). In the first stage, the CG sets a fiscal target for the RG, knowing the RG's expected fiscal capacity. The fiscal target is ex ante feasible. In the second stage, the RG decides whether to comply with the fiscal target based on expectations about its fiscal capacity and on whether the CG will enforce the fiscal target. In the third and final stage, the CG decides whether to enforce the target based on the RG's compliance decision in the second stage and its expected fiscal capacity. Nature reveals itself only at the end of the game in the form of a shock affecting the RG's fiscal capacity and, therefore, the feasibility of the fiscal target.[5]

Voluntary and involuntary fiscal noncompliance may also emerge as equilibrium outcomes under this game. Voluntary fiscal noncompliance occurs when the

[5] In practice, fiscal target assessments usually occur at a time when factors underlying fiscal capacity, such as nominal GDP, are still only estimates.

Figure 14.1. The Fiscal Noncompliance Problem

1. Sequencing

CG chooses target → RG chooses to comply or not → CG chooses to enforce or not → Shock

2. Voluntary Fiscal Noncompliance

CG chooses target → RG chooses not to comply → CG may enforce or not → Target ex post feasible

3. Involuntary Fiscal Noncompliance

CG chooses target → RG chooses to comply → CG chooses to enforce → Target ex post infeasible

Source: Authors' calculations.
Note: CG = central government; RG = regional government.

RG is not willing to comply with the budget balance target regardless of whether the CG is expected to enforce it, and even when fiscal capacity to comply with the target is highly expected. Under these circumstances, the shock can be assumed away, because the target is feasible both before and after the shock—that is, the target is both ex ante and ex post feasible—(panel 2 of Figure 14.1). Involuntary fiscal noncompliance occurs when the RG is willing to and ex ante capable of complying, but does not have the ex post fiscal capacity to do so (panel 3 of Figure 14.1).[6]

Voluntary Fiscal Noncompliance and Soft Budget Constraints

Voluntary fiscal noncompliance could be the result of soft budget constraints. RGs with soft budgets are not constrained to finance their spending from an approved budget. Therefore, they would not feel constrained to deviate from fiscal targets set in this budget if doing so will prevent them from providing a desired level of public goods and services. In the multilevel government context, the soft budget constraint problem arises from the CG's lack of a credible no-bailout commitment that allows RGs to overspend in the expectation of an eventual bailout.[7]

Soft budget constraints and voluntary fiscal noncompliance are interconnected. The theoretical literature models soft budget constraints as a sequential game (Inman

[6] Under an involuntary equilibrium, RGs must always be ex ante capable of complying with fiscal targets (that is, fiscal targets must be ex ante feasible). Ex ante infeasible fiscal targets could not be credibly enforced, fostering involuntary noncompliance.

[7] A bailout is broadly defined to account for not only resources granted to SNGs in the event of a fiscal or financial crisis, such as emergency liquidity funds and outright debt restructuring, but also less extreme situations observed outside crisis. For instance, it may take the form of a change in the allocation of formula grants or simply unconditional gap-filling transfers. A bailout may include situations in which SNGs' borrowing restrictions are lifted, allowing them to borrow to finance above-the-target fiscal deficit levels.

Figure 14.2. Soft Budget Constraint and Fiscal Noncompliance Problems

Sequencing				
CG sets transfer or target	→	RG expects bailout, overspends, does not comply	→	CG bails out, does not enforce

Source: Authors' calculations.
Note: CG = central government; RG = regional government.

2003; Rodden, Eskelund, and Litvack 2003; Vigneault 2007; Bordignon 2006). Actions in the voluntary fiscal noncompliance game described above are logical extensions of the soft-budget-constraint game (Figure 14.2). In the first stage, the CG announces its intergovernmental transfer policy and sets the RG's budget balance target. In the second stage, the RG does not believe the CG's transfer policy, expects a bailout, overspends, and thus deviates from the budget balance target. In the third stage, the CG fulfills the RG's expectation by bailing it out, thereby not enforcing the breach in the budget balance target.[8] Much like in the voluntary fiscal noncompliance game, nature's draw does not make a difference and the target remains feasible.

Bailout and overspending incentives complement each other to spur voluntary fiscal noncompliance. Two necessary but not sufficient conditions characterize soft budgets and noncompliant governments. The first is that the CG must find it optimal not to enforce the fiscal target and to provide additional resources to the RG in stage 3. It will do so if the economic and political costs of denying additional resources (see below)—thereby enforcing the target—exceed the bailout or nonenforcement costs in the form of administrative, legal, or financial penalties, or if the bailout (nonenforcement) is triggered by deviations from national or supranational fiscal rules as well as reputational losses against financial markets and the public at large. Under these circumstances, the bailout or nonenforcement strategy is ex post optimal. The second necessary condition is that the RG, knowing that the CG has an incentive to provide additional resources and not to enforce the target, finds it optimal to overspend and not comply in stage 2 (that is, overspending is ex ante optimal). An ex post optimal bailout will not lead to noncompliance if overspending is not optimal. This may occur, for instance, if a bailout comes with costly conditions attached (for example, loss of fiscal autonomy, unpopular reforms). At the same time, by construction, an overspending optimal strategy cannot exist in the absence of an ex post optimal bailout. In short, for voluntary fiscal noncompliance to occur, factors that raise both bailout and overspending incentives must be in place.

[8] A critical assumption here is that the compliance assessment takes place before the bailout (that is, in the second stage). Bailouts that occur before the compliance assessment period (for example, gap-filling transfers) would help avoid or mitigate fiscal noncompliance. This requires corrective fiscal noncompliance measures or controlling the impact of alternative factors on uncorrected measures so as to take gap-filling transfers into account.

Bailout and Overspending Incentives

CGs may choose to bail out RGs for economic and political reasons.

- *Economic motives.* A benevolent CG that cares for the welfare of the whole nation would choose to bail out a fiscally irresponsible RG to avoid the negative spillovers to other jurisdictions and to itself. Negative spillovers to other jurisdictions—referred to as horizontal spillovers—usually take the form of underprovision of health, education, and other essential services by the nonrescued RG to other RGs. Negative spillovers to the CG, or more broadly, to the general government—referred to as vertical spillovers—may occur if default of a nonrescued RG endangers the banking system or the corporate sector nationwide because of their exposure to RG debt, thereby increasing fiscal risks and lowering credit ratings at the central or general government level (Inman 2003). Bailout incentives are expected to decrease with bailout pecuniary costs for CGs and increase with bailout economic benefits. Pecuniary costs are expected to increase with the size of the region: the larger the region, the larger the cost of the public goods and services it provides. However, the impact of region size on bailout economic benefits is ambiguous and depends on assumptions about the "extensive" and "intensive" nature of the spillover. The larger the region, the larger the extensive nature of the spillover: the larger the number of regions and individuals benefiting from the public goods and services provided by that region, the larger the bailout economic benefits (Wildasin 1997). But the smaller the region, the larger is the intensive nature of the spillover, and the larger the amount of public goods and services appropriated by each citizen in the bailed-out region (Crivelli and Stahl 2013). Bailout incentives are, therefore, expected to increase with RG size if the bailout benefits from the extensive nature of the negative spillovers outweigh both the benefits from its corresponding intensive nature and the bailout pecuniary costs (Wildasin 1997). Otherwise, bailout incentives are expected to decrease with RG size (Crivelli and Stahl 2013).
- *Political motives.* CGs may also bail out RGs to create the conditions to govern, stay in power, and reelect their principals. Bailout incentives are greater if directed toward RGs that are well represented in the national legislature, and thus influential for government stability and the passage of critical legislation (Porto and Sanguinetti 2001). Similar motives may also lead CGs to bail out regions with which they are politically aligned—that is, regions where government incumbents are from the same party or coalition of CG incumbents (Grossman 1994).[9] The CG may also offer bailouts to ensure national unity

[9] CG preference for bailing out politically aligned regions could also reflect electoral strategies to target safe electoral districts, that is, regions that had previously largely voted for and elected the CG party or governing coalition (Cox and McCubbins 1986). Such preferences may not necessarily prevail if the CG follows a swing strategy, whereby it will attempt to target regions that have previously voted for the CG party or governing coalition by narrow margins (Dixit and Londregan 1996). In some cases, such narrow margins may not have been sufficient for CG politically affiliated regional partners to win the election and form a government.

(Leite-Monteiro and Sato 2003). As a result, bailout incentives are likely to increase in regions where representation at the national or subnational level of pro-autonomy parties is larger (Bolton and Roland 1997).

Flawed intergovernmental fiscal frameworks increase bailout and overspending incentives. They do so by raising expectations among voters and creditors that the CG must be accountable in the event RGs are not able to fulfill their spending mandates or debt obligations (von Hagen and Eichengreen 1996). Mindful of the political costs of not fulfilling those expectations, CG bailout incentives will likely increase, raising RGs' bailout expectations and increasing overspending incentives. Rodden, Eskelund, and Litvack (2003) and Ter-Minassian (2015) list a number of institutional flaws that can be broadly categorized as (1) limited fiscal autonomy, (2) lack of preconditions for market discipline, and (3) weak administrative controls and fiscal rules. Limited fiscal autonomy may be the result of RGs' limited taxing powers, spending discretion limited by minimum service standards or revenue earmarking, and overlapping and unclear revenue or spending assignment. Insufficient fiscal autonomy is usually reflected in large gaps between the RG's mandated spending and revenue assignments, that is, large vertical fiscal imbalances (VFIs). The capacity of financial markets to discipline RGs is undermined by regulatory incentives and lax prudential requirements on RG lending, RGs' access to noncompetitive financing sources (CG onlending, public and development banks, state-owned enterprises), and lack of transparent and comprehensive public accounts that blur RGs' creditworthiness. Administrative controls such as those guiding RG borrowing are usually not based on clear and objective criteria (for example, ability to service debt). Last, fiscal rules applied to RGs are often poorly designed and weakly enforced.

Common-pool financing provides incentives for overspending. When most RG spending is financed out of a common pool of resources with few strings attached, overspending—and by implication noncompliance—will become an attractive option. This will be the case because RGs will bear only a fraction of the marginal costs of providing regional goods and services (von Hagen 2005). Common-pool financing is usually provided in the form of general purpose, open-ended, and equalization transfers or through debt-mutualization schemes. The literature shows that excessive dependency on such transfers to finance subnational public goods and services exacerbates overspending.[10]

Involuntary Fiscal Noncompliance and Fiscal Stress

Involuntary fiscal noncompliance may become likelier in times of fiscal stress. These are periods marked by large negative fiscal shocks usually associated with significant economic downturns and large fiscal adjustment efforts. In combination, the two factors have been shown to undermine RG capacity to meet fiscal targets as follows:

- *Shocks and forecast errors.* Economic shocks commonly trigger fiscal stress, making ex ante feasible targets ex post infeasible. Shocks could be region

[10] See Ter-Minassian (2015) for a review.

specific (idiosyncratic shock) or they could affect the whole country (common shock). A common shock can affect regions differently depending on each region's economic structure (for example, a bust in housing prices would affect regions where preshock median property values had been higher) or exposure to fiscal risks (for example, size of explicit or implicit contingent liabilities assumed by RGs on behalf of public enterprises or regional banks). Large shocks are usually reflected in large forecast errors.[11]

- *Feasible targets and adjustment plans.* In times of fiscal stress, CGs, as guardians of fiscal sustainability, are under pressure from markets and supranational institutions to design and implement ambitious but credible fiscal adjustment plans. Such pressure often leads to ex ante feasible, but very demanding, fiscal targets for the general government (Beetsma, Giuliodori, and Wierts 2009). This is particularly the case for the so-called Stability and Convergence Programs of Europe's SGP. In such programs, fiscal targets need to show ex ante compliance with SGP fiscal rules. Ambitious but feasible general government targets in decentralized fiscal frameworks are, in turn, often reflected in ambitious but feasible subnational fiscal targets, as CGs try to shift part of the fiscal adjustment effort to regions by "passing the buck" (Vammalle, Allain-Dupre, and Gaillard 2012).[12] Involuntary fiscal noncompliance, as a result, is expected to become likelier as fiscal adjustment to meet a given fiscal target increases. RG adjustment efforts, in turn, may increase if fiscal targets are not revised following fiscal noncompliance in a given year, leading to persistent fiscal noncompliance patterns. Similar arguments explain why CG incentives to enforce RG fiscal targets also increase in times of fiscal stress. Failure to do so will increase the likelihood that general government fiscal targets will be breached and that markets and supranational institutions will hold the CG accountable for general government fiscal noncompliance.

THE SPANISH FISCAL GOVERNANCE FRAMEWORK

Numerical fiscal targets at the regional level go back more than two decades in Spain. They were subject to numerous changes before and after the global financial crisis:

- *Budget consolidation scenarios and the 2002 Budget Stability Law.* Regions were first subject to budget balance limits in the form of fiscal deficit

[11] Large forecast errors, as discussed in the introduction, could also be the result of strategic considerations to ensure ex ante compliance with fiscal rules. In the context of the recent global financial crisis, they have also reflected larger-than-anticipated fiscal multipliers (IMF 2015).

[12] This allows CGs to minimize the political costs of fiscal consolidations by preserving the provision of public goods and services under their mandate, while avoiding increasing the burden of their own taxes. CGs may also raise subnational fiscal targets to build buffers for possible noncompliance in different subsectors, RGs included.

ceilings as part of the Budget Consolidation Scenarios agreed to with the CG after 1992. Fiscal deficit ceilings at the regional level came into law four years later under the 2002 Budget Stability Law (BSL). The 2002 BSL set a single zero-deficit limit for all regions, that is, all regions were obliged to post a budget outturn that was either in balance or in surplus. It also envisaged an adjustment plan with corrective actions in the event of noncompliance. Throughout this period, fiscal deficit ceilings for each region were set as a percentage of national GDP.

- *The 2006 Budget Stability Law.* The reform of the first BSL, approved in 2006, entered in force in 2007 and was implemented as a consequence of an EU-wide reform of the SGP. The 2006 BSL enabled the CG and RGs to adapt their deficit and surplus targets to the economy's cyclical position. Specifically, it allowed the RGs to run a deficit of 0.75 percent of GDP if economic growth was below a certain threshold, to which a further 0.25 percent of GDP could be added to finance increases in productive investment.[13] Fiscal deficit ceilings were also set as a percentage of regional rather than national GDP. The 2006 BSL included a no-bailout clause. It also introduced monitoring and enforcement mechanisms. If a risk of noncompliance was detected by the Ministry of Finance, a warning could be made to the responsible government unit. In the event noncompliance materialized, the noncompliant government was required to draw up an economic and financial rebalancing plan over a maximum term of three years. Last, it stipulated that, if a deviation from targets were to prompt a breach of the SGP, the tier of government involved should assume the attendant proportion of the responsibilities that should arise from the breach. In addition, RGs that failed to meet the deficit target would require CG authorization to initiate any debt operations.
- *The 2012 Budget Stability Law.* Regional fiscal targets were subject to further refinements to comply with EU-wide fiscal governance taking place in the context of the Six Pack, Fiscal Compact, and Two Pack. A constitutional reform approved in 2011 enshrined the rules-based framework in the Constitution. A new BSL approved in 2012 introduced structural budget balance, expenditure, and debt rules at the regional level. The 2012 BSL refined rules-based monitoring and enforcement mechanisms to prevent, correct, and penalize deviations from fiscal rules and targets introduced in the 2006 BSL. Monitoring and enforcement were also reinforced through improvements in the quality, coverage, and frequency of intrayear regional

[13] Under the second BSL, fiscal targets were set in three stages. In the first stage, a report assessing the cyclical phase for the following three years was prepared. Taking into account the cycle, in a second stage, fiscal targets for the general government and subsectors (central, regional, and local governments as well as the Social Security System) taken together were set and submitted to Parliament. Once approved by Parliament and subject to the aggregate RG target, individual fiscal targets for each RG were set by means of bilateral negotiations between the Ministry of Finance and representatives of each RG on the Fiscal and Financial Policy Council.

and local budget figures and the creation in 2013 of Spain's independent fiscal council—Autoridad Independiente de Responsabilidad Fiscal. Fiscal deficit limits continued to be measured as a percentage of regional GDP.

UNDERSTANDING FISCAL NONCOMPLIANCE AMONG SPAIN'S REGIONS

Empirical Methodology

Alternative drivers of fiscal noncompliance among Spanish regions are assessed by looking at noncompliance frequencies and compliance margins. To gather some stylized facts, the analysis starts by examining noncompliance empirical distributions across a number of different potential determinants of voluntary and involuntary fiscal noncompliance. An econometric analysis is then performed to identify whether fiscal noncompliance is likely to be voluntary by looking at the determinants of compliance margins. The sample includes 16 out of 17 Spanish regions over the period 2002–15.[14]

Noncompliance events are defined as cases of negative deviations between fiscal outturns and fiscal targets for a given region and year. That is, $f_{it} - f_{it}^{*} < 0$, where f, f^{*}, i, and t are fiscal balance outturns, fiscal balance targets, respectively. Noncompliance events are sourced from the annual compliance report submitted by the Ministry of Finance to the Economic and Financial Council (CPFF).[15] The CPFF comprises the Minister of Finance and public finance authorities from each region. While the Ministry of Finance is the ultimate body in charge of overseeing regional finances, the CPFF plays a formal role in the approval of regions' fiscal balance targets.

Noncompliance frequencies are defined in equation (14.1) as the ratio of noncompliance cases to the total number of cases within a particular group X. Groups are partitioned by quartiles (q) if measured on the basis of a continuous variable.

$$P\left(f_{it} - f_{it}^{*} < 0 | X_q\right) \text{ where } q = 1, \ldots 4. \qquad (14.1)$$

[14] Spain has 17 regions (*comunidades autónomas*). Nevertheless, two different center-periphery financial arrangements are in place. A majority of regions, 15, share the Common Regime of regional finances (*comunidades autónomas de régimen común*), with partial devolution of expenditure and revenues, while the remaining two (Navarre and Basque Country) enjoy a special status referred to as the Foral Regime of regional finances (*régimen foral*) under which they enjoy almost full spending and revenue autonomy. Within the latter two regions, though, the Basque Country is further decentralized, with revenue-raising responsibilities distributed to lower government levels (*diputaciones forales*) broadly resembling the provincial structure within the region. The latter region is therefore excluded from the subsequent econometric analysis because of the absence of comparable data.

[15] Available at www.minhap.gob.es/esES/CDI/SeguimientoLeyEstabilidad/Paginas/InformesCompletos LEP.aspx. Two annual compliance assessments have been conducted since 2013. Noncompliance events are defined based on the second and final assessment.

Compliance margins, $f^e = f^* - f$, are measured in percentages of regional GDP. Officially, they were measured as differences between fiscal outturns and targets as a percentage of national GDP between 2003 and 2007 and as a percentage of regional GDP from 2008 onward. To allow compliance margins to be compared over the years and across regions according to a homogeneous metric that at the same time reflects differences in regions' fiscal capacity, official compliance margins have been reestimated in percentage of regional GDP using the latest nominal GDP series.[16] That was accomplished in two steps: first, nominal deficit values were uncovered by multiplying targets and outturns by the nominal GDP available around the time targets and outturns were, respectively, set and assessed; second, the difference between nominal deficit outturns and targets was divided by the latest nominal regional GDP series.

A dynamic panel regression analysis is used to examine potential determinants of noncompliance margins. Noncompliance margins are regressed on the same variables conditioning noncompliance frequencies. Estimates are derived using Arellano-Bond first-difference generalized method of moments (FD-GMM) estimators to allow for possible inertial patterns in noncompliance as well as endogeneity of dependent variables. Equation 14.2 summarizes the specification:

$$f_{it}^{e} = \alpha\, f_{it-1}^{e} + \gamma\, INVOL_{it} + \delta\, VOL_{it} + \eta_i + \rho_t + \epsilon_{it}, \qquad (14.2)$$

where *INVOL* and *VOL* are vectors with factors associated with involuntary and voluntary noncompliance events (hereafter referred to as voluntary and involuntary factors), respectively; η and ρ are, respectively, country and time fixed effects, α governs the degree of persistence of RG fiscal compliance and noncompliance, and γ and δ measure the relative contribution of involuntary and voluntary factors to fiscal compliance and noncompliance.[17]

The estimation strategy aims to identify operative economic, institutional, and political factors associated with voluntary and involuntary patterns of fiscal noncompliance. In light of the relatively short cross-sectional dimension, the identification strategy is implemented in a parsimonious way by individually assessing the impact of a larger set of variables expected to encourage voluntary fiscal noncompliance on a baseline that controls for lagged fiscal noncompliance and the more limited number of factors associated with involuntary compliance patterns. To address the problem of overfitting and biased estimates in small cross-section samples stemming from the proliferation of GMM instruments, only the lags t–2 and t–3 are used, and the instruments are combined into smaller sets by using the

[16] The regional GDP series used is measured in market prices and in accordance with the new European System of National and Regional Accounts (ESA 2010).

[17] The literature suggests that fiscal deficit at the CG level can encourage deficits at the RG level (see Molina-Parra and Martínez-López [2015] for the case of Spain) through the so-called copycat or yardstick effect. Nevertheless, this analysis did not find robust statistically significant evidence to support the hypothesis that fiscal compliance at the CG level influences fiscal compliance patterns at the subnational level. The results are excluded from the chapter for the sake of simplicity.

collapse option in Roodman's xtabond2 package for Stata. The robustness of the results are checked using two-stage least squares (2SLS) estimators.

Testable Hypotheses

The proposed multilevel governance framework developed in the second section can help us understand fiscal noncompliance among Spain's regions. It can do so by helping identify to what extent regional fiscal noncompliance is voluntary. Voluntary fiscal noncompliance can be the result of bailout or overspending incentives driven by welfare or political motives. The framework can also look at the role political, fiscal, and financial market institutions play in shaping such incentives. Fiscal noncompliance could have also been involuntary because of common or asymmetric shocks, and because of fiscal targets and adjustment plans that were borderline feasible. Drawing from this framework and empirical analysis referenced in the previous section, Table 14.1 summarizes some testable hypothesis that are relevant in the Spanish context.

Table 14.1. Fiscal Noncompliance Testable Hypotheses

		Expected Sign	
Channel	Variable	Noncompliance Frequency	Compliance Margin
I. Voluntary			
Spillovers	Region size	Negative/positive	Positive/negative
Fiscal Autonomy	Tax autonomy	Negative	Positive
	Expenditure discretion	Negative	Positive
Market Discipline	Financing costs	Negative	Positive
	Access to soft financing	Positive	Negative
Fiscal Rules	Fiscal rule strength	Negative	Positive
Political Representation	Size of parliament representation	Positive	Negative
	Congruence of regional and national government coalitions	Positive	Negative
Elections	Election year	Positive	Negative
Political Autonomy	Regional representation of pro-autonomy parties	Positive	Negative
II. Involuntary			
Shocks	Common or nationwide positive shocks	Negative	Positive
	Region-specific positive shocks	Negative	Positive
Fiscal Target Adjustment	Annual changes in fiscal deficit targets	Positive	Negative
III. Other			
Inertia	Compliance margin in previous year	—	Positive

Source: Authors' calculations.
Note: See Annex 14.1 for a detailed description of the variables. — = not applicable.

Facts and Factors

Fiscal noncompliance between 2003 and 2015 varied markedly across regions in both how frequently regions missed the target and by how much these targets were missed (Figure 14.3). Fiscal noncompliance frequencies appear to be stratified into at least three groups: (1) broadly compliers, (2) broadly noncompliers, and (3) largely noncompliers. The broadly compliers comprise regions that have stuck to their fiscal targets in at least half of the years during the analysis periods. This is a large and heterogeneous group demographically, economically, and historically. It includes the Canary Islands, Galicia, Madrid, Asturias, Castilla and León, Extremadura, Andalucía, Aragón, and the Basque Country. Navarra, Rioja, Castilla la Mancha, the Balearic Islands, Cantabria, and Murcia are among the broadly noncompliers—regions missing their targets in up to two-thirds of the years. Finally, Valencia and Catalonia missed their fiscal targets in three-fourths of the years during this period. Just like the first group, regions in the last two groups

Figure 14.3. Regions' Noncompliance with Fiscal Deficit Targets

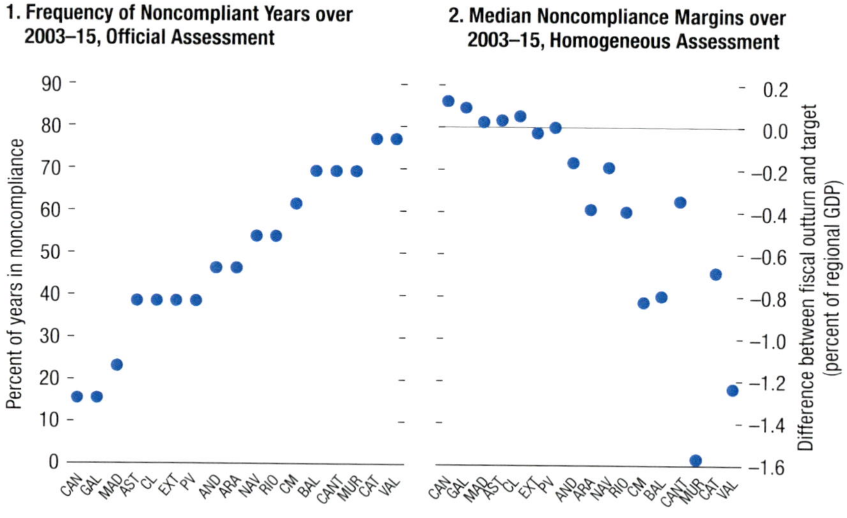

Sources: Ministry of Finance; and authors' calculations.

Note: Under the official assessment, fiscal noncompliance events are defined as differences between fiscal targets and outturns in percentage of national GDP between 2003 and 2007 and as a percentage of regional GDP from 2008 to 2015. Under the homogeneous assessment, fiscal noncompliance events are defined as differences between fiscal targets and outturns in percentage of regional GDP between 2003 and 2015 (see Annex 14.1). AND = Andalusia; ARA = Aragon; AST = Asturias; BAL = Balearic Island; CAN = Canary Islands; CANT = Cantabria; CAT = Catalonia; CL = Castilla and Leon; CM = Castilla La Mancha; EXT = Extremadura; GAL = Galicia; MAD = Madrid; MUR = Murcia; NAV = Navarra; PV = Basque Country; RIO = Rioja; VAL = Valencia.

Figure 14.4. Evolution of Regions' Noncompliance with Fiscal Deficit Targets

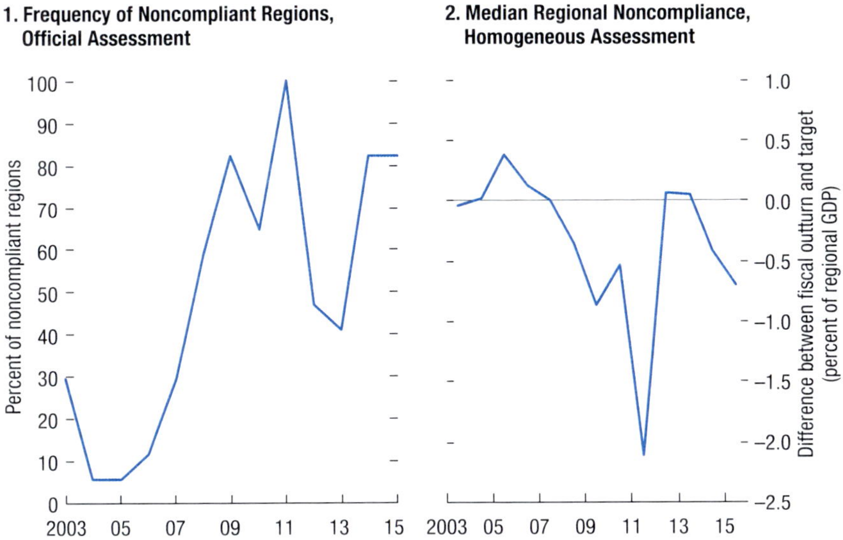

Sources: Ministry of Finance; and authors' calculations.
Note: Under the official assessment, fiscal noncompliance events are defined as differences between fiscal targets and outturns in percentage of national GDP between 2003 and 2007 and as a percentage of regional GDP from 2008 to 2015. Under the homogeneous assessment, fiscal noncompliance events are defined as differences between fiscal targets and outturns in percentage of regional GDP between 2003 and 2015 (see Annex 14.1).

have very distinct attributes. Noncompliance frequencies and margins appear to be broadly correlated in the sense that more-frequent noncompliers tend to breach their targets by wider margins than less-frequent ones.

Regions' fiscal noncompliance increased markedly in the postcrisis years. The number of noncompliant regions and their corresponding noncompliance margins also increased significantly following the global financial crisis (Figure 14.4). Noncompliance peaked in the post–EU sovereign debt crisis in 2011 when virtually all regions were unable to meet their fiscal deficit targets, most of them by very large margins. This deviation was corrected in the following years through more realistic projections of shared revenues advanced to the regions and supported by fiscal adjustment plans.

Involuntary Channels and Baseline Specifications

Fiscal noncompliance, common shocks, and forecast errors are linked. Common shocks are proxied by observed deviations between nominal (national) GDP

Figure 14.5. Forecast Errors and Regions' Noncompliance with Fiscal Targets

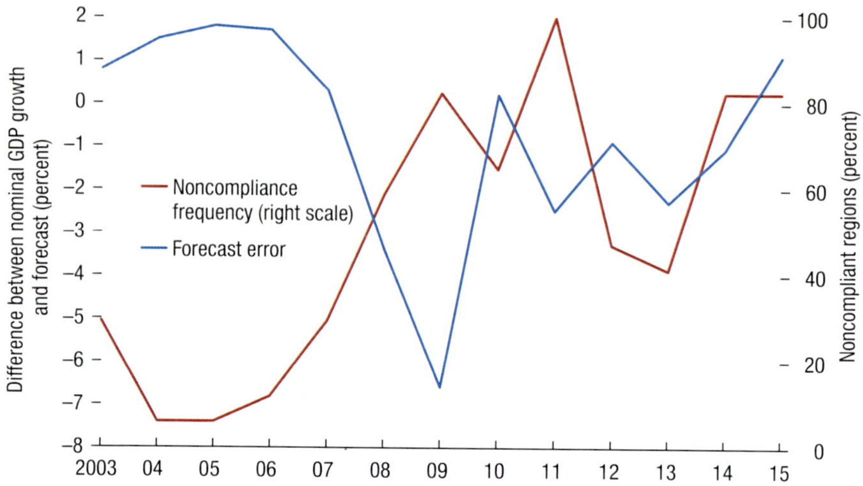

Sources: Ministry of Finance; and authors' calculations.

growth outturns and forecasts set in annual budget laws (forecast errors).[18] Negative (positive) forecast errors in nominal GDP growth should undermine (bolster) compliance with fiscal deficit targets through corresponding revenue shocks. Noncompliance margins and frequencies have clearly moved in tandem with forecast errors (Figure 14.5). Years when fiscal noncompliance was widespread (2008–11 and 2014–15) have usually been years when forecast errors have been negative.[19] Regression results provide support for the positive correlations between forecast errors and involuntary fiscal compliance, with positive and statistically significant estimates in about half of all estimated models (Tables 14.2 and 14.3).

Idiosyncratic shocks seem to play a limited role in determining fiscal noncompliance. Measured by differences between regions' real GDP growth, consumer price inflation, and house price inflation, and corresponding national averages, positive idiosyncratic shocks are expected to reduce fiscal noncompliance frequencies

[18] The key assumption here is that forecast errors are mostly driven by unanticipated changes in fundamentals and not by technical errors, weak or untimely data, or strategic motives (for example, overestimated nominal GDP growth forecasts to inflate revenue projections and make ex post excessive spending levels ex ante compatible with existing fiscal targets). Strategic motives and technical errors should play less of a role here to the extent that national growth forecasts are set by the center, where forecasting capacity and data quality are expected to be, on average, better than that of regions.

[19] 2010 and 2015 (widespread noncompliance and positive forecast error) were exceptions.

Table 14.2. First-Difference GMM Estimates of Fiscal Compliance Margins

	(1)	(2)	(3)	(4)	(5)	(6)	(7)	(8)	(9)	(10)	(11)	(12)	(13)
Lagged Noncompliance Margin	0.74*	1.09**	0.76*	0.83*	0.76	0.70***	0.37	0.91**	2.42***	0.31*	0.73*	0.49	0.24
Growth Forecast Errors	0.09*	0.04	0.09	0.10*	0.10*	0.12***	0.04	0.09	0.06	0.05	0.09	0.12***	0.04
Regional-National Growth Differential	−2.09*	−2.67*	−2.16*	−2.13	−2	−0.73	−0.6	−2.32*	−1.82*	−0.36	−2.17*	−1.19	0.24
Regional-National Inflation Differential	−0.36	−2.08	−0.39	−1.1	−1.28	−1.27	−2.41**	−1.23	−1.68	−2.83*	0.86	−1.29	−1.19
Fiscal Target Adjustment	−0.80**	−1.13**	−0.81**	−0.94**	−0.85*	−0.35	−0.82***	−1.02**	−0.99***	−0.51***	−0.68*	−0.52	−0.49
Execution Minus Budgetary Transfers (in regional GDP)		−0.48											
Regional Weight in National Population			3.86										
Regional Weight in National GDP				7.12									
Regional Weight in National Per Capita GDP					0.36								
Tax Autonomy						0.03							
Social Spending Share in Regional Government Spending						−0.33**							
Investment Share in Total Regional Spending						−0.24***							
Vertical Fiscal Imbalances							−0.15***						−0.13**
Fiscal Rule Index								0.05	0.02				0.01
Fiscal Rule Index × Lagged Noncompliance Margin									−0.06**				
Lagged Annual Change in Region Ratings										−0.09			
Lagged Annual Change in Implicit Interest Rates										1.03***			0.19
Ratio of Security to Loans										0.00			
National Election Dummy											−0.60***		
Regional Election Dummy												−0.36*	−0.50*
Party Congruence Dummy											−0.18	0.40	−0.41***
Proautonomy Party Share											−0.03	0.02	
Regions' Seats in National Parliament											−0.31	−0.86	

(continued)

Table 14.2. First-Difference GMM Estimates of Fiscal Compliance Margins *(continued)*

	(1)	(2)	(3)	(4)	(5)	(6)	(7)	(8)	(9)	(10)	(11)	(12)	(13)
Number of Observations	176	160	176	176	176	160	160	160	160	145	176	176	144
Number of Regions	16	16	16	16	16	16	16	16	16	15	16	16	16
Number of Instruments	16	15	16	16	16	15	15	15	15	15	17	17	14
Hansen	0.60	0.80	0.44	0.87	0.66	0.28	0.37	0.82	0.65	0.14	0.68	0.15	0.05
m1	0.12	0.11	0.13	0.15	0.23	0.02	0.09	0.10	0.06	0.14	0.12	0.20	0.00
m2	0.39	0.61	0.43	0.49	0.42	0.48	0.61	0.66	0.77	0.16	0.28	0.22	0.67

Source: Authors' calculations.

Note: The dependent variable is the difference between regions' fiscal deficit outturns and fiscal deficit targets. The larger this difference, the larger the fiscal compliance margin. Instrument set in all models includes the second and third lag of the explanatory variables. Hansen is the *p*-value of the test of the overidentifying restrictions (see Hansen 1982), which is asymptotically distributed chi square under the null hypothesis that these moment conditions are valid. A *p*-value equal to or greater than 0.05 indicates that the instrument set is valid, which is confirmed under all models. Note that m1 and m2 are the *p*-values of serial correlation tests of order 1 and 2, respectively, using residuals in first differences. The null hypothesis under both m1 and m2 tests is that there is no correlation between variables in the instrument set and the residuals. Observed *p*-values greater than 0.05 under the m2 test for all models indicate that there is no correlation with the instrument set defined in second lags. GMM = generalized method of moments.

$^{*}p < .1$; $^{**}p < .05$; $^{***}p < .01$.

Table 14.3. Two-Stage Least Square Estimates of Fiscal Compliance Margins

	(1)	(2)	(3)	(4)	(5)	(6)	(7)	(8)	(9)	(10)	(11)	(12)	(13)
Lagged Noncompliance Margin	0.49**	0.57**	0.49**	0.41**	0.39**	0.52**	0.75**	0.49**	0.46	0.14	0.30*	0.42**	0.79*
Growth Forecast Errors	0.04*	0.01	0.04*	0.05***	0.05**	0.03	−0.03	0.03	0.05*	0.07**	0.04**	0.05**	−0.02
Regional-National Growth Differential	−0.42**	−0.46**	−0.42**	−0.44***	−0.46***	−0.42**	−0.41*	−0.39**	−0.12	−0.26	−0.27**	−0.38**	−0.40*
Regional-National Inflation Differential	-0.47	-0.50	-0.45	-0.54	-0.55	-0.28	-0.50	-0.46	-0.17	-0.44	0.00	-0.51	−0.55
Fiscal Target Adjustment	−0.71***	−0.77***	−0.71***	−0.66***	−0.66***	−0.62***	−1.05***	−0.78***	−0.44***	−0.53***	−0.48***	−0.62***	−1.04***
Execution Minus Budgetary Transfers (in regional GDP)		−0.22											
Regional Weight in National Population			−2.59										
Regional Weight in National GDP				2.73***									
Regional Weight in National per Capita GDP					0.21***								
Tax Autonomy						0.02							
Social Spending Share in Regional Government Spending						−0.29***							
Investment Share in Total Regional Spending						−0.06***							
Vertical Fiscal Imbalances							−0.16***						−0.15***
Fiscal Rule Index								0.14***	0.04				0.07*
Fiscal Rule Index × Lagged Noncompliance Margin									−0.02				
Lagged Annual Change in Region Ratings										−0.15			
Lagged Annual Change in Implicit Interest Rates										0.26***			−0.07
Ratio of Security to Loans										0.00***			
National Election Dummy											−0.64***		
Regional Election Dummy												−0.2	−0.27*
Party Congruence Dummy											0.04	0.13	−0.19
Proautonomy Party Share											−0.00	−0.00	
Regions' Seats in National Parliament											−0.58**	−0.78*	
Number of Observations	144	128	144	144	144	128	128	128	128	131	144	144	128
Number of Regions	16	16	16	16	16	16	16	16	16	16	16	16	16
Hausman Test for Endogeneity	21.27	24.21	21.1	15.99	12.73	10.28	15.97	12.64	0.01	1.6	9.77	12.68	12.7
	(0.00)	(0.00)	(0.00)	(0.00)	(0.00)	(0.01)	(0.00)	(0.00)	(0.93)	(0.23)	(0.01)	(0.00)	(0.00)

Source: Authors' calculations.

Note: The dependent variable is the difference between regions' fiscal deficit outturns and fiscal deficit targets. The larger this difference, the larger the fiscal noncompliance margin. All variables are defined in level differences. The instrument set in all models includes the second and third lag of the explanatory variables. Standard errors allow for correlation within regions but not among regions (cluster robustness specification).

$^{*}p < .1$; $^{**}p < .05$; $^{***}p < .01$.

Figure 14.6. Fiscal Noncompliance and Regions' Idiosyncratic Exposure to Shocks

(Frequency of noncompliant cases over 2003–15, percent)

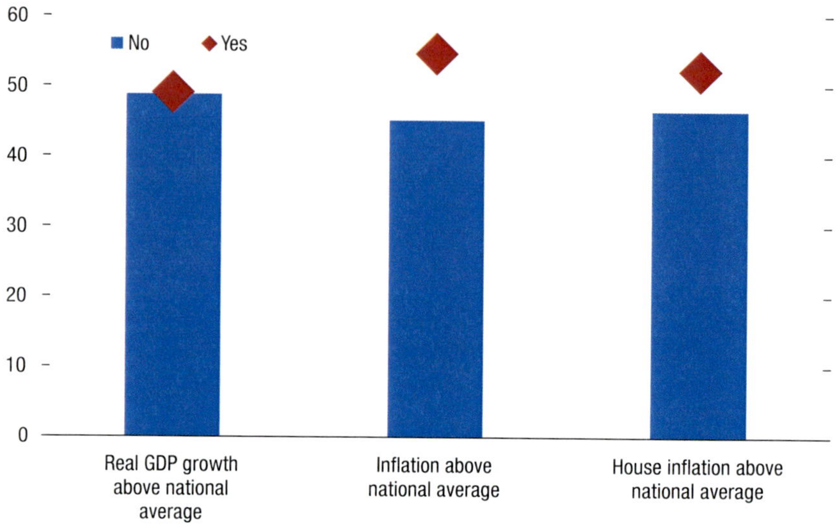

Sources: Ministry of Finance; and authors' calculations.

(Figure 14.6). Contrary to expectations, noncompliance frequencies were either the same (real GDP growth) or larger (consumer price inflation and house inflation) among cases in which idiosyncratic shocks were positive. Equally unexpected, positive idiosyncratic growth shocks seem to reduce rather than increase fiscal compliance margins. However, country-specific inflation differentials are not shown to be statistically significant (Tables 14.2 and 14.3). As discussed below, this finding may be explained by the relatively strong transfer dependency observed in most regions and, more specifically, by the fact that a significant share of regional finances comes in the form of transfers from the center allocated with the objective of equalizing regions' fiscal capacity to meet their spending mandates. Thus, reliance on equalization transfers mitigates the revenue impact of region-specific shocks, helping regions safeguard their fiscal capacity and meet their fiscal deficit targets.

Fiscal noncompliance has displayed some *inertial patterns*. In line with Leal and López-Laborda (2015) and Lago Peñas, Fernández-Leiceaga, and Vaquero (2016), fiscal compliance margins appear to be positively autocorrelated (Figure 14.7). As mentioned by Argimón and Hernández de Cos (2012), this could reflect budget rigidities due to incremental budget processes or multiyear expenditure commitments. Tables 14.2 and 14.3 confirm such inertial patterns under several specifications.

Figure 14.7. Inertia in Regions' Noncompliance with Fiscal Targets, 2003–15

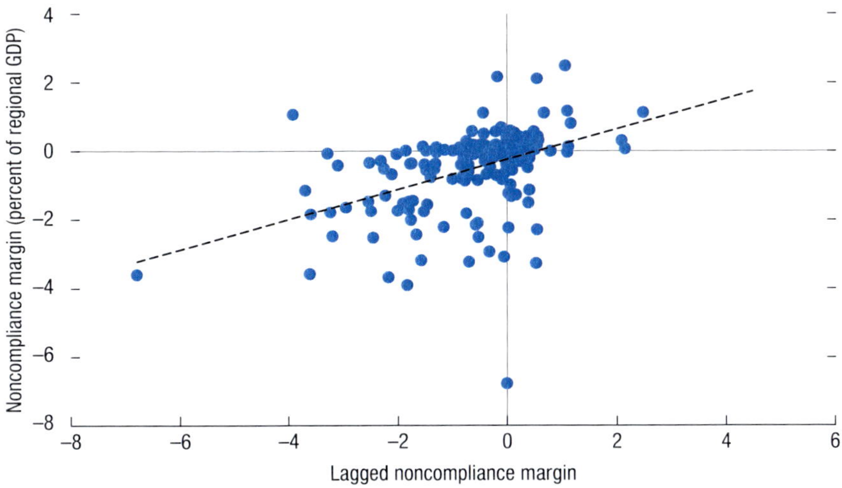

Sources: Ministry of Finance; and authors' calculations.
Note: Nominal GDP growth forecasts are set in the budget law.

Fiscal noncompliance increases with the required *adjustment effort*. Adjustment effort is measured by the difference between the fiscal deficit target in years t and t–1, both in percentage of regional GDP, a simple proxy for the required nominal adjustment.[20] Adjustment efforts have been quite heterogeneous across regions given that fiscal deficit targets, despite the existence of different starting fiscal positions, have been set uniformly across regions in most years. As expected, adjustment efforts are found to have a negative and statistically significant impact on fiscal compliance margins in most specifications (Tables 14.2 and 14.3). Estimated coefficients range from 0.5 to 1.0, implying that for each percentage point increase in RGs' fiscal deficit targets, compliance margins should be expected to decline between 0.5 and 1.0 percentage point.

Fiscal noncompliance may decrease if regions benefit from *gap-filling transfers* before the assessment date, as discussed in the second section. To verify that, we look at differences between actual transfers received by the RG from the CG and those originally budgeted. Noncompliance margins for an RG that receives more

[20] Adjustment effort could also be measured by the difference between fiscal deficit in year t and fiscal outturns in t–1. Unlike annual changes in fiscal targets, this measure is highly correlated with lagged fiscal compliance margins, and for this reason we have opted to exclude it from the baseline specification. Replacing it with our chosen adjustment effort proxy delivers qualitatively similar results at the expense of rendering lagged fiscal compliance margins statistically insignificant.

transfers than budgeted should be smaller. This hypothesis is rejected, with regression estimates not significant and with the wrong sign (Tables 14.2 and 14.3, model 2). One interpretation is that, while improving regions' fiscal capacity and thus helping stave off involuntary fiscal noncompliance, additional unbudgeted transfers reinforce expectations of further gap-filling transfers by end-year, thus boosting voluntary fiscal noncompliance and more than outweighing the initial deterrent effect.

Voluntary Channels

The analysis finds some tentative evidence of a positive impact of region *size* on fiscal noncompliance. Region size is measured according to the weight of a region's population, GDP, and GDP per capita in the corresponding national figures. Fiscal noncompliance tends to be more frequent among larger regions (that is, toward the end of the distribution) in all three measures, particularly with respect to GDP per capita (Figure 14.8). Fiscal compliance margins are shown to increase in a statistically significant way with regional GDP and regional GDP per capita only under 2SLS models (Tables 14.2 and 14.3, models 3 to 5).

Insufficient *fiscal autonomy* to adjust seems to play a role in determining regions' fiscal noncompliance. To assess the impact of fiscal autonomy, measures of tax and expenditure autonomy as well as of VFIs are estimated. Tax autonomy

Figure 14.8. Regions' Size and Noncompliance with Fiscal Deficit Targets
(Frequency of noncompliant cases over 2003–15, by quartile, percent)

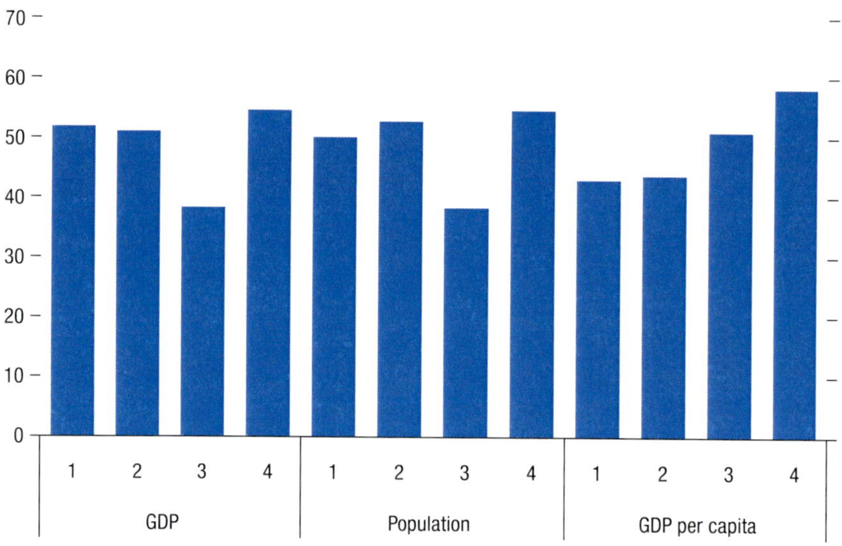

Sources: Ministry of Finance; Ministry of Public Works and Transport; National Institute of Statistics; and authors' calculations.

(in line with the terminology in the local public finance literature) is defined as the share of an RG's total tax revenues over which the RG has some degree of regulatory autonomy.[21] The larger this share, the greater a region's tax autonomy or fiscal coresponsibility, as it is often referred to in the Spanish empirical literature. However, in contrast with the local public finance literature, expenditure autonomy is defined here by the degree of discretion over mandated expenditures. With health and education mostly mandated to regions under center-imposed minimum standards, and social protection shared with the center, a larger share of regions' spending on these basic services limits regions' ability to adjust and comply with fiscal targets once their revenue-raising capacity is taken into account. That is, a region's autonomy to cut expenditures is expected to decrease as that region's spending share in basic services increases. With that in mind, the shares of regions' spending on essential public services (health, education, and social protection) and public investment in their total spending are computed.[22] Last, following Eyraud and Lusinyan (2013), VFI indicators are estimated for each region to capture the extent to which regions are unable to finance their own spending with own revenues, regardless of whether they have regulatory power of the corresponding tax bases.[23] As expected, noncompliance frequencies tend to be smaller among regions in the top tax autonomy quartiles (Figure 14.9), although the relation is not significant with respect to fiscal compliance margins (Tables 14.2 and 14.3, model 6). On the other hand, fiscal noncompliance frequencies are not necessarily the largest among regions in the top expenditure autonomy and VFI quartiles (that is, regions with greater social mandates and less own resources to fund them).[24] That said, as expected, fiscal compliance margins decrease as a larger share of regions' expenditures is allocated to social services and public investment—that is, as regions' expenditure autonomy decreases (Tables 14.2 and 14.3, model 6). Finally, regions with large VFIs tend to display lower compliance margins, as shown in Tables 14.2 and 14.3 (models 7 and 13).

The impact of stronger *rules* on fiscal compliance is not clear-cut. As described in the previous section, fiscal rules in Spain have become increasingly stronger over the years. They are currently among the strictest fiscal rules in Europe, as measured by the European Commission fiscal rule strength index. Stronger rules, however, have not always led to improvements in fiscal compliance, partly because of delays in implementing existing monitoring and enforcement

[21] Regions have regulatory autonomy over personal income taxes (schedules, allowances, credits), wealth and estate taxes and property transfer taxes (schedules, deductions, credits), gambling (exemption, base, rate, credit), and vehicle registration (rates). Significant tax decentralization took place following the 1997, 2002, and 2009 reforms of the regional financing system.

[22] Regions account for two-fifths of total general government spending on essential public services and more than 90 percent when it comes to health and education (Pérez García, Cucarella, and Hérnandez 2015), but about 5 percent with respect to social protection.

[23] VFIs are defined as [1 - *Own Revenue/Own Spending*]. Own revenue (spending) corresponds to a region's total revenue (spending) minus transfers received from RGs by the CG and other public entities (transfers paid by RGs to the CG and other public entities).

[24] Although for VFI, noncompliance frequencies tended to increase up to the third quartile.

Figure 14.9. Regions' Fiscal Autonomy and Noncompliance with Fiscal Deficit Targets

(Frequency of noncompliant cases over 2003–14, by quartile, percent)

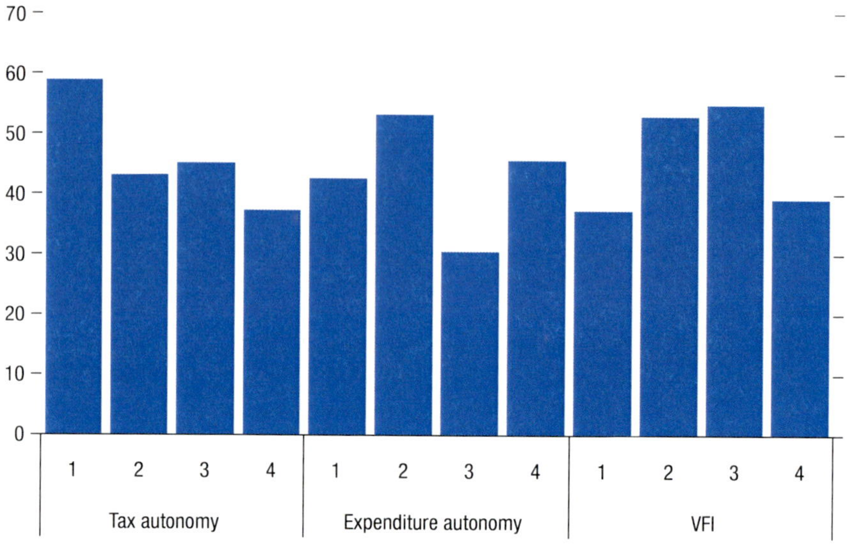

Sources: Ministry of Finance; and authors' calculations.
Note: Tax autonomy is defined as the ratio between a regional government's own tax revenue and total tax revenues. Expenditure autonomy is the region's share of general government spending on essential services. VFI = vertical fiscal imbalance.

procedures (Lledó 2015). The regression results seem to reinforce this point. Under the baseline GMM specification, stronger fiscal rules do not show any direct impact on fiscal compliance margins directly. Instead, they seem to have an indirect impact on compliance margins by helping reduce inertial patterns (Table 14.2, models 8 and 9). These results are reversed under the 2SLS specification, which shows fiscal rules having a direct rather than an indirect impact on fiscal compliance margins (Table 14.3, models 8, 9, and 13).

Financial markets seem to affect fiscal noncompliance through two different channels. On the one hand, fiscal noncompliance frequencies are larger among regions with lower (poorer) credit ratings and, to some extent, facing larger market-financing costs, which seems to provide some support to the idea that financial markets undermine fiscal compliance by raising the financing costs of regions that are not perceived as creditworthy (Figure 14.10).[25] On the other hand, fiscal noncompliance becomes less prevalent among regions where reliance

[25] Although one cannot rule out the possibility of reverse causality, with fiscal noncompliance leading to poorer credit ratings, higher risk premiums, and costlier market financing.

Figure 14.10. Financial Markets and Regions' Noncompliance with Fiscal Targets

(Frequency of noncompliant cases over 2003–15, by quartile, percent)

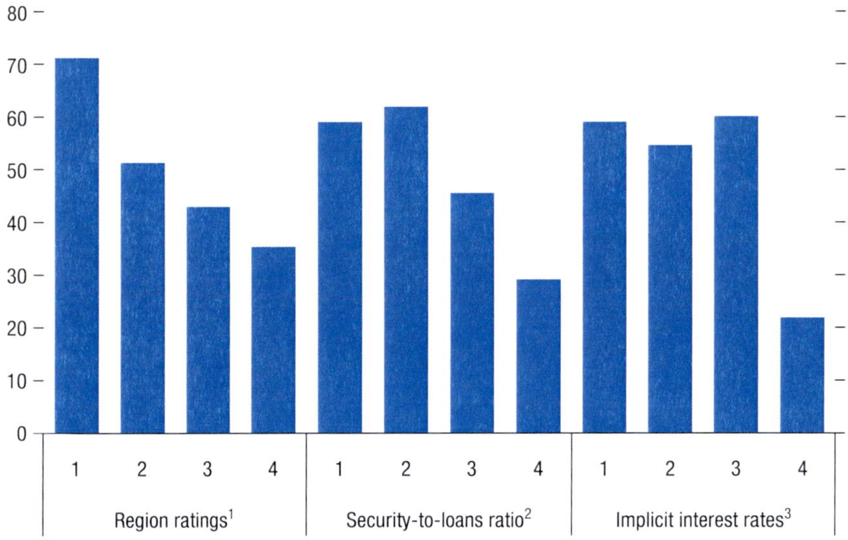

Sources: Ministry of Finance; and authors' calculations.
[1]Regional governments' credit ratings.
[2]Ratio of region's public debt in government securities to banking loans, percent.
[3]Region's interest payments in percentage of end-of-year regional public debt stock.

on market-issued securities, rather than softer bank loans, is greater. This finding indicates that greater market exposure helps deter fiscal noncompliance because regions internalize the impact fiscal noncompliance would have on credit ratings and market-financing costs. The regression analysis of fiscal noncompliance corroborates the latter channel: increases in the financing costs faced by regions in the previous year tend to increase rather than reduce compliance margins in the following year (Tables 14.2 and 14.3, model 10). However, greater reliance on market securities has no statistically or economically significant impact on compliance margins (Tables 14.2 and 14.3, model 10).

Fiscal compliance is weakened during election years, but the role played by politics in other areas is less clear-cut. Fiscal noncompliance seems to increase during *election years*. As expected, fiscal noncompliance is more frequent and displays wider margins during election years (Figure 14.11; Tables 14.2 and 14.3, models 11, 12, and 13). Unlike previous fiscal discipline analyses for Spain, but as expected in this framework, political alignment or *party congruence* between central and regional governments notably increases the likelihood of fiscal noncompliance. In particular, regions politically aligned with the center are shown to

Figure 14.11. Politics and Regions' Noncompliance with Fiscal Deficit Targets
(Percent)

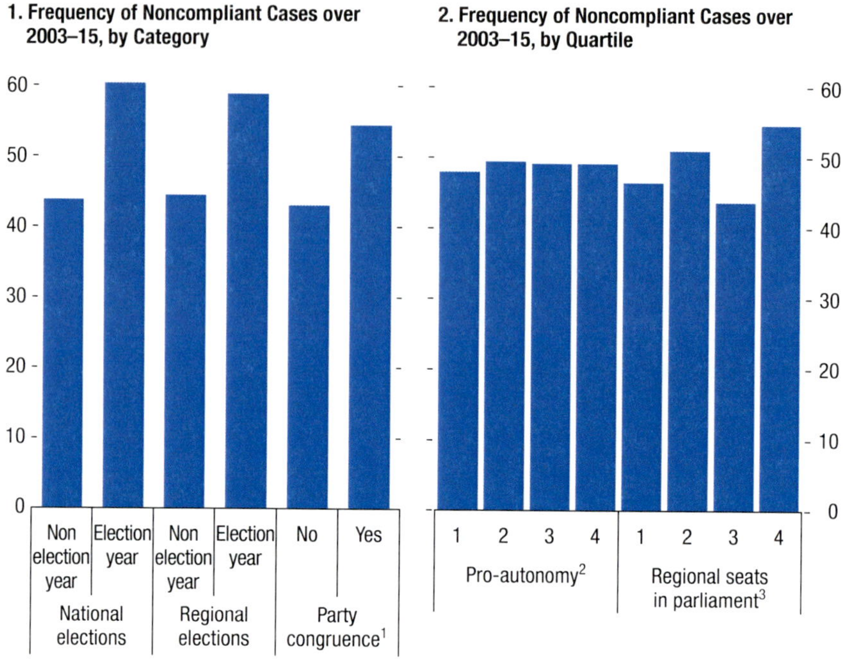

Sources: Ministry of Finance; and authors' calculations.
[1]Regional government led by the same party or by a government coalition leading the central government.
[2]Percentage of members of regional parliaments from regional pro-autonomy parties.
[3]Seats in national parliament (lower house) allocated to each region.

be nearly 1.5 times more likely to deviate from targets than nonaligned regions.[26] The regression results provide only tentative support to these hypotheses: regions aligned with the center presented smaller, albeit statistically insignificant, compliance margins under most specifications (Figure 14.11; Tables 14.2 and 14.3, models 11, 12, and 13). *Pro-autonomy* regions, defined by the percentage of members of parliament from regional pro-autonomy parties—expected to deviate from center-imposed fiscal targets—turned out to be only marginally more likely to deviate from fiscal targets than regions with weaker pro-autonomy preferences, with pro-autonomy regions presenting smaller but statistically insignificant margins under most specifications (Figure 14.11; Tables 14.2 and 14.3,

[26]As discussed in the section titled "Testable Hypotheses," this may be the result of the CG following a "safe" electoral strategy. Simon-Cosano, Lago-Peñas, and Vaquero (2012) show that strategy to be preferred by national incumbents running in national elections, as reflected in the distribution of transfers to regions where the incumbent performs better.

models 11, 12, and 13). Last, regions with the largest *political representation in the national parliament* are the most frequent noncompliers, albeit not necessarily with compliance margins that are statistically significantly smaller (Figure 14.11; Tables 14.2 and 14.3, models 11, 12, and 13).

CONCLUSIONS AND POLICY DISCUSSION

This chapter argues that in multilevel governance systems, SNGs tend not to comply voluntarily with fiscal targets the larger are their compliance costs as well as the costs the CG is expected to incur in enforcing these targets. It proposes a conceptual framework in which these costs can be, first, political and thus determined by factors directly undermining CGs' condition to be elected and form stable government coalitions (for example, the national or regional electoral calendar and RGs' political representation, affiliation, and political autonomy preferences). Second, compliance and enforcement costs are also linked to intergovernmental fiscal frameworks—fiscal rules, tax and expenditure assignments, borrowing controls—and, more specifically, to how these arrangements shape perceptions among voters, creditors, and politicians of SNGs' fiscal autonomy and whether they rather than CGs should be held politically accountable for any disruption in regions' fiscal obligations in the event of noncompliance. Lack of fiscal autonomy shifts political accountability to CGs—thereby raising enforcement costs—while stronger rules and access to financial markets tip the political barometer toward RGs—thereby raising noncompliance costs.

In this chapter's framework, involuntary fiscal noncompliance occurs when SNGs are unable to be fiscally compliant even when they are willing to be. This pattern becomes more likely in times of fiscal stress, defined as periods with large negative fiscal shocks. Fiscal stress times are also periods of increasing domestic or supranational political pressure on CGs to ensure that fiscal consolidation targets at the general government level are met. To minimize the political costs such pressures entail, CGs tend to "pass the buck" of the adjustment down to RGs. This leads to ambitious but feasible center-imposed SNG fiscal targets that become infeasible once the fiscal shock materializes.

Applied to Spain's regions, this conceptual framework shows that fiscal noncompliance displays involuntary traits. We find fiscal noncompliance to be driven by factors partly outside the control of Spanish regions, namely common macroeconomic shocks and large adjustment efforts. The latter is arguably attributable to ambitious and rigid fiscal targets set by the center as a result of national and supranational pressures for general government consolidation referred to above.

Fiscal noncompliance among Spain's regions has also been shown to have a voluntary dimension, with fiscal rather than political arrangements playing a somewhat more prominent role. Fiscal deficit targets were missed more frequently and by wider margins the lower a region's autonomy to cut spending due to expenditure mandates and the larger the gap between the resources they can raise to deliver these mandates and their actual costs (that is, the larger VFIs are). Contrary to expectations, stronger and well-enforced fiscal rules have not made fiscal compliance more frequent or compliance margins wider. The analysis has also identified some tentative support for the disciplinary role of financial markets, with increases in regions' market-financing costs reducing fiscal noncompliance margins. The frequency and margins of fiscal noncompliance have also been shown to increase during election years. Other political factors expected to induce voluntary fiscal noncompliance, such as political autonomy preferences, political alignment with the center, and political representation, demonstrate ambiguous or nonsignificant regression estimates.

The main policy lesson in this analysis is that enhancing fiscal compliance in multilevel governance systems requires a more comprehensive assessment of intergovernmental fiscal arrangements that goes beyond strengthening formal rules-monitoring and enforcement procedures. This assessment should include not only rules-based fiscal frameworks but also (1) the assignment of revenue-raising and spending mandates and (2) the burden-sharing of fiscal consolidation efforts and related setting of fiscal deficit targets. All that should be accompanied by a focus on making CG enforcement politically credible. In particular,

- *Rules-based frameworks.* To strengthen fiscal compliance at the national level, much emphasis has been placed on the need to bolster rules-based fiscal frameworks with formal enforcement procedures such as financial and administrative sanctions and automatic mechanisms that correct for past deviations from fiscal targets (Schaechter and others 2012). That has been the case in Spain, particularly after the most recent reforms, which, as discussed, introduced some of these procedures aimed at tackling regional fiscal noncompliance. Looking ahead, there is still some scope to further strengthen existing procedures by making their activation more automatic and by tightening the legal requirements to publicly explain deviations from fiscal targets (Lledó 2015). Such measures may come in particularly handy during election years when the political costs for the CG to enforce targets are more salient and noncompliance has been shown to be more pervasive than in nonelection years.
- *Intergovernmental fiscal responsibilities.* In line with previous work looking at the effectiveness of subnational fiscal rules (Kotia and Lledó 2016), this analysis stresses the need to revisit, and possibly reduce, existing VFIs by ensuring SNGs' revenue-raising and borrowing mandates are consistent with their spending mandates. These measures would help strengthen SNG fiscal autonomy and policy accountability, including for fiscal deficit targets. In doing so, it would make CG enforcement of SNG fiscal deficit targets politically less costly and more credible.
- *Fiscal consolidation burden sharing.* The negative impact of increases in fiscal targets on compliance margins warrants a review of how the burden of fiscal consolidation is shared across and within government levels and, correspondingly, how realistically fiscal deficit targets are set. SNG reputational costs for noncompliance with fiscal targets that are widely perceived as infeasible among voters, markets, and politicians are minimal, rendering even well-designed and well-implemented enforcement mechanisms toothless. In the case of Spain, this may call for the adoption of differentiated

fiscal targets across regions to balance adjustment needs with existing fiscal capacity. In light of the impact of negative growth shocks on fiscal compliance, a review is also warranted of how appropriate the technical capacity and procedures behind the formulation of macroeconomic forecasts informing central and subnational budgets and fiscal plans are.

Two additional qualifications are worth mentioning with regard to the normative proposals outlined above that go beyond the scope of this chapter:

- First, while the adoption of differentiated fiscal targets might be efficient when conditioning on a given fiscal starting position (that is, a given level of regional deficit and debt), in a more general, dynamic setting, moral hazard arguments dictate that SNGs may develop incentives not to conduct sound fiscal policies in good times. This might be the case when SNGs anticipate that additional room for fiscal maneuver is to be granted in crisis times to those governments with weaker initial fiscal positions. The strict implementation of fiscal rules is crucial for the development of ex ante fiscal margins against adverse shocks, and to guarantee that the heterogeneity of structural fiscal positions among regions in normal times is minimized.
- Second, international experience shows that the occurrence of subnational fiscal crises cannot be ruled out, even in a setting in which national fiscal rules are fully credible and intergovernmental fiscal responsibilities are set at an optimal level. In the latter regard, the recent Spanish experience indicates that granting to regions additional instruments to prevent liquidity crises is warranted, so that pressure on the CG to financially support or bail out SNGs is reduced. In particular, the possibility of designing rainy day funds with regular contributions during periods of economic prosperity could be studied, along with the development of tools that guarantee the regular access of regions to financial markets even in periods of fiscal stress (Delgado-Téllez, González, and Pérez 2016).

ANNEX 14.1. VARIABLES USED IN THE EMPIRICAL ANALYSIS

Annex Table 14.1.1. Variables Used in the Empirical Analysis

Variable	Description	Source
Fiscal Noncompliance Margin (official assessment)	Difference between fiscal deficit targets and outcomes in percent of national GDP between 2003 and 2007, and in percent of regional GDP from 2008 to 2015	Ministry of Finance
Fiscal Noncompliance Margin (homogeneous assessment)	Difference between fiscal deficit targets (homogeneous assessement) and outcomes in percent of regional GDP	Authors' calculation
Fiscal Deficit Targets (homogeneous assessment)	Equal to Fiscal deficit targets (official assessment) × Nominal GDP (CG budget)/Regional GDP between 2003 and 2007, and to fiscal deficit target (official assessement) from 2008 to 2015	Ministry of Finance (nominal and regional GDP); and authors' calculation

(continued)

Annex Table 14.1.1. Variables Used in the Empirical Analysis *(continued)*

Variable	Description	Source
Growth Forecast Errors	Real GDP Growth Outturn – Real GDP Forecast	National Institute of Statistics (outturn), Ministry of Finance (forecast)
Regional-National Growth Differential	Regional GDP Growth – National GDP Growth	National Institute of Statistics
Regional-National Inflation Differential	Percent Change in Regional CPI Growth – Percent Change in National CPI	National Institute of Statistics
Fiscal Target Adjustment	Difference between fiscal deficit target (homogeneous assessement) in the current and previous year	Authors' calculation
Execution Minus Budgetary Transfers (in regional GDP)	Transfers from CG (outturns) – Transfers from CG (budget)	Ministry of Finance and National Institute of Statistics
Regional Weight in National Population	Ratio of regional to national population	National Institute of Statistics
Regional Weight in National GDP	Ratio of regional to national GDP	National Institute of Statistics
Regional Weight in National per Capita GDP	Ratio of regional to national per capita GDP	National Institute of Statistics
Tax Autonomy	Ratio of regional own revenues (regulatory power) to total regional revenues	Ministry of Finance; authors' calculation
Social Spending Share in Regional Government Spending	Ratio of regional spending in basic social services (health, education, and others) to total regional spending	Instituto Valenciano de Investigaciones Economicas and Ministry of Finance
Investment Share in Total Regional Spending	Ratio of regional investment to total regional spending	Ministry of Finance
Vertical Fiscal Imbalances	[1 – Regional Own Revenues/Regional Own Spending], where own regional revenue (spending) corresponds to a region's total revenue (spending) minus transfers received by the CG and other public entitites (transfer paid to the CG and other public entitites)	Authors' calculation
Fiscal Rule Index	Numerical fiscal rule strength index	European Commission
Fiscal Rule Index × Lagged Noncompliance Margin	Interactions between the lag of noncompliance margin and the fiscal rule index	Authors' calculation
Region Ratings	Average rating numerical index, taking into account three rating agencies: Fitch, S&P, and Moody's	Authors' calculation using Fitch, S&P, and Moody's databases
Implicit Interest Rates	Regional interest payments in percent of end-of-year regional public debt stock	Ministry of Finance
Ratio of Security to Loans	Ratio of total outstanding government securities issued by the regions to outstanding loans from commercial banks	Bank of Spain
National Election Dummy	Dummy that equals 1 for the year of national parliament elections	Web pages of the national and regional parliaments
Regional Election Dummy	Dummy that equals 1 for the year of regional parliament elections	Web pages of the national and regional parliaments
Party Congruence Dummy	Dummy that equals 1 if regional and national government are led by the same party or party coalition	Web pages of the national and regional parliaments
Proautonomy Party Share	Percent of members of regional parliaments from regional pro-autonomy parties	Web pages of the national and regional parliaments
Regions' Seats in National Parliament	Share of members of the national parliament elected in each region	Web pages of the national and regional parliaments

Source: Authors.

Note: CG = central government; CPI = consumer price index.

REFERENCES

Argimón, I., and P. Hernández de Cos. 2012. "Fiscal Rules and Federalism as Determinants of Budget Performance: An Empirical Investigation for the Spanish Case." *Public Finance Review* 40 (1): 30–65.

Auerbach, A. 1999. "On the Performance and Use of Government Revenue Forecasts." *National Tax Journal* 52 (4): 765–82.

Autoridad Independiente de Responsabilidad Fiscal (AIReF). 2016. "Informe sobre los presupuestos iniciales de las administraciones públicas para 2016," April.

Beetsma, R., B. Bluhm, M. Giuliodori, and P. Wierts. 2013. "From Budgetary Forecasts to Ex-Post Fiscal Data: Exploring the Evolution of Fiscal Forecast Errors in the EU." *Contemporary Economic Policy* 31 (4): 795–813.

Beetsma, R., M. Giuliodori, and P. Wierts. 2009. "Planning to Cheat: EU Fiscal Policy in Real Time." *Economic Policy* 24 (October): 753–804.

Bolton, P., and G. Roland. 1997. "The Breakup of Nations." *Quarterly Journal of Economics* 11 (4): 1057–89.

Bordignon, M. 2006. '"Fiscal Decentralization: How to Harden the Budget Constraint." In *Fiscal Policy Surveillance in Europe*, edited by P. Wierts, S. Deroose, E. Flores, and A. Turini. Basingstoke, U.K.: Palgrave Macmillan.

Bruck, T., and A. Stephan. 2006. "Do Eurozone Countries Cheat with Their Budget Deficit Forecasts?" *Kyklos* 59 (1): 3–15.

Canuto, O., and L. Liu, eds. 2013. *Until Debt Do Us Part: Subnational Debt, Insolvency, and Markets*. Washington, DC: World Bank.

Cordes, T., T. Kinda, P. Muthoora, and A. Weber. 2015. "Expenditure Rules: Effective Tools for Sound Fiscal Policy." Working Paper 15/2, International Monetary Fund, Washington, DC.

Cox, G., and M. McCubbins. 1986. "Electoral Politics as a Redistributive Game." *Journal of Politics* 48 (2): 370–89.

Crivelli, E., and K. Staal. 2013. "Size, Spillovers, and Soft Budget Constraints." *International Tax and Public Finance* 20 (2): 338–56.

Delgado-Téllez, M., C. I. González, and J. J. Pérez. 2016. "Regional Government Access to Market Funding: International Experience and Recent Developments." *Economic Bulletin* [Bank of Spain] (February): 3–13.

Dixit, A. K., and L. Londregan. 1996. "The Determinant of Success of Special Interests in Redistributive Politics." *Journal of Politics* 58 (4): 1132–55.

European System of Accounts: ESA. 2010. Euroopean Comission: Luxembourg. http://ec.europa.eu/eurostat/cache/metadata/Annexes/nasa_10_f_esms_an1.pdf.

Eyraud, L., and L. Lusinyan, 2013. "Vertical Fiscal Imbalances and Fiscal Performance in Advanced Economies." *Journal of Monetary Economics* 60: 571–87.

Foremny, D. 2014. "Subnational Deficits in European Countries: The Impact of Fiscal Rules and Tax Autonomy." *European Journal of Political Economy* 34 (June): 86–110.

Frankel, J., and J. Schreger. 2013. "Over-Optimistic Official Forecasts and Fiscal Rules in the Eurozone." *Review of World Economics* 149 (2): 247–72.

Grossman, P. 1994. "A Political Economy of Intergovernmental Grants." *Public Choice* 78 (3–4): 295–303.

Hansen, L. 1982. "Large Sample Properties of Generalized Method of Moments Estimators." *Econometrica* 50 (4): 1029–54.

Hernández de Cos, P., and J. Pérez. 2013. "Sub-National Public Debt in Spain: Political Economy Issues and the Role of Fiscal Rules and Decentralization." In *Fiscal Relations across Government Levels in Times of Crisis—Making Compatible Fiscal Decentralization and Budgetary Discipline*, edited by European Commission, 186–216. European Commission Economics Papers 501, European Commission, Brussels.

Inman, R. 2003. "Transfers and Bailouts: Enforcing Local Fiscal Discipline with Lessons from U.S. Federalism." In *Fiscal Decentralization and the Challenge of Hard Budget Constraints*, edited by J. Rodden, G. Eskelund, and J. Litvack, 35–83. Cambridge, MA: MIT Press.

International Monetary Fund (IMF). 2015. "Crisis Program Review." Policy Paper, IMF, Washington, DC, November 9.

Jonung, L., and M. Larch. 2006. "Improving Fiscal Policy in the EU: The Case for Independent Forecasts." *Economic Policy* 21 (47): 491–534.

Kotia, A., and V. Lledó. 2016. "Do Subnational Fiscal Rules Foster Fiscal Discipline? New Evidence from Europe." Working Paper 16/84, IMF, Washington, DC.

Lago Peñas, S., X. Fernández-Leiceaga, and A. Vaquero. 2016. "¿Por qué incumplen fiscalmente las CCAA?," FUNCAS, Documento de Trabajo No. 784/2016, Madrid, Spain.

Leal, M. A., and J. López Laborda. 2015. "Un estudio de los factores determinantes de las desviaciones presupuestarias de las comunidades autónomas en el periodo 2003–2012." *Investigaciones Regionales* 31: 35–58.

Leal, T., and J. J. Pérez. 2011. "Análisis de las desviaciones presupuestarias aplicado al caso del presupuesto del estado." *Estudios de Economía Aplicada* 29: 909–32.

Leal, T., M. Tujula, and J.-P. Vidal. 2008. "Fiscal Forecasting: Lessons from the Literature and Challenges." *Fiscal Studies* 29 (3): 347–86.

Leite-Monteiro, M., and M. Sato. 2003. "Economic Integration and Fiscal Devolution." *Journal of Public Economics* 87 (11): 2507–25.

Lledó, V. 2015. "Coordinating Fiscal Consolidation in Spain: Progress, Challenges, and Prospects." In *Spain Selected Issues,* IMF Country Report 15/233, IMF, Washington, DC.

Molina-Parra, A., and D. Martínez-López. 2015. "Do Federal Deficits Motivate Regional Fiscal (Im)balances? Evidence from the Spanish Case." GEN Working Paper A 2015-3, University of Vigo, Santiago de Compostela, Spain.

Pérez, J. J., and R. Prieto. 2015. "Risk Factors and the Maturity of Subnational Debt: An Empirical Investigation for the Case of Spain." *Public Finance Review* 43 (6): 786–815.

Pérez García, F., V. Cucarella, and L. Hérnandez. 2015. "Servicios Públicos, Diferencias Territoriales e Igualdad de Oportunidades." Fundación BBVA, Bilbao.

Porto, A., and P. Sanguinetti. 2001. "Political Determinants of Intergovernmental Grants: Evidence from Argentina." *Economics and Politics* 13 (3): 237–56.

Reuter, W. 2015. "National Numerical Fiscal Rules: Not Complied with, but Still Effective?" *European Journal of Political Economy* 39 (September): 67–81.

Rodden, J., G. Eskelund, and J. Litvack. 2003. "Introduction and Overview." In *Fiscal Decentralization and the Challenge of Hard Budget Constraints,* edited by J. Rodden, G. Eskelund, and J. Litvack, 1–31. Cambridge, MA: MIT Press.

Sato, M. 2007. "The Political Economy of Interregional Grants." In *Intergovernmental Fiscal Transfers: Principles and Practice,* edited by R. Boadway and A. Shah, 173–201. Washington, DC: World Bank.

Schaechter, A., T. Kinda, N. Budina, and A. Weber. 2012. "Fiscal Rules in Response to the Crisis—Toward the 'Next-Generation' Rules. A New Dataset." Working Paper 12/187, IMF, Washington, DC.

Simon-Cosano, P., S. Lago-Peñas, and A. Vaquero. 2012. "On the Political Determinants of Intergovernmental Grants in Decentralized Countries: The Case of Spain." Working Paper 1230, International Center for Public Policy, Georgia State University, Atlanta.

Strauch, R. M., and J. von Hagen. 2009. "How Forms of Fiscal Governance Affect Fiscal Performance." In *Fiscal Governance in Europe,* edited by M. Hallerberg, S. Rolf, and J. von Hagen. Cambridge, U.K.: Cambridge University Press.

Ter-Minassian, T. 2015. "Promoting Responsible and Sustainable Fiscal Decentralization." In *Handbook of Multi-Level Finance,* edited by E. Ahmad and G. Brosio. Cheltenham, U.K.: Edward Elgar Publishing.

Vammalle, C., D. Allain-Dupre, and N. Gaillard. 2012. "A Sub-Central Government Perspective on Fiscal Policy in a Tight Fiscal Environment." In *Institutional and Financial Relations across Levels of Government, OECD Fiscal Federalism Studies,* edited by J. Kim and C. Vamalle, 17–44. Paris: OECD/Korea Institute of Public Finance.

Vigneault, M. 2007. "Grants and Soft Budget Constraints." In *Intergovernmental Fiscal Transfers: Principles and Practice,* edited by R. Boadway and A. Shah, 133–71. Washington, DC: World Bank.

von Hagen, J. 2005. "Political Economy of Fiscal Institutions." In *Oxford Handbook on Political Economy,* edited by D. A. Barry and R. Weingast, 464–78. Oxford, U.K.: Oxford University Press.

———, and B. Eichengreen. 1996. "Federalism, Fiscal Restraints, and European Monetary Union." *American Economic Review* 86 (2): 134–38.

Wildasin, D. 1997. "Externalities and Bailouts: Hard and Soft Budget Constraints in Intergovernmental Fiscal Relations." Policy Research Working Paper 1843, World Bank, Washington, DC.

CHAPTER 15

Budget Institutions in Low-Income Countries

SANJEEV GUPTA, SAMI YLÄOUTINEN, BRIAN OLDEN, HOLGER VAN EDEN, TERESA CURRISTINE, TOM JOSEPHS, ELIKO PEDASTSAAR, AND JOHANN SEIWALD

INTRODUCTION

All countries need to ensure fiscal credibility and sustainability. This paper presents a framework of budget institutions needed to support countries' fiscal efforts at three key stages of policy making: i) understanding the fiscal outlook and challenges; ii) formulating a credible fiscal strategy; and iii) implementing that strategy.[1,2] The framework underlying the paper has been applied to a wide range of advanced and emerging economies.

The purpose of this paper is to apply the same framework to seven low-income countries to assess the relative strength of their budget institutions and identify priorities for institutional reform. The low-income countries studied are Bolivia, Kenya, Mozambique, Myanmar, Uganda, Vietnam, and Zambia. As the application of the framework requires a deep understanding of a country's budget institutions, it was feasible to extend this analysis to only seven aforementioned countries. The results obtained are then compared with those from the G20 advanced and emerging market countries. This comparison of the weaknesses and strengths of country groups' budget institutions allows a better understanding of where low-income countries lag behind other country groups. The paper further discusses how budget reforms should be sequenced in low-income countries. Since the framework is applied to a small sample of seven low-income countries, the results should be interpreted with caution.

The paper is structured as follows. The second section begins by presenting twelve budget institutions that can support planning and delivery of credible

This chapter is reprinted from *OECD Journal on Budgeting*, Vol. 15, Sanjeev Gupta, Sami Yläoutinen Brian Olden, Holger van Eden, Teresa Curristine, Tom Josephs, Eliko Pedastsaar, and Johan Seiwald, "Budget Institutions in Low-Income Countries," ©2016, with permission from OECD.

[1] See Olden et al. (2010), IMF (2014).

[2] Budget institutions can be defined in broad terms as the laws, procedures, and conventions that influence budgetary decision-making and governance.

fiscal strategies at three key stages of the fiscal policy-making process. The third section applies the framework to seven low-income countries and compares the status of their budget institutions to the G20 advanced and emerging market countries.[3,4] The fourth section presents recommendations for designing and implementing appropriate reform strategy across countries, particularly in low-income countries. Particular attention is paid to prioritization and sequencing of reform efforts.

BUDGET INSTITUTIONS FOR CREDIBLE FISCAL POLICYMAKING

While many factors affect public finances, there is considerable literature that argues that the strength of budget institutions has a bearing on fiscal outcomes. A positive relationship between the quality of budget institutions and fiscal outcomes has been demonstrated in numerous studies covering different geographical regions and countries with varying political set-ups and income levels (e.g., von Hagen (1992), von Hagen and Harden (1996), Hallerberg et al. (2009), Hallerberg and Yläoutinen (2010) for Europe; Alesina et al. (1999), de Haan et al. (1999), Filc and Scartascini (2007) for Latin America; Gollwitzer (2011), Prakash and Cabezón (2008) for Sub-Saharan heavily indebted countries; and Dabla-Norris et al. (2010) for low-income countries in general). Generally, the empirical evidence emphasizes the key role played by comprehensiveness of the budget, its medium-term orientation and top-down decision-making in the budget processes.

Strong institutions can improve fiscal performance irrespective of country-specific economic and fiscal prospects. They can do this by highlighting the need for sustainable policies, exposing the full cost of public interventions, emphasizing collective responsibility over sectoral interests, and raising the cost of deviating from stated fiscal objectives. The framework lists 12 budgetary institutions and their key design features that can support planning and delivery of credible fiscal strategies at three key stages of the fiscal policy-making process (Box 15.1):[5]

- understanding the fiscal outlook and challenges
- formulating a credible fiscal strategy
- implementing that strategy through the budget process

The institutions included in the framework have been identified on the basis of their ability to support planning and implementing a credible fiscal strategy.

---

[3] Advanced G20 countries are Australia, Canada, France, Germany, Italy, Japan, Korea, United Kingdom, and United States; Emerging Market G20 countries include Argentina, Brazil, China, India, Indonesia, Mexico, Russia, South Africa, Saudi Arabia, and Turkey.

[4] Since the purpose is to provide a general overview of budget institutions in the three country groups, country-specific scores are not presented.

[5] For a more detailed discussion, see Olden (2012).

BOX 15.1 Twelve Budget Institutions

A. Understanding the Fiscal Outlook and Challenges
- Fiscal Reporting
- Macroeconomic and Fiscal Forecasting
- Fiscal Risk Management
- Independent Fiscal Agency

B. Formulating a Credible Fiscal Strategy
- Fiscal Objectives and Rules
- Medium-Term Budget Framework
- Performance Orientation
- Intergovernmental Fiscal Arrangements

C. Implementing the Fiscal Strategy
- Budget Unity
- Top-Down Budgeting
- Parliamentary Budget Approval
- Budget Execution

Source: IMF 2014.

However, while this framework allows one to analyze shortcomings and related reform needs in countries' fiscal frameworks, it should not be viewed as a generic guide to budget institution reforms. When applying this approach to low-income countries, attention has to be paid to starting conditions and sequencing of reforms, which depend on country-specific circumstances, including on their capacity to implement them. These issues are taken up in the final section.

Understanding the Fiscal Outlook and Challenges

A clear understanding of the current fiscal position and a realistic view of the medium-term fiscal outlook facilitates a formulation of appropriate fiscal policies. Government's decision on a fiscal stance depends crucially on the view of the economic outlook, and the more accurate economic forecasts are, the more informed the budget decisions will be. Full awareness of the current state and future evolution of the public finances is particularly important in the face of uncertain macroeconomic and fiscal outlook. In this context, the following institutions are important:

- *Fiscal reporting* that provides comprehensive, timely, credible, and transparent information is central to inform decision makers and the public about the state and outlook of the economy. Good practice requires fiscal reporting to be comprehensive and accurate, and include financial statements audited by an independent audit institution and fiscal statistics produced by an independent statistics agency.

- *Macroeconomic and fiscal forecasting* that is realistic and credible. In ideal circumstances, macro-fiscal forecasts have a multi-year focus, updated on a frequent basis and cover all fiscal aggregates together with a range of realistic economic assumptions.
- *Disclosure and effective management of fiscal risks* allow a government to deal with situations that threaten its fiscal position. This means main fiscal risks (macro-fiscal, guarantees, international commitments, social commitments, public-private partnerships, and legal claims) are disclosed in budget documents together with alternative medium-term budget scenarios. Similarly, new risks (contingent liabilities in particular) are subjected to scrutiny and approval as regular budget appropriations. This is particularly important during times of fiscal stress when the temptation to circumvent expenditure restrictions by resorting to guarantees and other contingent liabilities could become stronger.
- *Independent fiscal agencies* with a clear mandate can help to support the overall credibility of a government's fiscal strategy by assessing the integrity of the forecasts and the government's fiscal performance on a regular basis.

Formulating a Credible Fiscal Strategy

Addressing the fiscal challenges identified in fiscal reports and forecasts requires the formulation of a sound and comprehensive medium-term fiscal strategy. The credibility of that strategy depends in part upon the institutional arrangements which support it. The following four budget institutions are important in this regard:

- *Fiscal objectives and rules.* Comprehensive, transparent and stable fiscal objectives connect the medium-term fiscal strategy with numerical targets that will guide future decisions and against which performance can be monitored. Some flexibility, either by accounting for the cycle or by including explicit escape clauses, can enhance the credibility of fiscal rules.
- *Medium-term budget frameworks* are crucial to convert those targets into detailed and documented revenue and expenditure plans. Successful medium-term budget frameworks provide binding restrictions on multi-year expenditure and a clear and consistent statement of the government's medium-term priorities within a total expenditure ceiling. Such frameworks should cover most central government expenditure.
- *Performance-oriented budgeting* provides decision makers with information on how the budget contributes to the government's overall policies. Regular spending reviews can help to provide a strong evidence base for expenditure rationalization.
- *Intergovernmental fiscal arrangements* ensure the consistency of the fiscal stance within the different levels of government and allow coordinating and burden sharing of fiscal policy and spending between layers of government.

Implementing the Fiscal Strategy

Even the most robust consolidation plan can be derailed when confronted with the pressures and realities of the annual budget process. Unless supported by strong institutional arrangements for the preparation, approval, and execution of the annual budget, there is a risk that actual expenditure will turn out to be higher than forecast, or actual revenue lower than forecast. Four institutions are central in this regard:

- *Budget unity* ensures that central government expenditures are authorized under one decision-making process, which consequently makes the control over budget execution more effective. Most central government expenditure should be covered by the central government budget and authorized annually. Also major tax expenditures should be quantified and published.
- *A top-down approach to budget preparation* imposes limits on both aggregate and sectoral spending agreed by the government at an early stage in the budget preparation process. This approach increases the likelihood that the outcome of the annual budget discussions will be consistent with the government's *ex ante* fiscal objectives and fiscal plan. This is facilitated by limited earmarking of revenue and by ensuring that all major revenue and expenditure decisions are taken as a part of the annual budget process.
- *Constraints on parliamentary budget approval.* While parliament's formal powers over the allocation of public resources vary greatly across countries, experience suggests that pre-budget or budget orientation debates can help create parliamentary ownership of medium-term fiscal objectives in a range of legislative contexts. The political legitimacy of the overall fiscal strategy is further enhanced when parliament endorses the government's medium-term fiscal objectives before considering the government's annual budget proposal. However, greater parliamentary input into the overall fiscal strategy needs to be combined with legislative procedures that promote collective responsibility for its delivery. As in the cabinet, voting on the budget in parliament needs to follow a top-down sequence in which the legislature first approves the main fiscal aggregates, such as the budget balance, total expenditure, and total revenue, before voting the allocation of resources to different sectors, ministries, programs, or line items.
- *Discipline in budget execution* that maintains overall fiscal discipline, while recognizing that unexpected events will occur during the course of the budget year. Open-ended or standing appropriations need to be kept to a minimum. Overspending against budget totals should require the government to introduce a supplementary budget and, ideally, propose offsetting expenditure cuts.[6] Carry-over of expenditure—enabling budget agencies to exceed annual appropriations—should also be subject to restrictions. To avoid future expenditure room being taken up by binding contracts or future promises, controls on multi-annual commitments should also be in place.

[6] Also virements can be used to make in-year adjustments in budget appropriations.

EVALUATION OF BUDGET INSTITUTIONS

This section discusses the extent to which the above-noted 12 budget institutions are in place in seven low-income countries. In this regard, we transform the institutional features of countries' fiscal frameworks into a set of ratings (see Box 15.2). As the purpose is to provide a general overview of budget institutions in the three country groups, country-specific ratings are not reported in the paper.[7] In this context, a few caveats are worth mentioning:

- The analysis presents only a snapshot of the state of countries' current budget institutions. Many countries under review are engaged in ambitious reform agendas to strengthen their frameworks. Due to the static nature of the analysis, the discussion does not do justice to these efforts.
- Each institution included in the framework is assigned the same weight. A case could be made that not all institutions are equally important, particularly from a country-specific point of view. While this is justified, the approach is meant to keep the framework as transparent and simple as possible.
- Finally, as noted above, the sample of countries under review is small. While the discussion below gives a good overview on the state of these countries' budget institutions, the results are not necessarily representative of all low-income countries.

BOX 15.2 Methodology for the Evaluation of Budget Institutions

The 12 budget institutions and their key features described in the previous section are used to evaluate the institutional strength of each country in the sample. Each key feature is translated into a specific evaluation question. The number of questions by institution varies from three to six, and the assessment consists of 52 questions in total. The questions have been formulated in such a way that they are factually verifiable. A country is given a rating of 0 if the criterion is not met; 1 if the criterion is partly met; and 2 if the criterion is fully met. The evaluation questions and basis for each rating are set out in IMF (2014). For every country, the ratings against each question are averaged to produce an overall score of the strength of each of the 12 institutions. Each of the 12 institutions has the same weight in these averages, regardless of the number of questions used to rate the institution.

[7] The ratings are derived from detailed assessments by experts deeply familiar with the institutional setup in these countries.

Figure 15.1. Average Scores by Institutions

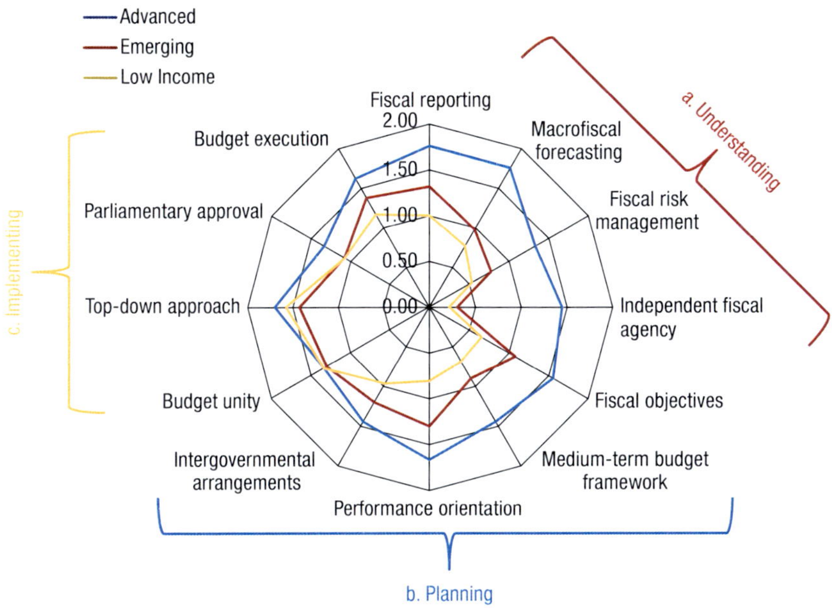

Source: Authors' calculations.

Based on the institutional scores, the following general observations can be made (see Figures 15.1 and 15.2):

- As one might expect, the budget institution scores are lower in low-income countries, compared to emerging market and advanced countries. This applies particularly to the understanding and planning stages, where the largest institutional gaps for low-income countries seem to be.[8]
- There seems to be a link between strength of institutions and economic development; institutional scores and GDP per capita broadly speaking move together in the country sample.[9]
- Low-income countries score, on average, the lowest among country groups in all categories except three, namely top-down budgeting (slightly higher than emerging), parliamentary approval (tied with emerging) and budget unity (tied with advanced), whereas advanced countries score, on average, higher than others in all other categories.

[8] This should not be interpreted to say that low-income countries have no weaknesses in budget execution. For example, Andrews (2013), based on PEFA scores, found developing countries had the weakest scores in budget execution among different stages of the budget process.

[9] Also, the recent crisis has played an important role in incentivizing the advanced countries to carry out institutional reforms. Reforms have been implemented at a rapid pace in advanced Europe in light of the need for fiscal consolidation in the aftermath of the financial crisis, contributing to a growing gap in institutional strength between advanced and emerging G20 countries (see IMF 2014).

Figure 15.2. Range of Scores by Institution

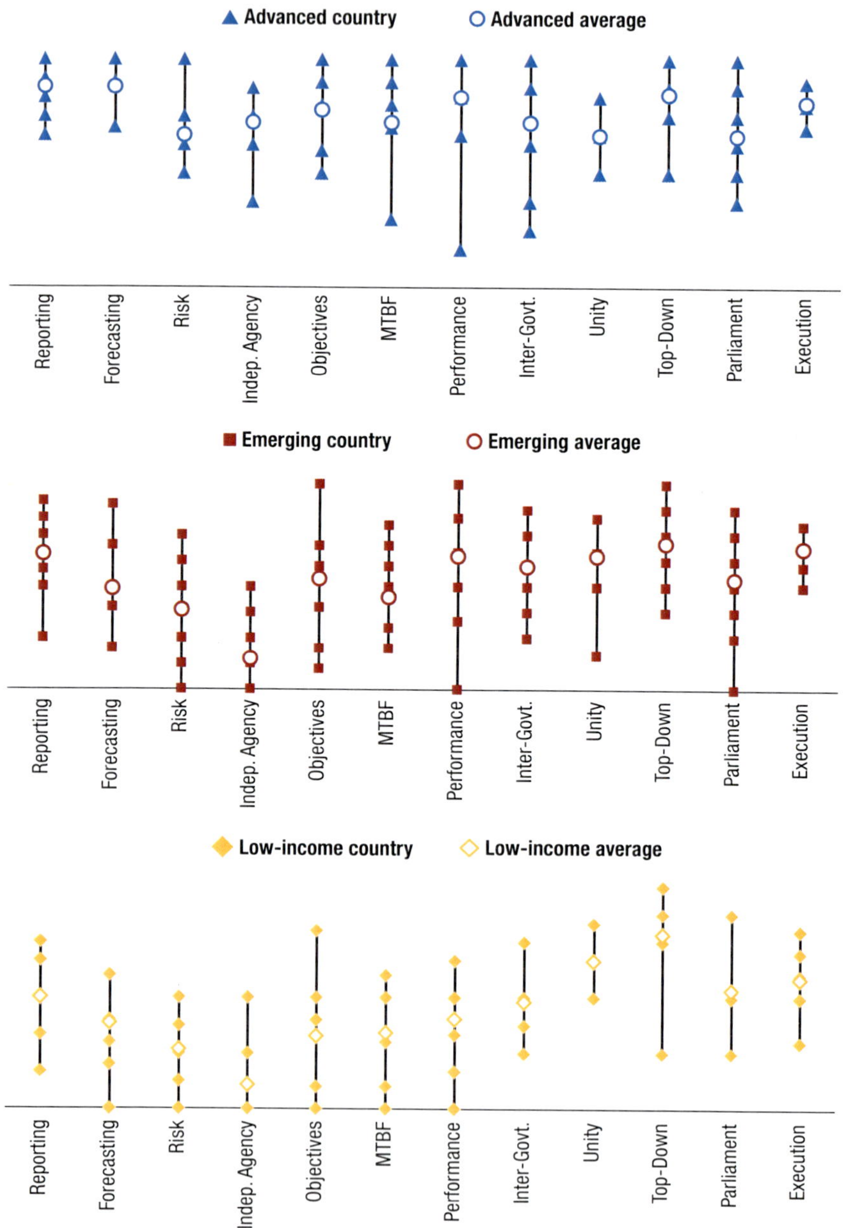

Source: Authors' calculations.

- The variance of scores by institution is generally speaking larger for low-income and emerging market countries, compared to advanced countries, indicating large differences between and among countries.[10] Particularly for the understanding and planning stages, many low-income countries scored zero on a number of individual institutions, indicating that these countries do not have basic arrangements in place.

Understanding the Fiscal Outlook and Challenges

Most low-income countries in the sample seem to have basic fiscal reporting practices in place which should give them reasonable information about the present financial position. However, arrangements concerning forecasting future fiscal developments and related risks are less robust. These are the areas where the gaps in the G20 advanced countries are also most pronounced (see Figure 15.3):

- *Fiscal Reporting*: All sample low-income countries produce financial statements which cover at least the budget, and in most countries financial statements are audited by an external auditor. Most countries produce a balance sheet, but generally speaking without including all assets and liabilities. About half of the countries produce financial statistics for central and general government but generally not for the whole of the public sector. In almost all countries financial statistics are produced by an independent office but generally not in line with international standards.
- *Macroeconomic and Fiscal Forecasting*: About half of the sample low-income countries publish medium-term forecasts in the budget documents with related assumptions but generally speaking without any quality control through ex post comparison of previous forecasts with actual outturn of key macroeconomic and fiscal aggregates. Also an update half-way through the budget year, with updated projections of key fiscal variables is missing in almost all countries. Long-term fiscal projections are also a rarity.
- *Fiscal Risk Management*: Main fiscal risks (macro-fiscal, guarantees, international commitments, social commitments, PPPs, legal claims) are not discussed nor quantified in the budget documents. Also alternative medium-term budget scenarios are not produced. In a majority of the countries, the government prepares a medium-term debt management strategy, including analysis of debt-related risks, but without including asset-related risks (for example, changes in the asset values or cash-flow they provide). In almost all countries, parliamentary approval is sought for new guarantees and in very few, for other significant contingent liabilities.
- *Independent Fiscal Agency:* With some exceptions, countries do not have independent agencies to assess the credibility of the forecasts and the government's fiscal performance on a regular basis.

[10] Here one should note that the sample sizes are different between the country groups: low-income countries (7), emerging market (10), and advanced countries (9).

Figure 15.3. Understanding the Fiscal Outlook and Challenges

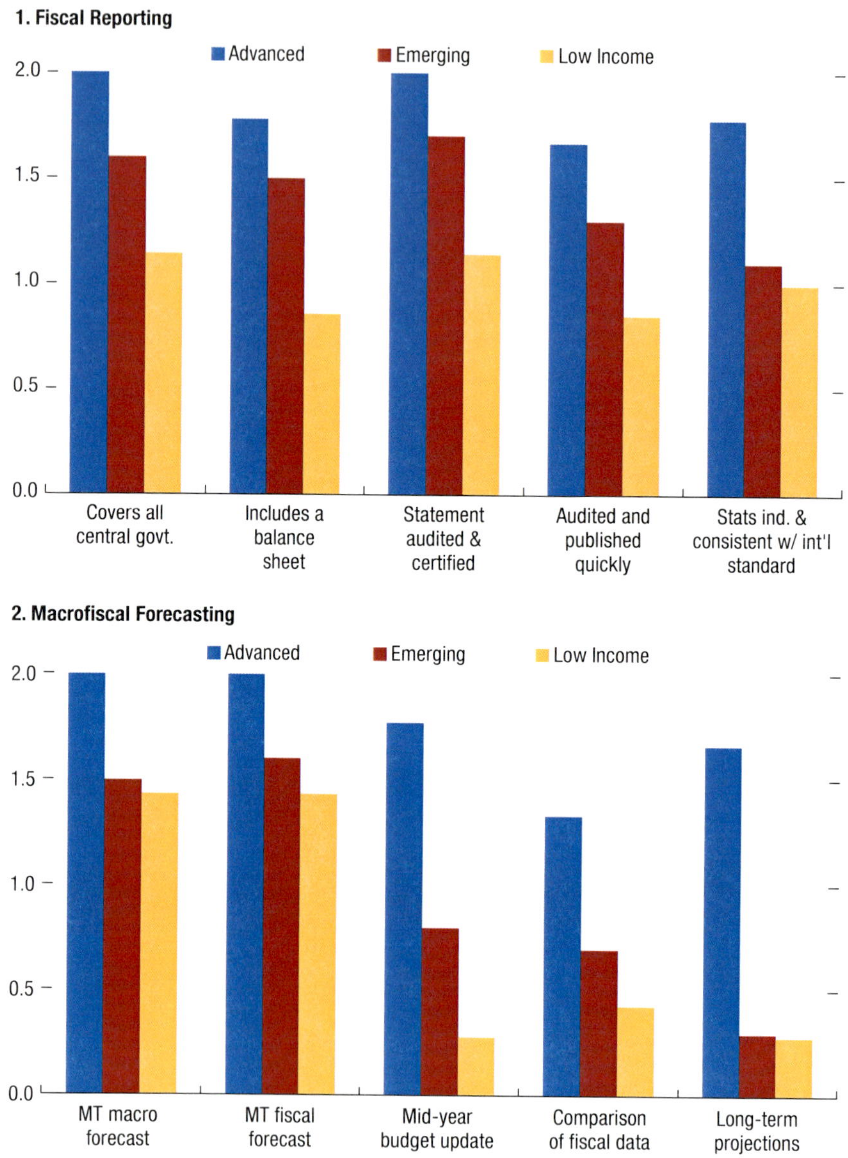

Source: Authors' calculations.

Figure 15.3. Understanding the Fiscal Outlook and Challenges *(continued)*

3. Fiscal Risk Management

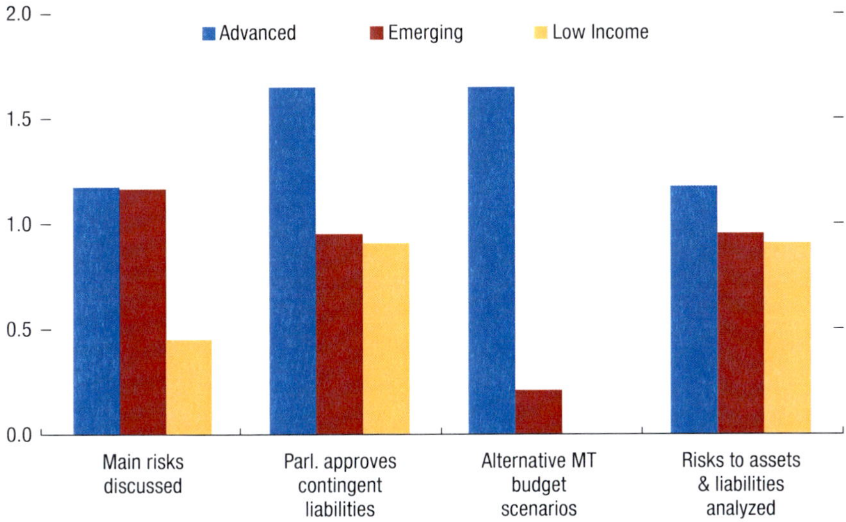

4. Independent Fiscal Agency

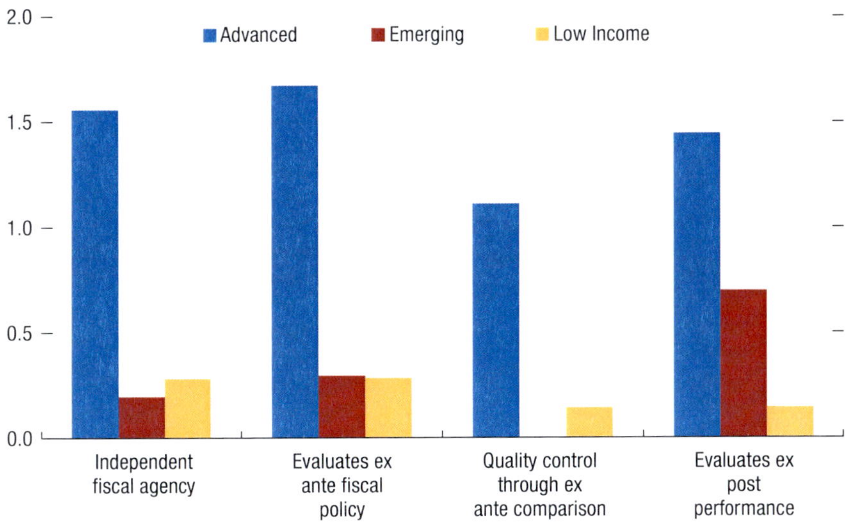

Source: Authors' calculations.

Developing a Credible Fiscal Strategy

Many institutions related to formulation of a fiscal strategy are relatively underdeveloped. Most countries in the sample have taken first steps in introducing some medium-term elements in their fiscal management but many challenges remain to be addressed; fiscal objectives and medium-term budget frameworks receive the lowest scores on average among the low-income countries. Also performance orientation is still at its infancy. Finally, intergovernmental financial arrangements are not clearly specified in many countries (see Figure 15.4).

- *Fiscal Objectives and Rules:* About half of the sample countries have specified some type of medium-term fiscal objective and regularly report performance against the stated objective. In very few countries, the objective has been enshrined in the law, and in almost all countries, exceptions to the rule are frequent. Fiscal objectives do not accommodate the impact of the business cycle.
- *Medium-term Budget Framework*: About half of the sample countries have some type of multi-year estimates for major categories of revenue and expenditure but they constitute only a non-binding restriction to future budgets. No reconciliation of changes in sectoral allocations from year to year is currently produced. Furthermore, budget documents do not present any consolidated summary of the fiscal impact of proposed new revenue and expenditure measures.
- *Performance Orientation:* About half of the sample countries include a program classification for information, and only very few of these form the basis for legislative appropriation. Many countries have established some type of performance targets or objectives but typically these are not systematically monitored. Comprehensive and systematic expenditure reviews are rare among the countries in the sample.
- *Intergovernmental Fiscal Arrangements:* About half of the sample countries produce a year-ahead or a medium-term forecast of the budget for the central or federal government but it is typically not broken down into the respective contribution of individual sectors/level of government (budget, social security funds, extra-budgetary funds, local government and state-owned enterprises). A majority of the sample countries have fiscal rules for sub-national governments in place but without centralized sanctions or enforcement mechanisms. Again, about half of the countries have a legal framework for coordinating and sharing the burden of fiscal policy between layers of government.

Implementing the Fiscal Strategy

Institutions related to implementing the fiscal strategy emerge as the strongest among the three key stages of the fiscal policy-making process included in the framework. Gaps in relation to the advanced G20 countries still persist

Figure 15.4. Formulating a Credible Fiscal Strategy

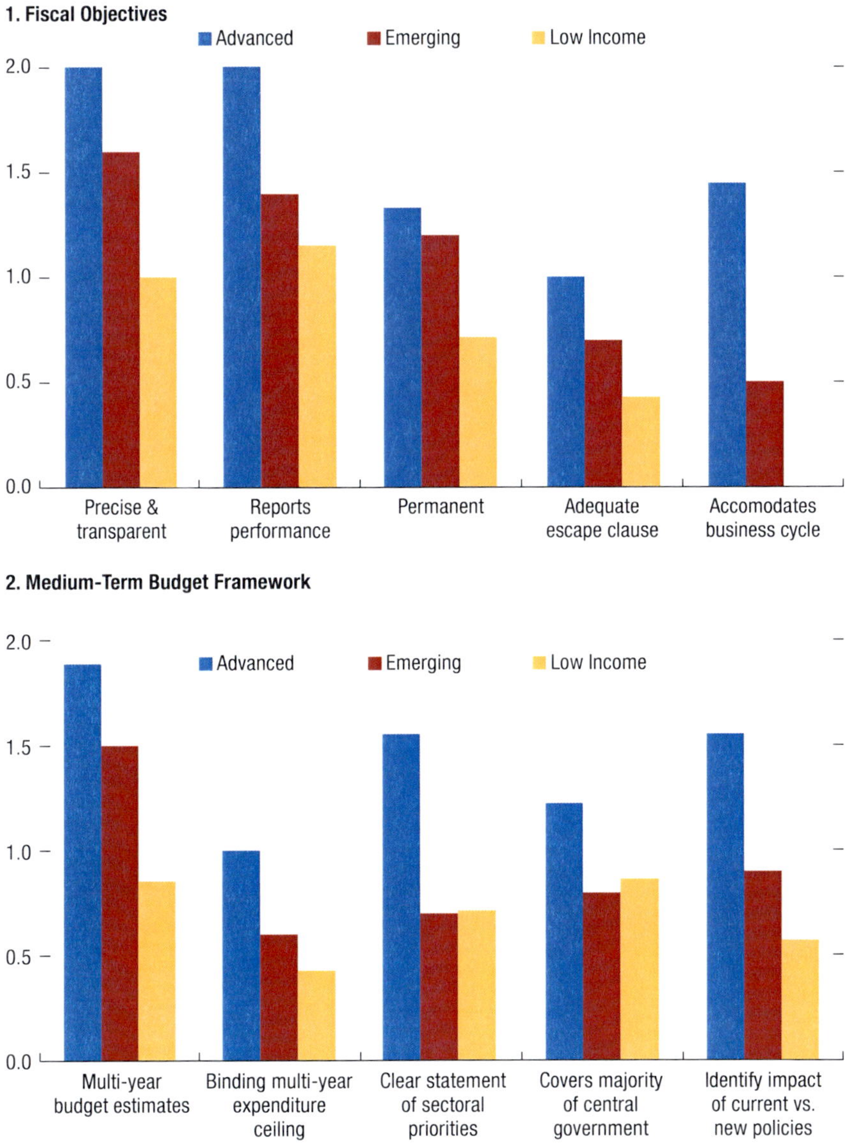

Source: Authors' calculations.

Figure 15.4. Formulating a Credible Fiscal Strategy *(continued)*

3. Performance Orientation

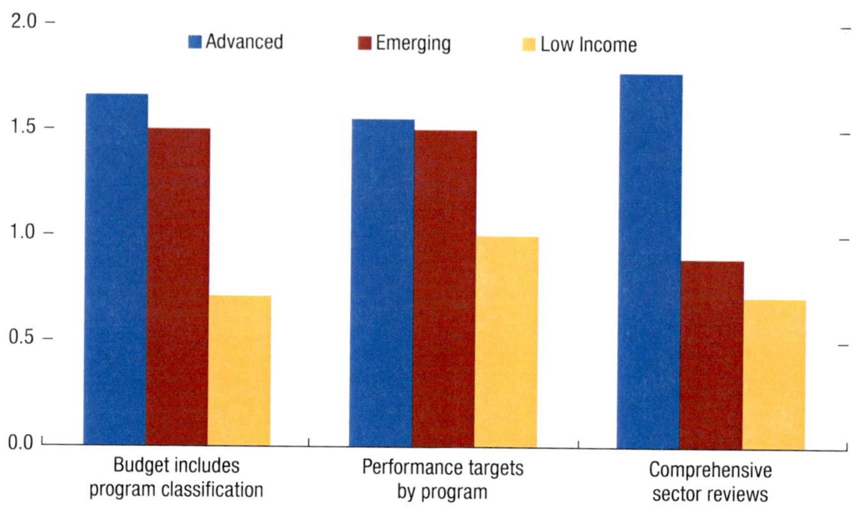

4. Intergovernmental Financial Arrangements

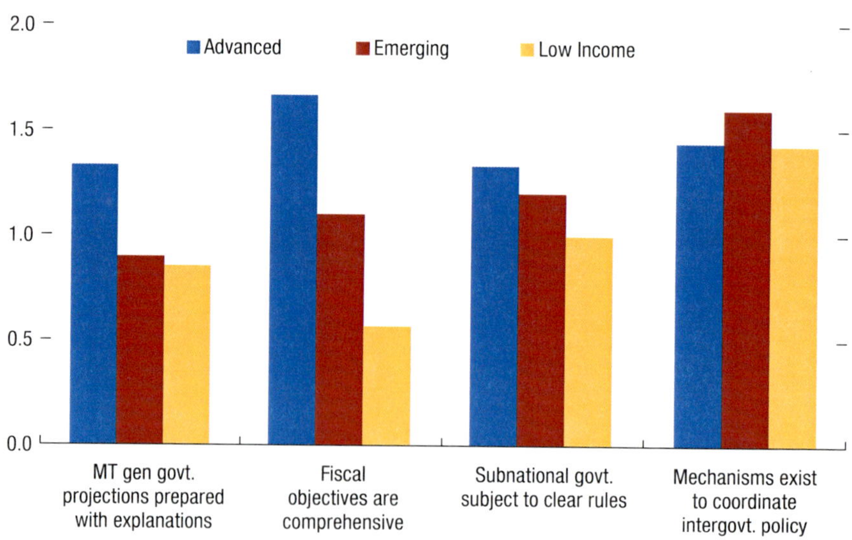

Source: Authors' calculations.

particularly in top-down budgeting and budget execution. In particular, while it is common to fix the ceilings at the early stages of the budget process, it is equally common that these restrictions are overlooked at the subsequent stages (see Figure 15.5):

- *Budget Unity*: Low-income countries in the sample receive equal scores on average on budget unity when compared to emerging market and advanced countries. In all of the countries, the budget, unemployment, and social security funds or spending cover at least 80%, and in many, more than 90% of central government expenditure. In all countries more than 90% of the budget spending requires annual authorization by parliament. However, arrangements regarding tax expenditures are less advanced; while most countries produce an annual quantification of tax expenditures, there is no control on their size.
- *Top-down Budgeting*: In almost all sample countries, there are ex ante limits on both aggregate and sectoral or ministerial spending provided in budget submissions, but importantly, in about half of the countries these ceilings are rarely respected. In almost all countries less than 10% of central government revenue is subject to earmarking or standing spending commitments. In about half of the countries, major revenue and expenditure decisions are often or sometimes taken outside the budget process.
- *Parliamentary Budget Approval*: Typically, the parliament does not endorse a medium-term fiscal target or objective. With some exceptions, there are limits on the legislature's right to amend the government's draft budget. In about half of the countries in the sample, the annual budget is not approved in a top-down sequence (i.e., parliament does not first approve an overall annual budget framework for total revenues and total expenditures). Typically, the legislature's right to amend the executive's budget proposal is rather limited. In a majority of the countries, there is a legal requirement in place that a budget has to be approved before the start of the fiscal year.
- *Budget Execution*: Most sample countries have restrictions in place on overspending during the execution of the annual budget. In particular, most countries require a submission of a supplementary budget to parliament. Typically, carry-overs are not allowed or the government imposes a ceiling on the size of annual carry-over or on carry-over draw-downs. Contingency arrangements for specific expenditure categories exist in all countries but in some cases access criteria to such funds could be specified more clearly. In most countries, the finance minister (the executive) can defer or cut expenditure, without prior approval of parliament, at least up to a certain limit. Finally, all countries lack comprehensive limits or controls on multi-annual expenditure commitments.

Figure 15.5. Implementing the Fiscal Strategy through the Budget Process

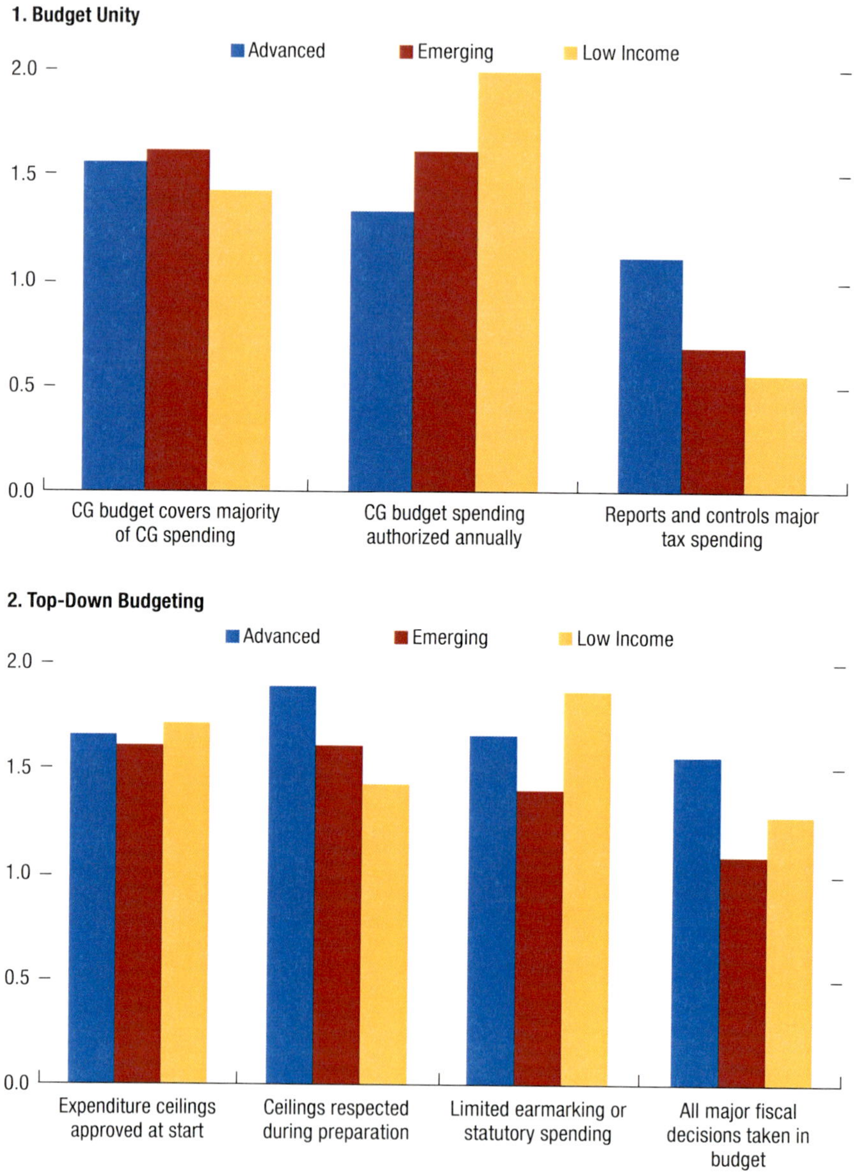

Source: Authors' calculations.

Figure 15.5. Implementing the Fiscal Strategy through the Budget Process *(continued)*

3. Parliamentary Approval

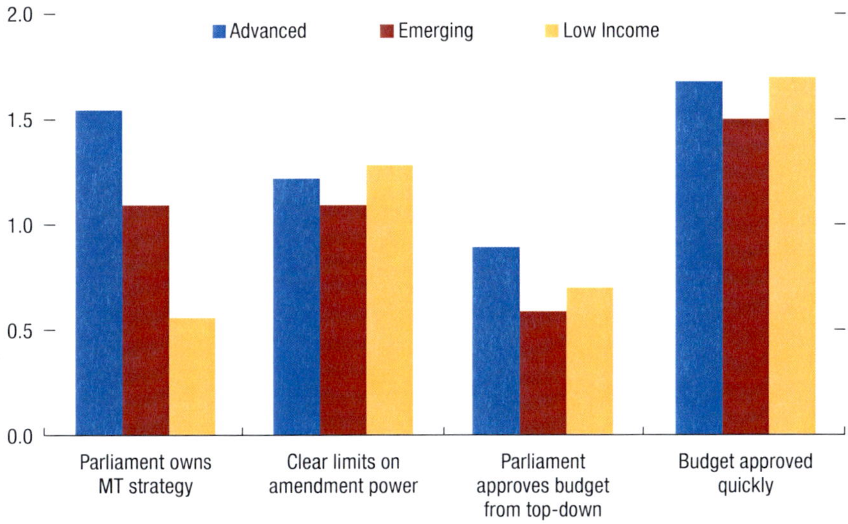

4. Budget Execution

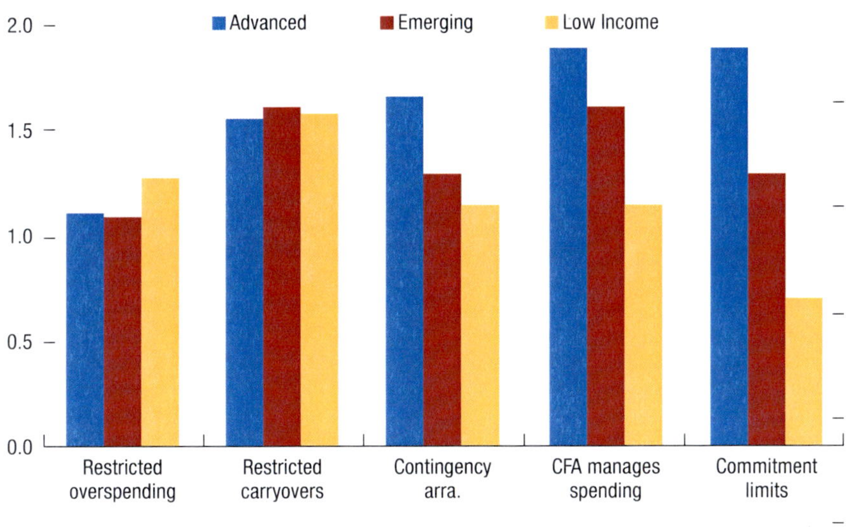

Source: Authors' calculations.

STRENGTHENING BUDGET INSTITUTIONS IN LOW-INCOME COUNTRIES

Prioritizing Reform Efforts

The above discussion suggests that in general low-income countries have substantial shortcomings in their budget institutions, which call for continuous reform efforts. The largest institutional gaps currently can be found from understanding and planning stages of the fiscal policy-making process, although some important challenges remain also in the implementation stage. Higher relative scores in the implementation stage may reflect a tradition of administrative and fiscal centralization among the countries in this group.

However, designing a reform agenda for low-income countries is a balancing act between ambition and realism. On the one hand, the reinforcing nature of the different institutions underlines the importance of taking a comprehensive approach to institutional reform. Indeed, institutional reforms in the above areas need to be coordinated across the budget stages and between branches and levels of government to maximize their impact on fiscal decision-making and performance. The impact of reform at any one stage of the process on fiscal behavior depends on the integrity of the system as a whole. But on the other hand, the design of a reform agenda has to take into account the low capacity of many low-income countries to implement reforms, as well as political economy constraints and weak governance systems. Therefore, it is not realistic to assume that all deficiencies identified above could be addressed simultaneously. Some prioritization and sequencing will be needed.

Indeed, reforms in budget institutions should address particular country-specific problems and should be placed in an appropriate order, i.e., be given the correct priority and sequence. The literature sets out some general principles (e.g., Diamond, 2013; Allen, 2013) but recognizes the difficulty of developing a set of operational rules that is applicable in all countries, in all contexts, and at all times. However, some guidance can be sought from the advanced country experiences.

Most advanced countries have reached decisions about the sequencing of reform in a non-structured fashion, but some important guiding principles can be identified:

- It is important to distinguish two kinds of sequencing: first, the order in which different initiatives within an overall PFM reform strategy (e.g., establishing a macro-fiscal forecasting unit, a treasury single account, a modern debt management agency) are introduced; and, second, the sequencing of individual tasks and activities within a single component of such a strategy, for example, the steps that are needed to convert the government's accounting and reporting system from a cash basis to an accrual basis, or to establish and make fully operational a unified revenue authority.
- Countries should not attempt too many reforms at one time. If too many reforms are attempted simultaneously, they are unlikely to succeed, e.g., because sufficient resources (human and financial) are not available, or the management capacity of the finance ministry is overstretched.

- Important basic elements of a budgeting system need to be put in place first before more advanced elements are incorporated.
- Many countries have tended to underestimate the complexity of the reform process and the need for careful handling of the implications for resources and staffing and supporting IT systems. A reform that is demanding in terms of skills and resources—such as introducing an MTBF, an accrual accounting system, or a Treasury Single Account—requires strong leadership, the development of a detailed action plan, a dedicated project management and communications team to implement the reform, and the active management of the human resource aspects of the reform. If these factors are given insufficient attention it is possible, if not likely, that the reform will: i) meet with substantial resistance inside and outside the finance ministry; ii) take longer than expected to implement; iii) cost more than necessary; and iv) deliver less than the full expected benefits, or fail completely.
- Reforms also need to take into account the views of stakeholders external to the finance ministry. Strong opposition may build up to reforms from line ministries, the president's office, or consumers of public services. There may also be opposition from managers and staff within the finance ministry.

Priorities for Institutional Reform for Low-Income Countries

In the context of the framework used in this paper, many budget institutions included in the framework can be seen as prerequisites to others. For example, binding medium-term budget frameworks have proved to be a useful and efficient tool for fiscal management in many advanced economies. However, implementing such frameworks is not an easy task: preconditions to a successful binding medium-term budget framework include credible and predictable annual budget, accurate medium-term macroeconomic and demographic projections, medium-term fiscal objectives and rules and a comprehensive, unified, top-down budget process (Harris et al., 2013).

Indeed, low-income countries would need to ensure that the basic PFM systems are in place before attempting to implement more sophisticated arrangements. The analysis presented above shows considerable variance in the strengths and weaknesses of budget institutions across and within the low-income countries. Given what has been discussed above, what institutional reforms should be seen as a priority? Two points are worth emphasizing:

- The connection between the institutional data presented above and the recommendations for necessary institutional reforms is not unambiguous: in other words, a low institutional score in some area does not automatically mean it should be seen as high priority. An example is the lack of independent fiscal agencies in low-income countries. Due to scarce resources, it is likely that establishing such agencies should not be seen as a priority in many cases.
- As discussed above, countries should not attempt too many reforms at one time, and instead address the institutional gaps in the basic elements of their budgeting systems before attempting more sophisticated reforms.

Therefore, appropriate reform strategies require country-specific reform programs and any generic advice is bound to be incomplete. With these limitations in mind, one can nevertheless highlight some common areas of institutional shortcomings countries should address.

Understanding the Fiscal Outlook and Challenges

Most low-income countries in the sample seem to have basic fiscal reporting practices in place but arrangements related to forecasting future fiscal developments and related risks are less robust. In order to improve understanding of the current and future fiscal position, low-income countries could consider:

- Expanding the coverage of their annual financial statements to central government, and ensure that there is a published external audit.
- Producing financial statistics by an independent office, in line with international standards.
- Including information about fiscal risks in their budget documentation, particularly in countries where PPPs, for example, are being used.
- Producing and publishing macroeconomic forecasts alongside related assumptions; and updating the forecasts in line with the budget process.
- Once the forecasting capacity improves, introducing medium-term forecasts with alternative medium-term budget scenarios, which would provide policymakers with a better sense of the country-specific vulnerability to uncertainty

Formulating a Credible Fiscal Strategy

Many institutions related to the formulation of a fiscal strategy seem to be relatively underdeveloped. While most countries have taken first steps in introducing some medium-term elements in their fiscal management, many challenges remain to be addressed. Where appropriate, low-income countries could consider:

- Adopting a medium-term objective in countries currently without such objective to provide guidance to fiscal planning, and once such objective is in place, regularly report on the fiscal performance against the stated objective
- In countries without any medium-term fiscal or budget framework, developing a simple framework, which would provide a projection of the fiscal balance, include estimates of government revenues and spending at a more aggregate level, and at the second stage providing guidelines (envelopes) to line ministries to prepare medium-term spending plans
- Once the prerequisites, such as solid macro-fiscal forecasting, credible budget, top-down budget process and medium-term fiscal objectives are in place, developing the framework into a more binding direction
- Ensuring proper interaction between central or federal government and subnational governments, at least by exchanging information regularly on fiscal policy, or ideally putting in place a legal framework for coordinating and sharing the burden of fiscal policy between layers of government

Implementing the Fiscal Strategy

While the institutions related to implementing the fiscal strategy seem to be the strongest among the three key stages reviewed, important challenges remain. These relate mainly to top-down budgeting and budget execution. In this context, low-income countries could consider:

- Issuing ex ante limits on both aggregate and sectoral or ministerial spending at an early stage in the budget preparation process, making sure that the size of the limits is realistic
- Changing parliamentary procedures to follow a top-down sequence where the parliament first approves an overall annual budget framework for total revenues and total expenditures and then discusses the allocation within these totals
- Putting in place appropriate restrictions for overspending during the execution of the budget and gradually introducing limits on multi-annual expenditure commitments

REFERENCES

Alesina, A. et al. (1999), "Budget Institutions and Fiscal Performance in Latin America", *Journal of Development Economics*, Vol. 59, pp. 253-273.

Allen, R. (2013), "Challenges of Reforming Budgetary Institutions in Developing Countries", in M. Cangiano, T. Curristine and M. Lazare (eds.), *Public Financial Management and Its Emerging Architecture*, International Monetary Fund, Washington, DC.

Andrews, M. (2013), *The Limits of Institutional Reform in Development: Changing Rules for Realistic Solutions*, Cambridge University Press, Cambridge.

Dabla-Norris, E. et al. (2010), "Budget Institutions and Fiscal Performance in Low-Income Countries", *IMF Working Paper*, No. 10/80, International Monetary Fund, Washington, DC.

De Haan, J., W. Moessen and B. Volkerink (1999), "Budgetary Procedures – Aspects and Changes: New Evidence for Some European Countries", in J. Poterba and J. von Hagen (eds.), *Fiscal Institutions and Fiscal Performance*, Chicago University Press, Chicago.

Diamond, J. (2013), *Good Practice Note on Sequencing Public Financial Management (PFM) Reform*, and *Guidelines for Sequencing PFM Reform*, PEFA Secretariat.

Filc, G. and C. Scartascini (2007), "Budgetary Institutions", in E. Lora (ed.), *The State of State Reform in Latin America*, Inter-American Development Bank, Washington.

Gollwitzer, S. (2011), "Budget Institutions and Fiscal Performance in Africa", *Journal of African Economies*, Vol. 20, No. 1, pp. 111-152.

Hallerberg, M. and S. Yläoutinen (2010), "Political Power, Fiscal Institutions and Budgetary Outcomes in Central and East European Countries", *Journal of Public Policy*, Vol. 30:1, Cambridge University Press, Cambridge, pp. 45-62.

Hallerberg, M., R. Strauch and J. von Hagen (2009), *Fiscal Governance: Evidence from Europe*, Cambridge University Press, Cambridge.

Harris, J. et al. (2013), "Medium-Term Budget Frameworks in Advanced Economies: Objectives, Design, and Performance", in M. Cangiano, T. Curristine and M. Lazare (eds.), *Public Financial Management and Its Emerging Architecture*, International Monetary Fund, Washington, DC.

IMF (2014), *Budget Institutions in G-20 Countries: An Update*, 7 April 2014, International Monetary Fund, Washington, DC.

Olden, B. (2012), "Fiscal Consolidation in Southeast European Countries: The Role of Budget Institutions", *IMF Working Paper*, No. 12/113, International Monetary Fund, Washington, DC.

Prakash, T. and E. Cabezon (2008), "Public Financial Management and Fiscal Outcomes in Sub-Saharan African Heavily-Indebted Poor Countries", *IMF Working Paper*, No. 08/217, International Monetary Fund, Washington, DC.
Von Hagen, J. (1992), "Budgeting Procedures and Fiscal Performance in the European Communities", *European Commission Economic Papers*, No. 96, European Commission, Brussels.
Von Hagen, J. and I. J. Harden (1996), "Budget Processes and Commitment to Fiscal Discipline", *IMF Working Paper*, No. 96/78, International Monetary Fund, Washington, DC.

CHAPTER 16

Fiscal Watchdogs and Sound Fiscal Policy: Is the Barking Loud Enough to Tame Politicians?

XAVIER DEBRUN, MARC GÉRARD, AND JASON HARRIS

This chapter revisits the potential contribution of politically independent fiscal watchdogs (fiscal councils, or FCs) to improving fiscal performance. A simple theoretical model first illustrates that FCs cannot credibly exert a direct constraint on day-to-day policy choices. However, by contributing to the broader public debate on fiscal policy—through the provision of unbiased quantitative and qualitative analysis, forecasts, and possibly recommendations—these institutions can reduce informational asymmetries hindering voters' ability to reward good policies and penalize bad ones. The chapter explores the empirical relevance of this argument by looking at the media impact of FCs in relation to real-time fiscal developments. It appears that FCs' activity and media impact increase in times of budget slippages or relative fiscal activism, a necessary condition for the validity of the theory. However, FCs' media impact is only weakly correlated with subsequent policy changes.

INTRODUCTION

The fiscal legacy of the 2008–09 economic and financial crisis brought to the fore serious concerns about the capacity of governments to meet their obligations in full. Several vulnerable governments came under severe market pressure, including in countries considered to be safe at the time. In the euro area, repeated and sometimes acute bouts of panic seized sovereign debt markets, raising the specter of widespread self-fulfilling solvency crises in countries with otherwise manageable public debt dynamics.

The need for improved fiscal governance quickly emerged as an essential part of any solution to mitigate elevated risks of fiscal crisis. A sound budgeting framework indeed conveys useful information about the likely range of future fiscal outcomes. Hence, by making bad states of public finances less likely in the

The authors are grateful to Petra Dacheva, Chifundo Moya, and Inna Remizova for outstanding research assistance, and to Bat-el Berger for help in the case studies. The views expressed in this chapter are those of the authors and do not necessarily represent those of the IMF or IMF policy.

medium term, markets are less easily spooked by adverse fiscal or macroeconomic shocks, while policymakers can respond more flexibly to such shocks. That is the magic bullet of fiscal credibility.

A considerable literature confirms the robust association between strong fiscal performance and good fiscal institutions. If the past is a good predictor of the future, institutional reforms could anchor a credible commitment to sound fiscal policies and reduce the short-term risk of a bad market equilibrium. Better fiscal governance comes at an additional premium in the euro area, where the risk sharing implied by crisis management measures calls for safeguards against moral hazard.

Fiscal institutions conducive to macroeconomic stability often come in the form of fiscal policy rules. Quantitative limits on debts, deficits, or spending have long been used to contain fiscal profligacy (for example, Fabrizio and Mody 2006; Debrun and others 2008). Yet experience has revealed serious limitations often related to the rules' inflexibility in the face of adverse or unusual circumstances, the lack of supportive budget procedures, or weak political commitment to effectively enforce them. Inflexibility ultimately threatens the credibility of the rule itself because the pressure of events can quickly lead to its suspension or even elimination.

Since the mid-1990s, a growing literature has argued that nonpartisan watchdogs—often dubbed fiscal councils or independent fiscal institutions—could shape policymakers' incentives in a more credible and effective way than numerical limits on budgetary aggregates. Through independent analysis, assessments, and forecasts, such bodies would raise voters' awareness of the consequences of certain policy paths, helping them reward desirable actions and sanction toxic ones (Kopits 2013; Debrun and others 2013). By barking loud enough in the face of undesirable behavior, fiscal watchdogs could foster democratic accountability and fiscal soundness. And instead of rigid rules, they could help devise an adequate policy response in most circumstances without undermining confidence in governments' ability to keep public finances on a sustainable track. The argument gains particular traction in times of extreme shocks and crises, when policy flexibility and credibility are both highly valued.

Establishing an independent FC now figures prominently in characterizations of sound fiscal policy frameworks well beyond the narrow circle of public financial management experts (Deutsche Bank 2016). Recent reforms of fiscal governance in the European Union (EU) now mandate independent institutions to assess the quality of budgetary forecasts and to monitor compliance with national fiscal rules. At the EU level, an Advisory Fiscal Board has been created to monitor implementation of the EU fiscal framework, advise the European Commission on the euro-area-wide fiscal stance, and facilitate coordination among national independent fiscal institutions.

Despite a long-standing and active debate in academic and policy circles, only recently has the economic analysis of FCs developed beyond sketchy and largely informal policy papers and opinion pieces (Calmfors 2010; Calmfors and Wren-Lewis 2011; Debrun, Hauner, and Kumar 2009; Kopits 2013; Debrun and others 2013). Economic theory discussing the desirability and effectiveness of such institutions remains in its infancy (Debrun 2011; Beetsma and Debrun 2016a, 2016b), and systematic empirical evidence exploring the link between these institutions and fiscal behavior is limited by the very short lifespan of most FCs (Debrun and others 2013). As a result, no definitive consensus exists with regard to the tasks FCs should be assigned, what institutional form they should take, and their complementarity with or instead substitutability for rules-based frameworks.

This chapter is an effort to fill some of those gaps. The second section sketches a highly stylized and purely illustrative model to anchor the debate on politically independent fiscal agencies. An important aspect is that the effectiveness of FCs rests on their ability to address the root cause rather than the symptoms of deficit bias. The third section gathers empirical evidence on the effectiveness of existing FCs, looking at two testable hypotheses emanating from theory. First, councils can only credibly affect policymakers' incentives and actions if they systematically influence the public debate on fiscal policy. In other words, does the watchdog bark when the risk of fiscal misbehavior looms large? Using data originally collected for case studies in Curristine, Harris, and Seiwald (2013), the chapter assesses the media impact of FCs at times when we would expect them to speak out, that is, in the aftermath of budgetary slippages or policy shifts. Second, the analysis tests whether desirable policy changes follow peaks in media impact, which would be consistent with FCs' ability to encourage better fiscal behavior. In other words, are political decision makers sufficiently impressed by the barking to correct undesirable actions? Finally, the chapter emulates other recent pieces—especially Calmfors and Wren-Lewis (2011)—by gathering more forensic evidence on what FCs do and achieve. Concluding remarks form the fourth and last section of the chapter.

FISCAL POLICY, FISCAL COUNCILS, AND DEMOCRATIC ACCOUNTABILITY

Since the late 1980s, a large literature has explored the reasons macroeconomic policies tend to deviate from a well-defined social optimum (see Kumar and Ter-Minassian [2007] for an extensive survey). On the fiscal side, the hypothesis of a deeply entrenched deficit bias emerged from the seemingly inexorable rise in debt-to-GDP ratios since the mid-1970s. Today's public debt levels are often unprecedented for peacetimes. While theories of deficit bias abound, empirical analyses have failed to identify a dominant explanation.[1] Because this literature has been surveyed elsewhere (for example, Calmfors 2010; Debrun and others 2008; Hagemann 2010), this chapter is limited to presenting a highly stylized

[1] Fragmented government coalitions (for example, Fabrizio and Mody 2006) and political instability (Debrun and Kumar 2009) emerge as more robust causes of excessive deficit. This may reflect common pool problems—that is, the failure to coordinate competing claims on finite budget resources—as well as the fear of not being reelected (implying myopia for politician); see, for example, Krogstrup and Wyplosz (2010).

two-period model of fiscal policy whose main virtue is to illustrate how FCs can help improve fiscal performance without assuming the delegation of policy instruments inherent to the theory of central bank independence (Wyplosz 2005).

A Simple Illustrative Model

Consider the two-period model of Alesina and Tabellini (1990), assuming constant and deterministic income levels. Identical private agents maximize utility U, which is separable over time and types of goods (private and public):

$$U(c,q) = E_0\left[\sum_{t=1}^{2}\beta^{t-1}\left(u(c_t)+v(q_t)\right)\right], \tag{16.1}$$

where c denotes the per capita consumption of private goods and q the per capita consumption of public goods. The term E_0 symbolizes the expectations operator conditional on information available at the beginning of period 1 (time 0), and β is a subjective discount factor. Assuming a constant proportional income tax rate τ, resource constraints simply write:

$$c_1 = (1-\tau)y + l$$
$$c_2 = (1-\tau)y - Rl$$

with R being the interest factor and l the stock of net private liabilities at the end of period 1.

Elected officials decide on public goods provision. They belong to one of two political parties (C or L) indexed by Q. Preferences are identical across political parties and to those of the population, but officials only value public goods when in office. These assumptions avoid the needless complexity of a partisan cycle in the conduct of fiscal policy, leading to a simple and well-defined deficit bias:

$$U_Q(c,q) = E_0\left[\sum_{t=1}^{2}\beta^{t-1}\left(u(c_t)+\rho^{t-1}v_Q(q_t)\right)\right];\ Q = C, L;\ 0 \le \rho \le 1, \tag{16.2}$$

with $v_C(q_t) = 0$ if party L is in office, and $v_L(q_t) = 0$ if party C is in office. Elections with uncertain outcome take place at the end of period 1, and the parameter ρ^{t-1} captures the probability of the incumbent party being in office at period t.

The government's resource constraints determine the amount of public goods per capita delivered in each period:

$$q_1 = \tau y + b - \delta_1, \tag{16.3a}$$

$$q_2 = \tau y - Rb - \delta_2, \tag{16.3b}$$

with b denoting the overall deficit at the end of period 1 (or equivalently, the principal of the debt to be repaid in period 2). The resource constraints are subject to random shocks affecting government efficiency. For a given amount of resources (tax revenue and borrowing), a positive realization of δ negatively affects public goods delivery. Concretely, δ could capture resource diversion by corrupt civil servants, the effect of poor administrative capacities, or unforeseeable policy mistakes. Of course, good surprises can also occur (more public goods being delivered with the same budgetary envelope). Hence, the shocks are nonserially correlated, with zero mean and finite variance: $\delta_t \sim N(0,\sigma_\delta^2)$. Also, we assume that fiscal policy decisions have no impact on income and, thereby, on private consumption since R is given and independent of b. Hence, these shocks capture the effect of good (or bad) luck on policymakers' performance.

In this model, a deficit bias[2] emerges because elected officials are uncertain about reelection. This result is immediately clear from a comparison of equations (16.1) and (16.2): any $\rho < 1$ entails policymakers' myopia (a policymaker discounts the future at a higher rate than a representative agent). While uncertainty is often exogenously given (for example, Beetsma and Debrun 2007), we argue that informational asymmetries between voters and policymakers can be instrumental in making election outcomes uncertain and are therefore at the root of the deficit bias. Specifically, this chapter makes the plausible assumption that voters cannot know for sure whether a given outcome for public goods delivery reflects the intrinsic competence of the elected policymaker or an exogenous event outside the policymaker's control affecting efficiency in public goods delivery (luck). The unobservable shocks affecting public goods delivery can thus lead voters to vote out (punish) competent officials or reelect (reward) undeserving individuals.

Characterizing the Deficit Bias

The socially optimal solution results from direct maximization of the representative citizen's utility (1) by a benevolent "social planner." To economize on notation, we set $\beta = R = 1$ (discount and real interest rates are equal to zero) and assume quadratic utility functions $u(x) = v(x) = -(x - \tilde{x})^2$. Decision makers dislike deviations from predetermined objectives, denoted by a tilde. The Euler equation under the social planner yields a balanced budget:

$$q_1^* = q_2^* \Rightarrow b^* = 0. \tag{16.4}$$

Before deriving the political equilibrium—that is, elected policymakers' choice—let us clarify the sequence of moves. First, "Nature" draws the governing party (C by assumption here). Second, party C officials prepare a budget, setting the deficit for period 1, and by extension, the expected time path of public consumption over the two periods. Third, an efficiency shock materializes during period 1, and finally, elections take place. In period 2, all debts are paid off after a new shock occurs. Solving this problem by backward induction rules out time inconsistency.

[2] The term deficit bias means that a utility-maximizing policymaker delivers a fiscal balance that is systematically weaker than one delivered by a representative agent who is directly in charge of fiscal policy.

As noted above, the probability of reelection is a central determinant of the budget deficit in the political equilibrium, denoted by a ** superscript:

$$b^{**} = \left[\frac{1-\rho}{1+\rho}\right]\tilde{b}, \text{ with } \tilde{b} = \tilde{q} - \tau y. \qquad (16.5)$$

Certainty about election outcomes defines two boundary cases. Certain reelection ($\rho = 1$) eliminates myopia, leading party C officials to opt for a balanced budget: $b^{**}\big|_{\rho=1} = 0 = b^{*}$. By contrast, certain defeat maximizes myopia to the point that party C is not bound by the intertemporal budget constraint and chooses a level of public spending consistent with the expected delivery of $\tilde{q}$ in period 1. The corresponding budget deficit is $b^{**}\big|_{\rho=0} = \tilde{b}$. All other solutions fall in the $\left[0, \tilde{b}\right]$ interval. Myopic policymakers generate a deficit bias only if $\tilde{b} > 0$, which requires that the appetite for delivering public goods (parameterized by $\tilde{q}$) exceed available tax money. This condition can be interpreted as the *common pool* problem inherent to budgetary decisions so that $b^{**} > b^{*}$. It is important to note that because voters' behavior remains purely exogenous, this deficit bias emerges in a political setting without formal democratic accountability.

Solving the Deficit Bias: Fiscal Rules versus Fiscal Councils

This section compares how fiscal rules and fiscal councils can affect policy outcomes.

Balanced Budget Rule

A straightforward solution to the deficit bias could be a balanced budget requirement. A fiscal rule affects policymakers' decisions to the extent that violating it entails a certain cost measurable in terms of utility. The costs can be merely reputational or result from a formal enforcement procedure with explicit sanctions (Beetsma and Debrun 2007). Under a fiscal rule, the "constrained" utility of the elected official would be

$$V_C = U_C - f(b - b^{*}). \qquad (16.6)$$

Policymakers now maximize V_C instead of U_C, as they internalize some costs of exceeding the deficit ceiling b^*. The optimal fiscal rule is such that $f^{*} = (1-\rho)\tilde{b}$ (the marginal cost of deviations), which implements b^* in the political equilibrium ($b^{**} = b^{*}$). The optimal rule thus imposes higher costs of breaching the deficit cap in countries where political instability (lower ρ) and the common pool problem (higher $\tilde{b}$) are more severe.

Of course, showing that an optimal rule exists does not mean that policymakers have any incentive to set it up in the first place.[3] In fact, it is straightforward

[3] This argument is analogous to McCallum's (1995) second fallacy of central bank independence, stating that if governments have the discretion to set up an independent central bank with the right incentives, they also have the discretion to revert to a dependent central bank with inadequate incentives. Jensen (1997) formally demonstrates in the Barro-Gordon-Rogoff framework that delegation does not matter if the no-renegotiation assumption is lifted.

to establish that the rule (f^*, b^*) violates the participation constraints of the policymakers as $E_0V_C(q^*) < E_0U_C(q^{**})$. Hence, even if policymakers inherit the rule from benevolent founding fathers, they will have an incentive to make it irrelevant or to scrap it altogether. Time inconsistency destroys the credibility of the rule (Debrun and Kumar 2009), which explains in part why these arrangements periodically come under intense pressure and are eliminated, substantially modified, circumvented, or temporarily ignored.[4]

Note that the time-inconsistency problem as characterized here may, a priori, be less severe in the face of supranational fiscal rules because such rules require international coordination to be changed. However, the experience with the Stability and Growth Pact in the EU suggests that supranational rules are not immune to change and circumvention. The pact has been thoroughly amended twice (in 2005 and 2010) since its introduction in 1997; its implementation has been uneven across countries, with large and influential member states seemingly benefiting from greater leniency;[5] and it has encouraged certain countries to mask the true state of public finances through sometimes egregious accounting manipulations.

Fiscal Councils

The main lesson from the above exercise is that any mechanism aimed at directly constraining fiscal discretion is bound to be resisted by policymakers and is therefore at high risk of being weakened or dismantled as soon as the opportunity arises. Now the question is whether nonpartisan fiscal agencies could at least appeal to policymakers (that is, satisfy their participation constraint) *and* help correct the deficit bias inherent to the political equilibrium.

The answer is arguably positive if we think of the FC as an institution that can induce meaningful rewards for policymakers who pursue policies closer to the social optimum. To illustrate this, the basic requirement that elected officials be accountable to their principal (the voters) is incorporated in the model. An immediate task is therefore to show that the deficit bias persists even if voters can credibly sanction inadequate policies and vote out an incumbent perceived to be unable to deliver enough public goods given available resources.

The failure of accountable governments to deliver the social optimum can be linked to informational asymmetries discussed earlier: voters' preferences may be hard to read, and the abilities and true agenda of those running for office are unobservable to voters. As a result, policy mistakes (or successes) can be difficult

[4] The problems for numerical fiscal rules have been documented and extensively discussed. However, in part because FCs can complicate attempts to circumvent rules—for example, by exposing accounting tricks and inadequate implementation of the rule—they are also exposed to attempts to reduce their influence. The abolition of the Hungarian Fiscal Council, created only two years earlier, is a vivid illustration of the inherent fragility of discipline-enhancing fiscal institutions. Beetsma and Debrun (2016b) formally model circumstances under which a country that has initially established an FC could eliminate it following elections.

[5] See Chapter 17, in this volume, by Gaspar.

to detect, interpret, and adequately sanction (or reward) because they are indistinguishable from the effect of luck.

Thus, for the sake of the argument, two basic assumptions are made. First, voters cannot observe the intrinsic competence of policymakers nor the shocks to public goods delivery. Second, opaque public accounts prevent voters from assessing whether observable outcomes are the result of either luck or competent policymaking. Formally, this means that the efficiency shocks δ_t and the true level of debt (deficit) are unobservable after the fact. Only tax revenues and actual output of public goods are perfectly observed. (Voters only know for sure what they pay and what they get.) The combination of unobservable competence and observable outcomes implies that voters will use the size of q_1 as a signal of competence.[6] In the stylized setup in this analysis, it effectively means that if they could observe δ_1, voters would interpret it as the incumbent's capacity to deliver public goods given fixed budgetary resources.

Rational voters can thus only observe a "subjective" budget balance—that is, the difference between the public goods they get and the tax money they pay. That measure reflects a shock (δ_1) and noise due to imperfect fiscal transparency (ξ):

$$q_1^C - \tau y = \xi - \delta_1, \tag{16.7}$$

where q_1^C denotes voters' perceived value of the public goods they consume—which also reflects the true budget balance. To infer the incumbent's efficiency or competence (which boils down to δ_1), voters solve a basic signal-extraction problem at the end of period 1:

$$E_1\left[\delta_1\right] = -\frac{\sigma_\delta^2}{\sigma_\delta^2 + \sigma_\xi^2}(q_1^C - \tau y). \tag{16.8}$$

Because voters' best guess of δ_1 reflects their assessment of the incumbent's competence, voters will form beliefs about the incumbent's competence on the basis of $E_1\left[\delta_1\right]$, which amounts to treating δ as persistent: $E_1\left[\delta_2 | Q = C\right] = \lambda E_1\left[\delta_1\right]$ with $0 < \lambda \leq 1$, while $E_1\left[\delta_2 | Q = L\right] = 0$.

The incumbent will be reelected if voters expect her to deliver more public goods given the remaining budgetary resources (which are the same for both parties). Formally, reelection occurs if $E_1\left[q_2 | Q = C\right] - E_1\left[q_2 | Q = L\right] > 0$. At time 0 (budget preparation stage for period 1), the perceived probability of reelection is therefore $\rho = \Pr\left(\lambda \frac{\sigma_\delta^2}{\sigma_\delta^2 + \sigma_\xi^2}(q_1^C - \tau y) > 0\right)$.

This shows that political incentives leading to a deficit bias remain even after explicitly introducing democratic accountability in the model. The difference with the section "Characterizing the Deficit Bias" above is that because the

[6] Cukierman and Meltzer (1986) and Rogoff and Sibert (1988) first introduced that type of conjecture in formal models of fiscal policy.

probability of reelection depends positively on the (ex post) realization of the budget balance, policymakers now face an opportunistic (ex ante) motive to run a deficit. Indeed, a deficit reduces the likelihood that voters will detect adverse efficiency realizations at the end of period 1, which they would interpret as a lack of competence, motivating them to vote against the incumbent.

What could be the role of an independent fiscal agency? The analysis above suggests that an institution able to clearly inform voters of whether the incumbent behaved consistently with an ex ante intent to produce q_1^* would solve the kind of asymmetric information problem described previously, and as a result, would contribute to eliminating the deficit bias that such asymmetry entails. For example, providing quantitative and qualitative analyses of fiscal policy (ex ante and in real time) could in principle help voters see through policymakers' incentives and fiscal accounts so as to better grasp the adequacy of the observed policy stance. By definition, such an institution should be politically independent and have a broad remit that could include elements of judgment on the nature of shocks to the budget. If voters are better equipped to distinguish between bad luck and bad intentions, they can make better decisions, thereby eliminating opportunistic motives and directly rewarding competent governments with greater reelection chances.[7]

In sum, a well-functioning FC, by becoming the main source of information on the underlying quality of fiscal policy, would allow democratic accountability to play its role. Of course, placing such a considerable amount of trust in an FC would require strict guarantees of independence from partisan influences, a clear definition of the policy objectives under the council's scrutiny (for example, fiscal sustainability), and a modus operandi genuinely "owned" by voters.

FISCAL COUNCILS, THE PUBLIC DEBATE, AND FISCAL POLICY

This section gathers empirical evidence on the effectiveness of FCs with a deliberate focus on the watchdog function, that is, the ability of the FC to signal fiscal misconduct. The focus is on two empirical questions: Does the watchdog bark when it should? And is the barking sufficiently impressive to deter misconduct and improve policy outcomes? To measure the impact of fiscal watchdogs in the public debate, this analysis uses the data set on the media impact of FCs compiled for the case studies in Curristine, Harris, and Seiwald (2013). This chapter thus complements the existing empirical literature, which relies mainly on thorough country case studies (for example, Calmfors and Wren-Lewis 2011; Coene and

[7] Beetsma and Debrun (2016a) demonstrate this in a simple Bayesian game with unobservable competence based on the same basic setup as in this chapter. They formally show that FCs contribute to improving average fiscal performance by (1) having competent governments elected more often and (2) encouraging incompetent governments to mimic competent ones.

Langenus 2011) and largely illustrative correlations between outcomes and specific features of FCs (Debrun and others 2013).

The Approach

The approach is twofold. First, we build on the theoretical sketch developed above to explore the influence of FCs on the public debate through direct measures of their media impact. Second, two short case studies analyze the media impact in greater details. The use of higher-frequency data (monthly instead of annual) allows for a more refined assessment of the noise-to-signal ratio of media reports.

The media impact variable is based on the number of times the official name of the FC appears in a country's national press (either in English or in national languages). Simple panel regressions are used to detect a relationship between the intensity of media reports referring to the FC and two real-time fiscal policy indicators expected to be of interest to the FC. The first policy indicator is the planned change in the cyclically adjusted budget balance (CAB) at the beginning of the year, which captures the degree of fiscal activism planned in the budget (stimulus or consolidation). The second is the first estimate of the deviation in the CAB with respect to plans. This variable is interpreted as a symptom (see Beetsma, Giuliodori, and Wierts 2009) of slippages (or overperformance) during the budget year, although its signaling power is affected by possibly large revisions in estimated output gaps.

Clearly, the results reported in the remainder of this section only constitute a first exploration, a potential enticement for further research that will be needed when the large number of new FCs will have gathered sufficiently long experience. One source of concern is the reliability of the underlying media data, which could create unwanted noise in the statistical analysis. For instance, it is difficult to assess whether the comprehensiveness of press coverage is comparable across countries. Another potential issue is that the straightforward measure of media impact that is used[8] could capture events only loosely related to the national budgetary debate, for example, political bickering about the appointment of a new FC member.

Data, Notation, and Testable Hypotheses

Data Sources and Notation

Real-time fiscal and economic data are collected from the European Commission's assessments of Stability and Convergence Programs (SCPs)—typically discussed in early spring on the basis of data transmitted by national authorities. To save on notation, country indices are omitted and time superscripts are used to denote the vintage of the commission's assessment of SCPs. As a result, X_t^t is the "real-time" forecast of X_t at the beginning of year t, and X_t^{t+1} is the first estimate of the

[8] All media data used in the case studies of Curristine, Harris, and Seiwald (2013) come from the Factiva database.

realization of X_t. The Δ operator symbolizes the first-difference of a variable over time. Hence, $\Delta X_t^t = X_t^t - X_{t-1}^t$ measures the planned "real-time" variation in X between t and $t-1$, while $\Delta X_t^{t+1} = X_t^{t+1} - X_{t-1}^{t+1}$ is the "first estimate" of the actual change. Finally, the "forecast error" of X is defined as $ERRX_t^{t+1} = X_t^{t+1} - X_t^t$.

Because of severe data limitations in the media data set, the sample only includes seven continental European countries—Austria, Belgium, Germany, Denmark, Netherlands, Sweden, and Slovenia—over the period 2003–10—years with comprehensive assessments of SCPs by the European Commission. To maximize the time dimension, the main fiscal policy indicator is the CAB instead of the more conventional cyclically adjusted primary balance, which was not consistently reported in SCPs by all countries in the early years of the sample. The set of control variables is necessarily parsimonious given the small size of the sample. It includes the gross public debt (*DEBT*) and the output gap (*OG*). The key indicator of media impact, *NEWS*, is the standardized number (z-score) of written press articles quoting the national FC (in English and national languages). It reflects the intensity of the news coverage of the FC's activity in each country and is thus taken as a proxy of its participation in the public debate on fiscal matters.

Testable Hypotheses

Theory points to two testable hypotheses. First, a necessary condition for the effectiveness of an FC is that it publicly reacts to fiscal developments, either because they signal a policy shift with a notable bearing on the realization of policy objectives or because undesirable deviations from planned outcomes call for an analysis of the causes—bad luck or bad budget execution. To the extent that these reactions contribute to the public debate, the FC will enhance democratic controls. In that case, a change in the *NEWS* variable *follows* variations in fiscal indicators. Second, an effective FC would be expected to make a difference in the conduct of fiscal policy, which would imply that changes in fiscal indicators would tend to *follow* peaks in FCs' media activity. The analysis focuses on the planned change in the CAB as a proxy for deliberate policy action, and on the forecast error, which could reflect unexpected shocks affecting the budget or policy slippages.

Results

We first document systematic differences in key fiscal dimensions between the seven countries that have FCs (hereafter FC7) considered in the analysis and the others, that is, countries that do not have FCs and those that might have introduced an FC more recently. The FC7 exhibit, on average, stronger fiscal balances than the rest of the EU (Figure 16.1). By contrast, while public debt was higher—by about 10 percentage points of GDP—in the FC7 before the crisis, it is slightly lower, on average, by the end of 2014. Because the stronger fiscal positions may in part reflect greater concerns about debt stabilization, market perceptions of sovereign risk for the two groups are also compared (Figure 16.2). Again, the FC7 enjoy much lower spreads, on average, than other EU countries, even after excluding the euro area periphery.

Figure 16.1. Fiscal Perfomance in EU Countries with Fiscal Councils (FC7) and other EU Member States
(Percent of GDP)

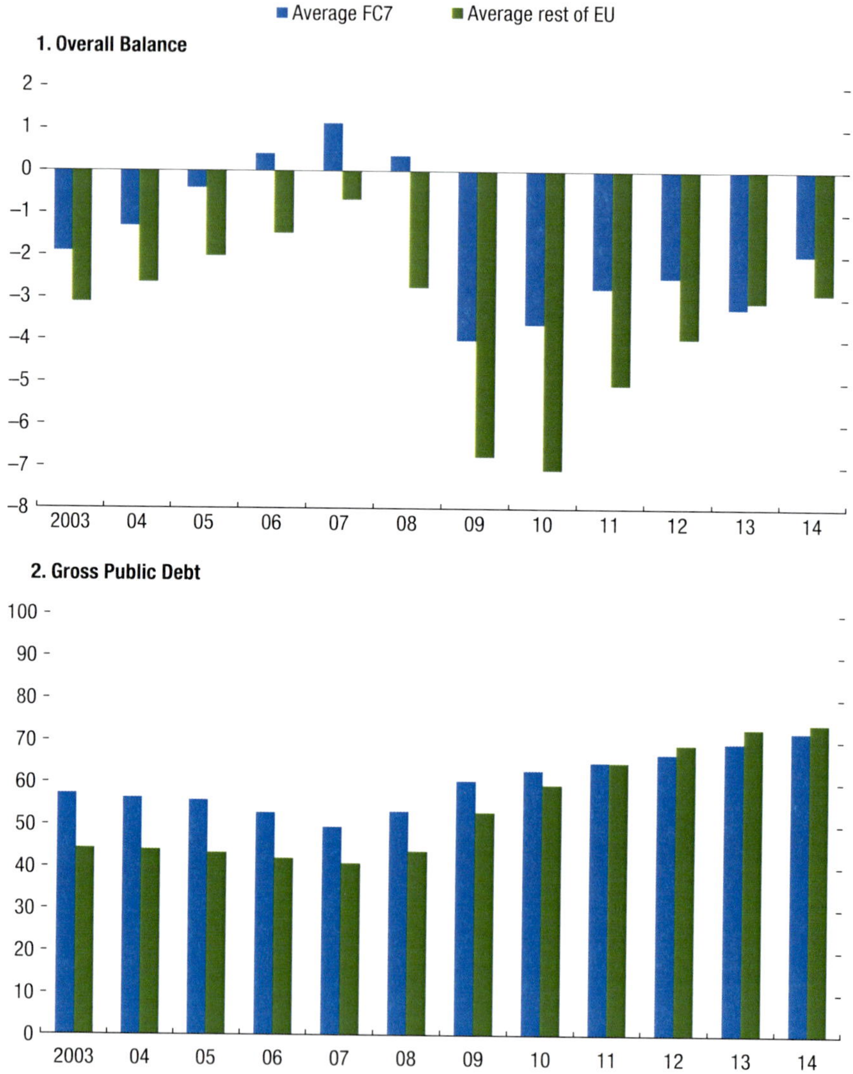

Sources: International Monetary Fund, World Economic Outlook database, and authors' calculations.
Note: EU = European Union; FC7 = European countries with fiscal councils: Austria, Belgium, Germany, Denmark, Netherlands, Sweden, and Slovenia.

Figure 16.2. CDS Spreads (Five-Year) in EU Countries with Fiscal Councils (FC7) and the Other EU Member States
(Basis points)

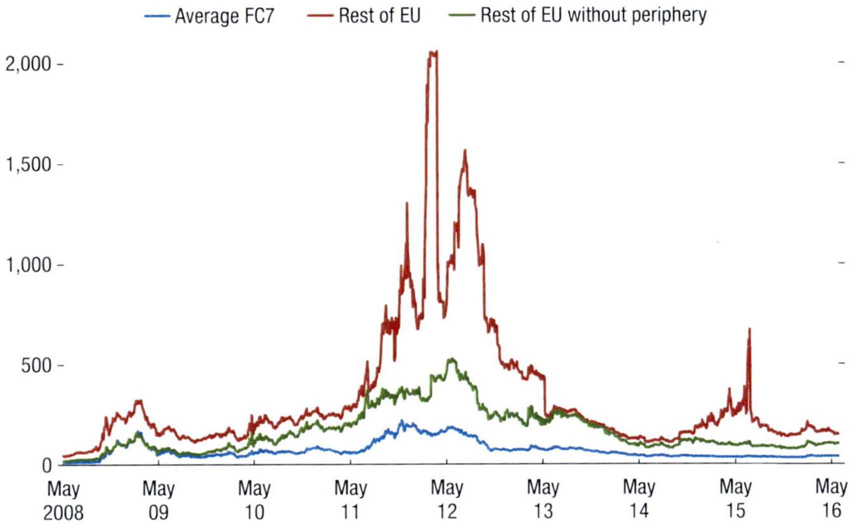

Sources: Markit; and authors' calculations.
Note: CDS = credit default swap; EU = European Union; FC7 = European countries with fiscal councils: Austria, Belgium, Germany, Denmark, Netherlands, Sweden, and Slovenia.

Do the Watchdogs Bark When Needed?

Using the seven-country sample over the period 2003–10, the following model is estimated: $NEWS_t = c + d_t + \alpha FISC_t^{t+i} + \varepsilon_t$, where *FISC* is a fiscal indicator, d_t is time dummies, and c indicates the use of country fixed effects. The fiscal indicator is either the planned variation in the CAB at the beginning of year t (so $i = 0$) or the first estimate (in early $t+1$) of the forecast error ($i = 1$), while *NEWS* captures the intensity of citations in the press during the entire year t.

The regressions reported in Table 16.1 detect a statistically significant correlation between the two fiscal indicators and the media impact of FCs. On average, the fiscal watchdogs seem to bark louder when large fiscal policy changes are planned, and they seem to be heard in the press. The FCs in the sample also tend to be more present in the media during years when forecast errors end up being greater, suggesting that they publicly reveal policy slippages or express concerns when unexpected shocks send budget plans off track. Interestingly, the negative signs obtained for the first differenced CAB and the raw forecast error suggest that deteriorations in the CAB lead to increased media attention to FCs' messages. This finding is consistent with FCs' primary role of promoting fiscal responsibility.

Table 16.1. Media Impact of Fiscal Councils and Magnitude of Fiscal Developments
(Dependent variable: NEWS)

	ΔCAB	|ΔCAB|	ERRCAB	|ERRCAB|
Fiscal Councils	−0.392***	0.721***	−0.217*	0.453**
	(−4.96)	(4.68)	(−2.25)	(3.42)
Constant	0.113***	−0.246**	0.207***	−0.176
	(5.17)	(−2.47)	(58.47)	(−1.51)
Adjusted R^2	0.08	0.16	0.05	0.13
Observations	51	51	51	51

Source: European Commission's Assessments of Stability Programs; and authors' calculations.
Note: All regressions include country fixed effects; robust *t*-statistics are in parentheses. CAB is the cyclically-adjusted balance, and ERRCAB represents the forecast errors of the cyclically-adjusted balance as defined in the text.
$*p < .1$; $**p < .05$; $***p < .01$.

Although these results provide an indication that FCs may be effective in sending the right messages at the right time, the limited size of the sample and the potentially weak signaling power of media activity call for caution. In particular, fiscal developments explain only a small fraction of the quantity of news reports referring to the FCs. Also, the introduction of time dummies severely reduces the precision in the estimated impact of fiscal indicators on FCs' presence in the media, suggesting that the results in Table 16.1 may capture developments—such as the global financial crisis—that jointly affect the budget and FCs' reported activity.

Do FCs Influence the Conduct of Fiscal Policy?

Following the earlier discussion, the underlying regression is as follows: $\left|\Delta CAB_t^t\right| = c + d_t + \delta NEWS_{t-1} + \beta_1 DEBT_{t-1}^t + \beta_2 OG_{t-1}^t + \varepsilon_t$. In contrast to the first set of regressions, several control variables known to be related to fiscal developments are introduced, namely the cyclical position of the economy (lagged output gap) and the (lagged) public debt level. With regard to the left-hand-side variable, meaningful correlations could be detected only between the absolute value of the planned change in the CAB for year t and FCs' media presence in year $t-1$.

As Table 16.2 suggests, stronger presence of the FC in the media in any given year is correlated with greater planned "fiscal activism" for the following year, regardless of whether the plans envisage a more ambitious fiscal consolidation or a greater stimulus. The results are fairly consistent across alternative regressions (fixed effects or pooled) and with the inclusion of the only two statistically significant time dummies (2007 and 2008). The control variables display the expected signs: a reduction in the output gap (less positive or more negative) encourages fiscal activism, whereas high public debt is less conducive to activism.

It may be tempting to conclude that more intense FC involvement in the public debate pushes governments to do the right thing; however, the paucity and quality of the data and the fragility of the results call for caution. In addition, simultaneity problems loom large, given that the plans for year t are prepared and discussed intensively in the second part of the preceding year. The results may thus reflect the fact that FCs are simply taking an active part in the debate

Table 16.2. Do Fiscal Councils Shape Policy Outcomes?
(Dependent variable: Absolute value of the one-year-ahead ΔCAB)

	Estimator				
	LSDV	**LSDV**	**LSDV**	**Pooled OLS**	**Pooled OLS**
NEWS	0.110	0.146*	0.153*	0.108**	0.108**
	(1.62)	(2.03)	(2.14)	(2.36)	(2.37)
OG	−0.347**	−0.271	−0.229*	−0.324***	−0.325***
	(−2.63)	(−2.27)*	(−2.08)	(−3.93)	(−3.96)
DEBT	−0.010	−0.022		−0.001	
	(−0.59)	(−1.28)		(−0.17)	
i2007	0.510*			0.492***	0.498***
	(1.99)			(3.30)	(3.33)
i2008	1.687**	1.306**	1.193**	1.601***	1.605***
	(3.46)	(2.93)	(2.75)	(5.10)	(5.22)
Constant	0.665	1.534	0.339**	0.178	0.147*
	(0.67)	(1.67)	(2.90)	(0.92)	(1.70)
Adjusted R^2	0.61	0.57	0.56	0.55	0.56
Observations	44	44	44	44	44

Source: Factiva; European Commission's Assessments of Stability Programs and Spring Forecasts; and authors' calculations.
Note: Robust *t*-statistics are in parentheses. NEWS is the standardized number (z-score) of written press articles quoting the national fiscal council. OG and DEBT are the first estimates of the output gap and general government debt, respectively. LSDV = least squares dummy variable; OLS = ordinary least square.
$^*p < .1$; $^{**}p < .05$; $^{***}p < .01$.

surrounding budget preparation, particularly when significant policy shifts are discussed. While this would be welcome and supportive of the evidence in Table 16.1, it might not necessarily reflect the council's actual influence on policy choices. Taking two lags to the *NEWS* variable did not help, suggesting that the distance between the council's message and actual decision making would then be too large.

Going Forensic: Fiscal Councils and the Budget Process

Although promising, the preliminary evidence on a link between FCs' media presence and fiscal indicators—which only conveys a clear policy signal at annual frequency—calls for a much more detailed analysis that goes beyond the scope of the present chapter. Insights can nevertheless be gained from a more "forensic" analysis involving higher-frequency data. In contrast to more comprehensive case studies of FCs (for example, the analysis of Sweden and the United Kingdom by Calmfors and Wren-Lewis [2011]), this analysis focuses on the link between certain fiscal episodes and FCs' media visibility.

Two case studies of long-lasting FCs are interesting in this regard: the Netherlands' Bureau for Economic Analysis, better known by its Dutch acronym CPB, and the Public Sector Borrowing Requirement Section of Belgium's High Council of Finance. The selection of two well-established institutions offers some guarantees that media quotes capture the actual impact of their routine work on the public debate. Analyzing new or failed institutions could distort the measure of media presence because the press could report on debates about the council itself—for example, public discussions about individual appointments or reports about personal or political conflicts preceding the FC's demise—rather than fiscal policy. Belgium and the Netherlands also provide the advantage of operating in contexts in which rules and numerical norms have typically played an important role. This facilitates the identification of specific "stress" episodes—for example, clear threat of breaking a rule or an official numerical target—during which the FC would be expected to communicate.

Case Study 1: The Netherlands

The Netherlands Bureau for Economic Policy Analysis—known by its familiar acronym of CPB, for Central Planning Bureau—is a veteran among FCs, beginning operations in 1945. It has been preparing economic forecasts since the 1950s, publishing reports on the state of Dutch public finances since the 1960s, undertaking election-commitment costing since the 1980s, and preparing long-term scenario analyses since the 1990s. The CPB also has a number of other roles, including cost-benefit analysis, and a fairly broad research agenda.

The CPB is formally a branch of the civil service within the Ministry of Economic Affairs and it is funded from the budget. Despite lacking a separate status for staff and being financially dependent on the budget, several elements contribute to the independence of the CPB, including a supervisory committee whose members are appointed by the cabinet for five years, and five-yearly independent evaluations (usually by academics, many of whom are not Dutch nationals).

Like most FCs, the CPB cannot bite: it has no explicit mandate or instrument that can directly influence fiscal policy. Also, it does not provide strictly normative assessments, not even against the government's own commitments and objectives. However, the CPB quantitatively evaluates the effect of government policies on public finances. Clearly, a positive statement saying that the continuation of a certain policy is bound to threaten fiscal sustainability is not materially different from a normative judgment that such policy should be changed.

Another positive way for the CPB to enter into normative territory at politically critical times relates to its role of costing electoral platforms before, and coalition agreements after, elections. That function has arguably improved the quality of public information and influenced the debate around elections, encouraging parties to tighten up their commitments in advance (so that costing can be undertaken) and to avoid making commitments to unaffordable policies (Bos and Teulings 2011).

The CPB is an insider working within the budget process. It provides the macroeconomic forecasts used for the budget. Those forecasts are produced behind closed doors and discussed with the government (initially through the Ministry of Finance, and later through the cabinet) before being released. While this means that the budget relies on independent forecasts, private discussions with the cabinet provide an opportunity for cabinet members to put pressure on the CPB (Bos and Teulings 2011). For the same reason, the CPB provides little public information about the evolution of the fiscal outlook during the year, allowing the government to change course, if necessary, without raising public awareness. Following meetings with the cabinet, the CPB publishes its forecasts four times a year, with more extensive updates in March and September than in June and December.

Overall, this set of attributes, combined with a long history of well-regarded analysis and forecasts, has given the CPB a considerable degree of public credibility. Although its specific contribution is difficult to identify, the Netherlands' fiscal performance since the mid-1990s has been relatively sound. In particular, there has been no apparent bias in macroeconomic forecasts, and ex post compliance with ex ante targets has been satisfactory.

Let us look at each of these three aspects in greater detail. Using data from the SCPs, we calculate the real GDP growth forecasting errors (at one-, two-, and three-year horizons) across countries over the period 2000–14. In the Netherlands, the average errors for the budget year have been, if anything, pessimistic; and while they appear slightly optimistic over the out-years, they remain well within one standard deviation of GDP growth in the sample. The same is true for the other countries whose FCs have within their remit providing independent macroeconomic forecasts for the budget (Austria and Belgium). This finding is in line with earlier results by Jonung and Larch (2006) showing that independent forecasting helps prevent an optimistic bias in GDP forecasts (Figure 16.3).

The discussion now turns to compliance with ex ante targets set over the political cycle. The Dutch budget system is governed by coalition agreements reached at the beginning of each parliamentary term. These agreements specify,

Figure 16.3. Real GDP Forecast Errors (Actual Minus Forecast), 2000–14
(Percentage points)

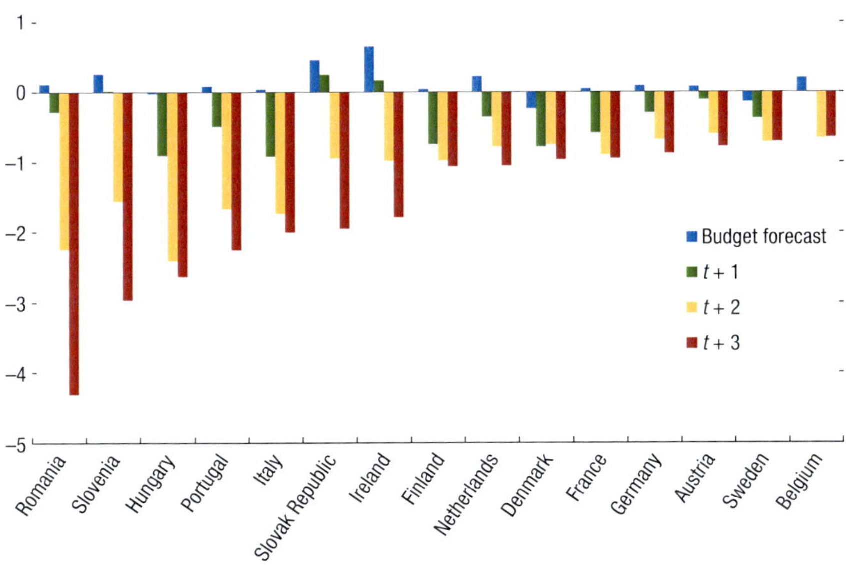

Sources: European Commission's Assessments of the Stability and Convergence Programs; and authors' calculations.
Note: The variable *t* indicates year.

Figure 16.4. The Netherlands: Fiscal Targets, Forecasts, and Outcomes
(Percent of GDP)

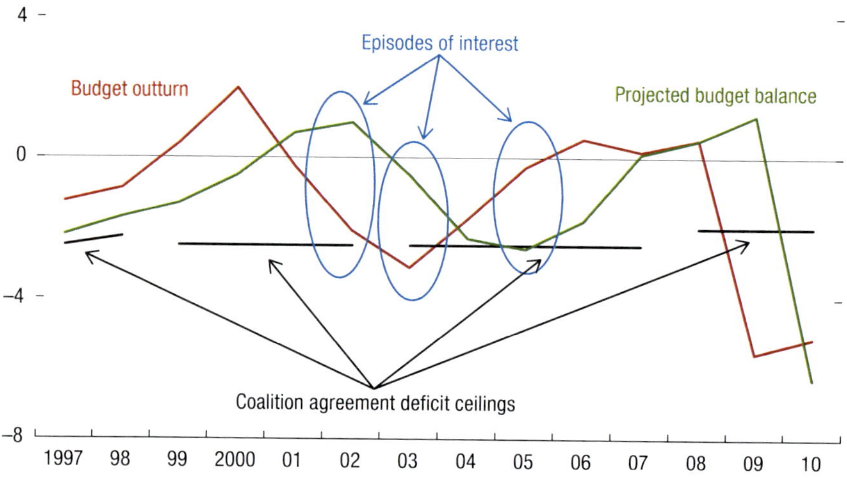

Sources: Netherlands Bureau for Economic Policy Analysis; and authors' calculations.

among other things, a deficit ceiling for the remainder of the term (bold black lines in Figure 16.4). Figure 16.4 also displays yearly forecasts for the budget balance (green line) and the final budget outcome (red line).

This comparison allows identification of episodes of interest characterized as follows: (1) either the budget forecast or fiscal outturn is exceeding the deficit ceiling, or (2) the fiscal outturn is significantly worse than the budget forecast. In either of these cases, the FC would be expected to raise awareness of these outcomes and make recommendations or suggestions to rectify the situation. Using the same media information as above (now at monthly frequency), we examine whether this did, in fact, occur.

The first episode was in 2002, when the fiscal outturn came out significantly worse than the budget forecast, and was in fact approaching the deficit ceiling set in the coalition agreement. The second episode occurred in 2003, when the outturn was again significantly worse than forecast, but this time actually breached the deficit ceiling. The third and final episode was in 2005, when the budget forecast exceeded the ceiling, even though the outturn ended up comfortably inside the ceiling. The events related to the global financial crisis are excluded because they represent a more significant, exogenous shock, with less control available to policymakers.

These episodes are now mapped in Figure 16.5, compiling the CPB's media presence calculated as the number of newspaper articles containing a reference to the CPB. We have adjusted and corrected that series for trend, looking at the number of articles relative to a four-year rolling average. The vertical bars in red

Figure 16.5. Media Presence of the CPB
(Number of press articles: relative deviations from four-year rolling average)

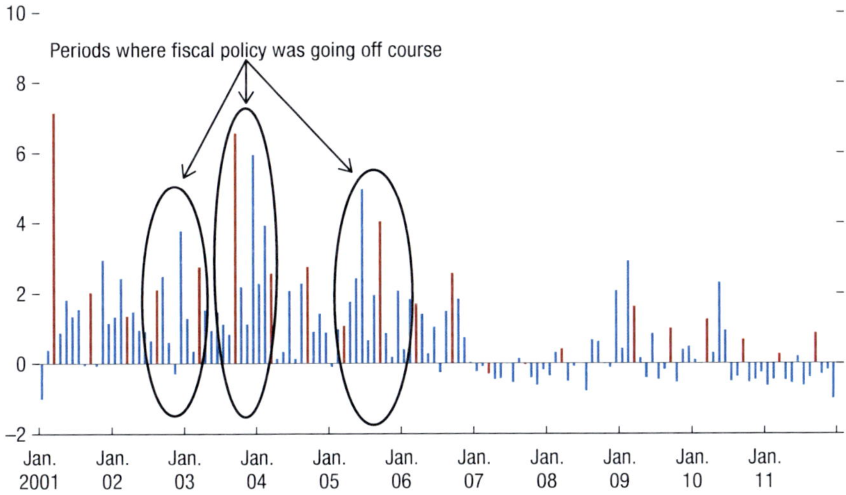

Sources: Factiva; and authors' calculations.
Note: CPB = Netherlands Bureau for Economic Policy Analysis (Centraal Planbureau).

refer to the months in which the CPB releases its public forecasts and fiscal assessments. Some of the spikes observed in the series refer to election periods, where the CPB featured heavily in the news.

The three episodes identified above coincide with a marked increase in media reports. It is useful to note that the major spikes, particularly in 2003 and 2005, relate to the timing of the CPB's release of its public assessments.

An examination of the contents of CPB reports at those times confirms this interpretation. In 2002, the slippage became apparent toward the end of the year, and the CPB noted in its December report that because of the worsening economy, the small surplus achieved in 2001 would turn to a deficit of 0.8 percent of GDP in 2002. In 2003, this continued deterioration was noted in the March report, where the projections in the Central Economic Plan of that year were revised downward and the CPB noted that "additional deficit-reducing measures are necessary to comply with the rules from the SGP [Stability and Growth Pact]." In the December 2003 report, the deficit forecasts were further revised upward, with the CPB noting that "even though the 3.35% deficit will be just above the 3% SGP ceiling, this does not mean that Brussels will determine this deficit to be 'excessive.' Netherlands will probably be able to call on exceptional economic conditions." In 2005, the forecast for the year exceeded the agreed-upon deficit ceiling, which prompted the CPB to warn in its December 2004 report that, "Regardless of the austerity measures of the government, the [2005] deficit stays dangerously close to the 3% SGP deficit ceiling."

Figure 16.6. Average Seasonal Pattern of the CPB Media Presence
(Percent of annual hits)

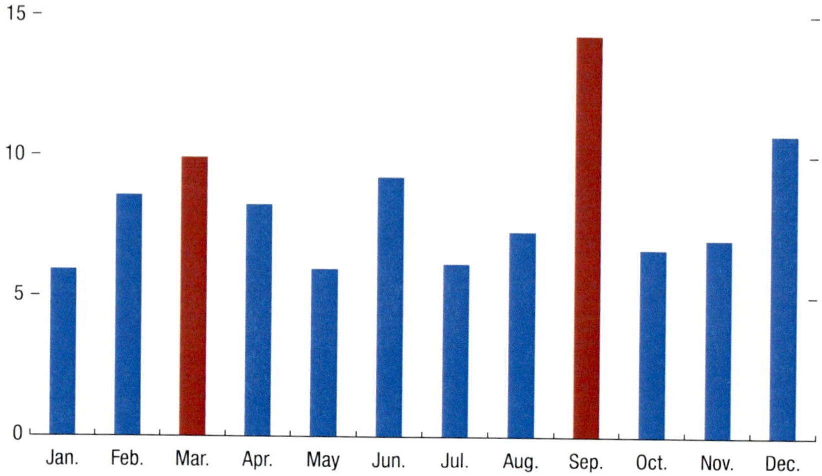

Sources: Factiva; and authors' calculations.
Note: The red bars correspond to the publication dates of the main reports. CPB = Netherlands Bureau for Economic Policy Analysis (Centraal Planbureau).

Beyond individual episodes, the CPB's ability to communicate to the public when it has something important to say and when it matters most during the budget process is important every year. Indeed, an FC constantly out in the public with a running commentary, disconnected from important parliamentary budget preparation deadlines, would raise doubts about its ability to add something important to the debate. We can assess this "noise-to-signal" ratio by plotting the average monthly seasonal patterns of media presence of the council (Figure 16.6). The spikes suggests that the CPB times its media interventions in a fairly systematic way, taking full advantage of the publication of its most extensive reports in March and September to influence the public debate.

The message emanating from this analysis is consistent with the broader correlations detected earlier in the panel of seven countries. Although it is difficult to identify a robust causal link between the activities of the CPB and improved fiscal performance in the Netherlands, the CPB's media visibility supports the idea that it actively contributes to the quality of the public debate and reduces information asymmetries between decision makers and the public. There is indeed no significant forecast bias, the messages of the council appear relevant and those messages are communicated in an effective and timely manner.

Case Study 2: Belgium

Two bodies provide independent fiscal inputs into the budgetary process in Belgium. Their responsibilities are split between the normative recommendations and assessments of fiscal policy from the High Council of Finance (HCF, and more specifically the so-called Public Sector Borrowing Requirement Section), and the positive, forecast-input role of the Federal Planning Bureau (under the umbrella of the National Accounts Institute)—see Lebrun (2009). The case of Belgium is of particular interest because it is one of only a few countries where an FC makes normative recommendations. Over the past two decades, the HCF has gone through periods of being highly influential, followed by periods where that influence has waned (Coene and Langenus 2011).

The HCF dates back to the 1930s, when it was formed to advise the Ministry of Finance. It assumed its current role in 1989 when it started issuing recommendations on public sector borrowing requirements. The main objective of Belgian public finances at the time was to reduce the high budget deficit and public debt ratios, which stood at 7 percent and 125 percent of GDP, respectively, in 1988. Much of the HCF's recommendations focused on monitoring and coordinating the fiscal effort across the different levels of government. Belgium's commitment to meet the Maastricht criteria provided an opportunity to expand the HCF's normative role with recommendations to comply with these criteria as well as with medium-term objectives.

Although the HCF does not have any direct instruments with which to shape budgetary choices, its recommendations, compiled in two reports, have often carried significant weight. The first report is published at the beginning of the budget process (June/July), when the HCF provides ex ante recommendations for fiscal targets. The second report provides an ex post assessment of the extent to which the government followed the recommendations and implemented the SCP of the previous year.

Unlike the Dutch CPB, the institutional setup governing the HCF is more that of an outsider looking into the budget. Its recommendations are developed in a fairly independent manner for the government to take on as it sees fit, rather than being worked out and negotiated behind closed doors. The HCF is staffed by experts from ministries, the National Bank, the Federal Planning Bureau, and academia. The HCF's members are appointed by the Minister of Finance for a five-year renewable mandate running across electoral cycles, which helps preserve independence. The chairperson is often an academic, although ties with political parties often exist. In addition, the political principal has at times let the HCF's influence wane. Over the mid-2000s, for instance, after a number of unfavorable assessments, the Minister of Finance let the chairman's mandate lapse without appointing a successor. Although this hiatus did not obviously reflect political interference—the composition of the HCF is subject to many constraints, which can cause delays in appointments—it prevented the body from providing fiscal recommendations, resulting in a significant loss of influence (Coene and Langenus 2011).

Overall, the performance of the HCF can be broken down into two periods: pre– and post–euro adoption (Coene and Langenus 2011). In the pre–euro adoption period, the Maastricht convergence criteria led to a good alignment of policymakers' objectives with the HCF's recommendations, which were largely followed. During that period, the structural primary surplus increased

Figure 16.7. High Council of Finance Budget Balance Recommendations, Forecasts, and Outturns
(Percent of GDP)

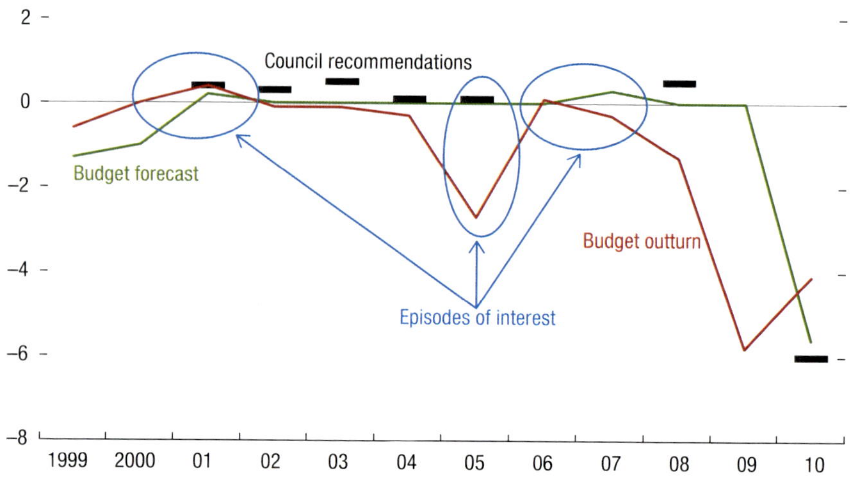

Sources: High Council of Finance; and authors' calculations.

by 5 percent of GDP, public debt started falling, and the budget moved toward balance. After euro adoption, the weight of convergence criteria in fiscal policy formulation was lost, and the appeal of the HCF's recommendations eroded. The primary balance deteriorated sharply because most of the savings on the interest bill were used to fund tax cuts and expenditure growth.

Because of data constraints, only the post–euro adoption period can be subject to an analysis similar to the one performed for the CPB. In Figure 16.7, the HCF's budget year recommendations for the fiscal balance are displayed in black, the budget forecast in green, and the outturn in red. A number of interesting episodes stand out. The first is the two years that follow adoption of the euro in 1999, when outcomes were broadly in line with the HCF's recommendations. The second episode is in 2004, when increasing divergences with the HCF's recommendations led to critical assessments of government policies. Finally, in 2005 and 2006, the HCF could not produce reports or recommendations because its chair was left vacant.

These episodes are now mapped into the measure of the HCF's media presence (Figure 16.8). In the initial period leading up to and during adoption of the euro, coverage of the HCF in the Belgian press was strong and sustained. Coverage tailed off as the 2000s progressed and the HCF clearly began losing its influence. In 2004, the HCF turned openly critical of the government's policies,[9] leading to

[9]The large deficit in 2005 was almost entirely due to a one-off debt assumption, related to the restructuring of the national railway company, which was attributed after the event.

Figure 16.8. Media Presence of the High Council of Finance
(Number of press articles)

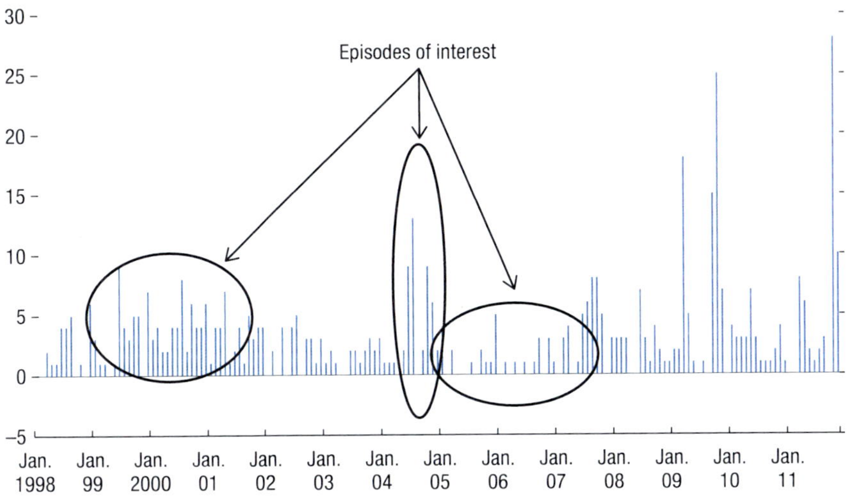

Sources: Factiva; and authors' calculations.

a surge in media reports. Finally, during the period when the HCF had no formal head and stopped reporting, its media footprint shrank substantially, despite emerging discrepancies between plans and outcomes in 2006.

Again, a more detailed analysis of the HCF's reports and press citations supports our reading of the data. In the early 2000s, when public finances were on track, press articles were relatively benign and the HCF reports noted with a fairly neutral tone minor deviations with respect to recommendations. For instance, the October 1999 report observed that "The deficit of the central government for 2000 is projected at 1 percent of GDP, which is 0.2 percent higher than recommended by the HCF." The tone of the HCF's reports changed drastically in 2004. In July of that year, it launched a stern warning in these terms: "The High Council considers these fiscal scenarios unrealistic in the medium-term," and "The High Council wants to point out that the deteriorating fiscal position is [not only] due to cyclical factors but also—and mainly—due to discretionary measures such as lowering taxes and a major growth in government spending." Of course, there is no report to quote for the last episode.

The monthly pattern of media reporting on the HCF is less clear-cut and incisive than in the Dutch case, pointing to a weaker ability to shape the public debate on fiscal policy (Figure 16.9). In particular, media presence is spread out more evenly over the year and is less concentrated around the times when the HCF published its key fiscal reports (in March and July). Such a pattern could also reflect a greater persistence of the HCF's message, for instance, because the

Figure 16.9. Average Seasonal Pattern of the High Council of Finance's Media Presence
(Percent of annual hits)

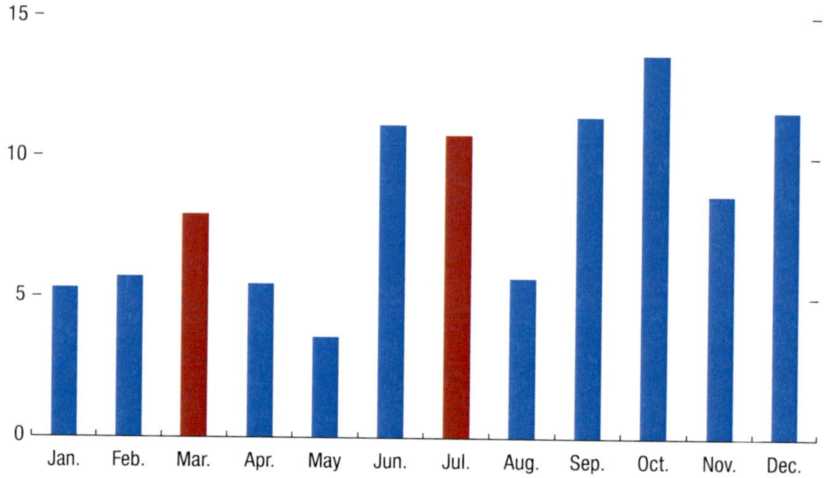

Sources: Factiva; and authors' calculations.
Note: The red bars correspond to the publication dates of the main reports.

media use the recommendations as a constant benchmark when discussing budgetary matters. Supporting that conjecture is the fact that despite less-pronounced monthly spikes than in the CPB case, a concentration of press articles cite the HCF in the latter half of the year, the period during which the budget is being negotiated and passed by parliament.

CONCLUDING REMARKS

The chapter discusses how independent fiscal institutions, even though they have no direct policy levers, can influence fiscal performance. From a theoretical perspective, the effectiveness of FCs depends on their capacity to deal with the root cause of fiscal policy biases, and, in particular, informational asymmetries between voters—the only legitimate principal in the policy game—and politicians. FCs do this by performing tasks that improve the quality of the public debate on fiscal policy (by providing analysis, recommendations, assessments, forecasts). This output allows the general public to properly process and interpret the often complex, opaque, and ideologically tainted signals received on the performance of policymakers. This line of argument means that FCs should behave and be perceived as serious watchdogs that bark when needed and are listened to.

The chapter offers an empirical assessment of this watchdog role. In line with the conclusions of the theoretical model, the analysis tries to quantify FCs' impact through their capacity to influence the public debate. We propose to proxy such influence with direct measures of media presence.

While this exploration of the statistical link between media presence and fiscal policy is promising, drawing robust conclusions would require a much broader sample. With only a handful of FCs with a sufficiently long lifetime, such exploration can only be considered a very first pass. Keeping these caveats in mind, it seems that, on average, fiscal watchdogs bark when expected. This is a necessary condition to ensure that FCs clarify signals about the appropriateness of fiscal policy, helping the general public reward good policies and sanction bad ones. If an FC can meaningfully improve policymakers' incentives, it can credibly strengthen fiscal performance. It nevertheless proved more difficult to find evidence of systematic policy corrections after peaks in FC media presence. One possible reason for these mixed results is that the repercussions of FCs' activity on the budget process might be more subtle and detectable only in specific inputs to the budget rather than in the aggregate fiscal stance itself. For instance, Debrun and Kinda (2014) show that the presence of an FC mandated to assess or produce budgetary forecasts leads to improvements in their quality (absence of bias and greater precision). Two case studies of well-established FCs lend support to the statistical findings.

An important avenue for future research would be to analyze FC design features that seem conducive to good capacity to improve the public's information about the quality of fiscal policy. The somewhat contrasting experiences of Belgium and the Netherlands suggest that strict independence from politics and recognized expertise in economics and public finance are key for the barking to be heard by all and taken seriously by policymakers.

REFERENCES

Alesina, A., and G. Tabellini. 1990. "A Positive Theory of Fiscal Deficits and Government Debt." *Review of Economic Studies* 57 (3): 403–14.

Beetsma, R., and X. Debrun. 2007. "The New Stability and Growth Pact: A First Assessment." *European Economic Review* 51 (2): 453–77.

———. 2016a. "Fiscal Councils: Rationale and Effectiveness." Working Paper 16/86, International Monetary Fund, Washington, DC.

———. 2016b. "The Political Economy of Fiscal Transparency and Independent Fiscal Councils: Theory and Evidence." Unpublished report.

Beetsma, R., M. Giuliodori, and P. Wierts. 2009. "Planning to Cheat: EU Fiscal Policy in Real Time." *Economic Policy* 24: 753–804.

Bos, F., and C. Teulings. 2011. "Evaluating Election Platforms: A Task for Fiscal Councils? Scope and Rules in Light of 25 Years of Dutch Practice." MPRA Paper 31536, University Library of Munich.

Calmfors, L. 2010. "The Role of Independent Fiscal Policy Institutions." Report to the Prime Minister's Office, Finland.

———, and S. Wren-Lewis. 2011. "What Should Fiscal Councils Do?" *Economic Policy* 26 (68): 649–95.

Coene, L., and G. Langenus. 2011. "Promoting Fiscal Discipline in a Federal Country: The Mixed Track Record of Belgium's High Council of Finance." Paper presented at the Workshop "Fiscal Policy Councils—Why Do We Need Them and What Makes Them Effective?" organized by the Austrian Government Debt Committee, Vienna, January 31.

Cukierman, A., and A. Meltzer. 1986. "A Theory of Ambiguity, Credibility, and Inflation under Discretion and Asymmetric Information." *Econometrica* 54 (5): 1099–128.

Curristine, T., J. Harris, and J. Seiwald. 2013. "Case Studies of Fiscal Councils—Functions and Impact." Policy Paper, International Monetary Fund, Washington, DC.

Debrun, X. 2011. "Democratic Accountability, Deficit Bias, and Independent Fiscal Agencies." Working Paper 11/173, International Monetary Fund, Washington, DC.

———, D. Hauner, and M. Kumar. 2009. "Independent Fiscal Agencies." *Journal of Economic Surveys* 23 (1): 44–81.

Debrun, X., T. Curristine, L. Eyraud, J. Harris, and J. Seiwald. 2013. "The Functions and Impact of Fiscal Councils." Policy Paper, International Monetary Fund, Washington, DC.

Debrun, X., and T. Kinda. 2014. "Strengthening Post-Crisis Fiscal Credibility—Fiscal Councils on the Rise. A New Dataset." Working Paper 14/58, International Monetary Fund, Washington, DC.

Debrun, X., and M. Kumar. 2009. "The Discipline-Enhancing Role of Fiscal Institutions: Theory and Empirical Evidence." In *Policy Instruments for Sound Fiscal Policies; Fiscal Rules and Institutions*, edited by J. Ayuso-i-Casals, S. Deroose, E. Flores, and L. Moulin. London: Palgrave Macmillan.

Debrun, X., L. Moulin, A. Turrini, J. Ayuso-i-Casals, and M. Kumar. 2008. "Tied to the Mast? The Role of National Fiscal Rules in the European Union." *Economic Policy* 23 (54): 298–362.

Deutsche Bank. 2016. "Better Budgeting in Europe: What Can Fiscal Councils Contribute?" *EU Monitor* (June 7): 1–20.

Fabrizio, S., and A. Mody. 2006. "Can Budget Institutions Counteract Political Indiscipline?" *Economic Policy* 21: 689–739.

Hagemann, R. 2010. "Improving Fiscal Performance through Fiscal Councils." Economics Department Working Paper 829, Organisation for Economic Co-operation and Development, Paris.

Jensen, H. 1997. "Credibility of Optimal Monetary Delegation." *American Economic Review* 87 (5): 911–20.

Jonung, L., and M. Larch. 2006. "Improving Fiscal Policy in the EU: The Case for Independent Forecasts." *Economic Policy* 21 (47): 491–534.

Kopits, G., ed. 2013. *Restoring Public Debt Sustainability: The Role of Independent Fiscal Institutions*. Oxford, U.K.: Oxford University Press.

Krogstrup, S., and C. Wyplosz. 2010. "A Common Pool Theory of Supranational Deficit Ceilings." *European Economic Review* 54 (2): 269–78.

Kumar, M. S., and T. Ter-Minassian. 2007. *Promoting Fiscal Discipline*. Washington, DC: International Monetary Fund.

Lebrun, I. 2009. "Fiscal Councils, Independent Forecasts, and the Budgetary Process: Lessons from the Belgian Case." In *Policy Instruments for Sound Fiscal Policies: Fiscal Rules and Institutions*, edited by J. Ayuso-i-Casals, S. Deroose, E. Flores, and L. Moulin, 320–345. London: Palgrave Macmillan.

McCallum, B. 1995. "Two Fallacies Concerning Central Bank Independence." *American Economic Review* 85 (2): 207–11.

Rogoff, K., and A. Sibert. 1988. "Elections and Macroeconomic Policy Cycles." *Review of Economic Studies* 55 (1): 1–16.

Wyplosz, C. 2005. "Fiscal Policy: Institutions versus Rules." *National Institute Economic Review* 191 (1): 64–78.

PART III

Supranational Fiscal Politics

CHAPTER 17

The Making of a Continental Financial System: Lessons for Europe from Early American History

VITOR GASPAR

INTRODUCTION

In the autumn of 2009, the global financial crisis mutated in Europe into sovereign debt crises in several countries of the euro area. Financial market participants were desperately seeking access to liquidity and safe assets. Credit risk became a relevant consideration for hitherto considered safe sovereign debt. The prospect breakdown of the euro area was a present threat for investors and populations. The situation started stabilizing only after political commitment to deeper integration was achieved in the European Council of June 2012. That was followed by the announcement of the Outright Monetary Transactions Program by the ECB in September 2012. One year after, in the summer of 2013, euro area fragmentation appeared to no longer be a relevant consideration in the financial calculations of international investors.

The history of financial politics in the early stages of U.S. history can provide insights into what can be done to build a robust and resilient European financial system and to establish the credibility of sovereign debt as safe assets. The U.S. federal government has never defaulted on its debt and the U.S. is a

This chapter is reprinted from the *Journal of European Integration*, Vol. 37, Vitor Gaspar, "The Making of a Continental Financial System: Lessons for Europe from Early American History," ©2015, with permission from Taylor & Francis.

The views expressed in this article are the sole responsibility of the author and should not be attributed to the International Monetary Fund, its Executive Board, or its management. The article benefited from comments, corrections and suggestions from Guillermo Calvo, Zsolt Darvas, Roger Gordon, Stephanie Hare, Heinz Hermann, Russell Kincaid, Sixten Korkman, Harold James, Johannes Lindner, Silvia Luz, Hans-Helmut Kotz, Maria Eugénia Mata, Laura Jaramillo Mayor, Yves Mersch, Ricardo Reis, Andre Sapir, Richard Sylla, Francisco Torres, Shahin Valée, Max Watson, Thomas Wieser, Guntram Wolff and Michael Woodford and participants in seminars at Bruegel, Brussels, at St. Anthony's College, Oxford, at the ECB, Frankfurt, at CFS, Frankfurt, at Columbia University, New York, and at a Conference at Eltville organized by the Bundesbank, the Bank of Japan, the Institute for Monetary and Financial Stability and the University of Hamburg.

well-integrated monetary union of continental dimension. Alexander Hamilton was the first secretary of the U.S. Treasury, from 1789 to 1795. He managed successfully the transition from a bankrupt federal government to a situation where the U.S. Treasury became the issuer of the ultimate safe asset. In the process, Alexander Hamilton laid the foundations for a modern financial system able to finance innovation and growth.

Alexander Hamilton appears as a rare combination of theoretical and practical reason; strategic and tactical thinking; and of audacity and realism. Building a Continental financial system in the aftermath of sovereign debt crises in the euro area is a priority in Europe. The aim of this article was to find out whether we can learn Hamilton's recipe for building a continental financial system in Europe.

The comparison of the challenges of Europe today and the early U.S. is the theme of Thomas Sargent Nobel Lecture (Sargent, 2013) that provided the inspiration for this article. Sargent draws on the general lessons from U.S. financial history, focusing on two episodes: the origin of the U.S. fiscal constitution in the late 1780s and the state debt crisis of the 1840s. James (2014) and Kincaid (2014) also interpret a much longer period of U.S. financial history. This article instead concentrates on a very specific period from late 1789 to early 1795 and looks at broader dimensions of finance. By concentrating on a briefer period, it is possible to examine in more detail how it was done. The paper closest to this one in scope is Sylla (2014).

The Hamilton moment illustrates the very strong threefold cord constituted by politics, fiscal policy and financial activities. As emphasized by Sargent (2013) it took a political transformation to make it possible to ground public finances on solid fundamentals. More generally, it is important to realize that changing policy outcomes systematically requires changing the rules and incentives of politics. For Europe a crucial question is: How can we (Europeans) design institutions in Europe so as to align political incentives with macroeconomic stability and financial integration? The experience of the first U.S. Secretary of the Treasury offers some inspiration.

Alexander Hamilton himself poses and answers some fundamental questions:

- Why is it important to honor public credit? Why not repudiate debt?
- By what means can public credit be maintained? How to ensure public credit? How to promote a smooth and quick transition?
- How to restore financial stability in the face of financial panic?

These answers are fundamentally relevant for Europe today. That much was clear from the summary presentation of the euro area crisis in this Introduction. The euro area and its member states are struggling to find timely answers. Those answers matter. They influence growth and employment prospects and the lives of millions of people. But there is one aspect that is crucial to stress. The only answers that can be relevant in the real world are political answers. Public finance and the financial system are part of a system of institutions in the political realm. Those institutions shape the relevant incentives and determine a set of possible outcomes. To repeat: the fundamental question is political: How can the rules of the political game, in Europe, be shaped in order to improve outcomes?

The article has a narrow focus. As already said, it looks at a well-determined episode: the experience of Alexander Hamilton as first secretary of the Treasury, from late 1789 to early 1795. The episode does not exhaust lessons from the U.S. for European financial integration. For example, the importance of politics in shaping the financial system is clear from the coalition between rural debtors, incumbent bankers, and state governments that led to a fragmentation of the U.S. national banking system through a myriad of local monopolies (see Calomiris and Haber, 2014).

The article is organized around the answers to the questions above. The history of the United States, in its early years, illustrates the importance of political institutional building. The replacement of the Articles of Confederation by the American Constitution of 1788 offers a perfect illustration. The history of subsequent decades also shows what institutional designs proved robust and which were not able to withstand political pressure.

The remainder of the article is organized as follows: the first section looks at constitutional politics in the U.S. in the 1780s. The second section presents Alexander Hamilton's vision of a modern financial system. The third section argues that the initial conditions were, according to standard indicators and analysis, very difficult. The fourth and fifth sections discuss specific actions by Hamilton. We discuss public debt management and crisis management, respectively. In the sixth section we conclude.

CHANGING THE RULES OF THE POLITICAL GAME

The challenge of building up U.S. public finances was daunting. The main problem was to ensure the service of debt accumulated during the War of Independence. At the end of 1789, total debt in the U.S. (federal and state) amounted to about $80 million (about 40 percent of GDP). Roughly speaking about one-third was States' debt and the remainder federal. In his First Report on Public Credit, Alexander Hamilton estimates the contractual interest rates as amounting to $4.6 million. Such amount compares with total operating expenditures of federal government estimates at $0.6 million.

In 1789 the U.S. was, in fact, in default. Bonds were perpetual debts (called consols). Therefore, default corresponded to the accumulation of interest arrears. Principal debt corresponded to bonds called "continental certificates" while accumulated interest arrears were named "indents." In 1789 these bonds traded at heavy discounts. At the lowest point the market value was about 20 percent for continental certificates and 12.5 percent for indents. To have a term for comparison the minimum market value for Greek 10-year bonds, in mid-2012, was about 15 percent. During the War of Independence, Congress also issued paper currency. Credibility was further undermined by the dramatic depreciation of paper money.

The situation in the 1780s still reflected the experience under the Articles of Confederation. Congress had the authority to incur debts. And, as explained in Federalist 30, the means to service these responsibilities were supposed to be provided by the States. However, the requests from Congress were left unfulfilled. The system in place was not effective. No State met its obligations in full; some did not comply at all or nearly so; and there is even at least one example of explicit refusal to comply (New Jersey). It was also the case that the attempt at reaching agreement for Congress to launch general taxation failed. The specific proposal was to launch a general import duty, whose revenue would be fully devoted to debt service. The proposal to amend the Articles of Confederation for this effect failed (first in 1781, vetoed by Rhode Island in 1782, and, second, in 1783, vetoed by New York). The proponent of these initiatives, Robert Morris, eventually resigned in 1784. Hence, it was clear at the launch of the Pennsylvania Convention that the framework of the Articles of Confederation left the debt accumulated during the War of Independence, for all practical purposes, unfunded. Congress did not have the power to tax. The inability to mobilize adequate revenue, to ensure debt service, translated into the deep discounts reported above.

The problem was political and financial. As much is clearly stated in Federalist 30:

> Money is with propriety considered a vital principle of the body politic (. . .) From a deficiency in this particulars, one of two evils must ensue: either the people must be subject to continual plunder (. . .) or the government must sink into fatal atrophy and in a short course of time must perish (. . .)
>
> (. . .) to depend upon a government that must itself depend upon thirteen others for the means of fulfilling its contracts, when once its situation is clearly understood, would require a degree of credulity, not to be often met in the pecuniary transactions of mankind, and little reconcilable with the usual sharp-sightedness of avarice.

The political solution involved having the 1788 Constitution substituting for the Articles of Confederation. The U.S. Constitution:

(a) Strengthened the ability of federal government to tax; and confirmed the ability of federal government to use public credit (Article 1, Section 8, Clauses 1 and 2).

(b) Gave the central government exclusive competence to regulate external trade and interstate commerce (Article 1, Section 8, Clause 3; "the commerce clause").

That was appropriate from the viewpoint of public finances as government revenue was—in the late 18th century—dominated by tariffs. To use an expression of Richard Sylla's, the 1788 Constitution created the "Constitutional Theater" where Alexander Hamilton acted as first U.S. Treasury Secretary. The Constitution made available the tools that would later be used by government (Sargent, 2013). The way this was done is the subject of what follows. Before doing so, next section will characterize Hamilton's financial program.

ALEXANDER HAMILTON'S FINANCIAL PROGRAM

Sylla (2011) and Sylla, Wright and Cowen (2009) characterize a modern financial system as having six main elements:

First, stable and sustainable public finances and competent public debt management;

Second, a stable currency;

Third, a central bank;

Fourth, a banking system;

Fifth, securities markets; and

Sixth, a process for incorporation of financial and non-financial businesses.

Sylla (2014) refers that these components were in place in the Dutch Republic early in the 17th century and that England introduce them shortly after the Glorious Revolution of 1688. These examples were known in the U.S. Alexander Hamilton referred to them with some frequency.

Sylla (2011) also documents that all of this information is contained in three letters that Hamilton wrote: two in 1780 (Robert Morris and James Duane, 1780a, 1780b) and 1781 (again to Robert Morris). These letters reveal a profound knowledge of financial history and institutions. According to the biography written by Ron Chernow (Chernow, 2004) Hamilton studied numerous authors including William Blackstone, Thomas Hobbes, Hugo Grotius, Samuel Pufendorf, John Locke, Malachy Postlethwaite, David Hume, Richard Price, and Adam Smith. It is clear from those writings that he was as impressed with the successful Dutch and British financial revolutions as he was with the demise of John Law's schemes in France. The latter experience may have been decisive for the First Treasury Secretary's acute sense of the importance of trust and stability in finance. From all of this Hamilton concluded that finance was key to state power and economic prosperity. The quote above clearly illustrates the link between public finances and state power. The importance of finance is made clear in the Third Letter:

> Most commercial nations have found it necessary to institute banks; and they have proved to be the happiest engines that ever were invented for advancing trade. Venice, Genoa, Hamburg, Holland, and England are examples of their utility. They owe their riches, commerce, and the figure they have made at different periods, in a great degree to this source.

When Alexander Hamilton started his tenure as Secretary of the Treasury none of the six elements, used by Sylla and co-authors to characterize a modern financial system, was in place. As we have seen in the "Changing the Rules of the Political Game" section, the Treasury was bankrupt. When he left the Treasury, all six components were in working order.

Rosseau and Sylla (1999) report estimates of average annual growth in per capita GDP, in the U.S., in the period 1790–1806 that of about 1.5 percent. This result must be put in perspective. First, it is important to recall that growth rates in per capita income before 1800 were about zero. Second, growth in per capita income in the U.S. has been persistently on a positive trend from 1790 onwards. The authors argue for a causal link between finance and growth in early U.S. history. In Rosseau and Sylla (2001), they widen the analysis to a panel of seventeen countries, in the period from 1850 to 1997. They especially examine the examples of the Dutch Republic, England, France, Germany and Japan. The authors suggest the possibility that both growth and globalization may have been "finance led." That would be in line with Hamilton's claim about: "banks . . . as the happiest engines ever invented to advance trade."

A CHALLENGING BEGINNING: WHY PAY FOR PUBLIC DEBT?

The Treasury Department was created in September 1789. It immediately got a mandate from Congress to prepare proposals to restore and maintain public credit. The urgency is clear; the First Report on Public Credit was presented in January 1790. One crucial first question was: Why pay for the public debt? Why not default?

The answer can be given at various levels. They are all present in different forms in the first Report.

First, at a very general level, public credit is a cornerstone of public finances and of financial development. Hence, it is vital for political government. It is also key for economic activity, that is, for trade, manufacturing, and farming, and, therefore, for economic prosperity. These points were systemically articulated. The structure of the argument is very close to that followed in recent research by Christoph Trebesch and co-authors (e.g., Trebesch, 2011 and Cruces and Trebesch, 2013).

Second, the debt was accumulated to finance the War of Independence. From the viewpoint of the United States, that was clearly a common good. Today we would label it a pure public (or collective) good. Therefore, the case for honoring the debt was strong on grounds of political (collective) cohesion.

Third, Hamilton was persuaded that the political coalition necessary to foster financial development involved the state and moneyed people. The latter were the main creditors of Congress. The viability of political support required an outcome compatible with the interests of creditors.

In the Introduction we have already documented that the U.S. Constitution provided the federal government with the powers necessary to fund public debt. Congress immediately approved a national tax, along the lines of the proposals that were blocked under the Articles of Confederation. Nevertheless, the starting conditions were dire.

In The First Report on Public Credit, the interests due (annually) under contractual arrangements were estimated at \$4.6 million. In 1790, the first complete year of operation of the new Constitution, total tax revenues came in at \$1.64 million (Sylla, 2011). Total operating expenses of the government amounted to \$0.825 million. So it turned out that tax revenues, while about twice operating expenditures, were only about one-third of interest payments due. We have already reported that when Hamilton took office, the U.S. was in default in its internal and international debt. It was accumulating interest arrears. Sylla (2011) further reports that in March 1790 Alexander Hamilton informed the President that the U.S. Treasury did not have enough funds to honor current expenditures and interest payments on Dutch loans. Authorization for a new $100,000 loan was sought. Within two days, Washington authorized the loan. The federal government was, in 1790, operating hand-to-mouth.

In these conditions, it was very difficult to establish trust and credibility. Nevertheless, from September 1789 when he took office, to March 1790 when the Dutch loan was obtained, the second market quote of Continental certificates and indents recovered substantially. The increase was from about 0.25 to 0.40 for the Continental certificates and from about 0.15 to 0.30 for indents. The secondary market discounts quickly diminished after that. How did he do it?

HAMILTON'S DEBT MANAGEMENT STRATEGY

Hamilton's debt management strategy aimed, first and foremost, at expectations management. It was based on two main elements: a market-based debt service reduction scheme (see Garber 1991) and a Sinking Fund.

U.S. debt was dominated, as was frequently the case in the 18th century, by consolidated perpetual annuities (consols). These bonds paid a percentage of their face value forever. The government, however, had the option to redeem, at any time, the consol at face value. That allowed the government to benefit from falling interest rates. If success in generating expectations of falling interest rates (increasing bond prices) was obtained, he could implement his market-based public debt reduction scheme. The idea is that by paying more than expected on existing debt, he would generate prospective savings that would more than compensate the costs.

Hamilton proposed to pay foreign debt in full. Surprisingly, this was not controversial. However, as Garber reports, even in the case of foreign debt, he did not allow for compound interest to apply to interest rate arrears. According to estimates in Garber (1991), the value saved as of January 1, 1790, represented about 2.3 percent of the total of foreign debt. The payment of external creditors made it possible for the U.S. to tap European bond markets. As described below, European finance played an important role in Hamilton's market-based strategy, through the use of the Sinking Fund.

For internal debt, the proposals and debated options were much richer (see Sylla, 2011 for a summary presentation and Garber, 1991, for the details). In the end, the Funding Act of August 1790 provided that domestic debt could be converted, under prescribed conditions, into new domestic debt instruments. The new bonds were 6 percent coupon bonds (the 6s), 6 percent coupon bonds with interest payments deferred 10 years (the deferred), and 3 percent coupon bonds (3s). The new bonds paid interest quarterly. The conversion offer treated principal and interest differently. For the principal, the offer was conversion at par into two-thirds 6s and one-third deferred. For interest arrears, the conversion was at par into 3s. There were specific provisions for the conversion of the debts of the States. The details are of no particular relevance for the line pursued in this article.

Garber documents that the market value of the offer was significantly below par. Hence, there was a substantial reduction in net present value of U.S. Treasury liabilities. On the same vein, Sylla shows that interest payments were reduced from about $4.6 million to $3.6 million. This was a substantial reduction.

The operation was very successful. At the end of 1794, when Hamilton was close to departing from the Treasury, 98 percent of domestic debt had been voluntarily converted. However, the take-up was gradual over time. By September 1791 only about $30 million in bonds had been converted. The response in bond market prices was much quicker.

The second important element of the plan was the Sinking Fund. The Fund was entitled to revenue generated by the operation of the Post Office. In the First Report on Public Credit, this revenue is estimated at $100,000. It was further asserted that the sum was likely to considerably grow over time. Hence, the Fund benefited from an important and reliable source of funding. The main ostensive argument for the Sinking Fund was the need to repay (to extinguish) public debt. However, the Sinking Fund could also use loans. That provided the Fund with considerable flexibility.

Therefore, the Sinking Fund was able to play three very important (and related) roles: first, to anchor expectations on a regime where Treasuries were properly funded; second, to accelerate the transition (increase) in bond prices to their new fundamental value ("true standard); and, third, to provide the Treasury with an effective instrument for bond market stabilization in case of disturbances. The latter role was not yet made explicit. It became clear through the actions of the Sinking Fund in stopping the financial panics of 1791 and, more clearly and importantly, 1792.

HOW DID HAMILTON RESTORE FINANCIAL STABILITY IN THE FACE OF FINANCIAL PANIC?

The success of the plan and the rapid development of financial markets and financial organizations led, in 1792, to a dangerous threat to financial stability. In a letter to William Seton, in early 1792, Hamilton expresses his grave concern with developments observed in securities' markets: "these extravagant sallies of speculation do injury to the government and to the whole system of public credit." Given that bond prices peaked in February 1792, a few weeks after the letter was written, the episode testifies how closely and accurately Hamilton observed financial market developments. Already in 1791 there had been a financial disturbance in August–September. The 1791 disturbance was associated with speculation in banks' stock. In that context, the Sinking Fund was used to stabilize bond markets.

However, it is the panic of 1792 that provides the paradigmatic example. Sylla, Wright and Cowen (2009) argue that these actions anticipate the classical lender of last resort doctrine.

The classical function of lender of last resort was articulated by Thornton (1802) and Bagehot (1873). An excellent presentation is Humphrey (1992). The lender of last resort function aims at protecting the financial system as a whole. It does not aim to save individual organizations. Only illiquid but solvent corporations are eligible for lender of last resort assistance. Insolvent entities should fail. The balance sheet and financial integrity of the liquidity provider are protected by adequate collateral. According to the doctrine, liquidity, through the lender of last resort function, should be available only at penalty rates.

In letters to William Seton, Hamilton defends the provision of very large amounts of liquid funds. Those liquid funds should be made available against the pledging of good collateral. The cost of funding suggested was 7 percent (that was the ceiling fixed in usury laws). Hence the interpretation of Sylla et al. that Hamilton was an early practitioner of the lender of last resort doctrine.

But there is an interesting question. What assets were identified as sound collateral? In the letter quoted in Sylla, Wright and Cowen (2009), Hamilton lists the 6s, the 3s and the deferred as the appropriate assets for the purpose. He suggests that the 6s should be accepted as collateral at par, the 3s should be accepted at 50 percent of nominal value, and the deferred at 60 percent. These values are below but close to the market prices that were to prevail in April 1792 (but clearly below those that had prevailed in early March). Sylla et al. also quote a remarkably clear message to William Seton where he urges the Bank of New York to ponder "how much more can be done in favor of parties who can pledge Public Stock as collateral security. This security of credit you are sure is a good one." It is hard to think how a case for U.S. Treasuries as safe and liquid assets could be made more emphatically. Perceptions of what are safe and liquid assets act as cornerstones in financial structures. Perceptions and expectations of assets as safe are shaped under financial stress. Hamilton used the 1792 crisis to promote the emergence of U.S. bonds as the ultimate safe and liquidity asset: a safe haven in times of distress.

There is another important point worth repeating. Alexander Hamilton was concerned with the stability of the system. Financial instability threatened the whole edifice that was being built. The economic consequences of financial instability are so far-reaching that they fundamentally influence the effects of financial systems on economic performance. These effects, in turn, have broader political consequences.

LESSONS FOR BUILDING A CONTINENTAL FINANCIAL SYSTEM IN EUROPE

The first lesson to be drawn is that politics, finance, and fiscal policy are co-determined and co-evolutionary. The process must be conceived and executed in a systemic way. What can be achieved in one dimension is determined simultaneously with the other two.

The U.S. is a monetary union backed by a well-integrated financial system and federal public finances. The euro area is an international monetary union backed by national (political) responsibility for fiscal sustainability. In the sovereign debt crisis in the euro area, financial fragmentation substituted for financial integration. Since mid-2012 the trend of financial disintegration was inverted. Europe is on its way to creating a banking union and a financial union.

The process of European integration has been driven to a very large extent by economic integration. The single market and the single currency are its most emblematic realizations. The European Union provides a pole of attraction and a role model favoring peace, democracy and human rights. Specifically, it shows the possibility of effective application of international law.

The second lesson is that there is a case to give priority to public credit; a case that is based on political, public finance and also on broader economic and financial arguments. The arguments put forward by Hamilton are in line with the implications of recent empirical research by Christoph Trebesch and coauthors. Alexander Hamilton managed to establish public credit while ensuring debt service at favorable terms.

To my mind this lesson is very general. It applies at the national level. It is also a precondition for successful financial integration.

The third lesson is that the fundamental foundation of public credit requires fiscal sustainability. In the U.S., that required the U.S. Constitution to substitute for the Articles of Confederation.

In the euro area after the failure of euro area governance to prevent the crisis, very significant progress was achieved. First, the fiscal governance of the euro area has been strengthened through the adoption of important EU legal acts (the six pack and the two pack). Second, and more importantly, in parallel, member states have also adopted the fiscal compact. Broadly speaking, the rules in the fiscal compact are in line with the six pack.[1] The important difference is that the fiscal compact aims at internalizing the European constraints into national governance frameworks. This aspect is decisive. In Europe, politics are dominated by the fundamental principle of the dominance of the national dimension of politics. Hence, European rules can only be fully effective once subsumed in the national frameworks.

The European rules prescribe a fiscal position close to balance or in surplus over the medium term. The effective operation of such rule ensures a slowly declining public debt-to-GDP ratio (assuming positive nominal growth of GDP over the medium term). Fiscal sustainability is guaranteed by compliance with European rules. Nevertheless, it is sobering to recall that government default in the early years of the U.S. had, at its root, political behavior not in line with the letter of the Articles of Confederation. At the end of the day, the responsibility

[1] The fiscal governance framework in the euro area has also become more complex, which gives rise to a number of other challenges (see Eyraud and Wu, 2014).

has to be national: in accordance with the principle of the primacy of the national dimension of politics.

Clearly it is possible to deny the primacy of the national dimension of politics and to advocate centralization. However, it seems to me that centralization is neither politically desirable nor politically feasible.

The fourth lesson is that smooth and quick transition requires active and skillful management. This is particularly so given the importance of perceptions and expectations. The transition must be so managed that perverse equilibrium paths are avoided.

In Europe, financial support has been made available in diverse forms. The European Central Bank (ECB) has signaled that "Within our mandate, the ECB is ready to do whatever it takes to preserve the euro" and Mario Draghi, the President of the ECB added, "and believe me it will be enough." The ECB announcement came in July 2012. One month after, heads of state or government reached a political agreement on deeper economic and monetary union. Since August 2012 quick progress has been achieved. In the autumn of 2013, the catastrophic risk associated with euro area fragmentation was no longer a salient concern for global investors. Nevertheless, a transition is never complete before the new framework is capable to prevent accidents and to minimize their effects in case they occur.

That leads to the fifth lesson: given that it is always possible that accidents will happen, public finance and the financial system must be robust and resilient. The institutional framework underpinning budgetary discipline and financial stability must be designed so as to be able to stem episodes of financial panic and to exclude perverse self-fulfilling equilibria. Alexander Hamilton proved more than equal to the task during the financial panic of 1792.

In 2009–2010, the euro area was not prepared for sovereign debt crises. The euro area was unable to prevent financial fragmentation and negative sovereign-bank credit risk feedback loops. Much progress has been made. But the job is not yet done. The priority is the realization of the banking union complemented by the integration and development of financial markets. The credibility of the banking union requires the existence of financial backstops of sufficient capacity to break the vicious sovereign-bank links and, hence, to ensure robust and resilient financial integration.

It is also important to bear in mind that financial transitions are dangerous moments. Liberalization and opening of financial systems is often associated with exuberance and excess. The local connection between politics and finance adds up to complexity. Financial crises, especially when associated with balance sheet vulnerability, have very long-lasting consequences, spanning generations. Therefore, the ability to maintain financial stability is key for the long-run consequences of financial architectures. Transition risks have also to be pondered. This is particularly important when building continental financial systems.

In the end, it is clear there is no recipe for baking a continental financial system. Institution building requires deep understanding of the specifics of the particular case.

To conclude: For Europeans, the most inspiring message may well be:

> Whoever considers the nature of our government with discernment will see that though obstacles and delays will frequently stand in the way of the adoption of good measures, yet when once adopted, they are likely to be stable and permanent. It will be far more difficult to undo than to do. Gazette of the United States, September 1, 1790.

Paraphrasing Thomas Sargent: That may well have been true of the U.S. then and it is certainly true for Europe now.

REFERENCES

Bagehot, W., 1873, *Lombard Street*, London: H.S. King in *The Collected Works of Walter Bagehot,* volume nine, edited N. St. John-Stevas, London: The Economist.

Calomiris, Charles and Stephen Haber, 2014, *Fragile by Design: the Political Origins of Banking Crises and Scarce Credit,* Princeton: Princeton University Press.

Chernow, Ron, 2004. *Alexander Hamilton,* New York: Penguin Books.

Cruces, Juan J. and Christoph Trebesch. 2013. Sovereign Defaults: The Price of Haircuts, *American Economic Journal: Macroeconomics*, 5 (3), pp 85–117.

Eyraud, Luc, and Tao Wu, 2014, "Euro Area Policies: 2014 Article IV Consultation Selected Issues", IMF Country Report No. 14/199.

Garber, Peter 1991, Alexander Hamilton's Market Based Debt Reduction Plan, *NBER Working Paper* 3597, January.

Hamilton, Alexander, 1780, Letter to Robert Morris, *First Letter,* Available from Alexander Hamilton, 1904, *The Works of Alexander Hamilton,* volume III, ed. Henry Cabot Lodge (Federal Edition), New York: G.P. Putnam's Sons.

Hamilton, Alexander 1780, Letter to James Duane, dated September 3, *Second Letter,* Available from Alexander Hamilton, 1904, *The Works of Alexander Hamilton,* volume I, ed. Henry Cabot Lodge (Federal Edition), New York: G.P. Putnam's Sons.

Hamilton, Alexander 1781, Letter to Robert Morris dated April 30, *Third Letter,* Available from Alexander Hamilton, 1904, *The Works of Alexander Hamilton,* volume III, ed. Henry Cabot Lodge (Federal Edition), New York: G.P. Putnam's Sons.

Humphrey, T., 1992, Lender of Last Resort, in P. Newman, M. Milgate and J. Eatwell (eds.), *The New Palgrave Dictionary of Money & Finance,* London: Macmillan.

James. 2014.

Kincaid, Russell, 2014, Comments on Vitor Gaspar's paper, "The Making of a Continental Financial System: Lessons For Europe from Early American History."

Rosseau, Pierre and Richard Sylla, 1999, Emerging Financial Markets and Early U.S. Growth, *NBER Working Paper* 7448, December.

Rosseau, Pierre and Richard Sylla, 2001, Financial systems, economic growth, and globalization", *NBER Working Paper* 8323, December.

Sargent, Thomas 2013. United States Then, Europe Now, *Nobel Lecture.* Chapter 10 in Thomas Sargent, *Rational Expectations and Inflation,* Third Edition, Princeton: Princeton University Press.

Sylla, Richard, 2011, Financial Foundations: Public Credit, the National Bank, and Securities Markets, in Douglas Irwin and Richard Sylla (eds.), *Founding Choices: American Economic Policy in the 1790s,* Chicago: University of Chicago Press, pages 59–88.

Sylla, Richard, 2014, Early U.S. Struggles with Fiscal Federalism: Lessons for Europe?, *Comparative Economic Studies,* Volume 56, Issue 2, 157–175.

Sylla, Richard, Robert Wright and David Cowen, 2009, Central Banker: Crisis Management during the Financial Panic of 1792, *Business History Review,* Volume 83, Spring, pp. 61–86.

Thornton, H., 1802, *An Enquiry into the Nature and Effects of the Paper Credit of Great Britain,* F. von Hayek, (ed.) London: George Allen & Unwin, 1939.

Trebesch, Christoph, 2011, Sovereign Default and Crisis Resolution, Ph.D. Dissertation, Berlin: Free University of Berlin.

CHAPTER 18

Fiscal Politics in the Euro Area

LUC EYRAUD, VITOR GASPAR, AND TIGRAN POGHOSYAN

INTRODUCTION

Like many other advanced economies, euro area (EA) countries have faced a significant accumulation of public debt in the past three decades. The public-debt-to-GDP ratio of the EA as a whole increased from an average level of less than 60 percent of GDP in the early 1990s to more than 90 percent of GDP in 2015. The surge in debt was particularly pronounced in 2009 and 2010 at the peak of the global financial crisis. Some countries were priced out of the market and contagion set in, with fiscal stress in some member states spilling over to others.

To explain the deterioration of fiscal positions, a large body of the literature has focused on the shortcomings of the institutional framework in Europe, in particular, the design of supranational fiscal rules and the incompletion of the Economic and Monetary Union (for example, Sapir and Wolff 2015; Benassy-Quere, Ragot, and Wolff 2016). Others have pointed to the role of the fiscal stimulus undertaken in the first years of the crisis and the materialization of contingent liabilities, including the rescue of the banking sector and the losses incurred by state-owned enterprises (IMF 2012). More recently, emphasis has been placed on the role of macroeconomic developments in general and low nominal growth in particular (IMF 2016a). Less attention has been paid to political economy considerations, although they can also account for deviations from sound fiscal policy and rising debt ratios.

This chapter takes a different approach and analyzes how political factors have negatively affected fiscal outcomes in the EA between 1999 and 2015. Its main contributions are threefold: from a conceptual point of view, the chapter extends the analysis of political economy factors and policy distortions, which are usually examined in the context of unitary countries, to the supranational level; from an

The authors thank for their comments Santiago Acosta-Ormaechea, Narcissa Balta, John Bluedorn, Lucas ter Braak, Nicolas Carnot, Paolo Cavallino, Xavier Debrun, Mark Flanagan, Sebastian Hauptmeier, James John, Will Kerry, Martin Larch, Johannes Lindner, Patrick Lunz, Adina Popescu, Philipp Rother, Murtaza Syed, and members of the National Bank of Belgium and the German and French Ministries of Finance. The authors are also grateful to Alessandra Cepparulo, Gilles Mourre, and Matteo Salto (all from the European Commission) for sharing the data sets on Stability and Convergence Programs and Excessive Deficit Procedure recommendations. Juna Luzi provided excellent research assistance.

empirical point of view, the chapter reviews a series of policy biases, including the relationship between country size and budget execution; and from a normative point of view, the chapter brings a novel perspective on fiscal governance reforms by focusing on how to correct incentives, while the literature has placed a greater emphasis on strengthening the economic rationale for the rules.

The purpose of the chapter is to document fiscal policy biases and compliance with existing fiscal rules. Whether the rules themselves are well designed is beyond the scope of this chapter. For example, the conduct of national fiscal policies when common monetary policy is constrained by the effective lower bound is not discussed here.

The remainder of the chapter is structured as follows: The second section argues that political economy factors affect fiscal outcomes at both the national and supranational levels in the EA, which creates a number of fiscal policy biases. The third section presents empirical evidence on these policy biases and shows that fiscal rules have not been effective in correcting them. The fourth section reviews past reforms and suggests options for the future. The final section concludes.

A POLITICAL ECONOMY PERSPECTIVE ON FISCAL POLICY BIASES IN THE EURO AREA

The European Union (EU) is a unique construct that cannot be described as a standard federal system. The specific institutional setup raises political economy issues, including some that are absent from unitary and federal states. In this context, this section documents policy biases in the EA at both the national and supranational levels.

This chapter adopts a broad definition of the notion of "political economy," understood to be the analysis of the interactions between the political environment and the economic system. In particular, we consider that the political economy field is not limited to the examination of political institutions per se but also covers tangential issues, such as cross-country policy coordination or the effect of fiscal reforms and fiscal developments on public confidence.

Policy Biases at the National Level

Policies conducted by rational and elected policymakers can produce suboptimal outcomes. The reasons for and nature of these deviations from optimality have been widely explored by the literature, and they apply to many policy instruments, including monetary policy (inflationary bias) and structural policy (status quo bias). In the fiscal area, deviations from optimal policy primarily take the form of excessive deficits and a tendency of fiscal policy to be procyclical (Figure 18.1). In principle, fiscal policy could be procyclical without exhibiting a deficit bias, but the deficit bias results in large part from a failure to control spending increases and tax cuts in "good times." Thus, the two biases are closely related in practice.

Figure 18.1. National Political Economy

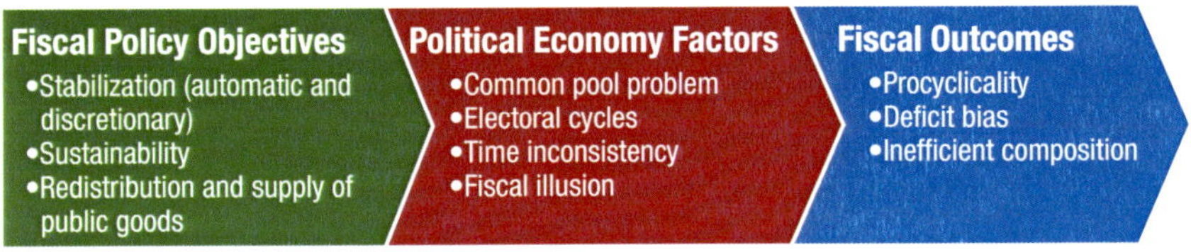

Source: Authors' compilation.

Although some economic arguments can account for fiscal policy biases, political factors are often the first ones to blame (Alesina and Perotti 1995; Eslava 2006; Debrun, Hauner, and Kumar 2009): politicians' reelection concerns and partisanship (leading to a short-term orientation for fiscal policy with opportunistic preelection spending as well as a tendency to produce optimistic revenue forecasts or unrealistic spending estimates); incentives to deviate from previous promises when economic agents have already adjusted their expectations and behavior (the "time inconsistency" problem, which could, for instance, occur with certain tax announcements); failure by heterogeneous groups such as line ministries, levels of government, or coalition parties to internalize the cost to the community of their competing claims on the government revenue pool (the "common pool" problem[1]); or the population's imperfect understanding of tax and debt finance combined with a misperception of the government's intertemporal budget constraint ("fiscal illusion").

Political economy considerations can also affect the composition of fiscal policy. In particular, in times of fiscal adjustment, public investment cuts and tax increases may be favored over current expenditure restraint for reasons that are not related to efficiency and equity. For instance, governments may be tempted to reduce public investment that yields benefits for future voters compared with the immediate political gains derived from protecting spending on transfers. In addition, public investment cuts are often less disruptive to the provision of public services. An excessive reliance on tax measures can be motivated by their smaller negative effect on economic activity in the short term (potentially offset by larger costs in the medium term), their concentrated impact on the electorate (at least for progressive income taxes), and their lower visibility relative to expenditure

[1] A common pool problem occurs when the benefits of spending accrue disproportionately to a particular group but the cost of taxation is spread over all groups. Because of this mismatch, individual groups do not internalize the full cost of expenditure (in terms of marginal taxation) and tend to overspend. In particular, common pool problems are prevalent when several decision makers (for example, spending ministers) compete for the public goods.

cuts (because broad tax bases can generate significant revenues from relatively small rate hikes).

Policy Biases at the Supranational Level

The EU is a unique entity that shares features of federal systems without properly falling under the definition (Moravcsik 2001; Hazak 2012). The EU lacks a number of legal and institutional elements that are present in federations. Unlike states in a federation, EU member states retain most of their sovereignty, and the national dimension of politics continues to predominate in the discussions at the European level (Gaspar 2012). Some argue that the EU construct lies between a fully federal system (such as the United States) and an intergovernmental cooperation system (such as the United Nations). Another important difference is that legislative powers are split between the European Parliament (EP) and the Council of the European Union—the latter represents the governments of the member states and is composed of national ministers. The vast majority of European laws are adopted jointly by the EP and the Council, although the EP involvement depends on which procedure the proposal is being adopted under.[2]

Focusing on the fiscal area, differences are apparent in all dimensions of fiscal policy (Cottarelli and Guerguil 2014). The size of the EU budget and its staff are very small compared with standard federal budgets and civil service; risk sharing and redistribution mechanisms are less developed; the EU does not have the ability to borrow for the general budget or tax citizens directly and draws its resources from member states' contributions; fiscal policy is subject to a very complex set of fiscal rules but enforcement mechanisms are weaker than in federations, and there are no direct controls from the center on member states' fiscal policies; and harmonization of spending and tax policies across states is very limited.

In the EA, another important aspect to consider is the existence of strong cross-country fiscal spillovers associated with trade linkages, confidence effects, the high degree of financial market integration, and the single monetary policy response.[3] Through these channels, fiscal imbalances in a given member state may affect the fiscal positions of other member states. These spillovers can go in either direction, either improving or deteriorating the fiscal position of neighboring countries. Empirical evidence of negative spillovers is provided by Caporale and Girardi (2013), who show that government yields of EA countries are strongly linked to each other. Therefore, deterioration in the fiscal position of a given country can be transmitted to the borrowing costs of other member states. Fiscal spillovers can also be positive, particularly when they are transmitted through the

[2] Under the "ordinary legislative procedure" (also called "co-decision"), the EP has equal legislative power with the Council. However, the EP's role is more limited under the other (called "special") legislative procedures, including consent and consultation.

[3] For instance, the European Central Bank may tighten monetary policy to contain inflation fueled by fiscal expansion in a specific country, particularly if it is a large one. Conversely, it can loosen the monetary stance in the EA as a whole if localized fiscal imbalances create risks of contagion, higher risk premiums, and disorderly market conditions.

Figure 18.2. Supranational Political Economy

Source: Authors' compilation.

trade channel: fiscal relaxation in one country may benefit its trading partners by raising the demand for export goods and services, as evidenced by several empirical papers (Giuliodori and Beetsma 2004; Beetsma, Giuliodori, and Wierts 2009). EC (2014) provides a comprehensive literature review of the spillovers in the EA by type of channel and type of shock.

All these specifics of the European institutional setup give rise to a number of political economy and policy coordination considerations that come on top of the ones prevailing at the national level (Figure 18.2):

- *Common pool problem at the supranational level.*[4] The process of fiscal integration in Europe may reinforce the common pool problem (and the related tendency to overspend), because it increases the number of constituencies and decision makers, and reduces transparency in the allocation of funds (von Hagen 2012). However, this concern should not be overstated given the small size of the EU budget and the fund allocation procedures (with each member state having veto power over individual budget items). A more serious common pool problem arises from the integration of bond markets. From the adoption of the euro until the global financial crisis, national bonds became quasi-perfect substitutes, with the process of financial liberalization resulting in a dramatic convergence of government bond yields.[5] Detken, Gaspar, and Winkler (2004) argue that the elimination of the exchange rate risk following the introduction of the euro rendered government bond markets close to perfect substitutes. Bond markets started

[4] The common pool problem could also be described as a type of fiscal spillover (because it creates an interdependence between the utility functions of individual states). Nonetheless, to simplify the discussion, this section separates the two issues to emphasize that the fiscal implications of the common pool are primarily borne by the country itself (in the form of overspending), while fiscal spillovers focus on the effects on other countries.

[5] Low credibility of the no-bailout clause of the Maastricht Treaty is another possible explanation for the convergence of sovereign yields.

functioning like a common pool of financing, which created conditions for localized credit booms and made contagion effects more likely (Bernoth, von Hagen, and Schuknecht 2012). Since the beginning of the crisis, the common pool has fragmented as a result of greater country differentiation of sovereign bond yields and the repricing of sovereign credit risk (Afonso, Arghyrou, and Kontonikas 2015). Nonetheless, nonfundamental and/or global factors continue to be important drivers of bond yields (ECB 2014).

- *Distorted incentives with respect to the fiscal stance.* In the presence of cross-country spillovers, the fiscal actions of individual countries have implications not only for their domestic economies, but also on the macroeconomic and fiscal conditions of other member states. If countries do not internalize the impact of their actions on others, distortions may arise. With positive spillovers, countries may have a tendency to conduct overly restrictive fiscal policies because they do not internalize the benefit of a fiscal expansion on other countries. With negative spillovers, the opposite bias materializes. For instance, individual countries may not fully internalize the costs of their fiscal profligacy in a common bond market. In equilibrium, with all governments making the same calculation, public debt and interest rates could rise compared with a situation of no interdependence across fiscal positions. Partly to address these issues, the EU has set up a yearly cycle of economic and fiscal policy coordination called the European Semester (which is supplemented by a review of national budget plans in EA countries), but this exercise cannot be described as a full-fledged cooperative approach meant to contain spillovers, given that fiscal plans are examined rather than negotiated between Brussels and the member states.
- *Biased enforcement of fiscal rules.* The unique surveillance and coordination procedures within the EU have posed challenges for enforcement. The responsibility for enforcement is shared between the European Commission (EC) and the Economic and Financial Affairs Council (ECOFIN), which comprises finance ministers of member states. The EC has the right and duty to monitor implementation of the Stability and Growth Pact (SGP) without having full power to take action in cases of noncompliance because ECOFIN has the final word on monitoring and enforcement decisions. This incomplete separation of powers between the two entities has long been seen as a weakness of the SGP for at least two reasons: First, the ECOFIN gathers officials responsible to their own countries' constituencies and with the mandate of advancing national interests. As a result, some have argued that the enforcement of the SGP has not been evenhanded, with preferential treatment granted to larger countries holding more voting rights (Cartenaro and Morris 2008). Second, ECOFIN members may have incentives to be lenient and avoid actions that are politically costly for other members because they might find themselves in a position of fiscal distress in the future. Otmar Issing, former Board Member and chief economist of the European Central Bank, described this implicit collusion situation as one in which potential sinners pass judgment on actual sinners. The

financial crisis has further accentuated this bias, with peer pressure becoming less effective when the number of fiscal delinquents rises.[6]

- *Deficit of democratic legitimacy and scapegoating of the center.* The deficit of legitimacy of the EU has multiple and complex roots. Among them is the limited remit of the EP, which creates a sense of "democratic shortfall." The EP has no right to initiate legislation, has no supervision over the Council of the European Union, and it may dismiss the EC only *en bloc* (not individual commissioners). Under special legislative procedures, the EP's legislative powers are more limited than those of the Council of the European Union, which is not a directly elected body (Kardasheva 2009). As a result, the European institutions are often perceived by the public as unelected and unaccountable entities. A second issue is the lack of transparency in the decision-making process: on many matters, decision making is intergovernmental (rather than supranational), which provides for less democratic oversight. For instance, with regard to the ECOFIN decisions, there are no minutes describing the discussions, only press releases with the content of the agreement that has been reached. Furthermore, the fact that the ECOFIN combines legislative and executive powers (with the ability to legislate on the fiscal framework and decide on its implementation) may result in excessive concentration of powers and undermine the system of checks and balances. Third, the complexity and sophistication of the governance framework, particularly in the fiscal area, make it difficult to understand. This problem is somewhat compounded by the multiplicity of monitoring schemes, which occasionally produce contradicting messages. All these factors have translated into a lack of transparency and ownership of the SGP. Exploiting this legitimacy gap, national policymakers have tended to attribute the responsibility for difficult and politically costly decisions to the center. During the global financial crisis, the fact that a number of assistance programs had been conducted under the surveillance of the EC reinforced the perception that fiscal austerity was imposed by Brussels rather than by the necessity to regain normal financial market access, rebuild buffers, and restore credibility after the crisis.

EMPIRICAL EVIDENCE ON FISCAL POLICY BIASES IN THE EURO AREA

As discussed in the previous section, political economy factors create policy distortions and can result in suboptimal fiscal outcomes. In particular, political considerations can lead to excessive spending in good times, eroding fiscal buffers and necessitating procyclical fiscal adjustments in downturns. During periods of fiscal consolidation, political preferences could be tilted toward preserving unproductive spending and increasing distortionary taxes, making fiscal composition less "growth friendly."

---

[6] This is because reputation costs decline, the "sinners judging sinners" incentive problem becomes more acute, and the difficulty of imposing sanctions increases with the number of delinquent countries.

Mindful of these risks, the SGP was designed to constrain fiscal discretion at the national level. The main objective of the SGP is to prevent national fiscal policies from having negative spillovers on other countries. Another objective is to help countries create fiscal buffers and allow fiscal policy to respond to country-specific shocks (euro-area-wide shocks are, in principle, left to the single monetary policy). To this aim, the SGP and the subsequent legislation has set numerical limits on various fiscal aggregates and developed a multilateral monitoring mechanism to ensure that deviations from the fiscal targets are corrected within a reasonable time frame (EC 2016b).

This section provides empirical evidence on the fiscal policy biases described above by reviewing macrofiscal performance under the SGP and the track record of fiscal rules. Its main purpose is to assess whether the governance framework has been effective in correcting policy biases. The analysis relies mainly on two databases, covering 19 EA countries over the period 1999–2015.[7] The first is the AMECO database maintained by the EC's Directorate General for Economic and Financial Affairs, which contains information on ex post outturns of macroeconomic and fiscal variables. The second is a real-time database building on various vintages of the Stability and Convergence Programs submitted by member states. These programs contain information on outturns of macroeconomic and fiscal variables at the time of the release as well as projections up to three years ahead.

Macrofiscal Performance under the SGP

Evidence of Procyclical Fiscal Policy

Although the main objective of the SGP is to prevent the buildup of excessive deficit and debt, it also leaves room for macroeconomic stabilization.[8] Stabilization can, in principle, take the form of automatic stabilizers and discretionary fiscal policy. The SGP puts emphasis on automatic stabilizers and tries to limit the scope for discretionary policy by imposing country-specific structural balance targets called medium-term objectives, or MTOs (Buti and Van den Noord 2004). If countries comply with these structural balance targets, their discretionary fiscal policy should, in principle, be acyclical, in the sense that their underlying fiscal stance would remain unchanged regardless of the cyclical position.[9] At the same time, automatic stabilizers would operate in full. The benchmark MTO is

[7] To ensure consistency, the empirical analysis is conducted since 1999, although some EA countries (Cyprus, Estonia, Greece, Latvia, Lithuania, Malta, Slovak Republic, and Slovenia) joined the single currency area later.

[8] IMF (2015a) provides recent empirical evidence on fiscal stabilization and reviews the relevant literature.

[9] Although compliance with MTOs is assessed using asymmetric fiscal balance *ceilings*, the legislation describes them as *targets*, in the sense that countries are expected to converge toward their MTOs and stay close to them. For instance, EC (2016b) states that "the country-specific medium-term objective corresponds to the structural budgetary position that Member States should achieve, and maintain, over the cycle." Therefore, complying with the MTO should limit the ability of countries to run a countercyclical policy. In practice, however, nothing prevents countries from overshooting their MTO targets, which could create space for a relaxation of the structural fiscal stance in bad times.

a structural deficit ceiling of 0.5 percent of potential GDP. Combined with the 3 percent nominal deficit ceiling, this should leave sufficient room for automatic stabilizers to operate during a normal cycle (Eyraud and Wu 2015).

In practice and despite these safeguards, the EU member states, like many other countries, seem to have pursued a procyclical fiscal stance and prevented automatic stabilizers from operating freely. The issue is widely discussed in the literature and the results are mixed depending on the sample period, the data source, and the empirical specification adopted. Some studies find that fiscal policy in the EA was acyclical until the beginning of the global financial crisis (Buti and Van den Noord 2004; Fatas and Mihov 2009), but most studies report evidence of procyclicality, especially in good times and following the introduction of the SGP in 1999 (EC 2004; Cimadomo 2005; Candelon, Muysken, and Vermeulen 2007; Deroose, Larch, and Schaechter 2008). The results also depend on whether the analysis is conducted ex post or in real time. In general, the evidence of procyclicality is weaker when real-time data are used, suggesting that there could be a difference between the ex ante intentions of fiscal authorities and ex post outcomes (Forni and Momigliano 2005; Cimadomo 2008; Golinelli and Momigliano 2006; Bernoth, Hughes Hallet, and Lewis 2008).

To investigate these issues, we first plot the changes in output gaps and changes in cyclically adjusted fiscal balances in EA countries over 1999–2015 (Figure 18.3).

Figure 18.3. Relationship between Changes in Cyclically Adjusted Balances and Output Gaps

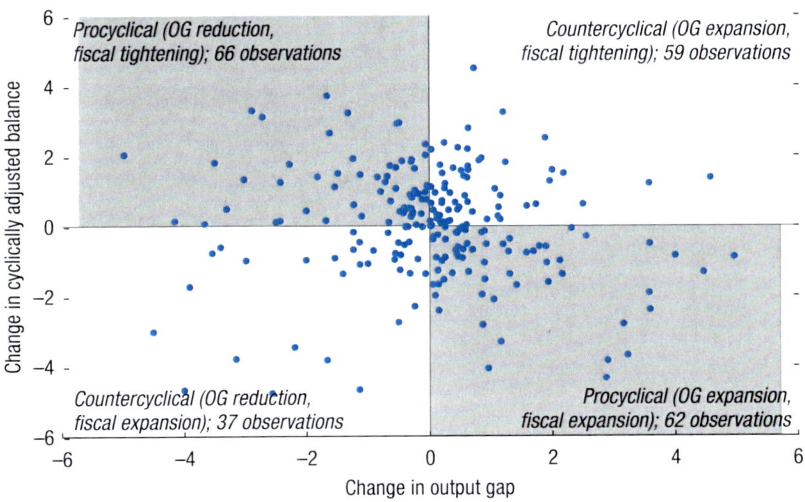

Sources: Annual Macroeconomic Database of the European Commission's Directorate General for Economic and Financial Affairs; and authors' estimates.
Note: The sample includes 19 euro area countries over 1999–2015. The figure reports the contemporaneous association between the variables (measured in percentages). Outlier observations (above 5 percent and below −5 percent) are excluded to improve the visual representation of the scatterplot. OG = output gap.

A procyclical fiscal stance would imply that observations should be concentrated in the upper-left or lower-right quadrants; a countercyclical stance would appear in the upper-right or lower-left quadrants; an acyclical fiscal stance would generate no systematic association between the two series. In practice, a negative association can be observed in more than half of the observations: in such cases, discretionary fiscal policy has loosened in periods when output growth exceeded its potential rate of growth (lower-right quadrant) and contracted in periods when output growth was below its potential (upper-left quadrant).

Various caveats apply to the descriptive analysis of Figure 18.3. The scatterplot does not show a strong negative relationship, perhaps because the variables of interest (output gap and fiscal stance) are subject to measurement errors. The bivariate correlation may also be spurious if it is driven by other factors that are not controlled for. In addition, Figure 18.3 does not tell whether the procyclical bias appeared at the planning stage or implementation stage of the budget. One possibility is that fiscal policy plans were already procyclical at the outset (despite the rules). Another possibility is that fiscal plans were acyclical or countercyclical, but procyclicality occurred through fiscal slippages during budget implementation.[10]

For all these reasons, a more formal econometric analysis is conducted to evaluate how fiscal policy responds to the economic cycle in the EA. Following the approach adopted in the real-time literature, we assess the respective contributions of policy *planning* and *implementation* to fiscal procyclicality by running the following regression for the sample of EA countries over 1999–2015 (see Cimadomo 2011 for a survey):

$$\Delta sb_{i,t} = \alpha_i + \beta \times \Delta gap_{i,t} + \gamma \times debt_{i,t-1} + \rho_t + \varepsilon_{i,t.} \qquad (18.1)$$

where i and t indicate countries and years, sb is the structural-balance-to-potential-GDP ratio, and $debt$ is the debt-to-GDP ratio. The main coefficient of interest is β, which measures whether discretionary fiscal policy is procyclical, countercyclical, or acyclical. A negative coefficient implies a procyclical fiscal stance (and a positive coefficient implies a countercyclical stance), while a statistically insignificant coefficient would suggest that the stance was acyclical. The regression also controls for the initial level of debt to capture a possible policy reaction aimed at ensuring debt sustainability.

Our estimations are performed using different vintages of the Stability and Convergence Programs (which include both plans and real-time realizations) and the latest AMECO database (ex post historical data as of 2016). Table 18.1 presents estimation results for three sets of variables: one-year ahead planned fiscal impulse and expected change in output gap (column (1)); real-time fiscal impulse and change in output gap as reported in the following year (column (2)); and ex post fiscal impulse and change in output gap using the latest vintage of the data

[10] These slippages may occur in a variety of contexts: countercyclical expenditure plans, based on overoptimistic revenue projections, could turn procyclical ex post when cyclical position and revenue outcomes disappoint; or ad hoc revisions of expenditure plans through supplementary budgets could also generate procyclicality.

Table 18.1. Fiscal Policy Procyclicality

	Fixed-Effects Estimator		
	Plans Δ(SB/GDP) $t\|t-1$	Actual, Real Time Δ(SB/GDP) $t\|t+1$	Actual, Ex Post Δ(SB/GDP) $t\|2016$
	(1)	(2)	(3)
Initial Debt/GDP	0.02	0.05***	0.04***
	[0.01]	[0.01]	[0.01]
ΔOutput Gap	−0.12	−0.27*	−0.55**
	[0.15]	[0.16]	[0.19]
Constant	−0.93	−3.88***	−3.27***
	[1.72]	[0.79]	[0.90]
Observations	105	102	224
Number of Countries	19	19	19
R^2	0.33	0.65	0.29

Sources: Annual Macroeconomic Database of the European Commission's Directorate General for Economic and Financial Affairs; various vintages of annual Stability and Convergence Programs; and authors' estimates.
Note: The sample includes 19 euro area countries covering the period 1999–2015. Columns (1) and (2) rely on stability program data, while column (3) uses the AMECO database. In the absence of structural balances in AMECO, cyclically adjusted balances are used for the pre-2011 period in column (3). Because of data availability, the analysis is performed using overall (rather than primary) structural balances as dependent variables. Estimations rely on the panel ordinary least squares estimator. All regressions include time and country fixed effects. $t|t-1$ indicates plans for period t reported in period $t-1$, $t|t+1$ indicates outturns in period t reported in period $t+1$, and $t|2016$ indicates outturns in period t reported in 2016. Robust standard errors are in brackets. SB = structural balance.
*$p < .1$; **$p < .05$; ***$p < .01$.

as reported in 2016 (column (3)). Estimations show that despite broadly acyclical plans (insignificant coefficient β in column (1)), real-time and ex post outcomes have been procyclical (negative and significant coefficient β in columns (2) and (3)).

The previous results may suffer from an endogeneity bias due to reverse causality effects. For instance, fiscal tightening (positive change in the structural balance) could widen the output gap (negative change) and generate a negative association between the two variables that is not related to procyclicality. Although this issue may not be too pronounced in the specification using the planned fiscal impulse (column (1)) given that expected changes in the output gap are typically used as "exogenous" inputs when formulating budget plans, the endogeneity bias may cause more problems in the other regressions. Annex Table 18.1.1 attempts to address this issue with a dynamic generalized method of moments (GMM) estimator, which uses, in addition to the lagged variables (in levels and differences), trade-weighted output gaps as an additional instrument (following Gali and Perotti 2003 and Jaimovic and Panizza 2007).[11] This approach substantially reduces the number of observations but confirms the evidence of procyclicality in all specifications.

Two additional sets of regressions are run as robustness checks. First, the effect of national political economy factors is explored by including in the specifications several political variables that are widely used in the literature (dummies for

[11] The GMM approach seems superior to the more widely employed approach using the lagged output gap (or the lagged change in the output gap) as a dependent variable in the equation. Although including the lagged variable is an easy fix to alleviate the endogeneity problem, it also makes the interpretation of the coefficient more difficult. For instance, a fiscal tightening in response to a positive change in the previous year's output gap would be interpreted as countercyclical, while it may in fact be procyclical if the macroeconomic conditions deteriorate in the current year.

legislative and presidential election years, and a measure of political fractionalization). Including these variables as additional controls does not materially affect the results (Annex Table 18.1.3). Whether the coefficient of the output gap (which is a measure of procyclicality) is affected by political factors is also tested by running separate regressions using interaction terms of the output gaps with individual political variables; the interaction terms generally do not come out significant.[12] Thus, the evidence of procyclicality found in the whole sample does not seem to be primarily driven by political considerations at the national level, suggesting that supranational factors may also be at play.

Second, procyclicality could be concentrated in the years of fiscal consolidation that followed the fiscal stimulus of 2009–10. To test the sensitivity of the results, alternative estimations excluding 2011–13 are reported (Annex Table 18.1.5). Results are not materially affected, meaning that procyclicality is not a crisis-specific phenomenon.

Evidence of Deficit Bias

An important question is whether procyclicality occurs throughout the cycle or only during upturns. If procyclicality happens in good times but fiscal policy is acyclical or procyclical in bad times, the asymmetric fiscal policy reaction results in a "deficit bias" and excessive debt accumulation (Balassone and Francese 2004).

Given that the main objective of the SGP is to prevent the buildup of excessive deficits and debt, it contains several provisions aimed at ensuring a symmetric policy response and mitigating the deficit bias. One is the ceiling on the deficit ratio of 3 percent of GDP. Another is the public debt anchor at 60 percent of GDP. Also, the SGP sets country-specific medium-term targets in cyclically adjusted terms (MTOs) and annual adjustments toward MTOs. Structural targets imply that fiscal buffers should accumulate in good times and be used to cushion shocks in bad times.[13]

Despite these provisions, the SGP has not prevented a steady deterioration in the member states' fiscal positions. Considering the sample of EA countries over 1999–2015, the deficit has exceeded the 3 percent ceiling in more than three-quarters of total country-year observations. Moreover, in 16 of the 19 EA countries, the average deficit over 1999–2015 was positive (in the range of 1.7 to 7.9 percent of GDP, depending on the country), exceeding the "close to balance" medium-term objective.

Nonetheless, the deficit bias does not seem more pronounced in the EA than in other advanced economies (excluding Japan) when taking a long-term perspective. Since 1999, the fiscal deficits of EA countries and other advanced economies (excluding Japan) have fluctuated around 3 percent of GDP, with the EA posting lower deficits than its peers since the beginning of the global financial crisis.[14]

---

[12] Results are not reported in the annex but are available from the authors upon request.

[13] As discussed above, although compliance with MTOs is assessed through fiscal balance ceilings, MTOs are medium-term "targets," which should be achieved and maintained by member states.

[14] The sample of advanced economies (excluding EA and Japan) includes Australia, Canada, Czech Republic, Denmark, Hong Kong SAR, Iceland, Israel, Republic of Korea, New Zealand, Norway, Singapore, Sweden, Switzerland, United Kingdom, and United States.

Table 18.2. Asymmetric Policy Response and Deficit Bias

	Fixed-Effects Estimator		
	Plans Δ(SB/GDP) $t \vert t-1$	Actual, Real Time Δ(SB/GDP) $t \vert t+1$	Actual, Ex Post Δ(SB/GDP) $t \vert 2016$
	(1)	(2)	(3)
Initial Debt/GDP	0.01*	0.06***	0.04***
	[0.01]	[0.01]	[0.01]
ΔOutput Gap*D(ΔOutput Gap >0)	−0.45***	−0.84***	−0.31
	[0.07]	[0.20]	[0.30]
ΔOutput Gap*D(ΔOutput Gap <0)	0.17	−0.13	−0.73***
	[0.26]	[0.18]	[0.22]
Constant	−0.48	−4.19***	−3.17***
	[0.66]	[0.66]	[0.94]
Observations	105	102	224
Number of Countries	19	19	19
R^2	0.39	0.67	0.3

Sources: Annual Macroeconomic Database of the European Commission's Directorate General for Economic and Financial Affairs; various vintages of annual Stability and Convergence Programs; and authors' estimates.
Note: The sample includes 19 euro area countries covering the period 1999–2015. Columns (1) and (2) rely on stability program data, while column (3) uses the AMECO database. In the absence of structural balances in AMECO, cyclically adjusted balances are used for the pre-2011 period in column (3). Because of data availability, the analysis is performed using overall (rather than primary) structural balances as dependent variables. Estimations rely on the panel ordinary least squares estimator. All regressions include time and country fixed effects. $t|t-1$ indicates plans for period t reported in period $t-1$, $t|t+1$ indicates outturns in period t reported in period $t+1$, and $t|2016$ indicates outturns in period t reported in 2016. SB = structural balance.
$^*p < .1$; $^{***}p < .01$.

We then test more systematically whether fiscal policy has reacted asymmetrically to the economic cycle in the sample of 19 EA countries by using a regression model over the period 1999–2015:

$$\Delta sb_{i,t} = \alpha_i + \beta_1 \times \Delta gap_{i,t} \times D(\Delta gap_{i,t} > 0) + \beta_2 \times \Delta gap_{i,t} \times D(\Delta gap_{i,t} < 0) + \gamma \times debt_{i,t-1} + \rho_t + \varepsilon_{i,t}. \quad (18.2)$$

Specification (18.2) is an extended version of specification (18.1), where the change in output gap is interacted with dummy variables for good times ($\Delta gap_{i,t} > 0$) and bad times ($\Delta gap_{i,t} < 0$). These interaction terms allow the asymmetric policy reaction to the cycle to be tested for. Similar to specification (18.1), coefficients β_1 and β_2 measure whether discretionary fiscal policy was procyclical (negative coefficients), countercyclical (positive coefficients), or acyclical (insignificant coefficients).[15]

Table 18.2 reports the estimation results for fiscal policy plans, and real-time and ex post outcomes. The estimations confirm the asymmetric response to the cycle and provide evidence of a deficit bias. Specifically, lax policies in good times have prevented countries from rebuilding buffers when their economies grew at rates above potential growth (columns (1) and (2)).

[15] A negative β_1 means that in good times (output growth is above its potential rate of growth, meaning Δgap>0), an increase in output gap is associated with fiscal relaxation, which denotes procyclical fiscal policy. Similarly, a negative β_2 implies that in bad times (output growth is below its potential rate of growth, meaning Δgap<0), a decrease in output gap is associated with a fiscal contraction, which is also a sign of procyclicality.

This finding is corroborated by GMM regressions that alleviate the endogeneity problem but at the expense of a large drop in the number of observations (Annex Table 18.1.2). The results are broadly robust to the inclusion of political economy variables (Annex Table 18.1.4) and the exclusion of the periods of fiscal consolidation after 2009–10 (Annex Table 18.1.6).

Evidence of Suboptimal Fiscal Composition

Political factors can have detrimental effects on fiscal policy not only through a suboptimal fiscal stance, but also through suboptimal budget composition (at unchanged stance). This is especially noticeable in periods of fiscal consolidation, when political preferences can be tilted toward preserving current spending and increasing distortionary taxes. These tendencies can ultimately undermine the growth potential of the economy (IMF 2015b).

To address this risk, the fiscal framework has been amended to create better incentives for countries to protect public investment. An "investment clause" was formalized as part of the flexibility guidelines issued in 2015, allowing countries to temporarily deviate from their MTOs (or convergence paths to MTOs) to expand investment in projects with positive, direct, and verifiable long-term budgetary effects on growth and on the sustainability of public finances.[16]

Although it is still too early to assess the effectiveness of this initiative, past evidence shows that fiscal composition has not improved during the global financial crisis. For instance, despite the already-high initial level of taxation in EA countries, fiscal adjustment during 2010–13 was tilted toward revenue measures compared with the United States and other advanced economies (Figure 18.4). A similar picture emerges when analyzing expenditure composition (Figure 18.5). The brunt of expenditure adjustment has fallen on investment spending instead of on current spending, which is less productive but often politically costlier to cut.

In theory, changes in tax and expenditure composition could well be driven by legitimate economic considerations and may not reflect political economy distortions. For instance, public investment cuts could be justified by a shift toward private sector provision of certain infrastructure services. Preserving current expenditure and social transfers could be optimal when consumers are credit constrained in an economy with considerable slack.

Nevertheless, in the EA, the case for lowering taxes on labor and capital and promoting public investment is very compelling (IMF 2016b). In fact, the disproportional cuts in public investment have led to a large investment gap, which we proxy as the difference between observed public investment and investment that would stabilize the ratio of the stock of public capital to GDP at its initial level.[17] Following Bogaert (2016), the capital-stabilizing net investment ratio is estimated as $y/(1+y)\times k$, where y is the real potential growth rate and k is the initial stock of

---

[16] The applicability of the investment clause is limited by strict eligibility conditions (Melyn, Van Meensel, and Van Parys 2015).

[17] In both cases, investment is expressed in net terms, meaning excluding depreciation. For the initial level, we use the 2013 stock of capital, which is the most recent data available.

Figure 18.4. Reliance on Revenue and Expenditure Measures in Fiscal Adjustment
(Percent)

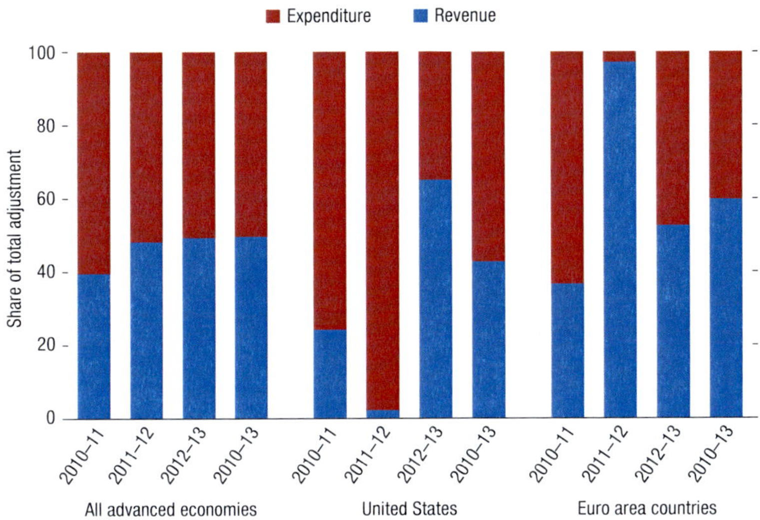

Sources: IMF World Economic Outlook database; and authors' estimates.
Note: The figure reports shares of revenue and expenditure measures in total fiscal adjustment.

Figure 18.5. General Government Expenditure Composition
(Rebased ratio to GDP)

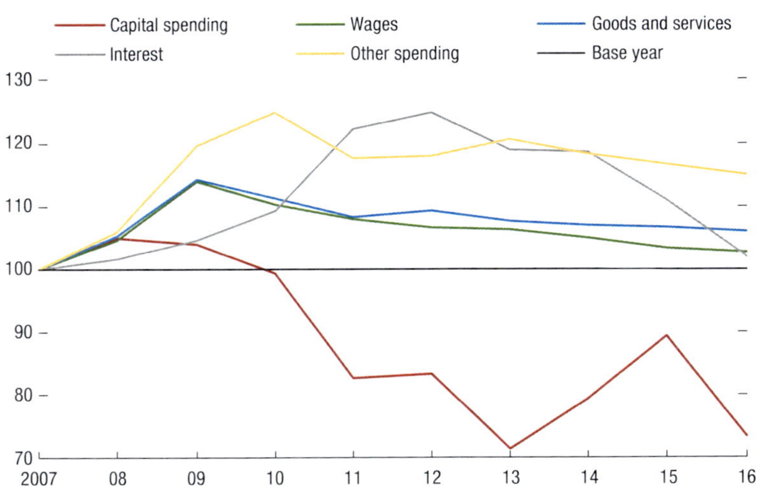

Sources: IMF World Economic Outlook database; and authors' estimates.
Note: The sample includes 19 euro area countries. GDP ratios are rebased using 2007 as the base year (= 100).

public capital as a ratio of GDP. The calculations show that in most EA countries, public investment is much lower than its capital-stabilizing level, resulting in a steady depletion of the capital stock over time. As of 2015, the investment gap ranged between 0.35 percent and 3.7 percent of GDP, depending on the country.[18] The erosion of public capital stock could, in turn, slow down the long-term potential of the economy, with adverse consequences on fiscal sustainability.

Compliance with Fiscal Rules

In the absence of a counterfactual, it is difficult to state that the SGP has failed in its objective of fostering fiscal discipline (fiscal outcomes could have been worse in its absence). However, it is clear that the SGP has not been sufficient to correct policy biases reflected in a suboptimal fiscal stance and compositional distortions. This section further analyzes the causes of this inability to correct policy biases. In particular, it assesses whether the mixed track record of the SGP is the result of poor ex ante compliance with the rules (at the planning stage) or poor ex post execution of plans. The analysis focuses on the issue of compliance without assessing whether fiscal rules themselves are consistent with their stated objectives, including ensuring fiscal sustainability or achieving economic stabilization.

What Has Been the Track Record of EA Countries with Fiscal Rules?

To prevent excessive deficits and debt buildup, the SGP has established a complex system of numerical constraints (EC 2016a). To simplify the compliance analysis, this section considers that the SGP includes four main numerical rules: the 3.0 percent of GDP nominal deficit ceiling, the 60.0 percent of GDP debt ceiling, the MTO in structural terms, and a benchmark fiscal effort of at least 0.5 percent per year in structural terms when structural balances are below MTOs or the country is under excessive deficit procedure (EDP).

Figure 18.6 compares fiscal outturns with these targets or ceilings since the adoption of the euro. This simplified exercise should not be considered a formal test of compliance for five reasons: first, it is based on ex post data (using the AMECO database) and does not correct for the classification changes that occurred following the transition from the ESA95 to the ESA2010 fiscal reporting formats; second, targets are assumed to be similar across countries, cover the whole period, and be constant over time; third, the assessment does not take into account the possible activation of escape clauses or other provisions granting some flexibility; fourth, the comparison is carried out for all 19 EA countries, comprising those that introduced the euro after 1999; and fifth, numerical deviations may not necessarily represent cases of noncompliance given that the EC also exerts economic judgment, on top of its quantitative assessment, in both preventive and corrective arms. In addition, the analysis covers the whole Economic and

[18] The analysis is conducted for 15 EA countries for which capital stocks are available from the IMF's public debt database.

Figure 18.6. Share of "Noncompliers" in the Euro Area
(Percent)

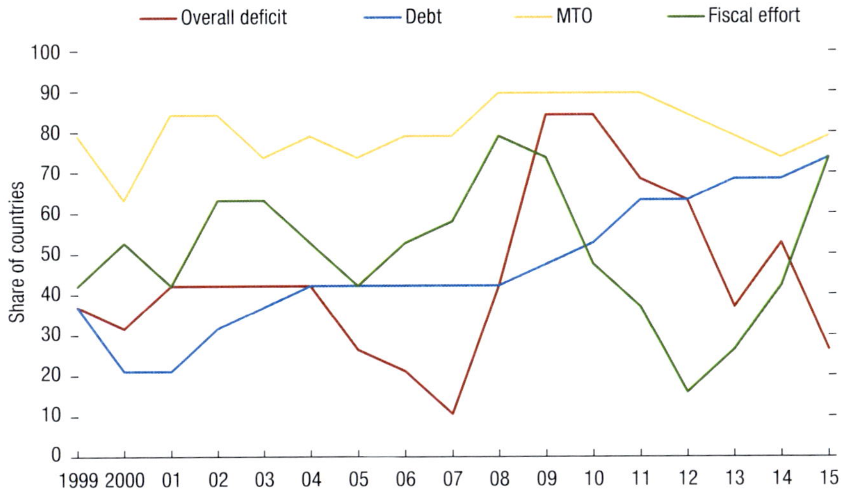

Sources: Annual Macroeconomic Database of the European Commission's Directorate General for Economic and Financial Affairs; and authors' estimates.
Note: The sample includes 19 euro area countries. Medium-term objectives (MTOs) are set uniformly to 0 percent for all countries until 2005 and to country-specific numbers from 2006.

Monetary Union (EMU) period, including the global financial crisis years when member states breached fiscal rules more systematically.

Figure 18.6 reveals a poor record of compliance with the key rules in EA countries over 1999–2015. For instance, the MTO was violated in 80 percent of observations under consideration, with almost two-thirds of countries exceeding the MTOs in every single year. Compliance particularly worsened during the crisis: in 2009, the MTO rule was violated by 90 percent of countries, the debt ceiling by 50 percent of countries, the deficit ceiling by 85 percent of countries, and the required fiscal effort by 75 percent of countries. In parallel, the share of countries with a debt ratio greater than 60 percent increased from 35 percent in 1999 to 75 percent in 2015. It is also notable that governance reforms implemented over 2005–13, such as increased flexibility, greater automaticity in enforcement, and greater ownership supported by revisions in national legislation, have not had an evident impact on compliance (without correcting for other factors).

What Are the Drivers of Weak Compliance?

The poor ex post compliance documented in Figure 18.6 could be attributed to two factors, as shown in the accounting decomposition below:

$$\underbrace{[\text{Outcome} - \text{Target}]}_{\textit{Ex post compliance}} = \underbrace{[\text{Plan} - \text{Target}]}_{\textit{Ex ante compliance}} + \underbrace{[\text{Outcome} - \text{Plan}]}_{\textit{Execution}}.$$

Figure 18.7. Decomposition of Deficit Rule Slippages

(Median across country-years)

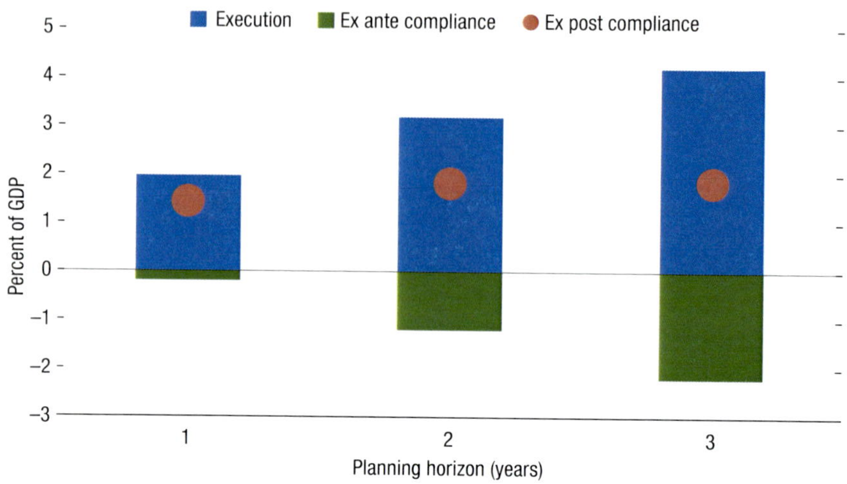

Sources: Annual Macroeconomic Database of the European Commission's Directorate General for Economic and Financial Affairs; various vintages of annual Stability and Convergence Programs; and authors' estimates.

Note: The sample includes country-years with deficit/GDP > 3 percent. In the decomposition formula, $t \mid t-i$ indicates plans for period t reported in period $t-i$, and $t \mid 2016$ indicates outturns in period t reported in 2016. Decomposition formula: $\underbrace{DEF_{t \mid 2016} - 3}_{\text{Ex post compliance}} = \underbrace{(DEF_{t \mid t-i} - 3)}_{\text{Ex ante compliance}} + \underbrace{(DEF_{t \mid 2016} - DEF_{t \mid t-i})}_{\text{Execution}}$.

A first possibility is that countries did not foresee complying with the numerical rules in their budget plans (poor ex ante compliance). Another possibility could be that planning was adequate, but ex post slippages led to consistent deviations from the plans (poor execution). The section above titled "Macrofiscal Performance under the SGP" analyzes the role of these two factors in determining the fiscal stance. The present section assesses their role in driving excessive deficits and debt in the subset of EA "noncompliers" over 1998–2013. The analysis below focuses on the two main rules capping the overall deficit and debt. The other rules are not examined because of the lack of data.

Figure 18.7 presents the results for the 3 percent deficit rule over the three-year planning horizon.[19] Consistent with the previous regressions, the analysis suggests that the main driver of poor ex post compliance was weak execution of plans. Given that the EC has not applied any fines or sanctions, this is also a sign of weak enforcement. Although the noncompliers consistently planned to reduce their deficits below the 3 percent threshold set out by the rules in each of the projected years, execution slippages more than offset these plans, leading to a

[19] The three components (ex post compliance, ex ante compliance, and execution) do not add up because of the use of medians.

Figure 18.8. Decomposition of Debt Rule Slippages
(Median across country-years)

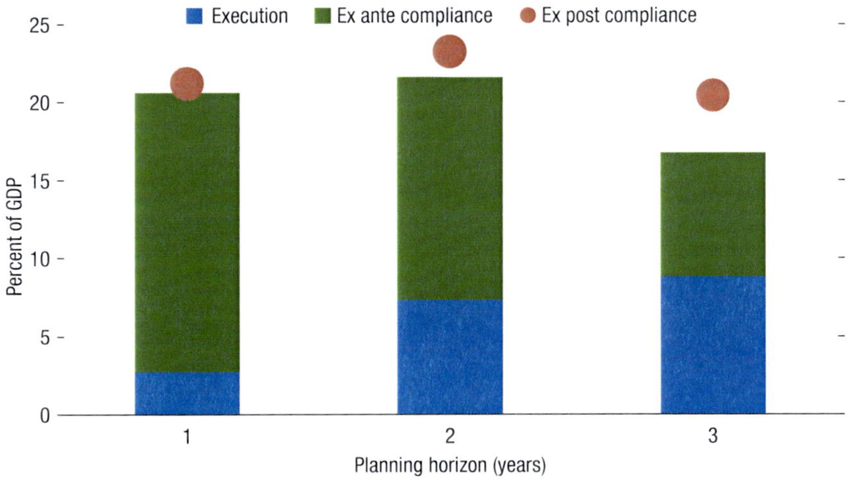

Sources: Annual Macroeconomic Database of the European Commission's Directorate General for Economic and Financial Affairs; various vintages of annual Stability and Convergence Programs; and authors' estimates.
Note: The sample includes 19 euro area countries, over 1998–2013. Reported are the medians. The sample includes country-years with debt/GDP > 60 percent. In the decomposition formula, $t \mid t-i$ indicates plans for period t reported in period $t-i$ and $t \mid 2016$ indicates outturns in period t reported in 2016. Decomposition formula:

$$\underbrace{DEBT_{t\mid 2016} - 60}_{\text{Ex post compliance}} = \underbrace{(DEBT_{t\mid t-i} - 60)}_{\text{Ex ante compliance}} + \underbrace{(DEBT_{t\mid 2016} - DEBT_{t\mid t-i})}_{\text{Execution}}.$$

median upward deviation from the ceiling of up to 2 percent of GDP at the end of the third year.

Figure 18.8 carries out a similar decomposition for the 60 percent debt-to-GDP ratio rule. Similar to the deficit rule, poor execution is the main culprit. While the noncompliers planned to reduce debt by about 10 percent of GDP—from about 80 to 70 percent of GDP on average (both numbers correspond to 60 percent plus the height of the green bars) within three years—the debt ratio remained broadly unchanged ex post (as measured by 60 percent plus the height of the red dots).

The fact that most of the deviations occurred at the execution stage should not necessarily be interpreted as evidence of unintended budgetary slippages. Actual outcomes can also deviate from plans because of an unexpected nominal growth shortfall, reflecting, for instance, a negative inflation surprise. Since the 2005 reform of the SGP, the assessment of effective action has focused on "conditional compliance" with rules by estimating and subtracting the contribution of economic factors to isolate the policy part. Other factors may also account for ex post deviations from plans, such as intentional biases (for example, deliberate underestimation of the fiscal deficit in the budget), valuation changes affecting the debt stock, or statistical adjustments in the perimeter of the fiscal aggregate (which would also be reflected in the "execution" term).

Country Size and Fiscal Outcomes

If deviation from plan is the main factor behind poor compliance, a natural question is whether these deviations, which may reflect poor enforcement of the rules, have affected all countries in a similar way or whether countries have behaved differently, perhaps because some benefited from more lenient treatment (Buti and Pench 2004; De Haan, Berger, and Jansen 2004). This section analyzes this issue of evenhandedness across member states using various approaches.

Is There a Relationship between Country Size and Deviation from Fiscal Plans?

First, the following regression is conducted for EA countries over the period 1999–2015:[20]

$$\Delta ob_{i,t|2016} - \Delta ob_{i,t|t-1} = \alpha_i + \beta \times Size_{i,t} + \gamma \times Controls_{i,t} + \rho_t + \varepsilon_{i,t}, \quad (18.3)$$

where the dependent variable is the difference between outcome and plan for the change in the overall-balance-to-GDP ratio.[21] As mentioned in Beetsma, Giuliodori, and Wierts (2009), using first differences instead of levels is preferable to mitigate the impact of potential changes in the deficit definition across data vintages.[22] The main explanatory variable is *Size*, measured as the share of nominal GDP of an EA member to total EA GDP. Various controls are included related to the forecast errors in macroeconomic variables (nominal and real GDP growth, output gap, openness, borrowing costs), initial fiscal positions (debt ratio, distance from the MTO), election cycle (dummy in parliamentary election years), and whether the country is under EDP. The coefficient of interest is β. If fiscal slippages are not affected by the country's size, then β should be insignificant.

The estimation results do not invalidate the hypothesis of a systematic difference of behavior between large and small countries in their deviations from fiscal plans (Table 18.3). Specifically, the coefficient of the size variable is negative and significant in most specifications, showing that overall balances in bigger countries tend to underperform relative to plan by a larger margin. For instance, column (1) shows that when the share of a country in the EA GDP increases by 1 percent, the fiscal slippage of the overall balance increases by about 0.3 percent of GDP.

---

[20] Estimations are performed using the panel ordinary least squares estimator with time and country fixed effects. The sample includes all observations, because restricting it to EDP countries would cut the sample by two-thirds of the observations.

[21] In this exercise, actual data are taken from the AMECO database, while plans are one-year-ahead forecasts from Stability and Convergence Programs (SCPs).

[22] Real-time data come from different data releases. If the definition of the deficit had changed across releases for methodological reasons (for instance, inclusion of public enterprises in the general government), then the comparison of deficit levels across data releases would not be possible. First differences largely cancel out the effect of such methodological modifications and allow data to be compared across releases.

Table 18.3. Country Size and Fiscal Plan Execution

	(1)	(2)	(3)	(4)	(5)	(6)	(7)	(8)	(9)	(10)	(11)	(12)	(13)	(14)
Country Size (GDP as a share of euro area GDP,	−0.32**	−0.30*	−0.29*	−0.23	−0.43***	−0.30**	−0.32***	−0.17	−1.64**	−0.63*	−0.30*	−0.35***	−0.32**	−1.99*
percent)	[0.13]	[0.16]	[0.15]	[0.18]	[0.13]	[0.13]	[0.10]	[0.43]	[0.59]	[0.31]	[0.16]	[0.10]	[0.12]	[1.02]
Dummy (= 1 for countries in EDP)		0.11												−4.11**
		[0.27]												[1.58]
Forecast Error: Real GDP Growth			0.10											1.21
			[0.19]											[0.86]
Forecast Error: Nominal GDP Growth				0.16										−1.02
				[0.15]										[0.92]
Dummy (= 1 for parliamentary election years)					−0.39									−0.75
					[0.31]									[0.59]
Initial Overall Balance/GDP (real time, SCP)						−0.05								−0.15
						[0.03]								[0.25]
Initial Debt/GDP (real time, SCP)							0.02***							0.13**
							[0.01]							[0.06]
Forecast Error: Output Gap								−0.01						0.03
								[0.16]						[0.38]
Initial MTO-SB/GDP (real time, SCP)									0.48***					0.64**
									[0.16]					[0.28]
Forecast Error: Lagged Change in OB/GDP										−0.23				−1.01**
										[0.18]				[0.35]
Real GDP Growth (ex post)											0.17			
											[0.24]			
Long-Term Bond Yields												0.03		−0.12
												[0.14]		[0.25]
Openness (ex post)													0.01	−0.08**
													[0.00]	[0.03]
Constant	1.90**	1.680	1.75*	1.310	2.61**	1.62*	0.020	0.690	8.88**	4.14*	1.410	2.36***	0.950	14.470
	[0.86]	[1.20]	[0.97]	[1.24]	[1.05]	[0.93]	[0.94]	[2.49]	[3.48]	[2.24]	[1.46]	[0.79]	[0.85]	[9.92]
Observations	187	187	187	182	154	185	182	159	84	150	187	166	187	54
Number of Countries	19	19	19	19	17	19	19	19	18	18	19	17	19	16
R^2	0.20	0.20	0.20	0.22	0.20	0.20	0.33	0.19	0.35	0.36	0.21	0.20	0.20	0.71

Sources: Annual Macroeconomic Database of the European Commission's Directorate General for Economic and Financial Affairs; various vintages of annual Stability and Convergence Programs; authors' estimates.

Note: The sample includes 19 euro area (EA) countries for the period 1999–2015. The dependent variable is the difference between actual and planned (1-year ahead) change in the overall balance-to-GDP ratio (in percent). Estimations are performed using the panel ordinary least squares estimator with time and country fixed effects. EDP = excessive deficit procedure; MTO-SB = medium-term objective–structural balance; SCP = Stability and Convergence Program. Robust standard errors are in brackets.

$^*p < .1$; $^{**}p < .05$; $^{***}p < .01$.

Nevertheless, caution should be exercised in interpreting the country size coefficient as evidence of uneven enforcement of fiscal rules. The negative correlation between size and fiscal slippages relative to plan could also be driven by other factors (Buti and Pench 2004). For instance, bigger countries may have larger fiscal multipliers, making fiscal adjustment costlier in terms of output if macroeconomic shocks force them to deviate from their initial budgets. Also, bigger countries tend to have deeper and more interconnected financial markets, making European Central Bank actions in response to developments in large countries more likely.

Are the Modalities of the EDPs (Length, Effort) Affected by Country Size?

To assess whether the previous correlation may be driven by an uneven application of rules, we test whether large countries have benefited from a more lenient treatment under the EDP. Figure 18.9 plots the relationship between the duration of the EDP and country size. Data from EC (2015) on EDP length are used. Originally, countries were expected to correct their excessive deficits within a year, and in exceptional circumstances, extensions of up to three years could be granted. However, in practice, some countries have taken up to eight years to correct their EDPs, and some countries entered EDP multiple times. Figure 18.9 shows that larger countries have tended to stay longer under EDP than smaller countries.

Figure 18.9. Relationship between Country Size and EDP Length

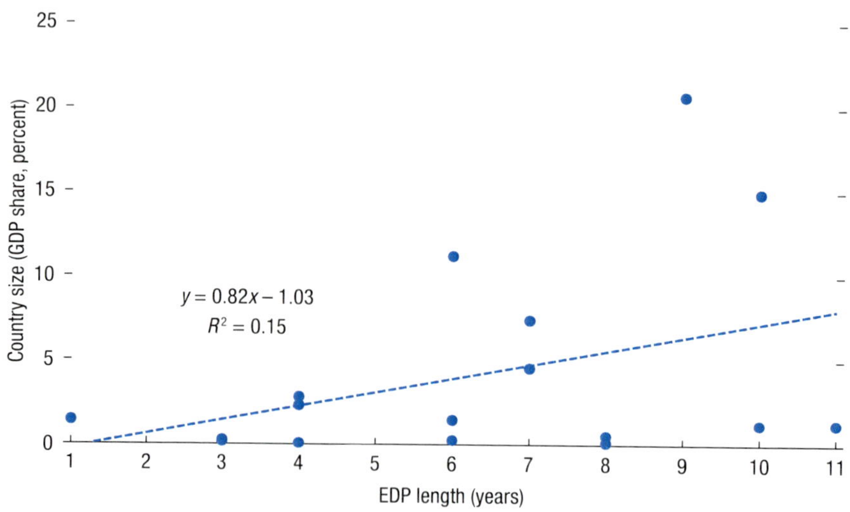

Sources: European Commission; and authors' calculations.
Note: The sample includes 19 euro area countries for the period 2003–16 (there was no EDP before 2003). The two extreme observations in the upper right corner are Germany and France. The slope of the line remains positive when these two observations are excluded. EDP = excessive deficit procedure.

Table 18.4. Country Size and EDP Recommendations

	19 EA Countries					
	(1)	(2)	(3)	(4)	(5)	(6)
Country Size (GDP as a share of EU GDP, percent)	−0.022*	−0.021*	−0.01	0.00	−0.01	0.00
	[0.01]	[0.01]	[0.01]	[0.01]	[0.01]	[0.01]
Public Debt (percent of GDP)		0.00				0.00
		[0.00]				[0.00]
Overall Balance (percent of GDP)			−0.054***			−0.036***
			[0.02]			[0.01]
Output Gap (percent)				−0.102***		−0.03
				[0.03]		[0.03]
Real GDP Growth (percent)					−0.135***	−0.115**
					[0.03]	[0.05]
Constant	1.147***	0.815**	0.734***	0.801***	1.156***	1.112***
	[0.14]	[0.36]	[0.15]	[0.12]	[0.11]	[0.31]
Observations	47	47	47	47	47	47
R^2	0.03	0.07	0.26	0.32	0.38	0.54
	28 EU Countries					
	(7)	(8)	(9)	(10)	(11)	(12)
Country Size (GDP as a share of EU GDP, percent)	−0.02	−0.02	−0.01	−0.01	−0.01	0.00
	[0.01]	[0.01]	[0.01]	[0.01]	[0.01]	[0.01]
Public Debt (percent of GDP)		0.01				−0.005**
		[0.00]				[0.00]
Overall Balance (percent of GDP)			−0.053***			−0.032***
			[0.02]			[0.01]
Output Gap (percent)				−0.095***		−0.02
				[0.02]		[0.03]
Real GDP Growth (percent)					−0.147***	−0.147***
					[0.03]	[0.04]
Constant	1.061***	0.725***	0.715***	0.837***	1.176***	1.266***
	[0.11]	[0.24]	[0.13]	[0.11]	[0.10]	[0.22]
Observations	68	68	68	68	68	68
R^2	0.02	0.06	0.18	0.26	0.39	0.49

Source: Authors' calculations.
Note: The sample includes 39 excessive deficit procedure (EDP) episodes from EC (2015). The dependent variable is the recommended average annual adjustment under EDP in structural terms. Estimations are performed using the pooled ordinary least squares estimator. Columns (1)–(6) present results from a sample of 19 euro area (EA) countries, while columns (7)–(12) present results from a broader sample of 28 European Union (EU) countries. Robust standard errors are in brackets.
$^*p < .1$; $^{**}p < .05$; $^{***}p < .01$.

We also test whether larger countries have been treated differently at the stage of the EDP recommended actions by running the following regression for 39 EDP episodes over 2003–15:

$$Effort_i = \alpha + \beta \times Size_i + \gamma \times Controls_i + \varepsilon_i, \tag{18.4}$$

where *Effort* is the average required annual fiscal effort (in structural terms) for EDP countries.[23] If larger countries were treated more leniently by the EC and ECOFIN, then the coefficient of the size variable β would be negative. The estimation results reported in Table 18.4 do not confirm this hypothesis: β

[23] The data on required annual fiscal effort used in EC (2015) was provided by EC staff. The required annual fiscal effort is defined as the total change in the structural balance required to eliminate the excessive deficit over the course of the EDP divided by the number of years.

coefficients are not significant in most regressions. In the sample of EA countries, the negative coefficient of the size variable is marginally significant in the specification without controls, but this significance vanishes when control variables are included and for the broader sample of 28 EU countries.[24] This outcome suggests that EC recommendations have not favored larger countries in the required size of adjustment at the planning stage.

To sum up, the evidence on biased application of the rules is mixed. On the one hand, bigger countries tend to deviate more from their fiscal plans than smaller countries, but this behavior could be unrelated to the rules. On the other hand, smaller countries under EDP are not requested to adjust excessive deficits faster than bigger countries, but the result should be treated with caution because it relies on a small number of observations.

PAST REFORMS AND POLICY OPTIONS FOR THE FUTURE

This section adopts a political economy view of the reform of the European fiscal framework. Despite past SGP reforms, the fiscal governance system continues to face a number of challenges, which points to the need to strengthen political incentives in the medium term and to introduce permanent changes to the EA architecture in the longer term.

Past Reforms of the European Fiscal Governance Framework

The previous section shows that the system of rules and procedures meant to foster fiscal discipline and mitigate cross-country spillovers has not been sufficient to eliminate policy biases. In fact, some of these biases have intensified in the past decade, such as the procyclicality of fiscal policy, public debt accumulation, and distortions affecting the budget composition. Although political economy factors are not the only reason for these suboptimal fiscal outcomes, the weakness of the fiscal governance framework has certainly not helped. The policy biases occurred despite successive revisions to the SGP that have attempted to mitigate political economy factors in four different ways (Figure 18.10):

- *Fostering evenhanded treatment of countries.* The "reverse qualified majority" voting system adopted in 2011 gives more power to the EC by ensuring that its recommendations or proposals are approved by the ECOFIN unless a qualified majority of member states vote against it. Because it is now more difficult for the ECOFIN to overrule the EC recommendations, the risk of collusion or uneven treatment of countries is somewhat reduced. In addition, the creation of the new European Fiscal Board—operational since October 2016—could also help in the future by providing an independent evaluation of execution of the fiscal governance framework.

[24] In both cases, the results should be interpreted with caution given the small number of observations.

Figure 18.10. Past SGP Reforms and Policy Biases

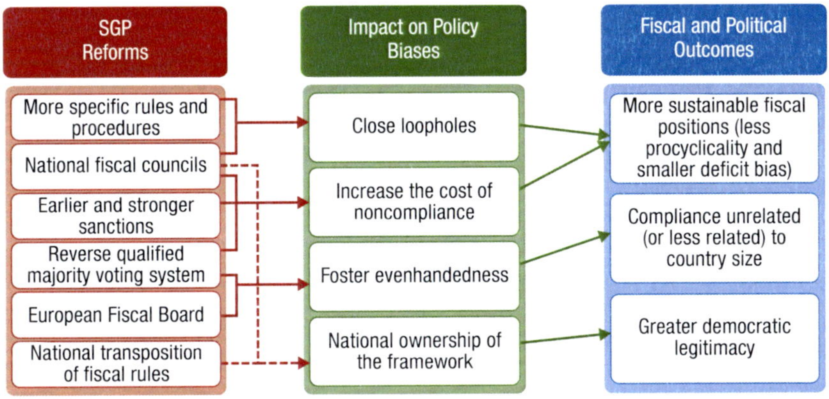

Source: Authors' compilation.
Note: SGP = Stability and Growth Pact.

- *Making deviations from rules more costly, both financially and politically.* Recent reforms have introduced the possibility of earlier and stronger sanctions for EA countries. The "reverse qualified majority" procedure may also increase the likelihood that sanctions will be applied. In addition, the 2012 Fiscal Compact has entrusted independent institutions, such as fiscal councils, with monitoring the implementation of fiscal rules. Among other duties, fiscal councils should protect the budget from political business cycles and expose to the public deviations from sound fiscal policy, raising their political cost for decision makers.
- *Bringing more specificity in the application of the rules.* Rules that are vague or ambiguous create margins of interpretation and loopholes that can be exploited by politicians and may result in uneven treatment of countries. Successive reforms of the framework have improved the specificity of the rules and of their conditions of application, including by laying out in detail the criteria for the use of flexibility within the framework.
- *Making the framework more legitimate and homegrown.* To foster national ownership of the system of rules, the Fiscal Compact has required countries to introduce structural balance rules (MTOs) in national legislation; these rules should be monitored by domestic independent institutions. Also, supranational surveillance has become better integrated with the national budget calendar to ensure that the EC's recommendations are timely incorporated into national budgets and policies.

Past reforms constitute important steps toward correcting policy biases, but they have fallen short of addressing the key issue of political incentives, probably because, in most cases, their primary objective was not to tackle political economy distortions. Reforms that made the framework more flexible and more growth friendly have created additional complexity, further reducing its transparency and making communication with the public more difficult. Fiscal councils have been presented as a way to address the shortcomings of fiscal rules by fostering transparency and accountability and triggering reputational effects. However, their influence should not be overstated, in part because they are not immune to political interference and because fiscal sustainability is not at the center of the public debate at the moment in many countries.

Finally, the most important procedural reform of the past years, the "reverse qualified majority" rule, may not be sufficient to guarantee evenhandedness and eliminate the perception that some large countries are treated more leniently. The EC has constant interactions with national authorities (including at the technical level), creating a risk that political considerations be internalized within the institution. The call for a more political EC by some European leaders also points in this direction. The newly established European Fiscal Board is intended to improve the legitimacy and evenhandedness of the EC recommendations. However, the board's effectiveness hinges upon its independence from the EC and other political pressures. Its stature in the European public sphere and its influence in debates about fiscal policy in Europe will also be key. They will depend, partly, on the board's communication strategy.

Taking into Account Political Economy Factors within the Existing Framework

Future reforms to the governance framework should try to reduce the hold of political economy factors on fiscal policy. Past reforms have focused mostly on enhancing the economic basis of the rules and upgrading their design to achieve the dual objectives of fiscal sustainability and economic stabilization. Less emphasis has been placed on ensuring that political incentives are well aligned with compliance. This approach may have reached its limits. If political incentives are not there, the most sophisticated revisions to the framework will not materially improve fiscal outcomes. Therefore, it is critical that new reforms also take into account the political economy dimension.

To make fiscal rules work politically, the incentive structure could be further strengthened on both sides—by establishing more credible sanctions and by creating more tangible benefits for countries complying with the SGP. Although this is a very difficult task in the absence of a political union, future reforms could be guided by two general principles:

- *Making sanctions more politically acceptable.* The current system of sanctions and "mandatory" remedial actions lacks credibility for two main reasons. First, financial sanctions for countries under EDP exacerbate the financial difficulties of already distressed governments, limiting the appropriateness of the sanctions and their scope for use in bad times. In the future, more emphasis should be placed on sanctions under the preventive arm, while nonpecuniary sanctions could also be considered under the corrective arm.

Administrative sanctions are, for instance, common in many federations (Eyraud and Gomez 2014). Second, and more important, elevated sanctions carry a stigma and a political cost that make their application very unlikely. A more gradual system could thus be envisaged. Initial and/or small deviations should entail small financial costs so that they face less political opposition, while repeated and/or larger deviations could be penalized more heavily.[25] In any case, the enforcement of sanctions is likely to remain a highly contentious issue as long as member states retain sovereignty over fiscal issues. The idea that sovereign states can be sanctioned is problematic in international law. A credible enforcement system will require further political integration (see below).

- *Creating tangible benefits for compliers.* The current fiscal framework is heavily tilted toward negative incentives in the form of sanctions and corrective actions. By comparison, the positive side of the incentive structure is underdeveloped. For member states, the individual benefits associated with complying with the SGP are not always clear in the short run. The main benefit should be to preserve access to low-cost financing, but market discipline was not effective in the EMU before the global financial crisis for various reasons (Allard and others 2013). As a matter of fact, rules were the most binding in the run-up to the euro when countries could see a clear advantage in complying with them (Ioannou and Stracca 2011). Once EA participation was guaranteed, the benefits of fiscal discipline became more elusive. Several options could be considered to reinforce the rule-benefits nexus in the eyes of member states and citizens. One possibility involves linking the volume of structural funds and other EU subsidies to compliance with rules.[26] The possibility of establishing stabilization capacity in the EA has also been discussed recently; in some variants, access to this central fiscal capacity could be conditioned on past compliance with rules (IMF 2016b). More generally, the fiscal framework should be designed in such a way that policymakers can establish a clear link between compliance and a well-functioning EMU that delivers price stability and robust growth. To support this macroeconomic objective, fiscal rules should be consistent with the conduct of ambitious demand- and supply-side policies that boost growth in both the short and medium terms.

In parallel with strengthening incentives, simplifying the framework is also essential (Andrle and others 2015). Successive legislative changes have made the

[25] In her analysis of collective action problems faced by individuals using common pool resources, Ostrom (1990) notes that in successful institutional arrangements, sanctions are generally graduated, with initial sanctions remaining relatively low. She also shows that successful peer enforcement requires two main conditions: (1) a perception that other players also comply (mutual trust) and (2) a perception that the collective objective associated with the pooling of resources is achieved.

[26] Since 2014, access to structural funds can be suspended if a country does not comply with the EDP recommendations under the corrective arm.

SGP increasingly complex. The initial pact included a few supranational rules, of which only the 3 percent deficit ceiling was truly binding. Later on, the fiscal crisis and the mixed experience with a small set of constraints prompted the adoption of additional rules—some of them to address the shortcomings of previous ones. Today, fiscal aggregates are tied together by an intricate set of constraints that makes the monitoring and communication of the rules very difficult. To enhance the SGP's democratic legitimacy, the framework should be simplified and made more transparent to the public. Doing so would also reduce the loopholes and limit the scope for interpretation—both of which induce political games in the negotiations between the EC and member states. Simplifying the framework may require rethinking its overall structure, including consolidating the preventive and corrective arms and eliminating some redundant or ill-designed rules (Eyraud and Wu 2015).

Toward a More Comprehensive Approach

In the long term, it is unlikely that reforms to the SGP alone will be sufficient to correct the policy biases that have plagued the functioning of the monetary union. The reason is that these biases are rooted in the overall architecture of the EA and, in particular, in the interplay between its various dimensions—fiscal, monetary, banking, and financial. Many argue that a partial approach focusing on the fiscal framework alone is not sustainable.

At the same time, there is no single comprehensive model toward which the EA should converge. Experience with existing federations suggests a range of options for alleviating the political economy pressures and fostering fiscal discipline. To simplify, these options can be arranged along a continuum structured around two polar models (Allard and others 2013; Wyplosz 2013; Cottarelli and Guerguil 2014). The first model would leave large autonomy to member states, while reinforcing market discipline. The model at the opposite end of the spectrum would rely more extensively on a center-based approach at the expense of a permanent loss of fiscal sovereignty for EA members. The ultimate scope and shape of the new architecture will remain a matter of social and political preferences.

Where Does the EA Stand Now?

At the moment, the EA framework combines elements of both models without bringing either of them to fruition. The provision enshrined in the Maastricht Treaty to ensure that member states do not assume other member states' fiscal commitments—often referred to as the "no-bailout" clause—was meant to give financial markets an incentive to discriminate among countries and price each member state's default risk. However, this clause has never been credible, and market discipline has not worked properly in the EMU (Moghadam 2014). With its set of supranational rules, the SGP also shares some similarities with the centralized model, but member states have kept most of their fiscal sovereignty, and the enforcement and control tools granted to the EC are very limited compared with what exists in other federations.

Decentralized Model with Stronger Market Discipline

In federations like Canada or the United States, states maintain a large degree of autonomy, including in the fiscal area. The center's controls over states' policies are relatively limited. Fiscal discipline is primarily achieved through financial markets, which limit the discretion of policymakers by imposing higher borrowing costs for imprudent policy. In these countries, bailouts of subnational entities are rare or nonexistent, and individual states are responsible for "honoring fully their own individual sovereign signature and all their commitments to sustainable fiscal conditions."[27]

Certain prerequisites are essential for making market discipline effective. First, mechanisms should be in place to manage state defaults in an orderly way, in particular by establishing clear rules for the involvement of private creditors. Bailouts of states by the federal level or by other member states should be either avoided or confined within the boundaries of a clear framework. In the EA, the scale of the global financial crisis has warranted the creation of risk-sharing institutions such as the European Stability Mechanism. Their interventions should be designed in such a way that market discipline is not weakened, including through proper use of conditionality. Second, market discipline requires that adequate information on the borrower's existing liabilities and repayment capacity be readily available so that potential lenders can correctly discriminate between borrowers. One lesson from the global financial crisis is that there is scope for enhancing fiscal transparency and improving the measurement and disclosure of government balance sheets. Third, the sovereign-bank link distorted the pricing of risk by markets in several EA countries during the crisis, in part because of the perception that weak banks may overwhelm national fiscal resources. A credible joint fiscal backstop at the EA level as part of a full-fledged banking union could substantially weaken bank-sovereign links (IMF 2013).

Because conditions for its effectiveness are seldom met, no federation relies on pure market discipline. Instead, institutional arrangements to constrain fiscal discretion, such as fiscal rules, are present in all federations. The countries where market discipline is strongest, such as Australia, Canada, and the United States, are those where subcentral rules are self-imposed. States establish these rules to signal to the market their commitment to fiscal discipline (Inman 1996). In Europe, relying more extensively on fiscal discipline does not mean that countries would need to pause or even reverse the fiscal integration process. Under the decentralized model, fiscal integration should continue with the goal of establishing "minimal elements" for the fiscal union to support robust growth and minimize the risk and severity of future crises (Allard and others 2013; Cottarelli 2013).

---

[27] This quote is taken from the letter written by J. C. Trichet and M. Draghi to Prime Minster Berlusconi dated August 5, 2011.

Centralized Model with Deeper Fiscal and Political Integration

Other types of federations, like Germany, rely on stronger central oversight and tight central controls over regional policies to achieve fiscal discipline and mitigate the extent of fiscal spillovers across states. For instance, the federal level may retain a large share of tax powers or impose stricter spending or borrowing limits on subcentral governments.

In the EA, moving toward this model would require that member states surrender some fiscal sovereignty in the long term. At present, the EMU incorporates some aspects of a fiscal union, but in the narrow sense of fiscal discipline. Fiscal governance reforms have so far aimed at enhancing policy coordination across members while preserving sovereignty over national policies. Transfers of fiscal authority to the center have remained very limited. The Five Presidents Report (Juncker and others 2015) argues that rules-based cooperation alone is insufficient to transit toward a genuine monetary and economic union, and greater sharing of sovereignty over time is inevitable. In practice, this approach would require EA countries to accept more resource pooling and joint decision making on elements of national policies, potentially supported by a stronger EC with more extensive powers.

A centralized model could also contribute to improving the management of the EA aggregate fiscal stance and achieving a better policy mix by mitigating the common pool problem, better taking into account the macroeconomic needs of the area as a whole, and internalizing the cross-country fiscal spillovers. Member states, including those enjoying some room for maneuver within the SGP, would be invited to contribute to the attainment of the desired aggregate fiscal stance. The distribution of fiscal effort among countries would be improved, notably by using fiscal space where it exists to increase public investment. This would contrast with today's suboptimal policy mix, where the burden of ensuring macroeconomic stabilization is largely left to the European Central Bank. Member states with negative output gaps have little or no room to support demand, whereas countries with fiscal space have no incentive to use it, resulting in a suboptimal aggregate fiscal stance (EC 2016a).

To underpin the legitimacy and accountability of a stronger fiscal center, political integration would need to advance as well (Issing 2016).[28] In its present form, the rules-based governance framework lacks a democratic feedback mechanism through which voters could more effectively influence the decision-making process in Brussels (Alcidi, Giovannini, and Piedrafita 2014). The EP is the only European institution consisting of directly elected members, but its influence over European policies and the governance framework is limited. Stronger political integration with elected policymakers accountable to the EP and European voters could help address this democratic gap and increase the resilience of the integration process to public discontent. As is the case at the

---

[28] Further political integration could take the form of a supranational political union or tighter intergovernmental coordination.

national level, citizens' support would then revolve around specific fiscal policies and actions rather than questioning membership and the European project as a whole.

Greater political integration could also help better shape, express, and defend matters of Europe-wide interest. As discussed above, the ECOFIN is composed of finance ministers of individual countries who are guided by national interests rather than EU-wide common objectives. This has created a number of issues, including a stronger say for big countries and perhaps more lenient treatment of them. Recent institutional reforms, such as the European Stability Mechanism and the banking union, have significantly increased the degree of risk sharing across member states, but this process could be further supported by a central executive authority, such as a Minister of Finance of EMU, which would act in the best interests of the union. Establishing a political union could provide legal grounds for such a central authority.

CONCLUSION

This chapter shows that some of the fiscal challenges faced by the EA are rooted in distorted political incentives—at both the national and supranational levels. Using real-time data from stability programs, the chapter provides evidence on a range of fiscal policy biases, including procyclicality, excessive deficits, and compositional distortions. The results also suggest that the presence of national and supranational fiscal rules has not successfully alleviated these biases, which have continued to prevail following recent reforms of the fiscal framework. The evidence of bias in applying the rules (as a function of country size) is not as conclusive.

The importance of distorted incentives is a very simple result, but it has far-reaching implications that have not yet been fully acknowledged in the reform of fiscal institutions. One extreme and dangerous manifestation of these distortions is the expressed perception by many analysts that European fiscal governance releases countries from their national responsibilities. Nothing could be further from the truth: fiscal policy is, first and foremost, a national responsibility. The combination of this misperception with the predominance of the national dimension of politics constitutes a dangerous mix.

One of the main lessons from this chapter is that the most sophisticated improvements in the design of the framework will not bear fruit unless they also garner political and public support. By strengthening the economic basis of the rules, reform of the SGP has made significant progress, but efforts should continue on two fronts—right design combined with right incentives. It is possible and desirable to have a stronger system of incentives, including gradual and proportionate sanctions and clear benefits for compliers. In the longer term, a lasting solution must combine market discipline and stronger fiscal governance. Fiscal union will, if it happens, be an aspect of a comprehensive architecture accompanying bank and capital markets unions. It would reflect political choices in Europe.

ANNEX 18.1. ADDITIONAL ECONOMETRIC RESULTS

Annex Table 18.1.1. Baseline Specification: Fiscal Policy Procyclicality

	Fixed-Effects Estimator			Dynamic Panel GMM Estimator		
	Plans Δ(SB/GDP) t|t–1	Actual, Real Time Δ(SB/GDP) t|t+1	Actual, Ex Post Δ(SB/GDP) t|2016	Plans Δ(SB/GDP) t|t–1	Actual, Real Time Δ(SB/GDP) t|t+1	Actual, Ex Post Δ(SB/GDP) t|2016
	(1)	(2)	(3)	(4)	(5)	(6)
Initial Debt/GDP	0.02	0.05***	0.04***	–0.02***	–0.04***	0.67
	[0.01]	[0.01]	[0.01]	[0.01]	[0.01]	[0.72]
ΔOutput Gap	–0.12	–0.27*	–0.55**	–0.90***	–0.56***	–0.57**
	[0.15]	[0.16]	[0.19]	[0.26]	[0.07]	[0.24]
Lagged Dependent Variable				–0.23***	–0.27***	–0.81**
				[0.07]	[0.08]	[0.40]
Constant	–0.93	–3.88***	–3.27***	1.85***	2.18**	8.60
	[1.72]	[0.79]	[0.90]	[0.54]	[1.03]	[10.08]
Observations	105	102	224	44	43	189
Number of Countries	19	19	19	15	15	17
R^2	0.33	0.65	0.29			

Sources: Annual Macroeconomic Database of the European Commission's Directorate General for Economic and Financial Affairs; various vintages of annual Stability and Convergence Programs; and authors' estimates.
Note: The sample includes 19 euro area countries covering the period 1999–2015. Columns (1), (2), (4), and (5) rely on stability program data, while columns (3) and (6) rely on the AMECO database. In the absence of SB in AMECO, cyclically adjusted balances are used for the pre-2011 period in columns (3) and (6). Because of data availability, the analysis is performed using overall (rather than primary) SB as dependent variables. Estimations rely on the panel ordinary least squares estimator. All regressions include time and country fixed effects. $t|t-1$ indicates plans for period t reported in period $t-1$, $t|t+1$ indicates outturns in period t reported in period $t+1$, and $t|2016$ indicates outturns in period t reported in 2016. Robust standard errors are in brackets. GMM = generalized method of moments; SB = structural balance.
$*p < .1$; $**p < .05$; $***p < .01$.

Annex Table 18.1.2. Baseline Specification: Asymmetric Policy Response and Deficit Bias

	Fixed-Effects Estimator			Dynamic Panel GMM Estimator		
	Plans Δ(SB/GDP) t|t–1	Actual, Real Time Δ(SB/GDP) t|t+1	Actual, Ex Post Δ(SB/GDP) t|2016	Plans Δ(SB/GDP) t|t–1	Actual, Real Time Δ(SB/GDP) t|t+1	Actual, Ex Post Δ(SB/GDP) t|2016
	(1)	(2)	(3)	(4)	(5)	(6)
Initial Debt/GDP	0.01*	0.06***	0.04***	–0.01	–0.04***	0.10
	[0.01]	[0.01]	[0.01]	[0.01]	[0.01]	[0.24]
ΔOutput Gap*D(ΔOutput Gap >0)	–0.45***	–0.84***	–0.31	–0.59	–0.68***	–2.31**
	[0.07]	[0.20]	[0.30]	[0.44]	[0.19]	[1.07]
ΔOutput Gap*D(ΔOutput Gap <0)	0.17	–0.13	–0.73***	–1.60*	–0.20	–0.93
	[0.26]	[0.18]	[0.22]	[0.85]	[0.38]	[0.77]
Lagged Dependent Variable				–0.23*	–0.22**	–0.67***
				[0.13]	[0.11]	[0.23]
Constant	–0.48	–4.19***	–3.17***	1.84**	3.07*	11.12
	[0.66]	[0.66]	[0.94]	[0.92]	[1.59]	[7.21]
Observations	105	102	224	44	43	189
Number of Countries	19	19	19	15	15	17
R^2	0.39	0.67	0.3			

Sources: Annual Macroeconomic Database of the European Commission's Directorate General for Economic and Financial Affairs; various vintages of annual Stability and Convergence Programs; and authors' estimates.
Note: The sample includes 19 euro area countries covering the period 1999–2015. Columns (1), (2), (4), and (5) rely on stability program data, while columns (3) and (6) rely on the AMECO database. In the absence of SB in AMECO, cyclically adjusted balances are used for the pre-2011 period in columns (3) and (6). Because of data availability, the analysis is performed using overall (rather than primary) SB as dependent variables. Estimations rely on the panel ordinary least squares estimator. All regressions include time and country fixed effects. $t|t-1$ indicates plans for period t reported in period $t-1$, $t|t+1$ indicates outturns in period t reported in period $t+1$, and $t|2016$ indicates outturns in period t reported in 2016. Robust standard errors are in brackets. GMM = generalized method of moments; SB = structural balance.
$*p < .1$; $**p < .05$; $***p < .01$.

Annex Table 18.1.3. Including Political Economy Variables: Fiscal Policy Procyclicality

	Fixed-Effects Estimator			Dynamic Panel GMM Estimator		
	Plans Δ(SB/GDP) $t\|t-1$	Actual, Real Time Δ(SB/GDP) $t\|t+1$	Actual, Ex Post Δ(SB/GDP) $t\|2016$	Plans Δ(SB/GDP) $t\|t-1$	Actual, Real Time Δ(SB/GDP) $t\|t+1$	Actual, Ex Post Δ(SB/GDP) $t\|2016$
	(1)	(2)	(3)	(4)	(5)	(6)
Legislative Elections	–0.11	0.11	–0.46**	–0.09	0.04	2.63
	[0.14]	[0.22]	[0.16]	[0.13]	[0.14]	[4.97]
Presidential Elections	0.05	0.72	0.71	–2.20**	0.6	2.19
	[0.51]	[0.46]	[0.51]	[0.93]	[0.45]	[3.00]
Fractionalization	0.68	3.1	2.38	–5.62	–0.82	0.00
	[1.66]	[2.95]	[4.47]	[4.48]	[5.69]	[.]
Initial Debt/GDP	0.02*	0.06***	0.04***	–0.03**	–0.04***	0.43
	[0.01]	[0.01]	[0.01]	[0.01]	[0.01]	[0.38]
ΔOutput Gap	–0.12	–0.28	–0.53**	–0.26	–0.50***	–1.14
	[0.18]	[0.17]	[0.20]	[0.38]	[0.15]	[0.75]
Lagged Dependent Variable				0.33	–0.32***	–0.61*
				[0.23]	[0.12]	[0.33]
Constant	–1.54	–6.43**	–5.20	6.51**	3.23	–29.93
	[1.72]	[2.29]	[3.62]	[2.86]	[4.69]	[23.35]
Observations	88	85	203	29	28	171
Number of Countries	18	18	18	15	15	17
R^2	0.36	0.7	0.3			

Sources: Annual Macroeconomic Database of the European Commission's Directorate General for Economic and Financial Affairs; various vintages of annual Stability and Convergence Programs; and authors' estimates.
Note: The sample includes 19 euro area countries covering the period 1999–2015. Columns (1), (2), (4), and (5) rely on stability program data, while columns (3) and (6) rely on the AMECO database. In the absence of SB in AMECO, cyclically adjusted balances are used for the pre-2011 period in columns (3) and (6). Because of data availability, the analysis is performed using overall (rather than primary) SB as dependent variables. Estimations rely on the panel ordinary least squares estimator. All regressions include time and country fixed effects. $t|t-1$ indicates plans for period t reported in period $t-1$, $t|t+1$ indicates outturns in period t reported in period $t+1$, and $t|2016$ indicates outturns in period t reported in 2016. The political economy variables are taken from the Database of Political Institutions compiled by the Development Research Group of the World Bank and are defined as follows: (1) legislative election = dummy variable taking the value of one in periods of parliamentary elections; (2) presidential elections = dummy variable taking the value of one in periods of presidential elections; (3) fractionalization = continuous variable between 0 and 1 measuring the probability that two deputies picked at random from the legislative body will be of different parties. Robust standard errors are in brackets. [.] refers to inability to estimate standard errors for the chosen set of instruments. GMM = generalized method of moments; SB = structural balance.
*$p < .1$; **$p < .05$; ***$p < .01$.

Annex Table 18.1.4. Including Political Economy Variables: Asymmetric Policy Response and Deficit Bias

	Fixed-Effects Estimator			Dynamic Panel GMM Estimator		
	Plans Δ(SB/GDP) $t \mid t-1$	Actual, Real Time Δ(SB/GDP) $t \mid t+1$	Actual, Ex Post Δ(SB/GDP) $t \mid 2016$	Plans Δ(SB/GDP) $t \mid t-1$	Actual, Real Time Δ(SB/GDP) $t \mid t+1$	Actual, Ex Post Δ(SB/GDP) $t \mid 2016$
	(1)	(2)	(3)	(4)	(5)	(6)
Legislative Elections	−0.1	0.05	−0.46**	−0.04	0.06	35.92
	[0.13]	[0.20]	[0.18]	[0.16]	[0.13]	[27.15]
Presidential Elections	0.07	0.73	0.70	−2.87**	0.55	0.48
	[0.54]	[0.46]	[0.50]	[1.31]	[0.50]	[1.89]
Fractionalization	0.67	3.57	2.19	−3.97	−2.85	0.00
	[1.56]	[3.00]	[4.26]	[6.28]	[5.64]	[.]
Initial Debt/GDP	0.02**	0.06***	0.04***	−0.01	−0.03*	−0.63
	[0.01]	[0.01]	[0.01]	[0.01]	[0.01]	[0.63]
ΔOutput Gap*D(ΔOutput Gap >0)	−0.51***	−0.89**	−0.25	−1.32**	−1.01***	3.05
	[0.11]	[0.37]	[0.34]	[0.52]	[0.29]	[3.30]
ΔOutput Gap*D(ΔOutput Gap <0)	0.15	−0.18	−0.72***	5.97	−0.21	−1.47
	[0.29]	[0.18]	[0.22]	[4.21]	[0.28]	[1.04]
Lagged Dependent Variable				0.11	−0.48***	0.96
				[0.24]	[0.12]	[1.22]
Constant	-1.11	-7.09***	-5.07	5.27	4.56	20.51
	[1.54]	[2.31]	[3.55]	[3.90]	[4.36]	[26.98]
Observations	88	85	203	29	28	171
Number of Countries	18	18	18	15	15	17
R^2	0.41	0.71	0.31			

Sources: Annual Macroeconomic Database of the European Commission's Directorate General for Economic and Financial Affairs; various vintages of annual Stability and Convergence Programs; and authors' estimates.

Note: The sample includes 19 euro area countries covering the period 1999–2015. Columns (1), (2), (4), and (5) rely on stability program data, while columns (3) and (6) rely on the AMECO database. In the absence of SB in AMECO, cyclically adjusted balances are used for the pre-2011 period in columns (3) and (6). Because of data availability, the analysis is performed using overall (rather than primary) SB as dependent variables. Estimations rely on the panel ordinary least squares estimator. $t \mid t-1$ indicates plans for period t reported in period $t-1$, $t \mid t+1$ indicates outturns in period t reported in period $t+1$, and $t \mid 2016$ indicates outturns in period t reported in 2016. The political economy variables are taken from the Database of Political Institutions compiled by the Development Research Group of the World Bank and are defined as follows: (1) legislative election = dummy variable taking the value of one in periods of parliamentary elections; (2) presidential elections = dummy variable taking the value of one in periods of presidential elections; (3) fractionalization = continuous variable between 0 and 1 measuring the probability that two deputies picked at random from the legislative body will be of different parties. Robust standard errors are in brackets. GMM = generalized method of moments; SB = structural balance.

$^{*}p < .1$; $^{**}p < .05$; $^{***}p < .01$.

Annex Table 18.1.5. Excluding Periods of Fiscal Consolidation during the Global Financial Crisis: Fiscal Policy Procyclicality

	Fixed-Effects Estimator			Dynamic Panel GMM Estimator		
	Plans Δ(SB/GDP) t|t−1	Actual, Real Time Δ(SB/GDP) t|t+1	Actual, Ex Post Δ(SB/GDP) t|2016	Plans Δ(SB/GDP) t|t−1	Actual, Real Time Δ(SB/GDP) t|t+1	Actual, Ex Post Δ(SB/GDP) t|2016
	(1)	(2)	(3)	(4)	(5)	(6)
Initial Debt/GDP	0.02*	0.05***	0.03**	0.00	−0.01	−0.05
	[0.01]	[0.01]	[0.01]	[0.01]	[0.01]	[0.06]
ΔOutput Gap	−0.08	−0.04	−0.46*	−0.35*	−0.56***	−0.29
	[0.22]	[0.19]	[0.24]	[0.21]	[0.05]	[0.48]
Lagged Dependent Variable				−0.38***	−0.18***	−0.50**
				[0.09]	[0.03]	[0.22]
Constant	−1.23	−4.34***	−2.25**	0.79	−0.23	5.50**
	[1.72]	[0.82]	[0.92]	[0.51]	[0.55]	[2.29]
Observations	59	57	173	31	31	141
Number of Countries	18	18	19	15	15	17
R^2	0.32	0.69	0.2			

Sources: Annual Macroeconomic Database of the European Commission's Directorate General for Economic and Financial Affairs; various vintages of annual Stability and Convergence Programs; and authors' estimates.
Note: The sample includes 19 euro area countries covering the period 1999–2015 excluding 2011–13. Columns (1), (2), (4), and (5) rely on stability program data, while columns (3) and (6) rely on the AMECO database. In the absence of SB in AMECO, cyclically adjusted balances are used for the pre-2011 period in columns (3) and (6). Because of data availability, the analysis is performed using overall (rather than primary) SB as dependent variables. Estimations rely on the panel ordinary least squares estimator. All regressions include time and country fixed effects. $t|t-1$ indicates plans for period t reported in period $t-1$, $t|t+1$ indicates outturns in period t reported in period $t+1$, and $t|2016$ indicates outturns in period t reported in 2016. Robust standard errors are in brackets. GMM = generalized method of moments; SB = structural balance.
$*p < .1$; $**p < .05$; $***p < .01$.

Annex Table 18.1.6. Excluding Periods of Fiscal Consolidation during the Global Financial Crisis: Asymmetric Policy Response and Deficit Bias

	Fixed-Effects Estimator			Dynamic Panel GMM Estimator		
	Plans Δ(SB/GDP) t|t−1	Actual, Real Time Δ(SB/GDP) t|t+1	Actual, Ex Post Δ(SB/GDP) t|2016	Plans Δ(SB/GDP) t|t−1	Actual, Real Time Δ(SB/GDP) t|t+1	Actual, Ex Post Δ(SB/GDP) t|2016
	(1)	(2)	(3)	(4)	(5)	(6)
Initial Debt/GDP	0.02**	0.06***	0.02**	−0.01	−0.01	−0.09*
	[0.01]	[0.01]	[0.01]	[0.01]	[0.01]	[0.05]
ΔOutput Gap*D(ΔOutput Gap >0)	−0.50**	−0.62*	−0.15	−0.62***	−0.44***	−1.41
	[0.24]	[0.32]	[0.42]	[0.09]	[0.04]	[0.91]
ΔOutput Gap*D(ΔOutput Gap <0)	0.07	0.01	−0.66**	−1.32**	−0.62***	−0.82
	[0.25]	[0.19]	[0.27]	[0.64]	[0.13]	[0.57]
Lagged Dependent Variable				−0.46***	−0.13***	−0.76
				[0.13]	[0.04]	[0.47]
Constant	−0.75	−4.68***	−2.04**	0.32	−0.33	8.56
	[0.70]	[0.68]	[0.94]	[1.40]	[0.65]	[8.55]
Observations	59	57	173	31	31	141
Number of Countries	18	18	19	15	15	17
R^2	0.36	0.7	0.21			

Sources: Annual Macroeconomic Database of the European Commission's Directorate General for Economic and Financial Affairs; various vintages of annual Stability and Convergence Programs; and authors' estimates.
Note: The sample includes 19 euro area countries covering the period 1999–2015 excluding 2011–13. Columns (1), (2), (4), and (5) rely on stability program data, while columns (3) and (6) rely on the AMECO database. In the absence of SB in AMECO, cyclically adjusted balances are used for the pre-2011 period in columns (3) and (6). Because of data availability, the analysis is performed using overall (rather than primary) structural balances as dependent variables. Estimations rely on the panel ordinary least squares estimator. All regressions include time and country fixed effects. $t|t-1$ indicates plans for period t reported in period $t-1$, $t|t+1$ indicates outturns in period t reported in period $t+1$, and $t|2016$ indicates outturns in period t reported in 2016. Robust standard errors are in brackets. GMM = generalized method of moments; SB = structural balance.
$*p < .1$; $**p < .05$; $***p < .01$.

REFERENCES

Afonso, A., M. G. Arghyrou, and A. Kontonikas. 2015. "The Determinants of Sovereign Bond Yield Spreads in the EMU." Working Paper 1781, European Central Bank, Frankfurt.

Alcidi, C., A. Giovannini, and S. Piedrafita. 2014. "Enhancing the Legitimacy of EMU Governance." CEPS Special Report 98, Centre for European Policy Studies, Brussels.

Alesina, A., and R. Perotti. 1995. "The Political Economy of Budget Deficits." *IMF Staff Papers* 42 (1): 1–31.

Allard, C., P. Koeva Brooks, J. Bluedorn, F. Bornhorst, K. Christopherson, F. Ohnsorge, T. Poghosyan, and an IMF Staff Team. 2013. "Towards a Fiscal Union for the Euro Area." Staff Discussion Note 13/09, International Monetary Fund, Washington, DC.

Andrle, M., J. Bluedorn, L. Eyraud, T. Kinda, P. Koeva Brooks, G. Schwartz, and A. Weber. 2015. "Reforming Fiscal Governance in the European Union." IMF Staff Discussion Note 15/09, International Monetary Fund, Washington, DC.

Balassone, F., and M. Francese. 2004. "Cyclical Asymmetry in Fiscal Policy, Debt Accumulation and the Treaty of Maastricht." Temi di Discussione (Economic Working Papers) 531, Bank of Italy, Economic Research and International Relations Area.

Beetsma, R., M. Giuliodori, and P. Wierts. 2009. "Planning to Cheat: EU Fiscal Policy in Real Time." *Economic Policy* 24 (October): 753–804.

Benassy-Quere, A., X. Ragot, and G. Wolff. 2016. "Which Fiscal Union for the Euro Area?" Policy Brief 2016/05, Bruegel, Brussels.

Bernoth, K., A. Hughes Hallet, and J. Lewis. 2008. "Did Fiscal Policy Makers Know What They Were Doing? Reassessing Fiscal Policy with Real-Time Data." DNB Working Paper 169, Netherlands Central Bank, Amsterdam.

Bernoth, K., J. von Hagen, and L. Schuknecht. 2012. "Sovereign Risk Premiums in the European Government Bond Market." *Journal of International Money and Finance* 31 (5): 975–95.

Bogaert, H. 2016. "Improving the Stability and Growth Pact by Integrating a Proper Accounting of Public Investments: A New Attempt." Working Paper 1-16 of the Federal Planning Bureau, Brussels.

Buti, M., and L. Pench. 2004. "Why Do Large Countries Flout the Stability Pact? And What Can Be Done about It?" *Journal of Common Market Studies* 42 (5): 1025–32.

Buti, M., and P. Van den Noord. 2004. "Fiscal Policy in EMU: Rules, Discretion, and Political Incentives." DG ECFIN Economic Papers 206, European Commission, Brussels.

Candelon, B., J. Muysken, and R. Vermeulen. 2007. "Fiscal Policy and Monetary Integration in Europe: An Update." METEOR, University of Maastricht, The Netherlands.

Caporale, G. M., and A. Girardi. 2013. "Fiscal Spillovers in the Euro Area." *Journal of International Money and Finance* 38: 84.e1–84.e16.

Cartenaro, M., and R. Morris. 2008. "Fiscal Policy and Implementation in EMU." In *Macroeconomic Policy in the European Monetary Union: From the Old to the New Stability and Growth Pact*, edited by F. Farina and R. Tamborini, 20–44. London: Routledge.

Cimadomo, J. 2005. "Has the Stability and Growth Pact Made Fiscal Policy More Pro-Cyclical?" Working Paper 247, Centre d'Etudes Prospectives et d'Informations Internationales, Paris.

———. 2008. "Fiscal Policy in Real Time." Working Paper 919, European Central Bank, Frankfurt.

———. 2011. "Real-Time Data and Fiscal Policy Analysis: A Survey of the Literature." Working Paper 11-25, Federal Reserve Bank of Philadelphia.

Cottarelli, C. 2013. "European Fiscal Union: A Vision for the Long-Run." *Swiss Journal of Economics and Statistics* 149 (2): 167–74.

———, and M. Guerguil, eds. 2014. *Designing a European Fiscal Union: Lessons from the Experience of Fiscal Federations*. London: Routledge.

Debrun, X., D. Hauner, and M. Kumar. 2009. "Independent Fiscal Agencies." *Journal of Economic Surveys* 23: 44–81.

De Haan, J., H. Berger, and D.-J. Jansen. 2004. "Why Has the Stability and Growth Pact Failed?" *International Finance* 7 (2): 235–60.

Deroose, S., M. Larch, and A. Schaechter. 2008. "Constricted, Lame and Pro-cyclical? Fiscal Policy in the Euro Area Revisited." Economic Papers 353, European Commission, Brussels.

Detken, C., V. Gaspar, and B. Winkler. 2004. "On Prosperity and Posterity: The Need for Fiscal Discipline in a Monetary Union." Working Paper 420, European Central Bank, Frankfurt.

Eslava, M. 2006. "The Political Economy of Fiscal Policy: A Survey." Working Paper 583, Inter-American Development Bank, Washington, DC.

European Central Bank (ECB). 2014. "The Determinants of Euro Area Sovereign Bond Yield Spreads During the Crisis." *ECB Monthly Bulletin* (May): 67–83.

European Commission (EC). 2004. "Public Finances in EMU." European Economy No. 3, Brussels.

———. 2014. "Cross-Border Spillovers in the Euro Area." *Quarterly Report on the Euro Area* 13 (4): 7–22.

———. 2015. "Report on Public Finances in EMU." Institutional Paper 014, Brussels.

———. 2016a. "Towards a Positive Fiscal Stance for the Euro Area." Communication from the Commission to the European Parliament, the Council, the European Economic and Social Committee, and the Committee of the Regions. https://ec.europa.eu/info/publications/2017-european-semester-communication-fiscal-stance_en.

———. 2016b. *Vade Mecum on the Stability* and *Growth Pact*. Institutional Paper 021, European Commission, Brussels.

Eyraud, L., and R. Gomez. 2014. "Constraints on Subnational Fiscal Policy." In *Designing a European Fiscal Union: Lessons from the Experience of Fiscal Federations*, edited by C. Cottarelli and M. Guerguil, 90–132. London: Routledge.

Eyraud, L., and T. Wu. 2015. "Playing by the Rules: Reforming Fiscal Governance in Europe." Working Paper 15/67, International Monetary Fund, Washington, DC.

Fatas, A., and I. Mihov. 2009. "The Euro and Fiscal Policy." Working Paper 14722, National Bureau of Economic Research, Cambridge, MA.

Forni, L., and S. Momigliano. 2005. "Cyclical Sensitivity of Fiscal Policies Based on Real-Time Data." *Applied Economics Quarterly* 50 (3): 299–326.

Galí, J., and R. Perotti. 2003. "Fiscal Policy and Monetary Integration in Europe." *Economic Policy* 18 (37): 533–72.

Gaspar, V. 2012. "The Urgency of the Long Run—European Politics during the Crisis." Pierre Werner Chair Lecture, Robert Schuman Centre for Advanced Studies, European University Institute, Florence, Italy.

Giuliodori, M., and R. Beetsma. 2004. "What Are the Spill-Overs from Fiscal Shocks in Europe? An Empirical Analysis." Working Paper 325, European Central Bank, Frankfurt.

Golinelli, R., and S. Momigliano. 2006. "Real-Time Determinants of Fiscal Policies in the Euro Area." *Journal of Policy Modeling* 28 (9): 943–64.

Hazak, G. 2012. "The European Union—A Federation or a Confederation?" *Baltic Journal of European Studies* 2 (1): 43.

Inman, R. P. 1996. "Do Balanced Budget Rules Work? U.S. Experience and Possible Lessons for the EMU." Working Paper 5838, National Bureau of Economic Research, Cambridge, MA.

International Monetary Fund (IMF). 2012. "Fiscal Transparency, Accountability, and Risk." IMF, Washington, DC. http://www.imf.org/external/np/pp/eng/2012/080712.pdf.

———. 2013. "The Functions and Impact of Fiscal Councils." Policy Paper, IMF, Washington, DC.

———. 2015a. *Fiscal Monitor: Now Is the Time: Fiscal Policies for Sustainable Growth*. Washington, DC: IMF.

———. 2015b. "Fiscal Policy and Long-Term Growth." Policy Paper, IMF, Washington, DC.

———. 2016a. *Fiscal Monitor: Debt: Use It Wisely*. Washington, DC: IMF.

———. 2016b. "IMF Article IV Consultation with Euro Area." Country Report 16/219, IMF, Washington, DC.

Ioannou, D,. and L. Stracca. 2011. "Have Euro Area and EU Economic Governance Worked? Just the Facts." Working Paper 1344, European Central Bank, Frankfurt.

Issing, O. 2016. "EU Superstate Would Have No Democratic Legitimacy, Warns Euro Architect." *The Telegraph*, March 3. http://www.telegraph.co.uk/business/2016/03/03/eu-superstate-would-have-no-democratic-legitimacy-warns-euro-arc/.

Jaimovich, D., and U. Panizza. 2007. "Procyclicality or Reverse Causality?" Working Paper 4508, Inter-American Development Bank, Research Department, Washington, DC.

Juncker, J.-C., D. Tusk, J. Dijsselbloem, M. Draghi, and M. Schulz. 2015. "The Five Presidents' Report: Completing Europe's Economic and Monetary Union." European Commission, Brussels, June 22.

Kardasheva, R. 2009. "The Power to Delay: The European Parliament's Influence in the Consultation Procedure." *Journal of Common Market Studies* 47 (2): 385–409.

Melyn, W., L. Van Meensel, and S. Van Parys. 2015. "European Governance Framework for Public Finances: Presentation and Evaluation." *National Bank of Belgium Economic Review* (September): 73–99. https://www.nbb.be/en/articles/european-governance-framework-public-finances-presentation-and-evaluation.

Moghadam, R. 2014. "Maastricht and the Crisis in Europe: Where We've Been and What We've Learned." Speech at the ECB/NBB Conference "Progress through Crisis?" Brussels, February 12. https://www.imf.org/en/News/Articles/2015/09/28/04/53/sp021214.

Moravcsik, A. 2001. "Federalism in the European Union: Rhetoric and Reality." In *The Federal Vision: Legitimacy and Levels of Governance in the United States and the European Union*, edited by K. Nicolaidis and R. Howse. Oxford, U.K.: Oxford University Press.

Ostrom, E. 1990. *Governing the Commons: The Evolution of Institutions for Collective Action.* Cambridge, U.K.: Cambridge University Press.

Sapir, A., and G. Wolff. 2015. "Euro-Area Governance: What to Reform and How to Do It." Brief 2015/01, Bruegel, Brussels.

Trichet, J.-C., and M. Draghi. 2011. "Letter of the European Central Bank to Silvio Berlusconi." Voltaire Network, Frankfurt, Germany, August 5. http://www.voltairenet.org/article171574.html.

von Hagen, J. 2012. "Common Pools—Why a European Fiscal Union Will Make Things Worse." *Bonn Journal of Economics* 1 (1): 65–73.

Wyplosz, C. 2013. "Europe's Quest for Fiscal Discipline." European Economy Economic Papers 498, European Commission, Brussels.

CHAPTER 19

IMF Conditionality and Revenue Performance

ERNESTO CRIVELLI AND SANJEEV GUPTA[1]

INTRODUCTION

Fiscal adjustment has been an important element of IMF programs.[2] Experience shows that expenditure reductions have generally been achieved while increases in revenues have fallen short in relation to program targets (IEO, 2003). This is despite the fact that reform of the tax system—including both tax policy and revenue administration measures—has been frequently subjected to conditionality, to support the implementation of needed structural tax measures.

Conditionality typically covers both the design of IMF-supported programs—that is, the macroeconomic and structural policies—and the specific tools used to monitor progress toward the program goals outlined by the country in cooperation with the IMF. The program's objectives and policies depend on country circumstances, but the overarching goal is to restore or maintain balance of payments viability and macroeconomic stability, while in low-income countries, reducing poverty. Until the early 1980s, IMF conditionality largely focused on macroeconomic policies. Subsequently, the complexity and scope of structural conditions increased, reflecting the IMF's growing involvement in low-income and transition economies, where severe structural problems hampered economic stability and growth. Over the years, program conditionality has become better tailored to individual country needs, more streamlined, and focused on core areas of IMF expertise (IMF, 2012).

This chapter is reprinted from *International Tax and Public Finance*, Vol. 23, Ernesto Crivelli and Sanjeev Gupta, "Does Conditionality in IMF-Supported Programs Promote Revenue Reform?" ©2015, with permission from Springer.

[1] International Monetary Fund, Washington D.C. 20431, United States. Email addresses: ecrivelli@imf.org (E. Crivelli; corresponding author); sgupta@imf.org (S. Gupta). We would like to thank the Editor Ron Davies and two anonymous referees for excellent suggestions. We are grateful to Santiago Acosta-Ormaechea, Celine Allard, Katherine Baer, Sabina Bhatia, Martin Cerisola, Karla Chaman, Francesco Columba, Ruud De Mooij, Jonathan Dunn, Nisreen Farhan, Katherine Ferry, Geoff Gottlieb, Michael Keen, Christina Kolerus, Svitlana Maslova, Masahiro Nozaki, Iva Petrova, Marcos Poplawski-Ribeiro, Saad Quayyum, and Philippe Wingender for many helpful suggestions on an earlier draft of the paper, and to Haoyu Wang for outstanding assistance with consolidating the data. The views expressed herein are those of the authors and should not be attributed to the IMF, its executive board, or its management.

[2] The average targeted fiscal adjustment in 133 IMF programs was 1.7 percent of GDP during the period 1993–2001 (IEO, 2003).

Conditionality can take different forms, including prior actions (PA), quantitative performance criteria (QPC), indicative targets (IT), or structural benchmarks (SB). Prior actions are measures that a country agrees to take before the IMF's Executive Board approves financing or completes a review. Quantitative performance criteria are specific and measurable conditions that have to be met to complete a review. Indicative targets are used to supplement QPCs for assessing programs. Structural benchmarks are reform measures that are important to achieve program goals and are intended to assess program implementation during a review.

Over the last 20 years, some form of revenue conditionality has been included in the 441 approved IMF programs, thus supporting the implementation of structural tax measures.[3] In recent years, the use of revenue conditionality has increased, partly reflecting greater reliance on the IMF's technical assistance and the desire of countries to implement this technical advice.[4] A quick glance at the data suggests that revenue conditionality in IMF-supported programs appears to have been associated with higher revenue collection in low- and middle-income countries. Figure 19.1 displays tax-to-GDP ratios in countries

Figure 19.1. Tax Revenue and IMF Revenue Conditionality
(Before and after a period of consecutive conditionality, 1993–2013)

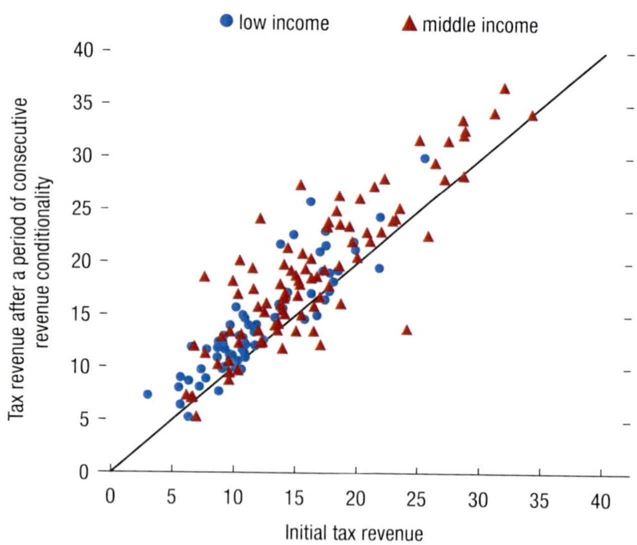

Sources: IMF, Government Finance Statistics and MONA database; and authors' calculations.

[3] An example of structural tax revenue reforms with a positive revenue impact is the move to replace harmful trade taxes with broad-based consumption taxes (Baunsgaard and Keen, 2010).
[4] Arezki et al. (2012) find that IMF technical assistance and training support structural reforms in the context of IMF programs.

Table 19.1. Tax Revenue Performance and IMF Revenue Conditionality
(Average annual changes, in percent of GDP, 1994–2013)

	1994–2013	1994–98	1999–2003	2004–08	2009–13
All Countries	0.13	0.03	0.29	0.34	−0.36
IMF Program with Revenue Conditionality	0.30	0.16	0.46	0.24	0.20
IMF Program without Revenue Conditionality	0.02	−0.22	0.40	0.21	−0.52
No IMF Program	0.12	0.11	0.15	0.41	−0.45
Middle-Income Countries					
IMF Program with Revenue Conditionality	0.33	−0.11	0.65	0.16	0.38
IMF Program without Revenue Conditionality	−0.09	−0.16	0.38	0.28	−1.66
No IMF Program	0.10	0.14	0.14	0.41	−0.57
Low-Income Countries					
IMF Program with Revenue Conditionality	0.36	0.51	0.18	0.33	0.12
IMF Program without Revenue Conditionality	0.14	−0.36	0.29	0.14	0.31
No IMF Program	0.01	−0.02	0.15	0.05	0.43

Sources: IMF, Government Finance Statistics and MONA database; and authors' calculations.

where tax reform was supported by a period of at least two consecutive years of revenue conditionality. In more than 75 percent of such cases, the tax-to-GDP ratio increased as compared to the year prior to the inclusion of the revenue conditionality.

One would expect an IMF program to contribute to improving revenue collection, regardless of revenue conditionality. This is because the government should be strengthening revenue collection as part of the agreed fiscal adjustment in the context of the program, so as to give a positive signal to creditors and investors (Przeworsky and Vreeland, 2000). Even in the absence of a Fund program, higher revenue collection would be needed to help deal with a severe fiscal crisis. A first key question then is whether there is a role for revenue conditionality in strengthening revenue collection.

Table 19.1 shows average annual changes in tax revenue for 1994–2013 for low- and middle-income countries. Revenue collection appears to have grown faster in countries with IMF programs that included revenue conditionality. Tax revenue increased faster in this group of countries as compared to the sample as a whole, and in particular faster than in countries without revenue conditionality either with or without an IMF program. This result is particularly strong for low-income countries in which average annual revenue growth in IMF program countries that included revenue conditionality is more than twice the observed revenue growth for the sample as a whole as well as for countries with no revenue conditionality.

The second key question relates to the design of revenue conditionality in IMF programs, and in particular the extent to which revenue conditionality has focused more on broad-based consumption taxes—such as the VAT—or income taxes, and their overall contribution to revenue. The recent work (Arnold et al., 2011; OECD, 2010) suggests a growth-hierarchy amongst taxes that favors broad-based consumption taxes for not discouraging savings and investment. Income taxes are believed to have the most adverse effects on growth as they interfere directly with economic decisions—in particular, labor force participation. Thus, an analysis of revenue conditionality in IMF programs can help better understand the contribution of IMF programs to economic growth (Dicks-Mireaux et al., 2000; Przeworsky and Vreeland, 2000). The final issue is whether the design of revenue conditionality—focusing on tax policy or tax administration; specific or more general in nature—makes a difference to revenue collection.

There are limited studies that have analyzed the impact of IMF programs on tax revenue collection.[5] Most prominently, Bulir and Moon (2003) studied fiscal developments in 112 countries during the 1990s and Cho (2009) in 93 developing countries during 1951–2000 and found that IMF programs had no effect on revenue collections. By contrast, Brun, Chambas and Laporte (2010) concluded that IMF-supported programs had a positive impact on total revenues in sub-Saharan Africa during 1984–2007. There is more extensive literature on the impact of IMF programs on the overall fiscal balance. Using alternative empirical methodologies these studies mostly conclude that participation in IMF programs improves fiscal outcomes (Conway, 1994; Evrensel, 2002; Dreher and Vaubel, 2004; Easterly, 2005; Atoian and Conway, 2006; Nsouli et al., 2006; Mumssen et al., 2013). However, there is no recent econometric assessment of the extent to which, conditional on other revenue-relevant developments, revenue conditionality contained in IMF programs has affected tax revenue collection—including its main components—nor of the underlying design factors of conditionality that may contribute to higher revenues.

This paper analyzes the impact of revenue conditionality in IMF programs on tax revenue collection in 126 low- and middle-income countries over the period 1993–2013. In doing so, it specifically addresses the questions raised above by using a newly assembled and broad (unbalanced) panel dataset on tax revenue—including all main tax components—and takes advantage of a database on IMF programs that includes detailed information on revenue conditionality. The essence of the empirical strategy is to examine the relationship between IMF programs—with and without revenue conditionality—and tax revenue performance as compared to countries with no IMF program, by looking at potentially differential effects on various types of taxes. Robustness tests are performed to account for differential characteristics in the design of revenue conditionality, to better understand potential differences related to the country's income level, or initial conditions, as well as the strength of institutions. Finally, cyclically

[5] Most of the literature has focused instead on the effects of IMF programs on the balance of payments (Reichmann and Stillson, 1978; Bird, 1996); on inflation (Edwards and Santaella, 1993; Killick, 1995); on public spending (Conway, 1994); social spending (Clements, Gupta, and Nozaki, 2013); on economic growth (Dreher, 2006a; see also Przeworkski and Vreeland (2000) for a review of the earlier literature); on sovereign risk (Jorra, 2012); and on the effect of IMF conditionality on trade openness (Wei and Zhang, 2010). See also Dreher (2009) for a review of conditionality in IMF programs and a discussion on its effectiveness.

adjusted revenues are considered to account for the effect of the economic cycle on revenues.

The paper is organized as follows. The next section describes the data set and presents the empirical specification and estimation strategy. The main results are presented in the third section, with further robustness analysis in the fourth section. A summary of the results and policy implications are presented in the last section.

DATA AND METHODOLOGY

Data

The dataset comprises an unbalanced panel of 126 low- and middle-income countries over the period 1993–2013. Data on tax revenues are drawn from three sources: the IMF's *Government Finance Statistics* (GFS), the IMF's *World Economic Outlook* (WEO), and the Organisation for Economic Co-operation and Development (OECD)'s *Revenue Statistics in Latin America*. These data comprise besides total tax revenue, taxes on goods and services[6], VAT, taxes on corporate profits (CIT), the personal income tax (PIT), and taxes on international transactions (Trade), all expressed relative to GDP. Full details of the dataset and summary statistics are provided in Annex 19.1. Figure 19.2 illustrates average tax revenue

Figure 19.2. Average Tax Revenue in Low- and Middle-Income Countries
(Percent of GDP, 1993–2013)

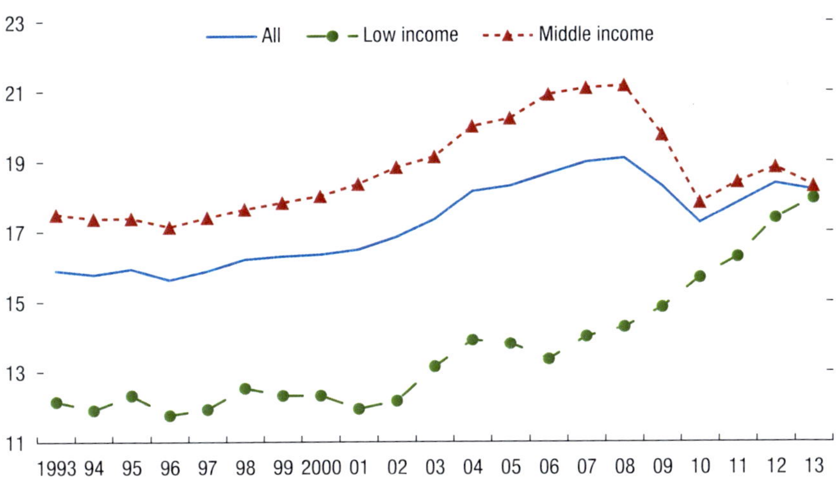

Sources: Country documents; IMF, Government Finance Statistics database; and authors' calculations.

[6] Includes VAT, excise taxes, and other consumption-related taxes.

performance for all countries in the sample, showing an average increase in tax revenue collection by about 2 percentage points of GDP, over the sample period. Until 2008, revenue collection in middle-income countries increased by around 3 percentage points of GDP, on average, about 1 percentage point of GDP more than in low-income countries. After 2008, however, low-income countries were able to strengthen revenue collection further, whereas in middle-income countries, the effects of the global financial crisis resulted in lower tax-to-GDP ratios. This translated into almost a convergence between the two groups of countries in observed tax-to-GDP ratios.

Data on IMF programs as well as on revenue conditionality included in these programs are taken from the IMF's Monitoring of Fund Arrangements (MONA) database, as explained in Annex 19.1. Revenue conditionality may be either quantitative (e.g., increasing the VAT rate to 18 percent) or structural (e.g., submitting legislation to parliament for introducing a VAT). At the same time, revenue conditionality can be related to tax policy or tax administration reform. Finally, revenue conditionality can be specific or general. Specific revenue conditionality can be identified with a tax type and is associated with a specific revenue target (e.g., increase the tax-free threshold under the personal income tax by a certain amount).[7] General conditionality, in contrast, cannot be linked to a specific tax type and its main objective is usually either to support the initial steps in a wide-ranging tax reform (such as submission to cabinet of a tax reform proposal) or to strengthen aspects of the revenue administration (e.g., adopt a new IT system in the revenue agency).

The incidence of revenue conditionality in IMF programs is represented by binary variables (including for total tax, and for each of the main taxes) that equal one if a country in a given year had an IMF program with met[8] revenue conditionality and zero otherwise. In cases in which revenue conditionality cannot be linked to a specific tax (general conditionality), it is assumed that the revenue conditionality applies to all taxes in that specific year. In most cases, the first lag of the revenue conditionality dummy is considered, to account for delayed reaction of tax revenue to the tax measure implied in the conditionality. This is particularly relevant for conditionality added during a program review taking place late in the year.

A large number of developing countries had IMF programs in the past twenty years. Since 1993, 96 of the 126 countries in the sample had such a program for at least 1 year. The number of years a given country had a program varied substantially. Over the entire sample, about 43 percent of the time, countries had IMF programs (Annex Table 19.1.1). IMF programs were more frequent in low-income countries (about 63 percent). Revenue conditionality has been an important component of IMF-supported programs. Since 1993, about 1,600

[7] Specific conditionality can also target revenue administration (such as create a large VAT taxpayers unit).

[8] If the revenue conditionality was not met, the dummy variable takes the value zero.

Figure 19.3. Years with Revenue Conditionality
(By country, 1993–2013)

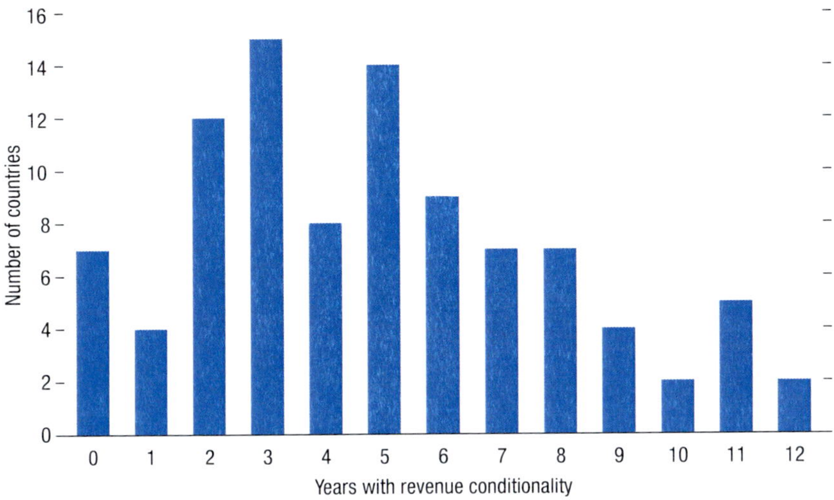

Sources: IMF, MONA database; and authors' calculations.

revenue conditions were included in the 441 newly approved IMF programs (about 20 percent of the total number of conditions). Figure 19.3 shows the number of years in which a Fund program included revenue conditionality. On average, countries had 5 years with revenue conditionality, which means those IMF programs included revenue conditionality in at least 5 occasions over the sample period (there might be more than one revenue condition in a given year, for example, applying to different taxes). In addition, countries had, on average, 3 years of consecutive revenue conditionality over the sample period. Finally, revenue conditionality has taken mostly the form of structural benchmarks (80 percent), with the remainder conditionality taking the form of prior actions.

The number of countries that included revenue conditionality in IMF-supported programs has varied over time. It increased during the 1990s—reflecting the structural nature of IMF programs in the former transition economies (Figure 19.4). As a result, more than 40 countries with an IMF program included at least one revenue condition by 2000. Subsequently, revenue conditions fell in the early 2000s with streamlining of conditionality in IMF programs (IMF, 2005). However, there was a resurgence of revenue conditionality after 2008, presumably reflecting challenges in implementing tax reforms and the need to shore up revenues in the aftermath of the global financial crisis. While during the 1990s, middle-income countries made up the bulk of the IMF programs with revenue conditionality (about 60 percent), more recently, low-income countries have increasingly included revenue conditionality (about 50 percent since 2006).

Figure 19.4. Countries with Revenue Conditionality in IMF Programs, 1993–2013
(By year and income level)

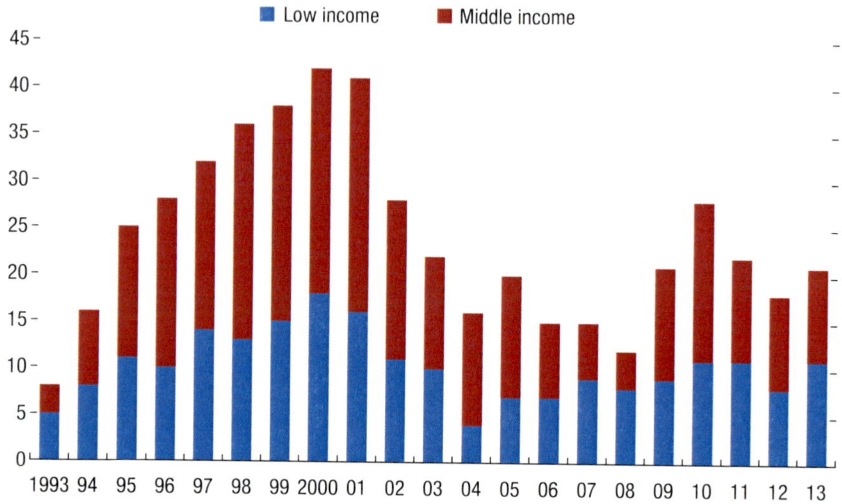

Sources: IMF, MONA database; and authors' calculations.

Noteworthy, the bulk of the revenue conditionality in IMF programs has focused on taxes on goods and services (56 percent), followed by conditionality on taxes on income (32 percent), and on international transactions (12 percent).

Finally, a closer look at compliance with revenue conditionality in IMF programs suggests that overall compliance has been close to 76 percent, with the strongest compliance observed for conditionality on taxes on goods and services (about 80 percent).[9] A low compliance record (including countries complying with 50 percent or less of the total number of revenue conditions) is mostly explained by noncompliance with conditionality on income taxes. Within this group, only 5 countries (accounting for about 2 percent of the total number of conditions in the sample) had a compliance record below 30 percent. In addition, countries with a low revenue conditionality compliance record were ranked very low in terms of quality of institutions (with a score below 2 in the ICRG ranking).

[9] While unmet conditionality is not likely to be equivalent to no conditionality in terms of its effects on tax reform, Annex 19.2 (available online only, at http://link.springer.com/article/10.1007/s10797-015-9379-7#SupplementaryMaterial) formally considers a revenue conditionality variable that equals one for all revenue conditionality regardless of compliance record and another variable measuring compliance with revenue conditionality. The results indicate that only met revenue conditionality has an impact on revenue collection.

Empirical Specification and Estimation

The impact of revenue conditionality in IMF programs on tax revenues is explored by estimating equations of the form:

$$T_{it} = \delta T_{it-1} + \beta_1 PC_{it-1} + \beta_2 PNOC_{it-1} + \zeta' X_{it} + \alpha_i + \mu_t + \varepsilon_{it} \quad (19.1)$$

where T denotes tax revenues in country $i = 1,\ldots,N$ at time $t = 1,\ldots,L$, expressed relative to GDP, in logs,[10] PC is a dummy variable for IMF programs including met revenue conditionality (equal to 1 if an IMF program with country i includes met revenue conditionality in year $t-1$ and 0 otherwise), and $PNOC$ is a dummy variable for country i having an IMF program in $t-1$ without revenue conditionality. X is a vector of controls, and country and time-specific effects are also included. The lagged dependent variable allows for sluggish response in the tax-to-GDP ratio. Eq. (19.1) is estimated separately for total tax revenue (Total Tax), as well as revenues from taxes on goods and services (G&S), the value-added tax (VAT), taxes on income (Income), taxes on corporate profits (CIT), the personal income tax (PIT), and tax on international transactions (Trade).

The control variables in X are drawn from previous studies on the determinants of tax-to-GDP ratios (Ghura, 1998) and tax effort (see, for example, Sen Gupta, 2007; Baunsgaard and Keen, 2010; Pessino and Fenochietto, 2010). In particular, the overall development of the economy, measured by GDP per capita, is expected to show a positive correlation with revenue reflecting a growing demand for public services with rising income per capita, and because of a higher degree of economic and institutional sophistication. A higher share of agriculture in value-added is expected to be negatively associated with revenue because agriculture is harder to tax. The degree of trade openness, measured as the sum of the shares of imports and exports in GDP, can present either sign. Rodrik (1998) argues that more open countries are vulnerable to risks and, given the need for social insurance, therefore tend to have bigger governments. Moreover, since trade taxes are easier to collect, especially in developing countries, a positive relationship between trade openness and revenues can be expected. However, higher trade openness could be the result of trade liberalization through tariff reductions. This would be consistent with a negative relationship between trade openness and revenue. Other control variables include inflation, which may have revenue effects through both unindexed tax systems and the generation of seigniorage; the level of external indebtedness, which reflects the need to generate revenue to service debt; and the quality of institutions as proxied by the Transparency International's

---

[10] Gujarati and Porter (2009) suggest that the log transformation may be of advantage since it may reduce the incidence of heteroskedasticity and skewness of the data. Auriol and Warlters (2005) suggest that the log transformation may help ensure that out-of-sample fitted values of the tax-to-GDP ratio lie in the 0–100% range. The results are, however, qualitatively identical when using the ratio in levels.

corruption perception index, which takes values from 0 (high corruption) to 10 (low corruption).

Eq. (19.1) is estimated using a system-Generalized Method of Moments (GMM) model,[11] allowing for an unbiased estimate of all variables, including the coefficient on the lagged dependent variable. The system-GMM takes Eq. (19.1) in differences and levels as a system, using lagged changes as instruments in the latter, and lagged levels as instrument for changes in the former. This estimator is best suited for situations with "small T, large N" panels as is the case in this paper with T=21 years and N=126 countries. As an alternative to the GMM results, we present main results using the Anderson and Hsiao (1981) instrumental variables approach.

Of major concern in this literature is the treatment of endogeneity of IMF revenue conditionality as IMF loans tend to be extended in response to economic imbalances (Conway, 2003). As such, countries with a low tax-to-GDP ratio—reflecting the underlying macroeconomic and structural weaknesses—may need to request IMF support to strengthen their fiscal position, thereby creating a potential problem of reverse causality. System-GMM models are well-suited to address cases in which independent variables are not strictly exogenous, meaning they are correlated with past and possibly current realizations of the error (Roodman, 2009a). Using second and deeper lags of the potentially endogenous variables (and their differences) makes them predetermined, meaning not correlated with the error term.

Also of concern is the possibility of sample selection bias associated with participation in an IMF program. With regard to tax revenues, countries that have an IMF program may not be directly comparable to those without one because the former must address macroeconomic imbalances that will influence fiscal policy and the ability of the government to collect taxes. This creates a potential selection bias problem. We address this issue by following the literature on the determinants of IMF programs (Moser and Sturm, 2011; Barro and Lee, 2005) that relies on identifying suitable instruments to isolate the effects of IMF programs on tax revenue. We instrument the IMF program variable in the system-GMM equations with economic as well as political variables that have been found to be well correlated with IMF program involvement.[12] For our main results, we use three variables: the lag of a five-year moving average of a dummy indicating whether or not a country was under an IMF arrangement, as in Przeworski and Vreeland (2000), which is a core political variable used extensively in the literature, indicating persistence in IMF involvement; the level of international reserves in months of imports, which in low level may indicate a higher likelihood

[11] The Blundell and Bond (1998) system-GMM estimator is used instead of Arellano and Bond (1991) difference-GMM estimator since the first one has much better finite sample properties in terms of bias and root mean squared error than the latter; the results are not qualitatively different.

[12] Moser and Sturm (2011) provide a very detailed survey of the literature on the determinants of IMF programs, including a description of the main economic and political variables. For further recent reviews, see for instance Steinwand and Stone (2008), Bird (2007), and Conway (2006).

of balance of payments difficulties and vulnerability to speculative attacks, thus making the country more likely to request and receive IMF assistance; and the Swiss Economic Institute's (KOF) index of political globalization, as a measure of a country's integration in the world politics, that may facilitate access to multilateral financing.

For robustness, we include additional political variables such as the index of political plurality and the chief executive years in office, from the World Bank's Database of Political Institutions; and the Freedom House polity indexes on political rights and civil liberties. Finally, Kuncic's (2014) indicator on legal institutional quality was considered. Full details of the dataset and summary statistics are provided in Annex 19.1.

These instruments, while likely correlated with the IMF program variable, are less likely to be directly correlated with tax revenue.[13] While our identification strategy is commonly used in the literature to address potential endogeneity and selection bias in the IMF program variable, such methodology implies a number of exclusionary restrictions for estimation of an IMF participation equation that clearly depends on the appropriate choice of instruments. These instruments may be correlated with other variables (besides tax revenue) that could ultimately be correlated with the dependent variable, other than via their impact on IMF conditions. As a result, the exclusion restriction may be violated, and the estimation strategy potentially biased.

To test the validity of the instruments in system-GMM we present not only the Hansen statistic[14] (Roodman, 2009b) but also the difference-in-Hansen test of exogeneity of the instruments (Bond, Hoeffler, and Temple, 2001). In addition, we test for under identification (Kleibergen and Paap (2006) LM test) and weak instruments (Cragg and Donald (1993) and Kleibergen and Paap (2006) Wald tests) following Bazzi and Clemens (2013) for both the levels equation as well as for the difference equation. Finally, due to the presence of heteroskedasticity in the data, robust standard errors are presented. Generally, the diagnostics performed on the estimations below are satisfactory, with a tolerable value for the Hansen test, and with the Arellano and Bond (1991) test for first and second order serial correlation (M1 and M2) suggesting that the former is present but the latter is not, which is consistent with the underlying assumptions. The difference-in-Hansen *p*-values imply that we cannot reject the hypothesis that the subset of instruments used is indeed exogenous. In addition, the Kleibergen and Paap (2006) reported *p*-values imply that we can reject the null hypothesis of under identification for the levels and difference equations. Also the diagnostics on weak instruments using the Cragg and Donald (1993) Wald test are generally acceptable, when compared

[13] Alternatively, other economic variables were considered as possible instruments without significant differences in the results, such as the level of external debt-to-GDP, inflation, the change in real GDP per capita, the change in the bilateral exchange rate to the US dollar, and the overall fiscal balance.

[14] The Hansen statistic's *p*-value should be high enough to reject correlation between the instruments and the errors but not too high because it weakens confidence in the test.

to the reported critical values from Stock and Yogo (2005) for the bias of the Instrumental Variable estimates greater than 10 or 30 percent of the OLS bias. Finally, we have tested for unit roots (due to the coefficient of the lagged dependent variable being close to one in some cases). For this we use Maddala and Wu's (1999) Fisher-type test[15] (suitable for unbalanced panels), using several alternative specifications (with/without time trend, demean) as proposed in Choi (2001). In all cases, the tests' p-values strongly reject the null hypothesis that the panels contain a unit root.

MAIN RESULTS

This section analyses the impact of IMF programs with and without revenue conditionality on total tax revenue and its main components. The question here is whether an IMF program with revenue conditionality has a differential positive impact on revenue collection as compared to countries with an IMF program that does not include revenue conditionality or to countries with no IMF program.

Table 19.2 reports the results for total tax revenue (Column 1), as well as four of its components: taxes on goods and services (Column 2), of which VAT (Column 3), taxes on income[16] (Column 4), and tax on international trade (Column 5).[17] In general, we do find support for the underlying hypothesis that revenue conditionality contained in IMF-supported programs has a positive impact on tax revenue. The effect of revenue conditionality on tax revenue is found to be positive and significant for the total as well as for taxes on goods and services, which includes VAT. In contrast, an IMF program without revenue conditionality has no significant impact on revenue collection. In addition, we formally test whether the coefficients of the two dummies (Program with and without conditionality) are significantly different from each other. The reported p-values for $\beta_1 = \beta_2$ suggest that both coefficients are statistically different from each other for total tax revenue, taxes on goods and services, and the VAT.

The estimated coefficient on total tax revenue implies that IMF programs with revenue conditionality could raise tax revenue by about 1 percentage point of GDP in a given year, with half of this revenue gain explained by the positive impact on taxes on goods and services. The lagged dependent variable captures the tax revenue gain over time for years with consecutive revenue conditionality. Taking this into account and recalling that countries had on average 3 consecutive years of IMF programs containing revenue conditionality over the sample period, it implies a revenue

[15] Using, alternatively, Augmented Dickey-Fuller or Phillips-Perron unit-root tests.

[16] Further disaggregation for taxes on corporate profits (CIT) and on personal income (PIT) was performed with no qualitative difference compared to total taxes on income.

[17] Annex 19.2 (online only, at http://link.springer.com/article/10.1007/s10797-015-9379-7#SupplementaryMaterial) presents the results after also controlling for the level of corruption (omitted here because it reduces considerably the number of observations), which are qualitatively identical to that in Table 19.2.

Table 19.2. IMF Revenue Conditionality on Tax Revenues[1,2]

	(1)	(2)	(3)	(4)	(5)
	Total Tax	G&S	VAT	Income	Trade
Tax, Lagged	0.9573***	0.9101***	0.9206***	0.7568***	0.9080***
	(0.0406)	(0.0512)	(0.0415)	(0.0807)	(0.1031)
IMF Program No Conditionality, Lagged	0.0054	−0.0656	-0.0184	−0.0433	0.0022
	(0.0282)	(0.0411)	(0.0347)	(0.0611)	(0.0600)
IMF Program with Conditionality, Lagged	0.0760***	0.1089**	0.1013**	0.0199	−0.0920
	(0.0349)	(0.0498)	(0.0509)	(0.0921)	(0.0835)
Trade Openness	0.0009**	0.0006	0.0007	0.0013	0.0010
	(0.0004)	(0.0007)	(0.0006)	(0.0013)	(0.0014)
Inflation	−0.0028	0.0614	0.4281*	0.1368	−0.1099
	(0.0021)	(0.1299)	(0.2604)	(0.1534)	(0.1280)
GDP Per Capita (log)	0.0054	0.0172	0.0089	0.0500***	0.0019
	(0.0120)	(0.0132)	(0.0100)	(0.0199)	(0.0118)
Agriculture Share in Value Added	0.0015	0.0006	0.0009	0.0001	0.0034
	(0.0013)	(0.0019)	(0.0016)	(0.0028)	(0.0040)
External Debt	−0.0005	−0.0003	−0.0001	−0.0025*	−0.0002
	(0.0006)	(0.0005)	(0.0007)	(0.0013)	(0.0009)
$\beta_1 = \beta_2$ (*p* value)	0.009	0.017	0.055	0.595	0.446
M1 (*p* value)	0.014	0.000	0.000	0.001	0.000
M2 (*p* value)	0.428	0.432	0.262	0.565	0.407
Hansen-Overidentification (*p* value)	0.646	0.825	0.513	0.389	0.797
Diff-in-Hansen-test of Exogeneity (*p* value)	0.363	0.608	0.368	0.303	0.510
For Levels Equation					
Kleibergen-Paap LM Test (*p* value)	0.000	0.000	0.000	0.000	0.000
Cragg Donald Wald F Stat	333.45	186.09	82.32	137.65	103.29
For Difference Equation					
Kleibergen-Paap LM Test (*p* value)	0.078	0.099	0.086	0.056	0.000
Cragg-Donald Wald F Stat	13.25	8.56	6.10	8.25	5.92
Observations	1,851	1,703	629	1,718	1,683
Number of Instruments	74	74	73	74	76
Number of Countries	122	114	81	114	114

Source: Authors' calculations.

Note: G&S = goods and services; VAT = value-added tax.

[1] Dependent variable is total tax revenue, and revenue from taxes on goods and services, VAT, income, and trade, respectively, relative to GDP. Full set of controls and year dummies in all regressions. Robust standard errors in parentheses; *** (**,*) indicate significance at 1 (5, 10) percent.

[2] One step, robust, with instruments based on first lag of differences in past IMF program (five-year moving average, lagged), international reserves (in months of imports, lagged), political globalization index, and second lags of their levels in the differenced equation. Stock-Yogo 30 percent maximum IV relative bias is 5.39.

gain of about 3½ percentage points of GDP by the third year of consecutive revenue conditionality, with half of the gain explained by taxes on goods and services.[18]

The highly significant impact of IMF revenue conditionality on taxes on goods and services—in particular on VAT—could be explained by the large share

[18] Alternatively, the impact of revenue conditionality on structural revenue performance can be analyzed by using a dummy on revenue conditionality that equals one during and after each IMF program. The results are qualitatively similar to those presented in the text and the coefficients imply similar revenue gains to those computed by the third year after the program started.

of revenue conditionality attached to these taxes as discussed in the Data and Methodology section. Besides their large contribution to tax revenue, the superiority of broad-base consumption taxes has been highlighted, not only in terms of efficiency and welfare gains (Keen and Ligthart, 2001) but also in terms of helping strengthen the tax administration, thus improving tax collection in the aggregate. The result on the VAT, in particular, also confirms previous empirical results on the positive relationship between the adoption of a VAT—which has been found to be positively correlated with having an IMF program—and improvements in tax revenue collection (Keen and Lockwood, 2010).

All in all, this result suggests that revenue conditionality has supported the development of growth-enhancing tax instruments (Arnold et al., 2011; Acosta-Ormaechea and Yoo, 2012). A proportional tax—such as the value-added tax—on all consumption, however, can have negative distributional impact. This effect is usually mitigated by exempting a few sensitive food and other items under the VAT, and adopting a turnover threshold that confers a competitive advantage to smaller and presumably less well-off traders who serve relatively poor customers; this is tantamount to a de facto exemption (Jenkins, Jenkins, and Kuo, 2006). Moreover, if revenues from the VAT finance increased social expenditures, then the net distributional outcome can be progressive (Muñoz and Cho, 2004). Empirical evidence for 140 countries shows that IMF programs have a positive effect on raising social spending (on health and education) in low-income countries (Clements, Gupta, and Nozaki, 2013).

The effect of IMF programs (with or without revenue conditionality) on taxes on income and on international trade is not statistically significant. In contrast to taxes on goods and services, the focus of conditionality on taxes on income has been less frequent due to their relatively low contribution to tax revenue.[19] The result can also be explained by the proliferation of tax incentives (including excessive allowances on the personal income tax or corporate income tax holidays, etc.) (Zee, Stotsky, and Ley, 2002). As for taxes on international transactions (trade taxes), the result is expected as trade liberalization has been generally supported in IMF programs to replace harmful trade taxes with broad-base consumption taxes (Baunsgaard and Keen, 2010), and as such, no impact—or even a negative impact—on trade tax should be expected.

Attention focuses now on identifying the differential impact on tax revenue from conditionality related to tax policy as opposed to tax administration measures; as well as specific as opposed to more general revenue conditionality in IMF programs, as defined in the Data and Methodology section. Table 19.3 presents the results for conditionality on tax policy and tax administration, whereas Table 19.4 presents the results for specific versus general conditionality.

Concerning the impact on tax revenue from conditionality on tax policy and tax administration, while the estimated coefficients in Table 19.3 show mixed results regarding the effectiveness of different types of conditionality on the

---

[19] Except perhaps for the tax on corporate profits in low-income countries whose share in total revenue can still be significant (IMF, 2013).

Table 19.3. Tax Policy vs. Tax Administration Revenue Conditionality on Tax Revenues[1,2]

	(1) Total Tax	(2) G&S	(3) VAT	(4) Income	(5) Trade
Tax, Lagged	0.9648***	0.8596***	0.9253***	0.8232***	0.8855***
	(0.0464)	(0.0528)	(0.0405)	(0.0812)	(0.0525)
IMF Program No Conditionality, Lagged	−0.0306	−0.0024	−0.0268	−0.0267	0.0427
	(0.0366)	(0.0476)	(0.0347)	(0.0641)	(0.0741)
Conditionality on Tax Policy, Lagged	0.1414**	0.0612	0.1433*	0.0628	0.0773
	(0.0687)	(0.0796)	(0.0889)	(0.1495)	(0.1499)
Conditionality on Tax Administration, Lagged	−0.0412	0.1691**	0.0534	−0.0719	0.0108
	(0.0690)	(0.0889)	(0.0816)	(0.0876)	(0.0858)
Tax Policy vs. Tax Administration (*p* value)	0.148	0.155	0.551	0.469	0.749
Constrained Coefficient	0.0505**	0.0602**	0.0959***	−0.0330	0.0456
	(0.0277)	(0.0312)	(0.0398)	(0.0692)	(0.0735)
M1 (*p* value)	0.013	0.000	0.000	0.000	0.000
M2 (*p* value)	0.519	0.460	0.315	0.636	0.545
Hansen-Overidentification (*p* value)	0.676	0.606	0.613	0.271	0.767
Diff-in-Hansen-Test of Exogeneity (*p* value)	0.434	0.368	0.518	0.254	0.565
For Levels Equation					
Kleibergen-Paap LM Test (*p* value)	0.000	0.000	0.000	0.000	0.000
Cragg-Donald Wald F Stat	51.85	37.39	22.13	20.07	12.22
For Difference Equation					
Kleibergen-Paap LM Test (*p* value)	0.006	0.000	0.014	0.003	0.000
Cragg Donald Wald F Stat	7.56	13.13	7.10	4.05	8.19
Observations	1,850	1,703	629	1,718	1,702
Number of Instruments	74	74	73	72	73
Number of Countries	122	114	81	114	115

Source: Authors' calculations.

Note: G&S = goods and services; VAT = value-added tax.

[1] Dependent variable is total tax revenue, and revenue from taxes on goods and services, VAT, income, and trade, respectively, relative to GDP. Full set of controls and year dummies in all regressions. Robust standard errors in parentheses; *** (**, *) indicate significance at 1 (5, 10) percent.

[2] One step, robust, with instruments based on first lag of differences in past IMF program (five-year moving average, lagged), international reserves (in months of imports, lagged), political globalization index, and second lags of their levels in the differenced equation. Stock-Yogo 30 percent maximum IV relative bias is 5.39.

different taxes, a formal test on the estimated coefficients suggests that the impact of conditionality on tax policy is not statistically different from the impact of conditionality on tax administration (with *p*-values well above 10 percent). The reported constrained coefficients also imply a similar revenue impact to that estimated in Table 19.2, with taxes on goods and services explaining about half the total revenue impact. This result also suggests that the impact on revenue collection can indeed be substantial when both types of revenue conditionality are present in a given year, which confirms that tax policy and tax administration complement each other in a successful tax reform.

Concerning the impact of specific versus general conditionality, while the estimated coefficients in Table 19.4 appear to favor specific conditionality, again a formal test on the estimated coefficients suggests that the impact of specific

Table 19.4. IMF Specific vs. General Revenue Conditionality on Tax Revenues[1,2]

	(1) G&S	(2) VAT	(3) Income	(4) Trade
Tax, Lagged	0.9116***	0.9198***	0.8155***	0.8854***
	(0.0536)	(0.0421)	(0.0565)	(0.0609)
IMF Program No Conditionality, Lagged	−0.0606	−0.0173	−0.0141	0.0823
	(0.0401)	(0.0379)	(0.0423)	(0.0608)
Specific Conditionality, Lagged	0.2517***	0.0928*	0.3038***	−0.3503
	(0.1041)	(0.0525)	(0.1162)	(0.4317)
General Conditionality, Lagged	0.0467	0.1020	−0.0383	−0.0593
	(0.0680)	(0.1652)	(0.0648)	(0.0853)
Specific vs. General Conditionality (*p* value)	0.154	0.956	0.0147	0.508
Constrained Coefficient	0.1185***	0.0933*	...	−0.0704
	(0.0458)	(0.0514)	...	(0.0837)
M1 (*p* value)	0.000	0.000	0.000	0.000
M2 (*p* value)	0.484	0.246	0.785	0.398
Hansen-Overidentification (*p* value)	0.730	0.528	0.447	0.892
Diff-in-Hansen-Test of Exogeneity (*p* value)	0.539	0.389	0.591	0.711
For Levels Equation				
Kleibergen-Paap LM Test (*p* value)	0.000	0.000	0.000	0.000
Cragg-Donald Wald F Stat	65.87	67.61	31.06	9.44
For Difference Equation				
Kleibergen-Paap LM Test (*p* value)	0.017	0.010	0.031	0.084
Cragg Donald Wald F Stat	6.84	6.21	7.51	1.10
Observations	1,684	620	1,699	1,683
Number of Instruments	74	73	74	74
Number of Countries	113	80	113	114

Source: Authors' calculations.

Note: G&S = goods and services; VAT = value-added tax.

[1] Dependent variable is revenue from taxes on goods and services, VAT, income, and trade, respectively, relative to GDP. Full set of controls and year dummies in all regressions. Robust standard errors in parentheses; *** (**, *) indicate significance at 1 (5, 10) percent.

[2] One step, robust, with instruments based on first lag of differences in past IMF program (five-year moving average, lagged), international reserves (in months of imports, lagged), political globalization index, and second lags of their levels in the differenced equation. Stock-Yogo 30 percent maximum IV relative bias is 5.39.

conditionality is not statistically different from the impact of general conditionality except for taxes on income, for which specific conditionality appears to have a positively significant and large effect on revenue collection. Again here, the reported constrained coefficients imply similar revenue impact to those estimated in Table 19.2 for taxes on goods and services and the VAT. For taxes on income, the revenue gain differential with respect to the overall sample—and in particular with respect to more general revenue conditionality—is expected and explained by the clearer link that exists between the revenue target and the specific conditionality added to help attain this target.

The results above having given a sense of robustness across different types of conditionality, the focus now is on alternative instruments within the system-GMM, as well as on alternative estimation methods. Table 19.5 presents the results for the impact of IMF programs (with and without conditionality) on tax revenues, when considering an extended set of alternative political economy instruments in system-GMM as indicated in the Data and Methodology section. As explained there, these instruments, while also correlated with the IMF

Table 19.5. IMF Revenue Conditionality on Tax Revenues with Alternative Instruments[1,2]

	(1)	(2)	(3)	(4)	(5)
	Total Tax	G&S	VAT	Income	Trade
Tax, Lagged	0.6825***	0.5085***	0.5672***	0.7474***	0.9159***
	(0.1703)	(0.1596)	(0.1784)	(0.2815)	(0.0951)
IMF Program No Conditionality, Lagged	−0.0226	−0.0838	0.0292	0.0328	-0.0996
	(0.0584)	(0.0874)	(0.0827)	(0.1133)	(0.1012)
IMF Program with Conditionality, Lagged	0.1566**	0.1638**	0.1835**	−0.0115	0.1209
	(0.0742)	(0.0796)	(0.0812)	(0.1448)	(0.1349)
$\beta_1 = \beta_2$ (*p* value)	0.068	0.092	0.057	0.809	0.204
M1 (*p* value)	0.044	0.034	0.006	0.014	0.000
M2 (*p* value)	0.635	0.657	0.384	0.760	0.317
Hansen-Overidentification (*p* value)	0.174	0.798	0.454	0.724	0.879
Diff-in-Hansen-Test of Exogeneity (*p* value)	0.584	0.715	0.844	0.878	0.409
For Levels Equation					
Kleibergen-Paap LM Test (*p* value)	0.000	0.000	0.000	0.000	0.000
Cragg-Donald Wald F Stat	81.46	44.08	25.85	36.95	28.69
For Difference Equation					
Kleibergen-Paap LM Test (*p* value)	0.000	0.018	0.012	0.000	0.000
Cragg Donald Wald F Stat	25.56	18.52	11.25	16.35	14.13
Observations	1,851	1,703	629	1,718	1,683
Number of Instruments	54	73	68	54	54
Number of Countries	122	114	81	114	114

Source: Authors' calculations.

Note: G&S = goods and services; VAT = value-added tax.

[1] Dependent variable is total tax revenue, and revenue from taxes on goods and services, VAT, income, and trade, respectively, relative to GDP. Full set of controls and year dummies in all regressions. Robust standard errors in parentheses; *** (**, *) indicate significance at 1 (5, 10) percent.

[2] One step, robust, with (collapsed) instruments based on first lag of differences in past IMF program (five-year moving average, lagged), political globalization index, political plurality index, chief executive years in office, polity index, legal institutional quality, corruption perception index, and second lags of their levels in the differenced equation. Stock-Yogo 30 percent maximum IV relative bias is 4.67.

program variable, are less likely to be directly correlated with tax revenue, with reported tests confirming the relevance of the chosen instruments.

The results in Table 19.5 are qualitatively identical to those presented in Table 19.2 above with a significantly positive effect of IMF programs with revenue conditionality on total tax revenue, as well as on taxes on goods and services and the VAT. Similarly, the reported *p*-values suggest that the estimated coefficients on IMF program with and without revenue conditionality are statistically different from each other for these taxes. After extending the set of instruments for the probability of being in an IMF program, however, the impact of revenue conditionality on tax revenue increases, which is reflected in larger estimated coefficients. In addition, Annex 19.2 (available online only)[20] presents the same results using the Anderson and Hsiao (1981) instrumental variables approach with

[20] Available at http://link.springer.com/article/10.1007/s10797-015-9379-7#SupplementaryMaterial.

an extended set of political economy instruments. The results are qualitatively similar to that in Table 19.2, though with lower estimated coefficients.[21]

FURTHER ANALYSIS[22]

A number of robustness analyses are presented in this section.[23] A first robustness check consists of trying to identify any differential effect of IMF programs with revenue conditionality on tax revenue based on the level of development of the country, or the strength and quality of the country's institutions. Table 19.6 presents the results for low-income countries that are eligible for IMF PRGT concessional financing (Column 1), as well as middle-income countries (Column 2) considered separately.[24] Table 19.6, Columns 3–4 present the results for countries grouped on the basis of the ICRG ranking of corruption, which is taken as a proxy for the strength of a country's institutions. For the analysis, countries with strong institutions are those with a score equal to or above 3, whereas countries with weak institutions are those with a score below 3.[25]

The estimated coefficient on IMF program with revenue conditionality for low-income countries (Column 1) is significantly positively related to tax revenue, implying a revenue gain of about 1½ percentage points of GDP— and with a coefficient that is statistically different than the coefficient for IMF program without conditionality. For middle-income countries (Column 2), however, while

[21] Alternatively, for further robustness, selection bias has been addressed using a fixed-effects model including Heckman's (1976, 1979) proposed two-stage estimation procedure. As a second alternative to GMM and fixed-effects estimators, we tried the inverse probability weight regression-adjustment method (Hirano et al., 2003). Results from these alternative models are not qualitatively different from those using system-GMM and have been dropped here to preserve space but are available from the authors.

[22] As in the Further Analysis section, the diagnostics here are satisfactory, with a tolerable value for the Hansen, Kleibergen-Paap, and Cragg-Donald tests, and with the Arellano–Bond (1991) test for first and second order serial correlation (M1 and M2) suggesting the former is present but the latter is not, which is consistent with the underlying assumptions.

[23] In addition, we have also included a dummy variable for oil exporter countries to capture potential negative influence of natural-resource revenues on domestic tax effort (Benedek et al., 2014). Alternatively, we have also used non-resource tax revenue only as in Crivelli and Gupta, 2014. The results being qualitatively identical to those in Table 19.2 are omitted to preserve space.

[24] Middle-income countries are classified according to the World Bank criterion. Seventy-two low-income countries are now eligible for concessional lending, which the IMF provides via the Poverty Reduction and Growth Trust (PRGT). It currently carries a zero interest rate on its loans. Eligibility for PRGT lending is based on a member country's annual per capita income and ability to access international financial markets on a sustainable basis. Concessional support credit lines under the PRGT include the Extended Credit Facility (ECF) and the Standby Credit Facility (SCF). Middle-income countries have been supported mainly under Standby Arrangements (SBA), but also under the Extended Fund Facility (EFF), the Flexible Credit Line (FCL), and the Precautionary and Liquidity Line (PLL). Prior to 2001, low-income countries received support under the Extended Structural Adjustment (ESAF) facility and the Poverty Reduction and Growth Facility (PRGF).

[25] This grouping is almost equivalent to considering the 50th percentile of the distribution with less and more corrupt countries, respectively, also on the basis of the ICRG ranking of corruption.

Table 19.6. By Income Level and Strength of Institutions[1,2]

	(1)	(2)	(3)	(4)
	Low-Income Concessional Financing	Middle Income	Strong Institutions	Weak Institutions
Tax, Lagged	0.8183***	0.8994***	0.8903***	0.8996***
	(0.1364)	(0.0117)	(0.0094)	(0.0351)
IMF Program No Conditionality, Lagged	–0.0570	–0.0992	–0.0113	–0.0215
	(0.0663)	(0.0837)	(0.0201)	(0.0294)
IMF Program with Conditionality, Lagged	0.1574**	0.1973*	0.0514**	0.0230
	(0.0709)	(0.1076)	(0.0250)	(0.0765)
$\beta_1 = \beta_2$ (*p* value)	0.042	0.106	0.045	0.637
Constrained Coefficient	...	0.0288	...	–0.0117
	...	(0.0267)	...	(0.0207)
Observations	1,034	1,470	1,106	974
Number of Instruments	40	31	82	80
Number of Countries	63	89	111	85

Source: Authors' calculations.

[1] Dependent variable is total tax revenue, relative to GDP. Full set of year dummies in all regressions. Robust standard errors in parentheses; *** (**, *) indicate significance at 1 (5, 10) percent.

[2] One step, robust, with (collapsed) instruments based on first lag of differences in past IMF program (five-year moving average, lagged), international reserves (in months of imports, lagged), political globalization index, and second lags of their levels in the differenced equation. Stock-Yogo 30 percent maximum IV relative bias is 5.39.

the impact of revenue conditionality appears to be also significantly positively related to tax revenue, the estimated coefficient is not statistically different from that for the IMF program without conditionality, and the resulting constrained coefficient is not significantly different from zero. This result shows how revenue conditionality in IMF programs can be instrumental in helping low-income countries address implementation challenges and capacity constraints in the adoption of tax reforms.

As for the analysis on the impact of IMF programs with revenue conditionality when considering the strength of a country's institutions, Table 19.6 (Columns 4–5) shows a clear indication that revenue conditionality in IMF programs will potentially have the largest impact on countries with the strongest institutions (or lowest corruption). The estimated coefficient on IMF program with revenue conditionality is only significantly positively related to tax revenue in countries with strong institutions. Also here, the reported *p*-values suggest that IMF program with revenue conditionality are statistically different than IMF program without conditionality for countries with strong institutions. This result confirms earlier results on the importance of institutions for fiscal policy implementation in low-income countries (Lledo and Poplawski-Ribeiro, 2013).

An additional robustness check consists in analyzing the differential impact of IMF programs with revenue conditionality once initial conditions are accounted for. For this purpose, the sample is split to include countries above and below the average tax-to-GDP ratio, as well as countries in the 25th percentile with the lowest and highest tax-to-GDP ratio, respectively, which is equivalent to tax revenue

Table 19.7. Initial Conditions: Measured by Tax-to-GDP Ratio[1,2]

	(1) Below Average	(2) Lower 25th Percentile	(3) Above Average	(4) Higher 25th Percentile
Tax, Lagged	0.9349***	0.8001***	0.8896***	0.8476***
	(0.0504)	(0.1348)	(0.0520)	(0.0503)
IMF Program No Conditionality, Lagged	−0.0214	−0.1197	0.0336	−0.0669
	(0.0355)	(0.1153)	(0.0379)	(0.0566)
IMF Program with Conditionality, Lagged	0.0709*	0.2063**	0.0803**	0.0966
	(0.0394)	(0.0938)	(0.0350)	(0.0606)
$\beta_1 = \beta_2$ (*p* value)	0.066	0.079	0.419	0.007
Constrained Coefficient	...	...	0.0584***	...
	...	...	(0.0222)	...
Observations	718	517	1,133	603
Number of Instruments	74	37	73	72
Number of Countries	78	59	102	70

Source: Authors' calculations.

[1] Dependent variable is total tax revenue, relative to GDP. Full set of controls and year dummies in all regressions. Robust standard errors in parentheses; *** (**, *) indicate significance at 1 (5, 10) percent.

[2] One step, robust, with (collapsed) instruments based on first lag of differences in past IMF program (five-year moving average, lagged), international reserves (in months of imports, lagged), political globalization index, and second lags of their levels in the differenced equation. Stock-Yogo 30 percent maximum IV relative bias is 5.39.

approximately lying below 10 percent of GDP and above 20 percent of GDP, respectively. The underlying hypothesis is that countries with a relatively low tax revenue collection may rely more on revenue measures supported by revenue conditionality to close the potential fiscal gap as opposed to countries where the tax effort is already high.

The results in Table 19.7 show a relatively small difference (not statistically different) in the revenue gain associated with IMF revenue conditionality for countries with tax-to-GDP ratios below and above the average. The difference is, however, much more pronounced for countries with the lowest and highest tax-to-GDP ratios. While the revenue gain associated with revenue conditionality in the first group of countries is close to 2 percentage points of GDP, there appears to be no significant impact on countries that already face the highest tax revenue ratio (above 20 percent of GDP).

A further robustness test consists of identifying changes in tax-to-GDP ratios that are not related to the current state of the economy when analyzing the impact of revenue conditionality in IMF programs, that is, the component of tax revenue that does not respond systematically to output conditions, but is instead the consequence of exogenous political processes or extraordinary non-economic circumstances. This analysis is particularly relevant in the context of IMF programs that are usually negotiated in the context of large macroeconomic imbalances and lower-than-potential economic growth. Following Fatas and Mihov (2003, 2006), cyclically-adjusted tax revenue (and components) are obtained by estimating for each country equations of the form:

$$T_{it} = \delta T_{it-1} + \beta \Delta Y_{it} + \zeta' Z_{it} + \alpha_i + \varepsilon_{it} \tag{19.2}$$

Table 19.8. Cyclically Adjusted Tax Revenue[1,2]

	(1)	(2)	(3)	(4)	(5)
	Total Tax	G&S	VAT	Income	Trade
Tax, Lagged	0.9400***	0.9033***	0.5026**	0.7620***	0.8265***
	(0.0520)	(0.0549)	(0.2336)	(0.0944)	(0.0871)
IMF Program No Conditionality, Lagged	−0.0059	−0.0176	0.1531	−0.0182	0.1494*
	(0.0343)	(0.0311)	(0.1240)	(0.0710)	(0.0850)
IMF Program with Conditionality, Lagged	0.1047*	0.0689*	0.1980**	−0.0461	−0.0999
	(0.0599)	(0.0415)	(0.0972)	(0.1026)	(0.0782)
$\beta_1 = \beta_2$ (*p* value)	0.084	0.054	0.067	0.811	0.053
Observations	1,712	1,492	516	1,507	1,491
Number of Instruments	55	87	53	55	55
Number of Countries	122	113	75	113	114

Source: Authors' calculations.

Note: G&S = goods and services; VAT = value-added tax.

[1] Dependent variable is the cyclically adjusted measure of total tax revenue, and revenue from taxes on goods and services, VAT, income, and trade, respectively, relative to GDP. Full set of controls and year dummies in all regressions. Robust standard errors in parentheses; *** (**, *) indicate significance at 1(5, 10) percent.

[2] One step, robust, with (collapsed) instruments based on first lag of differences in past IMF program (five-year moving average, lagged), international reserves (in months of imports, lagged), political globalization index, and second lags of their levels in the differenced equation. Stock-Yogo 30 percent maximum IV relative bias is 5.39.

where T is tax revenue (and components), expressed relative to GDP, ΔY is real GDP growth, and Z is a set of controls.[26] In order to control for possible endogeneity of tax revenue with respect to GDP, the instrumental variables (IV) estimator is applied, where $\Delta Y(-1)$ and $\Delta Y(-2)$ are used as instruments.[27] The residuals of Eq. (19.2) for each country represent the discretionary component of tax revenue and enter Eq. (19.1) as the dependent variable. The results in Table 19.8 are qualitatively similar to those in the Further Analysis section with a highly significant and positive impact of IMF programs with revenue conditionality on total tax revenue as well as for taxes on goods and services and VAT.

A final test considers the number of revenue conditions in IMF programs as an alternative benchmark to determine the impact of conditionality on tax revenue collection. While it is difficult to objectively measure the relative stringency of conditionality in IMF programs, using the number of conditions is a measure that has been widely accepted in the literature (see, for example, Dreher and Jensen, 2007; Copelovitch, 2010). In the analysis presented below, the IMF program with revenue conditionality variable is measured to account for the share of revenue conditions to the total number of conditions for each country/year during an IMF program.[28] The results in Table 19.9 on the impact of IMF programs with revenue conditionality are robust to this alternative indicator on

[26] Control variables include the current inflation rate to ensure that the results are not driven by high inflation episodes and a linear time trend.

[27] Overidentifying restriction tests (notably Wooldridge's 1995 score test) do not reject the validity of the selected instruments.

[28] Alternatively, qualitatively identical results were obtained when using the total number of revenue conditions.

Table 19.9. Share of Revenue Conditionality in Total[1,2]

	(1) Total Tax	(2) G&S	(3) VAT	(4) Income	(5) Trade
Tax, Lagged	0.9239***	0.8801***	0.8923***	0.7450***	0.8937***
	(0.0398)	(0.0596)	(0.0383)	(0.0828)	(0.0622)
IMF Program No Conditionality, Lagged	−0.0024	−0.0811	0.0099	−0.0467	0.0680
	(0.0317)	(0.0544)	(0.0301)	(0.0988)	(0.0678)
IMF Program with Conditionality, Lagged	0.1903**	0.4116*	0.2148**	0.0625	−0.0240
	(0.0926)	(0.2272)	(0.1166)	(0.3431)	(0.2112)
$\beta_1 = \beta_2$ (*p* value)	0.084	0.057	0.091	0.797	0.720
Observations	1,851	1,704	629	1,719	1,703
Number of Instruments	77	44	61	74	74
Number of Countries	122	114	81	114	115

Source: Authors' calculations.

Note: G&S = goods and services; VAT = value-added tax.

[1] Dependent variable is total tax revenue, and revenue from taxes on goods and services, VAT, income, and trade, respectively, relative to GDP. Full set of year dummies in all regressions. Robust standard errors in parentheses; *** (**, *) indicate significance at 1 (5, 10) percent.

[2] One step, robust, with instruments based on first lag of differences in past IMF program (five-year moving average, lagged), international reserves (in months of imports, lagged), political globalization index, and second lags of their levels in the differenced equation. Stock-Yogo 30 percent maximum IV relative bias is 5.39.

revenue conditionality. We find a significantly positive impact of IMF programs with revenue conditionality on total tax revenue, as well as on taxes on goods and services, and VAT. Similarly, the reported *p*-values suggest that the coefficients for IMF program with and without revenue conditionality are statistically different from each other. The main difference with the results reported in the Further Analysis section corresponds to the size of the estimated coefficients, suggesting a somehow larger revenue impact associated with revenue conditionality, particularly with respect to taxes on goods and services.

CONCLUDING REMARKS

In recent years, the number of revenue-related structural benchmarks in IMF programs has increased. This form of conditionality is agreed with the authorities and monitored by IMF staff, but is not a precondition for the continuation of the program. The question is whether this form of revenue conditionality has a positive impact on the revenue performance of a country. The evidence to date has been mixed. This paper revisits the issue by using more up-to-date and detailed data for 126 low- and middle-income countries during 1993–2013. The analysis extends beyond total tax revenues by disaggregating data by tax types. Since much of the conditionality tends to be related to a specific tax, the paper analyzes its impact on different taxes.

The results are revealing. Revenue conditionality indeed matters. It could potentially improve revenue performance by about 1 percentage point of GDP in a given year. It matters more in low-income countries than in middle-income ones, particularly those countries where revenue ratios are below the group average. It has the maximum impact on taxes on goods and services as well as the VAT—a tax which is relatively more friendly towards promoting growth. These results hold even after revenues are adjusted for economic cycle. Once conditionality is targeted to a specific tax, it affects revenue performance, particularly of income taxes. Unfortunately, in countries where corruption is high, revenue conditionality makes no difference to revenue performance.

Finally, notwithstanding the robust empirical evidence presented here on the positive impact of IMF conditionality on revenue collection, it might be that the focus on revenue conditionality in IMF programs is too narrow. A closer look at the effect of specific policy instruments or tax measures—possibly introduced or removed because of IMF conditionality—could provide a broader insight in explaining tax revenue performance. This subject is beyond the scope of the paper and needs to be explored in future research.

ANNEX 19.1. DATA

The countries in the sample are the following:

Low-income countries: Bangladesh, Benin, Burkina Faso, Burundi, Cambodia, Central African Republic, Chad, Comoros, Democratic Republic of the Congo, Eritrea, Ethiopia, The Gambia, Ghana, Guinea, Guinea-Bissau, Haiti, Kenya, Kyrgyz Republic, Lao P.D.R., Liberia, Madagascar, Malawi, Mali, Mauritania, Mozambique, Myanmar, Nepal, Niger, Rwanda, Sierra Leone, Solomon Islands, Tajikistan, Tanzania, Togo, Uganda, Zambia, Zimbabwe

Middle-income countries: Albania, Algeria, Angola, Antigua and Barbuda, Argentina, Armenia, Azerbaijan, Belarus, Belize, Bhutan, Bolivia, Bosnia and Herzegovina, Botswana, Brazil, Bulgaria, Cameroon, Cabo Verde, Chile, China, Colombia, Republic of Congo, Costa Rica, Côte d'Ivoire, Djibouti, Dominica, Dominican Republic, Ecuador, Egypt, El Salvador, Fiji, Gabon, Georgia, Grenada, Guatemala, Guyana, Honduras, India, Indonesia, Islamic Republic of Iran, Jamaica, Jordan, Kazakhstan, Kiribati, Lebanon, Lesotho, Libya, Lithuania, former Yugoslav Republic of Macedonia, Malaysia, Maldives, Mauritius, Mexico, Moldova, Mongolia, Morocco, Namibia, Nicaragua, Nigeria, Pakistan, Panama, Papua New Guinea, Paraguay, Peru, Philippines, Russian Federation, Samoa, Senegal, Seychelles, South Africa, Sri Lanka, St. Kitts and Nevis, St. Lucia, St. Vincent and the Grenadines, Sudan, Suriname, Swaziland, Syrian Arab Republic, São Tomé and Príncipe, Thailand, Tonga, Tunisia, Turkey, Ukraine, Uruguay, Uzbekistan, Vanuatu, República Bolivariana de Venezuela, Vietnam, Republic of Yemen.

Data on total tax revenue, taxes on goods and services, VAT, income tax revenue, and trade tax revenue are taken from three different sources: the IMF's Government Financial Statistics (GFS) database, the IMF's World Economic Outlook (WEO) database, and the Organisation for Economic Co-operation and Development (OECD) Revenue Statistics in Latin America database, relative to GDP. Data for the construction of the dummy variables on IMF program with and without conditionality are taken from the IMF's Monitoring of Fund Arrangements (MONA) database. Among the economic descriptors for conditionality in the MONA database, considered in this paper are those related to revenue conditionality, which are: revenue measures and revenue administration. Total revenue conditionality and only met revenue conditionality were considered separately. For IMF program without conditionality, the dummy takes the value one if the country has a program with no revenue conditionality in the year *t* and zero otherwise. The starting year of a program is defined as the year in which it was approved. The end year is the year in which the program expired. For IMF program with revenue conditionality, the dummy takes the value 1 if the country has a program that contains revenue conditionality for a given tax in year *t* and zero otherwise, as discussed in the Data and Methodology section. In cases in which revenue conditionality cannot be identified with a specific tax in year *t* (general conditionality), it is assumed that the revenue conditionality applies for each and all of the taxes in that country.

Share of agriculture in aggregate value added, taken from the World Bank's World Development Indicators (WDI) database. Trade Openness is calculated as imports plus exports in percent of GDP, taken from the IMF's International Financial Statistics (IFS) database. Per capita GDP is calculated in constant (2000) U.S. dollars, taken from the WDI database, expressed in logs. Inflation is the annual change in the CPI, taken from the IFS database. International reserves, nominal foreign exchange rate to the US dollar is taken from the IMF's IFS database. The overall fiscal balance, in percent of GDP, is taken from the WDI database. Foreign debt, relative to GDP, is taken from the WDI database. The ICRG corruption scores, produced by Political Risk Services Group, are assessments by staff and relate to actual and potential corruption in the following forms: excessive patronage, nepotism, job reservations, 'favor-for-favors', secret party funding and suspiciously close ties between politics and business. The scores range from 0 to 6, where 0 indicates the highest potential risk of corruption and 6 indicates the lowest potential risk for any country.

Other political economy variables include: past IMF program, measured as the lag of a five-years moving average of the IMF program dummy, taken from the MONA database; the KOF index of political globalization as in Dreher (2006b), measured by the number of embassies and high commissions in a country, the number of international organizations of which the country is a member, the number of UN peace missions the country has participated in, and the number of international treaties that the country has signed since 1945. Two indicators from the World Bank's Database of Political Institutions as in Beck et al., 2001: the index of political plurality, in which legislators are elected using a winner-take-all/first past the post rule, taking the value 1if this system is used or 0 otherwise; and an indicator for chief executive years in office, measured in number of years. Two indicators from Freedom House: one on political rights as a measure of free participation in the political process, including the right to vote freely for distinct alternatives in legitimate elections, compete for public office, join political parties and organizations, and elect representatives who have a decisive impact on public policies and are accountable to the electorate, taking the value 1 (most free) to 7 (least free); and the imputed polity index, which in addition to political rights, also measures civil liberties, allowing for the freedom of expression and belief, associational and organizational rights, rule of law, and personal autonomy without interference from the state. The imputed policy index takes the value 0 for least democratic and 10 for most democratic countries. In addition, Kuncic (2014) indicator on legal institutional quality is considered, taking the value 1 (high) to 0 (low). Finally, Transparency International's Corruption Perception Index has been considered, which measures the level of corruption in 152 countries, transformed to take the value 0 (high corruption) to 100 (low corruption). All these indicators are available online at www.qog.pol.gu.se, from Dahlberg et al. (2015). Annex Table 19.1.1 summarizes the data.

Annex Table 19.1.1. Descriptive Statistics

	Observations	Mean	Standard Deviation	Minimum	Maximum
Total Tax Revenue (percent of GDP)	2,211	15.30	1.62	0.34	60.94
Low-Income Countries	647	11.85	1.59	0.34	36.54
Middle-Income Countries	1,564	17.09	1.57	1.14	61.39
Tax on G&S (percent of GDP)	2,051	5.52	2.19	0.10	58.26
VAT (percent of GDP)	743	4.43	2.09	0.10	19.30
Income Tax (percent of GDP)	2,084	4.01	2.14	0.04	50.60
Tax on Corporate Profits (percent of GDP)	1,743	1.91	2.30	0.03	24.70
Personal Income Tax (percent of GDP)	1,648	1.36	2.44	0.00	13.30
Trade Tax Revenue (percent of GDP)	2,058	2.29	2.54	0.05	41.50
IMF Program Variable	2,646	0.44	0.50	0.00	1.00
Low-Income Countries	776	0.63	0.48	0.00	1.00
Middle-Income Countries	1,870	0.35	0.48	0.00	1.00
IMF Program without Revenue Conditionality	2,646	0.24	0.43	0.00	1.00
IMF Program with Revenue Conditionality: Total Tax	2,646	0.19	0.39	0.00	1.00
Low-Income Countries	776	0.28	0.45	0.00	1.00
Middle-Income Countries	1,870	0.15	0.36	0.00	1.00
IMF Program with Revenue Conditionality: G&S	2,642	0.17	0.37	0.00	1.00
IMF Program with Revenue Conditionality: VAT	2,646	0.16	0.37	0.00	1.00
IMF Program with Revenue Conditionality: Income Tax	2,642	0.15	0.36	0.00	1.00
IMF Program with Revenue Conditionality: Trade Tax	2,621	0.14	0.35	0.00	1.00
IMF Program with Specific Revenue Conditionality	2,643	0.06	0.24	0.00	1.00
IMF Program with General Revenue Conditionality	2,639	0.13	0.34	0.00	1.00
Share of Revenue Conditions in Total	2,647	0.53	0.13	0.00	1.00
Agriculture Value-added (percent of GDP)	2,379	20.55	14.62	1.33	93.98
Trade Openness (percent of GDP)	2,431	80.07	37.31	0.31	254.61
GDP per capita, US$2,000	2,434	1,312.90	3.03	49.89	14,764.78
Inflation (percent)	2,594	0.42	6.84	-0.10	244.11
Foreign Debt (percent of GDP)	2,551	59.98	57.14	0.00	753.62
ICRG Corruption Score	1,792	2.31	0.90	0.00	5.00
Political Globalization Index	2,263	55.88	20.70	8.86	94.72
Political Plurality Index	2,102	0.71	0.45	0.00	1.00
Chief Executive Years in Office	2,337	7.55	7.85	1.00	46.00
Polity Index	2,520	5.76	2.80	1.00	10.00
Legal Institutional Quality	2,143	0.47	0.14	0.07	0.90
TI Corruption Perception Index	2,141	29.59	13.41	0.00	79.00

Source: Authors' calculations.

Note: G&S = goods and services; VAT = value-added tax.

REFERENCES

Acemoglu, D., S. Naidu, P. Restrepo, and J. Robinson, 2014, "Democracy does cause growth," NBER Working Papers 20004, National Bureau of Economic Research.

Acosta-Ormaechea, S., and J. Yoo, 2012, "Tax Composition and Economic Growth," IMF Working Paper 12/257, (Washington: International Monetary Fund).

Anderson, T., and C. Hsiao, 1981, "Estimation of dynamic models with error components," *Journal of the American Statistical Association* 76, pp. 589–606.

Angrist, J., O. Jorda, and G. Kuersteiner, 2013, "Semiparametric Estimates of Monetary Policy Effects: String Theory Revisited," NBER Working Papers 19355, National Bureau of Economic Research.

Arellano, M. and S. Bond, 1991, "Some tests of specification for panel data: Monte Carlo evidence and an application to employment equations," *The Review of Economic Studies* 58, pp. 277–297.

Arezki, R., M. Quintyn, and F. Toscani, 2012, "Structural Reforms, IMF Programs and Capacity Building: An Empirical Investigation," IMF Working Paper 12/232 (Washington: International Monetary Fund).

Arnold, J., B. Brys, C. Heady, A. Johansson, C. Schwellnus, and L. Vartia, 2011, "Tax Policy for Economic Recovery and Growth," *Economic Journal*, Vol.111, pp. 59–80.

Atoian, R., and P. Conway, 2006, "Evaluating the impact of IMF programs: A comparison of matching and instrumental-variable estimators," *Review of International Organizations* 1, pp. 99–124.

Auriol, E., and M. Warlters, 2005, "Taxation base in developing countries," *Journal of Public Economics*, pp. 625–46.

Barro, R., and J. Lee, 2005, "IMF programs: who is chosen and what are the effects?" *Journal of Monetary Economics* 52, pp. 1245–69.

Baunsgaard, T., and M. Keen, 2010, "Tax Revenue and (or?) Trade Liberalization," *Journal of Public Economics* 94(9–10), pp. 563–77.

Bazzi, S., and M. Clemens, 2013, "Blunt Instruments: Avoiding Common Pitfalls in Identifying the Causes of Economic Growth," *American Economic Journal: Macroeconomics* 5(2), pp. 152–86.

Beck, T., G. Clarke, A. Gro, P. Keefer, and P. Walsh, 2001, "New tools in comparative political economy: The database of political institutions," *The World Bank Economic Review* 15(1), pp. 165–76.

Benedek, D., E. Crivelli, S. Gupta, and P. Muthoora, 2014, "Foreign aid and revenue: Still a crowding out effect?" *FinanzArchiv* 70(1), pp. 67–96.

Bird, G., 1996, "Borrowing from the IMF: the policy implications of recent empirical research," *World Development* 24, pp.1753–60.

Bird, G., 2007, "The IMF: A bird's eye view of its role and operations," *Journal of Economic Surveys* 21, pp. 683–745.

Blundell, R., and S. Bond, 1998, "Initial Conditions and Moment Restrictions in Dynamic Panel Data Models," *Journal of Econometrics*, 87, pp. 115–43.

Bond, S., A. Hoeffler, and J. Temple, 2001, "GMM Estimation of Empirical Growth Models," CEPR Discussion Paper 3048.

Brun, J., G. Chambas, and B. Laporte, 2010, "IMF programs and tax effort: What role for institutions in Africa?" Etudes et Documents E2010.33, Centre d'Etudes et de Recherches sur le Developpement International.

Bulir, A., and S. Moon, 2003, "Do IMF-Supported Programs Help Make Fiscal Adjustment More Durable?" IMF Working Paper 03/38 (Washington: International Monetary Fund).

Cho, H., 2009, "Do IMF Programs Discipline Budget Deficit? The Effects of IMF Programs on Government Budget Balance, Expenditure, and Revenue," *The Korean Journal of International Relations* 49(6), pp. 7–33.

Choi, I., 2001, "Unit root tests for panel data," *Journal of International Money and Finance* 20, pp. 249–71.

Clements, B., S. Gupta, and M. Nozaki, 2013, "What happens to social spending in IMF-supported programmes?" *Applied Economics* 45(28), pp. 4022–33.

Conway, P., 1994, "IMF lending programs: participation and impact," *Journal of Development Economics* 45, 365–391.
Conway, P., 2003, "Endogenous IMF conditionality: Theoretical and empirical implications," mimeo, University of North Carolina, Chapel Hill.
Conway, P., 2006, "The International Monetary Fund in a time of crisis: A review of Stanley Fischer's IMF essays from a time of crisis: The international financial system, stabilization, and development," *Journal of Economic Literature* 44, pp. 115–44.
Copelovitch, M., 2010, "Master or Servant? Agency Slack and the Politics of IMF Lending," *International Studies Quarterly* 54(1), pp. 49 – 77.
Cragg, J., and S. Donald, 1993, "Testing Identifiability and Specification in Instrumental Variable Models," *Econometric Theory* 9(2), pp. 220–40.
Crivelli, E., and S. Gupta, 2014, "Resource blessing, revenue curse? Domestic revenue effort in resource-rich countries," *European Journal of Political Economy* 35, pp. 88–101.
Dahlberg, S., S. Holmberg, B. Rothstein, F. Hartmann, and R. Svensson, 2015, "The Quality of Government Basic Dataset: Version Jan15," University of Gothenburg, The Quality of Government Institute. Available under: http://www.qog.pol.gu.se.
Dickes-Mireaux, L., M. Mecagni, and S. Schadler, 2000, "Evaluating the effect of IMF lending to low-income countries," *Journal of Development Economics* 61, pp. 495–526.
Dreher, A., 2006a, "IMF and economic growth: The effects of programs, loans, and compliance with conditionality," *World Development* 34, pp. 769–88.
Dreher, A., 2006b, "Does globalization affect growth? Evidence from a new index of globalization," *Applied Economics* 38 (10), pp. 1091–110.
Dreher, A., 2009, "IMF conditionality: theory and evidence," *Public Choice* 141, pp. 233–67.
Dreher, A. and N. Jensen, 2007, "Independent Actor or Agent? An Empirical Analysis of the Impact of US Interests on IMF Conditions," *The Journal of Law and Economics* 50, pp. 105–124.
Dreher, A., and R. Vaubel, 2004, "Do IMF and IBRD cause moral hazard and political business cycles? Evidence from panel data," *Open Economies Review* 15, pp. 5–22.
Easterly, W., 2005, "What did structural adjustment adjust? The association of policies and growth with repeated IMF and World Bank adjustment loans," *Journal of Development Economics* 76, pp. 1–22.
Edwards, S., and J. Santaella, 1993, "Devaluation controversies in the developing countries: lessons from the Bretton Woods Era," in: Bordo, M., and B. Eichengreen (Eds.), *A Retrospective on the Bretton Woods System*. University of Chicago, Chicago, pp. 405–455.
Evrensel, A., 2002, "Effectiveness of IMF-supported stabilization programs in developing countries," *Journal of International Money and Finance* 21, pp. 565–587.
Fatas, A., and I. Mihov, 2003, "The case for restricting fiscal policy discretion," *The Quarterly Journal of Economics* 118, 1419–1447.
Fatas, A. and I. Mihov, 2006, "The macroeconomic effects of fiscal rules in the US States," *Journal of Public Economics* 90, pp. 101–117.
Ghura, D., 1998, "Tax Revenue in Sub-Saharan Africa: Effects of Economic Policies and Corruption," IMF Working Paper 98/135 (Washington: International Monetary Fund).
Guitian, M., 1981, "Fund Conditionality: Evolution of Principles and Practices," IMF Pamphlet Series 38, (Washington: International Monetary Fund).
Gujarati, D., and D. Porter, 2009, "Basic Econometrics," McGraw-Hill Irwin.
Heckman, J., 1976, "The common structure of statistical models of truncation, sample selection and limited dependent variables and a simple estimator for such models," *Annals of Economic and Social Measurement* 5(4), pp. 475–492.
Heckman, J., 1979, "Sample Selection Bias as a Specification Error," *Econometrica* 47(1), pp. 153–161.
Hirano, K., G. Imbens, and G. Ridder, 2003, "Efficient Estimation of Average Treatment Effects Using the Estimated Propensity Score," *Econometrica* 71(4), pp. 1161–89.
Imbens, G., 2004, "Nonparametric Estimation of Average Treatment Effects Under Exogeneity: A Review," *Review of Economics and Statistics* 86(1), pp. 6–29.
Independent Evaluation Office of the International Monetary Fund, 2003, "Fiscal Adjustment in IMF-Supported Programs," Evaluation Report (Washington: International Monetary Fund).

International Monetary Fund, 2005, "Review of the 2002 Conditionality Guidelines," IMF Report, March (Washington: International Monetary Fund). Available via the Internet: http://www.imf.org/external/pubs/cat/longres.cfm?sk=18519.0.

International Monetary Fund, 2012, "2011 Review of Conditionality," (Washington: International Monetary Fund), June. Available via the Internet: http://www.imf.org/external/pp/longres.aspx?id=4692.

International Monetary Fund, 2013, "Issues in International Taxation and the Role of the IMF" (Washington: International Monetary Fund). Available via the Internet: http://www.imf.org/external/np/pp/eng/2013/062813.pdf.

Jenkins, G., H. Jenkins, and C. Kuo, 2006, "Is the VAT Naturally Progressive?" mimeo (Ontario: Queens University).

Jorra, M., 2012, "The effect of IMF lending on the probability of sovereign debt crises," *Journal of International Money and Finance* 31, pp. 709–25.

Keen, M., and J. Ligthart, 2001, "Coordinating tariff reductions and domestic tax reform," *Journal of International Economics* 56, pp. 407–25.

Keen, M., and B. Lockwood, 2010, "The value added tax: Its causes and consequences," *Journal of Development Economics* 92(2), pp. 138–151.

Killick, T., 1995, "IMF Programs in Developing Countries: Design and Impact," Routledge, London.

Kleibergen, F., and R. Paap, 2006, "Generalized Reduced Rank Tests Using the Singular Value Decomposition," *Journal of Econometrics* 133(1), pp. 97–126.

Kuncic, A., 2014, "Institutional quality dataset," *Journal of Institutional Economics* 10(1), pp. 135–61.

Lledo, V., and M. Poplawski-Ribeiro, 2013, "Fiscal Policy Implementation in Sub-Saharan Africa," *World Development* 46, pp. 79–91.

Maddala, G., and S. Wu, 1999, "A comparative study of unit root tests with panel data and a new simple test," *Oxford Bulletin of Economics and Statistics* 61, pp. 631–52.

Moser, C., and J-E. Sturm, 2011, "Explaining IMF lending decisions after the Cold War," *The Review of International Organizations* 6, pp. 307–40.

Mumssen, C., Y. Gunduz, C. Ebeke, and L. Kaltani, 2013, "IMF-Supported Programs in Low Income Countries: Economic Impact over the Short and Longer Term," IMF Working Paper 13/273, (Washington: International Monetary Fund).

Muñoz, S., and S. Cho, 2004, "Social Impact of a Tax Reform: The Case of Ethiopia," in *Helping Countries Develop: The Role of Fiscal Policy*, by Gupta, S., B. Clements, and G. Inchauste (eds.), pp. 353–84, (Washington: International Monetary Fund).

Nsouli, S., R. Atoian, and A. Mourmouras, 2006, "Institutions, program implementation, and macroeconomic performance," In: A. Mody, and A. Rebucci (Eds.), *IMF Supported Programs: Recent Staff Research,* Washington, D.C.: International Monetary Fund.

OECD, 2010, "Tax Policy Reform and Economic Growth," OECD Tax Policy Studies 20, (Paris: Organization for Economic Co-operation and Development).

Pessino, C., and R. Fenochietto, 2010, "Determining Countries' Tax Effort," *Hacienda Pública Española/Revista de Economía Pública* 195 (4), pp. 65–87.

Przeworsky, A., and J. Vreeland, 2000, "The effect of IMF programs on economic growth," *Journal of Development Economics* 62, pp. 385–421.

Reichmann, T., and R. Stillson, 1978, "Experience with programs of balance of payments adjustment: stand-by arrangements in the highest tranches, 1963–72," IMF Staff Papers 25 (Washington: International Monetary Fund).

Rodrik, D., 1998, "Why Do More Open Economies have Bigger Governments?" *Journal of Political Economy* 106, pp. 997–1032.

Roodman, D., 2009a, "How to do xtabond2: An introduction to difference and system GMM in Stata," *The Stata Journal* 9(1), pp. 86–136.

Roodman, D., 2009b, "A Note on the Theme of Too Many Instruments," *Oxford Bulletin of Economics and Statistics* 71(1), pp.135–58.

Sen Gupta, A., 2007, "Determinants of Tax Revenue Efforts in Developing Countries," IMF Working Paper 07/184 (Washington: International Monetary Fund).

Steinwand, M., and R. Stone, 2008, "The Fund: A review of the recent evidence," *Review of International Organization* 3, pp. 123–49.

Stock, J., and M. Yogo, 2005, "Testing for Weak Instruments in Linear IV Regression," In: *Identification and Inference for Econometric Models: Essays in Honor of Thomas Rothenberg*, Andrews, D., and J. Stock (eds.), New York: Cambridge University Press.

Thomas, A., and U. Ramakrishnan, 2006, "The Incidence and Effectiveness of Prior Actions in IMF-supported Programs," IMF Working Paper 06/213 (Washington: International Monetary Fund).

Wei, S., and Z. Zhang, 2010, "Do external interventions work? The case of trade reform conditions in IMF supported programs," *Journal of Development Economics* 92, pp. 71–81.

Zee, H., J. Stotsky, and E. Ley, 2002, "Tax Incentives for Business Investment: A Primer for Policy Makers in Developing Countries," *World Development* 30(9), pp. 1497–1516.

Index

Abed, G. T., 155
Accountability
FCs and, 401–7
for promise gaps, *34f*, 35–37, *36t*, 39*n*21
Acemoglu, D., 154–55, 282
on inclusive politics, 243
Adjustment effort
in economic shocks, 352, 371
for fiscal noncompliance, 365, 365*n*20
Advanced economies
elections in, 13, 140
ER in, 301–3
exchange rates of, 271*n*2
fiscal consolidation in, 13, 27, *28t*
forecasting in, 346
IMF and, 76*n*19
MTBF in, 314
optimistic forecasts in, 346
PBCs in, 7*n*13, 63
public debt in, 216–17, *217f*, 218
public investment in, 123
tipping points in, 241
wage bill in, 149
Advisory Fiscal Board, of EU, 400
Aggregate demand
full employment and, 8
government spending and, 178
from public investment, 111
Aidt, T., 113*n*4
Aizenman, J., 178*n*3
Alesina, A., 26, 27, 47, 94, 94*n*5, 96, 288
CAPB and, 285
on FCs, 402
on PBCs, 327
in public debt, 216–17
on status quo changes, 244*n*1
ALLHOUSE, 184, 184*n*12
Allocation, 5
for public investment, 123*n*27
Alter, J., 185
AMECO, 446, 448
American Recovery and Reinvestment Act, 184–85
Anderson, T., 493–94
Andrews, M., 383*n*8
Angelopoulos, K., 97
Annual Government Finance Statistics, of EUROSTAT, 140*n*3
Ardagna, S., 94
CAPB and, 285
Arellano, M., 68, 119, 119*n*21, 487
FD-GMM of, 356, *361t–362t*
Arezki, R., 262
Argentina
economic shocks and, 244*n*1
ER in, 305, 306
Argimón, L., 364
Armingeon, K., 181
Articles of Confederation, 429–30, 436
Arze del Granado, F. J., 153*n*3
Auerbach, A. J., 44
Auriol, E., 485*n*10
Australia
ER in, 306
promise gaps in, 49
taxes in, 84*n*1
Austria
promise gaps in, 49–50
SCM in, 291, *292f*
Autocratic regimes, Great Recession and, 179–80
Autonomous Communities, in Spain, 347

Baerg, N., 101
Bagehot, W., 435
Bailouts
of banks, 181*n*6
by CGs, 166, 351–52, 351*n*9
defined, 349*n*7
for fiscal noncompliance, 350, 350*n*5
overspending incentives and, 350, 351–52
for SNGs, 349*n*7

of SOEs, 166
See also No-bailout clause
Balanced budget rules (BBR), 100, 100*n*13, 104*n*18, 404–5
endogeneity and, 73
ER and, 301
rational voters and, 406
taxes and, 102*t*
Balance of payments
IMF and, 480*n*5
of LICs, 75*n*18
Banks
bailouts for, 181*n*6
crises of, taxes and, 95–96, 96*n*8
See also Central banks
Baqir, R., 155*n*6
Bartels, L., 179
Basinger, S., 98
BBR. *See* Balanced budget rules
Beck, N., 43
Beck, T., 500
Beetsma, R., 405*n*4, 407*n*7
Belgium
budget forecasts in, 420, 420*f*
debt sustainability in, 50
ER in, 303, 306, 308
FCs in, 413, 418–22, 420*f*–422*f*
HCF in, 413, 418–22, 420*f*–422*f*
media in, 420–21, 421*f*
promise gaps in, 50
public debt in, 419
SCM in, 291, 292*f*
Besley, T., 3–4, 3*n*3, 241
Bias
fiscal, 404–5
overfitting, 68
selection, 64–65, 486–87
See also Deficit bias
Biglaiser, G., 96
Bird, G., 486*n*12
Blackstone, William, 431
Blanchard, O., 181
Blinder, A. S., 181
Block, S. A., 64, 64*n*3
Blundell, R., 68, 119, 119*n*21
GMM of, 486*n*11
Bogaert, H., 452–53
Bohn, H., 311
Bond, S., 68, 119, 119*n*21, 356, 486*n*11, 487
Bonds
in EU, 443–44
in U.S., 17, 429
Bonfatti, Andrea, 15–16
Bordo, M., 271*n*2
Botswana, ER in, 309
Bover, O., 68, 119, 119*n*21
Brady, D., 244
Braendle, T., 11*n*20
Braütigam, D., 245
Brazil
economic shocks and, 244*n*1
ER in, 305
Brender, A., 63*n*1, 125, 127, 137*n*1
Brollo, F., 328
Brück, T., 197
Brückner, M., 99
Brun, J., 480
BSL. *See* Budget Stability Law
Buchanan, J. M., 5
Budget cycles
in LICs, 64–65, 68–69, 69*t*
proximity factor and, 6, 7*n*13
Budget deficits. *See* Deficits
Budget forecasts
in Belgium, 420, 420*f*
FCs and, 416
intergovernmental fiscal arrangements and, 388
of minority governments, 197
in Netherlands, 416, 416*f*
Budget institutions, 16
for credible fiscal policymaking, 378–81
defined, 377*n*2
evaluation of, 382–91, 383*f*, 383*n*8, 384*f*
fiscal outlook and, 385, 386*f*, 387*f*, 396
fiscal strategy in, 380–82, 386*f*–387*f*, 388–91, 389*f*–390*f*, 392*f*–393*f*, 396–97
in LICs, 377–97
in parliamentary systems, 381
strengthening, 394–97
Budget Law of 2003, in Italy, 330*n*4
Budget rules, 114
government spending and, 118
See also Balanced budget rules
Budget Stability Law (BSL), in Spain, 353–55, 355*n*13
Bulgaria, ER in, 306

Bulir, A., 480
Bureau for Economic Analysis, in Netherlands, 413, 414–18
Business cycles. *See* Political business cycles

CAB. *See* Cyclically adjusted budget balance
Cabezón, E., 378
Cabinet ideology
  fiscal politics and, 7–9
  public investment and, 13*n*21
  redistribution and, 8
Cahuc, P., 137*n*1, 139
Calmfors, L., 401, 413
Calvo, E., 99*n*10
Canada
  decentralization in, 30*n*8
  ER in, 306, 308
  promise gaps in, 50–51
CAPB. *See* Cyclically adjusted primary balance
Capello, D., 98
Capitalism, Socialism and Democracy (Schumpeter), 3
Capital spending
  elections and, 332, 332*f*
  fiscal rules and, 330
  in Italy, 331–32, 331*n*7, 332*f*, 336*f*
  outsourcing of, 331*n*7
  PBCs and, 16, 331
  public investment and, 130, 130*t*
  wage bill and, 139
Caporale, G. M., 442
Carcillo, S., 137*n*1, 139
Caro, L., 97
Cassidy, T., 327
CDS. *See* Credit default swaps
Cecchetti, S. G., 181
Center for Systemic Peace, 162
Central African and Economic Monetary Community, fiscal rules in, 73*n*15
Central banks
  exchange rates by, 275–77, 276*n*10
  Great Recession and, 194, 194*n*26
  independence of, 404*n*5
Central governments (CGs)
  bailouts by, 166, 351–52, 351*n*9
  DSP and, 328
  ER of, 256
  fiscal noncompliance and, 353, 353*n*12
  government spending by, 114*n*8
  macroeconomic forecasting for, 373
  MTBF and, 380
  SNGs and, 345
  soft budget constraints for, 345
  VAT and, 256
Centralization, 6, 437
  of EA, 468–69
  inclusive politics and, 243–44
  in LICs, 394
  of taxes, 256
Central Planning Bureau (CPB), in Netherlands, 414–18, 417*f*, 418*f*
CEPII, 168
CGs. *See* Central governments
Chambas, G., 480
Checks and balances, 250
  from DPI, 218
  in PBCs, 7*n*13, 192*n*22
  for public debt, 224
  veto players and, 218
Cheibub, J. A., 184*n*10, 202
Chernow, Ron, 431
China
  contract responsibility system in, 255–56
  SAT in, 256–57
  SOEs in, 242, 255–56
  taxes in, 254–57, 258*f*
  tax-to-GDP ratio in, 256, 257
  tax-to-GDP threshold of, 242
  VAT in, 256, 257
Cho, H., 480
Choi, I., 488
Cioffi, M., 327
CIT. *See* Corporate income taxes
Clements, B., 153, 161, 162, 163
Coady, D., 153*n*3
Coalition governments
  ER in, 300, 303, 305, 311
  Great Recession and, 198
  in Netherlands, 415–16
Cobb-Douglas specification, 157
Coelho, C., 328
Cohesion. *See* Political cohesion
Collier, P., 262
Colombia
  GDP per capita in, 260, 261*f*
  taxes in, 259–60, 261*f*
  tax-to-GDP threshold of, 242
  VAT in, 259–60

Combes, J.-L., 72
Commission on Growth and Development Report, 244
Common pool, 9, 14
  corruption and, 223
  in EA, 441
  in EU, 443–44
  government spending and, 441*n*1
  legislative periods and, 221*t*
  overspending incentives and, 352
  political fragmentation and, 214, 217–18, 222, 230*t*
  public debt and, 214, 222, 223*t*, 230*t*
  sanctions and, 465*n*25
  taxes and, 215, 441*n*1
Compliance. *See* Fiscal noncompliance
Conditionality
  endogeneity and, 486
  fiscal noncompliance and, 484
  GMM for, 486, 486*n*11, 487–88
  of IMF, 477–501, 478*f*, 479*t*, 483*f*, 484*f*, 489*t*, 491*t*–493*t*, 496*t*, 498*t*, 501*t*
  robustness tests for, 480, 494–98
  selection bias and, 486–87
  for taxes, 477–501, 478*f*, 479*t*, 480*n*5, 483*f*, 484*f*, 489*t*, 491*t*–493*t*, 496*t*, 498*t*, 501*t*
  tax-to-GDP ratio and, 496
  trade openness and, 485
Consiglio comunale (municipal council), 329
Consolidation promise gaps. *See* Promise gaps
Constitutive institutions, 243
Consumption multiplier, with wage bill, 139
Continental certificates, 429
Continental financial system
  in EU, 435–38
  in U.S., 427–35
Contract responsibility system, in China, 255–56
Control of parliament
  political cohesion and, 280
  in political fragmentation, 217
  public debt and, 223
Conway, P., 486*n*12
Cordes, Till, 15
Corporate income taxes (CIT)
  conditionality and, 481*f*, 485
  in EU, 105
  in left-wing governments, 98
  in OECD, 83, 84*n*1, 85, 86–88, 86*f*–87*f*, 103, 104*n*19
  in right-wing governments, 98
  tax competition for, 103
Correa-Caro, Carolina, 14
Corruption
  common pool and, 223
  DPI and, 123*n*25
  guide, of ICRG, 220, 500
  index, of Transparency International, 485–86
  political fragmentation and, 223
  public debt and, 223, 224*t*, 232*t*
  public social spending and, 158
  tax tipping points and, 248*f*
  World Bank and, 223
Council of the European Union, 442
Country size, fiscal rules and, 458–62, 459*t*, 460*f*, 461*t*
Covariance matrix, for PCA, 36*n*18
Cowen, David, 431, 435
CPB. *See* Central Planning Bureau
CPFF. *See* Ministry of Finance to the Economic and Financial Council
Cragg, J., 487–88
Credible leadership, 244
Credit default swaps (CDS), 411*f*
Crisis mode, for taxes, 95–97, 103–4
The Crisis of the Tax State (Schumpeter), 3*n*2, 241
Crivelli, Ernesto, 14, 17
Crowding-out effect
  for energy subsidies, 154, 164, 166, 169, 171
  on public social spending, 154
  right-wing governments and, 8
Crowe, C., 194
Cruz, C., 98
Cukierman, A., 194, 406*n*6
Currency unions, 274*n*8
Curristine, Teresa, 16, 407
  on FCs, 401
Cyclically adjusted budget balance (CAB), FCs and, 408–9, 411–12, 413*t*
Cyclically adjusted primary balance (CAPB), 27, 27*n*4
  exchange rates and, 285, 285*n*22

Dabla-Norris, E., 378
Database of Political Institutions (DPI), 98, 99, 99*n*11, 116, 118*n*17, 487, 500
  checks and balances from, 218
  corruption indicators in, 123*n*25
  on political fragmentation, 217
  on public debt, 216
Debrun, Xavier, 16, 328
  on FCs, 405*n*4, 407*n*7
  on Fiscal Council Dataset, 228*n*17
Debt. *See* Public debt
Debt rules (DR)
  in BSL, 354
  in emerging economies, 301, 307
  fiscal noncompliance with, 307
  in LICs, 64*n*4, 73*n*17
Debt-to-GDP ratio, 117, 119, 185
  deficits and, 213
  in EA, 448, 457*f*
  in EU, 436
  political fragmentation and, 226
Debt-to-GDP threshold, 226, 226*n*16
Debus, M., 97
Decentralization
  in Canada, 30*n*8
  in EA, 467
  in Spain, 30*n*8, 347, 367*n*21
  of taxes, 367*n*21
Deficit bias
  asymmetric response to, 451, 451*t*
  characterization of, 403–4
  defined, 403*n*2
  in EA, 450–52, 451*t*, 470*t*, 472*t*, 473*t*
  elections and, 402–7
  FCs for, 401, 405–7
  government spending and, 126
  incumbents and, 402, 406
  partisanship and, 402
  procyclicality and, 450–52
Deficit ceiling
  in EA, 455
  GDP and, 354
  in Netherlands, 415–16, 416*f*
Deficit of legitimacy, of EU, 445
Deficits, 8*n*16
  debt-to-GDP ratio and, 213
  EDP and, 454, 458–62, 459*t*, 460*f*, 461*t*
  ER and, 299–300
  in EU, 101
  fiscal noncompliance and, 358–59, 358*f*, 359*f*, 366*f*, 368*f*
  in Great Recession, 182
  minority governments and, 197
  PBCs and, 112
  political fragmentation and, 229
  quantitative limits for, 400
  SNGs and, 345
  in Spain, 356*n*17
De Gramont, D., 263, 264
De Haan, J., 7*n*13, 9, 137*n*1
  on budget institutions, 378
  on central banks, 194*n*26
  on political fragmentation, 198
Delgado-Téllez, Mar, 16
Democracy
  of EU, 445
  government spending and, 155*n*6
  in Great Recession, 179–80
  PBCs and, 7*n*13
  public investment in, 111–32
  See also Parliamentary systems; Presidential systems
Democratic Party, American Recovery and Reinvestment Act and, 184–85
Demographics, wage bill and, 141*t*–142*t*, 142, 145
Deng Xiaoping, 255
Denmark
  ER in, 306, 310
  promise gaps in, 51
  taxes in, 84*n*1
DeRouen, K., 96
Detken, C., 443
Developing economies
  exchange rates of, 271*n*2
  public debt in, 216–17, 217*f*
  tipping points in, 241
Devereux, M., 84
Devries, P., 26, 27, 27*n*5, 39, 47
Difference-in Hansen test, 487
Directorate General for Economic and Financial Affairs, of EC, 446
Direct taxes, in LICs, 67*n*9
Distribution, 5
Dobbins, J., 244
Domestic Stability Pact (DSP)

CGs and, 328
in Italy, 327–40, 333*f*, 334*f*
PBCs and, 333
Donald, S., 487–88
Downs, A., 3, 7*n*13
DPI. *See* Database of Political Institutions
DR. *See* Debt rules
Draghi, Mario, 437
Drazen, A., 63*n*1, 96, 112, 113*n*4, 125, 127, 137*n*1, 328
on status quo changes, 244*n*1
on wage bill, 139
Dreher, A., 76*n*20, 96–97
on central banks, 194*n*26
on conditionality, 500
Driscoll, J., 119, 282, 285
DSP. *See* Domestic Stability Pact
Duttagupta, R., 274*n*8

EA. *See* Euro area
Easterly, W., 217*n*5
Ebeke, Christian, 12–14, 72, 127
EC. *See* European Commission
ECB. *See* European Central Bank
ECF. *See* Extended Credit Facility
Eckhardt, S., 137*n*1, 139
Economic and Financial Affairs Council (ECOFIN), 444, 445, 462, 469
Economic and Monetary Union (EMU), 17
fiscal rules of, 85, 454–55
Great Recession and, 465
Economic shocks
adjustment effort in, 352, 371
automatic stabilizers of, 10
bank bailouts for, 181*n*6
fiscal noncompliance and, 352–53, 360, 364, 364*f*
reforms in, 244*n*1
stimulus packages for, 180
taxes and, 96–97
See also Great Recession
Economides, G., 97
Edin, P.-A., 197, 198
EDP. *See* Excessive deficit procedure
EEC. *See* European Economic Community
EFF. *See* Extended Fund Facility
Ehrhart, H., 67, 70
Elections
adjustments after, 64
in advanced economies, 13, 140
capital spending and, 332, 332*f*
country characteristics of, 123, 124*t*
deficit bias and, 402–7
descriptive statistics for, 129*t*
in EA, 99
in emerging economies, 140
endogeneity for, 71–72, 72*t*, 125–26
ER and, 301, 312
fiscal noncompliance and, 369–71, 370*f*
fixed-term, 125, 125*n*29
government spending and, 13, 66*n*7, 111, 130*n*34
in Italy, 331
in LICs, 63–78, 79*t*
monetary policy and, 137*n*2
non-endogenous, 125, 125*n*28
PBCs and, 113*n*3, 214–15
political horizon and, 280
in presidential systems, 64, 64*n*3
promise gap and, 25, 25*n*2
public investment and, 111–12, 112*n*1, 113*n*4, 117–23, 120*t*–121*t*, 122*f*, 123*n*27
scrutiny of, 72–77
selection bias in, 64–65
wage bill and, 13, 137–51, 146*t*, 147*t*, 148*t*
See also Incumbents
Electoral College, 127
Electoral proximity. *See* Proximity factor
Elites
energy subsidies and, 154, 154*n*5, 155–56, 159–61
imperfect information of, 154
middle class and, 14
public social spending and, 154
taxes and, 15
Emerging economies
DR in, 301, 307
elections in, 140
ER in, 314
IMF and, 76*n*19
public debt in, 216, 217*f*
taxes in, 70
wage bill in, 13, 149
EMU. *See* Economic and Monetary Union

Endegnanew, Yehenew, 13
Endogeneity
  BBR and, 73
  conditionality and, 486
  for elections, 71–72, 72*t*, 125–26
  for energy subsidies, 167–69
  for exchange rates, 285
  GMM and, 452
  OG and, 449
  reverse causality and, 449
Energy subsidies, 13–14, 153–72
  changes across regions for, 163*f*
  countries in study for, 172*t*
  by country, 164*f*
  cross-sectional specification for, 166–67
  crowding-out effect for, 154, 164, 166, 169, 171
  econometric analysis for, 165–66
  elites and, 154, 154*n*5, 155–56, 159–61
  empirical analysis of, 161–71
  endogeneity for, 167–69
  energy demand and, 157*n*13
  fragility index for, 162–63
  GDP and, 153, 154, 163, 167, 168
  IMF on, 154*n*4
  intensity around globe, 173*f*
  in MENA, 164, 174*f*
  middle class and, 154, 156
  political effectiveness and, 166, 169, 170*t*
  price gap for, 161
  SOEs and, 166
  synthetic index of governance for, 162
  taxes and, 160
  utility function and, 156*n*8
  VAT and, 155
  welfare effect of, 153*n*3
EP. *See* European Parliament
ER. *See* Expenditure rules
Escolano, J., 32, 32*n*9
  on public debt, 213*n*1
Eskelund, G., 352
Eslava, M., 112, 113*n*4, 328
  on wage bill, 139
Estonia, taxes in, 84*n*1
EU. *See* European Union
Euler equation, 403
Euro area (EA)
  centralization of, 468–69
  common pool in, 441
  debt-to-GDP ratio in, 448, 457*f*
  decentralization in, 467
  deficit bias in, 450–52, 451*t*, 470*t*, 472*t*, 473*t*
  deficit ceiling in, 455
  EDP in, 454, 458–62, 459*t*, 460*f*, 461*t*
  elections in, 99
  fiscal consolidation in, 445
  fiscal discipline in, 465
  fiscal noncompliance in, 454–58, 455*f*, 456*f*, 457*f*
  fiscal politics in, 439–69
  fiscal rules in, 17, 439, 454–58
  GDP in, 458
  government spending in, 452, 453*f*
  no-bailout clause of, 466
  OG in, 447–48, 447*f*
  past reforms in, 462–64
  policy biases in, 440–46
  procyclicality in, 450–52, 451*n*15, 470*t*–471*t*, 473*t*
  public investment in, 441, 452–54
  sanctions in, 464–65
  supranational fiscal policy in, 439
  taxes in, 441–42, 452–54
  VAT in, 85
European Central Bank (ECB), 437
  monetary policy and, 442*n*3
  Outright Monetary transactions Program of, 427
European Commission (EC), 463–64
  Directorate General for Economic and Financial Affairs of, 446
  fiscal rules of, 367–68, 444
  Great Recession and, 445
  reverse qualified majority rule for, 464
  SCPs of, 27, 47, 101, 353, 408–9
  Stability and Convergence Program of, 27, 47, 101, 353
European Economic Community (EEC), 251
European Parliament (EP), 442
  ordinary legislative procedure of, 442*n*2
European Safe Bonds, 17
European Semester, 444
European Stability Mechanism, 467
European Union (EU)

Advisory Fiscal Board of, 400
bonds in, 443–44
CIT in, 105
common pool in, 443–44
Continental financial system in, 435–38
debt-to-GDP ratio in, 436
deficit of legitimacy of, 445
deficits in, 101
democracies of, 445
ER in, 305–6
FCs of, 409, 410*f*, 411*f*
fiscal rules in, 11*n*20, 73*n*15, 85, 444–45
fixed exchange rates in, 290–93, 290*n*27, 292*f*
PIT in, 105
Six Pack in, 100, 105
taxes in, 100–101, 105, 442
Two Pack in, 100, 105
VAT in, 83, 100, 105
See also Stability and Growth Pact

EUROSTAT, Annual Government Finance Statistics of, 140*n*3

Excessive deficit procedure (EDP), 454, 458–62, 459*t*, 460*f*, 461*t*

Exchange rates
of advanced economies, 271*n*2
CAPB and, 285, 285*n*22
by central banks, 275–77, 276*n*10
of developing economies, 271*n*2
dynamic approach to, 274
empirical analysis and data for, 279–85, 280*t*
endogeneity for, 285
fiscal discipline with, 15, 271–96
MCD for, 280*n*16
outliers for, 285
PCA for, 280*n*16
political cohesion for, 272, 274–75, 277–88, 279*f*
political horizon for, 273–85, 278*f*, 288
public debt and, 277–78
robustness tests for, 285–90, 286*t*, 287*t*, 288*n*24, 289*t*, 290*t*
sensitivity of, 285–90, 286*t*
traditional argument for, 273
See also Fixed exchange rates; Flexible exchange rates

Executive committee (*giunta comunale*), 329

Executive polarization, in political fragmentation, 217–18

Expenditure rules (ER), 15, 299–317
adoption and abandonment of, 305–6, 305*f*
in advanced economies, 301–3
in Australia, 306
BBR and, 301
in BSL, 354
of CGs, 256
in coalition governments, 300, 303, 305, 311
compliance with, 306, 307–11, 308*f*–310*f*
deficits and, 299–300
design features of, 304*f*
details by country, 319*t*–323*t*
elections and, 301, 312
in emerging economies, 314
GDP and, 309
government size and, 314–16, 315*f*, 316*f*
for government spending, 300
Great Recession and, 306
index of, 312, 312*n*10
inflation and, 309
long-term sustainability and, 311–13, 312*t*, 313*f*
macroeconomic forecasting and, 299
in minority governments, 306
MTBF and, 316, 316*f*
panel regression analysis for, 318*t*
PBCs and, 300, 301
public investment and, 300, 313–14, 314*f*
reverse causality for, 311*n*9
types and design features of, 301–5, 302*f*, 304*f*

Extended Credit Facility (ECF), 494*n*23
Extended Fund Facility (EFF), 494*n*23
Eyraud, Luc, 17, 367

Falcó-Gimeno, A., 197
Fashola, Babatunde, 262–63
Fatás, A., 155, 272, 282
Favero, C., 94*n*5
Faye, M., 72
FCL. *See* Flexible Credit Line
FCs. *See* Fiscal councils

FD-GMM. *See* First-difference generalized method of moments
Federalist 30, 430
Federal Reserve, in U.S., 180
Fernández-Leiceaga, X., 347, 364
15-month forecast error, promise gaps and, 33*f*
Filc, G., 378
Financial markets
  fiscal discipline of, 26
  fiscal noncompliance and, 368–69, 369*f*
Finland
  ER in, 303, 306, 309
  promise gaps in, 52
First-difference generalized method of moments (FD-GMM), 356, 361*t*–362*t*
Fiscal autonomy, fiscal noncompliance and, 352, 366–71, 368*f*
Fiscal balance, in LICs, 70–71, 70*n*12
Fiscal balance ceilings, MTOs and, 446*n*8, 450*n*13
Fiscal bias, fiscal rules for, 404–5
Fiscal centralization. *See* Centralization
Fiscal Compact, MTOs and, 463
Fiscal consolidation
  absolute frequency of, 28*f*
  in advanced economies, 13, 27, 28*t*
  debt sustainability and, 50, 85
  in EA, 445
  fiscal discipline and, 49
  fiscal stress and, 32
  GMM and, 452
  in Great Recession, 473*t*
  procyclicality and, 450
  relative frequency of, 29*f*
  taxes and, 94–95, 94*n*5, 94*n*6
Fiscal Council Dataset, of IMF, 228, 228*n*17
Fiscal councils (FCs), 11–12, 14–15, 16
  accountability factor and, 401–7
  in Belgium, 413, 418–22, 420*f*–422*f*
  budget forecasts and, 416
  budget process and, 413–22
  CAB and, 408–9, 411–12, 413*t*
  CDS and, 411*f*
  for deficit bias, 401, 405–7
  effectiveness of, 401
  ER of, 304
  of EU, 409, 410*f*, 411*f*
  fiscal discipline from, 11
  fiscal rules and, 228*n*18, 406*n*4
  forecast errors and, 411
  Great Recession and, 399
  media and, 16, 407–13, 412*t*
  in Netherlands, 414–18
  OG and, 409
  political fragmentation and, 228
  public debate and, 407–22
  public debt and, 235*t*, 236*t*, 409
  strength of, 235*t*
  testable hypotheses for, 409
  weakness of, 236*t*
Fiscal crises. *See* Economic shocks; Great Recession
Fiscal decentralization. *See* Decentralization
Fiscal deficits. *See* Deficits
Fiscal discipline
  in EA, 465
  with exchange rates, 15, 271–96
  from FCs, 11
  of financial markets, 26
  fiscal consolidation and, 49
  from fiscal institutions, 11
  fixed exchange rates and, 273
  political strength and, 35
  robustness tests of, 294*t*
Fiscal horizon, primary balance and, 283
Fiscal institutions
  fiscal discipline from, 11
  fiscal rules for, 400
  political fragmentation and, 228
Fiscal noncompliance, 16
  adjustment effort for, 365, 365*n*20
  bailouts for, 350, 350*n*5
  CGs and, 353, 353*n*12
  conditionality and, 484
  deficits and, 358–59, 358*f*, 359*f*, 366*f*, 368*f*
  defined, 348
  with DR, 307
  in EA, 454–58, 455*f*, 456*f*, 457*f*
  economic shocks and, 352–53, 360, 364, 364*f*
  elections and, 369–71, 370*f*
  FD-GMM for, 356, 361*t*–362*t*
  financial markets and, 368–69, 369*f*

fiscal autonomy and, 352, 366–71, 368*f*
fiscal stress and, 352–53
forecast errors and, 352–53, 353*n*11, 360, 360*f*, 360*n*18
gap-filling transfers for, 365–66
GDP and, 356, 356*n*16
GMM for, 356, 361*t*–362*t*, 368
inertial patterns for, 361*t*–363*t*, 364, 365*f*
intergovernmental fiscal arrangements and, 16, 350, 352, 372
no-bailout clause and, 349
overspending and, 350
problem of, 348–49, 349*f*
reverse causality for, 368*n*25
soft budget constraints and, 349–50, 350*f*
in Spain, 345–73, 373*t*, 374*t*
taxes and, 366–67
testable hypotheses for, 357, 357*t*
two-stage least square estimates of, 363*t*

Fiscal outlook, budget institutions and, 385, 386*f*, 387*f*, 396

Fiscal politics
cabinet ideology and, 7–9
in EA, 439–69
effects in, 5–10
influences on, 10–12
political fragmentation and, 9–10, 9*n*17
proximity factor and, 6–7

Fiscal reporting, 11, 379–80, 385

Fiscal risk management, 380, 385

Fiscal rules, 10–15
capital spending and, 330
country size and, 458–62, 459*t*, 460*f*, 461*t*
in EA, 17, 439, 454–58
of EC, 367–68, 444
of EMU, 85
of EU, 11*n*20, 73*n*15, 85, 444–45
FCs and, 228*n*18, 406*n*4
for fiscal bias, 404–5
for fiscal institutions, 400
in Italy, 327–40, 330*t*, 341*t*
for LICs, 64, 64*n*4, 73–75, 73*n*15, 73*n*16, 74*t*, 77*n*22
numerical fiscal limits in, 346*n*4
in OECD, 100
for PBCs, 7*n*13, 327–40
political fragmentation and, 228*n*18
by SNGs, 15–16
for structural balances, 100
for taxes, 104
See also Balanced budget rules; Budget rules; Debt rules; Expenditure rules; Fiscal noncompliance

Fiscal space
in Great Recession, 178, 178*n*3, 185
in Italy, 331

Fiscal strategy, in budget institutions, 380–82, 386*f*–387*f*, 388–91, 389*f*–399*f*, 392*f*–393*f*, 396–97

Fiscal stress
fiscal consolidation and, 32
fiscal noncompliance and, 352–53

Fiscal watchdogs. *See* Fiscal councils

Fisher-type test, 488

Fiva, J. H., 112*n*1

Fixed exchange rates, 272–73
baselines for, 283, 283*t*
in EU, 290–93, 290*n*27, 292*f*
fiscal discipline and, 273
interaction terms for, 284, 284*t*
political cohesion for, 281*f*
political horizon for, 281*f*

Fixed-term elections, 125, 125*n*29

Fjeldstad, O.-H., 245

Flexible Credit Line (FCL), 494*n*23

Flexible exchange rates, 272–73, 274*n*7
political cohesion for, 281*f*
political horizon for, 281*f*

Forecast errors
by country, 415*f*
FCs and, 411
15-month, promise gaps and, 33*f*
fiscal noncompliance and, 352–53, 353*n*11, 360, 360*f*, 360*n*18
in Netherlands, 415
promise gaps and, 32

Forecasting, 380, 385
in advanced economies, 346
soft budget constraints and, 346
See also Budget forecasts; Macroeconomic forecasting

Foremny, D., 328

Forni, Lorenzo, 15–16

Fragility index, for energy subsidies, 162–63

France, promise gaps in, 52

Franco, Francisco, 251
Fritz, V., 243
Fuentes Quintana, Enrique, 251
Full employment, aggregate demand and, 8

G20, 195
  Great Recession and, 383*n*9
Gagliarducci, S., 327, 339
Gali, J., 185
Game theory, 198
Gap-filling transfers, for fiscal noncompliance, 365–66
Garber, Peter, 433–34
Gaspar, Vitor, 14–15, 14*n*22, 16–17, 443
  on public debt, 213*n*1
  on tax tipping points, 246
Gavin, M., 271–72
Gaviria, Cesar, 259
GDP
  debt-to-GDP threshold, 226, 226*n*16
  deficit ceiling and, 354
  deficit-to-GDP ratio, 185
  in EA, 458
  energy subsidies and, 153, 154, 163, 167, 168
  ER and, 309
  fiscal noncompliance and, 356, 356*n*16
  government spending and, 116*n*13
  Great Recession and, 178
  in Netherlands, 415
  PFA and, 29
  primary balances and, 30
  procyclicality and, 147
  promise gaps in, 26, 40
  public debt and, 216, 222, 223
  public investment and, 122
  RFA and, 29
  structural balances and, 30
  taxes and, 482
  tax tipping points and, 246, 246*f*, 247*f*
  trade openness and, 500
  VAT and, 103
  wage bill and, 140, 144*f*, 145, 146–47, 149*t*
  World Economic Outlook on, 32*n*11
  See also Debt-to-GDP ratio; Tax-to-GDP
GDP growth rate
  in LICs, 66
  taxes and, 93
  wage bill and, 142, 147
GDP per capita
  budget institutions and, 383
  in Colombia, 260, 261*f*
  in Nigeria, 262
  in OECD, 223*n*14
  in Spain, 253, 253*f*
  taxes and, 247
  tax-to-GDP threshold and, 246, 246*f*
  tipping points and, 241
Gehlbach, S., 84–85, 99*n*10
Generalized method of moments (GMM)
  for conditionality, 486, 486*n*11, 487–88
  endogeneity and, 452
  FD-GMM, 356, 361*t*–362*t*
  fiscal consolidation and, 452
  for fiscal noncompliance, 356, 361*t*–362*t*, 368
  for OG, 449, 449*n*11
  for public investment, 118–19, 119*n*21
  system-GMM estimator, 68, 486–87, 486*n*11, 492, 494*n*21
Gérard, Marc, 16
Germany, promise gaps in, 52
GFS. *See* Government Finance Statistics
Giavazzi, F., 94*n*5
Gillingham, R., 153*n*3
Gini coefficient, IRFs and, 44
Girardi, A., 442
Giunta comunale (executive committee), 329
Global financial crisis. *See* Great Recession
Globalization
  Great Recession and, 186
  stimulus packages and, 191
GMM. *See* Generalized method of moments
Goderis, B., 262
Gollwitzer, S., 378
Golosov, G., 9*n*17
Gordon, J., 245
Gorodnichenko, Y., 44, 193
Government
  lending rate of, Great Recession and, 194
  popularity of, promise gaps and, 40, 40*n*23, 41*f*–42*f*
  size of, ER and, 314–16, 315*f*, 316*f*

See also Central governments; Coalition governments; Intergovernmental fiscal arrangements; Left-wing governments; Minority governments; Right-wing governments; Subnational governments
Government debt. *See* Public debt
Government Finance Statistics (GFS), of IMF, 140*n*3, 481
Government spending
aggregate demand and, 178
budget rules and, 118
by CGs, 114*n*8
common pool and, 441*n*1
deficit bias and, 126
democracies and, 155*n*6
in EA, 452, 453*f*
elections and, 13, 66*n*7, 111, 130*n*34
ER for, 300
fiscal rules for, 100
GDP and, 116*n*13
growth rate of, 116*f*
of left-wing governments, 113
OG and, 185
partisanship and, 113, 113*n*5
political fragmentation and, 229
public debt and, 217*n*5
public investment and, 130, 130*t*
quantitative limits for, 400
in Spain, 367*n*22
wage bill in, 137
See also Capital spending; Overspending; Public social spending
Granger, C. W. J., 45
Great Recession (global financial crisis)
autocratic regimes and, 179–80
central banks and, 194, 194*n*26
coalition governments and, 198
deficits in, 182
democracies in, 179–80
EC and, 445
EMU and, 465
ER and, 306
FCs and, 399
fiscal consolidation in, 473*t*
fiscal space in, 178, 178*n*3, 185
G20 and, 383*n*9
GDP and, 178
globalization and, 186
government lending rate and, 194
IMF and, 195
incumbents and, 179
international policy and, 195
left-wing governments in, 197
minority governments in, 197
monetary policy and, 193–94
OECD and, 182
outliers and, 202
parliamentary systems in, 197
PBCs and, 198–200
political constraints in, 177–202, 201*t*, 203*t*–207*t*
political fragmentation in, 14, 198
presidential systems in, 197
stimulus packages for, 179–97, 183*t*, 187*t*–189*t*, 190*f*, 200, 202
in U.S., 184–85
Grembi, V., 327, 328, 331, 333
Griffith, R., 84
Grigoli, F., 315*n*14
Grilli, V., 9
Grotius, Hugo, 431
Gujarati, D., 485*n*10
Gunzinger, Fabian, 14
Gupta, Sanjeev, 12, 13, 13*n*21, 14, 16, 17
on energy subsidies, 155, 161, 162, 163
Gylfason, T., 262

Hallerberg, Mark, 13, 96, 99, 101
on budget institutions, 378
on ER, 300
Hamilton, Alexander, 17, 428–38
Hansen statistic, 487, 487*n*14
Hardin, G., 9*n*17
Harmonized Government Wage and Employment Data, of IMF, 140
Harris, Jason, 16, 407
on FCs, 401
Haver Analytics, 114
HCF. *See* High Council of Finance
Heavily Indebted Poor Countries (HIPC), 217*n*6, 223
Hendry, D., 44
Henisz, W. J., 184*n*12, 282–83
Hernández de Cos, P., 364
Hibbs, D., 7, 97
High Council of Finance (HCF), in Belgium, 413, 418–22, 420*f*–422*f*
HIPC. *See* Heavily Indebted Poor Countries

Hobbes, Thomas, 431
Horizon. *See* Political horizon
Horton, M., 182
Hsiao, C., 493–94
Hua Guofeng, 255
Human capital
public investment in, 113
public social spending and, 156*n*10
Hume, David, 431
Humphrey, T., 435
Hyde, S. D., 65, 75, 75*n*18, 127

Iceland, ER in, 306, 308, 309
ICRG. *See* International Country Risk Guide
Ideological approach, to PBCs, 112, 113
Ideology. *See* Cabinet ideology
IFS. *See* International Financial Statistics
Illera, R. M., 9
ILOSTAT of, of International Labour Organization, 140*n*3
Ilzetzki, E., 178*n*3
IMF. *See* International Monetary Fund
Impulse-response functions (IRFs), for promise gaps, 43–45, 45*f*, 46*f*
Inclusive politics, 243–44
Income tax. *See* Corporate income taxes; Personal income taxes
Incumbents
deficit bias and, 402, 406
Great Recession and, 179
in Italy, 331
reelection of, 63, 63*n*1
taxes and, 99
wage bill and, 145
Independent fiscal agency, 380, 385
India, 67*n*10
Indicative targets (IT), 478
Indirect taxes, in LICs, 67*n*9
Inertial patterns, for fiscal noncompliance, 361*t*–363*t*, 364, 365*f*
Inflation
ER and, 309
in LICs, 66
taxes and, 93
Institutions. *See* Budget institutions; Fiscal institutions; Political institutions
Intergovernmental fiscal arrangements, 380
budget forecasts and, 388
fiscal noncompliance and, 16, 350, 352, 372
public investment and, 11
International Country Risk Guide (ICRG), corruption guide of, 220, 500
International Financial Statistics (IFS), of IMF, 194, 194*n*25, 500
International Labour Organization
ILOSTAT of, 140*n*3
LABORSTA of, 140*n*3
International Monetary Fund (IMF)
advanced economies and, 76*n*19
balance of payments and, 480*n*5
conditionality of, 477–501, 478*f*, 479*t*, 480*n*5, 483*f*, 484*f*, 489*t*, 491*t*–493*t*, 496*t*, 498*t*, 501*t*
emerging economies and, 76*n*19
on energy subsidies, 154*n*4
Fiscal Council Dataset of, 228, 228*n*17
fiscal crises and, 96–97
GFS of, 140*n*3, 481
Great Recession and, 195
Harmonized Government Wage and Employment Data of, 140
IFS of, 194, 194*n*25, 500
LICs and, 65, 75–77, 75*n*18, 76*n*19, 76*n*20, 77*n*22, 80*t*
MONA of, 482, 500
PRGF of, 494*n*23
PRGT of, 66, 494*n*23
programs, 13, 17, 64–65, 72, 74*t*, 75–78, 80*t*, 85, 96–97, 102*t*, 104, 105, 106*t*, 107*t*, 108*t*, 187*t*, 188*t*, 191, 195, 196*t*, 198*t*, 201*t*, 203*t*, 204*t*, 477–501
revenue conditionality of, 17
taxes and, 477–501, 478*f*, 479*t*, 483*f*, 484*f*, 489*t*, 491*t*–493*t*, 498*t*, 501*t*
trade openness and, 76
See also World Economic Outlook
International policy, Great Recession and, 195
Ireland, promise gaps in, 53
IRFs. *See* Impulse-response functions
Israel, ER in, 311
Issing, Otmar, 444
IT. *See* Indicative targets
Italy
Budget Law of 2003 in, 330*n*4

capital spending in, 331–32, 331*n*7, 332*f*, 336*f*
DSP in, 327–40, 333*f*, 334*f*
elections in, 331
fiscal rules in, 327–40, 330*t*, 341*t*
fiscal space in, 331
incumbents in, 331
PBCs in, 327–40
promise gaps in, 53
RD in, 335–39, 335*f*, 336*f*, 337*t*, 338*f*, 339*t*, 340*t*

Jalles, João Tovar, 12, 15
Japan
ER in, 306
promise gaps in, 53
Jaramillo, Laura, 14–15, 14*n22*
on tax tipping points, 246
Jensen, H., 404*n*5
Jinjarak, Y., 178*n3*
Johnsen, C., 9
on common pool, 215
Jones, B. F., 244
Jong-a-Pin, R. M., 200
Jonung, L., 415
Jordà, O., 43
Josephs, Tom, 16
Jurado, I., 197

Kaasch, A., 9
Kahneman, D., 244*n*1
Kammas, P., 97
Katsimi, M., 115*n*10, 130*n*34
Katz, J., 43
Keefer, P., 98
Keen, M., 155
Khemani, S., 67*n*10
Kincaid, Russell, 428
Kinda, Tidiane, 15
on Fiscal Council Dataset, 228*n*17
Kiser, E., 245
Klein, N., 112*n*1
Klomp, J., 7*n*13, 137*n*1
KOF. *See* Swiss Economic Institute
Kontopoulos, Y., 9
on political fragmentation, 198, 218
Kopits, G., 100*n*12
Kosovo, ER in, 306
Kraay, A., 119, 282, 285
Kraft, J., 9
Kuncic, A., 487

LABORSTA, of International Labour Organization, 140*n3*
Laeven, L., 96, 96*n*8
Lago-Peñas, S., 347, 364
Lagos State, Nigeria. *See* Nigeria
Laporte, B., 480
Larch, M., 11*n*20, 415
Leal, T., 347, 364
Left-wing governments, 7–8
deficits of, 8*n*16
government spending of, 113
in Great Recession, 197
taxes in, 8
VAT and, 13, 98
Legal capacity, property rights and, 245, 249, 249*f*, 260
Lehman Brothers, 177, 181, 193
Lending rate, of government, 194
Levi, M., 245
LICs. *See* Low-income countries
Likelihood ratio test
for promise gaps, 35*n*14
for sphericity, 280*n*15
Lithuania, ER in, 309–10
Litvack, J., 352
Liu, Estelle X., 13, 328
Lledó, Victor D., 16
Locke, John, 431
Lockwood, B., 84
on energy subsidies, 155
Log transformations, for tax-to-GDP ratio, 485*n*10
López Laborda, J., 347, 364
Low-income countries (LICs)
balance of payments of, 75*n*18
budget cycles in, 64–65, 68–69, 69*t*
budget institutions in, 377–97
centralization in, 394
descriptive statistics for, 79*t*
DR in, 64*n*4, 73*n*17
elections in, 63–78, 79*t*
fiscal balance in, 70–71, 70*n*12
fiscal rules for, 64, 64*n*4, 73–75, 73*n*15, 73*n*16, 74*t*, 77*n*22
IMF and, 65, 75–77, 75*n*18, 76*n*19, 76*n*20, 77*n*22, 80*t*

PFM for, 395
taxes in, 66, 67, 67*n*8, 67*n*9, 69–70, 478, 481*f*
VAT in, 70*n*12
wage bill in, 13, 137–38, 137*n*1, 143, 143*f*, 149
Lusinyan, L., 367
Luxembourg, ER in, 303, 306

Maastricht Treaty, 195
Belgium and, 419
ER and, 305–6
Macroeconomic forecasting, 380, 385
for CGs, 373
ER and, 299
in Netherlands, 415
for SNGs, 373
Maddala, G., 488
Mahon, J. E., 93, 96
Malesky, E. J., 99*n*10
Mao Zedong, 255
Margin of majority, in political fragmentation, 217
Marinov, N., 127
Masciandaro, D., 9
Maurel, M., 72
Mauro, P., 155
Mayor (*sindaco*), 329
McCallum, B., 404*n*5
McCrary, J., 335
MCD. *See* Minimum covariance determinant
Meade, E. E., 194
Media
in Belgium, 420–21, 421*f*
FCs and, 16, 407–13, 412*t*
in Netherlands, 416–18, 417*f*
Medium-term budgetary framework (MTBF), 395
in advanced economies, 314
CGs and, 380
ER and, 316, 316*f*
overspending and, 11
Medium-term objectives (MTOs), 446–47, 446*n*9
fiscal balance ceilings and, 446*n*8, 450*n*13
Fiscal Compact and, 463
public investment and, 452
by SGP, 450
Meltzer, A., 406*n*6
MENA. *See* Middle East and North Africa
Menocal, A. R., 243
Messina, G., 327
Middle class
elites and, 14
energy subsidies and, 154, 156
Middle East and North Africa (MENA), energy subsidies in, 164, 174*f*
Mihov, I., 155, 282
Mills, Z., 137*n*1, 139
Milner, H., 125, 126*n*33
Minimum covariance determinant (MCD), 36*n*18
for exchange rates, 280*n*16
Minimum tax-to-GDP threshold, 241
Ministry of Finance to the Economic and Financial Council (CPFF), in Spain, 355
Minority governments
budget forecasts of, 197
deficits and, 197
ER in, 306
in Great Recession, 197
political fragmentation and, 10, 113
MONA. *See* Monitoring and Fund Arrangements
Moncloa Pacts, 251–52
Monetary policy
ECB and, 442*n*3
elections and, 137*n*2
Great Recession and, 193–94
Monitoring and Fund Arrangements (MONA), of IMF, 482, 500
Moon, S., 480
Moore, M., 245
Morris, Robert, 430
Moser, C., 486*n*12
MTBF. *See* Medium-term budgetary framework
MTOs. *See* Medium-term objectives
Mulas-Granados, Carlos, 9, 12, 13, 13*n*21, 14, 15, 328
Müller, W. C., 26*n*2
Municipal council (*consiglio comunale*), 329
Muthoora, Priscilla, 15

Nannicini, T., 327, 328, 333, 339
National Elections across Democracy and Autocracy (NELDA), 64, 65, 125

Navik, J. G., 112*n*1
NELDA. *See* National Elections across Democracy and Autocracy
Netherlands
  budget forecasts in, 416, 416*f*
  Bureau for Economic Analysis in, 413, 414–18
  coalition governments in, 415–16
  CPB in, 414–18, 417*f*, 418*f*
  deficit ceiling in, 415–16, 416*f*
  ER in, 303, 306, 309
  FCs in, 414–18
  forecast errors in, 415
  GDP in, 415
  macroeconomic forecasting in, 415
  media in, 416–18, 417*f*
  promise gaps in, 54
New Tax Management Procedure, in Spain, 252
Ngouana, Constant Lonkeng, 13–14
Niehaus, P., 72
Nigeria
  GDP per capita in, 262
  taxes in, 262–64, 264*f*
  tax-to-GDP threshold of, 242
No-bailout clause
  of EA, 466
  fiscal noncompliance and, 349
Noncompliance. *See* Fiscal noncompliance
Non-endogenous elections, 125, 125*n*28
Nordhaus, W., 112, 137*n*2
Nozaki, M., 161, 162, 163

Obama, Barack, 184
OECD. *See* Organisation for Economic Co-operation and Development
Office seekers, in partisanship, 26*n*2
OG. *See* Output gap
Ohlsson, H., 197, 198
Ölçer, Dilan, 12–13, 127
Old-age dependency ratio
  veto players and, 223
  from WDI, 218
Olden, Brian, 16
Olken, B. A., 244
OLS. *See* Ordinary least squares
Olson, M., 179
O'Mahony, A., 65, 75, 75*n*18
Opportunistic approach, to PBCs, 112–13, 139
Ordinary least squares (OLS)
  for conditionality, 488
  for energy subsidies, 154, 167
  for public investment, 118
Ordinary legislative procedure, of EP, 442*n*2
Organisation for Economic Co-operation and Development (OECD)
  banking crises in, 95–96
  CIT in, 83, 84*n*1, 85, 86–88, 86*f*–87*f*, 103, 104*n*19
  on conditionality, 481
  countries of, 85*n*5
  fiscal crises in, 96–97
  fiscal rules in, 100
  GDP per capita in, 223*n*14
  Great Recession and, 182
  PIT in, 83, 84*n*1, 85, 88–90, 89*f*–90*f*, 103, 104*n*18
  promise gap and, 26
  Revenue Statistics in Latin America of, 481
  tax competition in, 95, 103
  taxes in, 83–106, 84*n*1, 102*t*, 108*t*
  VAT in, 83, 84*n*1, 85, 91–93, 91*f*–92*f*, 103, 104*n*18
  wage bill in, 139
Osterloh, S., 97
Ostrom, E., 465*n*25
Outliers
  for exchange rates, 285
  Great Recession and, 202
  for PCA, 36*n*18
Output gap (OG), 33*f*
  calculation of, 32*n*10
  in EA, 447–48, 447*f*
  endogeneity and, 449
  FCs and, 409
  GMM for, 449, 449*n*11
  government spending and, 185
  primary balance and, 311
  promise gaps and, 32
  stimulus packages for, 185
  structural balance and, 449
Outright Monetary Transactions Program, of ECB, 427
Overfitting bias, 68
Overspending
  fiscal noncompliance and, 350
  MTBF and, 11
  PBCs and, 333

Overspending incentives
bailouts and, 350, 351–52
common pool and, 352

PA. *See* Prior actions
Panel regression analysis
for ER, 318*t*
for fiscal noncompliance, 356
for promise gaps, 37–39, 38*t*–39*t*, 59–60, 60*t*
for public investment, 118–19
Panel unit root test, for public investment, 129, 129*f*
Paradisi, M., 327
Parliamentary polarization, in political fragmentation, 217–18
Parliamentary systems
budget institutions in, 381
in Great Recession, 197
public investment in, 111, 116, 118*n*16, 118*n*17, 125–27, 128*t*
See also Control of parliament
Partisanship
deficit bias and, 402
government spending and, 113, 113*n*5
office seekers in, 26*n*2
public policy and, 26*n*2
taxes and, 13
Passalacqua, A., 217
Pastrana, Andres, 260
PBCs. *See* Political business cycles
PCA. *See* Principal components analysis
Pedastsaar, Eliko, 16
Pérez, Javier J., 16
Performance-oriented budgeting, 380
Perotti, R., 9, 94, 94*n*6, 288
on exchange rates, 271–72
on political fragmentation, 198, 218
Personal income taxes (PIT)
conditionality and, 481*f*, 485
in EU, 105
in left-wing governments, 98
in OECD, 83, 84*n*1, 85, 88–90, 89*f*–90*f*, 103, 104*n*18
in right-wing governments, 98
tax competition for, 103
Persson, T., 3–4, 3*n*3, 7*n*13, 9*n*17, 241
Peru
economic shocks and, 244*n*1
ER in, 305
PFA. *See* Planned fiscal adjustment
PFM. *See* Public financial management
Pina, A., 200
PIT. *See* Personal income taxes
Planned fiscal adjustment (PFA), 29
Plante, M., 155
PLL. *See* Precautionary and Liquidity Line
Pluralism, inclusive politics and, 243–44
Poghosyan, Tigran, 17
Political accountability. *See* Accountability
Political business cycles (PBCs), 112–13
in advanced economies, 7*n*13, 63
capital spending and, 16, 331
checks and balances in, 7*n*13, 192*n*22
democracies and, 7*n*13
DSP and, 333
elections and, 113*n*3, 214–15
ER and, 300, 301
fiscal rules for, 327–40
Great Recession and, 198–200
in Italy, 327–40
opportunistic approach to, 139
overspending and, 333
Political cohesion
control of parliament and, 280
for exchange rates, 272, 274–75, 277–88, 279*f*
for fixed exchange rates, 281*f*
for flexible exchange rates, 281*f*
primary balance and, 283
public debt and, 278, 279*f*
variables for, 280–82
Political constraints, in Great Recession, 177–202, 201*t*, 203*t*–207*t*
Political division. *See* Political fragmentation
Political effectiveness
energy subsidies and, 166, 169, 170*t*
public social spending and, 166, 169, 170*t*
Political fragility, 13–14
Political fragmentation
asymmetry of, 229
common pool and, 214, 217–18, 222, 230*t*
corruption and, 223
debt-to-GDP ratio and, 226
deficits and, 229

exchange rates and, 273
FCs and, 228
fiscal institutions and, 228
fiscal politics and, 9–10, 9*n*17
fiscal rules and, 228*n*18
government spending and, 229
in Great Recession, 14, 198
indicators of, 219*f*
minority governments and, 10, 113
promise gap and, 25, 25*n*2
public debt and, 213–29, 213*n*1, 219*f*
public investment and, 13*n*21
robustness tests for, 222–28
taxes and, 98–99
veto players and, 98, 214, 218, 222, 223*t*, 231*t*
Political horizon
elections and, 280
for exchange rates, 273–85, 278*f*, 288
for fixed exchange rates, 281*f*
for flexible exchange rates, 281*f*
public debt and, 278, 278*f*
variables for, 280–82
Political institutions, 241–65
for state building, 243–45, 243*f*
for taxes, 243–45, 245*f*
See also Budget institutions; Fiscal institutions
Political strength, 26, 35
POLITY IV, 127
Population growth, wage bill and, 147
Pork-barrel spending, 215
Porteba, J. M., 100*n*13, 180
Porter, D., 485*n*10
Portugal, promise gaps in, 54–55
Posner, P., 245
Postlethwaite, Malachy, 431
Potrafke, N., 115*n*10
Poverty Reduction and Growth Facility (PRGF), 494*n*23
Poverty Reduction and Growth Trust (PRGT), 66, 494*n*23
Prakash, T., 378
Precautionary and Liquidity Line (PLL), 494*n*23
Presidential systems
elections in, 64, 64*n*3
in Great Recession, 197
public investment in, 111, 116, 118*n*16, 118*n*17, 125–27
PRGF. *See* Poverty Reduction and Growth Facility
PRGT. *See* Poverty Reduction and Growth Trust
Price, Richard, 431
Price gap, for energy subsidies, 161
Primary balance
fiscal horizon and, 283
fiscal rules for, 100
GDP and, 30
OG and, 311
political cohesion and, 283
See also Cyclically adjusted primary balance
Principal components analysis (PCA)
for exchange rates, 280*n*16
for promise gaps, 32–37, 36*n*18, 39*n*21
Prior actions (PA), 478
Private sector, right-wing governments and, 8–9
Procyclicality, 447–50, 448*n*10, 449*t*, 470*t*–471*t*, 473*t*
deficit bias and, 450–52
fiscal consolidation and, 450
GDP and, 147
OG and, 451*n*15
Program countries. *See* International Monetary Fund programs
Promise gaps
accountability factor for, 34*f*, 35–37, 36*t*, 39*n*21
consequences of, 40–45, 59–60, 60*t*
defined, 27–30
determinants of, 32–39, 57*t*–59*f*
economic and political factors for, 33*f*, 37–39, 38*t*–39*t*
elections and, 25, 25*n*2
15-month forecast error and, 33*f*
forecast errors and, 32
government popularity and, 40, 40*n*23, 41*f*–42*f*
IRFs for, 43–45, 45*f*, 46*f*
likelihood ratio test for, 35*n*14
measurement of, 29–30
OG and, 32
panel regression analysis for, 37–39, 38*t*–39*t*, 59–60, 60*t*
PCA for, 32–37, 36*n*18, 39*n*21
political conditions for, 34*f*, 36*t*
political fragmentation and, 25, 25*n*2

political strength and, 35
proximity factor for, 34*f*, 35–37, 36*t*, 39*n*21
public debt and, 33*f*
sample selection for, 47–60
size of, 30*f*, 31*f*, 33*f*, 34*f*
strength factor for, 34*f*, 35–37, 36*t*, 39*n*21
structural balances and, 30
styled facts for, 32
sustainability factor and, 33*f*
Property rights
legal capacity and, 245, 249, 249*f*, 260
protection of, 3*n*3, 260
Proximity factor
budget cycles and, 6, 7*n*13
fiscal politics and, 6–7
for promise gaps, 34*f*, 35–37, 36*t*, 39*n*21
Public Choice school, 5
Public debt
in advanced economies, 216–17, 217*f*, 218
in Belgium, 419
checks and balances for, 224
common pool and, 214, 222, 223*t*, 230*t*
control of parliament and, 223
corruption and, 223, 224*t*, 232*t*
debt ceilings on, 216
decreases in, 227*t*
in developing economies, 216–17, 217*f*
in emerging economies, 216–17, 217*f*
empirical model and data on, 215–20, 220*t*
exchange rates and, 277–78
FCs and, 235*t*, 236*t*, 409
fiscal rules for, 100
GDP and, 216, 222, 223
government spending and, 217*n*5
high level of, 234*t*
increases in, 233*t*
indicators of, 219*f*
political cohesion and, 278, 279*f*
political fragmentation and, 213–29, 213*n*1, 219*f*
political horizon and, 278, 278*f*
promise gaps and, 33*f*
proximity factor and, 6–7
quantitative limits for, 400
reverse causality for, 216
taxes and, 94
in U.S., 427–38
veto players and, 10, 214, 215, 222, 223*t*, 231*t*
wage bill and, 143, 147
Public debt sustainability
in Belgium, 50
fiscal consolidation and, 50, 85
taxes and, 94
Public expenditures. *See* Government spending
Public finance theory, taxes in, 93
Public financial management (PFM), 316
for LICs, 395
reform strategy for, 394
Public investment, 13*n*21, 114*n*7, 115*n*10
in advanced economies, 123
aggregate demand from, 111
allocation for, 123*n*27
capital spending and, 130, 130*t*
country characteristics of, 123, 124*t*
in democracies, 111–32
descriptive statistics for, 129*t*
in EA, 441, 452–54
elections and, 111–12, 112*n*1, 113*n*4, 117–23, 120*t*–121*t*, 122*f*, 123*n*27
ER and, 300, 313–14, 314*f*
GDP and, 122
GMM for, 118–19, 119*n*21
government spending and, 130, 130*t*
growth rate of, 115–16, 115*f*, 116*f*
in human capital, 113
intergovernmental fiscal arrangements and, 11
MTOs and, 452
panel unit root test for, 129, 129*f*
in parliamentary systems, 111, 116, 118*n*16, 118*n*17, 125–27, 128*t*
in presidential systems, 111, 116, 118*n*16, 118*n*17, 125–27
Public policy, partisanship and, 26*n*2
Public revenue. *See* Taxes
Public social spending, 14, 153–72
changes across regions for, 163*f*
corruption and, 158
countries in study for, 172*t*
crowding-out effect on, 154
elites and, 154
human capital and, 156*n*10

optimal choice for, 159
political effectiveness and, 166, 169, 170*t*
Public spending. *See* Government spending
Pufendorf, Samuel, 431

QPC. *See* Quantitative performance criteria
Quantitative Easing programs, 200
Quantitative performance criteria (QPC), 478

Rational voters, 214–15
balanced budget rule and, 406
RD. *See* Regression discontinuity analysis
Realized fiscal adjustment (RFA), 29
Redistribution, cabinet ideology and, 8
Redoano, M., 84
Reelection, of incumbents, 63, 63*n*1
Regression discontinuity analysis (RD), in Italy, 335–39, 335*f*, 336*f*, 337*t*, 338*f*, 339*t*, 340*t*
Reinhart, C. M., 288
Reuter, W., 346*n*4
Revenue. *See* Taxes
Revenue conditionality, of IMF, 17
Revenue Statistics in Latin America, of OECD, 481
Reverse causality
endogeneity and, 449
for ER, 311*n*9
for fiscal noncompliance, 368*n*25
for public debt, 216
Reverse qualified majority rule, for EC, 464
RFA. *See* Realized fiscal adjustment
Riedel, N., 328
Right-wing governments
crowding-out effect and, 8
deficits of, 8*n*16
private sector and, 8–9
taxes in, 8–9, 98
Robinson, J., 243
Robustness tests
for conditionality, 480, 494–98
for endogeneity of elections, 125–26
for exchange rates, 285–90, 286*t*, 287*t*, 289*t*, 290*t*
of fiscal discipline, 294*t*
for political fragmentation, 222–28
Rodden, J., 352
Rodrik, D., 485
Rogoff, K., 112, 119, 123, 288, 406*n*6
Romer, C. D., 27, 27*n*5, 181, 185
Romer, D. H., 27, 27*n*5
Rose, A. K., 272
Rose, S., 64
Ross, M. L., 245
Roubini, N., 9, 198
Rousseau, Pierre, 431–32
Rousseeuw, P. J., 36*n*18, 280*n*16, 282*n*19
Rubio, Guillermo Perry, 259
Rules (institutional) approach, to PBCs, 112, 113

Sachs, J. D., 9, 198
Samper, Ernesto, 260
Sanctions
common pool and, 465*n*25
in EA, 464–65
Sarantides, V., 115*n*10, 130*n*34
Sargent, Thomas, 17, 428, 438
SAT. *See* State Administration of Taxation
SB. *See* Structural benchmarks
SBA. *See* Standby Arrangements
Scartascini, C., 96, 98
on budget institutions, 378
SCF. *See* Standby Credit Facility
Schaechter, A., 100*n*12
on ER, 300
Schena, Michela, 12
Schuknecht, L., 137*n*1, 139
Schumpeter, Joseph, 3, 3*n*2, 241
SCM. *See* Synthetic control methodology
SCPs. *See* Stability and Convergence Program
Seiwald, Johann, 16, 407
on FCs, 401
Seki, K., 218
Selection bias
conditionality and, 486–87
in elections, 64–65
Sensitivity, 450
of exchange rates, 285–90, 286*t*
Seton, William, 434, 435
SGP. *See* Stability and Growth Pact
Shepsle, K. A., 9
on common pool, 215

Shi, M., 70*n*12, 137*n*1
Sibert, A., 406*n*6
Sindaco (mayor), 329
Sinking Fund, 434
Six Pack, in EU, 100, 105
Smith, Adam, 3–4, 3*n*3, 431
SNGs. *See* Subnational governments
Social spending. *See* Public social spending
SOEs. *See* State-owned enterprises
Soft budget constraints
for CGs, 345
fiscal noncompliance and, 349–50, 350*f*
forecasting and, 346
for SNGs, 345
Solow, R. M., 10
Soto, Mauricio, 13
Spain
Autonomous Communities in, 347
BSL in, 353–55, 355*n*13
CPFF in, 355
decentralization in, 30*n*8, 347, 367*n*21
deficits in, 356*n*17
fiscal noncompliance in, 345–73, 373*t*, 374*t*
GDP per capita in, 253, 253*f*
government spending in, 367*n*22
promise gaps in, 55
SCM in, 291–93, 292*f*
taxes in, 251–54, 253*f*, 254*f*, 254*t*
VAT in, 252
Spence, Michael, 244
Spending. *See* Capital spending; Government spending; Overspending; Public social spending
Sphericity, likelihood ratio test for, 280*n*15
Spolaore, E., 180
Stability and Convergence Program (SCPs), of European Commission, 27, 47, 101, 353, 408–9
Stability and Growth Pact (SGP), 83, 195, 226*n*16, 346, 417, 444, 446–57
MTOs by, 450
past reforms in, 462–64, 463
Stabilization, 5, 5*n*5
Standby Arrangements (SBA), 494*n*23
Standby Credit Facility (SCF), 494*n*23
Starke, P., 9
State Administration of Taxation (SAT), in China, 256–57
State building
political institutions for, 243–45, 243*f*
tipping points and, 246–49
State-owned enterprises (SOEs)
bailouts of, 166
in China, 242, 255–56
energy subsidies and, 166
Status quo
changes to, 244*n*1
veto players and, 10, 14, 215
Stein, E., 97
Steinwand, M., 486*n*12
Stephan, A., 197
Stimulus packages
for economic shocks, 180
globalization and, 191
for Great Recession, 179–97, 183*t*, 187*t*–189*t*, 190*f*, 200, 202
for OG, 185
trade openness and, 178*n*3
Stock, J., 488
Stone, R., 486*n*12
Strand, J., 155
Strauch, R. R., 94, 94*n*6
on ER, 300
Streb, J. M., 192*n*22
Strength factor, for promise gaps, 34*f*, 35–37, 36*t*, 39*n*21
Strom, K., 26*n*2
Structural balances
fiscal rules for, 100
GDP and, 30
OG and, 449
promise gaps and, 30
Structural benchmarks (SB), 478, 483
Sturm, Jan-Egbert, 14, 486*n*12
on central banks, 194*n*26
on coalition governments, 198
Subnational governments (SNGs)
bailouts for, 349*n*7
deficits and, 345
fiscal rules by, 15–16
macroeconomic forecasting for, 373
soft budget constraints for, 345
Summers, Larry, 185
Sun, Y., 272, 274, 275
Supranational fiscal policy, 16–17
in EA, 439

Sustainability factor
defined, 32*n*9
promise gaps and, 32*n*9, 33*f*
See also Public debt sustainability
Svensson, J., 70*n*12, 137*n*1
Sweden
ER in, 303, 306, 310
promise gaps in, 55–56
Swiss Economic Institute (KOF), 194*n*26
Globalization Index of, 186, 191, 191*n*21, 195, 487
Sy, A., 262
Sylla, Richard, 428, 431–32, 433, 435
Symansky, S. A., 100*n*12
Synthetic control methodology (SCM), 291, 292*f*, 295–96, 295*f*
Synthetic index of governance, for energy subsidies, 162
System-GMM estimator, 68, 486–87, 486*n*11, 492, 494*n*21

Tabellini, G., 7*n*13, 9, 9*n*17
on FCs, 402
Tavares, José, 9, 15, 288
Taxes
balanced budget rule and, 102*t*
banking crises and, 95–96, 96*n*8
centralization of, 256
in China, 254–57, 258*f*
in Colombia, 259–60, 261*f*
common pool and, 215, 441*n*1
competition with, in OECD, 95, 103
conditionality for, 477–501, 478*f*, 479*t*, 483*f*, 484*f*, 489*t*, 491*t*–493*t*, 496*t*, 498*t*, 501*t*
crisis mode for, 95–97, 103–4
debt sustainability and, 94
decentralization of, 367*n*21
in EA, 441–42, 452–54
elites and, 15
in emerging economies, 70
energy subsidies and, 160
in EU, 100–101, 105, 107*t*, 442
fiscal consolidation and, 94–95, 94*n*5, 94*n*6
fiscal crises and, 96–97
fiscal noncompliance and, 366–67
fiscal rules for, 104
GDP and, 482
GDP growth rate and, 93
GDP per capita and, 247
incumbents and, 99
inflation and, 93
in left-wing governments, 8
in LICs, 66, 67, 67*n*8, 67*n*9, 69–70, 478, 481*f*
in Nigeria, 262–64, 264*f*
in OECD, 83–106, 84*n*1, 102*t*, 106*t*, 108*t*
partisanship and, 13
political determinants of, 97–99, 104
political fragmentation and, 98–99
political institutions for, 243–45, 245*f*
public debt and, 94
in public finance theory, 93
revenue volatility of, 248*f*
in right-wing governments, 8–9, 98
in Spain, 251–54, 253*f*, 254*f*, 254*t*
tipping points for, 241–42, 246–49, 246*f*, 247*f*, 248*f*
in U.S., 98
wage bill and, 97
See also Corporate income taxes; Personal income taxes; Value-added taxes
Tax state, 3, 3*n*2
Tax-to-GDP-growth, tipping point for, 14–15
Tax-to-GDP ratio, 479
in China, 256, 257
conditionality and, 496
log transformations for, 485*n*10
Tax-to-GDP threshold
countries crossing, 266*t*
GDP per capita and, 246, 246*f*
tipping points and, 241–42
Teräsvirta, T., 45
Ter-Minassian, T., 352
Thornton, H., 435
Time inconsistency problem, 441
Tinubu, Bola, 262–63
Tipping points
in advanced economies, 241
in developing economies, 241
GDP per capita and, 241
state building and, 246–49
for taxes, 241–42, 246–49, 246*f*, 247*f*, 248*f*
for tax-to-GDP-growth, 14–15
tax-to-GDP threshold and, 241–42

Tolosa, G., 274*n*8
Tommasino, P., 327
Torgler, B., 245
Tornell, A., 272, 274, 274*n*7, 275, 281
Torvik, R., 262
Trade and Development Report, of UNCTAD, 177
Trade openness, 165, 295
- conditionality and, 485
- GDP and, 500
- IMF and, 76
- measurement of, 220
- stimulus packages and, 178*n*3

Transparency International, corruption index of, 485–86
Trebesch, Christoph, 432, 436
Troiano, U., 327, 328, 333
Tsebelis, G., 98
Tversky, A., 244*n*1
Two Pack, in EU, 100, 105

UCD. *See* Unión de Centro Democrático
UNCTAD, 182
- Trade and Development Report of, 177

Unión de Centro Democrático (UCD), 251–52
United Kingdom, promise gaps in, 56
United Nations, World Population Prospects of, 140
United States (U.S.)
- bonds in, 17, 429
- Continental financial system in, 427–35
- ER in, 306, 308, 311
- Federal Reserve in, 180
- Great Recession in, 184–85
- promise gaps in, 56–57
- public debt in, 427–38
- taxes in, 98

Urgent Tax Reform Measures, in Spain, 252
U.S. *See* United States
Utility function, energy subsidies and, 156*n*8

Valencia, F., 96, 96*n*8
Value-added taxes (VAT)
- CGs and, 256
- in China, 256, 257
- in Colombia, 259–360
- conditionality and, 481*f*, 485, 488
- in EA, 85
- energy subsidies and, 155
- in EU, 83, 100, 105
- GDP and, 103
- in left-wing governments, 13, 98
- in LICs, 70*n*12
- in OECD, 83, 84*n*1, 85, 91–93, 91*f*–92*f*, 103, 104*n*18
- as regressive, 97–98
- in right-wing governments, 98
- in Spain, 252
- tax competition for, 103

Van den Noord, P., 99
Van Driessen, K., 36*n*18, 280*n*16
Van Eden, Holger, 16
Van Hooren, F., 9
Vaquero, A., 347, 364
VAR. *See* Vector autoregression
VAT. *See* Value-added taxes
Vaubel, R., 76*n*20
Vector autoregression (VAR), 43–45
Veiga, F., 113*n*4, 328
Veiga, L., 113*n*4, 328
Velasco, A., 272, 274, 274*n*7, 275, 281
Venes, N. M., 200
Venezuela, economic shocks and, 244*n*1
Verdier, Geneviève, 13
Vergne, C., 72
Vertical fiscal imbalances (VFIs), 352, 366–67, 367*n*23
Veto players, 99*n*10
- checks and balances and, 218
- legislative periods and, 221*t*
- old-age dependency ratio and, 223
- political fragmentation and, 98, 214, 218, 222, 223*t*, 231*t*
- public debt and, 214, 215, 222, 223*t*, 231*t*
- status quo and, 10, 14, 215

VFIs. *See* Vertical fiscal imbalances
Volverink, B., 9
Von Hagen, Jürgen, 13, 94, 94*n*6, 99
- on ER, 300

Wage bill
- in advanced economies, 149
- capital spending and, 139
- consumption multiplier with, 139
- cross-country variation in, 143–45, 143*f*

data on, 140–43, 140*n*3, 141*t*–142*t*
demographics and, 141*t*–142*t*, 142, 145
elections and, 13, 137–49, 146*t*, 147*t*, 148*t*
in emerging economies, 13, 151
GDP and, 140, 144*f*, 145, 146–47, 149*t*
GDP growth rate and, 142, 147
in government spending, 137
incumbents and, 145
in LICs, 13, 137–38, 137*n*1, 143, 143*f*, 149
in OECD, 139
population growth and, 147
public debt and, 143, 147
taxes and, 97
working-age population and, 140, 142*t*, 146*n*4, 148–49
Wagner, R. E., 5
Wagner's law, 144
Wallace-Wells, B., 185
Wälti, S., 96
Warlters, M., 485*n*10
Washington Consensus, 244*n*1
WDI. *See* World Development Indicators
Weber, Anke, 15
Weingast, B. R., 9
on common pool, 215
Weise, C. L., 180
WEO. *See* World Economic Outlook
West African Economic and Monetary Union, fiscal rules in, 73*n*15
Weyland, K., 244*n*1
Williams, L. K., 218
Windmeijer, F., 68
Wingender, Philippe, 14–15, 14*n*22
on tax tipping points, 246
Winkler, B., 443
Working-age population, wage bill and, 140, 142*t*, 146*n*4, 148–49
World Bank
corruption indicators of, 223
See also Database of Political Institutions; World Development Indicators
World Development Indicators (WDI), 66, 114, 118*n*19
on conditionality, 500
on energy subsidies, 162
old-age dependency ratio from, 218
World Economic Outlook (WEO), 114, 140*n*3
on conditionality, 481
on expenditure rule compliance, 307
on fiscal space, 185
on GDP, 32*n*11
on Great Recession, 182
for LICs, 66
on wage bill, 140
World Economic Yearbook, 127
World Governance Indicators, of World Bank, 162
World Population Prospects, of United Nations, 140
World Trade Organization, 256
World Values Survey, 253
on China, 257
on Colombia, 260
Wren-Lewis, S., 401, 413
Wright, Robert, 431, 435
Wu, S., 488

Yläoutinen, Sami, 16
on budget institutions, 378
on ER, 300
Yogo, M., 488
Yohai, V. J., 282, 282*n*19